The Radio Caroline Bible

The life and times of the world's most famous offshore radio station.

by Paul Rusling

Love, Peace and Good Music

Published by World of Radio Ltd, Hull, HU10 7TL, UK.
Printed by Biddles, Kings Lynn, PE32 1SF

First Edition, 2019.

ISBN Softback 978-1-900401-20-3
ISBN Casebound 978-1-900401-19-7
ISBN Epub / Kindle 978-1-900401-21-0

To my darling Anne
(47 years and counting!)
and our family

Thanks for all your help and support

Music & mayhem
from the most
Magical Maritime Mast

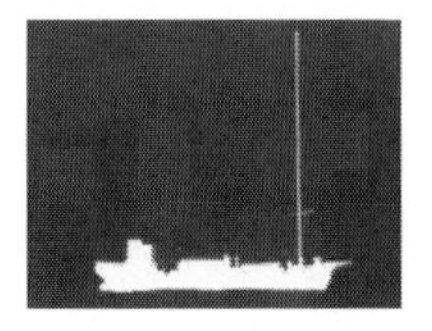

CONTENTS

INTRODUCTION

To those who've ever been involved with Radio Caroline, it can be infuriating to read some of the mythical stories and far-fetched fantasies, apocryphal misinterpretations or just complete works of fiction about the station.

This book adheres to authenticated aspects of the story of Caroline. It's a story of intrigue and mystery, one that that Caroline team have had to deliberately mask in places to protect those who didn't want their identities, nor the reasons for the radio station, to be exposed.

The book is simply a chronicle of the life of the world's most famous offshore radio station, that puts the major events into some semblance of order. This is NOT a gallery of DJs for enthusiasts; while many DJs are important to the Caroline story, their lives and habits have been omitted, mainly for brevity. Many have their biographies published and a bibliography of those is included. This is not a technical book either and while the reader is taken behind the microphone to explain some of the magic, the complexities of radio engineering and signal propagation are best explored elsewhere. Nor is this a political lecture nor a treatise of offshore or commercial radio.

Most of the story has been written or checked by those who were there; omitting the various popular tales that are simply myths, which most now realise were originally created to obfuscate the truth. Some spoof stories were put out as a smokescreen, what today would be called 'fake news' In mitigation, it must be remembered that, when operating on the edges of legality, one must take care to not to help one's enemies. In Caroline's first three phases, (at sea, from 1964 to 1991) staff often had to act covertly.

Caroline family members often knew only part of the story because information had to be controlled, on a "need to know" basis. Like any business the public's perception of Radio Caroline was carefully manipulated. Legally, no such thing as Radio Caroline existed, other than as a 'call sign' used on the air.

Several people were midwives at the birth of Radio Caroline, a few are still with us and clearly remember the fascinating events, related in these pages. Those founders with business acumen were enchanted by the idea of liberating the airwaves so they could bring about commercial radio in the UK assuming that, like ITV, it would be a licence to print money. Some in the Establishment enjoyed stirring things up a little; Radio Caroline was an ideal pastime or a gamble.

There are several different versions of the story of how Radio Caroline started, the who, where and when details are often confused, and sometimes it's been done deliberately. The story unfolded here is as close to the truth as possible and is based on the corroborated word of several of those who were actually there. They played active roles in the birth and the life of the "world's most famous" and certainly the most fascinating radio station – Radio Caroline.

ACKNOWLEDGMENTS

Material for the book came from a variety of sources; published articles and other books (see the bibliography on page 505) and from the personal reminiscences and research of so many friends and acquaintances, especially Colin Nicol, Sir Hans Knot, Ian Anderson, Kate Cary, Oonagh and Sonny Karanjia, Don Robinson, Keith Skues, Robin Adcroft, Ben Bode, Vincent Monsey, Steve Conway, Chris Edwards, Ronan O'Rahilly, Roger Day, Susan Calvert, Lion Keezer, Peter Moore and Dick Palmer. In particular I am most grateful to Hans Knot and Peter Moore for their many hours spent proof-reading. This book wouldn't have been possible without their valuable input.

Quotations are from correspondence, published articles, news reports, and recordings broadcast. All sources are acknowledged, where appropriate. The UK's National Archives at Kew were invaluable, as was help from the Dutch Nationaal Archief, the House of Commons library, the Office of Justice of Liechtenstein and Lloyds List Maritime Intelligence. I am grateful for their help.

Photographs are used in the book to aid the reader and are either from my own personal archives, or from those as acknowledged. Of special note are the images provided by Colin Nicol, Robin Adcroft, Lion Keezer, Rob Olthof, Martin van der Ven and Sir Hans Knot, plus Boudewijn Dom, Chris Edwards and François Lhote. Where the photographer is unnamed or the source is unknown, all rights are acknowledged. Items are used simply for informational purposes.

Paul Rusling
2019

Email: Paul@RadioCarolineBible.com

1. The Dawn of Radio Broadcasting

Radio Caroline has broadcast to the UK for over 55 years – that's over half a century, and indeed longer than a lifetime for many people. As radio broadcasting, certainly in Europe, is only really a hundred years old in 2019, and not until 2022 in the UK, that means that Radio Caroline has been around for over half the lifetime of radio.

To understand why it came about and what has sustained it one must look back even further than that, to where the magical tool of radio broadcasting began. We must also consider the existing radio landscape, and how its very firmament drove people to launch Radio Caroline, on board a ship!

Radio was developed as a communications tool, originally for the military but for general commerce too, particularly shipping. The use of wireless, as radio was then better known, cannot be attributed to any one individual; it was developed over a period by many eminent scientists of the late 1800s. Among the best known are Maxwell, Hertz, Faraday, Watt, Edison, Voltaire, most of whose names live on in today's world of wireless and electricity, some even in daily use as scientific units of measurement. Their discoveries of the natural phenomena, particularly those of electricity, often had limited use and commercial potential.

What was needed was a somewhat disparate group of inventors and entrepreneurs who could seize these many discoveries and bring them together in order to make useful tools of real benefit to mankind.

In the final years of the 19th century, several individuals were convinced that electricity was not limited to metallic conductors but could somehow escape into the air (commonly called 'the ether'). The effect of this could be used to convey information to more remote locations. The 1800s had brought great strides in communications by signalling over cables, which by then were reaching into all corners of the globe.

This radicalised both military and commerce, and huge fortunes were made by the cable companies who had armies of linesmen erecting vast networks to every tiny town and village, not to mention fleets of huge ships, busy laying the cables underwater. Messages that previously took days or weeks to travel could now be sent almost instantaneously.

Visionaries such as Professor Oliver Lodge (whose grandson Tom was later a leading light in the development of Radio Caroline), Guglielmo Marconi and Nicholai Tesla are just a few of those who saw potential in the ability of certain types of electricity to have an effect over a distance.

Professor Lodge was the first to publicly talk about radio waves in 1889, at a meeting of the Institute of Electrical Engineers (a learned society of budding electricians). For the next few years Professor Lodge demonstrated radio waves at various scientific meetings at the IEE in London and had many papers published, with his work widely reported, including in the leading newspapers such as the Times. He was never interested in commercially exploiting his work though.

Guglielmo Marconi was more commercially-minded and part Irish (his mother's family were the Jameson's whisky distillers) and over the next few years he demonstrated his equipment to the British Army and Navy in a series of experiments.

It's now clear that there were several entrepreneurs, each doing much the same thing but in different places and with slightly different equipment and usually for reasons. None of the participants seem to have any idea of exploiting the behaviour of radio frequencies for mass communications – almost all the experiments and development were aimed at developing point-to-point communications.

The first success of broadcasting was on a cable network, on which some performances from theatres in London were sent by telephone connections to homes. This also spawned a new style of entertainment establishment called an 'electrophone lounge'. There was one in Gerrard Street where the 'well to do' could be seen listening to concerts and shows on a telephone earpiece – the first instance of people kept "hanging on the telephone" perhaps?

Broadcasting by telephone never really caught on with the masses however, not many had a telephone of course. The business plan was flawed and they were soon mired in complaints about copyright infringement. The General Post Office decided to block any expansion of the embryonic broadcasting service. The GPO had been established in the 17th century and was the government tool used to censor all types of communications, whether sent by mail or broadcast.

Among the first radio transmissions to be made with a wider audience in mind (rather than a sole destination, as with communications link) actually came from boats of one kind or another. In the 1890s, Nathan Stubblefield had demonstrated broadcasting voice and music from a boat on the Potomac River in Washington. No recordings survive but the event was widely publicised in newspapers of the day.

In late 1905, the crew of one of the UK's warships decided to send Christmas greetings to radio enthusiasts in the Kent area while their ship was in Chatham dockyard. This happened in the same harbour where a Radio Caroline ship was later docked. The following year an American warship the USS Missouri also broadcast the tune 'Home Sweet Home' in greeting to its sister ships in the fleet.

Over Christmas the crew of the East Goodwin lightship used their ship's equipment to broadcast messages and fraternal greetings to their family ashore and sang them a couple of Christmas carols. Was this the first ever truly 'offshore' radio broadcast? They were officially reprimanded by their bosses at Trinity House the following week.

The radio waves however remained relatively silent and became used mainly for communications with ships, and military use in the Great War. Even on ships, the uptake of radio installations was slow. Help for the Titanic in April 1912 was slow in coming as nearby ships did not realise her peril. The radio operator on *The California* was off-watch and no one else understood the messages, which were transmitted using Morse and two different sets of codes were used.

There were some huge technical steps being made that would make broadcasting as we know it today feasible, such as the first thermionic valve, an '*Audion*' tube developed by De Forest in 1906. This enabled much easier modulation of the waves, particularly music. The development of radio was now undertaken by enthusiasts in their homes, but their activities were severely restricted and regulated by the authorities in many countries, to protect the communications messages to and from ships and the military.

Belgium seems to have had one of the first organised broadcast operations with performances from the Grand Opera House in Belgium being sent to receivers at the Royal Palace, but the equipment was very expensive and out of the reach of normal people. Only a small number of radio experimenters tuned in, on home-made equipment.

Manufacturers of electrical components began to recognise the increasing demand for their products and realised that even more demand could be generated, if only the radio enthusiasts had some reason to tune in. This involved in expanding transmissions beyond the bare utilitarian content of traffic to ships and technical remarks between general experimenters.

In the Netherlands, a Dutch experimenter called Hanso Henricus Shotanus Izarda began making regular transmissions from The Hague in 1919. These were regular concerts and his transmissions using the call sign PCGG are widely regarded as the first regular broadcasts in the world. As well as concerts, his early broadcasts contained a variety of performers, but these radio transmissions were made as a hobby, not a business.

This coincided with the American government removing many of the restrictions on radio in 1919. Many component manufacturers joined a 'talent pool' called RCA (Radio Corporation of America), ostensibly to share new technology, but in practice this became one of the largest groups manufacturing companies in the business.

The following year, 1920, the first American radio broadcast stations took to the air; among the best known is KDKA in Pittsburgh. It began when a keen radio amateur and inventor called Frank Conrad made the first commercial broadcasts, with sponsors paying the costs.

Marconi's company had become the leader in provision of communications equipment for ships and the First World War were boom years for his company. Development was by then based in several buildings in Chelmsford, a quiet market town in Essex. Expansion had been so rapid that several departments were housed in wooden huts jusy south of the town, in a village called Writtle. Their antenna design section remained in the huts until the 21st century!

Leading Marconi engineer Phillip Eckersley was convinced that 'broadcasting' audible programmes to everyone was worth pursuing and he organised experimental transmissions from the Writtle site. The transmissions were made using aerials hung from extended wooden posts, mostly built by Marconi engineers in their spare time. These proved very popular, especially with electrical suppliers who met the huge public demand for components to make suitable receivers.

To publicise the transmissions further, a world renowned vocalist, Dame Nellie Melba was invited to come and broadcast on the airwaves from Writtle. On arrival, she looked at the masts and wires and proclaimed that she would not climb up there AND sing!

Some of the manufacturers of components were by now offering kits of parts and even fully built receivers. They pressed the GPO (who regulated all post, newspaper and radio transmissions on behalf of The Crown) to licence them to broadcast programmes for general reception and in 1922 formed the British Broadcasting Company. The BBC as it was known received income from duty on the sale of complete receivers and by a reception tax, paid by listeners via a licence. Home construction of receivers was popular for many years due to these royalty payments and the imposition of "luxury tax" on them.

The Government brought the embryonic broadcasting company back under state control by nationalising it as the British Broadcasting Corporation, which it's been ever since. Despite the BBC's claims of being "independent of government" this ignores that it is still controlled by The Crown, a mysterious and nebulous body which had different powers depending on the context. The Monarch is the figurehead of The Crown, which permits a parliament to administer day to day affairs of state. The biggest group of elected members usually form the Government, but The Crown remains in charge of the monarchy and the government.

The BBC grew phenomenally as it had a monopoly in broadcasting, unlike many other 'western' countries such as the USA, Canada, France, etc. In those countries, private companies were allowed to operate radio stations. Their income came from the sale of airtime and involvement in other commercial activities.

In the UK, it was deemed that broadcasting was too powerful and sensitive to undue influence to allow commercial interests to profit from this valuable resource. The BBC had been licensed to primarily provide information and education, rather than entertainment. Its first Manager, John Reith, was a dour, strictly tee-total and God-fearing Scot who despised fun and frivolity. He hired a team of like-minded elitists and pillars of the Establishment who moulded its management, a trait that has continued even to the Corporations management today.

Among Reith's rules were that there would be no entertainment at all on Sundays, only hymns and sermons. The Sabbath, when most Britons had the day off and could tune in, should have seen the highest audiences, but most of the public didn't listen to the BBC. They tuned to a variety of foreign stations, broadcasting from continental Europe.

2. Commercial radio arrives

Most other countries had allowed commercial stations to operate and a British company, led by Captain Leonard Plugge, was set up to exploit this. He toured the continent discovering stations and arranged deals for his pre-recorded programmes to be relayed by them. Advertisers were very keen to reach the huge audiences that the IBS stations drew – up to seven million some weekends. The IBS had mobile studios which travelled the UK recording programmes in theatres. These were mainly variety shows, complete with audience participation, which helped promote the IBS radio stations still further.

One of their most successful stations was Radio Normandie, at Fecamp on the French coast, just across the channel from England. The Fecamp transmitter was ideally placed to put in a strong signal over most of southern England. Leonard Plugge (whose surname later became synonymous with getting airplay on the radio) also hired air time for his broadcasts on stations in Paris, Italy, Spain and even stations as far afield as along the Adriatic coast.

Plugge and his car antenna

Lenny, as he was known, undertook trips all over Europe in his grand tourer cars in the 1920s, monitoring the transmissions of various stations. He would then visit the stations and book his own programmes on them. These were recorded onto discs and sent over for transmission. Plugge's visits drew sizeable crowds and not simply because his trips invariably included four or five attractive female companions. His car was one of the first equipped with a radio receiver (he invented the car radio) and a loop aerial a big attraction in those days when visitors were rare.

With few stations broadcasting in those days, signals travelled much further, and medium wave reception after dark was possible between continents. Today, the levels of man-made radio fog (the electro-magnetic noise generated by computers and other electronic equipment) make reception very difficult on the MW band. A lot of broadcasting has fled to high frequencies, which may be more immune to noise and interference, but the signals can travel only very short distances.

Cross-frontier broadcasting has become known as 'border blasters'. Many such stations have broadcast into the USA from Mexico, offering grey products that were tightly-controlled by American regulators. The business continues today; one stations pumping 100,000 watts into southern California is now owned by Chinese interests.

One of the most powerful stations that Captain Plugge's programmes were heard on was Radio Luxembourg, located in the Grand Duchy – just over the border from Belgium. Its central location in the middle of Europe, combined with very high-power transmitters, made its transmissions were audible all over Europe Programmes comprising mainly popular entertainment meant it attracted millions of listeners, and consequently high levels of advertising.

Radio Luxembourg began in 1930 and copied the pioneering work done by Captain Pluggc. It had multi-lingual transmissions in English, French, German, Dutch and Italian and commanded huge audiences using several long wave frequencies. The BBC accused it of being a pirate as its frequency had not been internationally agreed and asked the GPO to block Luxembourg by severing its telephone connection. This stopped live programmes from London. They had to prerecord the shows, on a mixture of film and on large shellac discs.

During WWII the Germans took over the station but after 1946 it continued its multi-language output, with programmes in Dutch, English, French and German. Having so many languages time-sharing one Long Wave transmitter was not very satisfactory, so Radio Luxembourg built a powerful MW outlet in the early fifties. This could be heard over the entire UK after dark and within a few years it slowly dropped its spoken word and most of the variety shows in favour of music programming.

Huge tranches of Radio Luxembourg's airtime was bought in lengthy blocks as sponsored programming by the major British record companies, who show-cased their new releases by playing the first minute or so of each one. By doing so they hoped to encourage listeners to go out and buy them. Record sales figures suggest that the ploy may have worked, as the peak for the sales of single records was around 1963. The analysis may be flawed as it ignores some other factors: most record sales were of 45s, as 'long players' (albums) were not yet affordable, the lack of competition for the growing disposable income of teenagers and other reasons that caused record sales to rise in the early 1960s and then diminish.

In the early sixties, 45rpm singles gave only three minutes playing time per side and many cuts ran for less than two thirds that time. Singles were more popular among younger listeners than the 'long player' albums, as their attention span was generally much shorter, despite the lower speed and larger size giving around twenty minutes per side, LP buyers tended to be much older than fans of singles, something that didn't change much until the seventies.

There had been many plans to cover the UK from stations in the Irish Republic and the Isle of Man since the 1940s, however political pressure from London scuppered those projects.

The expansion of television in the early 1950s led to a pressure group of TV manufacturers pleading for commercial TV. The main constituents of the group were the TV receiver manufacturers, who were led by the Pye group and its enigmatic Chairman, C O Stanley. Pye Ltd had been making scientific and electrical components since the late 1890s. They led the development of radar and mobile telephony but yearned for a chance to broadcast in the UK.

Dutch electronics conglomerate Philips bought a majority shareholding in 1967 and took over Pye completely. Philips were a pioneer of radio valves and one of the first to operate an international radio station commercially, from 1927. They transmitted in English, Dutch and French as *The Happy Station* which became Radio Netherlands. Philips also introduced the *Compact Cassette* in 1963, which was to play a role in the survival of Radio Caroline when it made possible the transport of recorded programmes

Pye's demands for commercial broadcasting were partially met by the establishment in the UK when ITV launched in 1955, however it was only allowed to carry short advertising messages in spots of 15 or 30 seconds. The more influential 'sponsorship' of programmes was not allowed. As is implied by the ITA's full name, stations had to be seen to be wholly independent of advertising, in ownership and editorially.

The new ITV channel was immediately successful and was described by many as a 'licence to print money'. This was due to the ITV Network being the sole outlet for broadcast commercials. The only commercial radio heard in the UK around 1960s was from Radio Éireann, the Irish state broadcaster, which carried limited commercials, and the nocturnal Radio Luxembourg, only be heard by sky-wave.

The introduction of Independent television (ITV) hit the BBC very hard. Its share of viewing fell to only 28% within two years, despite ITV only reaching perhaps half the country and needing new TV sets to see the programmes, which were on a different band (VHF Band III)

In the late fifties, there had been a strong chance that the UK would get a commercial radio station, broadcast from Ireland. Transmitters in the Irish republic could reach much of the UK, even down into London. This was proven in the nineties when a joint venture between Radio Luxembourg and the RTE in Ireland operated a powerful long wave transmitter as *Atlantic 252.* That plan was about thirty years old and was originally proposed by two groups well before 1960.

Several organisations wanted to launch a TV station in Ireland and offered to do so free of charge if they could also have a licence for an international radio station powerful enough to cover the entire British Isles. The two keenest contenders were C O Stanley, the chairman of the Pye electronics group, and an American radio entrepreneur called Gordon McLendon. When Dublin dragged its feet over radio, McLendon got involved in launching a radio ship in the Baltic, broadcasting to Sweden from a ship that was to become Radio Caroline.

Pye's plan was to operate not only a national station, but a network of small local radio outlets too. This was based on an old WWII plan for the BBC to have similar number of local transmitters (called the 'Group H' chain) in the event of an invasion or other loss of the regional and national stations. Pye would manufacture a range of the necessary equipment.

Britain's first transistor radio, by Pye

They were also keen to sell receivers, a field in which Pye were undoubted leaders. Their PAM portable was extensively advertised as the country's first transistorised radio.

In the Ireland, the state broadcaster RTE (Radio Éireann) operated from the top floors of the GPO building in Dublin. The service was rigidly controlled by the government and the church, so Radio Éireann was very staid in its approach. Television in the UK was expanding rapidly and many in Ireland were clamouring for an independent commercial TV service.

Over a dozen companies made offers to the Irish government to run an Irish TV channel; two of them would do so only if they could also have a licence for a high-power radio station to broadcast commercial radio to the UK.

Among those who knew that the real money would lay in broadcasting radio across to the UK were Charles Murchison, a Frenchman who had run high power 'border blasters' into neighbouring countries in Andorra, Monte Carlo and Germany (*Europe No.1*).

Gordon McLendon
Legendary offshore radio pioneer

Gordon McLendon was a young Texan entrepreneur who had a group of radio stations based in Dallas who was easily able to match Murchison's expertise. He was very keen to broadcast to Great Britain and constantly sought ways of doing so.

When permission to broadcast from Ireland wasn't forthcoming, McLendon turned his attentions to putting a station board a ship off the Swedish coast. The station was called Radio Nord and, after the Scandinavians brought in legislation that made broadcasting in the Baltic difficult, his ship was moved and leased to an organisation that soon became part of the Radio Caroline empire. The ship was to become one of Radio Caroline's most famous ships ever, just a few years later.

Later, Gordon was one of the founding fathers of Radio London, Radio Caroline's biggest competitor in the sixties. Many aspects of Radio London were copied from Gordon McLendon's successful stations in Texas, the best known of which was KLIF in Dallas.

Pilkington Committee

In 1960, the British government set up a 'committee of inquiry' to look into the future of broadcasting. As is usual for such committees, it had no ordinary members, the usual assortment of 'the great and the good', who could be relied on to support the 'status quo' and block any radical changes. After two years studying radio and TV, the committee made some strange pronouncements.

The report said "the UK did not want commercial radio."

One of its conclusions was that the British public did not want commercial radio and that the BBC should extend its activities to include local radio to prevent the introduction of commercial radio! At that stage there were over a hundred companies formed to bid for commercial radio licences. The arrogant elite who comprised Pilkington's committee presumed that the entrepreneurs who formed those companies were all wrong? Their claims were absurd, as the majority of the British public were in fact already avid consumers of commercial radio, by the fact that over ten million of them tuned in daily to Radio Luxembourg.

"The Pilkingon committee were not just 10% wrong, they were 100% wrong," says Ronan O'Rahilly, who was about to play a major role in the development of commercial radio. "Their verdict was an affront to people. If that's the state of how a Government can get things wrong, this is surely it. British listeners had proved that they would listen to commercial radio with the most dreadful reception; they had never been given the opportunity to hear local commercial radio as the government had never permitted it."

"The Pilkington Committee got it completely wrong; there was clearly demand for hearing radio commercials. Millions of people were tuning to Radio Luxembourg every night, despite it having poor reception and only being available after dark. They ran spot commercials and sponsored programmes which the listeners enjoyed. There was certainly a demand for pop music on the radio, and certainly when presented in a different style to the BBC."

Many of the companies keen to operate local radio stations were associated with the Pye group and several looked at other ways to break the BBC's monopoly in radio.

BBC services in the early 1960s.
To understand one of the reasons for launching Radio Caroline, one must consider what the UK's sole radio broadcaster, the BBC, were offering listeners in the first half of the 1960s.

The BBC wasn't organised as radio stations but into several incongruous sections: Light Entertainment, Talks Department, Gramophone Dept, the Music Dept (classical music only) and so on. Each department made programmes for any of the three main networks of transmitters – the Home Service, the Light Programme and the Third Programme.

Those three were the only BBC channels officially audible in the UK, although the Home Service was for England while the other home nations had their own opt-out programmes of Radios Scotland, Wales and Ulster. The BBC also broadcast to the rest of the world Service for which they were funded (by an annual grant from the UK's Foreign & Commonwealth Office), but those transmissions were carefully arranged to make reception in the UK difficult.

Home Service
The main home for quizzes, drama, news magazines and similar programmes of mainly talk. The Home Service was often known as the BBC's 'senior service' as it was its oldest The station quite closely resembles the station that today broadcasts as Radio 4.

The Light Programme
A series of music and drama programmes, that was simply lighter than the talk-oriented and sombre Home Service. The channel had a very strict needle-time limit and most performances of pop music were by its own house bands, orchestras and artistes. It became BBC Radio 2.

Third Programme / Network Three
Created in the mid 1950s, this was a true 'network' in that it had a variety of services – the BBC Music programme which was a morning service of classical music and complete works. Many afternoons were given over to lengthy ball-by-ball cricket commentaries and the main Third Programme service took over for evening recitals of classical music and operas for over half its airtime, plus drama, talks and poetry.

Listeners to The Third were expected to listen and give each programme their undivided attention. This was made clear in its opening broadcast, a lecture by Joyce Grenfell. She also sat as a committee member of the Pilkington Committee. The Third was an overly highbrow collection of programmes appealing to a very tiny audience of the educated 'upper' classes.

Even when it was urged to lighten up the network to make it of broader appeal, the BBC management's answer was a few hours programmes of foreign language tuition, some further education, a sprinkling of jazz, science, archaeology and gardening, plus extra religious talks! After a programme on chess moves 'The Third' closed down for 15 minutes, before the more highbrow 'Network Three' programmes began their evening of serious music recitals and opera.

In summary, the BBC in the early 60s was worthy but dull and of little appeal to younger people. The demand for music was expanding rapidly, but to hear new music one had to tune to Radio Luxembourg.

Banned music

The BBC's Dance Music Policy committee sat in judgement of material and demanded several copies of the disc and a lyric sheet. These would be pored over by BBC staff, to weed out anything that may have sexual overtones, no matter how vague. Even artistes who had ever recorded anything slightly "off-colour" as the BBC called it then, would see all their subsequent releases excluded from airplay. Their guidelines was to "exclude sickly sentimentality which, particularly when sung by certain vocalists, can become nauseating and not at all in keeping with what we feel to be the need of the public." In other words, you only got what Auntie thought was good for you!

Henry Hall, George Formby and others who dared include any innuendo in their stage material had their music blocked by the BBC. Even in recent years, the Corporation has continued to ban singers such as Judge Dread who never ever used any profane language but still had his rhymes banned as the BBC producers could hear innuendo in songs where none existed! Judge Dread still enjoyed sales of millions, as did many artistes on labels connected with Radio Caroline.

The BBC also were keen to suppress any material that might contain not only sexual content but also political messages, references to the Royal family, politicians or another prominent people. They insisted that this was not strictly a 'ban' on the record, just an advisory to producers that the record should only be used "with great caution".

There were some other aspects of the BBC in the early 1960s that put it completely at odds with everyday life in the UK, especially of younger people. Its style of presentation, the pace of delivery, the attitude to 'ordinary people' are all now so evident.

John Reith's first directions have been upheld since by the senior management at the Corporation. He decreed that "Radio is too powerful a medium to be left in the hands of ordinary people." This has long been evident, given that the secret service were afforded offices in Broadcasting House and that all personnel records were scrutinised by them and indeed, all appointments were only made after MI5 approval. This was confirmed in several articles in leading Sunday newspaper in the eighties following which the BBC's appointments procedure was changed.

The BBC was organised along lines of the civil service with its contracts being cherished and often regarded as a "job for life'. Many of those recruited were on the school tie basis, a mushrooming 'old boy network' that prevails to some extent today.

The left-wing press was vehemently opposed to anyone else but 'the state' being given access to radio frequencies and made its position on commercial radio and pop music well known. The New Statesman was very dismissive of pop music fans as this sneering piece of editorial about young people illustrates:

> *What a bottomless chasm of vacuity they reveal . . bloated with cheap confectionery and smeared with chain-store makeup, the open sagging mouths and glazed eyes, the hands mindlessly drumming in time to the music, the broken stiletto heels, the shoddy, stereotyped 'with-it' clothes*

The dawn of broadcasting also brought about a huge change in the record business. Most record companies, such as Columbia, Regal Zonophone, HMV and Decca, had long been worried that the public wouldn't buy records if they could hear them on the radio. When commercial radio in Europe began in the early 1930s, some of the largest labels decided to band together and form a huge pressure group to fight radio and have it severely curtailed.

The BBC was always willing to accept draconian rules and limits on music, especially anything modern. Were it not for Captain Plugge and his International Broadcasting Company, it's certain that many artists of the thirties would never have been heard. The new group of record labels became known as EMI, which by the 1960s was the UK's largest record and electronics business with records sold all over the world.

3. Europe's early offshore stations

Some of the first broadcasts were made from boats at the very dawn of radio transmission, propagation was immediately found to be much greater over the sea. The first broadcasters used very primitive microphones on equipment that was designed for communications. Such equipment only needs a narrow band of frequencies to be intelligible and, while the resultant audio may be of low fidelity, it is quite sufficient to be understood. Broadcasting helped develop audio amplification, loudspeakers and especially microphones.

In the early days of the Cold War it became necessary to get western radio broadcasts heard in the centre of the Soviet Union. While Short Wave could achieve the coverage, the signals didn't reach many ordinary people as they didn't have suitable receivers. What was needed was to get a powerful signal "over the border" and into Moscow. The traditional 'border blaster' method using a transmitter in an adjacent country couldn't be used, as the Soviets had taken over all the countries adjacent to Russia; the closest ones were reluctant to allow political foreign transmissions from their soil.

Voice of America's radio ship MV Courier

To solve the problem powerful transmitters were installed on an American naval vessel, the *MV Courier* for use by the Voice of America. This was anchored off Greece from where its 150,000 watt MW signal, with an aerial held aloft by a helium balloon, could reach Moscow. Many of the programmes were received over short wave from the USA and then rebroadcast to the soviets on Medium Wave, which was available in almost every home in those days. The operation worked very well and didn't go unnoticed in other parts of the world.

World War II caused most of the European border blaster stations to close down. After the cessation of hostilities, only Radio Luxembourg reopened, after the intervention of Churchill. He felt the facility might be very useful if there was an east against west war in Europe. His vision was precise; as it became popular behind the Iron Curtain.

The UK wasn't the only country to limit broadcasting to a single state monopoly. The Benelux and the whole of Scandinavia too allowed only their state broadcasters on the air.

Offshore Broadcasting is lawful

Only sovereign nations are permitted to enact laws governing what can be done on their land. These laws also extend to a country's ships and aircraft, and in what are known as territorial waters. At the time in question, these waters extended three miles from the shore, based on how far a cannonball could be fired! Many countries have since increased their territorial waters, the UK increased to 12 miles in 1987.

Domestic laws apply to territorial waters, meaning that a radio transmission licence is needed for a radio ship anchored in the home or territorial waters. That law only applies to territorial waters while beyond their limits, the area becomes "international waters" often called the high seas. In theory, these are 'free' and ships are subject only to the laws and regulations of their flag state. The laws of many of the world's 184 countries are often vague and limited regards shipping and broadcasting, enabling a radio station to be lawfully established on vessels flagged in those countries.

The laws in the 1960s varied from country to country, but eventually new legislation to make offshore broadcasting unprofitable was dreamed up by the Council of Europe. This is a regional inter-governmental organisation, set up to harmonise democracy, human rights and the rule of law. The founders were the UK, France, Italy and the Scandinavian countries but it now includes Russia.

Secrecy of radio companies

Since the very earliest days of offshore radio, the ownership of the vessels used, the transmission equipment and of the radio station itself have invariably been invested in overseas companies, particularly where the 'veil of incorporation' is not easily lifted. The ships themselves were managed and operated by separate companies, with the only aspect being approachable being a small air time sales agency. Most offshore radio station's names existed only as an 'on the air' name, or station identification.

There are many reasons for domiciling the business in such odd jurisdictions: it gives some immunity from prosecution, it is a good way to protect assets and it avoids litigation in the case of copyright claims by music rights holders.

Radio Caroline was to use over two dozen such companies, including over twenty 'anstalts (trusts) domiciled in the central European country of Liechtenstein, usually run from Switzerland. An additional network of interlocking companies in such places as Panama, Honduras, the USA, Ireland and the Netherlands ensured the utmost privacy.

VHF FM

A curious oddity about *Radio Mercur* and two other Scandinavian offshore stations was their use of FM transmitters. While the VHF band was pioneered for broadcasting in the previous decade, it was still very rare in Europe. The BBC had some VHF-FM stations in the UK which eventually offered the three national services, however the choice of horizontal polarisation made reception difficult on car radios and portables. A horizontal antenna fixed at least 30 feet above ground level was recommended. Only those well-off could afford VHF / FM.

Even the BBC's experimentation with stereo (the first time it was used was on the Light Programme in 1960) did not seem to lure many new radio enthusiasts; if anything it drove some away as the pilot tone needed to switch receivers into the stereo mode made a hissing noise in many cases.

To achieve a strong signal, FM antennas need to be located as high as possible, which is somewhat impractical on board a ship! The advantage they do have is that by using suitable antenna, the power transmitted can be focussed towards the horizon. This often comes at the expense of the signal being stronger in some directions than others, but that too may be an advantage in some circumstances. It does avoid wasting signal in directions where it isn't needed.

Broadcast transmitters are not difficult to construct, the first one used by Radio Mercur was built by a Danish cycle repairer who was also a radio amateur.

Frequencies used for VHF / FM

Most countries of the world adopted FM frequencies only slowly, and many used only part of the internationally recognised FM Band, which was from 87.5 – 108 MHz. Many countries including the UK only used half the FM band for broadcasting, with the sector from 97 to 108 being used by the police, etc, for communications until the 1970s.

Some countries use a completely different band of frequencies for FM. The main countries using the lower band of frequencies from 65 to 74 are the former soviet / Russian satellite nations. These cover wider areas due to the lower frequencies, although they are narrower channels which gives slightly lower fidelity. Japan uses 76 to 90 MHz, as the higher frequencies are used for three extra TV channels.

Today the majority of countries have standardised on FM being from 87.5 to 108 MHz. Almost all countries use 200 kHz spacing, some have the final digits being odd digits, and some even.

Europe's first offshore commercial station

In Denmark a station was set up in the late 1950s emulating the VoA operation on the MV Courier. Radio Mercur covered the most populous parts of Denmark and later they transmitted a Swedish service too. This led to other broadcasters wanting to serve the lucrative Scandinavian market, where listeners had some of the highest disposable incomes in Europe. An ideal market for advertisers.

The first ship used for Radio Mercur was a very small vessel anchored in the Oresund, between Denmark and Sweden. She was the *MV Cheeta Mercur* and had a rotatable antenna enabling the signal to be focussed into particular areas, originally aiming them at Copenhagen.

There were newscasts in Danish and in English. Most programmes were recorded in Copenhagen and played out on board using professional Lyrec tape machines (locally built). Radio Mercur grew rapidly and made a fortune for its founders Peer Jansen and his uncle, Ib Fogh had to move to Spain as a tax exile.

They took over a huge old theatre in downtown Copenhagen and called it **Radio Mercur City**, after Radio City in New York. The venue featured the top artistes of the day including Cliff Richard. The theatre is still open today as the *Norrebro Teater* in the Ravensborggade, seating over 600 patrons, for whom it stages newly-written satire, comedy and music.

Radio Mercur – only broadcast on FM

Radio Mercur broadcast in English and Danish, but was soon to add an additional service for listeners in nearby Sweden who could also receive the ship's transmissions. The idea of broadcasting to two different countries in different languages on two quite separate frequencies was a business model that Radio Caroline would later undertake.

Skånes Radio Mercur

Radio Mercur began a second service in Swedish during hours that its Danish programmes were not being transmitted. The programmes of **Skånes Radio Mercur** were an initiative of Nils Svensson, a young radio enthusiast who had heard US radio during his trips to California.

The programmes that Nils ran were had more music than the regular Danish programmes which took the name *Dansk Radio Mercur*. The Swedish outlet became very popular as the state broadcaster limited music to just 60 minutes a day, meaning very little was actually played. *Skånes Radio Mercur* played non-stop music which was revolutionary in Scandinavia, so they quickly built up a large audience.

The Cheeta II

The original boat, the Cheeta Mercur, was soon pronounced to be too small for the job of transmitting two full time radio stations and so a second and larger vessel, the MV Cheeta II was acquired in January 1961. The Danish and Swedish services were then split completely; the ship transmitted both frequencies simultaneously.

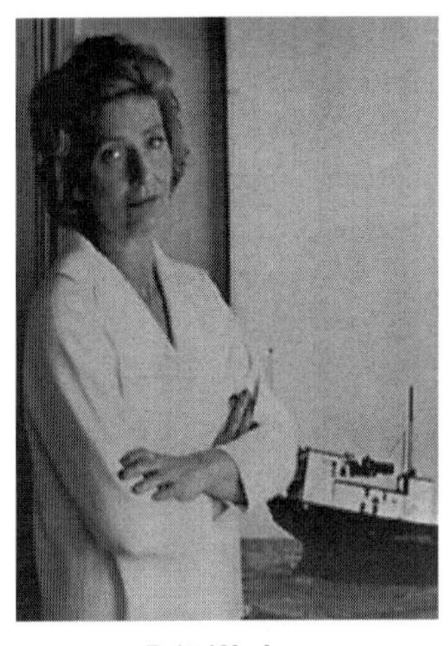

Britt Wadner

Later the original boat was restarted off another part of Denmark as Radio Mercur West. FM became very popular in Denmark and in southern Sweden, especially when Mercur began to transmit in FM stereo. They sold FM antennas in kit form to enable more distant listeners to hear the station.

By the end of the summer, Nils was tiring of his radio interest so he sold it to the sales manager of Skånes Radio Mercur, former beauty queen called Britt Wadner. She attracted a lot of interest in the station and a new outlet called Radio Syd.

When the Scandinavian governments introduced a new law in July 1962, DCR continued. The police needed to attend the 'Lucky Star' radio ship to investigate a murder on shore. They found that the ship had no papers, although the captain claimed it was registered in Guatamala, while flying a Lebanese flag.

An unregistered ship can be classed as “stateless” which is illegal in most countries, so the Lucky Star was taken into port to establish the facts. Newspaper reports of the ‘towing in’ action by the police were to have repercussions for Allan Crawford and Kitty Black’s project in England, although the British Government was unhappy about the development which potentially affected British shipping globally. The principle of International Waters being sacrosanct is vital to global trade and travel, although in 1990, they conveniently forgot this when introducing a new Broadcasting Act.

Action was taken against Radio Syd which also continued. The authorities could not stop the ship operating as it remained on the High Seas, so Mrs Wadner was sent to jail. This created some furore in southern Sweden and huge crowds of well-wishers besieged the courthouse and her home near Malmo. She was allowed to continue recording her own programmes for Radio Syd from her cell and gained lots of free publicity for the station.

The ship even played host to the Rolling Stones in 1964 and Brian Jones was especially interested. He hosted a programme and interviewed Mick Jagger and Keith Richards live on the air during a visit to the Cheeta II. When the tender took Mrs Wadner and The Stones ashore, they were greeted by several hundred fans; normally only a dozen or so would be waiting for DJ autographs.

Radio Syd’s ship, the Cheeta II was due to enter the Radio Caroline story quite dramatically in 1966. (Page 142)

Brian Jones of the Rolling Stones at the Radio Syd controls

The first steps of Radio Caroline
The first tentative steps to set up what was to become Radio Caroline were taken in early 1960 when New Zealand born music publisher Allan Crawford decided to leave the Australian company *Southern Music Group* and set up his own music publishing business, *Merit Music*, in London.

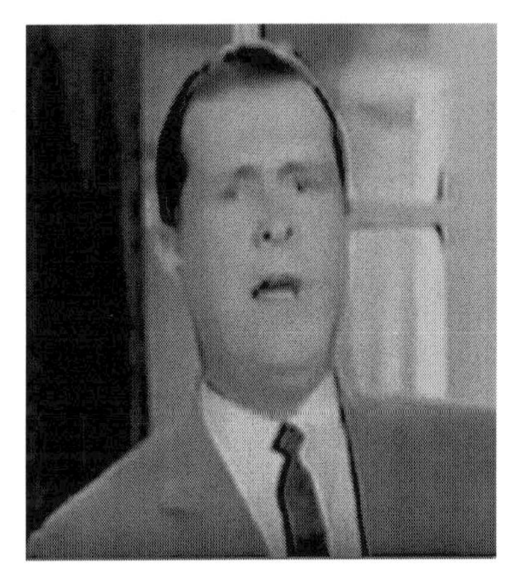

Allan Crawford

Crawford heard that Radio Luxembourg had gone into a joint venture with some of the large music publishers which would favour their own songs. The music company they had set up was called *Louvigny Music*, after the building in Luxembourg from where their English programmes were broadcast.

This incensed Allan Crawford as it would squeeze out independents such as he, so he requested a meeting with the BBC to discuss the problem. The senior BBC managers he met with didn't want to be involved in any further battles with radio Luxembourg (they had been fighting the station from the Grand Duchy since it began in the 1930s) but they seemed to think that it might help them if they could somehow discredit the idea of commercial radio. The BBC executives suggested to Crawford that he told the Pilkington Committee about the music publishing business of Radio Luxembourg.

Allan Crawford claims that this suggestion from the executives at the BBC was the very point that the idea for an offshore radio station off the UK was born in his head.

The BBC have long had a policy of getting involved in every kind of broadcasting possible, which they continue with today. It appears to be simply 'empire building', making their areas of interest as all-enveloping as possible. Of course, the more developments that they are involved in, the larger their net must become and all at the publics expense of course.

The BBC were very aware of developments in radio. They deployed two of their retired engineers to other offshore ventures to observe. These 'advisers' took on consultancy roles for Radio Veronica and for two embryonic projects set to broadcast to the UK, GBOK and GBLN.

Despite financial backing and the involvement of a major electronics company, neither UK station began broadcasting. Their plans were divulged to the authorities (GPO and various shipping regulators) who 'nipped them in the bud' stopping both ships in Scotland and later a lightship berthed at Sheerness.

The Pilkington Committee had been instructed to consider the idea of commercial radio, after intense pressure from the Pye Group. There were already over a hundred small companies throughout the UK formed to bid for commercial radio licences. Their final report and recommendations in 1962 were roundly condemned by all and sundry. People from both ends of the political spectrum denounced the recommendations.

Many of these were to be based in small towns throughout the UK; some already had low power MW transmitters installed. These had been installed as 'Group H' by the BBC during the war in case of invaded forces neutralised the main BBC stations but they had since been abandoned. The same engineers who designed that wartime plan for emergency radio were advising Pye and other prospective operators on a network of local commercial stations.

Even the communist paper the Daily Worker and the Daily Mirror, also pretty left wing, described Pilkington's denouncement of commercial radio as a "missed opportunity". The right wing Daily Telegraph said "This amazing document is motivated by a haughty conviction that anything which is popular must be bad", despite the fact that it probably had a higher percentage of readers who would have agreed with the report than any other newspaper.

Crawford had made a point of meeting with several broadcasters, the BBC and Radio Luxembourg of course as they were the two sources that most British listeners turned to for radio entertainment. He had also met two of the staff from *Ross Radio Productions Ltd*, a company which recorded programmes for Radio Luxembourg. They had a studio further along Dean Street from Crawford in Royalty House, later to become a secret Radio Caroline office.

Radio Veronica

Ross Radio had also been involved for a while with a Dutch offshore radio ship, Radio Veronica. It could be heard along the North Sea coast and it proved to be one of the catalysts of the Radio Caroline project. One that was to feature again several times in the life of station. Its name came from *Vrije Radio Omroep Nederlands*, VRON, which was shortened to Radio Veronica.

Three brothers, Dirk, Bull and Jaap Verweij, who had a textile factory in Hilversum had been early VRON investors. They took over the entire operation and brought in a former BBC engineer, Alfred N. Thomas, to help improve the transmitters and antenna. He later designed the Radio Caroline installation on its first ship. 'ANT' as he was known in the BBC was a Welshman with a long pedigree at the Corporation and had been involved in designing their high power MW regional stations.

ANT was brilliant at his job but could be difficult to work for and did not suffer fools gladly. Both ANT and another former BBC transmitter engineer, John H. Gilman, later mysteriously took up positions at the first British offshore projects that eventually became Radio Caroline.

Radio Veronica became very successful and, in 1964, bought a larger ship, the Norderney, which operated at sea until the end of August 1974, when the Dutch Government had to legislate due to the proliferation of radio ships on her coast. By then, Radio Veronica was making millions of guilders every year. The Norderney has been operating as a café in Amsterdam for some years now, while the radio station's name lives on as a channel aimed at middle aged men. Another station in the Talpa Media group is Radio 538, named after Veronica' last MW wavelength.

CNBC

Before it became such a huge success in the Netherlands, Radio Veronica pioneered offshore broadcasting to England. Late in 1960 a trio of British announcers were hired to make programmes in English for several hours a day. The DJ team was led by a Canadian DJ called Doug Stanley who had worked at the British Forces Network. He was assisted by fellow Canadian John Michael, now a leading TV chat show host in Canada, and well-known British DJ Paul Hollingdale, who has since worked for most of the biggest radio stations in the UK.

Many of the CNBC programmes were produced in Portland Place, just across the road from the BBC by Ross Radio Productions, although their main base was in Royalty House in Soho, close to where Crawford ran his music publishing business. The station styled itself as "Your Friendly host on the Dutch Coast".

The Ross Radio Productions directors were Monty Bailey-Watson and John Whitney CBE, who helped to launch the *Local Radio Association* pressure group in the1960s. Whitney's main partner at the LRA was John Gorst, who had been advertising manager at Pye and who later was elected an MP. He was very keen to promote the local radio plans and set up the Local Radio Association.

After a period writing scripts for TV, John Whitney joined the board of *Capital Radio* and was later recruited to join the IBA, the UK radio industry's regulator where he was Director General for seven years. In 2008 John was awarded the CBE for his services to the radio broadcast industry.

Monty Bailey-Watson was a Scouser, from the Crosby area of Liverpool and well connected to the Mersey Beat, including the Beatles and Brian Epstein. Their company made programmes for several months and broadcast them as CNBC (Commercial Neutral Broadcasting Company). Coverage from the Radio Veronica transmitter off the Dutch coast was not strong enough to win many listeners in the UK.

The trio of British DJs who hosted programmes on CNBC did bring about some big changes to Radio Veronica and were partly responsible for training some of their staff and the Dutch station becoming such a success later.

Allan Crawford met with John Whitney and his broadcasters Doug Stanley and Paul Hollingdale several time. He also visited Veronica's converted lightship, at its anchorage a few miles fromthe Dutch coast. Radio Veronica offered Allan Crawford a half share in their operation but he thought that its transmitter was too under-powered to attract an audience in the UK. He also felt that the price of £60,000 was too high and was sure he could assemble his own offshore radio ship much more cheaply and resolved to do so.

CBC Plays Ltd

Crawford was introduced to a theatrical agent called Dorothy Black, a fellow colonial, an accomplished pianist and a successful theatrical agent. "Kitty Black" as she was known throughout the industry was also a freelance French translator with a wide network of acquaintances in London and Paris in the theatre and the music business.

Among her friends were Vivian Leigh, John Gielgud, Richard Burton, Noel Coward and Margaret Rutherford. She regularly translated plays into English and ran the Lyric Theatre at Hammersmith. Shortly after they met, Allan Crawford and Kitty became founding board members of the first legal company of the Radio Caroline project. The company was called CBC (Plays) Limited; the name's originals and meaning is now forgotten, though it may have been formed from *Commercial Broadcasting Company* and is very similar to the Ross Radio company's CNBC subsidiary.

Dorothy 'Kitty' Black

The word "plays" could be taken as a link to Kitty Black's theatrical work, though some suspect that it refers Crawford's work of obtaining radio plays for his music material. The myths behind the *CBC Plays* name is typical of the 'cloak and dagger' methods used throughout the Radio Caroline story. There seems to have been deliberate shrouding of facts and obfuscation of the truth regarding many aspects. This is undoubtedly due partly to the possibilities of tax free income offered by operating an offshore radio station and to avoid the likely waspish response of the authorities and Establishment.

Kitty Black got involved with the Verweij brothers who ran Radio Veronica and who urgently needed extra funding. The Dutch authorities were actively discouraging advertisers and the station had problems with a rogue engineer who had skipped with a large amount of money he had been given to buy a larger transmitter in the USA.

The declared object of the CBC (Plays) company to the register of Companies in 1961 was "to launch an offshore radio station broadcasting to the UK." The UK had not been exposed to offshore radio at that time and few will have understood what it meant, or how it was to revolutionise radio in the UK over the next decade.

CBC (Plays) Ltd obtained legal advice on offshore operations from a Queens Counsel. This is a vital precursor to taking any new action that might be on the edge of being illegal, or unlawful. The formal legal advice in that document became invaluable in the next few years when it was used to persuade investors to finance the venture and the Bank of England to permit export of the funds.

An interlocking network of companies was created to operate the offshore radio station. The web of offshore companies, such as the *Atlantic Services Anstalt* of Liechtenstein and *Hanacon* of Panama, were to set up to protect the huge profits expected from offshore radio and as a cloak for the beneficial owners to hide behind. This complex set-up that had to be explained to each of the investors in turn; Kitty Black was concerned that any of them could have taken their ideas which had been so carefully planned and begin a venture of their own.

Permission was obtained by CBC Plays Ltd from the Bank of England to send its capital to a Liechtenstein ‘anstalt’ (a trust company). This was another vital step because currency restrictions still applied; it was illegal to take more than £25 out of the UK without permission. The agreement with the Bank of England, arranged by the Rothschilds, was to prove very useful and one of the company’s most valuable assets.

Two further figures were recruited first; they were broadcast engineers who were vital to launching any offshore radio station. They were both former BBC engineers, Arthur N. Thomas and John H. Gilman. Since retirement from the BBC and Marconi, both had been very active as consultants to a variety of projects, including Radio Veronica.

They advised on the aborted installation of equipment into two ships on behalf of stations that had been ‘still-born’ and were also engaged by Pye for their Irish radio project, and other work. Both were involved in transmission and had worked closely with Sir Hugh Carlton Greene, the Director General of the BBC on overseas projects. All BBC employees had to be security cleared by MI5 and it’s suspected that, after retirement, they continued their association with the BBC, who certainly had a mole in the world of offshore radio. Gilman was appointed as Head of Engineering at Radio Caroline after he and Thomas had worked on several other offshore projects.

C. B. C. (Plays) Ltd.

47, Dean Street, London, W.1

4. Bon Jour Mi Amigo!

While the CNBC experiment was taking on the Borkum Riff, another ship began broadcasting, that was eventually to see her become one of the most iconic Radio Caroline ships of all. The MV Bon Jour had been bought by the *Atlantic Services Anstalt* in Liechtenstain and the work to convert her to a floating radio station was done in Germany, then in Denmark and in Sweden as well as in Finland!

The architects of the project were a group of Texan businessmen: Bob Thompson, Clint Murchison and Gordon McLendon who owned several radio stations and had previously tried to broadcast to Great Britain from Ireland. They were keen to broadcast to any lucrative area of Europe and, in Jack Kotschak, they had a local movie buff who was willing to front such a venture.

An agreement was made with General Somosa, chief of staff of the Nicaraguan army, to register the ship. The Swedes put pressure on the Nicaraguans who withdrew the flag, so the ship was switched to the Panamanian flag and renamed the Magda Maria.

She boasted a pair of 10 kilowatt transmitters and no expense was spared in the design of the studio installation. Leading American radio engineer, John Mullaney, was engaged who developed an electrically short antenna that could be accommodated on a ship.

Instead of needing two masts hundreds of metres high, Mullaney's patented (and still 'top secret') design could operate with only one mast of 40 metres high and four large tuning boxes (see picture) of coils and capacitors. This device was difficult to master and needed proprietary knowledge to function really well. When it was properly installed, the Mullaney antenna allowed the station to use a very low frequency signal of 602 kHz, which gave very wide coverage even with modest power.

Sadly the Radio Caroline's engineers never got to grips with the system and opted for a much less efficient unipole.

The 602 frequency is thought to have been chosen to emulate the success of McLendon's KILT station in Houston, Texas, which was on almost the same frequency.

It took the Radio Nord team almost 18 months to get their radio station operational. The station was widely heard for over a year before the Swedish and Danish governments introduced new legislation that precluded obtaining supplies locally, or their countrymen advertising on offshore stations.

Allan Crawford and Kitty Black had by now joined forces with Major Oliver Smedley and were still working on their preparations to launch an offshore radio station to bring commercial radio to UK listeners. They had recruited theatrical supplier John Delaney as an investor and were planning to use another former light ship. The vessel was condemned by the Scottish coastguards as being totally unseaworthy.

One of Crawford's old chums from Australia arrived in London at just the right time; Ian Davidson had come to Europe and was planning to look for radio work. Crawford asked him to go to Sweden for him and check out the Radio Nord operation. Ian visited the Radio Nord offices and was very impressed by the calibre of their team and the quality of the broadcast-standard professional equipment they had installed. He reported back favourably to Crawford who flew to Sweden to try and buy the ship, which stopped broadcasting just weeks before the legislation came into force.

Crawford arrived just too late, as the ship's owners had sent her from the Baltic in case the Swedes seized the ship; they didn't want to risk losing their investment! They sent her to Spain for a survey and overhaul. During that summer of 1962, the ship was repainted and given yet another name, the Mi Amigo. The Texan owners charged their marine agent (Captain de Jong of Wijsmullers) with finding a buyer.

Radio Nord, at sea off Sweden

Magda Maria becomes Mi Amigo
The owners of the former Radio Nord ship already had one potential buyer lined up in Allan Crawford, who had sent Ian Davidson to visit her off the Swedish coast. Their shipping agent thought that the ship might also be of interest to Radio Veronica, the Dutch station which was finally becoming a commercial success and wanted to increase its power. It might also be interested in buying a newer ship as the Borkum Riff was quite compact and uncomfortable for the crew.

Before being offered to prospective buyers, it was decided to take the Magda Maria to be drydocked. The safest place that they could sail to with her two transmitters and an aerial mast was El Ferrol in Spain. While here she was given a new name, the *Mi Amigo*, which is Spanish for *My Friend*. This was to be her name for the next seventeen years, in a career more exciting than any other radio ship.

Radio Caroline did not yet exist, in anyone's mind, but by September, the newly painted and refurbished Mi Amigo was ready for action and, with a Polish and Dutch crew in command, delivered to the Thames estuary where she anchored in the Barrow Deep. The purpose of the visit was to prove her efficiency and so the ship secretly conducted various tests as Radio LN. The ship was under constant scrutiny of various arms of the British authorities.

The tests were done to impress two potential buyers who were keen to broadcast to listeners in England. The first group of buyers were the operators of the Dutch station Radio Veronica, the Verweij brothers, whose lightship off the Dutch coast with its low power transmitter was unable to get a decent signal into London. This had been proved with the CBC tests earlier. The Verweijs believed that, with a powerful station near London, they would be able to persuade the people at Ross Radio in London to pay more for the airtime.

The other buyer who had expressed a strong interest was Allan Crawford. Sadly, just before she moved to the Thames estuary, Danish police took action against another ship, a Radio Mercur ship, the MV Lucky Star. The police went to question a crewman about an offence on land and while there they saw problems with the ship's registration papers. They brought the ship into port as it would otherwise be under-manned. The finer details weren't widely known but the story ran in the UK press that a Danish pirate ship had been arrested and dragged into port! The British authorities were very annoyed as this 'extra territorial waters' action by the Danes could set an international precedent, which could affect British shipping anywhere.

The action in Denmark also spooked some *CBC Plays Ltd* investors who were still reeling from adverse press coverage of the reports of the Pilkington Committee who had just informed the British Parliament that "there is no demand for commercial radio in the UK." Crawford, Black and their CBC (Plays) Ltd company found themselves unable to complete the purchase of the Mi Amigo.

The Verweij brothers and Radio Veronica's shipping agent were invited over to England for a demonstration. The ship put a good signal into London according to Bull Verweij. As well as attending meetings with the owner's representative, Bill Weaver, at the Mayfair Hotel in London, Bull and his party sailed out to the Magda Maria via Brightlingsea, a small port on the Essex coast that was later to be very popular with trips to various radio ships.

While anchored off Brightlingsea for a couple of weeks, the ship drew quite a bit of interest. Some of the radio ship's Polish crew members mutinied at one stage and her Dutch captain set sail to Dutch waters. Whitehall was well aware of the ship's presence and purpose, although no action could be taken as, although she was in the Thames estuary, she remained safely in international waters.

With two potential buyers interested, the Mi Amigo's owners had placed a high price on the ship and its cargo of $450,000. Neither of the potential buyers seemed to be able to produce the necessary funds. Veronica didn't take the bait even when the ship was moved to their current anchorage off Scheveningen so she sailed to Ostend in Belgium.

Before she became the Mi Amigo

Newspaper reports in Belgium said that the Magda Maria was to replace the *MV Uilenspiegel*, a Flemish radio ship proved groundless, as did newspaper stories that she would be used for TV transmissions. The press stories all quoted Bill Weaver and Captain De Jong, who were the agents of another Liechtenstein company *Deco Anstalt* and who had selling rights to her.

Georges De Caluwé had operated a religious radio station in Antwerp intermittently for many years and had recently put it on a ship and anchored her near Zeebrugge.

Radio Uilenspiegel had the misfortune to run aground just days after 72 year old Georges was admitted to hospital and the project ground to a halt. The ship remained stuck hard aground on the beach at Cadzand for about ten years before the Belgian military blew it up in the 1970s.

Crawford pleaded with the Mi Amigo's American owners to come to an arrangement over leasing the ship instead of an outright sale. They hoped to sell her to the CIA for broadcasts to Cuba however, so in January 1963 the ship left Ostend for Brest in France and, after some modifications, set course for Galveston in Texas.

Among the major investors who had scaled back their investment into Crawford's radio ship venture in the autumn on 1962 were C.O. Stanley, the Chairman of Pye and William Harvey, the head of the British Print Corporation. Harvey had access to serious funds and various BPC subsidiaries held contracts to print many publications, including the Sunday Times magazine, Radio Times and Queen magazine. Harvey was also involved in several multi-million corporate takeovers in the early sixties, some of which proved almost as controversial as did MP Robert Maxwell's scandalous stewardship of the same company in the eighties. In 1963 he was literally 'awash with cash" and pouring money into several projects.

Other investors in the project included Mr RJ Deterding whose grandfather had founded the giant Shell Oil company and Mr CC Lomax, a name at Lloyds and whose family company was a leading publisher of technical journals.

Some of Atlanta's investors had been concerned that the British government might use some old legislation, known as 'hovering acts', designed to prevent ships waiting just outside territorial waters. These laws had been introduced in the 19th century to combat the once prevalent smuggling or 'running' business. Ships would wait just beyond British territorial waters, immune from action from the UK, so anti-hovering acts had been introduced. The 'QWC's Opinion' assured them that those laws had been repealed and posed no danger.

Among those that Crawford spoke to at the end of 1962 was Ronan O'Rahilly who was intrigued that Crawford had found a ready-made ship for the project, a method to get the funds out of the UK and had a legal opinion saying the project was lawful. He had heard about the idea from an Irish girl called Nicky Rogers who he had met at a party. She had seen the VoA ship The Courier at Rhodes in Greece, so the concept was not exactly new to him and he was keen to hear more.

RONAN O'RAHILLY

In 1961 another key participant in the launch and operation of Radio Caroline, Ronan O'Rahilly, arrived in London. His English born father, Aodagan, was an accomplished engineer who had married an American lady called Marion O'Connor. Aodagan's father Michael was a staunch Republican who died after a battle with British troops at the GPO building in Dublin during the 1916 Easter uprising. He was one of the founders of the Irish Volunteers, a predecessor of the IRA, and Keats wrote a poem about him, The O'Rahilly.

Ronan was one of five children; his brother Eoin and sisters Nuala, Roisin and Iseult. Always hyperactive, Ronan says that he found his school days tedious and that he yearned to live in London, the centre of the western universe. His father indulged him and Ronan arrived in London with a hundred pounds to make something of his life.

Ronan spent some time studying the 'method' technique of acting at the Stanislavsky studio which charged students £5 a week for a couple of hours tuition. Ronan had a circle of friends who decided they could duplicate this and they launched their own acting workshop. They called themselves Studio 61 and met in a rented room above a pub off Regent Street in London's West End for a short time.

In addition to the acting workshop, Ronan was increasingly active in music, promoting live acts in clubs and pubs. He would book the premises and artists, advertise the night; often by word of mouth among his expanding circle of friends, which was sufficient to attract a sizeable crowd. It could be a very lucrative business. Ronan would promote certain artistes at several venues, but usually at the Scene Club, in Ham Yard, just behind Piccadilly Circus.

Ronan sometimes stepped in to look after the place for its owner, Lionel Blake. Soon this quiet little jazz club became the hot focus of the mod world. Things really took off after they placed an advert containing admission vouchers in Record Mirror, promising the latest RnB records, played by DJ Guy Stevens. He played lots of organ instrumentals (especially those by Jimmy Smith) and lots of soul and Motown music, which had not yet taken off in the UK.

DJ Guy saw everything and knew everyone, sat in his booth in the wall at the bottom of the stairs (The Scene was in a basement) and he later ran the London office of the Sue record label. Guy admired the work of a bright young Irish lady who was then involved with a group at the top of the charts and suggested that Ronan contact her. He was looking for help with his music activities and found Oonagh in the *La Discotheque* club, where Ronan also worked, in the casino downstairs.

Ronan's PA, Oonagh Huggard

Oonagh had been in the music business for some time and was a Kerry girl, who'd gone to school in Dun Laoghaire, near Dublin. Being about the same age and Irish she and Ronan got on well. Oonagh was to play a key role in Ronan's business dealings and became his personal assistant and trusted confidant for over fifteen years.

"I lived in Thayer Street in Marylebone when they brought in parking meters, and I had nowhere to park, so we agreed that Ronan would drive my car during the week, dropping me off at home and I had it at weekends" recalls Oonagh. "We both enjoyed the same music so I accompanied Ronan to gigs, signed the artists, paid their expenses and generally administered their affairs, Administration wasn't Ronan's strongest point."

She and Ronan promoted live music nights at various venues featuring many as yet unknown artists such as Alexis Korner and Ginger Baker. Ronan was instrumental in The Animals moving down to London and also helped the Rolling Stones. They were being managed by Ronan's close pal, Giorgio Gomelski, who ran the Crawdaddy Club. The Stones were regulars at The Scene club off Windmill Street where Ronan and Oonagh ran weekly blues music nights. It was at the a weekly mod nights they ran, that the Stones polished their early performances.

"Ronan always had new ideas and could envisage things that were beyond the ken of most people," says Oonagh. "He wasn't a fantasist, far from it; his ideas were usually brilliant and he never wasted any time in making things happen. He would have done everything he did without my involvement, though without me he would have got ripped off a lot more. Despite being smart, he was a sucker for talent and never realised that he was being taken for a ride by musicians; very smart in business but very soft with anyone who could convince him they were talented, that was Ronan."

Georgie Fame

"We discovered many new groups and put them on at the Scene Club," Oonagh remembers. "They took Ronan's help, his backing and money, then signed up with bigger companies, once they were on their way. Many went off into the sunset without a word of thanks."

One artist often mentioned in Caroline's formation is Georgie Fame, who Oonagh spotted and brought to Ronan's attention. "Georgie was an absolute sweetie, who I found at the Flamingo Club. When he signed to Rick Gunnell's agency, Georgie insisted that Ronan should be part of the deal," recalls Oonagh.

The acting workshop had been one of Ronan's early ideas that became a cooperative. Called *Studio 61*, it specialised in 'method acting.' The core group was four strong and also included future Hollywood script writer, Michael Joseph, avid photographer Christopher Moore and 'Nicky' Henty-Dodd, whose double-barrelled surname was quite helpful when they were hustling and wheeler-dealing.

Nicky's full name was Cyril Nicholas Henty-Dodd, unusual for a Lancashire lad, although his family were quite well-to-do, owning a mill producing book-binding. His family always used their middle names so he was known as 'Nicky'. After Shrewsbury School he spent some time at Brighton College, but left with only one O-Level. He eventually had a five-year career in the RAF, some of it shrouded in secrecy. He made his broadcasting debut with a British Forces radio station in Iraq.

Nicky's RAF experience in reconnaissance and photography helped him get a job when he was discharged aged 23. Cameras and fashion were booming but he felt more drawn to the stage and even got a small speaking part in a play on ITV. He tried dozens of jobs and even became a door to door salesman, a job which he believes helped him become a radio salesman and a TV chat show host in later life.

"Charm and chat is vital when you are a salesman," 'Nicky' explains. "A bit of flattery and many women will believe anything. Always say to the older ladies the older ladies 'Hello Miss, may I see your mother?' It works every time, like a charm!" The acting project was under-capitalised, poorly managed and soon folded. Christopher Moore signed onto a cruise ship as a host while Nicky went to work in an estate agency.

Merit House

Ronan continued in music promotion. While hustling a record deal for one of Rick Gunnel's artists, Ronan visited Merit House, the Soho office of Allan Crawford's various record labels.

Ever on the lookout for pioneering investors, Allan Crawford told Ronan O'Rahilly about his plan to start an offshore radio station. Ronan responded that his father was involved in shipping in the Irish Sea and suggested that he might be interested in helping Crawford. A meeting was arranged with Ronan's father, Aodogán, at the family home, Moreen, a large country house near Clondalkin, Dublin. Crawford handed out copies of Project Atlanta's legal advice and the business plan, complete with all the financial projections.

Aodogán O'Rahilly wasn't in a position to invest money in the project but offered the use of a small port called Greenore that he had access to. Developed by British Railways in the 1800s, it was on the Cooley peninsular but had only an inadequate railway line to Dundalk. Unsuitable for modern travel, the whole site was for sale. Ronan's father thought that parts of it might suit one of his businesses, making plasterboard which he supplied to the UK. Always happy to indulge his children, Aodogán agreed to let them use it for fitting out the radio ship.

Greenore was the ideal location for the radio pioneers as the original plan was to locate the ship a few miles away, by the Isle of Man, from where transmissions could reach the industrial heartlands of northern England as well as Ireland. A key Atlanta backer, C.O. Stanley, had his family home and some businesses in Ireland too.

Crawford visited the Isle of Man formed a relationship with an electrical retailer called Harry Colebourn. As well as developing TV reception in the Island, Harry was rising to the top of the political tree in Tynwald, the Island's parliament, as a member of the House of Keys. The Island had long yearned for its own radio station and appointed Harry as chairman of a committee to press for a licence, which the UK controlled. Colebourn promised that he would bring an offshore radio ship to the Island if there were to be any further delays; he even imported his own MW transmitter to set up a station in Douglas.

In the first half of 1963 Allan Crawford continued to recruit further investors to fund the offshore radio project. The Bank of England were now dragging their feet over the transfer of the funds to foreign accounts to pay for the ship, the Mi Amigo, which was now berthed in

Belgium. Despite Crawford appealing to the courts and up to cabinet level, their capital remained stuck in the banking system. The ship's owners grew tired of waiting and so in early 1963 they ordered the Mi Amigo back to the USA where they hoped to sell it to the CIA for broadcasts to Cuba. By Easter 1963 she was tied up at Pier 37 in Galveston, where a lot of the radio equipment was removed and put in store at KILT, a Gordon McLendon station in nearby Houston. This was a major setback for Crawford and O'Rahilly's project.

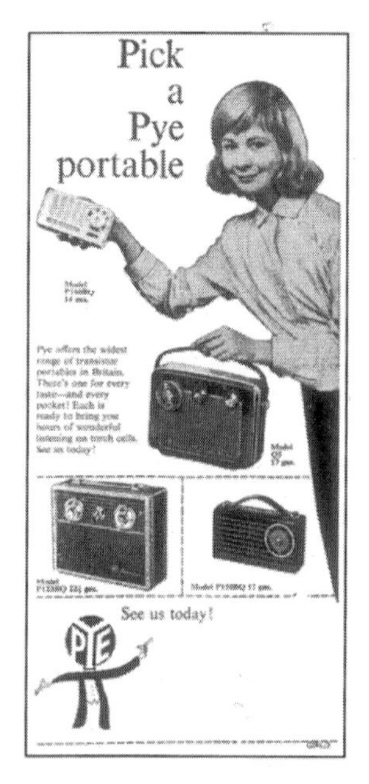

Success from a little radio

For the first forty years of broadcasting the only way to hear transmissions was a large and quite cumbersome receiver, often called 'a set" (it was indeed a set of different circuits, valves and other components). These were quite costly and shackled the listener to a mains power connection, unless one wanted to drag around bulky accumulators.

The lack of portability of radio receivers was changed by the invention of the transistor, a small solid-state device that meant radio receivers finally could be miniaturised. Duties and taxes in post-war Britain were still prohibitively high and the first all-British transistorised portable was made by PAM, which was a subsidiary of Pye. It was hardly miniaturised as the need for portability had not yet been pursued and sales were poor.

Transistorised radios had much lower power consumption demands. This enabled small dry cells of zinc-carbon to be used to provide the current. Ever Ready launched its popular PP series in the late 1950s, but both they and those first transistor radios were still expensive.

By the turn of 1960, the cost of mass production of the transistors themselves was tumbling. A claim was made in a radio trade paper at the time that, if the cost reductions of transistors continued to follow the downward spiral for another three years, the devices would soon be cheaper than buying hardcore!

Solid state integration, encapsulation and ever-cheaper resources has indeed meant that, item for item, the cost of transistors on chips has now surpassed the cost of hardcore – unit costs are miniscule, almost incalculable. The chips in the average smartphone, with its myriad of uses and mind-boggling processing power, cost just a couple of pounds. New technology means these prices are still falling.

The portable radio

As the decade dawned, Pye had begun to lose their lead in the market for small portable radios. Some manufacturers were still building 'portable' radios with low voltage valves inside them and even some car radios too still relied on valve technology. Needless to say, they were invariably expensive and not of wide appeal.
A four-man company in West London, Tellux, that normally made sun lamps, changed the radio landscape and made it ideal for the success of Radio Caroline. They acquired the UK distribution rights for Sony and launched the TR620 portable radio on an unsuspecting British public.

This tiny personal radio had a built-in loudspeaker, a leather carrying case, and an earpiece. It was completely self- contained, did not require a connection to an aerial or any mains power, so could be easily carried around.

SonyTR620

The most eye-catching thing about the Sony TR620 was not its range of colour schemes but the size. Measuring only 3½ by 2 inches, it could be popped into a jacket pocket or a handbag and so instantly became a true pocket radio. Those first models were not cheap; just under £20, which was almost a month's wages for most people. They were however the 'hot' new item that any self-respecting teenager wanted as they were somehow a link, however remote, with the other main topic of the day - the space race.

The transistor radio had a huge impact on the development of radio in a few years. The receiver went from being something that the family sat around in the evening to hear the latest variety shows, to a personal entertainment and information channel. To many listeners, their radio and the voices on their favourite station were to become a close friend.

One cannot over-state the importance of the portable radio to the success of Caroline. The station certainly didn't; they used transistor-toting young listeners in promotion and even fuelled the fire of its own success by selling radios 'on the air' with a series of commercials.

The pocket transistor radio was a highly personal item, it linked the owner with style and the hottest concepts, it was somehow a link to the trendiest strides being made. It looked good, it sounded great – the only problem was, there wasn't a great deal to listen to on it.

The Sony portable radio tuned the medium wave band, which had over a hundred channels – space for fifty radio stations – but the BBC offered only three programmes. The Home Service could be heard on half a dozen of these channels, but it was largely the same programme on all frequencies, peppered with a few regional news bulletins.

After dark however the band came alive with dozens of stations audible, thanks to the effect of 'sky wave'. Stations from all over Europe and even further afield could be heard, including the popular Radio Luxembourg on 208 metres. This is where most British teenagers heard the latest music, thanks to the station's programming policy. It offered sponsored programmes of 15 or 30 minute duration, which were mostly taken up by the major record labels.

The first satellites

Communications satellites were also a hot topic. No longer simply a vision of Arthur C Clarke (he first proposed the idea as long ago as 1945 in an amateur radio magazine), satellites were now a reality and carrying other traffic between the Britain and the USA as well as occasional TV pictures. It was only a few years since man had ventured into space and the whole concept of communications and a possible explosion of media was a hot topic of the day.

The Russians and Americans had been vying to put the first man into space, which happened in 1961, with cosmonaut Yuri Gagarin. Two months later President John F Kennedy proposed to Congress that "the USA should commit itself to achieving the goal, before this decade is out, of landing a man on the Moon and returning him safely to Earth."

Telstar

In 1962 the first live television pictures were sent by satellite, a huge step forward to making the world a global village, made possible by Telstar. This was a significant development for modern life and broadcasting, inspiring record producer Joe Meek to write and perform the first science fiction influenced hit. *Telstar* was played on a clavioline with some ethereal backing vocals; it hit the number one spot in the record sales charts late that year and went on to sell five million copies! Sadly, a claim of plagiarism blocked the royalties; the case wasn't settled until just three weeks after Joe's death. Telstar was on the charts in the UK for the next six months (and the first US chart topper by a British group). It was typical of the "anything is possible" thoughts now being suggested.

Allan Crawford continued trying to raise the money for his 'Atlanta' offshore radio project as 1963 progressed. He was also assembling a suitable team. A chance meeting with a contact from home led to him hiring Ken Evans, who had heaps of radio experience in Sydney. Evans was taken on to oversee the musical output of the station and he set about engaging a team of broadcasters for Atlanta.

Among those hired were another former colleague from Crawford's days in Australia, Tony Withers. He had a really deep voice and later became better known as Tony Windsor, or TW. Colin Nicol and Bryan Vaughan were two more Australians hired for the project, whose name was now referred to as Project Atlanta, rather than CBC Plays. Colin was taken on in late September 1963 by Ken Evans after a chance meeting in a pub where Colin was working. Offshore radio was to hire a lot of staff in pubs over the next few years!

In June 1963 Allan Crawford sent Ronan O'Rahilly over to Texas to try and reopen the discussions to buy the Mi Amigo and return it to Europe. He visited the ship in Galveston and the owners in Houston. By then the ships two transmitters had been removed from the ship and were being refurbished in Dallas by their original manufacturer, Continental Electronics.

Several high voltage components such an coils and connectors were made of copper and had corroded badly in the damp, salt-laden atmosphere found at sea. Continental experimented with some new bronze-based materials to slow down the corrosion.

They had some major clients who operated their equipment near the sea. Many high-power American stations actually build their antenna masts over sea water as, being a good conductor, it makes for a more efficient radiator. Continental's biggest client was the US Navy, for whom they also made super-power transmitters, many of them in the megawatt range.

While in Houston, Ronan met with Bill Weaver, the manager of KILT, one of McLendon's stations. Weaver was in charge of the ship so, together with chief engineer, Bill Cook, they went down to Galveston to see her. The Mi Amigo by now had only a small security team but Texans still had hopes of selling her to the CIA for use off Cuba. They showed some interest in new offers being made by Mr O'Rahilly and indulged him by answering the thousand and one questions that Ronan had about radio, transmitters, ships and studios.

A key adviser that Ronan met in Houston was Captain de Jong Lanau, from Wijsmuller's ship management section. He came from a long line of sailors and had worked in rescue and salvage operation in Scotland during the war. Wijsmullers had hundreds of mariners all over the world and there was little that he didn't know about ships. Sensing that the Mi Amigo might not be available and had lost a lot of the radio equipment, O'Rahilly asked whether De Jong could help find another ship in Europe. He said they could and help him to equip it. They would provide a crew, reducing the pressures on any new embryonic team.

Not long after Ronan flew back to London, Allan Crawford decided to visit Texas himself and took along a consultant radio engineer who inspected the Mi Amigo in great detail. This engineer was A N Thomas, who had previously worked for the BBC and then as a consultant to every other offshore radio project that had tried to broadcast to the UK. He had a long track record with the BBC going back to the thirties and had been involved in seizing the powerful German Wehrmacht stations at the end of World War II as well as being involved in a project to transmit to Europe from two radio ships near Heligoland.

On their return from Texas, Allan Crawford made an offer to the ship's owners to lease the vessel and her radio equipment. Having worked on the project for a couple of years now and with music publishing matters to manage, Crawford was not in a rush, which infuriated Ronan and encouraged him to see if he could raise the money himself.

Crawford was confident of getting a lease on the ship and new equipment. With the help of Ken Evans he continued building his team. One of their first appointments was Colin Nicol, who had just arrived from Australia with six years broadcast experience already under his belt, Colin busied himself with building a recording studio in Crawford's office at the top of Merit House. He was soon joined by fellow Australian Bryan Vaughan, a descendant of Sir Walter Scott

In August 1963 Crawford finally registered the project as a British limited company called *Project Atlanta Ltd*. The memorandum for the company's incorporation was presented to investors bound inside a turquoise green folder. The objects of the company specified setting up a commercial radio station broadcasting into the UK in partnership with *CBC Plays Ltd*. The documents were prepared by Major Oliver Smedley and his team at the registered City stockbrokers 'Investment and General Management Services'. The documents specified a capital of £150,000 but it was very vague on some important aspects. The proposed company would not own the ship, or any equipment; its main asset was simply the right to sell advertising on Radio Atlanta.

Crawford had recruited Major Oliver Smedley to chair Project Atlanta. He was a minor figure in the City and a keen Liberal party organiser who advised small investors where to put their money. The basis of the operation was that Project Atlanta Limited would collect commission on the sales of airtime and be responsible for all programming costs. The day to day operation of the radio station was dealt with by the *Atlantic Services Anstalt* (a trust) of Liechtenstein. If investors managed to lift the veil of incorporation, they would be led to yet another anstalt, called *Rajah*, which was chartering the ship from the owners, *Rosebud Shipping* of Panama.

Crawford told some staff that the initials PAL stood for "pal" which was a shortened English translation of the ship's name, Mi Amigo. Raising the funds was a long and laborious task and involved talking to hundreds of investors. Project Atlanta's seven directors put up 30% of the capital between them, with Allan Crawford's and Kitty Black's money invested in *CBC Plays Ltd.*

Behind the scenes and despite the many false starts of the last three years, the project to give Britain its first offshore radio station was beginning to take shape, but it was now split into two, for a short while anyway. Ronan O'Rahilly and Allan Crawford had both realised that they would be uneasy bed-fellows though both saw the attractions of continuing to have a loose working relationship.

It took the Atlanta group another three months, until early November 1963, before they had enough funds for a large down payment on the Mi Amigo. Crawford and Smedley returned to Texas and inked the contract with the American and Panamanian owners of the Mi Amigo at a lawyer's office in Dallas.

Ronan's own radio ship project

The incorporation papers for *Project Atlanta Ltd* prove that Ronan was not a member of Allan Crawford's team, despite him having made the trip to Texas on Atlanta's behalf in the Summer.

During that trip, it had dawned on Ronan that the Americans were not willing to sell the Mi Amigo and another way would have to be found. He saw that the Mi Amigo had already been stripped of most of her broadcasting equipment which caused him feel that Crawford's project was mired and unlikely to make much progress.

Ronan was already forging ahead on a mission of his own; he would start his own offshore radio station. He did not see the wide circle of CBC Plays making any progress who were much older and staider in their approach.

Carlton Tower Hotel

Ronan quickly assembled his own team, comprising some of his old acting pals and his faithful partner in the music business, Oonagh Huggard. She knew and understood the complex corporate structure needed and the various other administrative procedures so set up the necessary companies in the UK, Ireland and abroad.

The group's activities were conducted from the Carlton Tower Hotel in Knightsbridge, the newest and tallest of London's hotels with its swish £5 a night rooms being regarded as the most modern in town. The hotel's fashionable location, where Belgravia meets Kensington, was the perfect location to meet the kind of investors needed.

The Carlton gave easy access to telephones, meeting areas and the illusion of being high flyers. By befriending the genial Irish doorman and a few receptionists Ronan had a message service to create a good façade. As with all entertainment projects, appearance is importance. For this project, getting the well-to-do to part with money, appearances were vital.

Christopher Moore was Ronan's main crutch and foil and they worked closely together. American-born Chris had come to the UK while still young and had worked as a steward in the merchant navy for a while. Chris helped Ronan in some of his music business ventures and had worked as a club DJ.

Ronan was now gathering a group of wealthy individuals and who had the spare cash to put together a radio ship. This was largely thanks to his florid and over-detailed views of the station's financial potential. One of those who put money in clearly remembers being sold on the idea that the radio station would take in a million pounds per month, gross, and the likely dividends would be simply unimaginable.

Ronan's spiel was based on his knowledge of the music business, the legal opinion previously obtained by Alan Crawford and his recent trip to Texas. He was one of the few people in the UK who had actually stepped on a radio ship; few others even knew what sort of equipment was needed and happily accepted whatever he told them.

The main backers for the project were a small but eclectic number of the Establishment who each had their own different reasons for wanting a radio station free of official ties to broadcast into the UK:

1. Some of the backers wanted to use the radio ship project as a lever to force the government to licence commercial radio stations throughout the UK. This aim was not just their business, it had become a life's mission for them.

2. Some saw the radio station as a great way to make money quickly and were easily romanced by the young Irishman's predictions of very healthy revenue streams. They didn't know that the Business Plan had been constructed by Australian Allan Crawford; they assumed that the Radio Caroline team they were backing were experts in the field.

3. A third category of investor wanted "in" simply to cock a snook at officialdom, as that was their hobby. One particular member of the family at the very top of the aristocratic tree loved nothing better than acting outrageously and pricking pomposity. "All great fun, what!"

4. Some investors were keen to have a different kind of music heard in the UK. Some were promoters of new artists, some were pushing blues music, mainly American, which was never heard on the BBC, which rarely played American artists. The lack of music choice on the BBC didn't just help offshore radio get a huge audience, it was the thing that drove its birth.

Ronan and his close friends were in that final category and wanted simply to broadcast music by their favourite artistes. They felt that the BBC was letting British music and listeners in general down by not playing enough music. "I didn't mind rubbing shoulders with the nobs, as they were giving me all the money for this, I was happy to dance to their tune if we got the money for Caroline," he later explained.

"Money always comes to other money; simply giving the impression of wealth was convincing enough," claims Ronan, who borrowed £25 from a bank to buy a Savile Row suit, to go out and interest investors. "In London it's usually enough for people to THINK that you have money," he would often proclaim. His biggest asset was his confidence and he's sure his training as an actor prepared him well to raise the money: "I simply imagined myself to be an older man, I put myself into their head, so I could think like they do. It's a kind of method acting."

The Ross Family

One day, Christopher introduced Ronan to the man with whom he shared a flat in Chelsea. Ian Ross was what was called "a young man about town" who was looking for a purpose in life. He always seemed to have enough money to indulge his whims and fancies, but he was a worrier. "He anguished about spending £50 on some new boots for his girlfriend, but he and Chris usually spent all their time chasing girls up and down the Kings Road," remembers Oonagh.

Shortly after the introductions (in the coffee shop at the Carlton Tower Hotel) Ian took Chris and Ronan to meet his father at the family home near Haslemere, about an hour's drive down the A3, in Surrrey. Ian Ross's father was a New Zealander who had done well in the City of London; while never wearing the traditional bowler hat, nor being a member of the Establishment, he did mix with lots of stockbrokers and money people.

He immediately warmed to Ronan's youthful charm, his energy and the enthusiasm, with which he imparted details of the project. Over dinner, Ronan expounded the principle of the Caroline project and how it would "easily make a million pounds a month." Ronan produced a copy of the legal opinion, written by a QC for Project Atlanta. He also had Crawford's carefully costed business plan andled of his recent visit to a radio ship and transmitter manufacturers in Texas. Ronan knew how Crawford's corporate experts planned to set up inter-locking, 'front' companies in offshore jurisdictions.

While Ross senior's Christian name was Charles, many of his close friends and colleagues knew him simply as 'Jimmy'. He was fascinated by the multi-layered corporate structure of the project and assumed that Ronan must be an expert in Liechtenstein trusts and other offshore companies. The fast-talking young Irishman's had all the answers and his knowledge was impressive and Jimmy Ross hoped that a family involvement in this exciting new venture might give his errant son Ian something useful to do.

The near-rabid enthusiasm of Ian and Ronan encouraged Ross Senior to make a few phone calls that night. One was to his pal Jocelyn Stevens, the founder of Queen magazine, who was a wealthy and well-connected media baron. Ian Ross already worked closely with one of Stevens' partners, society photographer Patrick Armstrong-Jones, who had been created the Earl of Snowden after his marriage to The Princess Margaret. Ian's role was to coordinate photographic bookings and an element of sales.

Jocelyn Stevens

The doors to serious money were opening and beyond them lay all the money and support needed to make Radio Caroline a reality. While it had been Ronan who got the team together, he had little money, certainly nothing like the big boys had and they believed he was an expert in corporate matters and broadcasting.

It was Jocelyn Stevens who groomed Ronan's freewheeling public persona and convinced him that he could be the front-man or figurehead for the station. Ronan would coat Caroline's activities with his buccaneering spirit, peppering it with his trendy Chelsea speak, while Stevens polished it with a veneer of cool respectability. The new duo were a bankable proposition to the Caroline funders.

Jocelyn told Ronan not to worry about being young as "there is only two years difference in our ages." Ronan always kept very quiet about his age; despite his greying hair he continued 'thinking like an older man' when he was in fact only 24 years old while Stevens was 32! Although a bit of a rebel, Stevens was still part of the establishment. Jocelyn's grandfather, Sir Edward Hulton had sold him an old long-established fashion magazine called Queen, aimed at the aristocracy. Jocelyn would go on to edit the Daily Express, chair English Heritage and be ennobled as Sir Jocelyn Stevens CVO.

Over the next few days, Jocelyn Stevens and another friend of Charles Ross, John Sheffield, assembled a group of prospective shareholders. Many were keen to preserve their identities. It seemed to be simply 'racing money' for them, a bit of a game and they didn't want anyone to know they were involved.

An innovative entrepreneur, John Sheffield was the chairman of Norcros (named after Normanby and Crosby, villages on his family estate in Lincolnshire) and described as one of the most innovative financial minds of his generation. Eton and Cambridge educated John spent most of his life trying to find ways to save tax and helped many small businesses get "off the ground". He turned many small entrepreneurs into millionaires and helped raise funds for companies such as *Hygena Kitchens* and *Jensen Motors.* He was well known to Ian Ross's father Jimmy, who worked for the troubled car manufacturer which, by the sixties, was focussing on high powered sports cars. John is still one of the most venerated businessmen, particularly in the North, over ten years after his death. By grouping small dynamic companies in to one holding group, Norcros could more easily raise money on the stock market to back them. In the case of companies that were still considered risky, John Sheffield would find the money, often investing personally, although he was usually 'fronting' the funds for someone else.

John Sheffield

John Sheffield was also the father in law to Jocelyn Stevens, who had married his daughter Jane Sheffield. He was also good friends with Ian's father.

"Like many of his set, Jocelyn enjoyed being 'there' when new things happened but was always careful about getting too embroiled in things personally. He preferred to let others take the lead while he steered things from behind the curtain," said his chief assistant. "This is how he made so much money, he gave other people the chance to shine."

Jocelyn wasn't shy about publicity and, in the early days of the Caroline project, he was happy to be photographed with Ronan, the DJs or the ships. After Caroline launched, he took a back seat and soon bowed out altogether. The other investors stayed firmly in the background.

Jocelyn's wife, Jane, was Lady in Waiting to The Princess Margaret who was apparently one of the driving forces behind the 'escapade', which is how she described Radio Caroline to friends. She was good friends with Lenny Plugge, a regular at his famous house parties just off Park Lane, and knew a lot about his radio exploits. Years later, Plugge's daughter Gale was murdered when she became involved in trying to retrieve some 'indelicate' pictures of the Princess, stolen from a deposit box during a bank raid.

When Royal family advisers suggested that she was mixing in the wrong circles, the Princess supported the project even more. She and her husband, Anthony Armstrong Jones (Lord Snowdon), both took part in a 'home movie' produced by Peter Sellers at the Stevens' home, known as the Duchess of Caroline movie. Her status (she had been second in line to the throne before the Queen's children were born) meant that any friend and acquaintance was not only under the closest scrutiny by the security services, but also had considerable influence.

The security services were deployed to keep ensure that a tight lid was kept on many of the activities around Radio Caroline.

Several other high net worth individuals invested what they thought of as 'racing money' for this "bit of a punt" as John Sheffield called it to the many investors he advised. Among these was the Stanley family who were already investors in Project Atlanta and who had plans for their own Pye company to set up over a hundred local radio stations. Their intent was that the radio ships would force the government to negate the need for offshore radio by licensing local commercial stations.

Charles Orr Stanley

The source of this part of the funding has now been confirmed by former Pye employees as Charles Orr Stanley, their Chairman. He had a track record from several forays into radio, some via Pye subsidiaries. Among the stations he was involved in were *Radio LM* (in Lourenco Marques, East Africa), *Manx Radio* in the Isle of Man and a station in Morocco. He also bought large amounts of sponsored time on Radio Luxembourg for many years and visited many radio stations across Australia.

Stanley's Irish companies were also involved in one of the many bids to run a powerful radio station from Eire, serving the UK a couple of years previously. The Pye group's main intention was to press for a chain of several hundred local radio stations in the UK, to be equipped by Pye. They had also just put some money into the 'rival' Radio Atlanta project too and may have been simply hedging their bets.

Within days, the lion's share of the money needed to launch Radio Caroline was available in cash. Ronan and Ian fondly remember collecting large amounts of cash in two suitcases; they brought it back to the flat where they had "wad-fights' throwing bundles of the money at each other! This was an exhilarating moment as this was a huge sum of money. The average weekly wage was only £6 then.

Ronan always moved quickly to get things done and was fond of saying "the British dream and scheme, while we Irish get on and make the action." As soon as the first funding came in, he immediately instructed Captain De Jong Lanau of Wijsmullers to buy them a ship. Chris Moore as the only team member with experience of ships (working on a cruise ship) was sent to pay for it, in cash.

With his extensive contacts in the world of shipping, Captain De Jong knew of an ideal vessel, the MV Fredericia. A former passenger ferry that had just come out of service in Denmark, she was in good condition, despite being over thirty years old.

Kennedy Controversy

The story of John F Kennedy story affected Ronan deeply, becoming his favourite topic of conversation for the next fifty years. He claimed several times that Radio Caroline was named after Kennedy's daughter, but that myth in fact didn't start until a year after the station launched.

In November 1963 President Kennedy was assassinated in Dallas while being driven in a motorcade to a Democratic Party reception. The reasons behind the Kennedy shooting have been the subject of a hundred TV programmes and over a thousand books. There are several theories as to why he had been assassinated and who actually paid for the shooting.

One of the more fanciful stories was published in a book by Charles W. Weaver under the title *Triple Double Cross*. Weaver was a well-known Texan radio station manager who spent 38 years in the radio industry, including time at Gordon McLendon's large networks. For over a year, Weaver was involved with Radio Nord, the offshore station off the Swedish coast whose ship the Mi Amigo was about to become Radio Caroline's best-known vessel.

Weaver's book is part fiction, but much is built on fact and the days of the Mi Amigo, which was to become Radio Caroline from 1964 until 1980. Half the book cannot be corroborated and some of it is clearly nonsensical. What is not in doubt however is that the Mi Amigo is the ship at the centre of the controversy. It is the one that Ronan O'Rahilly visited in Summer 1963 and tried to buy on behalf of Alan Crawford.

Following JFK's assassination at the end of November, the FBI were closely watching the activities of everyone thought to have been implicated, no matter how remotely. That included some key radio people in Texas, who had oil exploration connections, which JFK was thought to be about to increase taxes on.

In November 1963 the Mi Amigo was moved to the nearby Todd's shipyard in Galveston and cleaned up, with her now shabby green paint being given a nice shiny new silver-grey colour. Just a few days before, *Project Atlanta Ltd* had managed to get the necessary funds cleared by the Bank of England and wired to ship owner, Rosebud Shipping, in Panama via a Liechtenstein anstalt.

All the vessel's machinery was fully-serviced, the radio equipment was re-installed and the stores replenished. The pair of reconditioned transmitters were hastily delivered over the Christmas holiday, along with a mixture of old and new studio equipment. KILT's transmitter supervisor Frank Maher was in charge of this work and he remembers that there was considerable official interest shown in the vessel after reports in local Galveston newspapers.

The local rumours suggested that the CIA were equipping the ship to broadcast to Cuba but the FBI were interested in the large number of links to the Kennedy assassination, just a month before. These were wrong, as the ship had been chartered by Project Atlanta, in a very convoluted arrangement that takes some untangling.

The ownership structure was deliberately complex in order to protect the identity of the owners. The ultimate ownership papers were in the name of *Rosebud Shipping* of Panama, she was then chartered to *Rajah Anstalt,* a trust registered in Liechtenstein, with a sub-lease to *Atlantic Services Anstalt*, also in Liechtenstein. That company had appointed as sole agents Crawford's new project Project Atlanta Ltd in London. There were two other 'foreign companies involved, which owned and sub-leased the transmission equipment

Although she was flagged in Panama, hidden in the Captain's day cabin at the aft end of the ship were another set of papers and a second flag to be flown if the ship's registry was withdrawn, or if she came under any other form of challenge.

This was a Bolivian flag, so the ship effectively had dual nationality. The Bolivians also flagged the Radio Veronica ship and they also had arrangements in place with a senior Nicaraguan government minister to flag the ship there if it became necessary. The owners wanted to take no chances of the ship being regarded as being stateless in case it was seized while at sea.

The Mi Amigo suddenly set sail on the very last day of the year, while almost no one was at work on the docks and wharves in Galveston. The official story was that she was going on "sea trials" pending a sale. This is a quite normal process where the engines, compasses, windlasses and other paraphernalia are given a 'shake-down' period of testing to ensure that no further work is required.

The Mi Amigo had on board not only her two previous transmitters as used for Radio Nord off Sweden, now refurbished by their manufacturers, Continental Electronics in Dallas, but a further two new units from the same manufacturer. Instead of returning to Galveston after the sea trials, as would have been normal, she set a course towards Cuba, and thence NE to the Bahamas.

She docked at Sun Cay, which had a private quay and airstrip, owned by the Murchinson, family. They were friends of Gordon McLendon and one of the original backers of Radio Nord. It's believed that the two new transmitters were trans-shipped here to go straight to Rotterdam, where the other ship, the Fredericia, was waiting.

The plan seems to have been to test the waters with the British Government, to see if they would act against a radio ship, as the owners of the Mi Amigo feared. None of the Americans wanted to risk their ship, the Mi Amigo, if there was to be official action by the UK against radio ships.

Some parts of the Atlanta and Caroline organisation were working very closely together, but many of the team had no idea how close the two organisations were. Secret talks had been held at the highest level to form a network, but the ink wasn't yet dry on any formal agreement so everyone was holding their cards tightly to their chest. Both Caroline and Atlanta used the same template for their corporate structure and there were even some common agents, in Vaduz (Liechtenstein) and in the Netherlands.

Oonagh was one of the few people that Ronan trusted to move around the large sums of money and made frequent trips to Holland and to Switzerland. It was there that the lawyer from Liechtenstein banked the funds and made all the necessary international payments in the names of the beneficial owners. He was the only person who knew all the intricate financial maneuvering. Almost every payment from the UK was made in cash, often tens of thousands of pounds at a time, carried in small packaged or secreted about the body!

MV Fredericia

Across in Europe, Wijsmullers, acting for an O'Rahilly company called *Cross Channel Container Services Ltd*, had by now concluded the deal to buy the former ferry boat *Fredericia* in Denmark. After the cash payment of £20,000 was handed over on the 30th December, she was taken to Rotterdam, where she arrived on the 8th January.

MV Fredericia, bought on the 30 December 1963, to become the MV Caroline

After acceptance by her new owners, Astrenic SA (a Panamanian company), the Fredericia was briefly named the 'Iseult'. Astrenic's respresentative, Ronan O'Rahilly, announced that the Iseult would be used for ferry services from Greenore to Preston in Lancashire. After being overhauled and cleaned, she had a powerful new Atlantis power generator and a pair of 10kW radio transmitters installed.

Meanwhile in London, Ken Evans, Atlanta's programme manager, was asked to train three of Caroline's DJs at the Atlanta studios in Soho; these were experienced actors John Junkin and Carl Conway and Ronan's old pal, 'Nicky' Henty-Dodd. Caroline didn't yet have any studios; indeed, the project had no offices and for a couple of months operated out of the upper floors of the *Queen* magazine offices in Fetter Lane, off Fleet Street.

The Mi Amigo was pushing on to Europe, but she could only make around 5 knots using her own under-powered motor. Arrived at El Ferrol in Spain three weeks later, she had taken a battering from a storm in the middle of the Atlantic. The short Radio Nord aerial mast and its complex guys and tuning boxes were severely damaged.

The Project Atlanta team were not unduly worried about the extra delays as they had been hatching their radio station plans for almost three years. What difference could a few more weeks delay make? While they knew that Ronan and his team were also planning a station of their own, Crawford believed that it would take them a similar amount of time to find a suitable ship and get operational.

Crawford and O'Rahilly had agreed on a programme of mutual assistance; Atlanta could use the port facilities in Greenore in return for allowing Caroline use of the Atlanta studios in London. There were many other ways in which the two companies would help each other.

Crawford didn't realise that, on the day before the Mi Amigo left the USA, Wijsmullers had bought a ship for Ronan as requested and it was on its way to Rotterdam. The former Danish ferry boat, the Fredericia, needed new generators which were easily obtained there. Two new transmitters had been rushed over from the USA and put on board in Rotterdam. The plan was to have them installed in Greenore by Arthur Carrington and his own company *Carrington Electronics*.

A Swedish engineer who had worked on Radio Nord was hired by Caroline to help install the transmitters and studio equipment. Ove Sjöstrom took along fellow countryman Jan Gunnarsson to assist in this huge task, which now had to be done in a hurry. With everything safely onboard, the Fredericia left Rotterdam and headed towards Ireland with a new name, the MV Caroline.

At a meeting in the Project Atlanta office in London while the Mi Amigo was crossing the Atlantic, Crawford thought he had agreed with O'Rahilly that the Caroline ship would take an anchorage in the north of the British Isles, while Atlanta would be moored off Harwich. In return, the vastly experienced Project Atlanta team would train the Radio Caroline DJs and provide studio facilities for them.

Transmitting Aerials

Harry Spencer

Aerials have to be properly matched to a transmitter's frequency in order to work efficiently. For MW they are pretty large and a tall mast was required to hold them aloft. John Gillman was engaged to design this vital part of the installation, with the erection carried out by Spencer Rigging of the Isle of Wight. The work had been commissioned by Wijsmuller's, who would also provide the marine crew for both vessels and ensure their compliance with the jungle of maritime laws.

Spencer Rigging's boss was Harry Spencer, a busy man who did not want to do the work in El Ferrol where the Mi Amigo had sought refuge from the Atlantic storms; Greenore was a little out of the way but far more convenient than Spain for his team and the essential supplies needed. A bigger problem, that the Radio Nord antenna had been damaged but the bespoke structure was not understood outside Mullaney's company. John Gilman set about designing a replacement but it would take a while to procure the materials. Erecting it in Greenore was ideal.

The contract engaging Spencer Rigging to carry out the antenna work was signed in the name of Merit Music Company Ltd, run by Allan Crawford. The contract states clearly that payment for the work was to be made by a Liechtenstein company, the *Rajah Anstalt*.

The frequency chosen for the radio ships is also a very important matter. One of the reasons quoted by the British government to exclude non-BBC radio stations was that there are no frequencies available. This is disingenuous of course and all that was needed was a political will to provide them.

The engineers used by the two groups were experienced BBC men with long careers in their craft. John Gillman and Arthur Carrington had selected frequencies at the high end of the medium wave band – around 1500 kilohertz, or 200 metres. Wavelengths of this magnitude allowed a shorter antenna to be used more easily, without resorting to custom made antenna as Radio Nord had done.

A folded unipole for 1500 kHz (200m) can be made to work with a mast only 100 feet high, practical for experienced riggers like Harry Spencer. It can be fed with its signal up the mast's guys, meaning the mast itself can be mounted onto the deck with no base insulator.

BANDSPREAD

Such was the influence of Radio Luxembourg that in 1963, some radio manufacturers began adding a 'Bandspread' facility to their radios. Most radios were made in the UK or in Europe in the sixties and manufacturers such as KB, Grundig, Perdio, Ecko, Sobell and Bush all offered the facility. Perdio's *Caralux* model was just one of dozens on the market.

This extra band focussed on a few channels at the very top end of the MW dial, from about 215 to 195 metres, which made it much easier to tune to Radio Luxembourg. The Great 208 could now be more easily found right in the middle of its own band, a boon to their audience. A third of the UK radio listeners now tuned to Luxembourg. It also became one of the reasons that John Gillman chose a spot at the high end of the MW band, so that they could also be found in the bandspread and right next to Radio Luxembourg.

British music had never been so good, so raw and so exciting, with thousands of groups of ordinary (and some not so ordinary!) teenagers making records. The Beatles had just had a record-breaking year and began 1964 with appearances on an American TV show that resulted in such an avalanche of record sales that they held the top 5 positions in the US singles chart.

The BBC Light Programme aired some of the pop music of the day but it was all the very 'safe' tracks selected by their producers in the Light Entertainment section, most of them quite elderly. They awarded live sessions to established artistes, who then performed 'covers' of the hits of the day. Sometimes one would even hear the actual hit records, if they had got past the censorial attitude of the Gramophone Department who were keen to ensure that nothing too risqué was broadcast, but this was only for a limited few hours a week.

That was the scene in late 1963, early 1964: millions of portable radios, mostly in the hands of young teenagers, all eager to hear the latest music. Radio listeners were ripe for the taking and there was lots of very low hanging fruit!

Various expedient moves were undertaken which resulted in two new transmitters being rapidly completed by the manufacturers, Continental Electronics in Dallas, Texas. These were the same model as those installed on the Mi Amigo for Radio Nord, a pair of 316B models, each capable of putting out ten kilowatts.

DJ Colin Nicol in the rigging

Captain De Jong of Wijsmullers met with Crawford and O'Rahilly in January 1964 where they agreed to share some resources. It was agreed that both ships would have their aerials rigged and installed on the ships by *Spencer Rigging* of the Isle of Wight.

Owner of the rigging company Harry Spencer had served a long apprenticeship in a ship yard and developed a firm rigging high masts on yachts so was the ideal man with the skills and expertise to install a high radio mast on board the Radio Caroline ship. His firm were later to install aerial masts on several other radio ships.

Spencer had insisted that the mast work wasn't done in Spain as obtaining supplies and communications were notoriously difficult. Ronan offered wharf space at Greenore, the former British Railways ferry port that was now controlled by his father. The work on the aerials and masts (the mast only holds up a cage of wires, which form the antenna proper) would be carried out just over the border in Ireland, convenient for travel but just out of sight of any prying eyes.

Former BBC and Marconi antenna specialist John H. Gillman had designed a suitable antenna for the Mi Amigo. This would be much simpler than the John Mullaney special one used by Radio Nord. It was agreed that a very similar folded unipole would be suspended from the mast that Harry Spencer would also build on the MV Caroline.

Alfred N Thomas, a retired BBC engineer, also worked for the Marconi's design team in Chelmsford. He was originally in charge of Atlanta's transmission arrangements but was rarely was seen on the ship. He put Gilman in overall charge of the Atlanta transmitter, who in turn recruited George Saunders, another young Marconi engineer.

"After meeting John Gillman in an Essex pub, I was flown over to Ireland to meet with his boss, A.N.Thomas," remembers George. "All his colleagues called him ANT, after his initials. The BBC were very big on initials in those days, departments and senior engineers were usually called by their initials. I took over the installation work from Milan Leggett who had sailed over in the Mi Amigo from Galveston. We also had another ex BBC engineer called Joe Neal who joined us."

MV Caroline transmitters
Two shiny new Dallas built 10 kilowatt transmitters were delivered to the ship while she was berthed in Rotterdam during February. They were installed by Swedish engineer Ove Sjöstrom who worked under the supervision of Arthur Carrington who had worked as an engineer at the BBC, ABC TV and at Pye. Two new Mercedes generators were also taken on board there but no antenna mast had been erected by the 13th February, when she left port, en-route for Greenore in Ireland.

Most of the installation work was done by electricians from the Dundalk Engineering Works, however this seems to have resulted in problems as, a couple of months later, radio engineer George Saunders was sent up to sort out the problems.

The port of Greenore was not only 'out of the way' and all but deserted but, being over the border was not subject to inspection by the British authorities. It was at the foot of the mountains of Mourne, where they go down to the Irish sea. An ideal place, away from prying eyes, where the work could be done without fuss or intervention. Both teams were based at a very discreet hotel, the Ballymascanlon, near Dundalk.

A company was formed in Dublin during February 1964 to sell the air time on the MV Caroline's radio station; called *Planet Productions Ltd* its shareholders included a variety of people, many of them British aristocrats who had been recruited by Stevens, Ross and Sheffield. Some of their one shilling shares were to change hands for up to five pounds each over the next few years, a great rate of return for those who sold at the right time. Many held on for even greater returns that had been envisaged by the founders.

Ronan O'Rahilly and his Dublin lawyer Herman Good from Rathmires led a small board of directors who were responsible for the executive operations of the company. The team included accountant Eugene Comech from Ealing, financial adviser Richard Corderoy from Upminster in Essex and London stockbroker Roger Trapnell.

Work on the MV Caroline took barely a month to complete, as some equipment had already been installed in Rotterdam. Only the aerial still needed to be installed as did studios and various other tasks. When the equipment was tested while at Greenore it blanked out radio and TV reception in the vicinity.

She was joined there by the Mi Amigo and both ships spent most of March alongside in Greenore. Space was at a premium and the Mi Amigo often had to lay away, just one example of many delays and more than a hint of jiggery-pokery. Some acts of mischief were nothing short of sabotage with various items being tampered with and even stolen as was to become evident later. Swedish engineer Ove Sjöstrom has since publicly admitted that he was one of the worst culprits for the pranks and japes played on the Atlanta ship. It was part mischief but also an expression of loyalty to his Caroline bosses.

Station Names

Allan Crawford had decided to call his project Radio Atlanta, a name that he and his associates had always used. Their UK company was Project Atlanta Limited, with over a hundred shareholders.

While Ronan's project was as yet unnamed, he later claimed that the station name was inspired by a picture of Caroline Kennedy as a toddler in the Oval Office, just before her father was assassinated.

Others claim that the name was chosen to honour Caroline Maudling, the daughter of a British cabinet minister, in order to get government support. Ronan did know Caroline Maudling and he was rather sweet on her. Allan Crawford however was always sceptical of both the Maudling and the Kennedy stories. "Caroline was quite a girl, a well-connected journalist who regularly had her copy featured in the Daily Mail," said Crawford. "She appeared on Juke Box Jury and was often seen on the town with John Lennon, until his wife Cynthia moved down from Liverpool. Ronan was smitten with her, some were even betting on whether they would get things together, but that all fizzled out. "

Allan Crawford believes that the name 'Caroline' was chosen by Jocelyn Stevens and his pals, who were all part of the same set of upper-class rebels. They were part of the Establishment but who loved pricking pomposity. They each told several friends that the name came from the style sheet of Queen magazine, where the station was based in the critical time before and after launch.

Beatrix Miller, the editor of Queen magazine who also went on to edit Vogue for twenty years, had pitched both publications at a particular demographic sector. Her writers were told to think of their target as a 'twenty something' year old promiscuous girl called Caroline.

According to Clement Freud, another Queen writer, "Beatrix Miller's targeted reader had long hair, was named Caroline, had left school when she was 16, was not an intellectual, but she was the sort of person that one ended up in bed with." This seems plausible and fits in well with the high level of Jocelyn's influence and the time frame.

Jocelyn Stevens firmly believed that the radio station should appeal to the same young woman – so it should be called Radio Caroline. As the representative of the major investors, his word was revered and the others, including Ronan, simply acceded to his suggestion.

Michael Parkin was adamant that it was Beatrix who had given the Radio Caroline its name. Her description of the target listeners was the crux of his sales pitch to prospective advertisers.

Michael had been hired by Jocelyn Stevens from Channel TV, the smallest ITV franchisee, to manage the new radio station. He remembers clearly that the name was only decided in February, the month before the station launched. Michael left Caroline in 1966 having by then earned enough money to start his own film company called *Caroline Films* and open an art gallery in Belgravia.

Michael Parkin

Although O'Rahilly and Crawford's group were effectively operating separately, both groups had been using the Radio Atlanta studios in Crawford's office in Soho to prepare programmes.

There was no company called simply Radio Atlanta, nor was there a registered company called Radio Caroline. The identities of both radio stations were deliberately enigmatic. *Caroline* and *Atlanta* existed purely as an "on air" identification for the nebulous and uncontrollable radio waves.

One thing the two camps did agree on was that they should carve the country up into two with one ship, the smaller Radio Atlanta taking a southern anchorage and the Caroline taking an anchorage off the Isle of Man, from where they could serve Ireland and northern England.

There was no written agreement to do this and Ronan has always maintained "Oh, it was just a verbal understanding, a gentleman's agreement." The Radio Caroline team knew that the first ship to get on the air would gain an enormous advantage, so in the weekend before the ship left, the directors decided to go for the Essex anchorage. None of the crew were told, even Simon Dee was in the dark until briefed by the Captain, after the ship left Greenore. "It really was a big surprise for everyone as no one had any idea that Caroline would head south, all the plans we made were to anchor off the Isle of Man. Things usually moved very fast at Caroline, it helped make it exciting."

5. Caroline Sets Sail

MV Caroline, ready to sail
Radio Caroline

The MV Caroline was ready first and she set sail in the last week of March 1964. Instead of heading towards the Isle of Man, where everyone expected her to drop anchor, Captain Baeker headed south and set course for the English Channel.

This was part of Ronan's plan; he planned to take the lucrative south-east market that Crawford had assumed was to be his. Ronan saw a huge advantage in being the first ship on the air "It's always the first in any business that people remember, no one remembers the second," was one of his mantras, so being first to get on the air was always deemed very important.

"The weather was horrendous and some of the crew were sick, but we were all charged with buckets of enthusiasm," remembers Nicky, one of only two DJs on board. "We had to shelter near the Isle of Man for a few hours as the weather was so foul, and then we sailed off, due south down the Irish Sea and told people who called us up on the radio telephone that our destination was Spain. I think everyone realised when we got to Land's End, and then headed due east, up the English Channel, that we were headed for the Thames Estuary."

The idea of a hip new music station having one of its announcers (no one used the term disc jockey then) speaking the clipped tones of the Queen's English with a double-barrelled name was absurd. Nicky was persuaded to adopt a mid-Atlantic twang and to change his name. The choice of 'Simon' was easy, it was his infant son's name. Dee was simply a short version of his own surname – Dodd. Soon even his wife Bunny was calling herself Mrs Simon Dee!

The MV Caroline's radio telephone calls while off Dungeness were all logged and government papers show that they included many details about the proposed start of programmes at Easter. The official papers confirm that the GPO in London knew of the plans for Radio Atlanta's ship the Mi Amigo, but the Government were taken completely by surprise when the MV Caroline appeared, even though the BBC's own mole was involved in the technical preparations.

Official logs of some of the later calls via the GPO station at North Foreland show the ship's location as being close to the lightship at the Cork anchorage, near Felixstowe.

Shortly after her arrival on Good Friday, 27th March, the radio engineers began their tests of the equipment. By 5pm it was all sounding fine and the message was sent ashore that all was ready to start the next day.

On board were the two DJs: Simon Dee and Chris Moore, plus a couple of studio engineers (Bob Hart and Frank Kemble), Caroline the ship's dog and a ship's marine crew of engineers and spare hands.

Anchored off Felixstowe at Easter 1964

Terry Field

On Easter Saturday morning, a press conference had been arranged by Planet Productions at the Old Cheshire Cheese, a Fleet Street pub.

The ship had been instructed to start transmissions at 12 noon but when the assembled journalists and friends tried to tune in, they couldn't hear anything! It soon transpired that the steel-framed buildings all around were blocking all the signal. Out in the street the signal was fine and so the Caroline team and the journalists heard the launch while stood out in the street, gathered around Ronan's huge Zenith portable radio.

"At five to twelve we played our signature tune" explained Simon Dee. "That was a Jimmy McGriff track called *Round Midnight*. Then, at twelve o'clock, we ran the announcements declaring the station open. These were done by Chris Moore, as Programme Director, but he wanted to pre-record his announcements as he was so nervous and afraid of making any goofs." The first record was, appropriately *Not Fade Away* by the Rolling Stones, which was dedicated to Ronan.

As the station's first programme director, Chris was in overall charge of proceedings. While Chris was very nervous, Simon Dee took to his new career like a duck to water. He chain-smoked his way through the first month on air, but was very averse to the food cooked by the Dutch crew so ate very little.

"I was often on the air for 7 or 8 hours a day as there were initially only two of us there who were broadcasters," says Simon. "Chris and myself just alternated, doing a couple of hours each, for the first few days. It was a while before any of the taped shows appeared and before we got some help out on the ship. We had a couple of Swedish guys who panel-mixed for us, but apart from them and the crew there was no one else on board."

The station played a lot of music not hitherto heard on the airwaves, particularly jazz and blues; by artists such as Ray Charles, a personal favourite of Ronan's. Simon and Chris were both into big band music: "Yeah, Count Basie and all that mob, marvellous!" enthused Simon. "Occasionally bits of jazz, Sinatra and all sorts of other groovy stuff. We played a lot of that on Radio Caroline you know, it was never just pop, pop, pop!"

Many of the pre-recorded shows made at Alan Crawford's studio in London by 'resting' actors Jon Junkin and Carl Conway were very laid back in tempo and content. Jon was an acting chum of Peter Sellers, a part of Jocelyn Stevens and Anthony Armstong's set. Both Carl and his wife Jenny became well known Caroline voices, not only recording commercials and programmes but interviewing visiting celebrities.

Rather than a reflection of the presenters' taste, the music content of the prerecorded shows was more in line with that which had been laid down by Beatrix Miller, Jocelyn Stevens' editor of Queen magazine who had set the style and tempo as well as the identity of the station.

Wavelengths

Radio Caroline originally broadcast from 6am to 6pm and then switched off for the night. It was thought that reception after dark would be much reduced due to incoming interference from the continent, via sky wave.

The first frequency used was 1520 kHz, which is 197.4 metres, although it was announced on the air as 199 metres. Ronan preferred using the 199 approximation of the station's wavelength as it rhymed with Caroline.

This was a practice that has been kept throughout Radio Caroline's life, with all declared wavelengths being said to be ending in nine, to rhyme with Caroline. This was the case no matter how inaccurate it was – the famous 1187kHz transmissions were always announced as 259m, even though 253 would be more accurate.

Listeners

Caroline's ten thousand watt signal gave good reception right across East Anglia and inland to well west of London, and along the south coast to Brighton. It was possible to hear the station even further afield, but listeners in the area shown shaded on this map received a good quality signal. The illustration is from the first advertising Rate Card issued by Radio Caroline in April 1964, two weeks after launch.

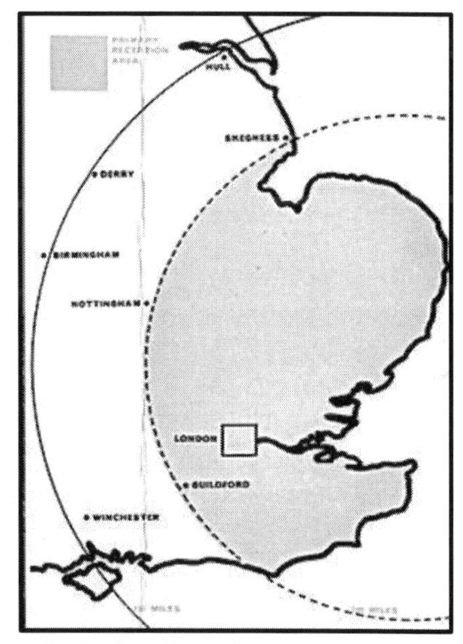

Radio Caroline's first coverage map

Within days, most newspapers had reported the arrival of this new radio phenomenon, playing music all day. Listeners had never heard anything like it before – here at last was a use for the many pocket personal radios that so many had been buying over the last year or so.

There were no organised or planned researched radio listening figures; these had never been needed as the only available time was on Radio Luxembourg. The BBC conducted some audience research, but this was more qualitative rather than quantitative and relied on a sycophantic response from its audience.

The BBC's staff would approach random people passing by in the street and ask "I'm from the BBC, would you tell me, did you listen to (programme name) yesterday". Always anxious to not offend anyone "from the wireless," the public invariably answered in the affirmative. The public went away happy to have met someone from the BBC while the Corporation's team member would report that everyone they met was highly delighted and avidly tuning in to whatever programme was the subject of the research.

In a bid to stir up more interest in the newspapers, Caroline's MD encouraged a friendly MP, Sir Eldon Griffiths, the member for Bury St Edmunds, to raise the question of Radio Caroline in the House of Parliament. It was an excellent way of getting press attention.

Soon after Caroline launched, the BBC's listeners were rewarded with an increase from 28 to 75 hours a week extra needletime, but this had to be shared across the Light, Home, and Third, giving each network about three and a half hours a day of records,

Government action

The British Government's Postmaster General, the cabinet minister responsible for broadcasting matters, was asked in Parliament about offshore radio. The questions were put by known associates of two Caroline investors who were keen to know the official government response, and to generate some publicity for the station and their quest for commercial radio.

"Such broadcasting contravenes many of the International Regulations and endangers agreements on the sharing of radio frequencies." answered Reginald Bevins, the Postmaster General. "It would almost certainly cause serious interference to communications. I am keeping a close watch on the position."

What the Minister didn't admit was that, while they had been aware of Project Atlanta and its plans for the Mi Amigo since she had first appeared off Essex in 1962, they had little idea about the Radio Caroline ship, whose arrival had taken almost everyone by surprise.

The claims of severe interference proved unfounded as Radio Caroline used professionally built transmitters that were adjusted and maintained to the highest standards. Initial complaints were that some coastguards could hear music behind their calls, but this was rectified almost immediately. In most cases it was found to have been generated inside the receiver at the coastguard stations and was resolved by proper alignment of the receiver.

Whitehall minions sent a flurry of paperwork flying in all directions, but were unable to take any direct action, despite the ship being in view of the beach at Felixstowe and audible on every radio in the south east. Official records show that many Whitehall departments were concerned at the arrival of Radio Caroline, and it was discussed at all levels of the BBC. While they made little or no mention of Radio Caroline on the air, the station was the hot topic of conversation and memos at Broadcasting House.

Senior officials at the BBC knew full well what was happening out at sea but were unable to share their information, even to the GPO, in case doing so exposed their mole in the two offshore projects.

Among radio listeners the arrival on the air of Radio Caroline was of immense interest and the local press was soon full of stories and readers' letters about the station. Many tried to cash in on the launch with some very odd offers. In Felixstowe, the local fishmonger began offering Radio Caroline skate' 'caught alongside the radio ship this morning' the sales tag said.

Press advert thanking listeners

Caroline are gentlemanly Pirates

Radio Caroline had offered to pay the Performing Rights Society (they represent song writers and music composers) royalties for use of music. "It's been very refreshing to find businessmen who have come forward voluntarily, despite their being under the smallest obligation to do so and offered to pay our fees," said Harold Walters, the general manager of the PRS. "These are very gentlemanly pirates."

Another copyright body who claim to represent the record companies also waded in, claiming that their members had not agreed for Radio Caroline to play music. "Public Performance Ltd" suggested that she stop immediately and issued a writ, which was sent to Jocelyn Stevens. In stark contrast, almost every individual record company sent boxes of their new releases to Caroline asking for airplay!

When in international waters a ship need only adhere to the regulations imposed by its flag nation. Panama had very few rules regarding broadcasting a slow administration and only vague documentation. The British Government claimed that they had sent a telegram to Panama suggesting that the ship's flag be withdrawn. Caroline had taken the precaution of obtaining a new flag for the ship which the Captain had instructions to fly only in an emergency.

The Government and the two largest record companies did consider jamming the Caroline broadcasts and the GPO worked out the costs of doing so, but their preferred transmitter manufacturer, Marconi, said it might take six to 12 months to build a suitable device and that the costs could easily run to six figures. Many in the Cabinet were supportive of the idea of commercial radio and voted to take no further action. Lobbyists for Pye and others were pressing the government to licence local commercial radio stations which they claimed would solve the problem and make offshore radio ships redundant.

The rumours of a second station (Radio Atlanta) getting ready to broadcast worried the British Government, but they were powerless to do anything about either ship. The GPO threatened that listeners could be prosecuted if they were found listening to anything but the authorised BBC stations. For many young rebellious listeners, labelling it unlawful would probably induce them to tune in and investigate this bright new sound that the Government didn't want them to listen to. The listeners were loving the fresh new sound of Radio Caroline.

Jocelyn Stevens

Two weeks after launch, Jocelyn Stevens confirmed that he was one of the financial backers of Radio Caroline. "Whenever anyone in this country gets a new idea, someone else gets up and says they can't do it and finally you have some in the Establishment inventing new laws to stop it."

"Radio Caroline is doing nothing illegal or harmful and I resent being accused of interfering with shipping when we have an Admiralty spokesman saying that we are not, said Mr Stevens from his office at *Queen* magazine in London.

"The only reason we are doing it from a boat is because it is not allowed on land. We are not trying to behave irresponsibly; we believe in commercial broadcasting."

Other directors had now joined the board of the Planet Productions company registered in Dublin, but it was proving difficult to register suitably named companies in the UK. Among the directors of Planet Productions were a stockbroker, a financial adviser and a chartered accountant.

Members of the Felixstowe Round Table chartered a boat to take them out to the MV Caroline so they could lobby the DJs to promote their forthcoming carnival. The ship's captain, 50 year old George Mackay from Manchester, invited them onboard for drinks. Apart from the two DJs, he had only a crew of foreigners to keep him company.

For the first few weeks the Caroline sales operation and Planet Productions were represented by Reg Cardew at the Queen office in Fetter Lane. Initially the salesmen worked from 54 to 62 Regent Street in the West End. This was simply a couple of rooms in a seven storey office building, which was also as a mailing address. Letters from listeners had already been arriving at the shipping agent in Felixstowe but a central London address was clearly essential.

Ronan and his PA Oonagh were busy trying to find suitable offices and set up a separate English company to do that, called Rosewood Limited. Other companies were set up to employ local staff and for Ronan's various music operations, such as ROAR Records.

A group of Caroline listeners in Ipswich led by Roger Beckwith began a petition in support of Caroline. "Everywhere we go we hear radio Caroline being played; it's something that has not been done before, a service the BBC does not provide," said Mr Beckwith. "People today obviously want to be able to listen to music throughout the day."

The Caroline ship's presence just off the coast was a boon to local fishermen and boat owners who happily ferried fans out to see the ship. Even small planes at a local airfield did brisk trade with trips out around the MV Caroline.

Four days after launch the supply boat brought out the first lot of mail that had arrived at Felixstowe Post Office – nine sacks of letters! "When we saw that lot coming out we knew there was no turning back, we were really overawed by it all," said Simon Dee.

The mail deliveries soon grew ever larger as the weeks then months passed by and the radio station became even better known. By the time Caroline was running major competitions 'on the air' such as Cash Casino and Partners in profit, up to a dozen girls were employed full time on mail duties.

All hands to the post room!

Les Perrin

How odd that the PMG should be against a company that generated literally thousands of extra postal items a day and boosted income for this government monopoly.

The Caroline Bell

It was customary in the 1960s for radio stations to use a sound effect as an interval signal; the BBC used the three notes B,B and C played on a piano, though mainly heard on the World Service, but also on BBC transmitters that were being warmed up each morning before programming feed was connected. Radio Luxembourg had a gong, which was played in (by pressing a button on the desk) regularly throughout the evening at programme junctions. At one of the main brain-storming sessions, it was decided that Caroline should adopt a ship's bell as its identification signal.

The 'bell' logo was also used on advertising and stationery. The first bell was recorded by two DJs but sounded weak, so Caroline engineer Ove Sjöstrum and Alan Turner re-recorded the MV Caroline's ship's bell. It was simple double clang, or 'ding ding' as it became known as on board, as that's what it said on the tape. It was played before and after each commercial and became the station's distinctive 'call sign' and is still heard on Radio Caroline, over 55 years later.

Tom Lodge rings the bell
Colin Nicol

Once on station, most offshore radio ships remained there as they needed to be outside territorial waters, i.e. on the High Seas, to be able to transmit with immunity from the law. All supplies and personnel transfers were done by local boat owners using pleasure or fishing boats. These were called tenders and to accommodate them, radio ships would hang a couple of large old tyres (unwanted tractor tyres proved best!) over the side, to act as fenders. These were essential as they cushioned the radio ship from the tender.

The normal practice was to tie the two vessels together with a couple of heaving lines, especially while fuel was being transferred. The different sized boats had a different profile to the current and, even while tied up tightly together, would move around differently in the tidal stream. Even in the calmest seas, it would appear as though the radio ship and the tender were behaving like two caged animals, struggling to be free of one another!

Crews and supplies had to negotiate the gap between the ships. Great care needed to be taken as a small slip could see someone falling between the two vessels, and either lost into the water, or crushed between the ships' sides. It's testament to the skills of the many crews over the years that not one accident ever occurred at tender times.

Mi Amigo readies for action

While the storms of melodrama raged around the mast of the MV Caroline off Felixstowe, work continued on the Mi Amigo in Greenore but with more delays. Radio engineer John Gillman fell off a gangplank and into the lough, almost drowning. Former BBC man Gilman had been recruited by his BBC colleague AN Thomas two years earlier. Both were involved with several projects after taking 'early retirement'.

The Mi Amigo left in the early hours of the morning, complete with a TV crew from Granada TV. They were shooting footage for a *World in Action* programme covering both Atlanta and Caroline. 'Destination Spain' was the message given to the coastguards and indeed the ship's log showed El Ferrol as being her destination. Quite plausible; she'd been there twice in the past 18 months.

As she rounded Lands End though it became clear her destination was a lot closer to home. Suddenly one of the stays holding up the mast snapped and the Captain had to put into Falmouth Bay and urgently call for assistance from Harry Spencer, the aerial rigger who had built the mast on the Mi Amigo as well as that on the Radio Caroline ship. He was based on the Isle of Wight, just along the coast. Within days the repairs were effected and she was ready to resume her journey to the Thames Estuary.

Advertising – the radio ship's treasure!

The purpose of the radio station was not simply to help publicise Georgie Fame's records, as had often been claimed, but to promote the case for commercial radio and to sell advertising. The GPO vainly hoped that they could deter advertisers from using Radio Caroline and for a few weeks, Caroline simply broadcast almost non-stop music, peppered with short announcements of a few seconds duration.

The first advert on Caroline was broadcast on Radio Caroline on 1st May; it was for Woburn Abbey. The actual commercial was recorded in London and features the voice of station founder, Ian Ross – his only appearance on the air was this commercial. The Duke of Bedford visited the Queen Magazine office often and liked Ian's voice, mainly because he could pronounce Woburn correctly while most people infuriated him by describing it as 'Woe Burn'). The Duke wrote his own commercial which promoted his new 'safari park' initiative. He was delighted with the response, which brought in over four thousand visitors the next day, despite wet weather.

More ad's followed the same day for local businesses in Essex and Caroline's first international advert for Bulova watches. National advertisers were broadcast on Caroline towards the end of the month for *News of the Wold, Reveille, Guinness* and their *Harp* lager brand.

At this time Radio Caroline claimed an audience of around 4 million. Originally the station asked for around £110 a minute for peak time advertising spots and although a Rate Card was published there was always considerable 'wheeling and dealing' done throughout the station's life. This extraordinary level of success was confirmed at the end of May when a Gallup Poll gave the station an audience of 7 million, out of just 20 million possible in the south east of England.

The Radio Caroline advertising rates were much cheaper than Radio Luxembourg, who at the time of Caroline's launch were charging almost £200 a minute. By the end of the month, Caroline had over £60,000 of advertising booked on the station.

Spot commercials on Radio Caroline followed the same rules and regulations as were used at ITV, this made it much easier for copy clearance purposes and enabled agencies to simply send their client's existing TV jingles, saving the costs of production. Caroline ran up to six minutes adverts per clock hour, just ten per cent of air time.

Government 'action'?
The first questions in the House of Commons about Caroline came only a week after launch when the Postmaster General made a statement to the effect that the government were contemplating their position, and that jamming the broadcasts was being considered. When asked by a Conservative MP who Radio Caroline was harming, the PMG suggested that listeners in Belgium had suffered some interference, as had shipping in the North Sea.

Caroline's engineers checked carefully and found there were no recorded reports of any such interference, no specific instances could be elicited from the GPO, but the Caroline engineers were instructed to keep a very strict check with hourly monitoring of the equipment.

The GPO then severed the ship-shore radio telephone link and ordered its staff who operate the facility at North Foreland not to handle any traffic to or from the MV Caroline, except in cases of emergency. The coast stations in Belgium and in the Netherlands continued to handle traffic, but this was used sparingly as the cost of international phone calls was very high.

Official visitors
A couple of days later Caroline's engineer Arthur Carrington took Bernard Jordan, a GPO engineer, to visit the MV Caroline to inspect the equipment. He returned satisfied that the equipment was of a professional standard and was not transmitting signals on any of the frequencies used for maritime communications.

On Wednesday the 6th May the MV Caroline was approached by the HM Venturous, a Customs cutter. In a bid to garner publicity, Radio Caroline claimed that permission was sought by the Customs men to board the radio ship and inspect her 'bonded stores' (goods being used without payment of any customs duty).

Radio Caroline say that their captain refused permission and the after a few minutes spent exchanging pleasantries, the cutter pulled away. In the House of Commons a few days later, the Chancellor of the Exchequer, Maurice McMillan, made a statement:

> *"The revenue cruiser "Venturous" which is in the service of Her Majesty's Customs and Excise approached the motor vessel MV Caroline in the normal course of operations relating to the safety of the revenue and the observance of Customs requirements."*
>
> *"The commander of the "Venturous" asked for, and was given, certain information about stores carried by the "Caroline"; there was never any question of boarding the vessel.*

That was the only occasion when an official British Government ship approached a radio ship while in international waters. The next occasion was to be in the late 1980s, all told in a later chapter.

HM Venturous was a small light fast V-Class patrol boat, delivered new in 1962. These vessels are not warships but simply customs patrol vessels, policing ships entering or leaving British ports. They are now deployed by the Home Office as part of the Border Patrol activities. The absence of a demand to board could reasonably be construed as acceptance of the claimed legality of the operation of radio ships.

While politicians and civil servants ashore made threatening noises to implement new laws to outlaw offshore radio, no action has even been taken by the British authorities while a ship has remained in International Waters. The Dutch are the only country to have taken action against radio ships on the high seas and beyond the limits of their territorial waters. They acted against TV Noordzee, Radio Paradijs and Radio 819 (when Caroline suffered collateral damage).

Legal action against the authorities in the cases of one 1980s case saw a return of seized radio equipment and a payment for loss of profit, while Radio Caroline, resumed transmissions just six weeks after it was raided and equipment seized. The equipment was later returned.

Jeremy Thorpe, the Liberal Party's MP for North Devon introduced a bill in the Commons that would force all radio stations to be registered with the GPO. He accused the government of condoning criminal action by failing to cancel the licences of people who listened to Radio Caroline. Thorpe suggested that with his bill, direct action could be taken on Radio Caroline by any warship and the seas quickly rid of them. "Caroline currently sings like an offshore siren," said the Liberal barrister who was later proven to be a pervert, a rapist and sodomist. "If taken over Caroline could quite easily start broadcasting inflammatory, seditious, obscene or undesirable material to an unprotected British public." The audacity and duplicity of the 'man'!

Thorpe continued to be a thorn in Caroline's side, forever speaking out against the station. He became leader of the Liberal Party and was investigated on many occasions by MI5 and the police over his relationship with a male model who he wanted shot. This affair led to his total disgrace when he faced criminal charges of 'conspiracy to murder'.
Karma certainly nailed him!

Thorpe

In just ten weeks of broadcasting, Radio Caroline had attracted seven million listeners, none of whom seemed to have been affected by the daily diet of music and good humour. Indeed, a report by a university lecturer said that factory workers seemed to be much more productive if they had some music to encourage them. The British Government limited its actions against Atlanta and Caroline to some sabre-rattling in Parliament and a refusal to list telephone numbers in the phone directories with the stations' names. Many in government also wanted commercial radio.

Ship's Anchorage

The MV Caroline had dropped anchor just east of Felixstowe. This was a little to the north east of the abandoned Roughs Tower and clearly visible from the beach. The Caroline's captain had only a general idea of where the best anchorage was supposed to be and he tried an anchorage a few miles north, just off the village of Bawdsey. The signal romped into Kent, Essex, London and East Anglia, but a good knowledge of the waters of the outer part of the Thames estuary was to prove very important , as will be seen overleaf.

6. Mi Amigo arrives on station

Towards the end of April the Mi Amigo finally arrived at her chosen anchorage, in the Wallet, just over three miles south of Frinton on Sea. This was selected by some experienced hands who were pilots from Trinity House. Sandy Horsley was the key man there who was also a shareholder in project Atlanta.

Trinity House are an ancient guild of master mariners who know the waters in their area extremely well. It's members are self-employed pilots who all ships must use when entering and leaving port. In some port areas the work has been taken over by the port authorities.

The local pilots in Harwich knew that "the Wallet" band of water, just off the Naze in Essex, was protected by a sandbank called the Gunfleet Sands. Although barely drying, even at the lowest tides, the Gunfleet sands did absorb the worst of the seas rolling in. As such, the Wallet offered a comfortable anchorage for small ships, like the Mi Amigo.

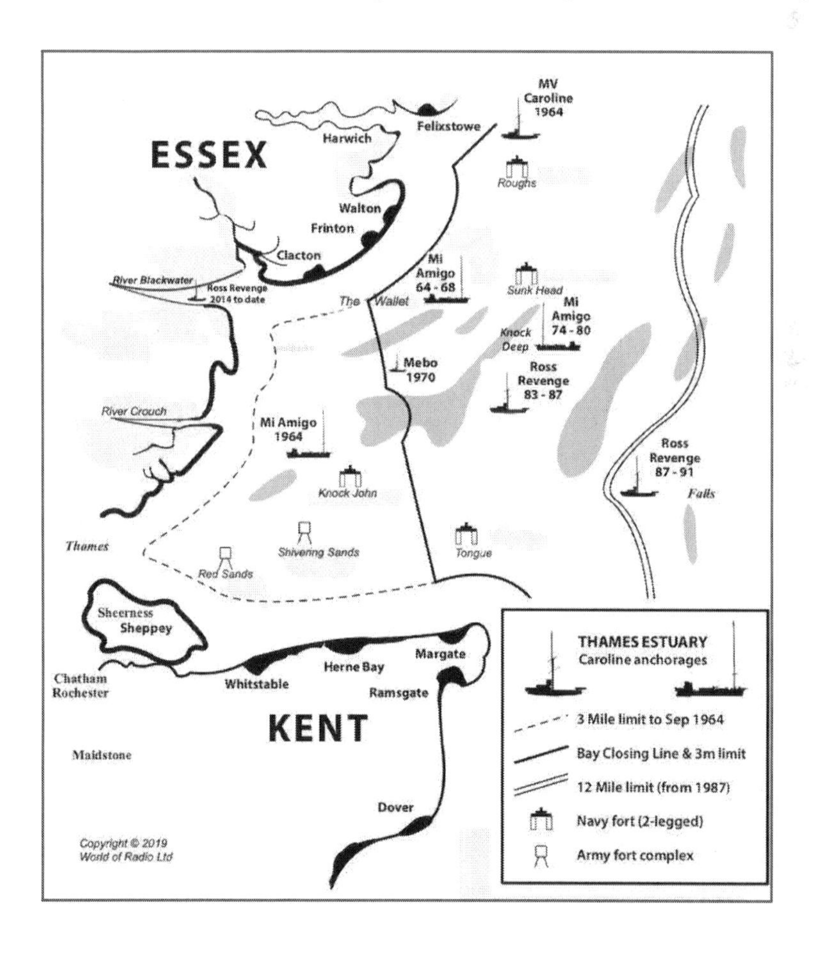

The Wallet was also conveniently close to Harwich, a full-time customs port. This was important as foreign ships anchored in international waters are treated as 'abroad', meaning that all shipments of supplies and personnel must be officially 'cleared' by many different government department, many only found in major ports. The smaller places, such as Brightlingsea, only have part time district officers.

First and foremost, the Wallet anchorage afforded an easy path for medium wave signals into London, meaning the UK's densest area of population would be able to hear the station. And, of course, the advertising agencies which were all located in the West End of London.

Once on her chosen station, the Mi Amigo engineers found that the correct transmitter crystals were missing from their transmitter. These are vital to originate the station's frequency and were specially made in the USA to lock the transmitters onto a particular wavelength. Atlanta had taken great care to select their wavelength of 201 metres but the Radio Caroline team on the Frederica had intercepted the delivery of crystals from the manufacturers as one of their tricks.

When the Radio Atlanta ship arrived on station in May, transmissions could not commence immediately as various essential parts were still missing. Swedish engineer Ove Sjöstrom has since publicly admitted that he took the transmitter crystals belonging to Radio Atlanta.

Simon Dee & Jan Gunnarson

Radio Caroline

Ove and his colleague Jan Gunnarsson sailed across from the Caroline to the Mi Amigo when she arrived off Frinton and mischievously re-arranged some wiring in the transmitter.

Jan had been brought over from Sweden by Ove Sjöström, the chief engineer recruited by Ronan O'Rahilly. "I was young and just wanted to help my bosses; delaying the launch of our competitor seemed like a fair thing to do," Jan told a radio conference in Sweden.

When Caroline intercepted the delivery, it left Radio Atlanta with only a solitary crystal for 1520 kHz, which was already used by Caroline. Atlanta had to wait until Caroline closed down at 6pm before starting transmissions. This opened them to accusations of trying to steal the audience, but it was in fact the fault of the Radio Caroline engineers that they had to do this.

Crawford admitted that he in turn had fed Caroline with erroneous technical information and even supplied them with a couple of hopeless engineers, who he knew would not be suitable. Despite rumours of rivalry and battles between the organisations, Ronan sent a "Good Luck" telegram to Crawford on Atlanta's first day.

There has been some conjecture that the American owners of the Atlanta ship would not allow the ship to start transmitting until they were convinced that the ancient 'hovering laws' would not be used by the British government to silence radio ships. The last thing they wanted was to have their valuable investment confiscated by the authorities.

The incident in which the Customs revenue cutter HM Venturous merely "spoke to" the Radio Caroline ship on the 6th seems to have allayed fears of official intervention; the Mi Amigo had made her first transmissions several days before but didn't start regular programming until the 12th May; a full three weeks after arriving.

After a week on board the Mi Amigo running Radio Atlanta on their own, son and father team Bob Scott and Johnny Jackson left, handing over the reins to a mainly Australian team led by Richard Harris and Tony Withers. Among their team was Keith Martin, who was disappointed to be billeted in the cabin up in the forepeak of the ship. This four berth cabin was dark and a bit noisy, being next door to the chain locker and only accessed down a vertical ladder.

Richard Harris
Colin Nicol

Richard was an Australian music and admin' expert had previously worked at Associate Television and at BFBS; he had heard of the Atlanta project some years earlier and set out to track down the mysterious music publisher who was setting it up. Eventually Richard left ATV and joined Project Atlanta to be station manager.

When a TV reporter asked if tales of sabotage were true and whether Caroline had stolen Radio Atlanta's ideas, Ronan responded that: "There have been eleven offshore radio stations in Europe so far and a been a number of people in England who have tried to put a station into operation on this basis."

Jocelyn Stevens told viewers to ITV's World in Action programme: "They are just being cry-babies. Radio Atlanta have had over four years to get on the air, trying to get their project going. Ronan and his team have got this together in six months. They just put it into operation."

Radio Atlanta Coverage

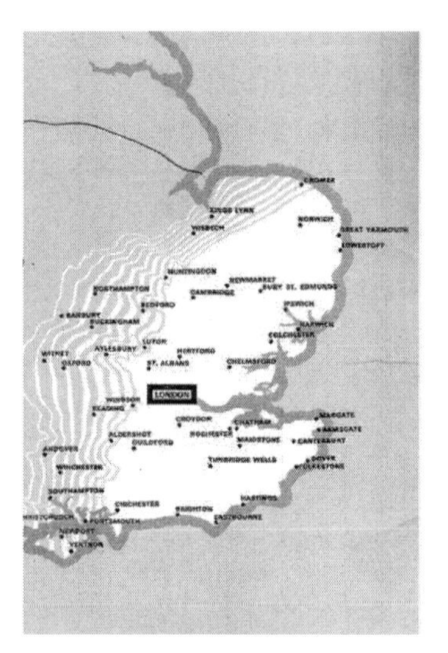

The launch of Radio Atlanta was on a much grander scale than Caroline's. It was held in the palatial Waldorf Hotel in London and attended by many advertising agents and people from the music business.

Allan Crawford told the assembled multitude that Radio Atlanta would provide a worthy alternative to the BBC Light Programme and be specially designed for family listening. News would be provided each morning, plus some guest appearances by celebrities.

Atlanta had a well organised base at Merit House, run by PAL's General Manager Richard Harris, an ex ATV man. He and Allan Crawford had recruited a small army of DJs and administrators including typists, clerks, secretaries and other office personnel. They worked over several floors of the Dean Street offices of Merit Music, while the top floor still had two recording studios.

Programmes

The first announcements on Radio Atlanta were not in English, but in French, courtesy of Alan Crawford's secretary. The first few days were a hybrid of pre-recorded programmes with live shows from a father and son duo on board the ship, Bob Scott and Johnny Jackson.

Or it could simply have been that a pattern of confusion was already being woven around the 'organisation'? "No one seemed to know what might happen next, or who was really responsible for anything," comments Colin Nicol, an experienced Australian DJ who hosted what became the first official show when Radio Atlanta started on the 12th May. "I was told that my programme was the first heard on the station, but I didn't hear it," says Colin. "The situation with Atlanta at the time was a bit chaotic; there was no real warning, not to me anyway, that the ship was going on air until after it had done so."

When Radio Caroline first opened, they broadcast from 6am to 6pm. Radio Atlanta had slightly extended hours not closing down until 8pm. Caroline quickly extended their evening hours to 8pm too, despite Michael Parkin, the Sales Manager, believing that television viewing would have decimated the potential audience by then.

Religion on the air

Initially neither Atlanta nor Caroline broadcast religious programmes, although sponsorship of entire segments was available and was soon taken up. A sponsorship advertiser could include several spots, some additional mentions and a guarantee that they had exclusivity in that period; i.e. no other advertiser's message would be heard.

Later Caroline began accepting some short religious programmes, often segments of just five minutes, such as the Oral Roberts, Voice of Prophecy. Others opened the floodgates by selling half an hour segments to Garner Ted Armstrong, of the California based Worldwide Church of God to air '*The World Tomorrow*'.

TWT programmes didn't include hymns, as did most other religious programmes, but was mostly quasi-political talk. Its programmes were not designed to gather in converts and money but they offered free literature. Armstrong was keen to warn the world of impending disasters, predicting a hellish 'third world war' before we arrived in a more utopian world. He spoke vehemently against the common market (EEC) and foretold of great problems from a 'United States of Europe'. Other topics that he discussed often included climate change and predictions of what might happen if the UK later left tried to leave any 'common European market'; BREXIT!

Garner Ted Armstrong
Radio 270

Armstrong claimed that the future is clearly foretold in the Holy Bible and often referred listeners to read the book of Leviticus. He offered free literature, post free, to reinforce the programmes.

Most offshore stations carried the daily 'World Tomorrow', the main exception was Radio Caroline South (though the programme was heard on the North ship). TWT paid enough to cover the entire running costs of even big stations, such as Radio London. There were many claims that the CIA were funding TWT and their Ambassadorial College, which had a large branch near St Albans.

Armstrong was not only a good customer, indeed a saviour to some stations, but he spoke out in favour of offshore radio, saying in print that "They are not illegal and violate no law of man. The British falsely call them pirate ships but they're not pirates, they are not marauders. They don't invade, pillage or steal and harm no one. They proclaim faithfully the Law of God. It's simply that most governments of man want to control what their people can hear or not hear."

PMG Reginald Bevins

The day after Radio Atlanta opened up, more questions were raised in Parliament. The PMG, Reginald Bevins, told members of the Conservative's radio and TV group that there would not be any immediate action against the stations. This was welcomed by the Leader of the Commons, Selwyn Lloyd, who was a strong supporter of commercial radio and who had led the fight for ITV. Mr Bevans said that he had no intentions to legislate against radio ships.

John Rodgers, the MP for Sevenoaks in Kent who also ran an advertising agency, told the PMG that the GPO had no right to intervene in offshore radio. Mr Bevans told the MPs that he was in favour of local radio and hoped to hold an inquiry into it. The following day, Mr Bevan confirmed to the House of Commons that Radio Caroline had not caused interference to the BBC.

Brian Harrison, the Conservative MP for Maldon in Essex urged the government not to take any action against Radio Caroline that would make itself a laughing stock. "This is the first decent programme the people of East Anglia have had for some time," he told the House.

The official minutes of Cabinet meetings at the end of May show that the Government couldn't decide whether to take action or not. Some wanted to permit commercial radio on land, while The Lord Chancellor warned that legislating against Brits running radio ships would leave the way open for foreign run stations. They decided to "wait and see."

MUSIC ROTATION

By the time Radio Atlanta took to the air, Ken Evans was already celebrating a year with the project and he went to the ship to oversee the music selections and the playlists more closely. The programmes needed variety, otherwise listeners could get bored and tune away.

"I had a system which I had operated at other stations previously," explains Ken. "We always had a big star name to open each show and then a big familiar standard. I would then have us play something that is exciting and maybe a little newer but still with an up-tempo and then bring in something new. Those slots are where Allan Crawford wanted his own releases played."

The running order in most clock hours on Radio Atlanta was
Standard | Recent | Oldie | Instrumental
and so on.

Over on Radio Caroline, things were done a bit differently: the system had a series of complex charts with different colours for each genre. Some records had only a week's worth of plays bought, some two and some up to four weeks. Each record would get ten to twenty plays a day, so it was more than once an hour, although the producers and whoever was making up that day's chart (later called a 'play list') tried to space these out so that it didn't become too repetitive for the listener.

Despite intricate plans being contrived for record plays, this didn't take into account the DJ's own personal preferences. If a particular DJ didn't really like a particular track he would usually just ignore the list, or arrange for the disc to be not available in the studio. This invariably meant using the record as a frisbee and chucking it over the side of the ship. The first to admit doing this was Simon Dee, who admitted doing so "on the air".

Across on Radio Atlanta their two DJs did the same, but eventually stricter playlists were drawn up that demanded that the DJs signed or initialled a sheet against each play. For a time, these were checked against copies kept at head office, but it was rare for the girls at Caroline House to get DJs into trouble for not playing the plug records.

In later years DJs such as Emperor Rosko and Johnnie Walker also confessed to pruning the lists of records for play, by tossing the worst ones over the side of the ship. This practice was being done in the best interest of keeping their shows flowing and Caroline sounding better on the air.

Sadly, it didn't do much for Caroline's reputation in the record business and there were many disgruntled publishers, artistes, their managers and record companies who paid hundreds of pounds yet never heard their music played.

After a few weeks, Bob Scott and his son Johnny Jackson suddenly left the Mi Amigo and Colin Nicol was sent out to supervise output live on the ship, along with Bryan Vaughan. They had been pre-recording shows for both the operations, Caroline and Atlanta, for over six months at Crawford's Soho office and seemed to work together very well as a team. Their role was to make sure that the pre-recorded shows went out on time and to fill in between them where none had been programmed.

DJ Colin Nicol

Radio Atlanta's first programmes had more polish and were better produced than had been the case at Caroline six weeks earlier. Shows on the first day included many taped greetings from celebrities and artistes. The Atlanta shows were of shorter duration than Caroline, but both stations used programme titles such as *Top Deck, Spin Around* and *All Systems Go*, not the names of the presenters. Both were still using a studio technician to operate the controls in the studio, as opposed to the 'self drive' style that became normal shortly afterwards.

Announcers on Atlanta and Caroline sounded more friendly and not scripted or rehearsed, as was the case on the BBC's Light Programme. The routine there was to rehearse each programme several times and not allow any personality or ad-libs (unless scripted!)

Radio Atlanta's advertising rate card looked very similar to Caroline's; it looked as though they had both been drawn up by the same team (in fact they had!). Atlanta's advertising was being sold by Leslie Parrish, a former Granada TV salesman but Caroline now had a team of six.

The basic rate for Atlanta's airtime was from £30 to £60 per thirty second spot, with the peak time being at breakfast. The other most expensive times were at lunchtime and then again in the evening, although the station initially closed at 8pm. Atlanta never continued its broadcasts into the night, although their rate card showed the full £60 per ad being charged for late evening transmissions.

While the stations had different identities on the air at first, there was still some sharing of resources. The joint use of Radio Atlanta's offices and recording studio in Tin Pan Alley plus Radio Caroline's friendly shipyard in Ireland were just the tip of the iceberg.

Project Atlanta's shareholders were mostly small businessmen, such as the Trinity House pilots. They had no deep pockets and were now being crippled by the leasing costs of the Mi Amigo.

The Radio Atlanta ship was run by Captain Meyer and his wife Irene, who served as cook to the ten man crew. Working together on Radio Atlanta was their first taste of married life together since their wedding. To the Meyers, the Mi Amigo really was home.

Captain Meyer, Irene and DJ Colin Nicol

The Caroline project had raised its capital from a much smaller number of wealthy individuals, including C O Stanley, the owner of Pye, who was keen to use the ships to demonstrate how commercial radio could become every bit as popular as commercial TV. They were better funded and had raised the money quickly, from fewer people.

The authorities had been investigating who else was funding the radio ships as rumours abounded, involving everyone from the royal family down to various widows and orphans that Major Smedley had been soliciting. A confidential internal report from the GPO to the Cabinet in May said: "It is said in Ireland that the strongest financial backer of both Caroline and Atlanta is Wilfred Harvey, the chairman of the British Printing Corporation who produced the BBC's Radio Times. Other BPC directors named were Max Rayne, a leading merchant London banker and Charles Murchison, who we believe ran several other radio stations in Germany, Monte Carlo and Tangiers." They omitted the holders of 86% of Caroline's shareholders and clearly had no clue!

While the Post Office were uncertain who was behind both ships, the BBC however knew exactly who was responsible as they had detailed information of exactly what was going on inside both Atlanta and Caroline. The BBC had one of their own as a mole. He had hired most of the engineers on the two ships and reported back regularly to his handler at Broadcasting House, Harman Grisewood, who was assistant to the Director General, Sir Hugh Greene.

To have the two ships double-serving the south east was diluting the effort and ignoring the riches possible by serving the north and Ireland. The original plan had been to share the territories and pool resources; talks on this continued throughout the first few months of operation.

There were rumours for some weeks that the two ships would merge and the Atlanta ship might steam north to anchor near the Isle of Man as Crawford had good contacts there. The Island had recently won agreement from the GPO for a low power local station to be tested in Douglas, but one House of Keys member said that if they didn't do so soon then he would float his own ship and call it *Radio Vannin.*

The MHK was Mr T. D. Colebourne, whose family had the island's main radio and TV shop; they were responsible for bringing television to the island. Colebourne had already met Allan Crawford some months previously and was keen to be involved in broadcasting. Crawford had sent two of his team to the island to gauge response from other politicians and the Island's businesses. They installed a one kiloWatt medium wave transmitter in the basement of a quayside hotel but it was never brought into use and in 1967 was gifted to Radio Caroline.

Tenders
In May, Radio Atlanta used an aggregates barge sailing out from Brightlingsea to ferry supplies to the ship. The DJs and crew hated the barge as it was used to carry sand and gravel and was very slow and dirty. Radio Caroline was supplied by Don Murrison from *Anglia Marine* in Harwich who used slightly faster ships, such as the tug *Hooligan*. Visitors faced an arduous climb up the side of the MV Caroline to get on board. Radio Atlanta's home, the MV Mi Amigo, was much easier to board as her gunwhales were low ; one could almost just step over the side!

The Radio Atlanta programming sounded brighter and more exciting than Caroline initially. It was more up-tempo and friendlier than Caroline, which was "laid back' and 'easy', as directed by Beatrixat Queen magazine. Atlanta's programmes were hosted by experienced and professionally trained DJs who would often drop in positioning statements, later called "strap lines."

- The Dolphin of the Sea, Radio Atlanta
- The Right side of Radio, Atlanta 201
- The Ship that Rocks The Ocean, Radio Atlanta
- Our Business is Show Business.

These catch phrases were used from the early days of Atlanta's test transmissions, when only father and son duo Bob Scott and Johnny Jackson were on board.

Programmes on Radio Atlanta were much shorter than Caroline, where the taped programming had all but dried up and programmes were mainly presented live, by DJs on board the Caroline ship. After several weeks alone on board, Simon Dee and Chris Moore were joined by new announcers, including Doug Kerr, Bryan Vaughan and Richard Harris.

The Radio Atlanta programmes were much shorter than Caroline's because it was only practical to get one hour of programme onto a reel of tape, if it was to have good audio fidelity. Atlanta did sound to have much brighter audio too, as it had one of the first audio processors, which Caroline didn't have originally.

Initially, neither ship had any station identification jingles. Crawford preferred a sound much closer to the BBC light programme and thought that the PAMS jingles that he had heard on a demo tape were far too American. Caroline didn't have any because they didn't have a studio set up ashore and the ship had no library music or sound effects.

Caroline House

At the time of launch, Ronan O'Rahilly had use of a large apartment on Eaton Square, Belgravia, but this was far too small for an office for the Radio Caroline operation. For a month or so, Caroline was run from Ian Ross's office at Queen magazine,but Jocelyn Stevens soon tiredof the venture and said he was not comfortable with some of the dubious practices. He was very concerned that when a writ arrived from the music copyright agents it was to his office.

A temporary mailing address in Regent Street was used, with just a secretary and the sales staff based there until Oonagh found a lovely seven storey townhouse in Chesterfield Gardens, the heart of Mayfair. It was just around the corner from Radio Luxembourg's London HQ and ideal. A company called Rosswood Ltd was set up to handle the £650 per week lease payments, with Ronan and Oonagh as directors.

The merger agreement with PAL was by then almost agreed and part of this was that both stations should share the same sales team, under a Radio Caroline (North and South) banner.

CAROLINE HOUSE 6 Chesterfield Gardens W1

Radio Caroline ordered a forty telephone lines service and was amazed to get them installed immediately as the 'waiting list' for GPO service then was around nine months. The lines were installed into the same ducts that served Leconfield House at the end of the street, the headquarters of MI5.

Most of the forty lines answered to the number HYDe Park 9721, though there were some ex-directory numbers added to the service and a few for subsidiaries.

Some conspiracy theorists assume that the unusually rapid service was a government instruction; things were pushed through quickly so that MI5 could monitor what was happening with Radio Caroline.

The GPO refused to list the number in their directories as Radio Caroline but, allowed a listing to be shown as 'Caroline Sales'. Most telephone operators would still give out the number if asked for Radio Caroline. Some days, Caroline House was receiving over 2,000 telephone calls a day and the telephone switch board soon became a two and then a three girl job.

"Caroline House"
6 Chesterfield Gardens, W1

The everyday business of the Radio Caroline operation was run from the basement. Chris Moore presided over two small studios, used for recording commercials, celebrity visitors and for auditioning broadcast staff. The business was known as *Radio Programme Planners*, which avoided using the name Radio Caroline on everything. The directors of the RPP company were Christopher Moore and Simon Dee.

The ground floor had a few service rooms which comprised a very comfortable reception area and the communications section which was a two girl operation with a large new switchboard and a Telex terminal.

The stairs had sea-blue carpet, reflected in huge mirrors covering the walls. On the first floor overlooking Chesterfield Gardens was a large open plan office that contained Ronan's huge desk, complete with a bust of J F Kennedy. That bust was to preside over Ronan's desk for the next forty years.

On the upper floors were more offices, which Oonagh would let out to friends in the burgeoning music industry. One of these was the Moody Blues and the other was for The Who. Their record company Track Records (which was also home to Jimi Hendrix as well as the Who) had its offices on the fifth floor of the building. On the top floor was a photographer's studio, run by a friend of Ian Ross from South Africa.

The Radio Programme Planners Ltd team down in the basement arranged commercials and playlists for Radio Caroline and was the official participant in deals to promote new releases on the station, a practice called 'payola' and quite legal.

Radio Programme Planners also trained new DJs into the 'Caroline' method, which Ronan and Chris had devised. Their initial belief was that the DJs should not develop their own personality on the air. They had an uphill battle with people like Tony Blackburn who was a bright cheerful DJ recruited in July 1964.

Tony, Norman St John and by Keith Skues, each had their own inimitable style, packed with catchphrases. Keith Skues arrived at Caroline House on the day of the merger but underwent Chris Moore's training before going out to the Mi Amigo at the end of August.

Tom Lodge joined Caroline a little earlier and said that he immediately felt completely at home on the ship. "As soon as my feet hit the steel deck, the smell of the ship hit me. A heady mixture of fresh paint, diesel oil and salt air enveloped me. It evoked so many memories of other ships that I had sailed on, that curious mixture of other people's vomit – but it was homely. It was still the ocean – and that meant freedom. This was where there is no end to the water. Where the horizon melts into the sky and the air tinges your lungs. A release from all of society's confinements."

Tom was to stay with Caroline for two years, being based mainly on the North Ship but, in 1966, he was drafted to the Mi Amigo in order to revitalise Radio Caroline South. Tom's wife Jeanine and their young family moved out to the Cotswolds. It was to be Tom who came up with the track that's become the Caroline theme tune, a single released by the Fortunes in January 1964.

Digging through the office record library one day, Tom unearthed up a Fortunes single released some months previously on Decca. "Caroline" was a typical teen idolatory song written by Tony Hiller that has usually been the station opener ever since. Hiller wrote almost 1500 songs in his long career, many chart-topping hits and jingles too. The Fortunes were a young unknown group managed by Reg Calvert, whose involvement with a Caroline subsidiary, was to end in tears, and be the excuse for bringing down the network of offshore radio.

Tom discovered another Decca single by Roy Hastings with the same name, *Caroline*. It was speeded up and the chorus - C-A-R-O-L-INE carefully extracted to make up a jingle that was much used throughout the sixties.

Two become one in a 'Merger'

Serious talks about the merger were made by Atlanta's sales team just weeks after their launch in May and it was predicted by The Times newspaper that the two ships must surely soon join forces. Finally, at the end of June 1964, agreement was reached during a meeting held in Vaduz, Liechtenstein. It was chaired by Dr Mercer, the lawyer acting for the companies owing the ships and equipment.

Allan Crawford and Oliver Smedley were accompanied by their lawyer, while Ronan, Jocelyn Stevens and their lawyer formed the other party. Also in attendance was the Wijsmullers' Captain De Jong Lanau of Wijsmullers, he firm who for serviced, supplied and crewed both ships.

Captain De Jong was a very precise man, loved fine detail and was almost fussy when it came to ships. Everything had to be double checked and absolutely correct. A portly man, he had a disconcerting habit of peering over his steel-rimmed spectacles and questioning every claim if he thought it might affect the trim or the stability of a ship.

The agreement was that the larger ship would sail north to an anchorage chosen in the Isle of Man while the other would remain in the Thames Estuary and broadcast to the south east and near continent. Ronan insisted that, being the larger ship, the North operation should have 55% of the income, and the Caroline South ship should only have 45% of the income.

The public announcement came on 2nd July with a joint statement issued on behalf of both Caroline and Atlanta by Leslie Perrin. While it was announced as a formal merger, in fact this was more of a takeover. Radio Caroline's company (*Planet Productions* Ltd of Dublin) had more funds available and had to bail out Project Atlanta Ltd. Radio Caroline was already looking to expand and considered an extra station off France, which would have been called *Radio Caroline Continental*.

Crawford would continue running the South ship as a separate business to the North ship, with both companies jointly selling the airtime and sharing the proceeds.

Ronan O'Rahilly and Allan Crawford

Radio Caroline

Radio Caroline

NEWS RELEASE

COMMERCIAL RADIO MERGER

The directors of Project Atlanta and Planet Productions Ltd today issued a joint statement announcing a merger between **Radio Atlanta** *and* **Radio Caroline***. The companies are responsible for the advertising and selling of time on the two offshore commercial radio stations. Mr Allan Crawford, Managing Director of Project Atlanta and Mr Ronan O'Rahilly, Managing Director of Planet Productions, will become joint managing directors of the new operation.*

The ship broadcasting the present Radio Caroline programmes, MV Caroline, will sail to the Isle of Man tomorrow morning (Friday) to a position five miles from Ramsey, Isle of Man It will continue to broadcast Radio Caroline programmes on the way to the destination and will remain on 199 metres medium wave.

The ship mv Atlanta will continue broadcasting from the present position to Greater London area and south east England under the national call sign, Radio Caroline.

In their joint statement Mr Crawford and Mr O'Rahilly said:

"The decision to merge was take in view of the enormous interest from the public and advertisers in other parts of England outside the original broadcasting area. This network will cover the most populous areas of Great Britain."

"It will specifically meet the demands from advertisers in the North and the Midlands and from existing advertisers who are already taking time on the two stations."

"All departments will merge to operate from one office. The Caroline Club and other land-based organisations will continue and be extended to cover the new broadcasting area."

Friday 3rd July was a frantically busy day on the North Sea with DJs on both Radio Caroline and Radio Atlanta being briefed on the plans. Radio Atlanta didn't make any announcement about the Caroline ship which was now anchored very close by. The crews were busy transferring equipment and personnel.

Radio Atlanta just closed down as normal that Friday night at 8pm and was never heard again; the next day she broadcast as *Radio Caroline South* with little fanfare, as though she had always been there.

New boys Tom Lodge and Jerry Leighton were chosen to form the DJ team for the Caroline ship and make the voyage north to the Isle of Man. They were assisted by studio technicians Alan 'Noddy' Turner and Terry Saunders who were needed as both ships had DJs sat in announcer booths and didn't self-drive the studio equipment.

The MV Caroline, left the MV Mi Amigo in the Wallet just after midnight on Saturday 4th July and sailed around the coast. She continued broadcasting as she went with many personal greetings from the crew, including Captain Hangerveldt. He eventually revealed his orders, live on the air: "On Monday, we reach our destination – The Isle of Man."

The ship with its unusually tall radio mast drew crowds of listeners to vantage points along the south coast, around Cornwall and Wales. Listeners used car headlights and mirrors to flash messages to the ship, which stayed just beyond the UK limit, in international waters.

Doug Kerr and Simon Dee elected to remain behind and broadcast as Radio Caroline South, to give the station some continuity and so joined Colin Nicol on the Mi Amigo. Few radio listeners would notice any difference as they tuned to Caroline that Saturday morning; some of the music was different as it now included more of Allan Crawford's cover versions of hits and did not have so many of the RnB albums that the MV Caroline was stocked with. She was now sailing along the south coast of England and picking up thousands of new listeners on the slightly different frequency.

Radio Atlanta's GM Leslie Parrish quit after the amalgamation, as his views were 'old style' TV sales and not 'Caroline style'. DJs Neil Spence and Mike Raven both quit the station too, but were both later heard on other stations. *Caroline* and *Atlanta* were soon joined by new stations that opened on the former army gun towers further upstream. Screaming Lord Sutch named a station after himself on Shivering Sands Fort, while a Kent company launched as *Radio Invicta* from the Red Sands Fort.

The merger in fact was only in name. Both Project Atlanta and Planet Productions would now be simply trading as 'Radio Caroline' which also didn't exist legally but was only a call sign used on the radio. Project Atlanta Ltd would continue to operate Radio Caroline South while Planet Productions ran Radio Caroline North.

Allan Crawford's team moved into Caroline House, which was large enough to accommodate everyone and still have room for the hangers-on from the music business who gravitated towards the station.

John Gillman, who had been in charge of transmitters on Radio Atlanta took over responsibility of engineering for both ships along with Kitty Black, a Project Atlanta director who acted as his secretary at Caroline House. John was also a director of a further subsidiary, *Hengown Limited*, which made all payments to the disc jockeys and other staff. The other directors of Hengown Limited included Radio Atlanta's programme manager, Richard Harris. Although registered in 1961, the company wasn't active until 1964.

Free Bracelet offer for Club Members

Both Caroline outlets sold various items to listeners, a range of jewellery, car pennants and other items were sold by mail order using any unsold airtime. Free bracelets were offered by Radio Caroline to listeners, who would be sent various other Caroline Club offers.

Others cashed in on Caroline's huge popularity. Merchandise of all kinds was produced by other firms with no connections with the radio station; one firm in Blackpool sold out of its stock of 8,000 T-shirts after just two mentions on the air!

On arrival off the Isle of Man, Caroline North began mentioning the Island's natural beauty and its many tourist attractions hourly, which Manx politicians and businessmen alike welcomed.

In Dun Laoghaire just outside Dublin, one local entrepreneur renamed his night club The Club Caroline and offered free admission to members of the real Caroline Club, a listeners organisation promoted on the air. David Martin ran the official Caroline Club from the Chesterfield Gardens office and sold items such as Caroline perfumes, necklaces and even clothes.

The announcement of a merger between the two ships generated copious press coverage all over the world. A businessman in Texas called Don Pierson read about it in his local paper in Dallas and flew straight to London, keen to put his own station on the air. He tried several times to meet with O'Rahilly and Crawford but they didn't want to encourage him, so he chartered a plane to fly over the ships to see for himself. Unimpressed by Caroline's output and its management, Don decided to set up his own station to show how it could be more successful. On returning to the USA, he formed a consortium, which became Radio Caroline's biggest rival, Radio London.

Two new offices

A PO Box was opened in Ramsey where, at its peak, the LDO manager reported that around fifty per cent of the mail they received in the town was for Radio Caroline. The "PO Box 3, Ramsey" address was one of the best known across the north and in Ireland.

Radio Caroline also opened an office in the middle of Liverpool to deal with the operations in the north. The base was at 61 Lord Street and became a mecca for listeners. Three airtime salesmen were based there as were a small team of PR girls and administrators. The Liverpool office was run by Kevin and James Duggan and Clive and Maria Silverton from St Annes. Their main work was running the successful Caroline Club and a team of salesmen for Spectre Promotions.

Radio Caroline's Liverpool office.

Caroline House in Liverpool is now the *Rococo* coffee shop, which mentions that it is in the former Radio Caroline Office on its web site and welcomes a steady trickle of radio enthusiasts. It's in the shopping centre, close to Liverpool One.

The Felix Restaurant, on Beach Station Road in Felixstowe changed its name to the Caroline Coffee Bar. Guest of honour for the opening was Caroline's latest DJ, Gerry Duncan. Gerry too was a sometime thespian who had appeared in a couple of plays and films and later helped produce the new Caroline, the 'Sound of the Nation' jingles.

The following week Simon Dee was in town to crown the Royalty Felixstowe Carnival Queen and was mobbed by fans when he arrived. Simon was now so popular he needed his own Fan Club, which was run by Olive Burgess of Chelmsford. The mother of five teenagers, Olive volunteered her services when Simon was crowning another carnival queen, in Basildon.

Established stars soon realised that by visiting the Caroline ships they could encourage the DJs to play their records more often. Adam Faith already had 19 consecutive hits under his belt when he made the trip out to the Mi Amigo with a copy of his 20th single, "I Love Being in Love with You". He went out to the ship on the *Agana* (a local Felixstowe tug often used to tender Caroline) and he too was met by hordes of female fans clutching autograph books when he returned to shore.

Programming Policy

One of the first things that Chris Moore did after the merger was to issue a Programming Policy document to try and homogenise the sound of the two stations. As well as the programme names, its key comments urged that the sound is to be kept UP TEMPO as much as possible. The order of the key numbers show priority on programmes. Each DJ should supply a carbon copy of his programme to the panel operator along with the stack of records.

When asked by the *Pirate Radio Hall of Fame* website if the Programming policy was strictly adhered to on the North ship, Chief DJ Tom Lodge, said:

> *We did at first try to keep to that format but Caroline House, where that Caroline North programme schedule came from, was so far away and out of touch with us on the Caroline North ship that we slowly moved away from all that.*
>
> *Caroline House could not hear us and the only communication was when someone came on board and maybe, rarely, a written communication. Plus, with the DJ shortage, nothing was tied down or regular. Sometimes no replacement DJs came and so we kept the shows going the best we could. Sometimes it was too rough for a boat to come out to the ship. And sometimes there were other personnel difficulties and so often we only had a few of us to keep the shows going.*
>
> *Chris Moore was a warm, friendly, gentle person, but with low energy. He wasn't the type who would be on top of us to follow his rules. Because of our isolation, I became the programme director for the North ship. Most of the papers on programming and so on were Caroline House creations for the advertisers. Most of the time we would receive a weekly log for advertising times and recorded adverts, or copy for us to produce adverts from - but on many occasions no boat came so we repeated the previous week's ad schedule.*
>
> *So you see, nothing was 'cut and dried'. Sometimes we did follow instructions and sometimes we didn't. And gradually we didn't. Plus our egos enjoyed creating our own shows.*

While Caroline South was now airing less of Allan Crawford's own label cover productions, it was a lot more chart music oriented than it had been previously and the DJs had almost a free hand in assembling their own play lists, provided the plug records were played.

Simon Dee continued with his daily music from films called Soundtrack while Carl Conway, now based ashore at Caroline House, interviewed dozens of film stars which were featured in many of Caroline South's other shows. By and large though, Caroline South played a lot more easy-listening music, while Caroline North was very chart oriented as Ronan preferred to give his DJs a freer hand in programme content.

As part of the merger, John H. Gillman became chief engineer of the Caroline network. He had recruited George Saunders from Marconi, who helped install the equipment on the Mi Amigo and others to man the ships. Each ship usually had two engineers on board at a time.

John hired Percy Scadden, a retired Police Inspector who lived on the seafront at Frinton, on the corner of Waltham Way, with his wife Jean. He could see the Mi Amigo from his garden and was an active radio amateur (G3CEB), well known in the area. Percy's main role was to be a local agent for the ship in Essex. He also operated a covert link to the Mi Amigo for urgent messages; nothing went out to the ship without his knowledge.

Percy (Bill) Scadden

As well as managing the physical deliveries via the Harcourt Shipping Agency in Harwich, he would maintain a radio rendezvous with the ship using his Yaesu FT200 amateur radio rig, using the call sign *Magda* (a tip of the hat to the Mi Amigo's former name). As a former CID Inspector in the Metropolitan Police, Bill (as he was usually known) Scadden knew the law well and had many useful contacts. The other authorities left him alone, his contacts and their discretion were useful as was his advice to the rest of the Caroline team.

Operations involving the North ship were handled by George Hare who joined Caroline while the ship was in Greenore. He ensured DJs and visitors were met at the Isle of Man's airport and taken to Ramsey for the short trip out to the MV Caroline, usually on the *Essex Girl* tender. He arranged all payments for supplies, repairs and the staff.

In mid-July Radio Caroline seemed to get some sort of official recognition when the Essex Police booked a series of adverts on the station for a sports event in Southend. It was Caroline's first adverts booked by an official body, though there were to be many more in futre; the Egg Marketing Board and even the GPO! In fact, the GPO in Blackpool even hired Radio Caroline North DJ Tom Lodge as compere for a function they were organising.

DJs Wanted

In June 1964, Radio Caroline placed a small advert in the New Music Express, at the time the best-selling weekly pop newspaper. It said the station was looking for disc jockeys and came to the eye of the lead vocalist with a group in Bournemouth, Tony Blackburn and the Rovers. 21 year-old Tony regularly scoured the pages of all the pop press, for news about the latest disc and tours. The simple lineage advert in the NME caught Tony's eye. It invited aspiring disc jockeys to submit a demo tape to Caroline House in London.

Tony promptly recorded a mini show on his reel to reel tape recorder featuring four Beatles songs interspersed with his cheerful banter and got it into the mail to the Chesterfield Gardens address. "As soon as I posted it I just knew that this was the job for me, and that I was the person that they were looking for," says Tony. He had wanted to be a DJ from an early age and had been practicing for the gig since he was 13. "I used to hook up a microphone to the radiogram and play records over a huge speaker we had in the hallway," confided Tony.

Within days he was up at Caroline House and being ushered into Chris Moore's office. "As the receptionist opened the door, I caught my first sight of the man on whom my entire broadcast future rested," remembers Tony.

"He was standing on his head throwing darts at a dartboard. It was just a taste of things to come, the wild world of offshore radio. I knew that I was at the right place!"

Radio Caroline PD Chris Moore

Tony's thirty-minute audition that morning wasn't impressive. "He told me that my voice was too flat and that I had to sound more exciting and put energy and laughter into it!" Fortunately, he gave me a second chance, liked what he heard and asked me if I could start the next day!

As an inexperienced broadcaster, Tony started on Radio Caroline at just £15 a week, but that was still twice the average weekly wage, and included all food and other requirements while on the ship. The on-board DJs worked a 'two weeks on board, one week ashore' schedule in those days so, all things considered, it was a grand life. The only downside for Tony was that his seven-year relationship with his girlfriend Sally didn't survive the periods afloat.

Tony, Chris Moore and Colin Nicol went out to the Mi Amigo together on Wednesday 25th July, with Tony replete in a hooped T-shirt that his mum bought him to celebrate getting the job, thinking it would make him look a bit nautical. “I was so excited when we got out to the ship and couldn’t wait to get on the air. This ship was to be the focus of my life for the next two years and I enjoyed my time on Caroline immensely!” Fifty five years later Tony would still be telling the world on the BBC, in the press and by social media how much his break at Radio Caroline meant to him.

Tony always tried to stayed out of the internal politics, in which most aspects of Radio Caroline was immersed when he first joined. “Ronan was supposed to be concentrating on the North ship, while Crawford was in charge of the old Atlanta ship, now called Caroline South.”

Tony Blackburn on the Mi Amigo with engineer Patrick Starling

Colin Nicol

“There was always plenty of confusion (Colin Nicol describes it as total chaos) and no one really knew what was going on.”

There was often some friction between the two Carolines. ‘Project Atlanta’ (south) and ‘Planet Productions’ (North) shared a lot of resources, particularly sales, but while young Ronan liked to be cool and groovy, his opposite number, Allan Crawford was older and more straight-laced. Ronan was a bit of a maverick and would often take a chance on new faces and slightly off-beat characters, while Crawford insisted that his broadcasters be experienced professionals.

Christopher Moore was officially the Head of Programmes for both stations but tended to spend more time on Caroline North business. Most of the music and programmes for the south ship were overseen by Ken Evans, who had heaps of broadcast experience in Australia before coming to London.

“Ken had an encyclopaedic knowledge of music,” remembers Keith Skues, who worked with him on the Caroline South ship, the Mi Amigo. “He loved all kinds of music, but especially show tunes and he produced an hour of this every afternoon at 2pm with Simon Dee hosting it. The North ship never carried that and was regarded as much hipper and groovier.”

DJ's spare time
Watching TV was one of the favourite activities for the team on board both Caroline ships, although this did not begin until late afternoon. Card games and scrabble were very popular and many DJs took to song-writing, or spending time replying to the hundreds of letters that each of them got with every tender. Visitors were always welcome and most weeks both ships were visited by new record stars to promote their latest discs.

While the core broadcast team comprised just five or so DJs and a newsman, the churn of broadcasting staff was immense; the station got through around 60 broadcasters in the first two years. One reason for this was the hardships endured by being away from home for two weeks at a time, many couldn't handle it.

The high wages paid to DJs when they came off on leave also posed problems for some individuals; they simply could not handle the life. In later years Ronan would ask the DJs how much they needed and he just paid them as little as he could get away with. That way he knew they would be keen to go back on board as soon as they had spent up.

Commercials
Even more important than the programming was the Traffic Department, which handled all materials broadcast as commercials. These might be simple read scripts, or recorded commercials, made either on board or, more usually in the studios in the basement at Caroline House.

Some of the big national commercials, such as those for products from the multinational companies such as *Unilever* might arrive 'ready-made' at Caroline House, having been produced by the client's own advertising agency. They still had to be 'trafficked into the system' which mean they needed properly logging and scheduling, to ensure each hour was carefully broadcast with them spaced throughout the period and avoiding too many commercials being bunched together, or 'heavily loaded' as it became known.

This meant logging of each commercial and ensuring that copies were sent to the two ships for transmission. After broadcast the Routine Sheet (which simply scheduled commercials to be aired) would come back to Caroline House. It had now become a proper log, and was signed by the DJ or whoever was responsible for playing the commercial on the air. Once back at Caroline House, administration staff would prepare the invoice and mail it, to ensure the commercials were paid for. This was the main revenue of Radio Caroline and needed careful management.

In August 1964 the Caroline South line-up included Mike Brown, Doug Kerr, Errol Bruce, Mike Allen, Keith Skues and Tony Blackburn. The breakfast show was usually hosted by Tony with Doug Kerr driving the desk. Doug had a receding hair problem, for which he took various pills and potions, and was very jealous of Tony's generous barnet. One morning he mentioned that Tony's hair looked like a tea cosy – and the name stuck! Everyone from Tony's Radio Caroline days still refers to him fondly as Tea Cosy.

"What made Radio Caroline so attractive to me was a couple of essential ingredients: youth, music and rebellion," says Tony. "It was bad news for us DJs that Ronan and Crawford never really got on well together and their constant factionalism caused much insecurity on board."

"We made so many hits in those first few months of Caroline," remembers Tony. "*Have I the Right* by the Honeycombs and *Terry* by Twinkle, who visited the ship and stayed overnight. We made those hits and a lot more too. Twinkle was quite a welcome change from the usually all-male crew, although two or three record librarians did come out from head office quite often."

Two of the girls had been hired by Radio Atlanta the previous year; Marion Cochrane and an ex BBC girl called Maureen Blackburn. They were joined by Dorothy Wright once the workload became so heavy. The girls usually went out to the ship in pairs every few weeks to keep the record library updated and other admin tasks complete.

One of Radio Caroline's recruits to the world of DJing that summer was Roger Gale, a budding actor, who was called by a former schoolfriend and asked to come in for an audition. He joined the station on August Bank Holiday Monday and flew up to the Isle of Man to join the North ship in Ramsey Bay.

That same weekend, Radio Caroline introduced its own chart of the Top 50 selling records of the week. The was presented as a countdown (it was later called the Caroline *Countdown of Sound*) opening with number 50 which, that first week, was The Ronettes' *Best Part of Breaking Up*. The show culminated with the number 1, North London's very own Honeycombs and their worldwide chart topper, *Have I The Right*. The chart closely followed the various UK sales charts published by the NME, Disc, the Melody Maker and Record Retailer and close perusal of the listings doesn't show much deviation from that used by the BBC.

A few months later, Caroline's new competitor Radio London broadcast a shorter chart; a Fab 40 which was introduced six weeks after they launched. Unlike the Caroline Countdown, Big L's chart was made up by its chief DJ. It often included plug records and formed part of the package of their 'paid for play' procedure. As a result, London's Fab 40 bore little resemblance to anyone else's chart, often dropping records from it before they ever made everyone else's chart.

Noble goes nutty

While listening to Keith Skues's programme in September that year, Paul Noble had heard Keith mention that he had worked in some outlets of the British Forces Broadcasting Network. Having also worked in the BFN, the comment prompted Paul to immediately apply for a job on Radio Caroline himself.

Paul Noble, Colin Nicol & Mel Howard

Colin Nicol

Paul's practical experience got him a job on Radio Caroline South as a technician, but he soon progressed to the microphone side of the operation. Paul's first programme was on Christmas Day 1964, Radio Caroline South's gift to listeners in the south? Paul eventually hosted the breakfast show where his 'Nutty Noble' character presided until the end of 1965.

Licence for commercial radio?

Caroline's investors had backed the offshore shenanigans in the hope that the Conservative Government would permit commercial radio, free of the BBC and able to accept spot advertising and sponsored programming. The Establishment was however split into two with Premier Minister Alex Douglas-Home's traditional style of government electing to take no action either way on offshore radio. This lethargy spelt a big disappointment to those lined up behind Jocelyn Stevens who wanted immediate action to licence commercial radio.

Simon Dee was featuring in many magazine adverts now and commercial radio was a major topic among candidates in the General election that Autumn. "Whatever happens, and however many stations become established, I hope nobody forgets how much they owe to Ronan O'Rahilly," said Simon. "He's the man who took the first risks and fought for something he believed in."

At the General Election in October 1964 the Labour party's ideological anti-Americanism and anti-commercialism brought an end to the hopes and aspirations that commercial radio on land might be licenced.

Those investors in Radio Caroline who had bet on existing stations winning licences realised this was hardly likely now and the new Postmaster General, Tony Benn lost no time in confirming the Labour Party's intentions to introduce legislation to thwart the offshore stations. It was to be almost three years before the socialist's ban on offshore radio came true, although it was unable to stop Caroline, which had a bright if somewhat faltering future ahead of it.

Caroline Annual

A popular Christmas gift for teenagers was once an 'annual' in the form of a hardback book. These were usually issued by large publishing houses on a franchise basis and as the station was by now a major brand name, a Caroline Annual was published. The contract went to the Manchester firm, World Distributors, who had Paul Denver edit this edition, which was printed in Norwich.

Some of Caroline's history is given in the book and it also has potted details of various personalities from both ships were included as well as a general inventory of the equipment. Over two thirds of the content however was of black & white pictures and articles about then current pop music stars, such as the Rolling Stones, Dusty Springfield, The Animals, PJ Proby, Manfred Mann and the Honeycombs. Many were closely associated with Radio Caroline

The book wasn't particularly up to date nor 'cutting edge'; it had a large number of articles about jazz music and artistes, for example. As with all annuals of this type, it was written in the Autumn, for the Christmas market but named as the following year, in this case 1965.

Among those featured in the book were Chris Barber, Johnnie Dankworth, Kenny Ball and Ella Fitzgerald, presumably as Caroline's music producer was Gerry Duncan, a keen jazz fan. There was even a 1940s shot of jazz trumpeter Bix Beiderbecke!

The Caroline Annual included articles on some of the DJs plus a description of the ships and the tortuous procedure one followed when going out to visit them. The annual also curiously referred to the DJs as "the disc spinners" and wrongly described certain staff as being American and Irish. It was however correct when it described two voices heard on Caroline as being "easy on the eye": Marilyn Richard who had previously worked as a secretary in Monte Carlo and Jenny Conway who appeared on stage in *Gentlemen Prefer Blondes*.

Cruising nearer London

One of the record librarian visits to the South ship was in late October 1964 and coincided with the Mi Amigo's experimental move further towards London, near the forts from where Radio Invicta and a new station, Radio City, were broadcasting. This was the same location as the Mi Amigo had used in 1962 to demonstrate its attributes to potential buyers, including Alan Crawford. The new anchorage was at the junction of the Prince's Channel and the Oaze / Black Deep; it was indeed a little closer to London but was more exposed, particularly to easterly running seas.

Offshore One tenders the Mi Amigo
Colin Nicol

Two months previously however, the territorial waters limit had been varied by the introduction of a 'Bay Closing Order' called the 1964 Territorial Waters Order in Council. An Order in Council is a regulation not debated in Parliament but having just as much weight in the courts. By measuring the surface area tidal waters inside a coastal indentation and comparing it to the area on an arc to the seaward side of that line, a new area of territorial waters could be brought within a state's jurisdiction.

One such 'Bay Closing Line' ran from near Clacton, due south across the Estuary down to the Kent coast, placing the proposed anchorage inside British waters, as well as three sea forts that were used for broadcasting (Red Sands, Shivering Sands and Knock John).

The new anchorage also exposed the Mi Amigo to much heavier seas: "We were very unlucky with the time of year, as there were high winds and the seas rushing inwards, they just tossed the Mi Amigo around all over," remembers George Saunders who was engineer on the ship at that time.

"We were only there a week, but it was a nightmare just keeping the station on air," said George. "The ship rolled dreadfully and made almost everyone on board sick. The transmitter didn't like it either, then we had a little fire in the engine room, that could have been dangerous but for some quick action. We were all pleased when we were ordered to return to the usual station, just off Frinton."

"We went through some bad weather off the Isle of Man too that winter," recalls Alan Turner. "The wind blew the windows in on the bridge and we dragged our anchor quite a few miles up the coast. We all had to muster in the mess ready to be evacuated if the abandon ship call came, which fortunately it didn't."

As well as record librarian duties, Marion, Dorothy and Maureen were also charged with promoting the station at various events. Marion was one of the few who really knew anything about music radio and had run two rock'n'roll stations in Australiaincluding 2SM in Sydney from where she imported the idea of calling the Caroline DJs 'Good Guys'.

The advertising industry had by now realised how powerful the two Radio Caroline ships had become especially among the lucrative teenagers and housewives demographic groups. Advertising began to come in faster and faster under the control of Michael Parkin, who had been recruited by Jocelyn Stevens. The ads were all pre-recorded on small reels of tape, which occasionally started with a slurring, wow on the big machines on the ships. Each commercial was preceded with a 'Ding Ding' of the Caroline bell, giving the station a signature sound. By late 1964 Caroline was attracting serious money from advertising and a wide range of other activities. In the December 1964, advertising for Radio Caroline peaked at £50,000 for the month.

Caroline's disc jockeys were now being paid at a rate of £30 a week and the organisation had the pick of the crop as there really was no other real competition. Radio Luxembourg's programmes were all sponsored and they invariably hired known names, experienced DJs, such as Pete Murray, David Jacobs and so on. The only other stations were two small operations (Radio City and Radio Invicta) who transmitted from abandoned gun forts in the Thames estuary; both those paid either the average wage of £7 a week, or even less!

Many of the DJs were excellent communicators, such as Mike Raven – a very well-respected blues and soul fan. He had given up a promising career on the stage to join Radio Atlanta but wound up running KING Radio on a nearby fort with very low power. Mike later joined the BBC's supposed replacement for the radio ships, Radio 1, but so many of his contemporaries simply faded into obscurity to follow other careers.

Caroline coverage of both radio ships
Radio Caroline

Tony Blackburn went from strength to strength and developed his own inane cheerful character. His programmes were crammed with one-liners: “So what, if my jokes produce a collective groan among listeners? It’s a lot better to be loved (or loathed) rather than have an audience that was indifferent to you,” says Tony. “At least it meant that people were talking about you.”

At first Tony’s jokes were all made up, usually about things such as their mast and the portholes. He began collating them into exercise book. “Later I subscribed to the Robert Orbin comedy service after reading one of his books. Many great comedians use services like this – Ken Dodd and Bob Monkhouse for example.”

One of Tony’s colleagues on Caroline South was Keith Skues, who had learned the broadcasting craft with various outlets of the British Forces Network. His voice entertained the troops in such far-flung bases as Germany, Kuwait, Aden and Kenya. With five years broadcasting experience under his belt when he joined Caroline, Keith already had the nickname ‘Cardboard Shoes, Keith Skues’ and quickly used his spare time on the Mi Amigo to invent more. And more!

Tony Blackburn too had a catchphrase on Caroline, essential fodder for all self-respecting disc jockeys. Tony’s was “Lets Away” which he even manged to slip into the opening of BBC Radio 1. Most memorable moments though are probably Tony’s use of an old tape of a dog barking which he found in a sound effects library on the Mi Amigo. He called the dog Arnold, even though the poor creature only had two Woofs. It became ever more widely known on subsequent stations that Tony broadcast on, including Radio London and Radio 1.

“We had a well-equipped studio, considering its location,” says Tony. “The main console had two excellent turntables and a professional Gates mixer that had come over with the ship from the USA, as well as a good quality AKG microphone plus some monitor speakers that the music sounded great on. We also had a couple of open reel Ampex tape recorders, mainly used for playing commercials but they also had plenty of back up music available, ready to play, in case the seas got too rough to play music off disc.”

"In the studio, we also had a great new piece of equipment called a Cart Player; this had a short endless loop of tape onto which we recorded our station ID jingles and other bits that we used regularly, Arnold lived inside one of those. I still have the original bit of tape somewhere!"

"On the face of it, jingles were just another form of station identification but to me they were a crucial programme element, vital to create a cohesive, smooth-running radio show, explains Mr Tea Cosy.

"We had a rumbling generator outside and, to make matters worse, the studio was very close to the waterline. As soon as the seas got rough, so did our shows! We would place heavy coins on the turntable's tone arms to stop them slipping across the discs," explains Tony. "To ham things up a bit we would often throw things like ash trays about and make it sound as though we were really braving it against all odds!" (For more of Tony's more dangerous escapades on the Mi Amigo, see the 'On The Beach' chapter on page 139).

Chris Sandford had appeared in several films and on Coronation Street for six months. His part was Walter Potts, Minnie Caldwell's window cleaner. (He had been signed up by Dennis Tanner who played the part of a music agent in the programme). Chris's single 'Not Too Little' became a Top 20 hit. Chris left Caroline to pursue his movie career and appeared in over fifty films and is now a renowned expert in fly fishing.

Initially, there were no attempts to sell merchandise by Caroline. The market for T-shirts and other garments emblazed with a station's logo was unknown in Britain. An enterprising company, *Slater & Tortoiseshell* of Blackpool offered to produce these for just 12/6d (62 pence). They had a simple logo of the words 'Radio Caroline' curved around a skull and cross-bones, with '199m' at the bottom.

Chris Sandford 'mikeside'
Radio Caroline

Within a week they had sold several thousand. They soon became 'the' trendy item to wear.

First Caroline T-shirt

"Our external contractors were soon totally inundated with orders and unable to cope, so we had to bring the operation back into Caroline House," remembers Oonagh, Ronan's PA. "I set up a complete new department on an upper floor in Caroline House where I had six typists doing nothing but dealing with T-shirt orders. This section was run by Delia Zimmerman, who was my assistant. She was a very capable secretary and good organiser, especially at the time we had to bail out Caroline Products and bring that all work in house."

Caroline House was now home to over fifty staff, although Ken Evans professed that he didn't know what most of the people did, except sit around and read the press all day. "The building was a magnet for people in the music business and we had a constant procession of new artists, eager to get some publicity for their new records."

Musicians were invited to send in their raw recordings to Caroline with the possibility of being signed up by Ronan's own music company, *ROAR Music*, which Allan Crawford had helped him set up. They released about a dozen singles with publishing by ROAR Music Ltd; usually production was handled by a friend of Robert Stigwood, Simon Napier-Bell. Stiggy was a friend of Crawfords who was becoming a media magnate. Many of his releases were plugged heavily on Caroline, such as the first BeeGees release, *Spicks and Specks*.

The Caroline Club magazine announced to its readers that a Caroline perfume was already in production and would be available shortly. The first batch was a complete sell out. Prizes offered in the competitions included tape-recorders, radios, T-shirts, shavers and even trips out to both ships! Caroline was also the first in the UK to offer a range of James Bond clothing, with sweaters, ties, and special Bond perfume, all on sale to Caroline Club members only.

Radio Caroline was now setting the music world on fire and every day new venues were announced for Caroline Disc Nights that invariable were sell outs. Simon Dee and fellow DJ Chris Sandford were very popular at these sessions and were often mobbed by fans eager for autographs or simply to wish them and Radio Caroline well.

Chris Sandford & Gay Shingleton
Radio Caroline

Gay Shingleton was recruited from the *Ready Steady Win* TV show (a spin off from Ready Steady Go) as a DJ. She had already worked as a DJ for a year in clubs around the West End and proved very popular with male fans who queued up for a chance to dance with her. She made a record of a Jackie de Shannon song (*In My Time of Sorrow*) was heard on several radio commercials and often seen around Caroline House.

Gay went on to have a successful TV and film career – her tragic story is about to be told in a book and probably a film by Simon Farquar.

The tremendous success of Radio Caroline attracted Don Pierson, a successful Texan businessman to look it over, but Ronan O'Rahilly wouldn't talk to him. Don thought the Radio Caroline operation was staid and not very commercial at all, so decided to set up his own station. Within a few weeks he had assembled a group of investors who stumped up around half a million dollars to buy a converted minesweeper and fit it out in Miami. After delays in Madeira and Lisbon, it arrived in the North Sea, equipped with a 50,00 transmitter.

London or Continental?

Within a few days of Radio London's ship *The Galaxy* arriving, Ronan called them and suggested a merger, with their newer ship replacing Caroline South. The Mi Amigo could move abroad to become *Radio Continental.* Caroline had already had a lot of interest from advertisers and listeners there and Radio Veronica were doing so well they had just bought a new ship, the Norderney and a larger transmitter.

Ronan met Radio London's Tom Danaher at Heathrow Airport who drew up a draft agreement, which would see the three stations pooling revenue with the Caroline North owners (Planet) take 36%. Danaher spoke for a quarter of the investors, but the others rejected the idea.
Radio London was managed by Philip Birch, a calmly spoken man who had cut his teeth at J Walter Thompson, then the world's biggest advertising agency. One error that London made was to initially moor near the army forts, as close to the capital as possible, enabling them to be served from Sheerness. The 'Bay Closing Order' had moved the 3 mile limit further out just weeks before. Ronan warned Birch not to broadcast there, as he didn't want offshore radio getting a bad name.

They then moved the Galaxy up the coast to anchor in the Wallet too, just a mile from the Caroline South ship, the Mi Amigo but the ship was silent for another month while they battled with technical problems and a boardroom battle that saw two key station builders sidelined.

London recruited a team of highly professional DJs, most with experience in the USA, Canada or Australia. The exception was a bright young Liverpudlian broadcaster called Kenny Everett. Most ear-catching of all was a package of polished station-ID jingles, made by PAMS, the leading jingle imagineers! Radio Caroline too had jingles, but these were all home-made efforts, mostly done on board the ship by DJs in the station's 'down time' overnight. By comparison, the Radio London sound simply sizzled.

"As soon as Radio London began test transmissions, I thought the game was up for Caroline," says Tony Blackburn. "they kept playing this one particular jingle *Wonderful Radio London*; it was slick, it sounded commercial and so professional. Great sounding adverts too, but those jingles were just the best thing I had ever heard." Caroline DJs immediately began stepping up the recordings of their own jingles but they were clearly a lot more amateurish than the polished PAMS sets that Radio London had bought. Some of the Caroline jingles were made by artistes in return for airplay of their commercial releases.

"The other big thing that Radio London had going for it was, their music format was constant and coherent," explains Tony. "On Caroline, we began our day with a fresh pop sounds, such as on my show. Then for the rest of the day it went all over the place with show-tunes, big band, jazz, everything! London played non-stop pop, I think the listeners liked that a bit more than Caroline's disjointed mish-mash."

Radio London chose a dial position of 266 metres, conveniently between the BBC's Light Programme on 247 and London Regional Service programme on 276 metres. Radio Caroline's two ships were both on 197 and 201 (both announced as 199), close by Veronica and Luxembourg, all easy to find in the 'Bandspread' part of the MW.

In December 1964 Radio London was still silent and Caroline offered to bareboat lease the ship. A draft agreement was drawn up by lawyers in the Bahamas, where Radio London was officially domiciled. The rates were suddenly hiked to £5,000 per week for the charter hey also demanded and onerous personal guarantees from all the Caroline board, and other terms which were not acceptable to Radio Caroline.

Caroline PD Christopher Moore asked Ken Evans, the music controller on the south ship, to visit the North ship. His task was to make a complete inventory of the record library and the get rid of all the music they had that was not on the South ship. This was an effort to make Caroline sound like a one national network.

This was such a huge task that Ken had to hire in some local help from the Isle of Man to simply do the basic cataloguing, so voluminous was the record library of the Caroline North ship. "It was absolutely impossible, they had records up there which the southern ship didn't have and the southern ship had records which the northern ship didn't have," Ken explained in an interview with Colin Nicol. "We would have to scrap hundreds of records."

Christmas 1964

Simon Dee and Ronan O'Rahilly conceived a plan to stage a 'Black Christmas' for 1964, to give Caroline a new, fresh, youthful sound as it seemed certain that London would start transmissions over Christmas. This idea didn't go down well with many of the south ship's laid-back team and despite some feverish preparation the idea was dropped.
A request was made to the BBC for a copy of the Queen's Speech to broadcast on Caroline on Christmas Day, but the Corporation refused.

Caroline also took on a permanent representative in New York and opened an office at 1697 Broadway, in the 'Ed Sullivan Theater' block in midtown Manhatten. George Bernard was a Brit who ran a trio of companies, including the (*Trans-Atlantic Entertainment Corporation)* which supplied programming for both the Radio Caroline outlets. George also wrote a lot of scurrilous stories for the *National Enquirer*. A few Radio Caroline DJs were flown over to New York in an attempt to get more publicity for the station among the advertising fraternity around Madison Avenue. They met the stars of Roulette Records and held a couple of press conferences which got lots of coverage.

Memo header from Caroline's US rep', George Bernard

One George Bernard success was his arranging a major national TV appearance for not one, but three "Ronans" on American TV. The identity of the MD of Radio Caroline was a mystery in an episode of *What's My Line*, where four panellists had to question and then match the correct person to the role. Only one (Kitty Carlisle) correctly named Ronan, the others all assumed that the Daily Mail's imposter Nigel Dempster was the real man.

Miss Caroline 1965, Denine Fiore

Among George Bernard's betst stunts was the appointment of a Miss Radio Caroline in New York. The winner was Denine Fiore, who was a leading New York model who had never entered a beauty pageant before. She was introduced to various media outlets and advertising agencies.

Simon Dee was now based at Caroline House and in charge of programming, although that meant he had to become the station's face at many events and in press features. He announced that "Radio Caroline will soon evolve into much more of a radio station, rather than a floating juke box. We shall have regular news bulletins, interviews with famous sports people, conducted by me personally and an increased variety of music." In answer to the Big L Fab 40, Radio Caroline introduced a *Sound 65* but it proved difficult, squeezing 65 records into a three hour show.

One of Simon's last recruits was Roger Gale, who had been working on the Caroline North ship for six months but had fallen out with the PD, Chris Moore. "Simon called me up around Easter and said that he had heard I was no longer on Caroline North," remembers Roger. "Simon invited me to join his team on Caroline South, but by the time I got there, Simon had left, to join the BBC." Roger did join the South ship where he spent six months, before leaving to join Radio Scotland which launched at Hogmanay 1965.

Roger Gale on Caroline

After his time in Scotland, Roger acted as a midwife on the Radio 270 ship Oceaan 7, a small boat off Scarborough, before being snapped up by the BBC. He worked at Radio One and Radio London and before he was elected Member of Parliament for Thanet North (Margate) and Herne Bay.

Caroline Newsbeat

The South ship began to lose lots of listeners following the arrival of Radio London and to regain them Caroline South began its own News service. The initiative was one from Australian, Graham Webb, who had just joined the station. Ronan gave Graham his head to develop this and made him Head of News. He had arrived in the UK only a few months earlier with a wealth of radio experience.

Graham hired two newsreaders for each ship; generally these were DJs who could annunciate well, not sound too English and have a mid-Atlantic inflection. Among the newsreaders in 1965 was Colin Berry, soon promoted to programming. A large receiver was installed in a newsroom on the ship where news readers could prepare bulletins. Graham 'Spiderman' Web was one of the station's first news readers, but many well-known broadcasters also fulfilled the role over the next few years, including Colin Berry, Dave Williams, Gerry Burke and Howard Rose. The news service was later extended to the North ship.

Among the rules that Graham set out for his colleagues were that "The Radio Caroline News Service is not to be called "The News" but always referred to as *Caroline Newsbeat.* This was announced by a strident jingle with pounding drums and a blast on a ships horn. It did sound very dramatic and for some people probably made the news actually sound interesting, a real production and a catchy presentation.

The new Labour government made more threats of new laws to outlaw offshore radio. Radio Caroline responded by promising to fight any new legislation in the European Court of Human Rights, and a lot of legal advice was taken.

A cub reporter at a Kent newspaper was approached by Caroline DJ Carl Conway to organise a petition to 'Save Caroline'. David Hughes was a superb target for this as not only was he a keen Caroline fan, but he became editor of the music paper Disc & Music Echo as well as a leading record company MD too, at EMI and Polydor, who was to play an important part in helping Radio Caroline.

Among those who joined Caroline as a newsreader was Londoner Nick Bailey. Only just 18, Nick had begun a theatrical career, running some promotion events at the Mermaid Theatre when the chance to be a Radio Caroline North newsreader arose. Nick is a seasoned broadcaster having spent time in Australian radio as well as being the voice that launched Classic FM. Nick remembers his time on the Radio Caroline North ship fondly: "Sometimes when reading the news I'd see sky through the studio window during one story and sea the next." There are more details in his autobiography, *Across The Waves.*

Sponsored Programmes
The many sponsored programmes that Caroline was airing at this time are thought to be a root cause of the inability of Caroline South to match Radio London's audience. These short shows were produced by advertising agencies on behalf of their clients and Caroline had little or no editorial control over the content, which was often incongruous. Worse, they were often hosted by old established names from light entertainment, who were not exactly very trendy or "with it".

Pete Murray was acceptable (he was still on the Top of the Pops rota on BBC 1 TV) but the likes of Anne Shelton and Charlie Drake were never going to attract many young listeners. Nor indeed was Vera Lynn, who hosted a programme on make up!

Radio Caroline North too had some sponsored programmes, though not so many as the south ship. There was also no competition, just the BBC Light programme and Ireland's RTE, which had only one channel aimed at all the family. Radio Caroline North's coverage was good across rural areas, while the main cities of Liverpool and Manchester got a strong signal.

Kennedy's greeting to Wilson
A special greeting was recorded by Robin Leach, another of Radio Caroline's associates in the USA, from Bobby Kennedy, who had been the US Attorney General but was by then a senator. He was tricked into making the recording by George Bernard with the story that the station had been named after his niece, Caroline Kennedy. The recording was played out at a St Patricks Day lunch at the London Hilton Hotel in the presence of Prime Minister Harold Wilson and Ronan O'Rahilly. This was the first public suggestion that the name was in honour of Caroline Kennedy.

Sen. Robert Kennedy
Terry Dixon

In his speech, Kennedy said "I want to first thank Ronan O'Rahilly, the managing director of Radio Caroline for the opportunity to extend my greetings to the Hon. Harold Wilson, the Prime Minister. I want to tell you what an honour it is to say a few words to you."

This linking by Kennedy of Harold Wilson to Radio Caroline caused something of a furore as it had been obtained by deception. It was the first time that the tale had been used publicly and began a self-perpetuating myth, often misquoted as the origin of the name.

Caroline South recruited more antipodeans, including Jon Sydney, who was as Australian as his name. He had worked in radio 'down under' but his real interest was the theatre and he trod the boards in the West End after leaving Radio Caroline.

As Radio Caroline's first birthday approached, a series of special promotions were undertaken. One such star-studded event was at the Fairfield Hall in Croydon, South London, where the Moody Blues topped the bill along with the Yardbirds and Jimmy James. Many of the day's top stars recorded special greetings for Caroline which were then played on the air. Among those heard were Dusty Springfield, Smokey Robinson, Martha and the Vandellas, The Supremes, Tom Jones, Dave Clark, Stevie Wonder, Donovan, Roy Orbison and Cliff Richard.

A number of awards were presented – the **Caroline Bell Awards.** Among the recipients for the first Bell Awards were Petula Clark for her single *Downtown*, Tom Jones for *Its Not Unusual* and the Animals for *House of the Rising Sun.* Petula Clark had enjoyed her first big hit for three years with 'Downtown' after heavy plugs on Caroline, as indeed had many of her stable mates such as the Honeycombs, the Kinks, Donovan, The Searchers and Sandie Shaw. The Beatles too were given a Caroline Bell Award, presented by Caroline's first DJ Simon Dee during the filming of their second movie, *Help*.

The awards were presented by Simon Dee, who remembers the Beatles one well; "All the shows had names and George Harrison slipped me a copy of their latest single and said: "When are we going to hear this on *Top Deck* then Simon?" That was a lovely moment as here were the most famous guys in the world who not only knew about me and my shows on Caroline, even its name, but were keen to have their music included on it."

Simon presents The Beatles with a Caroline Bell
Radio Caroline

"Pirate radio, particularly Radio Caroline, is a really exciting part of all our lives," said Paul McCartney. "It is part of the spirit of our lives, culturally and musically. I don't understand why they don't just let them bring the Caroline ship into Liverpool and broadcast from there, or London. They aren't doing any harm and are doing a lot of good."

Paul McCartney was a big radio fan and had quite a collection of radios. He had a specially tuned radio fitted in his car in the sixties and took a personal interest in the airplay that groups got, especially his seventies group, Wings. John Lennon was also a keen Caroline supporter and later persuaded George Harrison to support Caroline's fight for free radio. Ringo tried for his own station, with Cilla Black.

Since Caroline's first days, disc jockeys on both ships would work two weeks on board, followed by two weeks paid leave. They were increasingly expected to participate in events and other activities during their leave and when Caroline switched the shift pattern to two weeks on and one week off, some thought this was an imposition and left. Among those unable to face shorter shore leave were Roger Gale, Gary Kemp, Doug Kerr and Mike Allen, all from the South ship.

Caroline Good Guys
Record librarian Marion Cochrane had previously worked at radio station 2SM in Sydney which had copied New York station WMCA and called its DJs "Good Guys". This promotion was adopted by Caroline for a short while; it saw all the DJs dress in a uniform of blue check shirt, grey slacks and dark double-breasted yachting blazers at the many promotional events that they had to attend when on their shore leave. These were provided ad part of a deal with Burton's tailors, then a much bigger operation than their chain of shops today.

The team then on Caroline South was Tony Blackburn, Gary Kemp, Mike Allen, Keith Skues, Don Allen and Bob Walton. Promotions featuring the *Radio Caroline Good Guys,* were only short-lived.

Don moved to the North ship later in 1965 and took a lot of the Good Guys style with him. The younger audience was not impressed by uniforms however and most of the DJs sold their own branded T-shirts. These were very successful and were each professionally drawn with pretty life-like caricatures of the DJs. Tony Prince (yer Royal Ruler) is proud that his T-shirt still fits him fifty years later! Don Allen hung on to his Caroline 'Good Guys' blazer and with its embroidered badge pocket depicting the Caroline ship and logo.

The Radio Caroline schedules still used generic programme names, such as *All Systems Go, Spin Around* and *Traffic Jam* for most of its programmes, but on the North Ship some DJ names were creeping in. These were mainly for the better known and longer established DJs; Tom Lodge was hosting the breakfast show and Mike Ahern was mid mornings. Mike joined after writing to the station claiming to be the north of England's best DJ, after the station initially rejected him saying they received an average of 4,000 applications for jobs every week!

Since arriving off the Isle of Man, Caroline North had kept to the previous broadcast schedule of 6am to 8pm, staying open later only for some religious programmes that aired after 8pm. The reasons for the closedown at 8 were two-fold: Ronan believed that most of the hip and groovy 'Caroline crowd' were out to dinner, watching gigs or going to the pub after 8pm. Those who were older stayed home and watched TV. He believed that there really wasn't much of a radio audience available and what there was followed Radio Luxembourg anyway. Their big problem was the sky wave fading after dark.

Caroline North introduced some shows after midnight including a 'Surf Party' that ran from 12am-2am. It was usually presented by Jim Murphy, a Texan DJ whose big claim to fame seems to have been squatting at the top of poles for several days at a time, to get a place in the Guinness Book of World Records! Jim's programme attracted sponsorship from Cossack Vodka but he left the station a year later.

Another new development was the daily airing of the Jack Spector Show, a pre-recorded show from New York, over both Radio Caroline North and South. His style and delivery was a little strident for many Brits, with him whooping and hollering, yelling and shouting, amidst a cacophony of sound effects and up-tempo tracks. It did however attract Caroline South's biggest audience.

Jack Spector covers the UK on Caroline

Jack's show had the latest records that were hits stateside, and became cult listening for those who wanted to keep up to date with US music trends. Jack was one of the original WMCA 'All American Good Guys' and carried on broadcasting until dropping dead from a heart attack in 1994. Jack's daily show could be sponsored for just £750 an hour on both Radio Carolines, but sadly, there were few takers for the opportunity.

Caroline Sales

Advertising sales on Caroline were in hands of some accomplished media salesmen, led by Michael Parkin who had been hired from TAM who conducted TV audience measuring metrics by Jocelyn Stevens in early 1964. He had recruited Anthony Welch who specialised in sponsored programming and the team was held together by Josie Scudder. She lived in Whitstable where her parents ran a public house and began her marketing career at Unilever. After a spell representing Grampian TV in London, she joined Caroline at the station's launch. She ran the sales department at Chesterfield Gardens until it closed when she went to work for the new Yorkshire TV where her old boss Gwyn Ward-Thomas had just won the franchise.

Some aspects of Radio Caroline's sales operation were run by Robin Courage, whose family were leading brewers and some by William Fielding who was the eleventh Earl of Denbigh – he married a lady called Caroline in 1965. They were joined by another member of the Chelsea set, Major Murray Robb.

Live from Radio Caroline

Ronan O'Rahilly had persuaded one of his favourite jazz organists, Jimmy Smith to go out the ship and play live. Originally this was to have been on the North Ship, but Smith's busy schedule meant that he couldn't fit it in. He was only in town for a few days, to finish some tracks for the film *Where the Spies Are* and an appearance at the Royal Albert Hall. The south ship, was chosen for this inaugural performance.

Smith and two backing musicians (Tony Crombie on drums and guitarist Tony Thorne) on arrived at the ship, complete with their instruments, however it proved impossible to get the Hammond organ into the studio. The doorways were dimply too narrow – the live gig would have to be played out on deck. The first number was: *Hip Ship Blues* and the second was Satin Doll. It was too cold to play much more out on deck – listeners could hear the wind whistling past the microphones. After that experience, Caroline stuck to playing records.

Jimmy Smith later recorded some jingles that were often played on Radio Caroline North. While not selling enough to break into the singles chart, Jimmy is much revered among jazz artists. Ronan's favourite artiste Ray Charles credits him as being among his biggest influences. Jimmy's material on the Verve label is even today being avidly sought out by record collectors and jazz aficionados. The live performance on the Mi Amigo was introduced on air by Simon Dee who remembered later in an interview that "It was so cold out on deck in the wind that Jimmy had to keep plunging his hands into a bucket of warm water to be able to play the organ."

This was to be one of Simon's last appearances on the air as the following week, Simon skipped over to the BBC where he became an instant star, not only hosting record programmes on the Light programme but as a TV interviewer on *Late Night Line Up*. He was a natural for the role with his method acting training from the early 60s, his various jobs in sales and hospitality and of course 15 months presenting on board Radio Caroline. Simon was the first BBC programme host to not work with a script, although the BBC were very nervous about it at first. "We had never worked with scripts on Caroline, just occasionally a few notes perhaps, and I didn't want to change who I was," said Simon.

Many sponsored programmes were being broadcast on Caroline in Summer 1965, such as a regular fifteen minute show each morning sponsored by the appropriately named Anchor Cigarettes. Chappell Pianos also sponsored a daily show of mainly music from the shows, while the North Ship carried several religious programmes. Both ships carried many national advertisers, including Bulova watches who sponsored time checks on many offshore stations and a half hour sponsored programme on Caroline.

The Mi Amigo became a royal residence for a couple of days when Prince Richard of Gloucester, a cousin of Queen Elizabeth, spent some time on the ship with some student friends while researching for a piece in his university's magazine (Magdalen College Cambridge). The Prince, who lives at Kensington Palace, is now Duke of Gloucester and undertakes engagements roles for the royal family.

Frances van Staden was Oonagh's elder sister who joined as a switchboard operator. She soon began doing increasingly more administration jobs and had good contacts with the press and took over the supply of information to newspapers and magazines, to get more publicity for the stations. Frances later began to take over selection of music too and she stayed with the station until 1968. She had several girls on her team looking after reception, communications and the press, including Caroline Irving and Mary Josephine.

Frances van Staden
Doug McKenzie

Frances later became one of Ronan's personal assistants and a key organiser at Caroline House. There was a seemingly endless procession of pretty "dolly birds" who came and went, some after as little as a few days; nepotism was rife, Caroline really was a family!

The British Government continued to occasionally make threatening noises against radio ships but also had its own battle to fight in various far-flung corners of the world. More parts of the British Empire were being given independence and one problem country was Rhodesia, whose all-white government was led by Ian Smith. They threatened a Unilateral Declaration of Independence from the UK and the matter was extensively discussed in Parliament. The story was picked up via a foreign radio station by Radio Caroline's *Newsbeat* team, who re-broadcast it many hours before the BBC.

The suggestion was made that a radio station run by Britain should broadcast to Rhodesia from a Royal Navy ship, to which Harold Wilson, who was at that time the UK's Prime Minister, responded: "If we have to borrow from the experience of Radio Caroline, then we shall have no hesitation in doing so." Oliver Smedley, as Chairman of Radio Caroline South wrote to Downing Street offering whatever help Caroline could give. Ronan wrote to the Labour Party offering to help but didn't even get the courtesy of a reply, though official records show his letter did go to Downing Street.

Radio Caroline did help the British Government in a couple of ways: a more powerful (50,000 watt) transmitter had been ordered to beef up the south ship. These were custom built and usually took about three months to finish. In order to help the Government, Caroline agreed to release theirs which was almost complete. It was flown to Africa where it was installed near Francistown, Bechuanaland, as a cross-border station beaming into Rhodesia.

Two engineers who knew the Continental Electronics equipment well were supplied by Radio Caroline; George Saunders and John Gillman from the Caroline South ship. As part of the Diplomatic Wireless Service, the transmitter carried BBC World Service programmes. After being flown back to the UK, it was later used to jam Radio Caroline.

John Bloom takeover?

A takeover of Radio Caroline by John Bloom, a well-known financier and businessman, almost went ahead. The retailing and wholesale guru knew how to squeeze a profit from anything. He was perhaps best known for importing washing machines from Holland for half their usual price in the UK and recruited a team to sell 'door to door'.

John Bloom's main schemes revolved around coupons and the resale of HP deals. He is often credited as the person who did most to remove the burden of 'retail price maintenance' from the UK, which was stifling sales of consumer goods.

John Bloom could certainly afford to buy Radio Caroline, he knew exactly how the station operated and was a radio enthusiast. He had trained as a radio technician in the RAF and even enjoyed taking a spell at the turntables at parties. He was also very keen on boats and owned a large yacht called the *Ariane* which was about the size of the Mi Amigo and was later sold to Adnan Koshaggi.

Bloom also had considerable background information on the radio station, courtesy of his wife Anne; she was one of the partners that ran 'The In Place', a night club that was a favourite haunt of Ronan O'Rahilly and a confidant of several of the Radio Caroline team. She had engaged David Bowie to play at one of her famous parties in their home on Park Lane, where the Beatles met him and helped him find an agent.

John Bloom set off to Switzerland and to Liechtenstein with Ronan O'Rahilly to seal a deal but they couldn't find the true owner of the ships, well hidden by the "cloak of incorporation'. Ronan had only been there once and couldn't remember the details, so Bloom eventually pulled out as he wanted to be certain of a watertight sale.

It was common for artistes to visit both Caroline ships to promote their records. Many big stars of the day such as Gene Pitney, the Rolling Stones and Twinkle braved the seas to plug their records. Vivacious vocalist Marie Vincent was just one of several French artistes who visited the DJs on the Radio Caroline South ship to plug her single *Chip Chip*.

Marie Vincent plugging her single to Bryan Vaughan in the Caroline South studio

David Kindred

The two ships had a combined audience of around ten million, so the exposure gained by getting airplay on Caroline was superb. Established artistes and new faces alike were prepared to make the trip out from Harwich or from Ramsey. A list of the many lesser known artistes who visited the Caroline ships could fill a book. Gene Pitney had been a keen radio constructor when young and he described his trips to Caroline and Big L as "Fascinating and very memorable."

In September 1965, Sylvan Mason went out to the Mi Amigo to plug her single about Romeo and Juliet. "The BBC had banned it and we needed some publicity, so a trip out to Radio Caroline one Friday morning was perfect," she remembers.

Sylvan Mason

"When it was time to return, I could not be found and worsening weather meant that the tender had to leave me behind. I had to stay on board until the tender came back on the Monday. The crew were all complete gentlemen and treated me very well. I was, after all, a stowaway and it was a problem even finding somewhere for me to sleep! The young engineer, Patrick Starling, was the nicest of them all, but Tony Blackburn and Roger Gale were very kind too and invited me to help on their programmes."

Sylvan appeared on the air during several shows, including Roger Gale's *Party Time*, which Sylvan still has a tape of. She even made the station closedown announcement on the Saturday and identified herself as 'the Stowaway Girl'. Sylvan's record was a minor hit and she became a songwriter for many artistes. She wrote the theme music for Morecambe and Wise's 1970 TV show.

Sylvan also wrote the theme music for Morecame and Wise's TV show and married Barry Mason, the writer of such hits as "Delilah", "Love Grows (Where my Rosemary Goes)". Her banned record "We Don't Belong", has since been re-released on two compilation CD's, vinyl, and recently as a double A side with her latest composition, "There's An Ache In My Heart".

Audience Problems

A new opinion poll released in early Autumn suggested that Caroline South's audience had plummeted while Radio London was attracting around 15%. This was a huge turnaround in the fortunes of Caroline South and their sales team had a battle to attract advertising. Earlier in the year, a steady drift downwards had been halted and revenues were still around £50k a month at Easter. It was during the summer that revenues had slumped.

This wasn't a problem in the north, where Caroline had no competition and had endeared itself to listeners by playing lots of local music. Caroline North was a younger sounding station, with groovier DJs. There were no interruptions of its programmes on the North ship for "older people's music" such as show-tunes and jazz, as were heard on the south station. It was pure unadulterated pop, with a loose sprinkling of country music. Teenagers didn't mind that much, as the C&W sound was more prevalent in the north and especially in Ireland.

The North ship had a strong loyal following and was involved in several initiatives. One of the most unusual, but very apt, was promotion of special life-vests. These were developed by a Manx firm, *Nicki Clothing* of Union Mills. After being demonstrated on BBC TV's 'Tomorrows World' programme these were sold by Caroline House's merchandising team and by chandlers at the Island's five ports.

In the south of England, music tastes were quite different. Crawford had tried to fill the Caroline South playlist with a lot of music on his own record labels, comprising what later became called "covers". These were hit songs but performed by sound-alikes, minor artistes or session musicians. They sold well in supermarkets as collections of hits, but most pop fans preferred to hear hits by the original artistes.

Radio London had a fast upbeat delivery style of young-sounding DJs, playing mostly hits, punctuated by brash zingy jingles generating an overall coherent sound of continuity, which listeners in the south east were flocking to in their droves.

Radio Caroline South had a faster turnover of disc jockeys than the North ship and probably used twice the number of its biggest competitor, Radio London, although Caroline was on the air almost a year longer than Big L. Caroline South got through 72 DJs plus another 8 who usually featured only in pre-recorded programmes.

Tony Blackburn almost left Caroline in 1965, when Tony Windsor (who had worked on the ship in its Atlanta days and was now in charge of DJs over on Radio London) sent a message across on the tender inviting 'Tea Cosy' to join Radio London. "I did go to a meeting with their man in charge of programming, Ben Toney, but he was determined that I should change my name to Mark Roman," remembers Tony. "He came up with the name to match a programming concept he had dreamt up, but I was a bit partial to my own name and had built up a following so I declined their kind offer." This was a common practice in the States (where Ben Toney was from) that when a DJ switched stations then he usually left his name behind.

Advertisers were not slow to realise this and those who wanted to maximise their audience soon discovered the best radio policy was to use Radio London whose powerful transmitter gave widest coverage in southern England. Caroline North was the best bet for rest of the country – Ireland, Scotland, Wales and northern England.

8. Caroline South expansion

Alan Crawford and his Caroline South team had to make huge cuts to their operation by Summer 65. They were unable to negotiate any reduction in the lease payments for the Mi Amigo, nor for the supply runs from Harwich by Wijsmullers. The only way to cut costs was to reduce the DJ roster. Reduced numbers meant that everyone was now expected to work longer stints on board. The two weeks break was now reduced to just one week and several DJs quit in protest.

The marine crew on the two ships could not be cut as safety was of paramount importance. Wijsmullers, who operated the two ships on behalf of the owners, would not accept any drops in manning levels. The only other cuts possible were the Caroline House staff in Mayfair. The team of 66 was slashed down to 35, although that was still twice as many as were employed at Radio London.

The 'merger' deal in June 1964 had pooled the advertising revenues, with Caroline North getting a slightly bigger share, 55%. South was still being run by Project Atlanta Ltd. They were paying huge leasing costs for the Mi Amigo and, as a result, they were going bust!

Listeners to Caroline South didn't notice many of the changes as DJs often came and went. Some would go on extended shore leave and then re-appear weeks or even months later, as though nothing had happened. Some DJs were also rotated between the North and South ship; Don Allen began his career on the South ship but was soon sent up North where his relaxed style and knowledge of country music was very popular, especially among Irish listeners.

Keith Skues confided that he often followed up mail from housewives and visited them unannounced. "I just drop in for a cup of tea and a chin-wag but they never believe it's me! Sometimes their husbands are home, they welcome me too. They wouldn't be so pleased to see me if they knew what their wives had written to me in the first place!"

"I am known to my audience as 'Cardboard Shoes' and Mr Fantasmagorical. I call my car the 'Skuesmobile' but I rarely get the chance to drive it, as we often spend many weeks at a time out on the ship. It does drive you mad after a while because, sharing a cabin with others so you get no privacy at all. That and having the station's output relayed all over the ship on loudspeakers," said Keith.

Keith Skues
'Cardboard Shoes'

Tony's first release

Many of Radio Caroline's DJs were making names for themselves with club appearances, opening stores and one young man from the Caroline South ship had always wanted to make records. Tony Blackburn had a good singing voice and had fronted a band in Bournemouth before his DJ career. He was signed by Jack Baverstock of Philips records for their Fontana label.

He recorded half a dozen sides which were arranged by Les Reed and released over the next year or so as singles, but none ever made the charts for Tony. This was partly because his colleagues on Caroline and his rivals on other stations wouldn't play them. Tony did finally make the charts in a small way in 1968 and has now released over two dozen singles, some of which are surprisingly good.

"We made a great record called *Don't Get off That Train*," remembers Tony. "It was a great thrill to hear it played on the Light Programme as a new spin. I pushed it as hard as I dare on Caroline, but for some reason it wasn't a hit. After my second release also flopped, I almost gave up the singing; well, for a little while!" Tony became a bit disenchanted by the music business for a while, especially after a song that he discovered was filched by other artists at the label.

South ship expansion plans

Michael Parkin had recruited a strong team of sales executives plus commercial production men Gerry Duncan and Canadian Bill Hearne. Their advert spots were of good quality but Michael's team often had problems closing sales as Radio London's signal was much stronger that Caroline South. The PAL board agreed that some way must be found to remedy their signal shortcomings.

A more powerful transmitter was considered and eventually a 50 kW rig was ordered but, due to lack of funds, the unit was diverted for use by the British government in a propaganda exercise in South Africa against Ian Smith's government in Rhodesia who had declared UDI. Both Allan Crawford and Ronan O'Rahilly each offered to help the Government in the plans to establish a powerful station broadcasting into Rhodesia.

The PAL board, who ran Radio Caroline South, felt it would be better to expand operations by using another of the abandoned gun-towers in the Thames Estuary and send the Mi Amigo to broadcast to another part of the UK to broaden their coverage area and pick up more listeners and thus advertising that way.

Radio 270 ship, Oceaan VII

G W Proudfoot

Talks were held with Don Robinson, who was keen to start a service covering the North East. Don was a Yorkshire-born showman and had success as an entrepreneur as well as a performing wrestler. If the Mi Amigo was stationed off the River Tees, coverage of the industrial north east, around Newcastle and Middlesborough would be assured and well down into Yorkshire.

Don often worked with legendary boxing promoter Jarvis Astaire who was a minor shareholder and was reputed to be joining the Caroline board. Talks continued slowly but Jarvis and Don decided not to proceed with the Caroline invitation. Jarvis had persuaded the government to licence sporting events to be shown live by closed circuit TV in various venues and he brought boxer Mohammed Ali to London

Don decided to set up his own offshore radio station. Originally to be called Radio Yorkshire, this project became Radio 270 and launched the following year from the Oceaan 7 moored off Scarborough.

Using the Forts

Using one of the abandoned military forts was an idea that had been suggested to the Caroline board by Colin Nicol in early 1964, when there had been delays getting the Mi Amigo across to the UK. He had thought that the abandoned army forts would make a good transmission site and avoid jumping through so many maritime 'hoops'.

The Caroline South management now returned to Colin's idea and selected the Knock John tower, a former naval gun emplacement, mounted on two concrete pillars and about 30 feet above the high water line. The structure had been colonised by seabirds since being abandoned and had been plundered for its copper and fittings.

The Knock John Fort's location was perfect; just to the seaward side of the army gun towers used by Radio City and KING Radio, it offered a much easier path for the radio signal to London than the ship. It was close to the location that Mi Amigo had tried the previous year but had found too exposed for an anchored ship. Caroline sent two men onto the Knock John Fort in the Summer to prepare it for use.

Knock John fort – a new home for Caroline South?

Roy Bates was a local fisherman who also had his eyes on the fort after his own previous attempt to take over Radio Invicta on the nearby Red Sands fort had failed.

Hearing that Caroline had put men onto Knock John, Bates took a team of heavies out to 'the Barrows' (the channel in which the fort was sited). They soon removed the four Caroline caretakers. As soon as Bates left the fort, Crawford and Smedley sent out a new team to clean up the fort and prepare it for transmissions of Radio Caroline South. Bates was soon back and turfed the Caroline men off the fort once again; the Caroline board did not wish to get involved with a series of violent takeovers as this might bring bad publicity to the offshore radio business. They abandoned the plan to use Knock John and left it to Roy Bates, who started a low power station there, Radio Essex.

The Caroline South board thought that the nearby Red Sands Fort, housing KING Radio, might be inside British Waters. Oliver Smedley, who was chairman of Caroline South, had a cousin (Mike Raven, who had previously been a Radio Atlanta DJ before it became Caroline South) who worked there, so he had inside knowledge. The Caroline South board then turned their attentions to Radio City, which was located on the Shivering Sands fort, just a couple of miles away.

Caroline take over RADIO CITY

In August 1965 Allan Crawford and Major Oliver Smedley invited Reg Calvert, the owner of Radio City, to a meeting at Caroline House. Reg was impressed by the apparent opulence and sheer size of the Chesterfield Gardens headquarters, not to mention Radio Caroline's apparent success, which was in stark contrast to the much shabbier and 'down at heel' Radio City office in Denmark Street.

The idea that Crawford pitched to Calvert was for a three station triumvirate: Caroline North was to remain off the Isle of Man serving the north west and Ireland, Caroline South to sail up the coast and become Caroline East, and Radio City to become Caroline South. Reg Calvert suggested that a Caroline West near Bristol and Cardiff might be a good alternative, anchoring near the Isle of Lundy.

The plan called first for the Radio City facility to be beefed up to a stronger signal. The fort-based station operated with a couple of home-built transmitters, that could only pump out a couple of kilowatts of power. Reg Calvert had by now invested £22,000 into Radio City, which was a tiny amount compared to the amount that Project Atlanta had now spent on Radio Caroline South.

PAL's chairman, Major Smedley, offered to buy a new transmitter for Radio City and administer all the advertising sales. After costs, Calvert would get 50% of the profits plus a salary of £1500 a month.as well as to take charge of programming and technical arrangements.

The Caroline South directors and Calvert shook on the deal and said that the Radio Caroline lawyer, Michael Simpkin, would prepare a contract shortly. They promised Calvert that, if the deal did not succeed for Caroline's fault, the Radio City could keep the transmitter.

It was almost the perfect deal for Reg, who wanted to spend more time with his wife Dorothy and their young daughters, Candy and Susan Calvert. He also had a busy stable of artistes to manage, including the Fortunes, which often took him abroad on business trips.

The merger was announced to the press by Radio Caroline's PR representatives on the 22nd September and Reg Calvert visited the Caroline South ship, the Mi Amigo, the following day. Radio City was at that time just a year old, Reg having bought it from Screaming Lord Sutch, a rock'n'roll vocalist who Reg managed.

From that time, Radio Caroline's London office took in all the income of Radio City, then running at around £800 a week. With running costs of only £400 a week, Radio City was a profitable business. Keeping the two Caroline ships afloat cost around £12,000 each week.

Reg & Dorothy Calvert by Shivering Sands fort

Susan Calvert

A few days later, another new station opened up on the nearby Red Sands Fort, previously used by Radio Invicta and KING Radio. The new station broadcast mainly easy listening music and was squarely aimed at older listeners. Called Radio 390, it had no raving up-tempo disc jockeys, just calm and professional announcers – it sounded just as though the BBC was running it. The new station also had a huge radio antenna which made its 10kW signal sound much stronger – the BBC monitoring station at Tatsfield, just south of London, said that it was certainly the most powerful signal of all the offshore stations at that time which worried the Caroline South team even more.

The appearance of two new stations (Radio 390 and Radio Essex) and the proposed expansion of Radio Caroline onto Shivering Sands elicited a threat from the Labour government that they would begin to clear the ex-military installations in the Thames of radio stations "very soon". They claimed that new legislation (the Bay Closing order of 1964) placed them firmly inside British Waters as, as such, subject to UK laws. In particular the 1949 Wireless Telegraphy Act which made operation of any transmitter without a licence from the GPO a criminal offence.

Major Smedley flew to Houston and met with an equipment broker, called Besco International, run by Dick Witkowski who could supply a used transmitter for less than a thousand pounds, plus carriage. The unit that was supplied was however was a five kW unit that had seen service for quite some time at KCUL, a country station in Texas. It was sold as a ten kilowatt unit with an upgraded PA section but was very old, probably around 20 years and quite inefficient. It would need a lot of power to generate 10kW output, which Caroline South would need to compete with Radio London.

The 'new' transmitter was shipped over in three enormous crates and BESCO's engineer Milan Leggett dismantled the unit transmitter prior to it being shipped to Rotterdam. He had worked on the Mi Amigo the previous year helping to get it ready for the launch as Radio Atlanta and sailed with the ship when she left Galveston at the end of 1963. Leggett was previously the Chief Engineer at KILT and KLIF in Dallas and worked at several other McLendon stations, so he knew all about old transmitters. He worked as a radio engineer for almost 70 years and died in California in 2015.

Engineer AD Person after lifting a PA tube from a transmitter on the Mi Amigo

Soon, Radio City was running commercials being sold by the Caroline South sales team and relaying news broadcasts from the Mi Amigo as *Caroline Newsbeat*. Payments to Radio City were remitted to Caroline, and two of their engineers Carl Thomson and Ted Walters sent to install the 'new' transmitter on the Shivering Sands fort. They were both engineers from the South ship and well experienced with equipment of that power level.

Reg Calvert grew increasingly concerned about the deal as the promised payments did not materialise. He decided to hedge his bets and set up another station on the nearby Knock John Fort, not realising the problems that Caroline were already experiencing with Roy Bates over occupation of the structure.

Bates soon turned up and turfed the Radio City team off Knock John Fort, seizing the small transmitter and generator they had started to install there. A few weeks later he launched Radio Essex from there, using some of the Radio City equipment.

From Rotterdam, the KCUL transmitter was loaded on the Caroline South tender, the Offshore One. She took the three crates of equipment across the North Sea to the Shivering Sands fort, arriving on Tuesday 12th October, 1965, Columbus Day! One of the crates was dropped into the sea while loading it onto the fort and had to be retrieved the next day with help from the East Kent Sub Aqua Club.

After a thorough cleaning and drying the Radio City team were unable to get it working. Sadly, the dunking in the sea had soaked not only the components, but some paper labels too, which led to the re-assembly job taking far longer. Once the equipment was thoroughly cleaned and dried, it placed an enormous load on the struggling Radio City generators. They were simply unable to power the transmitter, which being quite old was terribly inefficient and needed a supply of around double that available on Shivering Sands.

Radio Caroline agreed to provide the necessary generator; a 100 kVA model was ordered from *George Cohen Machinery*, a long-established East End scrap metal company who, during the sixties, were the largest machine hire company in the UK. Arrangements were made to ship the Rolls Royce generator out through Burnham on Crouch but the move was blocked by the Customs at Harwich who controlled the area. Allan Crawford arranged to have the monster plant shipped by professional cargo handlers via Whitstable on the 6th December. In the meantime, Project Atlanta ran out of money and they had to sell Radio Caroline South to the North ship operators, Planet Productions.

"We had invested quite heavily in the Radio City partnership and we simply ran out of money before we could get it fully operational," explained Allan Crawford. "Our income and costs had always fluctuated widely; our bank balance was a bit of a roller-coaster. One month we were rich, the next we hadn't enough for wages! We borrowed some extra funds to cover part of the Radio City expansion from Jarvis Astaire who had been an original investor in Atlanta," continued Crawford. "Suddenly, he recalled the loan, as he wanted to invest in Don Robinson's project off Yorkshire. That was the end for us as we had major cash flow problems."

Project Atlanta had now run out of enough money to keep Radio Caroline South operating;' Ronan O'Rahilly was forced to step in and rescue the operation before Caroline South's problems got the entire Radio Caroline operation a bad name. All Project Atlanta Ltd rights to the Mi Amigo were transferred to Planet Productions, and their debts settled. The Atlanta shareholders got their money back but only just.

Radio Caroline North's ship, the MV Caroline, was not subject to high lease payments, having been bought 'outright' for cash in December 1963. They had the same 'service and supply' agreement with the Wijsmuller organisation and it was quite punitive. Wijsmuller's contract to obtain and deliver everything to the two ships had never been negotiated and even the supply of items as small as a crate of milk was very lucrative for them, charged at 18 times the shore prices! Many supplies could be obtained 'duty free', so were cheaper still.

Caroline North's operating costs too were lower than the sister ship, which had been lumbered with a high sub-rental for its use of Caroline House in London's West End. Radio Caroline North simply used a Post Office Box number in the Isle of Man, a small cottage to house visiting disc jockeys travelling to and from the ship and a modest office in Liverpool. The North ship used the part time services of a small fishing boat, *Essex Girl,* rather than the full time use of a bigger tender, the *Offshore One* that serviced the Mi Amigo.

Some of the large property in Chesterfield Gardens was sublet to others by the company which Ronan and Oonagh headed, Rosswood. Tenants included several people from the music business such as the Moody Blues and Track Records. Some offices were let to photographer friends of Ian Ross who had a studio on the very top floor of Caroline House, where the natural light was best.

Caroline's Irish HQ

There was also a Caroline House in Dublin, although this was a more modest suite of rooms in townhouses in Molesworth Street, just opposite Leinster House in the middle of town. Originally at number 12, this was an old building and the station's base moved across the street to number 27 in 1966. The Irish headquarters was run by James Craig who handled administration and some sales.

Caroline House in Dublin

Planet Productions' investors had always had much deeper pockets, although the original investors brought in by Ian and Charles Ross were now refusing to put any further money in, as the much promised "million pounds a month" projected by Ronan in his spiel for the funds had not come to fruition. Radio Caroline was turning over just over half a million pounds a year.

The two main shareholders were John Sheffield of Norcros and Charles Ross, Ian's father. Between them they held over 80% of the shares in the Caroline North operation. A total of £250,000 had been paid for shares in Planet Productions, which in turn had loaned most of its capital to several overseas companies. Jocelyn Stevens had only a modest holding and had since sold off about half his shares.

Planet Productions had now acquired Radio Caroline South from Project Atlanta, although Smedley, Crawford, Kitty Black and some of the Atlanta team still held onto a small shareholding. To achieve this, Planet Productions Ltd had just received a large cash injection bringing in more shareholders but more was soon to be needed! Planet now effectively owned the whole of the Radio Caroline sales operation in the UK. It was the only commercial station offering national coverage.

Also joining the Caroline family at this time was London-born **Barry Ainley**. He had studied at the Sorbonne in Paris and in Madrid before meeting his wife Elizabeth at the London School of Economics. Barry became a merchant banker and worked for a leading private merchant bank in London one, Close Brothers. A Radio Caroline shareholder brought him in to help manage Radio Caroline which was now the largest commercial radio station in the world in terms of listeners but it urgently needed to bring some order to its business operations.

MD Barry Ainley
Keith Skues

"I was asked by an investor to step in and run Radio Caroline, which was odd as I knew nothing at all about pop music," admitted Barry. "I was introduced to John Sheffield, who was another big investor in the company, who offered me a senior role in his business if I could sort Radio Caroline out."

Barry tussled with the chaotic circus that was surrounding Caroline House and was made General Manager of Planet Productions before being was promoted to a board position. Barry hated the term 'radio pirate' and frequently pointed out that Radio Caroline pays royalties for playing records.

Barry's new management regime brought some sweeping changes to the Caroline empire. The first task was to find out what the 60 or so support workers actually did. Many of them couldn't even describe what their own jobs really entailed! Within a week around two dozen 'jobs' were axed, though this still left twice the number of people as were working at Radio London around the corner.

The big problem was that Ronan's team were all much younger than Crawfords and had very little business experience. Caroline House was a hotbed of euphoric chaos, where almost any madcap idea was given its head. The building and the Caroline operation was almost a template for some of the Beatles' Apple Corps exploits just two years later. Pandemonium was a good description, of the quiet days!

Staff on the Caroline South ship had heard rumours of the changes for some time but Caroline staff were often fed on the 'mushroom principle – kept in the dark! They suddenly received a memo from Bill Hearn, a Canadian who had been producing commercials etc on the North ship:

> *There's been a sudden swing in the 'high command' at Caroline House which finds Ronan as Supreme Commander and Allan is on the out. Things are all just a bit vague at this writing but, it seems there was a big board meeting this last weekend which wound up with these changes. He wants the station to swing more than it is presently doing. well, it had been my opinion for some time that the sound of the nation is dropping off and it is my intention to work on it after the New Year.*
>
> *There is a little too much individuality instead of a team feeling and obviously the policy which I went to lengths to prepare is gathering dust . . . it also needs 100% co-operation of all the DJs aboard and I regret to say it, if their cooperation is not forthcoming, we'll have to go looking for those who will adhere to format and policy.*
>
> *Bill Hearne*
> *Programme Director.*

The right to operate the Radio Caroline South ship had been bought from Project Atlanta in a "pennies in the pound' deal by Planet Productions. Ronan's team was finally in charge of the entire Radio Caroline operation. While Radio Caroline North was very profitable, it wasn't enough to cover the South ship's operation nor could it sustain the profligacy of the plush offices in Mayfair.

The North ship was really swinging at this time and much hipper than the much more laid back South ship. The Caroline Club held its Annual Ball at the New Brighton Tower Ballroom on the Wirrall, where the Beatles had been regulars and perfect reception of the North ship was guaranteed!

For the Radio Caroline Club Ball, called *Zowie 1*, the headline stars were most of the top charts and live acts of the day. Caroline Club members could travel on the same train as the stars from Euston Station and be entertained by them during the journey.

Tom Lodge was one of the first who was drafted in from the Caroline North ship to make the output of Radio Caroline South sound more "trendy and switched on" or swinging, as Ronan had ordered. He introduced several new DJs to make Caroline South a much more swinging station.

TV on the Radio!

Among Tom's first recruits was Englishman Tommy Vance who had run away to sea and then worked in American radio for some years before being threatened with the dreaded draft into the American Army. He fled back to England was taken on straight after Christmas 1965 where his knowledge of the latest sounds in Los Angeles were just what Tom Lodge wanted to bring the station more up to date.

Tommy became known as *TV on the Radio*, a nickname he kept for the next 40 years as he worked his way through the BBC and Virgin Radio. "Going from the middle of Los Angeles to being sat in the middle of the North Sea within five days was a bit of a culture shock!"

All change for Caroline South DJs

Keith Skues was one of several DJs who didn't quite fit in "the all new sound of 66". In a magazine feature, he later said: "Zingwise, you have to face it a lot of the older DJs are getting past it these days. They're not exactly switched-onsville are they? What viewers want now is a bit of zip and sparkle from their DJs and they find some of the older fellows rather dull."

Keith was only 26 at the time but had been on the air with Radio Caroline for 18 months and had a further four years experience of DJing with the British Forces Network, which made him quite a veteran broadcaster. "I was one of the original Caroline Good Guys and think of myself as zany, saucy and quite mad, but I'm basically wholesome."

The official story put out by Caroline House was that about ten DJs had quit because of seasickness. The real reason was their style just didn't fit the direction that Tom Lodge had to take the station to win back listeners from Radio London which had just celebrated its first year on the air with a survey that gave them over 8 million listeners, the same amount as both Caroline ships combined.

In a newspaper interview published over the Christmas / New Year holidays, Ronan said that he found the Government's threatened action against offshore radio as "Frightening, it is so scary what they are planning doing to British people and so terribly petty. The Government can't bear the thought that we've got a mass communication medium with millions of listeners, over which they have no control."

"Contrary to what Anthony Wedgewood Benn says, we have never interfered with rescue signals nor provided any hindrance to any shipping transmissions," said Ronan to the Sunday Express correspondent Clive Hirschhorn. "What right has the PMG, Wedgewood Benn, to deprive millions of Britons from their considerable enjoyment. He's not doing a service to Britain, but a dis-service to housewives who like the music we play because it happens to be around when they want cheering up."

When asked if the word pirate was perhaps a problem, Ronan said that many famous Britons were pirates, Sir Francis Drake and Walter Raleigh to name but two. "Radio Caroline is simply a throwback to the good old buccaneering days; the public love us for that very reason," said Ronan.

"The Irish breed rebels where the English breed gentlemen. I'm a rebel I suppose. I rebelled against authority and was thrown out of seven schools. I came over to London in 1961 to try and make it on my own." "I looked upon that move as a challenge, but I found English people very difficult to get on with at first. I found them stuffy and their total lack of involvement and their standoffishness in whatever they did, that upset me."

"Like most of the Irish I'm a bit of a garrulous cat and I involve myself totally in whatever I do. I like talking to people and being friendly, even with strangers. I have this uncanny sixth sense of knowing what the public want. And I have the necessary drive to turn my dreams into reality."

Ronan said that his ambitions were to build his own modern city somewhere in Ireland and become President of the USA. He also had some overly generous and philanthropic ideas that he harboured for many years; Ronan wanted to solve two huge social problems, homelessness and more money for the music sector of culture. "The government give lots of money to high row arts and culture like classical and opera, but not a penny to real people's music. That's what most kids are into; we should be encouraging them to make music."

Two New Voices?

At the end of 1965 a new voice was heard on Caroline South, or was that two? Colin Berry had worked in TV before joining Radio Caroline the previous year, in the traffic department (scheduling commercials). He was pressed into service as a newsreader on the Mi Amigo in December when Colin Nicol got ill and needed a holiday.

Some of the crew on the Mi Amigo renamed him Robin Berry, a somewhat appropriately festive name, with Christmas approaching! Having worked in Caroline House for over a year, Colin's voice was already well known on both the stations from various commercials. He was also the main announcer for the now very popular *Partners in Profit* promotions.

Colin Berry

Colin didn't like life at sea much and was soon shore again. He later worked as a music plugger and then joined the BBC where he was one of the main continuity voices on Radio 1 and Radio 2.

9. On the beach

Some of the older sounding DJs on Caroline South were now replaced by younger, hipper DJs in Tom Lodge's revitalisation project. Among the new intake of DJs was Emperor Rosko, the son of a famous American film maker who had begun his career by broadcasting to 6,000 sailors on board a US Navy aircraft carrier.

The Admiral Robbie Dale was part of the new line-up, as was the self-proclaimed "best DJ in the North of England", Mike Ahern. He had been lured from the North Ship to add his zaniness to Radio Caroline South. They were joined by American Keith Hampshire, who became known on the air as 'Keefers' and on board as Mr Happy. He could always raise a smile, even things looked bleak.

One of the biggest voices on Radio Caroline of all belonged to Dave Lee Travis, well-known in many Manchester night clubs and to Caroline listeners all over the North. Dave was huge bear of man with a luxuriant beard and a heart as big as his gigantic ego.

DLT adopted the nickname "Your Dinner Record Spinner" on Caroline South, which inspired Roger Day to become "Your Thinner Record Spinner" as he was so skinny, that his usual nickname was Twiggy. A great lover of practical jokes, Dave's lunchtime show on Caroline South became very popular. Like his colleague Tony Prince, Dave preferred the more homely and certainly more comfortable Radio Caroline North ship off the Isle of Man and returned there later in 1966.

Despite the cuts, Caroline realised they had to pay top rates for the best DJs; by the end of 1966 the pay for some of the real stars had risen to £70 a week. This was to avoid them moving to rival stations, as by doing so they were likely to lure across some of their listeners. Coupled with free board, including free beer and cigarettes for only a shilling (5p) a packet, this was the good life, even if the hours were long and being confined to a small ship drove some of them crazy!

In mid-January, some ferocious north easterly gales were blowing into the Thames estuary. On Wednesday the 12th, the Radio London ship, a former minesweeper called the MV *Galaxy*, lost her anchor; the chain had snapped just below the surface of the sea. She ended up about four miles to the south, off Clacton.

The following week the weather was even worse and this time it was the turn of the Mi Amigo to fall foul of the weather. The records in the top three are pretty poignant “Keep on Running”, “My ship is coming in” and “A Must to Avoid.” On the 19th January, Radio Caroline South closed down at 8pm that night as usual and the crew were all watching TV. Walton Coastguard just four or so miles away though were keeping watch and realised that the Caroline ship was moving.

The ship didn’t keep a radio watch and calls went unheeded so the coastguards called the local Caroline agent, Percy Scadden who lived just two miles away in Frinton. He went down to the shore and tried to contact the ship by flashing his car headlights, but there was no response. In desperation, Mr Scadden called ITV who interrupted the normal programmes to put out an urgent message. The crew saw it and came on deck, to find the lights of Frinton pretty much all around them. The Mi Amigo was just a few hundred yards from the beach.

The crew were unable to start the ship’s engine but help was on the way from the Offshore One tender, which was usually stabled at Harwich and the Walton lifeboat. It was however too late; with a sickening crunch, the Mi Amigo hit the beach at Cheveux de Fries Point, near the Frinton Golf Club, just after midnight on the 20th. As if Radio Caroline had a guardian angel watching over her, she had run aground in the only stretch of the beach that she would fit, without hitting one of the large unforgiving groynes that run down to the sea every hundred yards or so.

It was too dangerous for the lifeboat to get alongside the Mi Amigo so the local lifeguard rescue company quickly swung into action. They set up a ‘breeches buoy’, by firing a line over the stricken ship with a rocket. This is a system with a bosuns chair, pulled along a line with those being rescued sat in it. It a well proven method that has saved hundreds of lives and is still in use, very useful for transferring crew between ships at sea when it’s too rough to get alongside.

“It had long been a standing joke that we would one day end up on the beach at Frinton, but we quickly realised this was very serious and we were in great danger,” said Tony Blackburn. “I came off to the glare of what seemed like dozens of press photographers who had been alerted to the drama by the TV newsflash.”

Tony usually went to be early to be fresh for his breakfast programme. He shared a cabin with Norman St John: “I went to tell him that we were adrift and he had to get up, but that was a joke that we had played on many new boys, and he didn’t believe me at first.”

Walton coastguards rescue the crew by breeches buoy

"The beach was covered in snow, I remember that and a burly policeman almost carrying me to an ambulance, says Tony. "It was freezing cold and beginning to snow, there was snow on the beach."

Eventually the rest of the DJ team were brought off, including Dave Lee Travis, Norman St John, Graham Web and Tom Lodge along with radio engineer Patrick Starling – better known as the Child Scientist. Tom Lodge arrived on the beach clutching the only picture that he had of his wife.

Captain Willy Wrury and six of his crew elected to remain on board but the others were all were taken to the Police Station for mugs of steaming hot tea and then to a local shop. This was opened up specially to give the shipwrecked mariners a change of clothes, a common practice in such events. They were then put up in the Gables Hotel in Dovercourt for the night after "some refreshments" to help them sleep.

Meanwhile, back on the beach, the Dutch Captain and his crew were joined by two of the Coastguards to keep watch as the tide fell away, leaving the ship high and dry. When the tide came back in it almost pushed the Mi Amigo onto the nearby groyne. The Wijsmullers tug *Titan* arrived soon afterwards and a five-inch thick rope was taken out to her, about 500 yards offshore. After half an hour of heaving, the 470 ton Mi Amigo's still hadn't moved much, if anything it seemed to have become embedded even deeper into the beach. Suddenly with a dull twang the rope parted after getting tangled on a piece of wreckage, and everyone grew disconsolate of ever saving the Mi Amigo.

Captain Wrury then lowered one of the ship's anchors onto the beach, then had it dragged a distance from the ship and secured. When the swell next rose the captain called for full power from his engine and windlass and dragged the ship along the length of the chain to be closer to the seas, a procedure known as kedging. As the propeller churned and thrashed at the beach, it dislodged many tons of material from around the stern of the ship, that had been holding her fast aground.

Eventually, with a bit more heaving from the tug, the captain managed to get the ship into deeper water – he had saved her! She moored about a mile offshore to allow divers to inspect her hull over the weekend, but the visibility was so poor that it was decided to take her to dry dock. The ship's engine, a 240 horse-power unit made by Deutz, had been damaged by sand and gravel getting onto the engine and the sand had blocked the sea chest causing the engine to seize. She also needed several emergency pumps as some plates had shifted and were letting in sea water.

Ronan O'Rahilly, who had been watching from the shore, turned to Percy Scadden and hugged him, saying "what a wonderful sight, free at last to fight another day." Ronan told everyone for many years afterwards that it was a miracle that the Mi Amigo had now been wrecked. She had come ashore on the only section of beach for a couple of miles where a groyne had been removed. Had she stranded across one of the groynes she would most likely have been wrecked.

The Mi Amigo was taken to Zaandam, on the River Ij, just outside Amsterdam, where she was drydocked on Sunday 23rd January and repairs were started immediately. While the Mi Amigo was in the drydock she had her bottom scraped and her hull repainted a deep red colour. She was also given a new set of anodes to help protect from corrosion.

Diesel engineer Tony Visscher with the new generator in Zaandam

Carl Thompson

The ship was also given a new 50 kilowatt transmitter making her as powerful as neighbour Radio London. To power it, the Mi Amigo needed a new generator. A new German model was to last well and still running in 1973 when it was jettisoned over the side.

The top section of the mast was removed as she would need a longer extension to cope with the longer wavelength. It had been decided that she would leave the high end of the MW band, the old 199 wavelength and move to a slot close to Radio London and the Light Programme.

Radio Caroline South however was "off the air", which was a disaster to the organisation. They had only just taken over operating the Caroline South ship from Project Atlanta. The huge headache of having no station audible in London could not have come at a worse time, and they needed to be back on the air urgently. Help was also soon as hand and once again it came from Scandinavia. A station called Radio Syd (it means south) had just been forced to leave the Baltic Sea as a result of abnormally thick pack ice in the area.

Radio Syd's owner, former Swedish Beauty Queen Britt Wadner, was a very trendy lady and friend of the Rolling Stones. As soon as she heard of Radio Caroline's plight she offered her ship to the station. Ronan had written to her the previous year when she was sent to prison for breaking broadcasting laws, so she was returning his friendship. It wasn't exactly a charitable gesture however – Radio Syd was paid £750 a week for the hire of the ship.

The Radio Syd ship was called the Cheeta II and she made her way down to the Thames Estuary, arriving on the last day of the month. Radio Syd broadcast on FM however so a medium wave transmitter was required.

Wijsmuller's tender, the Offshore One, sailed over to Holland and brought back one of the 10kW transmitters from the Mi Amigo. There had to be a complete switch around of equipment in the ship's hold anyway, to accommodate the huge new fifty kilowatt unit that was on its way from Dallas. Getting one of the Mi Amigo's 10kW units out of the way was convenient.

The medium wave transmitter was installed in the Cheetah II's for'ard hold, almost under the foremast. The ship had a transmitter cabin built out on the forepeak but this was already full of FM and TV equipment, leaving no room for a medium wave rig.

The Cheeta II didn't have a suitable MW antenna either as she had previously only broadcast on FM and UHF TV in her days off Malmo Sweden, so an extra one had to be built, making her probably the only five-masted radio ship!

The MV Cheetah, with five aerial masts anchored off Frinton.

Colin Nicol

Caroline's longest serving DJ, Colin Nicol, transferred onto the Cheeta II to get the ship ready for Caroline programmes. "It was a lovely old former ferry boat and their Swedish crew were really helpful and made us feel at home. I stayed on board her for over a month, helping to set up studios on the ship." The studio and record library were at the stern of the ship, on the top deck, with large windows so you could see almost right around the ship.

The ship succumbed to some rough weather but eventually broadcasts were resumed; Caroline South was back on the air on 199, and most of the DJs transferred to there.

The Cheeta II could only transmit for about six hours a day however as her generators were not powerful enough to run much longer than that without a rest. At best, the station was only making less than 5 kilowatts and it sounded very weak in London. After a few weeks of on-off broadcasting the Cheeta II was forced to sail to Lowestoft for vital repairs to a leaking pipe below the waterline.

The Cheeta period was to be the last time that Colin Nicol was heard. Such a shame as he was the voice of offshore radio, having joined Radio Atlanta in 1963. "I'd really had my lot by then," says Colin. "I was not only the longest serving person at that point, but I was also the only one left of the originals, and the whole thing was going in a way I didn't like. There was a certain type of person and they had a philosophy which wasn't quite me." Colin joined Radio Luxembourg, a sad loss to the Caroline family.

The extra expenditure on new transmitter, generators, aerial and studios now being installed onto the Mi Amigo meant that more money was needed. Some members of a well-known Irish family, the Solomons, were already modest investors and were very interested. Philip Solomon and his family were well-entrenched in the music business. His father Maurice and his Uncle Harold (Peres) had been one of the largest shareholders in Decca records, while his brother Mervyn owned Emerald Records, a leading outlet for Irish and Scottish music. Emerald Music had the rights to many well-known musicians of the day, including Rory Gallagher and Van Morrison.

After moving to London, the Solomon family expanded their empire and were soon representing many famous names, including Gene Pitney, and Jim Reeves. They ran a ticket agency and a management company that looked after many acts, such as the Bachelors, who also became investors in Caroline in their own right.

The Solomons were ideally placed to benefit from the Radio Caroline ships, even if no other advertising was sold. The benefits to their own businesses from plays on Radio Caroline were potentially huge. They agreed to pump in a six figure sum provided that Philip was made joint MD and controlled the programming. Solomon claims that he was led to believe that he was buying into the ownership of the two ships, the entire Caroline organisation. All he got was a shareholding in an Irish company that had the rights to sell advertising time on the stations.

“Solomon wasn’t ever interested in Caroline,” remembers Oonagh. “He just wanted to promote his own music. He just hung around the building and the moment Ronan left, Solomon would start to change things around and generally cause trouble.”

Ronan’s companies in the UK included a few acting and music related limited companies, which were run solely by his PA, Oonagh, and he. The real money continued to be channelled by them personally through Ireland, Switzerland and Liechenstein and was often carried out of the UK in cash hidden about their person.

Philip Solomon
Radio Caroline

A new Sales Manager was appointed at the same time, Brian Scudder, recruited from the world of TV airtime sales.

Ramsey lifeboat had to be launched to the Radio Caroline North ship after a crewman was badly scalded by hot coffee in the mess. He was treated in the Ramsey Cottage hospital for a week.

At the shipyard in Zaandam (north west Amsterdam) work to repair and refurbish the Mi Amigo was pressing ahead. In the drydock, the hull was scraped and surveyed, but there was found to be little damage. New anodes were fitted and a new lindane-based protective coating was applied, to inhibit the growth of barnacles and seaweed, known as a ship's beard. She also had a new generator, a full engine overhaul and a new section to the mast raising the height to 162 feet.

The new 50,000 watt transmitter had arrived but was not installed until the ship was outside Dutch waters, near IJmuiden. A gantry had to be installed on the ship to winch the kit into the hold, identical to one on the Radio Veronica ship, Norderney. Its presence on photographs helps date them as being post March 1966.

The ship was staffed by Caroline engineers the whole time, John Gillman had left the organisation two months before as he was really a part of the Project Atlanta regime. Gillman was really missed at this point as he had designed the antenna on the ship in 1964. George Saunders, who had by now been with Caroline almost as long, and who had been shipwrecked from her in January, had also left after the beaching and joined the other 'old hand' John Gillman out on a secret project for the government, setting up a 'border blaster' beaming British signals from Francistown into the breakaway Rhodesia which had declared UDI.

Only young Patrick Starling (also known as Child Scientist) and some new engineers were available to go to Amsterdam and supervise installation of the all new Caroline South kit. A new generator, transmitter, aerial mast, refurbished studios and a new aerial were all being renewed, in order to handle the more powerful 50 kW signal on the new wavelength.

Patrick Starling (aka Child Scentist) teaches DLT and Mike Ahern to play poker

Colin Nicol

Fab Four meet Caroline's Chief DJ

Chief Caroline DJ Tom Lodge got a call to leave the Cheeta II immediately and travel to London for a secret meeting. "When I arrived I didn't know what this was all about, but I was given a tape recorder and asked to wait in a room," remembers Tom. "All of a sudden the door flew open and four of the most famous musicians in the world burst in. It was the Beatles: John Paul, George and Ringo."

Tom's ensuing interview contained much tomfoolery by the Fab Four. They were on a sparkling form, ribbing Tom with their scouse humour. John Lennon' had a few things to say about the ship's captain, "He's stirring up a fine old brew in the captain's cabin". This was a popular extract from the afternoon's recordings which was often played out on Caroline North.

Tom Lodge joins The Beatles!

The boys expounded their view on commercial radio with Ringo Starr saying "The more stations the merrier, that's what I always say. You've heard me say it before?" A few years later Ringo and Cilla Black joined *Liverpool Broadcasting Ltd*, a company formed to bid for a commercial radio licence in Liverpool.

George Harrison told Caroline listeners that: "If the BBC can be legal on land, then so can everybody else. They should either have nobody doing it, or everybody doing it!" George became a staunch supporter of Caroline in ensuing years and helped the station in many ways, especially financially. Paul too was a big radio fan and had a collection of Caroline recordings on tape, whereas John preferred American stations.

The interview with the Beatles was mixed with some other messages from star names such as Dusty Springfield, Spencer Davies and the Walker Brothers and pressed onto a disc by Lyntone, all organised by the Beatles' Public Relations man, Tony Barrow.

When the Beatles left on a tour of North America a while later, Caroline North's breakfast DJ *Jerry 'Soopa' Leighton* accompanied them and sent back regular reports on the Fab Four's progress every day. The reports were read on Caroline South as well as the North ship. During one conversation, John Lennon asked Jerry Leighton why he didn't move to the south ship as he couldn't hear him on Caroline North as he didn't live in Liverpool any longer!

Easter 1966 saw Caroline celebrate her second birthday with special greetings from stars given away on a free disc to listeners. Copies of the disc could be obtained by redeeming tokens in the first four week's issues of DISC AND MUSIC ECHO, a new weekly newspaper. It was an amalgamation of the weekly pop paper 'Disc' with a Liverpool publication that had previously been known as Mersey Beat.

Cilla, Spencer Davis, Dusty and the Bachelors at Caroline House

Radio Caroline

The new paper was relaunched on St George's Day and heavily promoted on both Radio Caroline and Radio City which had been jointly selling airtime.

The fully refurbished Mi Amigo had to moor for a few days off IJmuiden for her new 50,000 watt transmitter to be installed. This had to be done just outside Dutch territorial waters and was accomplished by the erection of a gantry above the transmitter room hatch covers which remained in place until early 1973.

By the second week in April the Mi Amigo was anchored off Frinton, close to the Cheeta II and was soon able to start transmitting on her new frequency. There were problems with a loose connection at the top of the antenna which no one would dare climb. It was even higher than the old one as it had a new section inserted. Percy Scadden sent a message out to the ship that the boss was on his way out, after spending the morning shopping for suitable rubber soled shoes. On hearing that, Tony Blackburn shinned up the mast to remake the dodgy connection. "Ronan offered me £50 when he arrived out there for climbing the mast," remembers Tony. "I refused the money, more out of bravado really. He never did pay me though!"

The new frequency that had been chosen was 1169 kHz, which was to be announced as 259 (though in reality was 256m) between the BBC Light programme and Caroline's arch competitor Radio London.

The high power caused some insulators to fail and there was a danger that the mast might collapse. Harry Spencer's expert rigging team were urgently summoned from the Isle of Wight to complete the job. After a day on 256m, the frequency of transmissions from the Mi Amigo was changed to one a little further down towards the Light, and the new frequency 1187 kHz selected, 253m.

Three Radio Carolines!
Both the Mi Amigo and the Cheeta II were now broadcasting as Caroline, one on 199 and the other on 259. For a couple of weeks listeners could hear three Radio Carolines on the air: two off Essex and the original ship, the MV Caroline, off the Isle of Man. New boy Robbie Dale remained on the Cheeta II with only Tony Prince to help and urge listeners to retune to the new Caroline service on 259 metres. They ran separate programmes most of the time but did conducted some live link-ups between the two ships by simply having a portable radio playing the other on air in the studio.

When the Mi Amigo began full broadcasts on Wednesday 27th April, she stayed on air from 6am to 12 midnight, and later until 2am. There were still some engineering adjustments that needed to be done with the equipment off, but after a couple of months the station was running 24 hours a day. She now had a spare 10 kilowatt transmitter in the hold that could be quickly switched on during emergencies and as a result, transmissions became more reliable and 'down time' very rare.

The Cheeta II continued on 199m until May, although she remained on station off Frinton until mid-July. Talks were held with several parties to use her for broadcasts to another part of the UK. A *Radio Caroline West* was mooted for a while, in the Bristol Channel and talks were very advanced with Don Robinson, the founder of Radio 270, for the Cheeta II to move to Yorkshire and provide a service in the North East.

Radio 270's own ship the Oceaan 7 had been dismasted on April Fools Day, a rather foolish date to be advertised for any launch! The mast on Radio 270 was replaced during an urgent refit in Grimsby docks in May. Her return put paid to the *Caroline North East* idea, while the seas were judged to be too rough in the St Georges Channel for a station serving Bristol and Cardiff. In the end, Mrs Wadner sailed her to Gambia and broadcast there for some years.

In the first half of 1966 there had been talk of many new stations, not just the three concerning Radio Caroline. Scotland too now had its own radio ship. The *MV Comet*, a former lightship, was equipped with a pair of 10kW transmitters made by RCA. Radio Scotland had problems and lost money as they could never decide on a suitable mooring.

Several locations were tried, but none got a reasonable signal into both Edinburgh (the capital) and Glasgow (Scotland's biggest city). Each time they moved the ship, tugs had to be chartered and the station incurred huge costs. A move from the east coast to the west meant a long tow north and back, with loss of signal for a week while the crew endured some appalling weather.

The west coast anchorage of Radio Scotland off Ayr was very poorly researched. It was intended to get the signal into Glasgow, as the Black Mountain near Shots was impenetrable from the east coast anchorages. Using the location on the west coast resulted Radio Scotland being fined in court for broadcast from a location 36 miles inside territorial waters! This was the result of the 1964 Bay Closing Order in Council which had added lots of straight lines to the new line of territorial waters. Radio Scotland had believed that the old three-mile limit measured from the low water mark was still in effect.

They tried a location off the Ulster coast and changed the station name to *Radio Scotland and Ireland* for a few weeks. Reception was then so weak in Edinburgh that Radio Caroline considered establishing a new station on Scotland's east coast. A launch of *Radio Caroline Scotland* was discussed with radio engineers and the crew of the Cheeta II, however the return of the Comet to the east coast made that much less viable and expansion of Caroline north of the border was dropped.

Not only was the downtime of Caroline South a problem but the costs of upgrading the ship to 50 kilowatts were very expensive. The new transmitter needed aerial improvements and more powerful generators to run it. While the station was now heard much more clearly and Tom Lodge's format was certainly a lot hipper and cooler, they still had huge competition in the form of London, 390 and the two stations on the MV Olga Patricia, *Swinging Radio England* and *Britain Radio*.

The new Caroline South DJ team included Tony Prince, Tony Blackburn, Tom Lodge, Mike Ahern and Emperor Rosko, a hot fast-talking, high-energy DJ from California. They also now had some great new jingles, courtesy of Swinging Radio England.

Action was taken by the BBC against disc jockey Pete Murray, whose sponsored programme *Call In At Currys* was aired on Radio Caroline in early 1966. The BBC mandarins axed Pete from his Light Programme job, although he continued as a member of the roster of DJs who hosted Top of the Pops on BBC TV.

100 kW for the North ship?

Philip Solomon told the press that Radio Caroline North would also get a larger transmitter, 100,000 watts! This would enable it to be heard right down in the south of Ireland as well as over the whole of Scotland. Nothing ever came of the plan, although the crew and DJs were told that some mysterious boxes in the hold were the new transmitter, which would be connected up 'soon'.

As Project Atlanta was no longer running Caroline South, the deal with Radio City had ended too. Reg Calvert carried on operating Radio City alone, but he was now tiring of the hurly-burly of offshore radio, which he and his wife Dorothy were running as a family concern. They also ran several dance hall venues and managed some beat groups, including the Fortunes and Pinkerton's Assorted Colours. This was quite demanding, especially as the Fortunes had begun to take off in popularity and had many TV and foreign engagements to fulfil.

Calvert was disappointed that the Radio Caroline arrangement had fallen through without him properly being reimbursed, as had been promised by Project Atlanta's chairman, Oliver Smedley. He began discussions with Caroline's greatest rival, Radio London to see if they might want to merge with Radio City. After long discussions between the two organisations, a deal was done.

The draft agreement proposed setting up a company, Sweet Music Limited, to be owned jointly by Reg Calvert and Radio London. This company would operate Radio City as a new station, to be known as UKGM (*United Kingdom Good Music*). Two Radio London DJs, Keith Skues and Duncan Johnson, along with engineer Martin Newton, visited Shivering Sands fort in early June to see what extra studio equipment might be needed to launch the new station there. Keith had previously been on Caroline South but had now joined Big L and now he was to be Chief DJ on the new UKGM station.

Radio London's plan was to take over Radio City on Shivering Sands fort, install a larger transmitter for their new station UKGM. This would then release the *Galaxy* to sail north to become Radio Manchester. *Big L* had never managed to make their 50kW transmitter work for long at high power and had a shocking signal after dark when incoming interference from Yugoslavia resulted in a loud and very annoying heterodyne whistle over their programme.

A company promising radio and TV services had been set up on the nearby Sunk Head fort. Radio Tower made a few weeks test transmissions but it gradually faded, seemingly very under-capitalised. The promised TV Tower had insufficient power to be seen ashore.

Radio Caroline's increase in power to 50kW had another effect on Radio London – the Caroline signal was so strong that it got into the studio equipment of Radio London. Her listeners could her the Big L programmes fine, but they could also hear the Caroline programme faintly in the background. This situation continued for around a year, until Radio London finally closed down the following year.

Radio London then claimed to advertisers that it was broadcasting with a signal 50% higher than Radio Caroline. Its claims of 75 kW were simply hyperbole, as the station had only a 50kW transmitter on board, plus a standby 10kW unit. It was impossible to increase the power of the London transmitter and in fact they were usually running at only 35kW due to other technical problems on their ship. Their antenna was not fed properly and would not accept full power (much less the mythical 50% increase)

In late May 1966 Radio London came knocking on Tony Blackburn's door again. They were keen to engage new DJs as their planned sweet music venture on the Shivering Sands fort was taking shape and they would be taking quite a few Radio London names. They wanted Tony to drop his jokes and his voice a few octaves, which terribly offended him at the time. He soon adopted a much lower pitched voice, but hung on to the jokes, and joined the Big L.

He was joined on Radio London by former Caroline shipmate Keith Skues, who had left the Radio Caroline South ship previously for a land-based job at Radio Luxembourg but relished a chance to get his feet wet once again and reside "four miles off the Frinton, Essex coast."

Radio Caroline South was by now, without any doubt, the most powerful offshore station. The radio battle in the south east was really heating up now. Caroline were now capable of pounding out their full power and on a good wavelength close to the Light programme. To build audience as rapidly as possible, Caroline slowly increased hours in order to provide an 'around the clock' service, which local station Radio Essex had pioneered a few weeks earlier.

No sooner had Radio (and TV) Tower disappeared than another newcomer was heard – Swinging Radio England. She arrived on 2nd May on board the *MV Olga Patricia* and began transmitting tests straight away with three energetic American DJs well experienced in Top 40 radio and three British DJs, who had no experience of radio at all. The British 'rookies' took the names Johnnie Walker and Roger 'Twiggy' Day and soon became well-known and much-loved, although their real fame came when they crossed over to Radio Caroline South.

SRE had not one but two 50,000 watt transmitters; they offered a sweet music service on one channel as Britain Radio and 'Boss Radio, Hot Top 40' on another. The ship's accommodation was incomplete and its management were simply hopeless –SRE closed within six months and transmitted a Dutch station instead, Radio Dolfijn.

Jingle Jingoism!
As station identification, SRE ran a brand-new jingle package that it had ordered from PAMS, the biggest creative audio company in Dallas. These were even more sparkling and zingy than Radio London and known as 'The Jet Set,' featuring sounds of planes tearing across the sky and the repetitive strap line "the fastest thing in the air"!

The Caroline DJs began recording them off the air (their ships were only two miles apart). Tony Blackburn and Rosko eagerly set to with their razor blades and splicing tape, mixing them in with Radio Caroline IDs. Within hours they were going wild with delight, with 'their' new jingles; Tony Blackburn had never played so many jingles! The Radio England DJs were furious! When they began regular shows with their jingle package, listeners had already heard them on Caroline, and thought SRE were now pirating Caroline's new jingle package!

SRE had to buy another new package which turned out to be even better. Their new package known as *ThatMan* sounded as though the jingle singers were saying Batman, which at that time was the biggest show to hit the TV screens. Plenty of ZAP! and POW! interspersed all over them, their strap line would be 'All the boys are boy wonders!"

The *ThatMan* package contained lots of instrumental beds that the DJs could use under their dialogue over. It was extensively used on other offshore stations, particularly Radio 270 off the Yorkshire coast.

Swinging Radio England was huge competition because it too had a 50 kW transmitter, the same model as Caroline's. Half its disc jockeys were Americans, from hot radio stations in Miami, hip-talking, "in your face" and professionally trained. They took the name 'Boss Jocks' and while they were perhaps a bit too brash and strident for some older people, younger listeners loved the station.

The Olga Patricia had something else that helped seal the fate of easy listening music on Radio Caroline; they had an extra 50 kW transmitter, which could simultaneously transmit a second station. This became sister station, Britain Radio. Tagged 'the Smart Set', it also had a special jingle package that was copied even by the BBC who ordered the same package and used it on Radio 2 outlet for fifteen years!

Swinging Radio England and Britain Radio were the brainchild of Don Pierson, one of the Texans who had been behind the launch of Radio London. Upset that his board wouldn't run the station the way he wanted to, Don simply went away, put together a new team of backers and built another one. This time he doubled up, installing not one but TWO stations, on the same ship!

10. Buccaneers do battle

The Chairman of Project Atlanta, the company that had previously ran Radio Caroline South was Oliver Smedley. Now he had lost all control over Caroline South he turned his eyes to Radio City, which he thought should still be part of his empire. He suggested to his colleagues in Project Atlanta Ltd that they might be able to recoup some of their money from Radio City, where they had installed a transmitter, the one that fell into the sea and had not yet been got working. Smedley proposed taking the Radio City fort by force and then do a deal with Radio London, who were apparently keen to take it over.

Smedley's former colleagues in Caroline South, especially Allan Crawford, were not at all keen on this idea to use violence and blackmail to take over another man's radio station. He refused to be involved and left Smedley and former Caroline South director Kitty Black to get on with it. They recruited some out of work dockers as 'muscle men', stormed Radio City's fort at 3am and then called a meeting with Radio London.

Later that day Reg Calvert called at Smedley's home to discuss the removal of the raiding party when Smedley suddenly shot him at point blank range. Within minutes Calvert was dead - shot down in cold blood. It was the turning point for offshore radio in Britain.

The story made headline news all over the world. Millions first heard of the raid during a 'Caroline Newsbeat' bulletin, whose headline was:

> *Thirty seven year old Reg Calvert, manager of many pop beat groups, including the Fortunes and owner of the offshore radio station Radio City, was shot dead in a country mansion near Saffron Walden, Essex, early this morning.*

Suddenly offshore radio had its first death. As the story unfolded and the reasons for the takeover emerged, it became clear that the business of offshore radio wasn't only one of music and entertainment. It had some seedy characters, shady plots and gangsterism.

This was a total disaster!

A man who, until recently, was the chairman of the company running world's best-known offshore station, Radio Caroline South, had shot dead the owner of a rival station, with whom he had been a business partner. It brought the whole field of offshore radio into disrepute – how could anyone now claim this wasn't 'pirate' radio?

The police arrested Smedley but he was immediately given bail. Officers visited Shivering Sands fort and interviewed the armed raiding party who were still holding the Radio City team hostage. The police claimed they couldn't act as the fort was outside territorial waters and was therefore outside their jurisdiction.

Radio Caroline immediately issued a statement disowning Major Oliver Smedley who'd had no connection with Radio Caroline for over six months. The magistrates in Essex sent Smedley for trial but the charge was reduced to one of manslaughter. He was later acquitted on the grounds of self-defence, but Reg Calvert's widow Dorothy was appalled when the police didn't call any witnesses to dispute this and prove their case. He was able to wriggle off all charges 'Scot free.'

"When Smedley's Project Atlanta failed and they lost Radio Caroline South, he had offered to find my father a backer for Radio City," explains Susan Calvert, Reg's eldest daughter. "When Smedley heard about the deal my father had arranged with Radio London, he just took over Radio City by force and blackmailed Radio London."

"Smedley's former partner in Atlanta, Allan Crawford, tried to talk Smedley out of the raid but he went ahead in the middle of the night with a bunch of thugs. Both Radio London and my father refused to have anything to do with the blackmail attempts or Smedley and demanded that he remove his men from the fort."

Rather mysteriously, the police didn't produce any real evidence against Smedley and reduced the charge from murder to manslaughter. He was then found 'not guilty' and awarded costs! One of the most amazing travesties of justice and perpetrated against a man widely known to be of the utmost integrity. The full story of the background to Radio City is in Susan Calvert's book

The Government prepare legal action

The hijacking of Radio City, the attempts at blackmail culminating in the killing of one station boss by the chairman of another radio company, brought matters to head. The Government had to act. Tony Benn, as Minister for Technology, promised new legislation to starve out offshore radio.

Only weeks later, a cabinet reshuffle saw his post being taken by Edward Short. He announced a new law that would make it an offence for British subjects to work for, or supply, an offshore radio station. It would mirror the legislation that had discouraged offshore radio from other coasts, such as Scandinavia.

Within weeks of the events surrounding Radio City on Shivering Sands fort, the new PMG published the Marine and Broadcasting (Offences) Bill. It would make broadcasts from British ships or aircraft illegal anywhere without a licence and criminalise any British person working on an offshore radio station, wherever it was registered. More difficult, it made advertising on an offshore radio station by British companies illegal, as was the act of ferrying goods or people to and from an offshore radio station, except in an emergency.

While the BBC and other opponents of offshore radio were pleased, the majority of people were not at all happy at the plans. The proposals were variously described as "a hammer to crack a walnut'. *The Economist* magazine summed up the views of many when it said, in an article in its July 30, 1966 edition:

> *The bill to put down the "pop pirates" was published on Thursday. It has a ripe cartload of needless rubbish. The unlicensed commercial broadcasting stations around Britain's coasts give a good deal of harmless pleasure and do very little practical harm*

The bill was roundly condemned in many newspapers and the public at large. If the Economist, The Times and the Sketch were against the draconian new laws, surely it wouldn't be passed by parliament?

Caroline from Cambridgeshire?

In August 1966, traditionally a slow news period, some of the popular press reported that Radio Caroline was exploring was to set up on land. It had been offered a site in Reach, a small village in Cambridgeshire by Leonard Warren, who was the 'Overlord of Reach'. This was an ancient Kingdom set up the issue of a Rogation charter by King John in 1201.

Radio Caroline lawyers studied the paperwork for some months before pronouncing that the initiative was unviable as the independent sovereignty had not been constantly maintained and so its powers to do things like issue licences had lapsed.

The summer recess of Parliament gave the impression that, despite the sabre-rattling in July in response to the business surrounding radio City and the death of station owner Reg Calvert, no action was after all going to be taken. Audience levels for the two Caroline ships and the consequential advertising revenues continued to grow

Audience Survey

There was some good news for Caroline staff in late Summer 66 when a National Opinion Poll survey credited Caroline as having the highest number of listeners of all the offshore stations, almost 9 million. That was the same number as were tuning to Radio Luxembourg each week. The nearest competitor was almost a million behind Radio Caroline, whose adult audience had nearly doubled from 15 to 28% over the previous four months.

This was all partly due to the South ship's new DJs, revitalised programming and 'hipper' style of presentation, and of course the hike in power. The new 50kW transmitter and new '259' wavelength resulted in listeners and response from areas where the station didn't previously reach well. The Midlands region saw an increase from 11 to 19% of all adults tuning in, while corresponding figure for the 'west of England and South Wales;' area was almost trebled, from 4% to 11%.

Caroline's new programming initiatives gave the station a brand new 'feel'. The pace was more upbeat, the DJs sounded warmer and friendlier combining to give a more convivial station sound. In particular, the daily programmes of Jack Spector live from New York gave the station's listeners a fresh sound not previously heard in the UK.

The press had now got a taste for stories about the friendly 'radio pirates' off the coast, that listeners loved. There were daily calls to the station's PR officer, Francis van Staden who, along with her assistant Carolyn Irvine, handled all media enquiries for Radio Caroline, South and North.

They were kept busy not only simply answering questions from journalists, but arranging an ever-increasing itinerary of events for Caroline DJs to attend and visits to both ships to arrange for media and for listeners chosen to be so honoured by competitions. The visits involved complex arrangements clearing customs and other official checks that were made each time a supply ship went out.

Radio Caroline also now had its own admiral, albeit a self-appointed one. The Admiral Robbie Dale was working in a club DJing one day when he was talent-spotted by one of the girls from Caroline House. She invited him for an audition and he was soon shipped out to the Cheeta II, Caroline's temporary home early in 1966. "The first week or two were dreadful, I spent a lot of time in bed with sea-sickness, but one I had found my sea legs, I loved it," remembers Robbie.

Robbie's fan club was called The Beat Fleet and soon had some well-known names among its crew. Among those who accepted commissions were Ray Davies, Jimi Hendrix, Georgie Fame and Geno Washington. Four of the Rolling Stones became special ratings!

The Admiral Robbie Dale
R Robinson

By the late Summer, with Caroline now blasting out a 50kW signal on 259, Robbie's mailbag was topping a thousand letters a week. These all got a response, usually from the two girls who ran the Beat Fleet for him.

Robbie was always very fashion conscious and loves to be on stage; even in 1966 he had ambitions to do TV work, which he achieved three years later at Radio Veronica.

Joining the Caroline team in 1966 was Rick Dane, who hosted the late-night slot. An unwanted slot when Caroline didn't bother broadcasting, Rick soon made it popular, capable of attracting one of the biggest mailbags for any DJ. The new wavelength and five times as much power as previously made overnight broadcasting much more viable.

When Rick left Caroline in November he hosted the *Lucky Birthday Bonanza* competition and promoted concerts at Brian Epstein's Saville Theatre. After a shirt stint on Radio One he moved to Florida installing equipment in bars and clubs in Miami, Florida. Rick was succeeded by Johnnie Walker, a new Caroline recruit who had left *Swinging Radio England* just before it closed, the previous month.

By late 1966, disc jockeys on Caroline were being paid on a variety of wage structures, mainly according to their results. Tom Lodge had over-achieved his goals of making the South ship not only hip cool and trendy, but also it was very high profile and firmly a part of the music business in London; he was paid over £100 a week.

Life as a Radio Caroline DJ was one of the most exciting roles for a young man (they were all male in those days). Well paid, plus all food and lodging paid for on the ship, feted as a celebrity and all the real stars were keen to be your friend. Being a disc jockey on Radio Caroline was undoubtedly one of the best jobs in the music business.

A Caroline Wedding

An idea was hatched for the ultimate story that would endear everyone to Radio Caroline: a wedding would be held on board one of the ships and broadcast live.

Gipps & the happy couple
Manx Press / RC

The best-known relationship among the Caroline team was between Canadian William Brown (better known air as DJ Mick Luvzit) and the Janet Teret, the sister of a former Caroline North DJ Ray 'Ugli' Teret. Mick was a pure romantic who would often sing to his girlfriend on the air (he was a great singer too and made some records for Philips). When he wasn't singing to Janet, Mick would be writing her love poems, often reading them live during his programme.

They agreed to be married 'on the air' by the ship's Captain, Martin Gips, with the whole ceremony broadcast live and all paid for by station boss Ronan O'Rahilly. The event took only three weeks to organise. Special papers had to be obtained from the Panamanian Embassy and the Captain had to borrow a special uniform from the Isle of Man Coastguard office.

Mick and Janet's big day dawned on Saturday 20th September, but some of the ships bringing guests out to the MV Caroline got lost in Ramsey Bay which was enveloped in a thick fog! The ship's fog horn was sounded every two minutes to help visitors find their way across Ramsey Bay. Radio Caroline North listeners got a front seat with a running commentary as the visitors arrived on board.

Finally, at 5pm Captain Martin Gipps performed the ceremony, assisted by the Royal Ruler, Tony Prince. Radio Caroline's Head of News, Graham Webb commentated on every step of the ceremony that took place in the ship's saloon. Mick's best man was Jerry Leighton and Janet was given away by her brother Ray as her parent's plane was late due to fog at the airport.

The celebrations continued on into the evening, while Mick and Janet went off onto the Isle of Man to start their honeymoon in a small cottage at Crosby. Newspaper readers all around the world carried news of the Wedding in reports that probably got more publicity for Radio Caroline than the station had ever received.

Mick revisited the Isle of Man in 2002 for the first time since he left Caroline in 1967. He was astonished to find that the Island's museum had no less than 300 reports of his wedding from the world's newspapers press, as well as a large portfolio of photographs of the ceremony. These even including Mick buying the rings from a Douglas jeweller, accompanied by his bride's parents and visiting his brother in law's boutique on the town's North Quay.

Mick and his bride moved to Canada where they brought up their daughter, Jelisee. Sadly, the marriage didn't last but they remained close friends until Mick's death in 2012.

Missing from the wedding was Austrian radio engineer, Manfred Sommer. He was a popular crew member on the ship and got his fair share of fan mail too. One day while showing some visitors the engine room he announced: "This is the fan that keeps the engine cool," and stuck his arm into it! Despite a tourniquet, the bleeding wouldn't stop and he had to be taken off by lifeboat to Ramsey's Cottage Hospital.

Summer 66 saw Caroline introduce a strict policy of playing only chart records, i.e. songs in the *Caroline Countdown*, or approved 'plug records'. Managers, record companies, music publishers or the artistes themselves were offered 5 plays per day for £100 a week, which went to the station owners and so was not payola.

The biggest cause of dissent among Caroline's DJs was the strict implementation of the playlists. Solomon had bought a part of the Caroline operation and wanted his releases and artistes plugged incessantly. Many DJs didn't approve, not only of the frequency some records were scheduled for play, but they felt strongly that the preponderance of country and Irish music didn't match the Radio Caroline image, especially in the South.

Tom Lodge was now growing tired of the battles between the two Caroline MDs who would give contradictory orders. Many of Solomon's orders were ignored and his bans reinstated by Ronan that it could be a confusing time for some of the staff, although some DJs would play off one boss against the other when they could.

MV Caroline 'dressed overall' for Mick and Janet's wedding.

The very loose 'pay for play" system was now a formal arrangement. The DJs began revolting over the imposition of forced plays into their shows, which they felt attracted listeners by the music that THEY chose, not Caroline House. Since the station's early days, when Simon Dee had first jettisoned the worst records over the side, some plug records had been subjected to the wrath of DJs.

Philip Solomon launched a new record label at the end of 1966 called *Major Minor*; its releases enjoyed extensive airplay on Radio Caroline, once the DJs stopped using them for frisbee practice. Many of the Major Minor releases were from the existing Solomon stable of artistes but some were licensed from foreign labels, with whom Radio Caroline had formed an alliance.

Among these were Barclay Records in France and Roulette Records in New York. Run by Maurice Levy, Roulette had run its own daily programme on Radio Caroline, hosted by leading WMCA disc jockey, Jack Spector, which was heard on both the North and South ship. One of the artists that Radio Caroline got firmly behind was Tommy James and the Shondells. After a minor hit in 1966, they slowly increased their profile, culminating with a UK number one in 1968, *Mony Mony*.

Tommy James is generous in his praise of Radio Caroline. "The BBC wouldn't play our records at all," rues Tommy. "The BBC hated '*Hanky Panky*' which, had they listened closely they would have found that it is in fact simply about dance steps. Radio Caroline played us quite a bit and without their help it wouldn't have sold at all. They also got behind my other 45s, including "*I Think We're Alone Now*."

After returning to the UK early in 1966, Tommy Vance had left Caroline as his wife didn't like him being away at sea for so long. Tommy then hosted shows for Radio Luxembourg for a while and then embarked on a career in the music business with an old pal from Seattle, Jerry Dennon. After two singles (*You Must Be The One* and the Stones number, *Off The Hook*) both flopped he was back out on the radio Caroline South ship in December.

Caroline North was a vital part of the music scene in Manchester (where the TV programme Top of the Pops began) and in Liverpool, home of the Beatles and many more major world class artistes. Caroline's northern office in Liverpool was heavily involved in management of the Cavern Club, by then a magnet for fans and even styled its logo on the Caroline Bell. It reopened after a major refurbishment and upgrade with CCTV in July 1966

The Dynamic Duo revitalise Sales

Radio Caroline still needed more revenue, so ramped up the battle for sales revenue by importing two advertising salesman with experience of Canadian radio and TV sales. Terry Bate was British-born but had achieved great success in radio and TV air time sales with Canada's top radio promotion consultancy.

Terry's associate, Allan Slaight, had risen through the ranks of small town radio stations in Canada. Eventually he became Programme Manager and then MD of CHUM. Under his control CHUM became the top station in Toronto. On his return to Canada Alan built Standard Broadcast into the country's largest network. He has since sold the company for over $1 billion, another Caroline success story.

Terry and Alan decided to offer their services in England which they saw as being a radio market with huge potential. They were offered a contract by Radio Caroline to provide sales, merchandising and advertising expertise. Their introduction of several new advertising initiatives brought in hundreds of thousands of pounds. They soon became known as the Dynamic Duo. Terry Bate was also responsible for arranging the commercial sales for Caroline TV but in the 1970s he set up a consultancy with Beaverbrook Newspapers to apply for local radio franchises across the UK.

The first of the Dynamic Duo's initiatives was *Caroline Cash Casino*, which began in October 1966. Each competition would have a series of clues, which led to a mystery sound, or a well-known person or item. Listeners had to guess what it was by noting down a series of clues read out only on Caroline. All entries had to be sent by mail along with a proof of entry from the sponsoring product. Each time a new clue was read out the cash jackpot would increase by £10 for each incorrect answer drawn. With prizes up to £4,000 (worth about £70,000 today) tens of thousands of entries poured in during the first week.

Competition draws were recorded at Caroline House by Canadian Bill Hearne whose vocal style and delivery were ideal for the competition. Cash Casino was a huge success and advertisers vied to be one of the four sponsors heard each day. Caroline had proof that their advertising worked as they had thousands of proofs of purchase of the sponsors' products in every mail. Among the products sponsoring the Caroline Cash Casino were *Galaxy* chocolate, *Findus* frozen foods, *Alberto VO5* shampoo and *Weetabix*. The price of participation was £7,500 for each advertiser and there were usually four sponsors at a time.

There were over five and a half million entries received for Cash Casino from listeners, over the 39 weeks that the 13 flights of Cash Casino ran. There had never been such a high value competition heard on the radio before and it was the talk of millions of people. This was due to the relatively valuable prize on offer, previously the best that one might expect was a book token, but Caroline Cash Casino changed that forever.

Caroline profited enormously from Cash Casino, expanding its audience enormously. A National Opinion Poll in May 1967 showed the stations were now reaching 19% of the population. Many sponsors who could not participate (there was a waiting list, it really was fully booked) and most of them booked other advertising slots on the station.

Even the Post Office benefited from Caroline Cash Casino: by the time it had its four millionth entry, £67,000 had been received by the Post office in the form of the 4d (less than 2p) paid for the postage stamps, over £1 million in today's money. The station received over 100,000 entries within two weeks of launch. By the time it finished over five million entries had been received.

Cash Casino was so successful that some advertisers wanted their own exclusive promotion. For Weetabix, Caroline ran *Partners in Profit*, where listeners had to circle one of the letters from the end flap of a packet of Weetabix. During each drawing, two entries would be selected. If they both selected the same letter, they shared the prize pot, and if not an extra £10 went into the jackpot for the next drawing.

Just as with Cash Casino, *Partners in Profit* began each flight with £100 in the kitty. The *Partners in Profit* drawings were also made in London and played out on both Caroline North and Caroline South. A month later, Colgate Palmolive's AJAX cleaning solution signed up as joint sponsors.

Another 'audience participation promotion' devised by the Dynamic Duo was *Birthday Bonanza*. This ran six times a day and was hosted by Tommy Vance and Rick Dane. Listeners sent in their birth date and the winning entries drawn had their birthday checked against a list of prizes.

The main sponsors of Birthday Bonanza were Golden Wonder peanuts, Nescafe and Helix toothbrushes, with the daily draws presented by Colin Berry. The sales team had a much easier time selling advertising time on Caroline South now she had such wide and strong coverage from the improved facilities on the Mi Amigo.

One of the most popular DJs on Radio Caroline was Tony Prince who had been seconded to the south ship to brighten up the programming earlier in the year. He was soon back on his beloved North ship, but only after a run in with Phil Solomon. “He fired me and then two days later Ronan took me back on,” says Tony. He had joined Caroline at Christmas 1965 after a spell introducing *Discs a Go Go* on TWW, the ITV franchise in Bristol. Tony was originally a singer in a band, *Rory Storm and the Hurricanes*, whose drummer was Ringo Starr.

Tony got his break as a DJ with the Top Rank ballroom circuit but originally he was a real life jockey. “I shared rooms at the stable in Middleham with Willie Carson when we were apprentices but had problem keeping my weight down,” explains Tony. After leaving Radio Caroline, Tony managed Radio Luxembourg for many years and then ran the DMC - Disco Mix Club and his own *Wedding TV* channel

The 50 kW transmitter on the south ship brought Radio Caroline to a huge new audience on the continent and particularly across France. The enhanced Caroline South signal could be clearly heard all day across the whole of northern France and into Paris too.

“The biggest reaction to Caroline wasn't from England, it was from France,” said Ronan in an interview in the nineties. “The French went berserk about Radio Caroline. I mean, they really went really potty, they were all dead keen and enthusiastic. We had French TV, French magazines and French newspapers giving us wall to wall coverage for a long time.

“One of the biggest movements, who are all total fanatics and are incredibly enthusiastic, are the French Radio Club.” says Ronan. “Their magazine covers every aspect of Caroline, and they also run boat tips. There’s a massive number of French young people who come over to visit Caroline.”

Ronan reads an FRC magazine
Offshore Echos

Rosko, Le President of France!
H Henroid

When Jean Provoust, the owner of the trendy *Paris Match* magazine, bought a shareholding in Radio Luxembourg he contacted Radio Caroline for advice. Caroline were given a daily slot on RTL to try and to popularise its French service.

Ronan seconded Radio Caroline South's top DJ, Emperor Rosko to go to Paris and host the new programmes. Rosko adopted the name 'Le President Rosko' for the show, which were called *Mini-Max*. RTL even commissioned a special custom set of PAMS jingles to Rosko's and Caroline's specification.

"The French had the first Revolution, before the Russian Revolution, the Irish Revolution, in fact all the revolutions," said Ronan. "It must be part of the French character to support liberty, fraternity and equality." Offshore Echos is unique in being the only truly international publication devoted to the world of offshore radio. Just like Radio Caroline, it has customers and followers in several dozen countries.

When a tip of coal mine slurry engulfed the Welsh village of Aberfan, killing 109 primary school children in October 1966, Bessie Braddock, the Labour MP for the Liverpool Exchange constituency launched an appeal for the families on Radio Caroline North. Almost £10,000 was given by the generous Caroline listeners who responded to the appeal, which was broadcast many times on Caroline North.

In October 1966 Radio Caroline wrote to over a hundred North ship listeners about the signal strength and asked them if they would participate in an experiment to help find a more favourable anchorage for the ship. The plan was to sail the MV Caroline around the Irish sea for a few days, broadcasting as she went and then collate listener reports to see which location enabled transmissions to get out best.

The trip was suddenly cancelled and a frequency change made. Tests went out overnight on 1169 kHz, a frequency in use only by the Ukraine and which the Mi Amigo had tried in April. The overnight transmissions continued right throughout November. In December, some daytime tests found the 259 signal to be superior to the 199. The station received many more reception reports for the 259 wavelength than had ever been had for 199 and it was believed that the daytime coverage was up to 50% greater.

The change to 259m permanently, obviated a planned purchase of a 50kW unit for the North ship; it no longer seemed to be necessary. From the week before Christmas, Radio Caroline North stayed on the 259 slot and was never heard again on 199. The station had been advised to stay on 199, at the top end of the band by certain engineers no longer with the station. Had they given the frequency advice to help the BBC and suppress Caroline's coverage?

Now both ships were broadcasting as *Caroline on 259*, things were a lot easier when promoting the brand to national sales clients. Terry Bate's *Caroline Cash Casino* competition was by now hugely successful with over a million entries having been sent to Caroline House. Within a month the Caroline HQ in London would be receiving over two million entries a week!

Caroline's Christmas Caper

For Christmas, the Head of News on the South ship decided to stage a caper (a radio pantomime) for listeners. Bob Larkins was also known around the ship as the Tasmanian Devil and had been an actor in Australia as well as at the Mermaid Theatre in London. He recruited DLT to provide the music and sound effects for his production. It focussed on the big craze of the year – Batman! The lead role was played by Keefers (Keith Hampshire) while Steve Young played Robin, the Boy Wonder.

An extra tender trip was laid on for the extra bags of letters and gifts for the DJs just before Christmas. It also took out three huge turkeys, some superb wines, untold amounts of chocolates and sweets from various record companies and a huge Christmas tree, which turned out to be too big to get into the messroom!

Stores were a very important part of life on both Caroline ships. The Mi Amigo was served by the Offshore One, a Wijsmuller tender that usually sailed from Felixstowe and also ran to the Radio London ship, less than a mile away. The MV Caroline off the Isle of Man was tendered by the Peel fishing boat *Essex Girl* running out of Ramsey and later the Offshore III that brought supplies from Ireland. Being a larger boat, the cook on the MV Caroline began rearing his own chickens on board, so a supply of fresh eggs was usually available!

The station's DJs were among the best-known names in the UK, some of them on the continent too. Many companies were keen to buy into the Caroline 'brand'.

The South ship's own pet Admiral, Robbie Dale, was adopted as 'Ships Mascot' by one of Her Majesty's warships, HMS Hydra. A newly built deep ocean hydrographic ship, her pennant number was A144 when newly commissioned in Summer 1966 and served twenty years in the Royal Navy, surveying waters all over the world. Many marine charts still current today use the work done by HMS Hydra. Robbie was invited to several functions on board but sadly was not able to persuade her Commanding Officer, Captain John Paton to work for Radio Caroline, although she did give a salute as she passed by the Mi Amigo while *en route* to Chatham for stores.

TV on the radio

R Hope-Weston

Tommy Vance had left the ship for a while, had a lonely period out in Luxembourg (his wife didn't want to join him there either!) and seen both his records not get the sales that everyone had hoped for. He made his way back out to the Mi Amigo and within days his programmes *TV on The Radio*, were once again a part of the daily ritual for millions of listeners. A rock music expert, Tommy was a wonderful fount of knowledge on American bands, he was like a walking encyclopaedia of music.

The rest of the Mi Amigo's line up was by now very settled and there was not so much 'churn' in the DJ team as previously. Johnnie Walker had taken over the 9 to midnight slot, with Mike Ahern, Robbie Dale, Steve Young, DLT and Keith Hampshire all being regular fixtures in the daily schedule.

The second book to focus on Radio Caroline was published by the Landmark Press. The author was John Venmore Rowland who had served in the Special Operations Executive with John Gilman in the war and had broadcast on commercial radio in Australia. Every assistance was afforded to the author by Frances van Staden and her team as the book was supposed to brief MPs in the debates on the radio ship legislation in the Houses of Parliament. Sadly, the book was delayed and didn't appear until June, when it was heavily promoted on the air with a single by The Gibsons of an early Roger Cook and Roger Greenaway song called The Magic Book. Packed with facts and details of the DJs, it consolidated the case for and against Radio Caroline.

Payola Pays for Plays

In February 1967 Radio Caroline admitted to the press that it was possible for record companies, publishers and artistes to buy plays on both the Caroline stations. For a payment of £100 a record would be played regularly on the air; once a record became a hit it would be played free of charge.

Often called 'payola', this was not illegal and in fact 'pay for play' was quite common in the radio industry. Radios Luxembourg and London also practiced this and even took a cut of records that became hits. They both held publishing rights to records they played often through their own publishing companies, Pall Mall Music and Louvigny Music.

Among those who regularly bought time on Caroline for their releases was Don Arden, who was the manager of well-known groups the Small Faces, The Move and later Black Sabbath and the ELO. Don Arden cut a record himself called 'Sunrise, Sunset" and had to pay for plays to have it heard on Radio Caroline. One of the plugs was scheduled between 10 and 11pm but DJ Johnnie Walker thought it was the most dismal track he ever heard. He remarked on this to listeners and played it at different speeds before stopping it. Sadly, Don Arden had invited a few dozen of his friends around to hear it being played on Caroline; he was not best pleased and threatened to break Johnnie's legs over his comments!

Micky Most too was very aware of the value of regular airplay and took his own boat out with his brother David and their artists. They always entertained Caroline DJs rather regally whenever they were in town and vied with Janet Martin and her team from Polydor to be most extravagent. Other independents too did much the same were Ed Kassner's President label who were often very generous as were Larry Page (Page One), Chris Blackwell (Island) Jeff Kruger (Ember). Lee Gopthal and Graeme Goodall who launched dozens of small reggae labels were also close friends of Caroline, as were the three Palmer brothers who all bought plays.

Battles with Bates

Just as the battle for advertising revenue was won, than another fort battle broke out, this time with the former Radio Essex operator, Roy Bates over Roughs Tower, a former Navy fort just a few miles east of the Mi Amigo. Caroline management thought the fort might make a good base to stage supplies for the Mi Amigo as she was a relatively small ship and unable to store large quantities of fuel and other stores on board. Roughs Tower seemed ideal, or it might even be useful as a site for transmission.

Caroline workmen visited Roughs Towers and some time was spent cutting down the superstructure of the installation. This made it possible to land a small helicopter on the platform.

Roy Bates' own station, Radio Essex, had closed the previous December after losing a court case brought by the GPO about its use of Knock John Tower, twelve miles to the south east. That fort was held to be well within British territorial waters, by virtue of the Bay Closing Line rules introduced in 1964. Bates now eyed Roughs Towers as a replacement to restart his offshore station. He waited until the Radio Caroline team left the fort on leave and then simply clambered onboard and seized possession.

For some weeks, rivals from both Caroline and Bates tussled over occupation of Roughs Tower until, eventually, a truce was arranged. For a while the two teams worked together, until someone injured a hand while lowering gas bottles on a winch and was taken off for treatment. It set the scene for a later stage in the battle

Parliamentary spoil sports

The new Post Master General was Labour MP Edward Short, who was very robust in his dislike for offshore radio. His bill progressed slowly through both Houses of Parliament in the spring of 1967 during which he took every opportunity to spread the most outrageous lies about the stations. The Newcastle based MP was accused of acting as a banker for bribes in the Poulson scandal.

PMG Edward Short

Short adhered to the Harold Wilson line, that radio should not be commercialised in any way. Never given to levity, in public he was very authoritive, perhaps as hark-back to his occupation of school headteacher? He even banned his teenage daughter Jane from listening to the radio, confiscating her transistor radio! No wonder that radio people called this PMG *Spoil Sport Short.*

While Radio Caroline limited its campaigning to supporting organisations like the *Broadside Free Radio Movement*, Radio 270 stepped up the 'Fight for Free Radio' into a battle against the government. They urged listeners to bombard MPs, the PMG and the Prime Minister with letters. The station carried sponsored programmes paid for by local councillors and York University's Conservative Club. These programmes attacked the government's Marine Broadcasting Bill and included contributions by Patrick Wall and other Tory MPs.

Caroline plans to continue
"We intend to stay on the air, even if it means moving our offices outside the country," promised Radio Caroline's Frances van Staden in the press in April. "While the new broadcasting bill will make it illegal for anyone British to work for Radio Caroline, in whatever capacity, it makes no attempt to make our ships illegal, because they are, without any doubt, beyond British territorial waters."

"By moving our offices to a foreign country, employing disc jockeys and other personnel who hold foreign or Commonwealth passports," said Frances. "Obtaining advertising from abroad, we intend to, continue broadcasting without moving either of the boats and without breaking the law.

There were hopes that the Caroline North ship could continue exactly as she was when the Isle of Man Parliament rejected the legislation that extended the Marine Offences Bill to cover the Island. The Island is home to the world's oldest parliament, Tynwald and UK legislation applying to the tiny crown dependency must be approved there. The Labour Government (who have no members in the Manx Parliamant) decided to ignore the pleas of the Manx and impose the law on the Island, which started a constitutions crisis.

The two dozen or so British staff of Radio Caroline were told in April that they had to choose between British citizenship or Caroline. Two of them said immediately that they had already decided to become stateless rather than citizens of a country that could impose what they termed an undemocratic law. Liverpool born DJ Mike Ahern was one of Caroline South's most popular names and now held the 9 to mid-day slot. Mike's mail bag was over a thousand letters a week. His colleague Gerry Burke, the main newsreader on the south ship was also one of the first to declare his allegiance to the station.

"It wasn't easy asking everyone to make up their minds on such an important issue as this, said Ronan O'Rahilly. "We must look to the future and are now in the middle of signing up new non-British staff. These are mainly Canadian and Americans, like Keith Hampshire and Ian McRae who have quickly become very popular with our listeners."

Caroline had already begun its transfer to the continent and had opened an office in the Netherlands. The sales team were already talking to several international clients and an agency agreement had been agreed with a top advertising agency in Paris. "In a year's time we will be choc-a-bloc with advertisements for Japanese transistors, South African oranges and many other products that have nothing to do with Britain," promised Ronan.

Terry Bate, the head of advertising on Caroline was just as confident and said "We doubt that the government will act against foreign advertisers by trying to block imports of goods from companies who advertise with us. How can they find out which adverts have been paid for before their Bill comes into law?"

"Religious programme can't be banned and its widely known that we charge for playing certain new releases, but not all of them. How can the Government know which records have been paid for?" asked Mr Bate when questioned by David Hughes, who then was a journalist at the Kent messenger newspaper. "People blithely say that the British Government will not allow us to apparently flaunt the law, it's not that stupid. Well, I say it IS that stupid!"

The new law only made it illegal for British subjects to work on Caroline and, in not acting against the ship, effectively recognised Caroline to be international. To make the station truly international was no great hardship from a legal point of view; the ships were already owned by a complex web of Liechtenstein, Irish and Panamanian companies and trusts. They were operated by a Dutch shipping company, none of whom had any legislation such as that which the UK was introducing. Their crews could continue manning the two radio ships as normal and supplies could easily be run from Holland and Ireland to the ships without changing their anchorages – it would just involve a longer journey.

The station operators knew that they had to fight the impending legislation and were happy to support various pressure groups formed to take up the Fight For Free Radio, including the Broadside Free Radio Movement, the Free Radio Association and a dozen or more local groups. In Yorkshire the 'Commercial Radio Supporters Club' was formed in Hull by schoolboy Paul Rusling, a keen Radio 270 fan. The CRSC organised a petition which collected over 60,000 signatures, which was taken over by the 'Free Radio Association'.

The CRSC continued as a DJ fan club for some of the Radio 270 DJs and, for several years, ran a series of discos in local clubs, with guest offshore DJs. These included Radio Caroline DJs Don Allen from the North ship and Spangles Muldoon from the South Ship.

By the end of April 1967, the Caroline Club had achieved membership of over 60,000 members. Members paid five shillings each (25p) for membership which gave them a regular newsletter and priority in getting requests played on the station.

There was a surge in interest from the public following the passage through Parliament of the Marine Offences Bill which sought to prohibit British subjects having anything to do with Radio Caroline. The same month Caroline opened its first continental sales office. Located on the Koninginnweg in Amsterdam, the new base was initially run by Basil von Rensburg, a South African born sales executive.

Visitors to the Caroline ships

Both ships were often visited by tourists from nearby holiday resorts. “Enterprising fishermen and other boat owners would fill their craft with holidaymakers who wanted to come out and visit the ships and meet us on board,” says ‘Tatty’ Tom Edwards, who joined Caroline from Radio City when the fort-based station closed in February 1967. “The captain didn’t want anyone on board who was not officially approved but quite a few did come on board while he was sleep.”

It could pose problems if visitors were openly welcomed. Both Caroline ships were in international waters and any visitors from the UK should have gone through customs and various other regulatory bodies both on departure and arrival back in the UK. Apart from being in breach of their regulations, it could be dangerous as even getting between the ships could be quite hazardous. There were also dangerous voltages on exposed wires on deck which worried the Insurance companies who covered the radio ships and those ferrying out visitors.

Nevertheless, many visitors have, over the years, been welcomed on to all the Radio Caroline ships. Mini-skirted girls helped brighten up life for many of the DJs and were entertained to visit the cabins while their boyfriends usually seemed more interested to see the contents of the transmitter room or the ship’s engine room.

Until the new law came in, supplies continued to be ferried out to both Caroline ships from nearby ports. The North ship was looked after by the Ramsey Steamship company while the South ship was serviced by local agents Harcourt Shipping. Originally in Harwich, they had moved across the estuary to Felixstowe.

Most visitors took the train from Liverpool Street station to Ipswich where Caroline’s minibus would meet them. Percy Scadden, Caroline’s local agent, would ensure the usual formalities were dealt with before the Offshore I (usually) would set off from Felixstowe for the Wallet and the Caroline South ship, the Mi Amigo. The trip out to the ships (Radio London and Radio England were moored close by) usually took about an hour.

Boarders Repelled

At the end of June, the battle for Roughs Tower, the former naval fort near the Caroline South ship, flared up once again. Radio Caroline's local agent Percy Scadden from Frinton led their team. They sailed out aboard the Offshore II and attempted to retake the fort from two of Roy Bates men who were holding it.

On this occasion, the Radio Caroline staff met with a ferocious defence from Bates' men who threatened the Caroline team climbing up the ladders. When they got halfway up the legs of the fort all hell broke loose and they were bombarded with home-made Molotov style cocktails. These were also thrown at the boat that had delivered the Caroline staff to the fort and it had to withdraw to a safe distance. Negotiations to rescue to Caroline boarding party, now clinging desperately to the fort's legs, continued for over two hours.

Bates' security men on the fort lowered a wooden crate containing blankets and left one of their men hanging 20 feet above the sea. The raider clung on for three hours before being rescued by the Walton lifeboat which was also threatened.

Roughs Fort, the scene of several skirmishes

M Bates

Not wanting to do battle with Bates again, the Caroline team abandoned the plan to use Roughs fort. "We intended to reboard the fort as we understood that it had been abandoned by the other team," explained Ronan O'Rahilly. "Very simply, we have had people on there for over two years now. Our previous caretakers had gone off to get medical treatment for one of their colleagues. The fort seemed to be derelict with the rope ladder just dangling down but suddenly we were ambushed."

"Our plans for the fort are nothing to do with radio," explained Ronan. "I'm looking at turning the structure into a retreat or a health farm, the ozone out at sea is very beneficial for health. I want to turn the place into a sort of fun palace."

"I do not intend to use violence, that's not the way we do things," affirmed Ronan. "Love is stronger than hate, but the Radio Essex security team were armed with knives and an air gun, plus home-made fire bombs." Ronan said that he planned to send Roy Bates some flowers but was adamant he would have to leave the fort. “It’s my property. I doubt he will be out there very long.”

Ronan did send Roy Bates a huge bunch of flowers (this was the height of flower power, and the ‘summer of love’) but Bates was very concerned at this gesture. Thinking it may be a comment on his masculinity he quickly gave the flowers to his wife, Joan.

Roy’s son Michael, a 15 year old schoolboy, was living on the fort and usually in the thick of any skirmishes. He was an excellent climber and could handle a gun or Molotov cocktail better than most men. Just weeks before the Marine Offence Act came into force, Harold Wilson called a meeting of his senior ministers, the GPO and armed forces, commanding them to find a way to remove any trespassers from Roughs Fort and demolish it. The plan was to offer Bates £5,000 to give up possession but he demanded £90,000.

A team of crack naval personnel then approached the fort with police officers and tried to trick Michael and his mother, the only ones on the fort at that time. They told them that Roy Bates had sent word to hand it over. Michael refused after a discussion and two choppers full of Marines, waiting near Harwich were stood down.

Prince Michael Bates

Sealand Corp

While Ronan dreamt of a health farm and growing mushrooms in the legs of Roughs Tower, Terry Bate admitted: “We were hoping to put a large tower with TV transmitters and a radio station on there. There was certainly enough room and being well outside the three mile limit, there was nothing the government could do. This proved to be true as no action has ever been taken against Roy Bates and his family who continue to occupy the fort today.

The plan to build a TV and radio station on there was revived in 1985 and discussed on the Terry Wogan chat show, on prime-time TV. Two members of the aristocracy had joined the board and a former Caroline manager was supervising construction of the equipment in Holland. Suddenly the funders withdrew and the equipment was sold. It appears that someone had been bought off!

The *Fight for Free Radio* was continuing in parliament as the Labour Party pushed its anti-offshore radio bill. It cleared its final parliamentary hurdle in July meaning it would become law at midnight on Monday 14th August as the Marine Broadcasting (Offences) Act (MOA).

Most offshore stations assumed that the legislation would be rigidly enforced and it would be impossible to operate after August. So, one by one, they announced they would close down. This was later to prove a fallacy and several have since found ways to circumvent the punitive legislation. Most British radio listeners regarded the law as undemocratic and quite draconian, taking away harmless entertainment and a useful public service.

Only Radio Caroline had planned to continue with the other stations, no longer having any interest in the fight for free radio happy to surrender. Many were consigned to the scrap heap, although some found work at the BBC's new stations designed to replace the ships. Caroline advertising supremo Terry Bate found a new office on the side of the Singel canal in Amsterdam. A few desks and some office supplies were delivered but no staff were actually working in the building until August. With some DJs now leaving, Caroline began recruiting new voices for both ships.

Roger Day was a new Caroline recruit who cut his teeth on Swinging Radio England. He was now working in night clubs for Billy Walker, the boxer. As a lifelong Caroline fan, Roger was an obvious choice. "I remember it well, going to work for the world's greatest radio station," says Roger. "It felt great and I still think that. It was such a magical feeling going on board the Mi Amigo for the first time, the ship had a magical aura about it. I never took drugs but I knew what the feeling was as it was in the air around the ship, you couldn't describe it."

At the end of July, Ronan O'Rahilly announced Radio Caroline's plans to continue broadcasting from both the North and South ship after the Marine Offences Act became law. "We are going to be around for quite a while," declared Ronan. "We shall broadcast one or two fake adverts, nobody will know which advertisers have genuinely paid and which ones are the fake ads."

"My team are also planning to broadcast an exposure on the Prime Minister, Harold Wilson and maybe his colleagues too." The tape of 'The Truth about Harold Wilson' programme was held in the safe on board the Mi Amigo and never did get aired, out of respect for Mr Wilson's family. The original aim was only to scare him and make him realise how much hurt he was inflicting on others.
With the new Marine Offences Act due to come into force in mid-August, Radio Caroline opened news offices in Amsterdam, Paris, Dublin and in New York and Toronto, although some were just small sales bases. The majority of the Radio Caroline operation was slowly switched to offices in Dublin and Amsterdam; by August almost no one was left at Caroline House in Chesterfield Gardens. The board of

directors had now all resigned from the company with all the investors finally repaid their investment with a decent profit.

Ronan invested several hundred thousand pounds into his film company, *Mid Atlantic Films*. It seemed to use most of its capital in funding Marianne Faithfull's first film, *Girl on a Motorcycle.* It was the first movie to attract an X certificate in the USA where it was called "Naked under Leather."

Faithfull appeared clad in an all-over costume of leather, which set the trend for motorcyclists for decades to come. It was the sixth most popular film in the UK at the box office that year. Music for the movie was composed by Les Reed.

Ronan decided that he would continue operating both Radio Caroline ships as though the new law didn't exist. Philip Solomon was also prepared to continue funding too as he had been doing well from the operation and planned to take over even more of the station's air time for his records and acts.

"It was Ronan's determination to beat the new act that I just fell in with," admitted Philip Solomon who was the one with a strong business head. "All the other investors just went off into the night with their money. I decided to use my dividends to buy as much of the airtime as I could in advance and, to be honest, I got a very good deal."

"Ronan was over the moon when he heard that Robbie and I would stay and fight on," says Johnnie. "There was never any doubt for me, I just felt that the government's decision was so wrong, it was against what most people wanted. Literally depriving them of their right to have a bit of music on the radio, so it just occurred to me that it was a matter of principle. I think most of the others felt the same way, I know Robbie did. My Mum was really supportive, she had run my fan club and sent out thousands of 'Kiss in the Car' licences."

As DJs Johnnie Walker and Robbie Dale travelled out to the Mi Amigo on the 14th August, they were mobbed by adoring teenage fans. They were met on board the Mi Amigo by the sight of the entire complement of DJs all packed, ready to leave the ship. DJs who had promised that they would stay and fight on, including Tom Edwards, Keith Hampshire and Steve Young all left. Roger Day also went ashore to renew his passport, but was back on board a week later.

Carl Conway had been with Caroline since the station's early days and he was asked to move to Holland and continue work there but he declined due to some promises of theatrical work. Colin Berry was also invited to continue with Caroline but he was worried about being away from his family so long, so declined the offer and joined the BBC.

Australian DJ Ross Brown was hired to replace Colin as newsman on the Mi Amigo and he travelled out with Johnnie and Robbie but only stayed for a few weeks. The following month, Ross was persuaded to move to the North ship which had faced a similar exodus of DJs. He became known there as "On the air Freddie Beare", or 'Frantic Freddie' and stayed with Caroline North until the ship was towed away in 1968.

The departing DJs had reached the conclusion that it might be too dangerous to disobey the law and decided to desert instead, although all had previously pledged their allegiance to the station. Tom Edwards would later find fame and fortune with the BBC and London Weekend TV where he became a well-known continuity announcer. Mike Ahern went to Australia for a couple of years but returned to the UK and worked at several local stations. Keefers flew back to Canada and released several hit records before retiring to raise horses.

Station boss Ronan O'Rahilly travelled out to the Mi Amigo on the morning of the 14th August, along with advertising guru Terry Bate but they were unable to persuade the British DJs to stay and fight on. That left only Robbie and Johnnie to take the station into a new phase of broadcasting, in contravention of the Marine Offence Act which became law at midnight.

That Monday afternoon, Caroline South solemnly paid tribute to its neighbour and rival Radio London; they bailed out of the battle and closed down for good at 3pm. Ross Brown was in the hot seat but it fell to the Admiral Robbie Dale, to comment on the demise and make an important announcement, with considerable emotion and conviction:

> *"We would like to welcome back to all those Radio London listeners who just joined us as Big I closed.*
> *Welcome to Caroline, now the one and only, your future in commercial radio."*

Clearly very emotional, Robbie played the Beatles "All you need is Love" before handing back to Johnnie Walker. Most of his colleagues, the departing Caroline South DJs heard this as they were sailing back to shore, while north of the border, Radio Scotland's final programmes were still playing out, as were those on Radio 270 off Scarborough.

Off the Isle of Man, half the Caroline North DJ team also deserted the ship, rather prematurely. Dave Lee Travis, Tony Prince and chief newsreader Dave Williams said tearful goodbye to their listeners on the air and left the ship at 6pm for the short tender ride into Ramsey.

It was hoped that the police would have to prosecute "innocent" advertisers and force them to prove that they had not placed adverts on Caroline. Among the fakes would be spots promoting the Labour party, in a bid to embarrass the government. No action was taken against advertisers on Caroline though some were sent a letter by the GPO, warning them that their advert could be illegal.

On the Caroline South ship, as the evening wore on the excitement grew and as the clock ticked towards the midnight hour both men realised that although they were now almost alone out at sea there were as many as 25 million listeners tuned in.

Radio Scotland, back now off the Fife coast and Radio 270 off Bridlington in Yorkshire closed down at a minute to midnight. Millions of extra listeners tuned over to the distant Caroline South, to see what would happen at this important moment in radio history.

Was it all just a publicity stunt?
Would Caroline too, meekly switch off, like all the others?
Would the police appear, ready to clap the DJs in leg irons?
Would naval gunboats be sent to put the last stations off their air?

Departing DJs who had left the two ships that Black Monday probably wondered if they had done the right thing. They had left Radio Caroline, the station that had brought them to prominence in Britain's media landscape, and their colleagues, all alone at sea in their hour of need.

Many who achieved more further fame with the BBC and Luxembourg have said they rued leaving the Lady at that time, but they were afraid of their futures and knew how intent the government were to get the stations off the air. Even many who left the radio industry for other pastures have professed to having an aching and yearning in their hearts to have carried on the Fight for Free Radio.

11. Caroline Continues

On the stroke of midnight Johnnie Walker played in the civil rights folk anthem *We Shall Overcome*, followed by the *Caroline* theme song by the Fortunes and then *All You need Is Love* by the Beatles. He then announced to an estimated audience of 22 million that the station was now known as *Radio Caroline International* and announced:

> *"Radio Caroline would like to extend its thanks to Mr Harold Wilson and his Labour Government for at last, after over three and a half years of broadcasting, recognising this station's right to be here, it's right to be broadcasting to the people of Great Britain and the Continent which we have been doing since Easter Sunday 1964."*
>
> *"We in turn recognise YOUR right as our listener to have freedom of choice in your radio entertainment and of course, Radio Caroline belongs to you. It is YOUR radio station, even though it costs you nothing. And, as we enter this new phase in our broadcasting history, you have our assurance that we intend to stay on the air, and . . we love you. Caroline Continues!*

It was Ronan's idea to thank Harold Wilson, to emphasize to listeners in the UK that the station was in international waters over which the government had no control but Johnnie ad-libbed the announcement.

Robbie Dale had been looking out of the studio porthole at thousands of car headlights and hand torches that were flashing out from the surrounding clifftops at the ship. He said: "It really is amazing to see all those cars out there and to know that we're not alone in this, our most important moment."

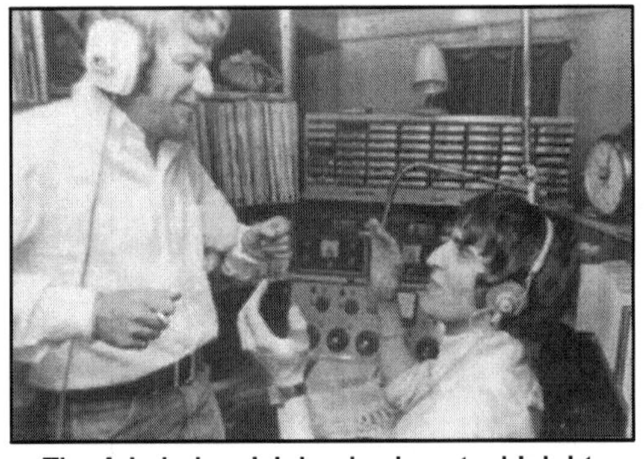

The Admiral and Johnnie sing at midnight

"Of course we're not alone," said Johnnie, who went on to thank many of the people who had made Radio Caroline possible:

> *"A few other people we want to thank now . . . Robbie and I want to say thanks to our leader, Mr Ronan O'Rahilly, Mr Philip Solomon and all who work for Radio Caroline, to make it possible for us to sit here and speak to you now. Also to thank the many, many people who have been with Caroline since that Easter Sunday way back in 1964. We are still here because you have given us such tremendous support."*

Spangles

A young club DJ and TV technician called Harry Cary had arrived late in the evening of the 14th August, having travelled down from Lancashire. On hearing that he had no broadcast experience, Robbie Dale sent him to bed for a few hour's sleep. Young Mr Cary he was so exhausted that he missed the 'Caroline goes International' moment at midnight. His initial appearances were as Chris Anthony, spinning in the near non-stop music overnight, but he was soon promoted to a mid-day show which he christened 'The Lunchtime Loonabout'.

Chris used quite a few different names on Caroline: Chris Anthony, then Spangles Muldoon and, for a few weeks, he used the name Herb Oscar Anderson. He had found the name on a jingle demo tape and thought it sounded a bit grander than the mad monicker of Spangles Muldoon. He later became Dave Kaye but when he became Caroline's station manager in 1972, he reverted to his own name, Chris Cary.

The 'Spangles Muldoon' character was a parody on a Peter Cook character, Spotty Muldoon, from the mid-sixties who wore a bag on his head to hide his spots while listening all the time to Radio Caroline. Cook wrote a song about him, *The Ballad of Spotty Muldoon*, which had been a minor chart hit.

Also recruited to the South ship was Stevie Merike, who had just left Radio Scotland which closed down that fateful day, Black Monday, 14th August. The previous year Stevie had tried to get a singing career off the ground when he left the RAF. He managed just one week as Tony Merrick on the chart at Number 49 with a version of the Stones song *Lady Jane*. He became popular on Caroline South in the afternoon slot from 3 until 6pm and later joined BBC Radio One.

Stevi Merike

"We were so pleased to see some help arrive," says Johnnie Walker. Robbie showed them around and sorted out cabins then joined me on the air for midnight. We couldn't put everyone on the air at that important time and Robbie thought it would be better that they get some sleep, as they would be thrown in 'at the deep end' the next day.

Johnnie and Robbie were not exactly alone in the studio; a posse of journalists had come out on a late-night tender with two new DJs to witness the most momentous of occasions. Champagne flowed for couple of hours in what was certainly a party atmosphere.

Johnnie staggered off to bed at 2 am and was asleep before his head hit the pillow. "When we got up on the Tuesday morning, we fully expecting to see a couple of warships ready to board us and close us down, but there was nothing – just the empty sea." said Johnnie.

While Robbie and Johnnie were having breakfast there was the sound of shouting outside. A man had come out in a dingy from Frinton to bring some newspapers and see if the DJs wanted anything bringing from the shops! It was the listeners part in the defiance of the punitive Labour government that had tried to suppress freedom."

"Despite having only an outboard motor, our 50 year old errand boy disappeared back to shore and re-appeared later with sweets, a fishing rod that Robbie Dale had requested and more newspapers. We were bowled over by his courage and spur of the moment spirit to do his bit to help," said Johnnie. "He was a great morale booster in those first few days of illegality. We now knew someone still loved us wanted to stick their neck out and support us!"

Terry Bate had hired Basil van Rensburg to front the Amsterdam sales operation. Meanwhile he and Ronan cleared Caroline House of all the papers and equipment. "I hosted a dinner party for eight at the Savoy Hotel in London," he remembers. "It was there at midnight we toasted the introduction of the Marine Broadcasting Act. George Brown, a Minister of the then Wilson government was at the next table and, at my invitation, joined us in the toast!"

"At 7.00 am the next morning I flew seven staff members and myself to Amsterdam in my own plane and we opened the new **Radio Caroline International** office by the side of the Singel canal at 9.00am."

Singel 160 in Amsterdam

Rob Olthof

The Amsterdam office was run by Pinky Siedenberg. Pinky was assisted by Nan, the wife of Don Richardson who was an engineer on the Caroline South ship. Nan Richardson would sort out the sacks full of listener mail that arrived daily and take them to the tender in her Citroen van.

Don Richardson

Nan Richardson tried to convince some of the DJs that she knew all about every event and happening on the boat because she and Don had telepathic mind conversations. Johnnie Walker got up one night to find the studio lights ablaze and Don passing messages over the regular 259m transmitter! Apparently he did this regularly, to keep his wife up to date on the situation, so she always knew what was happening on board.

Both Caroline ships continued playing the usual commercials, for Weetabix, Coca Cola, and Maclean's toothpaste. The grey 'men from the ministry' scurried around the advertising agencies demanding to know what was going on and why Caroline were still running adverts. The advertising agencies didn't know what was happening and protested to the GPO investigators: "We would like to contact them and tell them to stop running our adverts, but you've closed them down in London and we don't have any way to get in touch now."

Caroline ran many new adverts too; one was placed by garage in Norwich and for a device to 'beat the breathalyser'. It was designed to cash in on another new Government initiative, to stop drink-driving.

The Caroline North ship, anchored just off the Isle Of Man was in a stronger position than ships anchored off the UK. The Manx had resisted pressure from London to introduce the Marine Offences Act, as they objected to the imposition of UK laws. A group of local politicians led by Sir Charles Kerruish visted Whitehall to demand that they be given clearance for the Island to have its own station heard nationally. The plan was for Radio Caroline to take over the Island's own local station, Manx Radio and operate it at high power.

The new law was forced on the Isle of Man by London with an 'Order in Council, issued using the signature of the Queen, to force it through, without any parliamentary debate. This Order in Council could not take effect until midnight on 31st August. Caroline North therefore got an extra two weeks of freedom, become the new act took effect.

Almost the entire Radio Caroline North DJ team had decided to leave on the 14th however, along with newsreader Dave Williams. DJs Tony Prince and Dave Lee Travis met with cheering but tearful fans on the quayside at Ramsey when the last tender came ashore that teatime, before an impromptu wake at the Mitre Hotel, that lasted well into the early hours of the following morning.

Chief DJ on the North ship, Don Allen, was Caroline's longest serving disc-jockey. As a Canadian, he was unaffected by the law which applied only to British subjects. A new team however had been recruited and the station continued, broadcasting from its lonely mooring by the Bahamian bank in Ramsey Bay. Supplies would now have to be run across from Ireland, a run that would take about 10 hours, rather than the 45 minute trip into the Isle of Man.

There were still two more weeks of complete legality when Caroline North could run supplied from the Isle of Man with immunity. The Radio Caroline North football team played its last game ever, against a GPO team in Lancashire, just days before the new law came in.

James Dunn, the Labour MP for Liverpool Kirkdale, visited the ship and was interviewed on the air by Don Allen. He said that his visit was to thank listeners personally for supporting a charity of which he was a founding member for their support in a recent campaign. Mr Dunn apologised for the Marine Offences Act: “I personally have my own views but the Government has decided this and I have to follow the party line. I do regret that it has happened, it’s such a shame. I don’t agree with the Act in its present form.”

The boys on the North ship were now missing the care and attention of Caroline’s local agent, George Hare. It was his job to ensure that visitors and the team were met at Ronaldsway Airport in the south and brought to the harbour in Ramsey.. He also oversaw supplies and payments for Radio Caroline North.

Before the MoA came into force on the 15th August, there was a daily tender service from Harwich to the Mi Amigo using the Offshore One. Sacks and sacks of mail which in those days was the only way to get any feedback from listeners. Now suddenly that supply of mail wasn’t there and the tenders were much rarer events. It took some time to get the lines of communications opened up properly but the DJ team continued their cheerful banter with tremendous stoicism.

Neither station had broadcast an address that listeners could write to until September, so the mail simply dried up. It took some listeners to realise that the delay in getting mail to the ships was a lot longer than previously; many continued to write to the station’s previous addresses. P O Box 3 in the Isle of Man accumulated four huge trolleys of mail which were retained for some months. Mail continued to be delivered to Caroline House in Mayfair for some weeks after the act, until they suddenly stopped.

The UK activities of Caroline now had to be carried out covertly as no one knew what action might result. Many of the station's affairs were handled by the London office of Major Minor Records by Phillip Solomon's PA, Joan Thirkettle. Joan, a keen Radio Caroline listener in the early days, was a big Simon Dee fan.

Joan Thirkettle

She had worked as a researcher for Radio Caroline before joining Solomon at Major Minor. Later, she joined ITN where she was one of the first female journalists seen 'in vision'. Joan moved to the BBC for a while before becoming one of the founders of the UK's first commercial radio station in 1973, LBC.

Most of the action was now in Amsterdam with north American sales coming from the Toronto office, which was managed by Allan Slaight and his company, *Marich Associates.* Caroline also had a mailing address on Madison Avenue in New York which generated a lot of press enquiries but no sales revenue.

Joan realised that someone was 'ratting' on Caroline and informing about Caroline's 'underground' supplies. It has later proven (in government records, kept in the National Archives at Kew) to have been a song plugger at Pye Records just the street in ATV House. GPO investigators were told how Major Minor's office was the base and about the speedboat used to take records out to the ship.

Pye Records had spent money plugging its releases on Radio Caroline before the law changed. One of their staff was now seeking to stop anyone else getting airplay. Pye artistes continued being heard on Caroline as their managers or the song publishers bought airtime. The Foundations, the Kinks, Status Quo and Long John Baldry are a few Pye artistes that flourished as a result of relentless airplay on Caroline.

Solomon took legal advice and concocted a tale that he had severed all links with Caroline and asked them not to play his records. He met with Robin Scott, a senior BBC controller at Radio One and assured him that he had no links with the ships. They didn't believe his claim and continued banning Major Minor product from plays on the Radio One.

New London base

The London sales operation had now closed as had all the support services, at least on paper. Caroline House was all but deserted, although mail continued to be delivered for some weeks. Ronan had switched his base to a secret office in Soho from where he ran *Mid-Atlantic Films.*

Royalty House in Soho

This was just a couple of rooms in Royalty House in Dean Street, Soho, just a hundred yards along the street from Merit House, where the first Radio Caroline shows had been recorded in early 1964.

Royalty House is the same building where *Ross Radio Productions* recorded many of their programmes for CNBC a few years earlier – the first offshore broadcasts into the UK, which Ronan thought was ironic. Only he, his secretary and his PA, Oonagh Huggard, were present and providing covert support for the station. This was more practical than everyone converging on the office in Amsterdam and it was vital to have some vestige of a presence in London.

Very few people knew that Ronan was based there. Only he, his PA Oonagh Huggard and a secretary were to be found at Royalty House, conducting the business of *Mid Atlantic Films.* Some of the work of finding DJs for and other Radio Caroline matters were conducted from there, but very covertly. Contacts with the music industry (obtaining new music and arranging payola deals) were done by Philip Solomon from his office on New Oxford Street by his assistant Joan Thirkettle.

Link man Percy Scadden continued to provide the South ship with some succour by way of a daily rendezvous over the air from his home on Frinton seafront. An emergency link was available with the North ship, courtesy of Sir Charles Kerruish but this was top secret and for use only in an emergency as he held a very senior role in the Manx Parliament, Tynwald.

Mrs Dale joins Caroline

Towards the end of August, and without the usual daily tender bringing mail and newspapers, the ship's DJs minds turned to mischief with more time on their hands. One day an engineer found that by changing a few cables around in the studio, the BBC's FM transmissions could be rebroadcast over Caroline with good quality. The Light Programme ran a daily soap opera called Mrs Dales Diary and Johnnie decided that, as Robbie Dale had gone on leave, he would relay the BBC 's Mrs Dale instead, especially as they probably didn't have as many listeners as Caroline.

Government destroy Sunk Head Tower

The following week, a party of fifty Royal Engineers sappers travelled out to the Sunk Head Fort, a few miles south of the Caroline South ship. This structure had been used by Radio Tower the previous year and was going to be part of an offshore TV station. The army lost no time in laying about 2,000 pounds of gelignite around the tower which exploded with a blast that could be heard on the coast fourteen miles away. Their action, which cost many thousands of pounds, was designed to prevent the fort being used as a base for offshore broadcasting.

Sunk Head and the nearby Roughs Tower, just a few miles to the north east of the Mi Amigo, were the only remaining offshore forts that were safely outside the three miles limit and in international waters. They could have been used by any non-UK based station for transmission.

Roughs Towers was still being occupied by Roy Bates, who had recently offered to give up possession for a large sum of money. As Caroline were not willing to pay his demand, he turned the fort into an independent nation, called Sealand. Roy's immediate family have occupied the fort ever since; it's manned by a team of security personnel, led by former Radio Caroline DJ and engineer Mike Barrington.

While the new law now made it illegal to run supplies to and from a radio ship on the high seas, it did not preclude people just going out to take a look. A HM Customs official in Harwich said "the operation of pleasure boats out around Radio Caroline is something that we are well aware of. So long as they don't deliver anything or people to the ship, then it's all perfectly legal, but there must be no physical contact between the ships." Supplies now had to come from other countries, which meant a long trip to the Dutch coast for Caroline's small tender, the Offshore 1. After the MOA took effect, it ran to the seaside town of Scheveningen and Wijsmuller's HQ in IJmuiden.

Over in the Isle of Man, the law didn't take effect immediately; the last few weeks were spent stocking up the Caroline with additional food supplies, spares, fuel and 70 tons of water. Ronan O'Rahilly was on board the last tender from Ramsey, to wish the team well and urge them onwards. The depleted team of DJs included Martin Kayne , hired from the recently closed Radio 355, Jason Woolfe and Lord Charles Brown whose arrival on the ship was announced on the air with due pomp and ceremony.

A Manx Adieu

On the last day of legality, 31st August, almost two thousand revellers embarked on the Isle of Man ferry *The Manxman* in Douglas. They sailed the 20 miles up the coast to Ramsey Bay, the anchorage for the last three years of Radio Caroline North.

As the captain of the Manxman sailed around the radio ship, his passengers shouted greetings and a final farewell to the ship that had brought the Island so much favourable publicity over the last three years. DJ Mark Sloane who had just joined Caroline North went up to deck with a microphone and did a commentary but was drowned out in some parts by the sound of the two ships horns greeting each other.

Later that night the last tender run to Caroline North left Ramsey taking Ronan O'Rahilly out to the ship to thank those remaining and offer some encouragement. When that tender left, the North ship was quite alone and wouldn't see any visitors for over six weeks. At midnight Chief DJ Don Allen played *O Land of my Birth*, the Manx National Anthem and announced:

"This the northern voice of Radio Caroline International on 259m, the continuing sound of free radio for the British Isles."

Daffy Don Allen's fan club postcard

The next morning the station continued to broadcast as normal, with the first 'illegal' commercial being for Kellogs Corn Flakes (made in Manchester, where Radio Caroline North was played in the factory). It was to be six weeks before another tender reached the Caroline North ship again. Supply runs were eventually organised via Dundalk in the Irish Republic.

Two days into September, Caroline DJs Mark Sloan and Don Allen announced they were starting to swim to Ramsey for a few beers. Ramsey lifeboat was despatched to search for the stir-crazy jocks, but as they neared the ship they were told that the MV Caroline's Captain had stopped the DJ's swimathon to shore. Swimming around the radio ship was a popular pastime but usually in the summer months. The Irish sea can be very cold in winter.

The extra plugs for records on Philip Solomon's Major Minor label didn't sound too out of kilter with regular programming on the North ship, as they always played a lot of country and easy listening music. The music of the Dubliners, Danny Doyle and David McWilliams went down very well with listeners all over Ireland, and in northern England too where many Irish showbands were popular on the night club circuits.

In late August, Brian Epstein, the manager of The Beatles, died at his London flat. The Fab Four were pretty rudderless after this devastating loss; 'Eppy' had not only made their worldwide fame possible, he handled every aspect of their business life. The Beatles urgently needed a manager, someone they trusted. John Lennon approached Ronan O'Rahilly and the pair spent almost three days debating the group's future. John persuaded George Harrison that Ronan was the right man for the job.

Brian Epstein

It was Ronan who suggested that the Beatles should set up different companies to appeal to young people, a boutique, record company, film company, etc; ideas that eventually begat Apple Corps. Paul McCartney however wanted his girlfriend's father, John Eastman, to take care of business and he recruited Ringo as an Eastman supporter. Despite the deadlock, the prospect of running the world's biggest group took Ronan's eye off the Caroline ball, allowing Solomon to take over more aspects of the Caroline organisation.

Ronan later helped George Harrison set up his record company (*Dark Horse Records*) and a film company (*Handmade Films*) at Sloane Square in Chelsea. George was always very grateful for the help Ronan gave him in the late 60s and early 70s. After Handmade Film's fifteenth release (and only three flops) George confessed that much of his success was down to two people, Ronan and Denis O'Brien, who was his partner in the film company.

In September, Granada TV's "World in Action" programme decided to make another episode about Caroline. The GPO now had a special team to kill off Caroline which reported back daily to the Prime Minister's office. They warned Granada TV and its regulator, the ITA, that they would prosecute if the programme went ahead, claiming it might publicise Radio Caroline. Other government departments were ordered to "pull out all the stops" to halt the programme by blocking Granada TV's visit to the radio ship.

When Granada's film crew set sail on a chartered Grimsby trawler, the Ross Dainty, GPO said that they would be prosecuted if they landed them on the radio ship. The company that owned the harbour and their manager, Edward Hall, were also threatened, although Customs said that this would be beyond their authorisation. The *Ross Dainty* laid to off the Mi Amigo for a couple of days, while Granada TV's lawyers "arm-wrestled" with the GPO mandarins in Whitehall.

The pantomime of lawyers arguing over a journalist's access to DJs playing records became big news and was covered in press around the world. "I can't believe what I'm reading in the newspapers today," exclaimed Ronan O'Rahilly. "The British government is going bonkers over press coverage of a radio station! When will it dawn on people how far this man Harold Wilson will go just to stamp out pop music and freedom. Freedom of the press is about the last freedom we have."

One solution was for Granada's team to board the Mi Amigo, film the DJs in exile and then sail to a port in Holland and back. Cameraman Paddy Seale and producer Mike Hodge went on board and made the film which featured Robbie at his most candid while on the air.

"We can't allow ITV to give Radio Caroline any publicity," said Harold Wilson. "We made it clear that we want this station stopped and we shall see it stopped." He issued a 'D Notice' to silence any press coverage of the episode, which served only to make his government look mindless, vindictive, stupid and ineffectual. It was good publicity, reminding over fifteen million ITV viewers that Radio Caroline was still out there and still broadcasting.

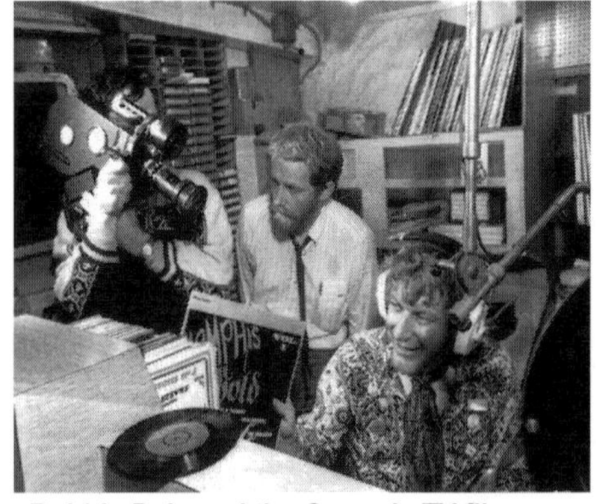

Robbie Dale and the Granada TV film crew

Radio 1 launch

Radio 1 was the BBC's answer to Government demands that it found a way to replace the offshore radio stations. A part time pop music service using one of the Light Programme's old frequencies, 247 metres was chosen. Reception was poor in many places, and dire after dark when interference from a station in Albania marred reception.

Sadly, Caroline South was off the air that Saturday morning with a technical problem, but it's likely everyone wanted to sample the BBC's new offering anyway. The Caroline South DJs listened to the somewhat starchy BBC output with occasional hoots of laughter. The Mi Amigo was soon back on the air later that day. On the Caroline North ship reception was almost impossible of the new BBC service as the Caroline North's own transmitter on 1169 kHz was only 5 channels away from Radio 1 on 1214 and came from the distant Moorside Edge transmitter. A small infill station on the Lancashire coast made reception across at the Isle of Man even worse.

The BBC hired about forty DJs from the 200 who applied, including five former Radio Caroline DJs. They were Simon Dee who had been at the Light Programme for over two years now, Tony Blackburn, who had also been at the BBC for a couple of months, having left Radio London prematurely to be one of the first inside Broadcasting House.

Tony too could be rebellious at times. He sneaked in the Move's single "Flowers in the Rain" in as the first Radio 1 played, even though they were embroiled in a legal battle with Harold Wilson. The Move had published postcards of Wilson in the bath with his secretary, Marcia Falkender, in response to a suggestion from Ronan made to his pal Tony Secunda who rented offices at Caroline House. The group settled out of court, handing all the royalties to the Prime Minister.

Another former Caroline DJ, Keith Skues, hosted Radio 1's first mid-morning show, followed by two more shipmates Emperor Rosko and Mike Ahern. While Radio Caroline stars were well represented that first morning, the majority of the BBC's hirings came from Radio London, even the jingles were re-sings of an old Big L package.

Newspaper coverage

Caroline DJs listening in to the station's launch were not impressed, but the biggest disappointment to them was the huge coverage the station got in newspapers and magazines. Caroline was rarely mentioned at all, it was almost as though she had ceased to exist.

The problem was that the GPO had written to every newspaper editor pointing out to them that any press coverage even mentioning Radio

Caroline would be construed as being intended to publicise the station, and so in breach of the Marine Offences Act. Newspapers tended to shy away from mentioning Caroline for a long time, except when the station was of high news interest.

They were happy to run front page stories when there was a whiff of controversy. The problem was that many newspapers saw commercial radio as stealing their advertising revenue, which they had long had a monopoly over. The only newspapers in support of Radio Caroline were those that also had radio companies formed and ready to operate commercial radio stations themselves, such as the Daily Express.

On the Mi Amigo and the MV Caroline, the DJs went about their programmes as though the Act hadn't happened. Commercials still ran; some of these were dummies but most were being paid for, using subsidiary companies outside the UK, however no attempts were made by Caroline to run supplies or people into the UK. Both ships had visitors, but unofficially. The Wijsmuller crews still operated the two ships "by the book".

Plug records still had to be played; Roger Day began slotting them in very early in his programmes so that after 7am, when audiences were at their largest, he could still play what the listeners wanted.

The mixing panel in the main studio (see below) was custom built by Caroline engineer, Pete Posthumus and worked very well in the fierce 50kW field (Big L was plagued by audio breakthrough)

In October Johnnie wrote a short presentation about the current predicament and their aspirations for the future. He set it to a stirring piece of music, the *Ballad of the Green Berets* that had been a hit for an American GI, Barry Sadler, two years previously.

The trailer has been a favourite of Caroline fans ever since and Johnnie has given permission for its inclusion here, as it indicates how feelings were running on the Mi Amigo in late 1967

Johnnie Walker in the studio with the playlist on the desk

Mans Fight for Freedom

By Johnnie Walker

This is the Story of Mans Fight for Freedom. The beginning is in the past, the middle is now, the end is in the future. It is a story of sadness and of triumph

August 14th as DJs Robbie Dale, Johnnie Walker and Ross Brown leave Liverpool Street station. Spurred on towards the sea by hundreds of cheering people. See them now as they stand on the tender; There are tears in their eyes as their families, their homes and their loved ones are left behind.

Three o'clock on this Monday afternoon and on 266 Big Lil is heard for the last time. Caroline is alone. These three men prepare for midnight, for in a few hours time they are to challenge the might and the power of the British Government. They will become criminals. Midnight approaches, it is August 15th.

Johnnie Walker announces that Caroline belongs to you, that she loves you and she will continue. The Beatles sing "All You Need Is Love". These men sound happy but underneath they are sad, for they now know that they have passed the point of no return. They are not sad for long as they are joined by other men who also gave up so much to fight for freedom.

The seas are rough and cruel, life is hard, but as each day passes the moment of triumph draws nearer. The British people rally round, they send food, they send comfort and they send their love. All you need is love. And Love overcomes. The British government relents, Caroline raises her anchor and heads for England.

See her now majestically and proudly, sailing up the river towards the capital that has welcomed so many victors in British history. But none as victorious as these men. They stand on the deck waving to the millions of people who line the Thames, this time the tears flooding from their eye are tears of happiness. The insurmountable odds have been surmounted. They reunite with their families, with their friends with their loved ones.

We are near the end of our story. London's skyline has a new landmark pointed towards the heavens – Caroline's aerial, at least beaming out its love and music to a free and peaceful nation. We have overcome. The battle is over. Free Radio becomes a way of life, but never taken for granted. For no man will ever forget Monday, August 14th, nineteen hundred and sixty seven.

Man's Fight for Freedom describes the events of August 14th 1967 when Caroline stood alone to continue bringing free radio to Great Britain. It talks of the months of solitude and desolation out at sea and how it affected the crew. As the music suddenly changed tempo, you can hear Johnnie's spirits lift as he predicts a triumphant return to Britain, with Caroline sailing up the Thames. Johnnie was there to see the Ross Revenge, enact part of the script in the 1990s when she visited the London docks for a few months.

Anxious to stem the flow of listeners to Radio 1, Chief DJ Robbie Dale made some changes to the schedules. As Tony Blackburn seemed to be getting the biggest share of publicity at Radio 1, Robbie talked his star DJ, Johnnie Walker, into trying out the breakfast slot, up against Tony Blackburn in November. This was no criticism of Roger Day, Caroline South's regular breakfast show host who was one of the stations brightest sounding DJs. It was just a question of maximising the station's attraction at peak time. After a couple of weeks on the breakfast shift Johnnie moved back to his regular slot when the Twiglet returned to ship after a holiday.

New Yorker Howie Castle enjoyed offshore radio on hearing it while on holiday in the UK. He packed up and came to join Caroline in late 1967 – arriving the same week as Andy Archer. He chose a pseudonym, that of a broadcaster who he admired on WOLF in New York; Bud Ballou. He usually hosted the early evening show on Caroline and the *Billboard Hot Hundred* at weekends.

Bud Ballou on Caroline South

Morris Brown

Caroline dropped many of the short programme names used since her early days and used the main DJs name, such as the Stevie Merike Show. Regular DJs had their own named slots and other DJs acknowledge them sitting in while they were on a week off, or ill. It was quite normal to hear the main incumbent referred to, even more often than the DJ actually hosting the show.

Other DJs however gave their show a different title, unconnected with their own name. Some of these were very descriptive: Spangles Muldoon referred to his midday session as "*The Lunchtime Loonabout*" while New Zealander Glenn Adams presided over *The Two-Ton Mustard Seed*. This psychedelic name was typical of those heady days of flower power and was an idea Glenn had picked up while at the Broadcasting School in San Francisco. Glenn shared the forecastle (often abbreviated to the focs'l) cabin, which could only be reached down a vertical ladder at the very front of the ship. It was a four man cabin, and in those days was also the domain of Spangles Muldoon. Right next door was the ships chain locker – a noisy place where the ships anchor came into the ship and clanked away in the slightest seas. It had purple walls and was known as the Bag O'Nails; all the cabins on the Mi Amigo were named after London clubs.

Alive, Alert and Aware
In September, Caroline International began promoting the ideas of Justice and Fairness. "Being a free radio station we cannot be deterred in fighting for anything that has right on its side. Radio Caroline International, with its new campaign to help man in his fight against unfairness and victimisation."

Disc Jockeys also announced that " We at Caroline International want you to know that the products we advertise are the best on the market. We only advertise first class products. We believe in the goods we advertise and stand by them because we ourselves use them on board the ship, and on shore, and because they are also tested at great length very carefully by experts in the manner of the magazine Which, produced by the Consumers' Association. Products advertised Caroline International are known as the most superior in their field."

The Caroline schedules in Autumn 1967 were full of Phillip Solomon products, particularly releases on the Major Minor label. Among the tracks most frequently heard were those from David McWilliams' first album. His iconic *Days of Pearly Spencer* has become one of the tracks most associated with Caroline, although it was originally a B side; Harlem Lady was promoted as the A side for a month.

Despite extensive Caroline airplay, Pearly Spencer never became a UK chart hit, although the other side, *Harlem Lady,* had been in the 'breakers section of the chart for four weeks. In the Netherlands, where Caroline had many listeners too, the single made it to number eight in the Veronica Top 40 and number ten in Belgium. Marc Almond revived the song in the 1990s, but the David McWilliams version will always be one of the most memorable Caroline sounds.

David's much superior track *Can I get there by Candlelight* was also a hit in Holland after being Radio Veronica's *Tip for the Top* on four different weeks. One reason touted at the time for 'Pearly Spencer's' failing to get higher in the charts was that you could hear it played so often on Caroline, there was no need to buy a copy. In fact, it was due to the BBC virtually banning it, due to its close links to Caroline

One of Johnnie's favourite performers, Otis Redding died in December 1967 and on Friday 22nd, Johnnie devoted the whole of his programme to a tribute to the man. His shows were also supported by Otis' record company, Atlantic.

Johnnie was never a shrinking violet and always told his listeners exactly what he was feeling, elated or disappointed. When times were really hard Johnnie used his programme to tell the Caroline management ashore exactly how he felt about the lack of water, lack of heating, fresh food and most of all mail from listeners and seeing new faces. The Admiral Robbie Dale persuaded Philip Solomon to promote Johnnie and give him more responsibility, so he better understood the problems of keeping Radio Caroline going.

The winter of 67 – 68 was a harsh one with lengthy periods between supply tenders for both ships. To the credit of the two teams of DJs, Caroline still sounded quite bright and playing plenty of the latest releases. Christmas sounded to be a lot of fun on the ship, when what few commercials there were ended up being read backwards!

Encouraged by Dutch gin cocktails, the DJs all invaded the studio as Christmas Day dawned to help Carl Mitchell along with his programme by singing an assortment of carols.

The DJs were all in real party mood, possibly delighted by the fisherman's ganseys (a seaman's sweater, usually smelling of natural oils) that Philip Solomon had sent out as gifts.

Radio Caroline's *Countdown of Sound* continued as a main daytime show, while an overnight Billboard Hot 100 was also very popular as it was packed full of the latest American releases, largely ignored by the BBC.

a rare sight that winter – Offshore 1 tender alongside

One psychedelic group from south London called Traffic Jam had tried many times to get a hit record, using a variety of names including The Sceptres and Traffic Jam. Just before Christmas they had laid down a self-penned number, *Pictures of Matchstick Men*, complete with wailing organ and electronic effects, bearing their new name, Status Quo. Their manager, Pat Barlow who was subsidising the band from his work at the gas board, decided to give the record a final push and invested £200 for some plugs on Radio Caroline.

Andy Archer made the Quo's record his *Caroline Sureshot* for a week which gave it an extra push, though it probably didn't need it; the DJs on both the ships loved it. The platter wasn't chucked out of the porthole, a fate that many plug records endured but the DJs gave it extra spins. It received extensive play on Caroline all over Christmas and, within weeks, it had made it up into the Top Ten.

A similar success was happening to several former plug records heard on Caroline, that were all but ignored elsewhere. Artistes like Felice Taylor and the Equals had their product released on Ed Kassner's President record label and Tommy James and the Shondells were part of the Roulette Records roster, represented by Major Minor. Incessant plays on Caroline also turned many other Major Minor records into hits, not just the Dubliners, Danny Doyle and David McWilliams, but unlikely chart material such as those by the Raymond Lefevre Orchestra!

Scadden's Yaesu rig

While the schedule of tenders was a problem, comm's to the ship continued much as before, thanks to Percy Scadden's amateur radio station at his home on the seafront in Frinton. He made a rendezvous with the Mi Amigo on an unused frequency at 9:30 each day and used a neighbour's telephone to pass messages on. The rig he used was a Yaesu FT200, a reliable SSB transceiver capable of operating on all the short wave bands.

The GPO never expected Radio Caroline to survive more than a few weeks so, the fact that both ships had survived to 1968 worried them. A task force was set up to investigate and Ronan and Phillip Solomon were questioned. When asked if he ran Planet Productions, Ronan denied it, claiming that the company does not exist in the UK as it had been moved abroad. Asked by Special Branch officers why Caroline played his records fifty times a day, Solomon said that he subcontracted the promotion to an agency in Holland and claimed that they must be they who were booking the time themselves.

The team of GPO investigators traced and interviewed everyone who had been a director of any of the Radio Caroline companies. Each said that they had sold their shares in Caroline to a Bahamian millionaire when the Marine Offences Act became law. Philip Solomon wrote to the Head of the BBC's Radio 1 and Radio 2, claiming that he had written to Radio Caroline and asked them not to play his records so often as it was embarrassing him in London!

Chris Cary was persuaded to move to the Caroline North ship. After a holiday with his family and pals from the clubs in the Midlands, he set off to Dundalk in Ireland for a tender to the Caroline North ship. Before he could reach the ship out in Ramsey bay, the Dutch tug 'Utrecht' was to beat him to it.

During Saturday 2 March, Caroline South DJs announced that they would be late on the air on Monday as some essential work had to be done on the generator cabling down in the depths of the engine room.

Johnnie Walker was senior DJ and on Saturday 2nd March, finished his programme at midnight. He sat up chatting with the Dutch crew until 3am and then went to bed.

The last programme of the day was hosted by Andy Archer. Andy hailed from a little village near Kings Lynn. As *Terrible Terry Dawson,* Andy had worked on Radio City for a while before a stretch in the RAF. He came out to Caroline South in late 1967 and became a very popular DJ. Andy was a pretty unusual guy, with an ancestral tree that included Sir Robert Yallop, a leading Jacobite and friend of King Charles II, who was arrested for plotting against King William.

A young Andy Archer.

Despite his penchant for the good things in life, Andy was enjoying his time on Caroline South and was looking forward to a great year as he played the last record of the broadcast day in the early hours on that Sunday morning. It was *Cinderella Rockerfella,* by Esther & Abi Ofarim, then at number one in the charts. As it faded at 2 am Andy closed down the station for the night; he had no idea what a momentous occasion it was, nor of the most dreadful disaster about to befall the station, and in fact the entire Caroline Organisation.

This was to be the end of Radio Caroline's first phase!

12. An unexpected trip to Amsterdam

For various reasons, the Wijsmullers had not been paid for a couple of months and the bill for crewing and supplying the two ships had now built up. The south ship, the Mi Amigo, was still subject to lease payments to her owners, but an agreement had been reached to freeze these for a year.

The costs of manning, servicing and insurance for both ships still were due from the station however, as these had been met in the normal way by the ships' management company, Wijsmullers. This arm of the company was run by different part of the family and its' said that the others in the company resented Radio Caroline being allowed to run up so much credit with the company.

A demand for immediate payment of £30,000 was made in February 1968 and this went ignored as both Philip Solomon and Ronan O'Rahilly were away on holiday at the time. Wijsmullers had good connections with various British Government agencies and valued the work they got from this for their towing and salvage divisions.

Ronan O'Rahilly claims that one of the Wijsmuller brothers was approached by the British Government, or by agents acting for Harold Wilson in a personal capacity, to find a way to remove the two Caroline ships. "There's no doubt in my mind that a deal was done with one of the Wijsmullers who were promised more lucrative contracts with the British Government if the Caroline ships were removed," says Ronan. "Such dirty tricks are often practiced, usually on the excuse of it's in the national interest."

Already having their crewmen on board both the ships would mean that the ships were already under the Wijsmullers' control. There could be plenty of reasons to take the ships into port for servicing, repairs and other work required by the insurers, although to do both at once, without any notice, would be more difficult to explain.

The most plausible reason is that the secret task force charged with stopping Radio Caroline simply handed over a bundle of cash to have the ships brought in. They would gamble that, once in port, the momentum to relaunch would never happen. It was likely that, having had both ships brought into port, Radio Caroline might never find a way to get the ships back to sea again. Today, with Wijsmullers' key 'movers and shakers' of that period now infirm or departed, it's unlikely that the true reason will even be known.

What we do know is that, on Saturday 2nd March 1968 the powerful Dutch tug Utrecht dropped anchor a mile from the MV Caroline, it showed no signs of wanting to communicate with the MV Caroline. The following morning, just after 2am, a loud bump was felt throughout the ship. Before anyone could go and investigate, a group of Dutch seamen burst into the lounge.

The ship's captain, the chief DJ and the chief engineer were summoned to the lounge and a letter was read out from the Wijsmuller tender firm. Its aid simply that all broadcasting was to cease immediately, the studios were to be sealed off and the crystals removed from the transmitters.

After heated discussions the staff on the MV Caroline complied with the order to avoid any possibility of violence. The Dutch marine crew all worked directly for Wijsmullers anyway and were colleagues of the tug crew. All the crew were left in the dark regarding their future and didn't know if the ship would be taken to Greenore for repairs or if they were to be taken to the Essex coast to replace the Mi Amigo.

Unknown to the crew on the Caroline North ship, the same events were happening on the MV Mi Amigo, the Caroline South ship.

Nothing had seemed untoward that Sunday morning on the Mi Amigo; at 5am Ray Glenister began the usual routine of spinning non-stop music for half an hour, until Roger Day started his breakfast show at 5:30. Suddenly the Wijsmullers tug 'Titan' came alongside and her master gave identical orders to the Mi Amigo's crew and the broadcast team to those handed to the crew on the North ship.

Ray tried to broadcast an urgent message to listeners on shore but the microphone was snatched away by a burly tugman and Ray was ordered out of the studio. He hurried downstairs to wake senior DJ Johnnie Walker; the DJs were then given just ten minutes to clear their personal items from the studio which was then locked up. The DJs were confined to the ship's mess-lounge while work continued to cut the anchor chain so the tow to Amsterdam could begin.

The transmitter was switched off at 5:20 and work began severing the anchor chain. "This confirmed my worst fears and told me that this was the end," explains Johnnie. "They just unhooked the anchor chain and let it fall into the sea, no buoys were attached so that it could later be found and used again. Nothing! We thought then that this was it, we were not coming back."

The coastguards at Walton on the Naze could not see what was going on due to a mist that shrouded the east coast that Sunday morning, but the Galloper lightship sent a message to them mid-morning to say "We just observed the Mi Amigo pass by and it's chasing a Dutch tug!"

The Titan towed the Mi Amigo to a rendezvous with two more tugs off East Anglia before crossing the North Sea to IJmuiden. They then went along the North Sea canal towards Amsterdam where Pinky Siedenberg who ran the office was waiting on the quayside. They had no idea of what was going one and didn't know how or when the ships were going to get back to sea.

On arrival in Holland the Wijsmullers issued a short statement to the effect that the ship would undergo some repairs and a survey prior to re-insurance before being returned to her moorings off the UK.

The Wijsmuller Company said the ships needed surveying, a condition of their insurance. They were also owed around £30,000 for the tender services to both Caroline ships but there were sufficient funds in the station to pay the bills.

"I don't think any of us really believed that," confides Roger Day, whose Sunday morning breakfast show had been so rudely stopped by the tug's arrival. "We knew that once we were in port anywhere, the British Government would put pressure on and we would not get out again. It really was the end of a dream."

The DJs were paid off, given air tickets back to the UK and told to await further instructions. Some of then decided to stay on in Holland, fearing prosecution on arrival back in England. In fact, there was no action taken against any of the Caroline DJs, several of whom had travelled back and forth into London regularly. Roger Day had been stopped only once, by a customs officer who asked him to play a request when he got back to the ship!

Chief DJ "the Admiral" Robbie Dale was on holiday in Spain at the time; the first he knew about the seizure of the ships was via a telegram sent by Johnnie Walker from Amsterdam advising him. On returning to Holland he found there was nothing he could do personally to get the ships freed.

LAS MERCEDES TORREMOLINOS
X 28 AFS835 LONDONLB 22 10 2200
CAROL GON FOR GOOD SORRY CANT JOIN YOU SEE YOU AROUND THE 25TH PETER

"All commercial trading companies owe money and run on credit," explained Ronan. The amount was trifling compared to the value of the ships as a 'going concern'. They effectively slashed our value by taking the ships off the air." The timing of the siezures was simply unfortunate with both of the Caroline bosses being away on holiday and no one having sufficient authorisation to release the money.

Bart Wijsmuller had wanted to continue providing the two Caroline ships with service while his brothers did not, for some reason. They had instructed two of their ocean-going tugs to bring in the Caroline ships to Amsterdam. It's strongly suspected that an arm of the British secret service, perhaps even someone acting for Harold Wilson in a personal capacity, had got to the Wijsmuller brother in charge of ocean operations and persuaded them to have the ships towed away at that particular time.

Back off the Isle of Man, it took all day to complete preparations on the North Ship. Manx journalist Terry Cringle got a speedboat out to the Caroline to see what was going on and he interviewed some of the DJs at the ship's rail that Sunday afternoon.

While none of the DJs knew what was really happening, Cringle realised that this was a big story. He hurried back to land with his scoop and tried to reach Ronan O'Rahilly but he was on holiday as was the station's local representative, George Hare. Terry's copy to the national press resulted in the front page stories that broke the news to millions of anxious listeners the next day.

MV Caroline under tow
GPO Archive

It took until late Sunday afternoon for the tug crew to cut the anchor, which is still out there in Ramsey Bay. By teatime the anchor systems had been cut away, a tow line had been fixed between the MV Caroline and the tug Utrecht and a long, slow tow southwards to the English Channel began.

At various times on the voyage at least two vessels of the Royal Navy were seen following them. It took four days for the Utrecht to tow the Caroline North ship around Lands End and on to the Netherlands. Just outside IJmuiden she was joined by the tug 'Nestor' for the final tow up to to Amsterdam, to be tied up alongside the Mi Amigo.

When Solomon arrived back from his holiday he insisted that the Wijsmullers return the ships to their anchorages at their own expense before he would pay the outstanding bills. The two parties remained in stalemate, refusing eventually to even meet and discuss the problem.

Sisters at the Amsterdam quayside
Dutch Naionaal Archives

Radio Luxembourg were quick to act on the disappearance of the two Carolines from the air. They had seen their audiences dwindle a little as the BBC launched Radio One, and wondered if perhaps this was a chance to fight back?

Luxembourg hired five of the best-known voices from offshore radio – Tony Prince from the Caroline North ship and Roger Day from the Mi Amigo. Their news service was given a boost with the booming voice of Paul Kaye from Radio London on news and then they added Paul Burnett (Radio 270) and Bob Stewart, also from Caroline North.

Robbie Dale didn't have quite so far to travel; he signed up for nearby Radio Veronica, pre-recording his shows in Hilversum which were well received and a welcome sound for Radio Caroline listeners.

Robbie's late night shows on Veronica didn't bring the expected audiences in the UK, but his specially recorded shows for Radio Veronica International in Majorca were popular. Soon he was active in record production, even releasing a single himself (Soul Mama) and then branched out into television.

Robbie's *Jam on TV* programme attracted over 2m viewers some weeks, a remarkable figure for a small country like Holland and the show's timeslot. There were plans to show the programme in London, or have Robbie launch a similar one but these were mysteriously dropped after initial discussions with the UK producers.

Radio 270 to the rescue?
In an interview with the weekly music paper Disc & Music Echo in April, Ronan O'Rahilly said that he was confident of getting Radio Caroline back on the air by Easter weekend, though they wouldn't be using the Mi Amigo or the MV Caroline.

Ronan had reached an arrangement with the owners of Radio 270, which had lain unused in Whitby for over six months and was available for sale. She had even been advertised quite extensively by local estate agent Denys Tuckley. The Oceaan 7 was still fully equipped and a Caroline engineer had been on board and inspected the equipment. A team of DJs from both the Caroline ships were to be used in this small-scale return which would still be heard strongly in London.

Four Radio Caroline DJs, moved for a week into rooms in the Hayburn Wyke Hotel at Cloughton, just north of Scarborough in a secluded part of the North Yorkshire Moors. It's a quaint little 18th century hotel that few frequent in the off-season, so its seclusion was perfect.

Ronan's right-hand man, Jimmy Hoolihan visited the Lord Nelson pub in Scarborough and other harbourside haunts of seamen, to try and muster a crew for the ship. The DJs meanwhile headed over into Whitby with Ronan (using the name Mike O'Connor) to look over their new home. While in the town they bought hundreds of records from Headlam's record shop in the town (now the *Magpie Kitchen* shop). Owner Alf Headlam had been in the merchant navy and was delighted that records from his shop would soon be heard on Radio Caroline.

Ronan knew Radio 270's managing director, Wilf Proudfoot, well. At one time there had been talks about Radio 270 (or Radio Yorkshire as their project was then called) becoming part of the Radio Caroline network and, while that proposal was never consummated, the two had stayed in close touch.

Among the DJs selected to appear in the relaunch were Andy Archer, Don Allen, Mark West and Roger Day. Four of the DJs travelled up to Whitby and waited in the Hayburn Wyke hotel with Ronan, ready to await the departure of the ship.

Radio 270's ship was a brave little vessel, only marginally smaller than the Mi

Amigo, but with a relatively powerful engine (240hp). Less than thirty years old, she was in good condition having been well maintained. Her two captains ran all items of equipment daily and sailed the ship in and out of port regularly. She had been stored at the shipyard in Whitby since closedown and was now replenished with diesel, food and other essential supplies and some equipment was upgraded.

An interview with Andy Archer in a newspaper was however run a week too early, alerting the authorities, who descended on the home of Radio 270's former Managing Director, Wilf Proudfoot. He was told that supplying the ship to Radio Caroline would breach the Marine Offences Act. A meeting with Wilf's co-directors decided that the risk was too great, especially as the required deposit for the ship which had been promised by Geoffrey Pearl of the FRA, had not yet materialised.

Talks and meetings were going on elsewhere to find a replacement ship including with the representatives of the Radio London ship, the Galaxy. The former US minesweeper had been taken to Hamburg following its closedown the previous August. It had a 50 Kilowatt transmitter and modern studios. The owner's representative Don Pearson however had strong hopes of selling the facility to an Italian consortium, said to include King Constantine of Greece. They held out for a higher price than Radio Caroline could muster.

Phillip Solomon refused to meet any of the Caroline team, who were astounded to see a report in Billboard magazine in May revealing a new plan. It said that Solomon was the owner of a new 200,000 Watt version of Radio Caroline being built on an Island off the British coast!

This was understood to be Manx Radio; whose owners were keen to have a strong voice covering the whole of Britain and had promised a licence to anyone who was able to get the international permission for a suitable frequency. The article wrongly described Solomon as the founder of Radio Caroline and concerned a new deal he had struck with Maurice Levy at Roulette Records in New York.

Some weeks later, one of the ships, the Mi Amigo, was put into dry dock during exploratory talks to free her. She was surveyed, but no work was found necessary; the report said 'fine condition', which was not surprising as she had been drydocked only two years previously.

Andy Archer and Jimmy Hoolihan moved onto the Knock John Fort in June and prepared to broadcast from there. They were visited by a TV crew from Southern, the ITV operator. After a couple of weeks however, the idea was suddenly dropped and the small crew of five taken off the fort.

Marianne: The Girl on a Motorcycle

Mid Atlantic Films

Ronan put a brave face on the situation and pressed on with his attempts to find a replacement ship but he was also busy with his film projects. The distributors and *Mid-Atlantic Films* were almost ready to release Marianne Faithfull's debut movie, which was called *Girl on a Motorcycle*.

The previous year, Caroline had a large Board of Directors and several dozen staff who would have attended to matters, but now Solomon was running things on a shoestring with just he and his PA.

The Wijsmuller brother who had been responsible for the hijacking of the two ships flew to London for a meeting with Ronan to see what might be done to release the vessels, which were now becoming an embarrassment and a burden. As he walked through Heathrow Airport's labyrinth of terminals, the brother who had ordered the ships be seized collapsed and died a short time later of a heart attack. Ronan would tell everyone that the bad feelings of the British listeners descended on the Wijsmuller who had taken away their radio stations.

Ronan always maintained that The Lady, as he called Caroline, had a charmed life and someone or something was always watching over her. So many uncanny 'coincidences occurred, right from the early days of the station that gave his claim substance; so many unexpected events for which there was no rational explanation. Perhaps Karma was at work, protecting the Caroline spirit?

With the two ships in port for the foreseeable future, many of the Radio Caroline DJs busied themselves working in nightclubs and some, such as Caroline North's Martin Kayne began selling tapes of their old programmes and the station's jingles and other assorted highlights. Andy Archer continued to work in night club DJ on his return to the UK and was also taken on by a club in the Black Country. Indeed, so did many more of his colleagues, especially those from the North ship.

Martin Kayne

Andy Cadier

Bring Back Caroline T-shirts

Martin's shipmate Don Allen had a strong fan club to fall back on, the wonderful world of Daffy Don Allen, run by one of his most enthusiastic listeners, 'Nutty' Norah Swallow in Illingworth near Halifax. Much later, Norah embarked on her own career as a country music presenter on the radio.

Don Allen in his special Bring Back Caroline t-shirt

Don produced a special T-shirt whose logo read *BBC - Bring Back Caroline, RADIO that is Number ONE*! They sold well, especially when he appeared at various clubs and ballrooms all over the north of England. It wasn't long before Don was back on the air, this time at Manx Radio in the Isle of Man. He also joined RNI before moving to Ireland.

Spangles Muldoon too signed with an agent and became a gigging DJ travelling far and wide but moved to Wolverhampton where he worked at the Oasis Casino for a while. The following year he was back at sea spinning records! Sadly, there was no transmitter to bring Spangles' shows to a wide audience as he was DJing in the nightclub on a ferry from Immingham on the River Humber across to the continent. He also appeared at the CRSC radio nights in Hull, as did Daffy Don Allen

Instead of heading straight to the BBC, Johnnie Walker had a change of career for a year driving a van in London before being head-hunted by Radio One. His first interview with Johnny Beerling took place, appropriately, on a canal barge on the Regents Canal.

The Free Radio Association and smaller groups around the UK, (e.g. CRSC in Yorkshire) strived to keep the Caroline name in the public eye and ensured that Caroline's name was not forgotten; their unlikely bed-fellows included John Witney and his Local Radio Association. The Conservatives, still in opposition, listened and made plans for local commercial radio. The FRA had by now expanded to absorb Broadside The Free Radio Campaign run by Alex McKenna of Romford delivered a coffin full of redundant radios to Harold Wilson at 10 Downing Street.

In various polls of readers, Radio Caroline DJs were still well supported despite the station being off the air. Robbie Dale joined Radio Veronica to host a late-night programme and was invited by the British Embassy in The Hague to be their judge at the National Song Festival!

Status Quo were now enjoying worldwide success with their single, 'Pictures of Matchstick Men' thanks to plugs on Caroline. They threw their weight behind the campaign and organised their own protests outside 10 Downing Street.

Status Quo - always big Caroline supporters

"We have always acknowledged that the success of *Pictures of Matchstick Men* was due to the exposure Radio Caroline gave us," said manager Pat Barlow. "We feel that Caroline should still be there to help other new artistes. We're going to have a protest march as soon as we have organised support from the fans."

The group never did forget Radio Caroline and were always happy to reciprocate the station gave them at the dawn of their career. In 1971, Francis Rossi wrote a song called 'Caroline,' originally as a blues song. The Quo's rocked up version was included on their 1973 album *Hello*. As a single and made the Top 5 in the UK and Sweden and the number became Quo's set opener at almost every gig for twenty five years. The only memorable time it wasn't was at Live Aid, where it was demoted to second number by the anthemic R*ockin All Over the World*.

Status Quo acknowledged Radio Caroline again in the eighties. Their Christmas 1981 'Rock'n'Roll' single, includes a couplet reminiscing about the days when it was so hard to get radio play.
:

Waiting all the time to find . . .
'radio plays' on Caroline

As the first anniversary of the Marine Offences Act approached, Radio Caroline remained silent. The ships still lay at an Amsterdam quay. They had been moved from Houthaven near the Centraal station across to the Zaandam yards where the Mi Amigo had been repaired previously. Here they were in a difficult to reach area and had some security, although the most determined fan could still get access. The doors into the ship's superstructure were never locked and it was possible to wander around. Sadly, some disrespected the radio station and the ships and vandals had soon plundered the record libraries and strewn DJ mail around in some areas.

An Aberdeen university student, Paul Harris, had spent a year finding a publisher for his book *When Pirates Ruled The Waves*. The Post Office wrote to every large book publisher in the UK, claiming that they would be acting illegally if they were involved in the book or gave any help to Paul Harris at all. After being thwarted for a year, Paul decided that the only route open to him was to self-publish. He set up his own imprint, called Impulse Publications.

Paul Harris

When Pirates Ruled the Waves was the first publication to tell the story of offshore radio and it went on sale in bookshops in August 1968. Radio Caroline and its story featured prominently in the book, which was reprinted six times. Paul went on to write about Swedish offshore station *Radio Nord* which broadcast from the Magda Maria (the ship that became Caroline South's 'Mi Amigo') and he was a co-founder of *Capital Radio*, which launched its own ship in 1970.

Some Radio Caroline DJs planned to mark the Anniversary of the MOA with some illegal broadcast as *Radio Free London*. This activity was not new and various individuals had made short broadcasts from their homes, etc, since the 1930s. Most of these 'land pirate' operations had been political in content, to promote some campaign or other, or simply kids messing about and experimenting with equipment. Few had ever produced programmes designed to appeal to radio listeners.

The team behind the launch of Radio Free London were different. About half were former Radio Caroline DJs looking to promote the Caroline cause but only in a responsible manner. Spangles, Andy Archer, Jason Wolf and Stevie Merike had all broadcast on Caroline's north or south ship in the previous year so had prominent names that would be known to many listeners.

It was decided to set the station to coincide with a big rally planned to be held in Trafalgar Square in August. A transmitter was constructed by a south London radio amateur called Peter. He was to join another radio ship two years later and be renamed Peter Chicago, by DJ Duncan Johnson, for no other reason than his mild manner was the least like someone from the windy city than you could imagine!

The RFL transmitter was of good quality and was installed at a flat in Addison Gardens, in Shepherds Bush. The apartment was leased by Robin Adcroft, but was also home to an endless stream of radio enthusiasts, including Caroline's Spangles Muldoon.

A young Robin Adcroft

Robin Adcroft had been a Caroline supporter for many years and was also the main photographer for the FRA. He was working as a film and audio engineer in the RFL days but soon became an accomplished radio technician. His flat in Addison Gardens, near Shepherd's Bush, was a rendezvous for Radio Caroline supporters and DJs too in 1968. It was the base for the UK's first widely heard unlicensed radio station, Radio Free London.

The RFL team strung out a long wire antenna across the railway lines behind the flat and tied it up to a convenient fire escape opposite. The transmissions on 203m medium wave got out very well and could be heard all over the city, even down in the underground!

The DJ line up made it sound like a Radio Caroline tribute as it included Spangles Muldoon (who by then had also moved into the flat with girlfriend, Kate), Andy Archer, Stevie Merike and Jason Woolfe.

The aerial termination on a fire escape was unfortunate as the office building it served was used by the BBC. The station was raided at teatime while Spangles was on the air. Despite the offer to say a few words to listeners, the GPO sleuth declined his opportunity at stardom and confiscated a dummy transmitter!

Robin Adcroft broadcast on Radio Free London, as Robin Lane and a few years later joined Radio Caroline. He moved across to the Mebo II (with yet another name, Robin Banks) when the Caroline International 389 station closed. He was working as a film and audio engineer in the RFL days but soon became an accomplished radio technician.

Spangles made good use of the airtime on Radio Free London to relaunch the Caroline Club. It was advertised in the 'classified' columns of various music papers. The membership fee seemed to vary weekly, and the promised merchandise often took weeks to appear. Members received a free book with details of many of the Radio Caroline Disc jockeys, as well as a 7inch record containing many of the station's jingles and Johnnie Walker's epic *Man's Fight For Freedom* speech.

The disc sold so well that stocks ran out quickly and the disc had to be repressed, several times. Plans for T-shirts and other memorabilia came to nothing, but the Caroline Club continued to flourish.

Sadly, due to a printing error, the Caroline Club booklets did not have any photographs in them which led to a lot of demands for refunds. Spangles and his girlfriend Kate moved to Chesterton Hall Crescent in Cambridge where they were married. They continued organising Caroline events including a variety of disco nights across East Anglia, but the audiences were diminishing with every month that Radio Caroline remained off the air.

The book for the Caroline Club rapidly became a 'collectors item' as it was never completed, the photographs of the DJs were missing from all the copies however, when they do surface they can sell for as much as £100 each at radio enthusiast meetings.

Caroline Club Members handbook

More 'land pirate' stations opened and closed regularly the following winter and Caroline enthusiasts grew ever more despondent. South London was a hotbed for stations, one of which featured Don allen and Jason Woolf, but the stations were only heard for a few hours, mainly at weekends. The GPO were zealous in their persecution of these part time broadcasters.

March 1969, first anniversary of the ships being towed away, was a sombre time as many listeners began to think that the Radio Caroline they loved might never again be heard on their radios.

Andorra revival hour

A pre-recorded *Caroline Revival Hour* was broadcast on Radio Andorra on the first Saturday in March, to commemorate the first anniversary of the night when the two Caroline ships had been snatched from their moorings.

There had been considerations to use the Radio Andorra MW outlet two years previously by Caroline; George Saunders, one of the longest serving engineers, suggested then that it might be called *Radio Andorra, the technical horror*! George had researched the possibilities of signals quite closely, using the trusty Oxford Advanced Atlas, which describes ground composition in great detail, on which George rightly based his expectations.

The 'Caroline Revival Hour' was a test to see if it was feasible to get an audience from the station, which had some spare night time hours available.

There was a possibility of running a Radio Caroline service from midnight to 4am each day from Radio Andorra's transmitter. Due to its location high in the Pyrenees, the signal on 428 metres Medium Wave (701 kHz) was not very well heard in northern Europe. This was due to the ground composition which is not favourable, just as Caroline engineer George Saunders had predicted, a few years previously.

DJ Don Allen played a selection of Radio Caroline favourites, some recordings of Caroline South becoming 'international' and some adverts for the Free Radio Association. The other Radio Caroline voices heard in the hour long programme were Bud Ballou and Stevie Merike.

13. Caroline TV

In April, John Lennon and Yoko One agreed to participate in TV programmes to be transmitted as Caroline TV from an aeroplane flying over the North Sea. Often ridiculed, this was a serious project. It was announced at a press conference in New York at the end of April.

Super Constellation aircraft used by the American Air Force to broadcast over Vietnam had become available so Ronan placed a deposit on them and set about organising Caroline TV, along with advertising man Terry Bate and wealthy banker George Drummond.

The first discussions about Caroline TV had been in May 1966 when it was proposed to broadcast a TV service from the *Cheeta II*. The ship was already equipped with a UHF colour TV transmitter that had only been used for a very short time off the Swedish coast. She had on board as small TV studio. The plan was to carry promotional films for new record releases. These would take place for five hours at lunchtime, and again late at night.

“The Super Constellations are great planes and there are many of them still flying. They lost favour when jets came in as they are slow, but that’s ideal for an aerial TV transmitter,” explained Ronan. He said he had leased one and taken an option on a second aircraft. “The plan is to broadcast a mixture of live music concerts and some old pop movies every day from 6pm until midnight, and until 2am at weekends.”

“The aircraft will be used alternately, flying at 20,000 feet in a figure of eight above the North Sea,” said Ronan. “Tito has given us permission to base them in Yugoslavia and; he is not scared of the UK’s views. The planes have special tanks in the wings that were installed for trans-Atlantic flights so they can stay in the air for over 26 hours. We only need them to be ‘on the air’ for 8 hours, so there is no problem.”

The first Caroline TV logo

Caroline stayed in the news when the ships were seen on the ITV children’s programme *Magpie*. Programme host Susan Stranks pointed out the two ships to her colleague Pete Brady during one programme. Pete hosted the breakfast programme on Caroline South’s neighbour, Big Lil. Susan told Magpie viewers that the ships were being overhauled and would be back at sea.

A few weeks later, Johnnie Walker was approached by Radio 1 producers and offered a short-term contract presenting a weekly programme. After a year of driving vans in the capital he was eager to return to the air, just as much as his legions of fans were keen to hear him and he accepted the engagements, even though it would mean working with a producer and having precious little needle time.

Johnnie claimed to speak for quite a few radio "fans" when he dismissed the idea of a return for Caroline. "We need to realise now that there is no chance at all of Radio Caroline ever being heard from a ship again," he said in an interview in the *Outasight* magazine, published by Polydor Records. Thankfully, not everyone believed him or followed the somewhat pessimistic and defeatist stance.

Johnnie was joined in the Radio 1 studio by well-known Radio Caroline South DJ and newsreader Gerry Burke, who often called himself Henry Morgan. On Johnnie's show he masqueraded as 'Bill the Boilerman' in a couple of sketches. These were designed to pad out the lack of needle time available on the BBC.

Gerry was working with Caroline colleagues Guy Blackmore and Ross Brown as record pluggers that summer when they enjoyed their first success with OC Smith's only hit single, *Son of Hickory Holler's Tramp*.

Later in 1969 Radio Caroline's first DJ, Simon Dee agreed to be interviewed for the launch of Caroline TV. "I might even be persuaded to join Caroline TV and bring my successful TV chat show *Dee Time* back to Caroline, which is where my broadcast career began. My current contract runs out at the end of the year and from then onwards I shall be a free agent. If Caroline TV has a normal, mature format I see no reason why I should not be involved."

Ronan told journalists that "The TV project is being financed by a group of international investors to the tune of £600,000. It will be run from offices in Switzerland, New York and Holland. Our main investor is a wealthy young banker called George de Vere Drummond." He was a very wealthy aristocrat. A godson of King George, his father was the chairman of Drummonds Bank, now a part of RBS. He shared an apartment in Eaton Square with George Lazenby, who Ronan also managed.

At a presentation to prospective advertising agents in November, Terry Bate revealed that advertising was already being booked on the station. The rates would be just £300 for 30 seconds, which was a bargain compared to ITV which was charging £5,500 for the same amount of time.

The reaction of the Labour government was one of horror. They thought they had seen the back of Radio Caroline and now it would be returning to TV sets across the UK! Their counter-action was intense; they organised a team of over twenty civil servants and Labour Party apparatchiks to fight this “threat to national security”. They held two press briefings themselves simply to claim to the world’s press that they considered that the proposed Caroline TV project was illegal!

They also bought adverts in the trade press warning companies not to support the Caroline TV venture as it would be bad for young people to have a non-stop flow of music on the TV. This dissuaded many backers, causing more problems for the fledgling project.

One of Caroline’s directors, George Drummond, went to the GPO and met with the Minister of Posts and Telecommunications, John Stonehouse. Despite George maintaining that the Caroline YTV project was completely legal, would always remain so and operate lawfully, the British Government machine swung into action. Instructions were given to most embassies in Europe and staff spent hour searching aerodromes and airfields across the continent looking for ‘The Two Connies’ which Ronan had christened the aircraft. Even the RAF was involved with pilots briefed to report all visual sightings of Super Constellations, and air traffic control were instructed to report all unknown flights over the North Sea.

“I know my tails (from the secret service) were back on from about then,” remembers Ronan. “The phone in my flat would sound odd, peculiar clicks and echoes, that sort of thing. People would follow me in the street and into bars and hotels.”

Ronan's risks a call

“I had lots of friends in restaurants and hotels all over London and I soon learned that most staff were happy to help me slip out the back door again. I never really had a problem with them and could usually shake them off.”

Harold Wilson had personally set in motion large contingents of the British Government to try and stop Caroline TV. He worked closely with his close friend the Minister of Post and Telecommunications, John Stonehouse.

The UK Government's team to stop Caroline TV included ten men from the Ministry of Posts and Telecommunications, five from the Foreign Office, three from the Board of Trade and over a dozen assorted flunkeys and pen-pushers from the Ministries of Technology, the Treasury, the Home Office, the Board of Trade, the HM Customs & Excise and other agencies.

Tailplane logo

Wilson received regular reports from the various meetings which discussed all aspects of the proposals, advertising and Caroline TV's own team, which numbered only less than a dozen, about a quarter of the size of the official teams agonising how to stop them.

The Treasury Solicitor's department advised that even if Caroline TV's planes landed in the UK, it would not be possible to hold them, so long as they were foreign registered aircraft. It would be difficult to prove any individuals had taken part in the transmissions and might take a long time to get warrants prepared. "The difficulties of obtaining adequate evidence should not be under-rated," warned the officials.

Jamming was dismissed as posing too many technical problems and needing many stations throughout the UK. The option of using a British aircraft to jam it was dismissed as impractical. The Minister of Defence warned that the RAF might not be willing to participate, as a matter of policy. They certainly had no suitable aircraft available for this kind of work. The Caroline TV aircraft could not be forced to land in the UK without endangering life and the safety of the aircraft. The possibilities of preventing anyone flying over the North Sea was a non-starter,

At that time the two Caroline ships were still tied up in Amsterdam. The Mi Amigo had been dry-docked, recertificated and was ready to go back to sea again, as soon as the outstanding bills were settled. Some equipment had been stolen from the Caroline North ship, the Fredericia but the Dutch police were now guarding both vessels. Ronan visited the ships on several occasions, on one occasion he was accompanied by John Lennon and his driver.

At another news conference held in December in Mayfair, the Caroline TV logos were shown to journalists as some huge theatre style back-drops with psychedelic patterns of vibrant, lurid colours. The channel chosen for the first Caroline TV broadcasts would be one of the low ones below 30 in the UHF band and Christmas Day had been set as the first day. Tests of just just 20 minutes of IDs and announcements, with regular programmes now set to commence in Spring 1970.

Feb 1970 launch of RNI

Radio Caroline fans had heard many rumours of a German offshore station planning to start in late 1968 which would have several hours a day English programmes. It seemed plausible although its rumoured ship, the MV Galaxy as previously used by Radio London, was now looking the worse for wear having spent two years in harbour.

Early in 1970, Swiss radio entrepreneurs Erwin Meister and Edwin Bollier finally got their *Radio North Sea International* station (RNI) on the air. The main DJ they hired in the early days was Caroline South's Thinner record Spinner, Roger Day. He soon brought in some old shipmates from the Mi Amigo in the form of Andy Archer and Carl Mitchell, the Weird Beard. Roger also hired two more offshore names, Mark Wesley and Alan West, who had both served on Radio 270.

RNI had borrowed money from Radio Veronica but agreed to not broadcast off the Dutch coast. A few weeks later they moved their ship, the Mebo II, to the UK. The anchorage chosen was about five miles south of Clacton, but action was taken by the British GPO to jam the ship's signal.

Disgraced PMG and soviet spy John Stonehouse

The jamming of the radio ship's signals was undertaken under the personal orders of Prime Minister Harold Wilson and his PMG, John Stonehouse. A few years later, Stonehouse was caught trying to fake his own death by leaving a pile of clothes on a beach. He was jailed and later discovered to have been a soviet spy working directly for the Czech government for about seven years, including during his time as a British government minister. He had lied to journalists and to the House of Commons, falsely claiming that many European countries were prone to interference from the radio ship. A dirty trait that other 'socialists' and officials were to repeat over the years.

The anchorage chosen for the Mebo II was was about five miles south of Clacton, just outside British territorial waters. Direct action was taken by the GPO to jam the ship's medium wave signal from a government site at Bluebell hill near Rochester using a transmitter loaned by the BBC. A 'cat and mouse' game ensued with RNI dodging from one frequency to another, as the GPO jamming followed, minutes later. This was a very controversial move as Britain had never jammed another radio station, even during the war.

Caroline returns for the General Election

Prime Minister Harold Wilson called a 'snap' General Election in June and Ronan O'Rahilly helped orchestrate a campaign to unseat the Labour Government. He persuaded the Swiss owners of RNI to allow Radio Caroline to take over the RNI transmitters for the duration of the election campaign.

The ship already had several old Caroline DJs on board anyway, such as Andy Archer, Carl Mitchell and Roger Day. Mitchell announced to astounded listeners on the 13th June: "Stand by for an important announcement," followed minutes later by "the unbelievable has happened, welcome to the return of Radio Caroline."

The 'All New Radio Caroline' immediately began airing the "Fight for Free Radio" messages of 1967 and the DJs reminisced about the old Radio Caroline days. Nostalgia flowed in buckets along with many favourite Radio Caroline jingles.

An office was established at Beacon Records, an independent label owned by Milton Samuel who was very sympathetic to offshore radio and delighted to get air time for his releases. His first Beacon single, *Aint Nothing but a Houseparty* by the Showstoppers, was plugged by Caroline in her last two weeks on the air in 1968 and he was anxious to help and repay the favour.

One of Milton's Samuel's best friends was former Radio Caroline DJ Emperor Rosko, now at the BBC's Radio One, but showing considerable flair as a record producer too. "It was such an exciting time," says secretary Brenda Pidduck who also handled reception and promotion for Beacon and helped out with the radio work too.

She was one of many voices heard on a special parody of a TV theme "*Who do you think you are Kidding Mr Wilson*" played extensively during the election campaign that was now swinging into action and masterminded by Ronan O'Rahilly. The track was laid down at IBC (International Broadcasting Company), Lenny Plugge's old studio, bang opposite the BBC's Broadcasting House in Portland Place!

Ronan's campaign was centred around urging listeners to vote Conservative. The telephone numbers for many local Conservative Associations and campaign offices were given out on the air and listeners encouraged to call for more detailed local information.

A specially decorated Caroline campaign bus toured the marginal; constituencies in south east England, covered in posters depicting Harold Wilson as Chairman Mao, and staffed by a bevy of attractive young ladies giving out political leaflets. Ronan uncharacteristically spoke at a rally in Hyde Park and led a protest march on Downing Street, telling supporters: "During the War, the government did not even jam Lord Haw Haw but British lives were at stake. Today, all that's at stake today is a little freedom and pop radio."

Ronan and Radio Caroline's first DJ Simon Dee often manned the bus, giving press interviews and urging on the many Radio Caroline supporters who turned out to help.

Ronan and Simon manning the bus

This was the first General Election at which under 21s were allowed to vote. Over a million new voters, aged 18 to 21 years old had been 15 to 18 three years previously when Harold Wilson and his Labour Government had closed down the offshore stations. Now they were again dictating what kind of radio station the people should be allowed to listen to, by jamming out the latest pop radio ship.

The posters depicting Harold Wilson as Chairman Mao, was simply a 'tit for tat' reflex of the Prime Minister's own personal battle with Radio Caroline. His Marine Offences Act was widely regarded as an offence against democracy. Now he had taken a further step of jamming – an undemocratic move to drown out any word against his policies.

Simon had recently been hosting a Sunday night chat show on ITV but his contract had been terminated after an interview with George Lazenby (another of Ronan's proteges) became 'embarrassing'. George's film career as the new James Bond had recently become a short one; just one film, *On Her Majesty's Secret Service*! Ronan had persuaded Lazenby there was no future in the Bond franchise and that he should get out immediately for the sake of his career.

"Ronan and Simon worked incredibly hard every day, out promoting the campaign in all weather, but George didn't play much of a part at all," remembers Oonagh. She had now married architect Sonny

Karanjia and was in charge of Ronan's office at Hayes Mews. "George would just sit around the office all day. It was Ronan and Simon who did all the leg work, they were both very enthusiastic."

Urs Emmenegger

Special Branch turned back a visiting Swiss director of the Mebo company at Heathrow. Urs Emmenegger claimed he had flown in only to pay for printing of the posters and to do some sightseeing!

In fact he was the key connection between Mebo and Sir Paul Bryan, Conservative MP for Howden and shadow minister for broadcasting matters. Some meetings had been set up between them by Ronan O'Rahilly and Wilf Proudfoot. Emmenegger was smuggled into the UK a few days later via ferry by the Radio Caroline fixer, Jimmy Hoolihan.

The new Radio Caroline, now broadcasting from the Mebo II, stressed the dictatorial attitudes of the Labour MPs on the air every ten or fifteen minutes and suggested that listeners should vote Conservative. Labour however were a long away ahead in the opinion polls and most political pundits were certain that Wilson would retain control. They reckoned without the great loss that so many people felt after their 1967 MOA closed so many radio stations.

Radio Caroline focussed on all the marginals in the South and East and visited many towns within them using the Fun Bus. The strangely decorated ex-LT bus was seen in many marginal constituencies and pictures were used in dozens of newspapers to illustrate stories about the return of Radio Caroline.

Ronan and Simon would often appear at events, astride the *Harley Davidson Electroglide* motorcycle, ridden by Marianne Faithfull in the now famous movie (see below). With Caroline DJ Andy Archer, they became the star attractions at a rally held at Speaker's Corner on June 14th, just days before polling day.

Simon and Ronan on the Electroglyde

A crowd of over five thousand supporters marched down Whitehall to Downing Street where the protestors played Caroline loudly on their radios. Ronan managed to stuff leaflets and posters into the letterbox but the chants for Wilson to come out went unheeded.

The jamming was not proving very effective; many Radio Caroline listeners soon learned that they could null out the worst effects of the jamming if they rotated their radios a little to one side. Reception was also perfect on FM close to the coast and on Short Wave in the rest of the UK, in fact it could be heard all over the rest of Europe. The Mebo II was equipped with two Short Wave transmitters as well as MW and FM, the first time that Radio Caroline had broadcast on any other wave bands but the Medium Wave.

Just hours before polling day, the Government set up a much larger transmitter near Southend. It was the 50kW Continental Electronics transmitter that had been built for Radio Caroline in 1965, that Radio Caroline had allowed to be diverted to a British Government DWS site to broadcast propaganda into Rhodesia, which Caroline engineers Gillman and Saunders had commissioned. It had been kept mothballed at Crowborough for a few years but was now housed in a tent at Canewdon in Essex and tuned to wreak havoc on the Radio Caroline wavelength.

The jamming transmitter was protected around the clock by a small army of private security personnel and the Military Police. The strong jamming signal became known as "Wilsons Wail" and it now transmitted not only over the programmes of Radio Caroline, but also over BBC Radio 1. It even interfered with neighbouring TV sets and turned the jamming escapade into the biggest f*aux paux* committed by Wilson, as it drew the public's attention to his own personal hatred of Radio Caroline, something that most people thought of as being simply a harmless service of music and fun.

The day after polling dawned bright and blue, literally. Wilson was defeated and the Conservatives were returned to power. In talks before the election they had promised that commercial radio would be licensed in the UK. Among the new MPs were Paul Brown, a former investor in Radio 270 and that station's former MD, Wilf Proudfoot. They both helped steer an 'Independent Radio' bill through Parliament that brought about commercial radio in the UK a few years later.

Conservative PM Edward Heath appointed a new Postmaster General, Chris Chattaway, who took charge of the Post Office and its jamming operations. While he immediately closed down the largest transmitter he was unwilling to stop the jamming completely. Radio Caroline had now closed down, its job done. The Mebo II was once again broadcasting as RNI - Radio Nordsee International.

One must assume that, once in office, the new PMG had access to top secret briefings from the intelligence services (MI5) about the background of the owners of the ship and decided that it was not in the UK's national interest to allow it to broadcast off the UK. Some documents about this have been released under the thirty years rule and can be found at the National Archives at Kew however, many other have been suppressed for 60 years.

The response of young voters surprised many people in the media who, being remote from pop and rock music, had little idea of how important the radio issue was so many voters. For those aged 18 to 25, this was their first opportunity to demonstrate their voice in a General Election.

A few days afterwards, the Mebo II sailed off to a new anchorage off Holland, defeated by the jamming. Clearly, they could not build an audience and make any money while the jamming continued. As soon as the ship was back off the Dutch coast, the jamming stopped.

Radio Caroline had just demonstrated how powerful the message of offshore radio could be, although the circumstances were exceptional. It may have been the magic and memories of the Caroline name, the enthusiasm of the station's DJs and the adverse feeling of so many people; they were sold the idea that their freedom had been eroded by the Labour government.

New legislation was swiftly introduced (the *Representation of the People Act*) covering activities such as broadcasting immediately prior to a General Election, although this still wouldn't apply to radio stations outside British territorial waters.

After the General Election, RNI reverted to its original name and Radio Caroline was once again all but forgotten by most people, even some of its die-hard fans. Many of them wrote to the music press etc and admitted that they didn't expect Radio Caroline to ever broadcast again. Such comments had been made after the two ships were towed away two years previously. They were to be made again many more times during the roller coaster life of the returning Radio Caroline.

Ronan O'Rahilly returned to his quest to get Caroline TV onto the air and two weeks after the election, the press once again had plenty of material, announcing the new start date of the flying TV station.

"*The Captain of Seaborne Sounds turns to Airborne images*" ran the flash headline in DISC & Music Echo. "BBC Television, that grand old institution of visual living room entertainment is in for the shock of its life on July 1st. Not only will Ronan O'Rahilly's swashbuckling Caroline TV be blasting on to our screens on that date … but it is entirely due to the BBC that the most exciting venture since John Logie Baird invented the TV machine is happening at all!"

Ronan explained to DISC's editor David Hughes that "It happened about 18 months ago. I'd been asked to appear on a BBC 2 programme, *Late Night Line Up*, about commercial radio and its effects on British broadcasting. I especially checked that I wasn't going to be cut and they assured me it was fine. Then two hours before I was due in the studios, the phone rang and the man said 'I'm sorry Ronan but .."

Alter lunch with a friendly newspaper journalist Ronan said: "I never realised how censored and controlled BBC-TV was. The only way to get around the censorship was to start my own TV station." That was the throwaway remark that sowed the seed of Caroline TV.

The article in DISC revealed that Caroline TV was now due take to the air on Wednesday July 1st. "If Radio Caroline had remained alone, it would still be running today. It was only because so many other, poorly organised stations got in on the act that the pirate radio scene collapsed," said Ronan. "Caroline TV will be the best thing ever to happen to pop music in Britain. There is virtually no other outlet for pop, especially progressive pop, on TV as we will give time to all comers. We're not just interested in 'Top of the Pops' type performance, we can screen home movies too."

"Another feature we shall have is the only uncensored daily chat show called 'Out of Your Mind' which will be filmed in London. This show will not revolve around the personality of the interviewer, so each programme will succeed or fall on the merits of the people talking. It could be fantastic one day and terrible the next, but at least it will be free!"

The Sunday Times followed that up with a lengthy piece the following week which explained that the staffing alone would cost between £300,000 and £800,000 every week. The Marine Offence Act, passed in 1967 to deter offshore radio stations also applied to aircraft of course, but Ronan explained how he would avoid problems with that.

"We have had to approach firms abroad and have backers around the world. We can probably get American record companies, German and Japanese tape recorders and transistor firms, and so on. This thing will eat money and we can only start when we have the money; at any other point it is total insanity."

The Sunday Times described Ronan as "a heady blend of idealism and materialism" who was now making a pop film called 'Gold', followed by a film about his hero, Robert Kennedy. Ronan was quoted as saying "Left wingers call him a capitalist pig but you don't get America's President Nixon flying out to talk to students in South Africa."

"O'Rahilly has always believed in giving people what they want," claimed the Sunday Times, which said that his first big thing was smuggling *Spangles* sweets over the border into the Irish Republic. Ronan was quoted as saying "It's hard to think that it was then the big 'high', like marijuana is today. I was on the 'Why Not?' trip even then. Everyone likes Spangles!"

The long-promised John Lennon and Yoko Ono interview was to form the start of broadcasts. Two press conferences were organised by advertising guru Terry Bate and former banker George Drummond. They explained to journalists that landing rights had been agreed with a private airfield in France. One of two Super Constellation planes was about ready to take to the air and was just awaiting a connector for the antenna, which hung below the plane when in flight. Terry Bate said that he had now got over one million US dollars' worth of advertising lined up from one company alone, a cola distributor.

The optimistic dates given seem to be more designed to appeal to a group of investors who were dithering on the side-lines. Their money was needed to secure the second aircraft which was still languishing in the USA. The projects main assets were the transmitters which had been ordered six months previously and a room full of promotional materials in Ronan's Mayfair flat. The service would use the planes alternately and use an empty channel on the UHF band every evening, from 6pm until late. Caroline TV's programming policy would be of light entertainment, with the schedules comprising old movies and videos of artistes performing their latest releases.

Ownership of the Radio Caroline ships had now been transferred to *Tesman Investments* of Panama, and *Kernan Corp* of Liechtenstein. More changes were made, but still the ships remained incarcerated.

Israeli businessman Abie Nathan, who wanted to set up an offshore station called The Voice of Peace had also visited but did not have enough money for the $250,000 then being asked for the Mi Amigo. He bought instead an old coaster called the MV Cito in the north of Holland and took it to New York to be converted into the Peace ship, with some financial help from John and Yoko. They hit many problems and it took over three years to get the Peace ship on station.

In December vandals broke into the Mi Amigo and opened some taps connected to the sea chest. The ship began filling with water and almost sank at the quayside in the Houthaven, a small dock just west of Amsterdam's Centraal Station. Crewmembers of a tug belonging to the Amsterdam Port Authority saved the ship by jumping on board and installing some emergency pumps.

A proper guard was then put on board the ships in the form of Dave Fletcher from the UK. He told Dutch radio journalist Hans Knot that Ronan still had plans to restart Radio Caroline soon. Fletcher was a pseudonym for a former Radio Caroline engineer who told visitors that Ronan and others had visited the ships several times. He told them that he was on a six week contract to keep watch on the ships.

"Mr O'Rahilly was here a few weeks ago with an engineer and they made a full list of all the machinery and the studio equipment. I got the impression they had agreed the release fees for harbour dues with the shipyard and at least one, if not both, the ships were free to leave."

MC5 kicking out the jams

Ronan was now also busy managing an American rock group called MC5. He arranged for them to come over and plan a festival called *Phun City* which was being staged at Worthing on the South Coast by Mick Farren, who had been the editor of the underground magazine *International Times*.

"Ronan and the MC5 band showed up with a huge outside Broadcast Unit, complete with a pair of massive television cameras, that did look very impressive at each side of the stage," Mick Fallon remembers in his memoirs. "He also had a mobile home about the size of a villa, all protected by Tom Keylock, who was the Rolling Stones' minder and Jimmy Houlihan, Ronan's own security man."

Moves to get Caroline back on the air switched to the Irish Sea as Ronan had several lengthy meetings with the Manx Government who owned Manx Radio outright having bought out Richard Meyer and Pye.

The team now in charge of Manx Radio was led by Bill Quayle MHK, a long term Radio Caroline fan. He had Caroline North DJ Daffy Don Allen in charge of programmes at the station and felt the time was right for the island to broadcast to the UK and Ireland. He announced that Ronan would be joining Manx Radio and they bought a 10 kilowatt solid state transmitter which was installed at the Foxdale site, replacing the smaller 1kilowatt unit that Pye had built there ten years earlier. After some cajoling from Ronan, Manx Radio's new RCA transmitter was quietly commissioned and they ran the full 10kW for a week, with good reception all around the Irish sea. before the BBC complained along with the Post Office. They had some clout as, a short time later they had to stop. The Island's Governor, who is the Queen's agent in the Island who answers to The Home Office, was forced to insist that Manx Radio cut the power back to 1 kilowatt.

Caroline TV film launch raided

On New Years Day 1971, a timber-built motor torpedo boat called the *Eidolon* from Chichester was apprehended after it broke down at sea. Post Office officials, assisted by the local constabulary, arrested the crew and took them to a police station for questioning. Lawyers acting for *Mid Atlantic Films* immediately lodged objections that the vessel was not being used for anything illegal but had been purchased six months previously for use as a mobile film unit.

The vessel was equipped with video recorders and other studio items but no TV transmitters nor aerials. A surveyor confirmed that the MTB was in no condition to go to sea nor was it habitable and bore signs of having been partly submerged recently. After a thorough search of the vessel it was handed back to a representative of Mid-Atlantic Films a week later.

In January 1972, Ronan arranged an extensive tour of the UK for American rock band MC5. Their American manager had become embroiled with the White Panthers, a far-left anti-racist collective, supported by John Lennon and Yoko Ono. They asked John to look after the band in the UK and, in between gigs at the LSE, in Cambridge, Liverpool and in France, they also wrote and recorded the soundtrack for Ronan's forthcoming movie, Gold.

By March 1972 the two ships had lain in Amsterdam for exactly four years, deserted except for pilgrimages made by radio fans. The security watchmen had been withdrawn long ago which enabled some visitors to pilfer the equipment and record library. When the old Caroline office in Amsterdam had closed in 1968, sacks of mail been put onto the Caroline North ship; this had been rummaged through and scattered around in cabins and the lounge. The promised new funding never arrived and Wijsmullers decided it was time to move both vessels on, so they instructed the firm R W Buis to put the two radio ships up for auction.

14. The ships are sold

On Monday 29th May 1972 the MV Caroline was sold at a public auction for 26,500 Guilders. The buyer was Frank Rijsdijk from the *Hendrick Ido-Ambacht* company. The price included not only the ship, but all the contents left on board. Frank Rijsdijk sold the Caroline ship on to Rinus van Marel of Ouwerkerk in Zeeland who had a ship-breaking business. Before she could be moved to the scrapyard the 160 feet mast needed to be taken down, so the ship could be towed through the Dutch canal system.

Sisters chained up for auction

Her final resting place was on a mud bank called Het Keeten. The ship's 1350 horse power motor seemed to be in good condition and in August the ship was driven on the high water into a small creek. There, the upper structure that housed the studios was removed, however the rest of the work on scrapping the hull of the ship was difficult. She had been ice-strengthened to withstand the winters in Scandinavia.

It was decided to burn out the interior of the ship whereupon the breakers found that the ballast on the ship for her time at sea were almost a hundred tons of old ships anchors – scrap steel. Rinus van der Marel kept one relic of the Radio Caroline North ship – the ship's bell, which he hung proudly in his office and was always happy to show it to the many Caroline fans who made a pilgrimage to his scrap yard. He took the bell with him when he emigrated to Africa.

On the same day that the MV Caroline was sold, auctioneer RW Buis also sold the Mi Amigo. The highest bidder was the Hofman Shipping Agency who offered 23,000 Guilders. They were bidding for an undisclosed client who was in reality Bart Wijsmuller. Bart was the oldest of the four Wijsmuller brothers who ran the shipping company that had seized the ship. Bart was sympathetic to Radio Caroline's ideals and willing to release the ships but was over-ruled by his family, who would not release them until *Vagabund* (a Liechtenstein company that owned them in1968) paid the outstanding bills.

For the sake of family harmony, Bart could not disclose his identity as the new owner of the ship, so he arranged for it to be put in the name of two radio enthusiasts, Rob Vermaat and Gerard van Dam. Most people assumed she would also be broken up however, just two weeks later, the Dutch branch of the Free Radio Campaign announced that, following lengthy discussions with the new owners, they had agreed to convert the Mi Amigo into a free radio museum.

Gerard was already well known in Holland for his radio activities. The previous year he formed the *International Society for the Promotion of Free Radio*. With his friend Hans Verbaan, Gerard ran several radio fan groups, including the Dutch branches of the FRC and the FRA. Gerard was also a chauffeur of Radio North Sea DJs, ferrying them from the harbour at Scheveningen to the RNI office in Bussum.

Work began to restore the Mi Amigo's studios and the cabins, so that visitors could stay on the ship. Orders were taken for these activities by the BBC, cheeky initials for the *Bell Broadcasting Company,* which was simply a name on a letterhead. To try and pressure radio fans to book their time on the Mi Amigo, Gerard said that if bookings were not sufficient, then the owner of the ship would be forced to scrap the Mi Amigo.

Gerrad takes the Helm
Hans Verbaan

Over the Summer, a small army of 'radio freaks' worked hard on the Mi Amigo. It was very tiring as nothing much had been done since she was in the dry dock in 1968; papers and small items of equipment were scattered everywhere. Three huge loads of rubbish was removed from the ship and attempts made to get the water and the central heating working again, but this used valuable fuel. The tanks for the generators seemed to have mysteriously emptied – they had been over half full when she came in on 4th March 1968.

Some equipment from the MV Caroline had been transferred before she was moved to the scrapyard, including one of the 10kW transmitters, but it proved to be suitable only for spares. The parts were useful to keep the original 10kW Radio Nord unit operating.

When Peter Chicago arrived at the ship, Gerard confided in him that the plan was to take her back to sea to broadcast once again as soon as possible. As engineer on the Mebo II, Peter was able give lots of useful advice on the equipment.

Even some of the equipment removed over the last few years mysteriously found its way back on board, as it had been removed purely by enthusiasts keen to ensure its safekeeping! Most of the volunteers believed that the ship was going to become a museum and a training ship for radio DJs.

Ronan arrived on board to give his advice just two weeks later and persuaded Gerard that the money was available to carry out the repairs and have her broadcasting again. His plan was to return her to an anchorage at the English side of the North Sea.

Mi Amigo readies to leave
Rob Olthof

"I had to keep everything under my hat in the early days as you could never be sure who some of the volunteers were," said Ronan. "You never knew who they talked to about our intentions. We did have one Dutch guy who would go straight round to the RNI people and tell them what we were doing, all innocently, I'm sure. But no one knew who the RNI people were with."

"There was a man from the British Embassy in The Hague who came along every few days and took lots of pictures but we didn't let him on board," said Ronan, who stayed out of sight usually, afraid that his presence could alert people to what was really happening."

A tug belonging to *Iskes Shipping* took the Mi Amigo from her berth in Amsterdam on the 2nd September. The only DJ on board was Crispian St John. She was supposedly heading for England where, it was claimed, there might be a greater interest in a pirate radio museum. There was indeed a lot of interest in MW radio in the UK that day as the BBC re-organised of their network, to squeeze in twenty local radio stations and the long promised chain of nineteen commercial stations (the ones that a few years previously had been blocked as there was no space left on the MW band for more radio stations!).

Mi Amigo - back at sea.
In the early hours of the next morning the Mi Amigo dropped anchor off IJmuiden for a few hours, before Koos van Laar picked up the ship's line and towed her south. Just after 5am she arrived at a new position off Scheveningen, just 500 meters from the RNI and Veronica ships. Listeners to RNI heard about the new arrival when, at 5:20 that morning, DJ Tony Allan played the Fortunes record *Caroline*, for the crew of the Mi Amigo which he said had just anchored close by. The news of their new neighbour was also carried by Radio Veronica later that day and in the British national press two days later.

Several conflicting reports appeared in the Dutch press about the Mi Amigo's plans. By the middle of the month the stories emerging were very confusing; one front page story in a national newspaper claimed that the Mi Amigo would become a new casino ship (gambling at tables was still illegal in Holland).

At first, the Mi Amigo had no electrical power, the crew had to use torches when moving around after dark. Peter Chicago connected up a fluorescent tube to the Mi Amigo's antenna. Using the power from the nearby RNI ship caused that to illuminate the ship a little.

The first day the Mi Amigo anchored off the Dutch coast, a keen radio fan Lion Keezer heard the news and went out to see the ship with a journalist. They hitched a lift on RNI's inflatable dingy for the last few hundred yards as the fishing boat that took them out was wary of customs problems; the ship was proudly flying a Panamanian ensign as well as a *Skol International* pennant! They were welcomed on board by the crew, including Peter Chicago and Gerard van Dam.

The ship was still very incomplete, especially the studio area, with the turntables not yet mounted into their plinths. A *Gates Studioette* mixing console from the MV Caroline was in the studio though; it had been taken from the North ship by Chicago, during one of his many visits. It had been well cared for, lovingly restored and would form the main mixing desk in the Radio Caroline studio for many years.

Gerard van Dam on the Mi Amigo, first day at sea in September 1972
Lion Keezer

Other equipment had arrived over previous weeks and was awaiting installation, but it was evident that there was a lot of work yet to do.

Ronan O'Rahilly finally popped his head above the parapet again a fortnight later and visited the Mebo II, home of RNI. He persuaded ex Caroline DJ Spangles Muldoon, at that time working on RNI, to join him and Gerard to relaunch Radio Caroline. During his show on RNI that night, Spangles referred to his imminent move and dropped hints by referring to RNI's wavelength and linking it to Caroline's 259 slot.

By the end of the month, he had recruited RNI shipmate Andy Archer to join Crispian St John on board the ship. Others shanghaied were Graham Gill as well as the former Radio City DJ and Radio Netherlands newsreader, Allan Clark.

Ronn had his hands full at the time with the film *Gold* in post production, management problems with the MC5, Caroline TV and now the Mi Amigo about to go back to sea as Caroline – but he still found time to help and cajole his friends at Manx Radio, still arguing with the Home Office in London over their power increase.

First day back at sea, on the 3rd September 1972
with the 1966 pole mast still standing and the bell logo on her port quarter.

Lion Keezer

Wavelength Day
The first transmissions from the Mi Amigo came on the last day of September, which was quite an active one on the Medium Wave and. Over in England it was BBC Radio 1's fifth birthday but in the Netherlands, Radio Veronica was changing its wavelength. It moved from 192m at the high end of the and right down to 538m at the other end. Here the station's signal travelled much further and gave them near national coverage. RNI tried to steal some of Veronica's limelight, and listeners, by opening up with a second transmitter on Veronica's old 192 slot, but the biggest surprise of all was on 259 meters.

Using only the 10 kW transmitter, Caroline joined in the radio party on the Medium Wave and was widely heard, although no announcement identifying the station was made. There were however quite a few hints and some people twigged what was happening when '259' played different versions of the Neil Diamond song, *Sweet Caroline*.

The Admiral Robbie Dale visited the Mi Amigo the following day and it was an emotional scene as he greeted former Mi Amigo shipmates Andy Archer and Spangles Maldoon, who had worked on the ship as Radio Caroline International four years previously. Robbie didn't join the reborn Radio Caroline but he did dedicate a record to all the crew during his weekly show on Hilversum III, the state pop station.

Captain Dick Palmer on the Mi Amigo
Bob Noakes

The equipment on the Mi Amigo was in poor condition, particularly the mechanical items such as the ship's engine, the generators and windlass, etc. Spangles talked his old friend Dick Palmer into coming out to the ship, where he spent a year immersed in diesel and engine oil, repairing almost every part of the ship. Dick had been building up a successful garage business since his work for Roy Bates on the two forts off the UK. An accomplished diesel mechanic, his sanity, and persuasive personality made him the ideal ship manager.

It took several more weeks to get basic equipment working, and the ship made habitable. Bedding and mattresses needed replacing, the water system needed a lot of work and the main electrical power generator needed an overhaul. Eventually though things were coming together as Ronan found more money for the ship.

Spangles brought his young wife Kate across from Birmingham to help organise a new office for Radio Caroline office. It was set up in a small private hotel on the Zeekant in Scheveningen. The hotel was run by Mr and Mrs Pleitter who have given Caroline the use of the top two floors which doubled as an office and overnight crash pad for staff.

Kate Cary on board a tender
Lion Keezer

Chris and Kate both worked tirelessly to build a new Caroline organisation from the ground up, a gargantuan task that had been done by dozens of administrators only a few years earlier. Kate was very organised with lots of clerical experience; she was fun too, bubbly, cheerful and always keen to join in the fun and games.

While 'Spangles Muldoon' was well-known from his days on Radio Caroline and RNI, he decided to revert to his name Chris Cary. It was through Chris that the RNI owners made an approach to buy the `Mi Amigo. He referred them to Ronan O'Rahilly, who refused their bid of a quarter of a million guilders. They threatened that he would regret turning them down and said Caroline would not last the winter.

By early November the station had made several test transmissions at varying power levels. These were usually non-stop music, with the occasional announcement but reception reports were now coming in from all over Europe, although the power level was less than ten kilowatts. The pop press and daily newspapers in the UK carried announcements that Radio Caroline was about to return.

It had been intended to transmit a new service in Dutch aimed at the western part of Holland using the 10kW transmitter. The English service of Radio Caroline would be carried on 259m by the 50kW transmitter.

Aerial mast problems

In the early hours of the 13th November, a bad storm hit the Netherlands, the worst weather since 1921. The Mi Amigo's anchor chain snapped and the engine was inoperable, leaving her to drift for about three miles, at the mercy of the waves. The motion of the Mi Amigo, jiving around on the heavy seas did not help the mast and with a loud crack the entire structure came toppling down, just as the crew were dropping the emergency anchor.

Mi Amigo's pole mast
Lion Keezer

The Mi Amigo's mast was a unique hybrid of three different structures. The lower section (about 51 feet) was from the Radio Nord days. It was lengthened in Greenore for Radio Atlanta with a 91 feet length of *Sparlight* yacht mast. In early 1966, it was lengthened again by inserting a 20 feet section in the middle of these, making the entire length 162 feet.

The mast had stood firm ever since the rebuild but no maintenance had been carried out on the stays, a network of steel guy wires that hold it firmly in place. These needed re-greasing at least once a year and kept under tight compression, otherwise strain imbalance can snap guys and buckle the mast.

The Mi Amigo crew managed to drop an emergency anchor and the ship was saved but was now dismasted. It fell along the length of the deck and was hanging over the side of the ship with the extensive network of rusted steel guy wires and antennae feeder tangled around everything on deck. Captain Taal and crewman Peter van Dijken went out on deck to secure the remaining pieces to the side of the ship, but it was impossible to re-erect even a short part of it.

This made the ship a very dangerous place for a week or so; the old mast had to be cut away and jettisoned, leaving only a short stump. A temporary aerial was lashed up between that and the aft mast just in front of the bridge. Just enough to transmit a much reduced signal.

Chris Cary had met an Englishman called Barry Attersal-Smyth, who ran a company in the Dutch town of Den Bosch. Barry was a Caroline enthusiast and, on seeing the sad news about the Caroline mast on the TV news, immediately offered to build a replacement.

Within two weeks the short lattice structure was out and standing proudly on the top of the ship's superstructure. It became known as the 'Mickey Mouse' mast as it was only about 60 feet long and a bit 'bent' but it did enable Caroline to get back on the air. Only a small team of DJs were living on board the ship, mainly Andy Archer, Crispian St John and engineer Peter Chicago.

Spangles announced the test transmissions at the end of the month and urged listeners to write in with reception reports. Over two thousand letters were received in the first week at the *P O Box 2448 in the Hague*, address given out on the air. The reports proved that the station was being heard as far as Scandinavia, Belgium Germany and the UK, despite having no high mast. Only low power was possible, with the short mast so modifications were made allowing it to be reinforced.

In the middle of December Caroline reappeared on its first wavelength, 199 metres. The first advert was for Ronan's film, *GOLD*, which was just opening for a short run at the Classic cinema near Piccadilly Circus in London. Caroline was identified as Radio 199 and regular output began in earnest in December. On the DJ roster, were several Dutch voices such as Mike Storm and Lion Keezer who did mornings followed by Jeremy Bender, and Paul Dubois in the afternoon. On the winter solstice, the Captain of the Mi Amigo, Dick Palmer made his Radio Caroline debut, although somewhat reluctantly. He would become one of the most memorable Caroline characters.

The crew was growing all the time, with Tony Allan and Graham Gill having joined from RNI and Allan Clark with some Dutch colleagues also arrived on board. On 1st December however there were still only two DJs on board, Spangles and Crispian St John, who had joined before the ship left Amsterdam, plus a few engineers, including Dutchman Jan Troost. All took turns to host the test transmissions.

On most days, Caroline stalwart Andy Archer and another RNI recruit, Crispian St John, could both be heard doing breakfasts while Peter Chicago restricted his bouts of presentation to the evening hours. The station even had some shows presented by the man who had made the return of Radio Caroline possible, Gerard Van Dam (sometimes called, rather appropriately, Gerard van der Zee). Not only was he a key worker, but he and his mother had invested too. He was good at persuading people to invest in 'The Lady' however and earned his stripes as one of the real saviours of Radio Caroline.

Gerard was much quieter than most of his Caroline colleagues and always seemed somewhat in awe of some of the big star names, despite having mixed with most of them for some years. Andy Archer wanted to do more than non-stop music shows. He wasn't happy playing simply chart hits and set his heart on hosting a rock show combined with talk. His late-night shows featured interviews with such luminaries as Alice Cooper, Barry of the Golden Earring and some guys from Frank Zappa's Mothers of Invention!

Erection of the triangular mast begins
Lion Keezer

Caroline urgently needed a decent radio tower to be able to get back on the air with the full power. Dutch DJ Lion Keezer found a magnificent three-sided lattice structure, tapering up to the top. It would be the highest mast on any of the ships and emit a huge signal.

The triangular shaped mast was originally designed for a cable TV receiving station. It arrived at Scheveningen harbour for delivery and Ronan flew across personally from London to pay for it, with funds provided by George Harrison. The first sections were shipped out to the Mi Amigo during December and by Christmas the bottom section had been erected.

Not only did Lion Keezer find the new mast but he collected the steel foundations and insulators from the NDSM shipyard in Zaandam using a Ford Transit van, that almost collapsed under the weight! On land this type of mast was self-supporting, needing no guy wires.

Chris was quite a competent engineer as well as being fearless; he would attack any job with great gusto. He brought relentless enthusiasm to everything; it was infectious and he convinced many that they could achieve anything if they worked away at it long enough. He drew up a simple guying plan for the mast, but not all of the steel cable needed was readily to hand.

The first Caroline telephone number was that of the hotel. Landlady Mrs Pleitter, by now in her late sixties, was easy to convince that, as the station used an extension at the top of the hotel, the calls would be charged to someone else. She got quite a surprise when the bills for international calls began to arrive the following quarter for thousands of guilders! Ronan paid the bill of course, as the station's office could not function without a telephone!

The station was however on the air and making money as Radio 199. DJs Andy Archer, Crispian St John and some Dutch DJs were now broadcasting all day, most days. Some advertising was forthcoming, however it was mostly retailers such as Gerard van Dam's mother's fashion boutique, *Inca,* which paid 20 ,000 NLG in advance.

The limited amount of funding from the *Inca* boutiques wasn't enough to pay everyone. The English DJs didn't mind, they were there to be a part of Radio Caroline, which was still a legend in the UK and world famous. They wanted only to enjoy the huge exposure and promotion that this might bring their broadcasting careers, so they would happily broadcast for free.

To the Dutch crewmen on the ship it was a different story. To them this was just another job and they worked only for their weekly wages to support their families. They resented the erratic wage procedures due to sporadic contributions from Ronan, Inca boutiques and Cor de Ruyter.

In the early hours of Christmas Day morning, RNI and Radio Caroline both broadcast Christmas greetings to each other in a special Christmas link-up. There was considerable Love and Peace sent over the airwaves for Christmas Day but the peace was to be shattered in a few days with more dramatic events on board Radio Caroline.

On Boxing Day, Andy had to apologise to listeners for all the banging that could be heard on the air. "We have a gang of workmen on deck outside the studio who are erecting a new antenna mast," he said. This was the foundation and bottom section of a new triangular mast that had recently arrived on board.

Some of the first Radio Caroline team bound for the ship in 1972
Allan, Andy, Ronnie, Lion, Graham, Paul Dubois, Angelique, Henk, Capn Wil & Henk's wife.
Martin Stevens

A few days later, the station began announcing that Caroline would change frequency shortly. The plan was to leave 199 metres and return to 259. Thursday 28th December Andy Archer told listeners that they had some trouble out on deck and he was going to investigate.

Captain van der Kamp said that he intended to take the ship into port and threatened the English DJs who would not cooperate. The crew began fighting English DJs Andy Archer, Peter Chicago and Crispian St John for control and the Captain holed up on the bridge with a rifle. He had been persuaded by the promise of money from neighbours Radio North Sea who wanted to see Radio Caroline 'off the scene'.

A Dutch naval destroyer, the D814, was standing by, to intervene when it seemed that the ship and her crew may be in danger. The destroyer sent a small launch across to the Mi Amigo and enquired if the Captain needed any help. Captain van der Kamp told them that all was cool, it was just a small problem with some crew who were annoyed at the lack of pay while they were away from home over Christmas.

A large press contingent witnessed fighting and a bit of a struggle on deck thanks, to RNI's Trip Tender which brought out a party of journalists who had been tipped off that something big was about to happen. A new Caroline crew with Gerard van Dam and Lion Keezer also came out on board the launch *Seanews* and the Dolfijn.

Oil feeder pipes had been sabotaged interrupting transmissions so Captain van der Kamp was dismissed and he left the ship with his crew on board RNI's Trip Tender, giving press interviews on the short trip to port. TV footage appeared on Dutch and British TV that evening as well as on all the BBC radio news bulletins. DJ Crispian St John was injured and the following day all the British national papers carried the story, although Radio Caroline continued normal programming.

Piracy on the High Seas

The mutinous crew crept back on board the Mi Amigo at 3am, after Caroline had closed down for the night. They took over the ship and severed the anchor chain.

Lion, Andy, Ron & Peter Prisoners in the Mess

Dory Vinkesteyn

The four DJs on the boat (Peter and Andy, plus Dutchmen Ron Dolman and Lion Keezer) were awoken by the old crew members and locked in the cold messroom.

The mutineers sabotaged the antenna as the tug Eurotrip from RNI's tender company took the Mi Amigo in tow. Dick Roos and RNI's Trip Tender did most of the tow and the flotilla was escorted by a Dutch warship, arriving off IJmuiden at first light. Ronan arrived on board the Vrolijk ship, *Dolfijn* and tried to prevent the Mi Amigo being taken into Dutch waters but the police ordered them to sail into port.

The harbourmaster there said there was no quay space for the Mi Amigo, so she was towed to Amsterdam. Radio officials then boarded but made no seizure as the crystals having been removed by Chicago as the ship entered Dutch waters. Ronan O'Rahilly told the authorities that he had dismissed all the crew, who tried to get an injunction that would have impounded the Mi Amigo until their wages were paid.

The Dutch shipping inspectorate pronounced that she was not seaworthy and ordered urgent repairs to collision damage caused by the tender before she could sail again. On New Year's Day 1973, the most urgent repairs were done and by early evening, two tugs began towing the ship along the North Sea Canal towards the sea. The crew continued their protests in IJmuiden but the authorities didn't believe some of their wild claims and the Mi Amigo was allowed to pass.

Captain van Der Kamp and his crew shouted abuse at the Mi Amigo as she sailed through the locks; Ronan hurled a few choice phrases in response from the deck of the ship as she sailed serenely seawards, under the command of her new master, Captain Jan Harteveld.

As the ship left IJmuiden, another claim came in; it was one final dirty trick from the RNI tender firm, the *Trip Tender Company*, whose Captain Dick Roos now had the affront to ask for payment for towing the ship in!

The Mi Amigo took five hours to sail back to the anchorage; everyone was exhausted after the long New Year's weekend and hassle of getting the ship out. Ronan stood up at the forepeak, enjoying the sea breeze and the smell of freedom. As he closed his eyes for a few seconds, DJ Lion's girlfriend, Dory Vinkesteyn, caught him in this unique picture, by the base of new triangular mast.

Ronan contemplates freedom

Dory Vinkesteyn

During the brief trip along the coast, new DJ Steve England, Chicago, Tony Allen and Gerard van Dam repaired the aerial so transmissions could resume. Radio Caroline was finally free once again.

Ronan drops the Mi Amigo's anchor New Year's Day, 1973

Dory Vinkesteyn

As soon as the Mi Amigo was back off Scheveningen, Ronan personally dropped the new anchor and Radio Caroline began broadcasting again immediately. The first DJ on the air was Gerard van Dam, who was followed by new recruit, Tony Allan and Ron Dolman.

The Mi Amigo was now under the command of engineer Dick Palmer. He was a level headed and sensible guy, an ideal leader and just the sort of steadying influence that many of the hotheads and young DJs needed to control them. He was also quite a philosopher and could talk sense and peace to bot h the DJs and depleted ship's crew.

As well as revenue from commercials, there were donations too from well-wishers in the music business who wanted to see Radio Caroline succeed. Key among these were contributions from John Lennon and George Harrison, of the Beatles. George now had his own record label with plans to expand it rapidly and needed an outlet to promote his product. Micky Most and his label RAK were supportive too, as was the Dutch *Red Bullet* production company whose roster of artistes included Shocking Blue, Focus and Golden Earring. Red Bullet is owned by DJ Joost De Draaijer who had recently left the RNI fold.

Most other music business promoters however were wary of the Caroline brand as the station was not reliable in either signal strength due to all the technical problems encountered, nor in programme consistency with the constant changes and format swings. This had recently become a little more predictable with pop during the day and heavier rock at night. DJs forming links with newer recording artistes, especially some in the Netherlands, managed to secure a limited amount of record plugging.

Radio Caroline began a news service too with bulletins being read on the half hour, when other stations didn't normally carry any news.

Kate Cary, along with Chris and their daughter Louise, lived in the hotel on the Zeekant in Scheveningen. Kate's role was doing all the Radio Caroline administration as well as recruiting a team of DJs, engineers and sailors for the ship. One of Kate's best hirings was Dennis King, who was a first class blagger. Dennis could negotiate the supply of almost anything the station needed and do a trade (known in the Caroline organisation as a "contra deal") in return for commercials on the air. This made the station sound very 'busy' which could snowball and make Radio Caroline sound very important.

Communications with the ship were easily accomplished with a small radio telephone hidden in a cupboard; the Mi Amigo was anchored only four miles away and could be seen from the windows of the hotel. The ship-shore station (Scheveningen Radio) wouldn't handle calls to radio ships unless in an emergency. It was vital to be in touch with the ship as Caroline was offering commercials on the air within an hour of taking an order. A succession of CBs, amateur rigs and taxi radios were used.

New Caroline financial guru?

It was a constant hassle paying the bills for the rapidly growing team and a lot of ingenious hustling was the order of the day. In one heated meeting, hotelier Mr Pleitter had protested that he knew about finance as he had been a financial adviser; Ronan explained that Caroline's regular Finance Director was very ill, which is why bills were late in being paid. Perhaps Mr Pleitter might help out with this for a while? The hotelier was in fact a convicted fraudster and probably thought he might get his hands on Caroline's likely millions, so quickly agreed and soon forgot about the overdue rent.

The Caroline teams didn't realise that Mr Pleitter was on 'weekend release' from a jail sentence and one day the police arrived to arrest him. While searching for Mr Pleitter in the Caroline office, a muffled voice emerged from a small cupboard "Mi Amigo to office, hello, are you there?" The Police recognised this as an illegal radio link and Mr Pleitter was charged with a radio offence as well as 'absconding'. The Pleitter's teenage son, Michael, was upset at the police raid so he deflated the tyres on the police car. Mrs Pleitter feigned a heart attack, so an ambulance was called too. Also in attendance were two transvestites from Germany seeking airplay plus several DJs and a journalist from a trade magazine. The Zeekant was usually such a quiet place in winter, it had never seen such a circus!

After that incident, Chris installed a radio link in his car and any necessary communication with the ship was done from a different location each day. The Pleitters and Caroline management agreed that the time had come to find a new office for the radio station!

Caroline House, Den Haag

More suitable premises were found in a back street close to the Hague's Holland Spoor railway station. It was conveniently located and in the middle of the city's 'red light' district!

Caroline House, The Hague, Holland

The entrance was a smart glass door, with an inner vestibule behind and a small store cupboard. A flight of stairs led up to the main reception where Kate welcomed visitors and a large open-plan office, with the station name picked out in large white letters on the pale blue wall. It was equipped with new Adler electric typewriters and a chilled drinks machine.

By now there were a dozen people working on board the ship, all on a "two weeks on, two weeks off" basis, meaning Caroline had as many staff on shore as on the boat. Fortunately, many were transient and moved quickly onwards to their homes, etc, for weeks off. Some crew and DJs often simply slept on the floor overnight

Chris and Kate Cary found a place to live on the Waalsdorperweg, a well-to-do area. The luxurious four-bedroom apartment was soon a crash pad for arriving and departing DJs on their way to and from the ship. Most of the Caroline team didn't bother with the formalities of the front door and simply climbed in through the ever-open window. After two weeks on board ship, they wanted to party, all night and every night, so life there became a little hectic.

Work started building studios on the top floor where commercials were produced and some of the DJs could pre-record shows. Visiting stars were not usually taken out to the ship due to its dilapidated state.

It could not be Caroline without jingles of course, and self-confessed jingle freak Steve England set to work on a stack of PAMS demo tapes. Before long he had assembled a decent set of new 1970s Caroline jingles, although with only one serviceable cart player on the ship, they were not heard very often.

Steve England in the 389 studio

Archer's Anoraks

Andy Archer in his red anorak!
Lion Keezer

Radio Caroline's programmes now settled down to a mixture of Dutch and English programmes with a slightly heavier feel than the pop that RNI and Veronica peddled. Norman Barrington, a former trainee bank manager and Steve England, a first-class Top 40 DJ were added to the station's line up while the Mi Amigo was in Amsterdam. The only real problems that were encountered now were the regular breakdown of the power generators.

Radio Caroline listeners are often very enthusiastic and, despite the remote location of the ships over the years and the difficulties imposed by the authorities, many of them have moved heaven and earth to visit the ships. Very few BBC listeners or indeed listeners to other radio stations have such all-consuming interest as to go to such extraordinary lengths to see "where it all happens". But Radio Caroline is no ordinary radio station!

Boat operators in south east England and off the Dutch coast have, for many years, become quite used to groups of Radio Caroline listeners wanting to make the pilgrimage out to the ship and it has become quite good business. Since 1964 when the Lady of Kent first took a party of sightseers to see the good ship Caroline, to today, when the Razorbill and others ferry a dozen enthusiasts at a time out to the Ross Revenge on the River Blackwater.

In early 1973 things were settling down well. Caroline was on the air more or less continuously and radio enthusiasts would come to pay homage at the radio ships. Some of those with a jaded view of the fans would pelt them with rotten potatoes or whatever was to hand, which the fans would gleefully collect and take home in their duffle bags (a forerunner of today's sports hold-all). The visitors were, rather disparagingly, often called wankers.

On one such occasion in early 1973, Dutch DJ called Ron Dolman was on the air. His lack of English was made up by his overt enthusiasm and he eagerly announced on the air that "the biggest wanker boat in the world was coming alongside, and its full of wankers!"

His exclamation at three o'clock in the afternoon was most unfortunate and, over dinner that evening, the crew decided that a new name had to be found for the radio enthusiasts who braved the elements to visit the ship.

It was Andy Archer who coined the word: Anoraks! "They all seemed to wear anoraks, with lots of pockets to bring their tapes that they swapped with fellow enthusiasts" explains Andy. "We just began calling them all collectively *anoraks* and the term stuck."

The term 'anoraks' became more widespread in the radio industry in the seventies and eventually crossed over to mainline life. It was applied to any group of keen and eager enthusiasts who were a little bit obsessed with technical things, from railway engines to aircraft. The metonym was adopted by a group of radio fans in the 1980s for a weekly report of trivia from the radio world as *Anoraks UK*. Later Princess Diana helped to popularise the term when she told Chris Tarrant that "I'm very keen on radio, I have it on all the time and can name most of the DJs, but I'm not yet a full-on anorak."

A contract to advertise cigarettes was discussed with Marlborough, but it was not welcomed by Ronan who referred to their product as 'cancer sticks'. The company did however sponsor a car in the Caroline racing team, which had some success in races at Zandvoort. The ship was well stocked with their product and many of the DJs proudly wore the bright red Marlborough anoraks.

The *Caroline Countdown of Sound*, a weekly Top 50 was reintroduced as a corner stone of programming. The chart was usually presented by Steve England and Ron Dolman, though other DJs had to step in at times. Run by Chris Cary and a few DJs it was a good mixture of the charts from both Holland and the UK, with uncool tracks eliminated, in line with the new cool and groovy International service that it was intended to run.

The Caroline Club was revived with a membership fee of ten guilders (just under £2 in 1973) and new members sought. This was a valuable revenue arm, necessary to keep Caroline afloat. Unlike the heady days of the 1960s, the ship and station was now owned not by a consortium of rich backers, but largely by Ronan alone.

Most of his money had been invested in yet another film venture that was yet to pay any dividends. The movie was called GOLD, but it was not to be a huge box-office success. Commercials were played on Caroline for the film, but it could only be seen at just a few cinemas in the West End.

Other income came from commercials that Caroline ran for small businesses in the 'Randstad' area of Holland (The Hague, Rotterdam and Amsterdam) where the station could be clearly heard. While Caroline broadcast mainly in English, most people there understood the language well, the Dutch being a lot more cosmopolitan and business-aware than the British. Radio Caroline's Dutch DJs filled most of the daytime hours and the English DJs took over after dark, when reception could include a much wider area.

The station had a new strap line, or positioning statement in 1973:

> *Serving the European continent from the North Sea*
> *This is the new Radio Caroline.*

This simple voice line was topped and tailed with many effects and other snippets from other jingles and is so memorable that it is still in use now, 45 years later!

Another memorable icon of those days is a visual that replaced the bell as the Caroline logo for a while. It was an outline of a young girl eating an ice-cream, modelled on Chris & Kate Cary's daughter Louise. The logo appeared on letterheads and car stickers and gave the 'young and giggly girl' image that Ronan claimed had been the intention for Radio Caroline when she began.

Louise had by now started nursery school in The Hague and her Dutch was quite proficient, certainly among the English members of the new office, also called Caroline House, in de Van Hoogendorpstraat in the Hague. When Kate received a call that was in Dutch and she couldn't understand it, she would hand the phone to Louise who could usually translate. It's amazing how quickly children can become bilingual.

Louise Cary in the Radio Caroline office

On Sunday the 25th March disaster struck when the last remaining generator failed mid record, leaving the station off the air. Without electrical power the station was not only silent but in darkness too. For several days the ship was lit by paraffin hurricane lamps and by the tried and tested method of connecting a fluorescent tube to the antenna cable. Chicago had previously discovered that enough power was picked up from one of the neighbouring ships to light it. This 'borrowed power' sufficiently illuminated the Mi Amigo, so she wasn't a danger to other ships while unlit.

Candy Magazine

One potential saviour for Caroline emerged in the form of Peter Muller, organiser for *Actie 68*. They ran a magazine from some garages in Haarlem called *Candy*. Salesmen Kes Koppenoll Kees and Will van der Steen (aka DJ *Bill Stones)* sold Muller three hours of air time to the magazine to promote its various 'products and services'.

The first *Nationale Candy Show* was "in the can and ready to broadcast," Will told colleagues later. It was recorded at the Candy editorial office in Haarlem and featured the voices of celebrities such as GJ Lindenboom, assorted call girls, lesbians and some very freaky people, as well as some rather suggestive music.

There was some disquiet in the Radio Caroline office that carrying adverts for Candy Magazine might deter some of the more genteel advertisers that the station was trying to court so Ronan forbade their transmission. Failure of the generator and a storm avoided that little dilemma, for a while.

The immediate generator needs were solved by a gentleman from Rotterdam called Carl Bart who provided a succession of generators. These had been removed from various sources as scrap, but with a bit of ingenuity from Dick Palmer and a few taps from a sledgehammer, they could usually be made to struggle on for a while longer.

After they left Caroline, Kate and Chris Cary went into business in the UK with Carl. "He was our friend for life after we went back to London" remembers Kate. "He contributed to Chris making a fortune during the power cuts in the UK. He sold Chris knackered generators and we employed Dick Palmer to renovate them. We rented these 'recycled' generators to companies who were determined to have power on during the 'three-day week' caused by a coal miners' strike."

Veronica on the Beach

On 2nd April 1973, hurricane force 12 winds hit the Dutch coast. They were reported to be the worst storms in living memory, particularly near Scheveningen where the three radio ships were anchored. The Mi Amigo rode out the storm with few problems.

During the night the Radio Veronica ship the MV Norderney lost its anchor, drifted and grounded on the beach, just a hundred metres from the stone pier at the south of Scheveningen harbour. In the cold light of day, it was evident that the ship was stuck firmly in the sand and could be there for some time.

Radio Caroline offered its help to Radio Veronica; this was typical of Ronan's generosity. He had helped rival stations in the past and would continue to do so in the future. Veronica urgently needed help as they had an important event coming up in their political battle for a full on-land licence and needed to rally support from their listeners. They were not talking to the RNI people following a battle that had resulted in three men jailed for taking part in a fire attack on the RNI ship.

The Veronica engineers looked at the Mi Amigo and were pessimistic that anything could be achieved as the facilities on board were very sparse and could not easily replicate Veronica conditions. For example, there were no working tape recorders in the studios, only one microphone and only the very short 'Micky Mouse' mast.

The Radio Veronica presenters were by now very big names in the Netherlands and usually operated with a technician driving the desk. Their programmes carried lots of high-cost commercials, personalised DJ jingles and other material. It was deemed vital to be on the air to garner support for a demonstration outside the Dutch parliament buildings on the 18th which was expected to be the pivotal date in the debate.

A deal was quickly done, money changed hands and the Radio Caroline crew of Chris, Chicago, Dick Palmer, Norman Barrington and a few others worked feverishly for several days to put out Radio Veronica programmes from the Mi Amigo.

Chris Cary, ready to sell

Radio Veronica's programmes were mostly pre-recorded at their plush studio centre in Hilversum. They were then taken out to the Veronica ship every day on their own tender, the *Ger Anna*. It was a very slick and usually foolproof operation.

The first priority was a new generator; one was rushed out to the Mi Amigo the following day as two new studios were built for Veronica broadcasts from the vessel. These would enable Caroline engineers to offer a full 'Veronica style' service, with both Radio Caroline and Radio Veronica technicians driving the controls for the big-name Radio Veronica broadcasters, some of whom came out to the Mi Amigo.

Caroline had promised to transmit Radio Veronica programmes at 11am on the 11th April. Veronica's biggest DJ, Rob Out, was standing by with an emotive heart-tugging script in hand in the Mi Amigo's Studio 2 as the clock ticked past the appointed start time. He was waiting for the cue from Veronica studio technician Freek Simons and Caroline man, Norman Barrington, sat in the studio next door. The transmission actually started one minute late; well, this was similar to a marriage and the bride should always be a few minutes late!

The programmes of Veronica went out from the Mi Amigo with hardly a hitch. On the day of the big demonstration in The Hague, 18th April, over 100,000 listeners thronged the streets around the Binnenhof, next to the Dutch parliament, where politicians were discussion whether or not to introduce legislation similar that the UK Marine Offences Act from 1967. Earlier in the day the Veronica ship had finally been wrenched free from the beach and was under tow back to her regular anchorage. Transmissions began immediately on her regular slot of 538m and continued in parallel on Radio Caroline's 259m facility for a few more days.

The Caroline - Veronica 'hitch' wasn't really a marriage, but more of a short-term fling, but it's one that produced considerable mutual respect. Caroline and Veronica remained firm friends at a time that no one who was there at the time regrets or will ever forget. Certain members of the Veronica crew continued the relationship with Caroline and would often pop across and pick up Caroline staff and bring them to their ship for lunch or other social occasions.

The programme made by the Candy magazine was scheduled to be broadcast on 13th April, but Radio Veronica was using the ship and had contracted for all the airtime on 259, so Candy's programmes had to be delayed. The programmes attracted a lot of publicity in newspapers and on rival radio stations. Religious broadcaster the EO complained: "The Netherlands will soon be covered by a wave of filth, broadcast by the pirate ship Caroline in collaboration with the soft porn magazine Candy!"

The adverse publicity and the bigger deal with Veronica caused problems between Caroline and the magazine publisher, who sent their lawyers around with a writ, demanding the programme be aired. Support for Radio Caroline came from the national *De Telegraaf* newspaper who refused Candy's front page advert promoting the programmes, as work continued on board to build the new mast.

Threats were made by associates of the magazine and security on the Mi Amigo was increased to repel any physical action against the ship but nothing more was heard from Candy's publishers.

The new facilities donated by Radio Veronica and the handsome transmission fees paid meant that Radio Caroline was finally able to erect the new triangular mast on the deck of the Mi Amigo. It needed three huge insulators to cope with the compression (it weighed over 8 tions) and be fully stayed.

The triangular mast is born!

The work had to be undertaken at sea but riggers would not come out so it was all done by a small group of engineers and DJs: Norman, Peter, Dick and Robin all took turns erecting the structure, which should have reached around 180 feet into the sky. Although one section was inadvertently installed upside down, this wasn't noticed until most of the mast was completed. It seemed to look OK, so was left as it was. Some guy wires were missing from the mast and some of the turnbuckles and other fastenings had gone missing. The 'Tirfor' hand winch that tightened the stays up until they were 'bar hard' had developed a fault, but eventually it was up.

Peter Chicago had been developing his skills at diplexing, the method of feeding two radio signals on different frequencies into one antenna. He and Chris Cary had plans to transmit two Caroline channels from the ship, using the 50 kW unit on 259, and a smaller 10kW on 199m. The higher frequency would not provide good coverage over the 'Randstad' area (Rotterdam, Utrecht, Amsterdam and The Hague) so was dropped.

Ronan's plan was to move the ship to the English coast as soon as possible, but it made sense to get everything totally in order while close to a supply port (tenders could be run legally from Scheveningen) as many replacement parts were needed for the ship.

To run two radio services needed some parts of both transmitters refurbishing, extra studio equipment and a more reliable generator. There wasn't enough money in the kitty to achieve all those, but there was a tower and a replacement generator on the way.

Over the winter months it had been found that the 199m channel (1520 kHz) had poor reception after dark due to a couple of Czechoslovakian stations sharing the same frequency. They didn't pose a problem during daylight, but after dark, medium waves are reflected down from the 'D' layer and the interference was very annoying and, at times, reception was impossible. A higher power transmitter could overcome it, but Caroline had only one 50kW unit which was tuned to 259m and a 10kW unit on 199m.

Chicago knew that to get the best coverage would mean going down the medium wave band, as Veronica had done some months before. They had moved from 192m to 538m – one end of the band to the other. He calculated that by moving to the old Radio 390 frequency (773 kHz) the signal could be heard over a much wider area, perhaps as much as three times the distance.

He did a lot careful monitoring all along the MW band and found a couple of better frequencies farther down the band. By adding an extra section of aerial from the top of the new mast down to the stern mast, 773 was found to load up pretty well.

The first tests proved that this was so with what Spangles called a 'broadside coverage up and down the English coast. "It blasts into the UK like a shotgun, were getting coverage from Dover all the way up to Scotland and a long way inland too," he told the Daily Mail. "We shall soon have a full time English service with some of the best DJs in the Europe." Chris told the press that interest was already being shown by international advertisers keen to reach the millions of listeners that Caroline would soon be attracting once again.

Daybreak at the Mi Amigo in May 1973.
(The new triangular mast is almost complete and has some 'toploading' to the stern)
Lion Keezer

Caroline International on 389

The 773 frequency (389 metres) was shared with a station in Cairo but that would not prove a big problem. After some long and laborious calculations, Peter found that the Mi Amigo aerial could operate on 389 almost as well as 259.

This required a long antenna, helped considerably by the triangular mast being just over 180 feet high. By top loading it with a cable stretching towards the aft mast, it would give a reasonable match on 389m. In the sixties, Radio England has achieved good results for the on 355 meters with a similar arrangement.

When the 10kW transmitter was retuned to 389m it managed about 7 kilowatts of power and reception was good right along the east coast of England. A very usable signal was possible in cities such as Norwich, Hull, Newcastle and even up to Edinburgh. The 389 signal also reached quite well into London, which was important to attract any advertising.

Peter Chicago plugs 538m!
Paul Rusling

After some long nights of longhand calculation and careful tuning, Chicago's work bore fruits and both 259 and 389 worked together fine. Now carrying the same Radio Caroline music, the acid test was to be able to drive each transmitter with separate programming. By mid-May it worked and the two were being identified as *Radio Caroline 1* and Radio *Caroline 2*.

It was during May that Radio Caroline was finally able to transmit separate music on 389m and 259m through the new triangular tower, the first time that had ever been possible. It wasn't quite complete and still needed a few more stays attaching, and the last section on the top, which for now was sat on the roof of the ship's superstructure.

Paul Alexander was a new DJ who had been recruited for the new sound of Caroline and he made his first ever broadcast on *Radio Caroline 2* during the early transmissions on the channel. A long-time radio enthusiast, Paul was in the middle of training to be a ships radio officer and had been working as a club DJ to pay his way through college. Sounding like a young Yorkshire version of Tony Prince, he spoke at breakneck speed and had an inclination to do the perfect "talk up" to the vocal of every record he played. Chris Cary and Ronan both claimed Paul as 'their' discovery.

Back onshore, Ronan had persuaded advertising guru Terry Bate to come back onboard for a while and help to bring in some advertising revenue but he was unable to do so unless there was a station to sell. There were still some of the team not yet in place, some DJs had promised to rejoin Caroline but had not yet arrived.

While still conducting test transmissions in May, new Caroline International DJ Paul Alexander was heard appealing:

> *"Calling all cooks and radio engineers;*
> *the Caroline organisation is now expanding and we urgently need new recruits to work on board the radio ship. Engineers with American radio experience are particularly intended to apply.*
> *Write to Caroline House, the Hague, in Holland"*

Radio Caroline very lucky to be able to use simply "Caroline House, The Hague, Holland", especially as most listeners were not Dutch and would never have been able to spell the correct street address, (van Hoogendorpstraat, not the easiest word for non-Dutch listeners). The other radio stations used P O Box numbers in those days, but those cost money to rent and simply added another number for those writing to have to remember and for many listeners to get wrong!

Since her earliest days, Caroline had always been so well known that the full address was deemed unnecessary. The local post office knew exactly where to deliver the Caroline mail and by the middle of 1973 the station was attracting four to five thousand letters a week.

Caroline Curry?

There were some odd responses to the pleas for a cook; Kate selected the most qualified (on paper) applicant and brought him out. Dave arrived attired in a suit and waistcoat, a bowler hat, carrying a briefcase and a rolled up umbrella!

Dave didn't last long as the Mi Amigo's cook as he just never fitted in. His white chef's jacket made him stand out like a sore thumb, but he did add an element of elegance to the proceedings as he served dinner. When Chris Cary demanded that Chef Dave make him a chicken curry, he refused as he had just cleaned down the galley (that event was a bit of a first!). Chris then told him he was fired and sent him to his cabin.

The next day, Mike Phillpot, a taxi driver cum engineer from Hull, devilishly told Dave, the new chef, that he was going to be made to walk the plank, or killed, cut up and used for food! The obviously naïve Dave was easily convinced that being pirates and on a Panamanian ship, the crew could do as they pleased.

The next day while the tender was alongside, everyone was busy helping pass over the supplies, a cry rang out and all the crew saw was Dave, topped by his bowler hat and carrying his brolly and briefcase flying across to the tender and freedom. That was to be the last the crew saw of Dave, so Jimmy Hoolihan had to continue treating everyone to his culinary skills.

Snap launch for Caroline International

During a visit to the ship on Sunday 3rd June, Chris Cary suddenly decided that the station must start regular broadcasts the following day. Advertising contracts were ready to run thanks to Terry Bate. Veteran Caroline breakfast DJ Roger Day was due to rejoin to host the flagship programme but hadn't arrived yet. Paul Alexander was instructed to take the breakfast slot; an unexpected move, especially for a first timer on the radio. There was no time to be nervous about the important step he was about to make.

The morning of Monday 4th June dawned bright and sunny. Quite a few of the crew were up and about as Andy Archer had convinced everyone that the Dutch TV and journalists would be coming out to cover the big event. Young Paul fell for it, hook, line and sinker and sat at the 389 desk in the studio in his best three-piece suit and a floral tie. He spent hours scanning the horizon for the mythological press boats!

Not only was Caroline International launching its Top 40 service on 389m, but a new Dutch language *Radio Caroline* would be launching at the same time over on 259. The Dutch version of Caroline would play easy listening music and be programmed by Andy Archer, who would also double as a DJ on the 389 service until more voices arrived.

Both the Caroline channels played a religious programme from 7 to 7:30 hosted by a well-known evangelist from the Hague who became the new station's first advertiser, Johan Maasbach.

After the morning ministrations from Reverend Maasbach, Paul Alexander launched his first ever radio show with the latest release by the Four Seasons, "Walk, Don't Look Back". Andy Archer took over at 9am, perched uncomfortably on the antique dining chair which was the only seat in the 389 studio.

Paul Alexander and Robin Adcroft

Bob Noakes

The big studio used for 389m programmes was quite large, with a huge wrap-around counter, like the servery in a fish shop, surrounding the DJ. Visitors could come in and stand there watching the DJ, were they so inclined. The studio also had large square portholes at opposite sides; Paul found he could squeeze through them quite easily and indeed he often performed links "half in and half out" the porthole, to the surprise of others on the ship. "Working five nights a week in a large dance hall gets you used to performing," said Paul "Sitting sedately in a chair was more than a 19 year old could manage."

On the DJs left was a double glass window, installed about twelve years previously, in the Radio Nord Days. It gave a good view into the smaller studio, from where the Dutch language '259' was broadcast.

On that first day the line-up on Dutch Caroline included Henk Meeuwis, an Amsterdammer with a very dry sense of humour and superstar jock Joop Verhoof who had started his radio career in March and quickly become popular with Dutch listeners. Many programmes came out to the ship from studios that had by now been built on the top floor of Caroline House.

Henk Meeuwis,
Rob Olthof

The on-board studio used for the 389 service was only sparsely equipped – a very odd mixer that had been purloined from a night club, two Garrard SP25 turntables and an old Grundig reel-to-reel tape machine that was sat on the floor at the DJs feet. There was no cart player for jingles and commercials – the tape recorder was used for everything, which made for ambidextrous and alert DJs, if nothing else.

The microphone was a good one though, an AKG D202; Paul almost made Chief Engineer Peter Chicago cry one morning when he disassembled it during his programme, while on the air! It never did go back together again but still sounded great! The microphone was mounted in a typically Chris Cary way: a hole was cut into a block of polystyrene that had been previously used to encase one of the transmitter valves. Very rudimentary and not very pretty (a lot like most of the Caroline DJs!) but it worked and saved the hundred pounds that a professional microphone mount would have cost.

The mixing panel is the heart of any radio studio; the 389 studio sported a unique specimen of doubtful parentage, but using some parts of a Rodec mixer, made in Antwerp and seen in many Belgian bars. Most audio mixers have either vertical or rotary faders to control levels; the 259 studio had a *Gates Studioette* console, which had rotary "pots' as they are called.

Modern studios have short throw faders, where a button zooms along a linear track. The 389 audio mixer was a home brewed job that had three or four vertical faders, plus a large rotary one on the left that controlled the studio LS monitor level.

The DJ's microphone in the 389 studio however only had a simple on or off toggle switch. When the studio microphone is live, it's important to silence the monitor loudspeaker, which lets the DJ hear the output of the desk. If this doesn't happen, an acoustic path will 'howl around' getting increasingly louder.

The 389 studio microphone switch left the microphone momentarily live to the speaker as it was switched on, so each time the DJ opened the mic, a short squeaky sound was heard, which could make the DJ sound unprofessional.

Mariners adrift

While Andy Archer was delighting his listeners that morning, Chicago decided to check how strong a signal was being radiated from the ship and whether there were any harmonics or spurious emissions getting out. He and Paul Alexander put off the from the Mi Amigo in the ship's lifeboat, tied to the 'mother ship' with a very long rope, coiled up on the floor of the craft.

They rowed out for half an hour, monitoring various frequencies and, wanting to go further, Chicago asked Paul to pay out all the rope, meaning right to the end of its travel. Misunderstanding the instruction Paul foolishly threw it all over the side, including the end! It promptly disappeared into the depths, of around 40 metres of water; that's 140 feet or over twenty fathoms!

Some frantic rowing ensued; at one stage an oar was lost and Chicago went over the side of the boat to retrieve it. Fellow crew on board the Mi Amigo wondered what they were doing, not realising they were adrift.

The rope was pulled back to the Mi Amigo, tied to a float and then sent off to Peter and Paul, by now drifting helplessly, further away from the ship. Fortunately, it was a fine day but it took two hours to get the intrepid mariners safely back on board.

Johnny Jason on the new Radio Caroline International -389

On the English service that first week, Andy Archer's mid-morning show ran from 9 until 12, following which the Caroline International service had a pre-recorded show from Spangles Muldoon. His *Lunchtime Loonabout* was a joy to hear on the air and often humorous. Recorded in two new studios on the top floor of Caroline House they were driven an engineer, having been set up that way for Dutch DJs, in the style of Radio Veronica, whose DJs were unable to drive a desk. The shows were played in by whoever hosted the next programme, usually Robin, Peter or Johnny Jason.

In several of his shows in the first week, Spangles explained that he was changing his name back to his 'real' name of Chris Cary, as his mother was becoming very confused as to who exactly he really was and she still called him Spangles!

Chris' Lunchtime programmes often under-ran, with only about 55 minutes of programme on the one hour reels, meaning whoever was tape watching on the Mi Amigo had to dart inside early and pop some filler music on when the programme abruptly ended, to get to the top of the next hour when the next programme started.

Mothers had always played a big role in the Caroline hierarchy; Kate Cary's mum, Mary, came out to visit the ship on one occasion. She was very sweet and gave some advice. As she left, Mary promised the DJs she would get various things sorted out, taking with her quite a shopping list of things that the DJs wanted sending out. Few of the promised supplies materialised but, the mere fact that someone promised to try, certainly raised morale for a few days.

Among those who responded to the advert for an engineer was Bob Noakes who arrived on board later in June as a technician and later became a DJ on Radio Seagull.

Some new jingles were introduced, largely edited from PAMS demo tapes, such as the "*Coffee and Music with – Radio Caroline*". This was a sung excerpt from a PAMS demo of the Harry Harrison programme on WABC tailed with the deepest, most strident voice that Chris Cary could muster.

The afternoon show was sometimes hosted by engineer Peter Chicago, who had a nice relaxed style and an excellent choice in music. He was followed at teatime by Robin Adcroft, who had originally come out as a studio technician, helped erect the mast and shown that he was a first class programme host. One of Robin's party pieces was his shrill call emulating a female FRA committee member he knew; a comical impersonator with a wicked sense of humour.

The Dutch media did not come out to visit the Mi Amigo on that eventful first day, though two of the Radio Veronica team came over to pass on their greetings and toast the Caroline International launch. There was not much beer on the Mi Amigo that day, so the Veronica crew took three Amigos back over to their ship, the Norderney. Radio Veronica had equipped their crew with a fast little dingy that took only a few minutes to cover the mile or so. Soon, Norman, Robin and Paul were sat in the 538 studio, helping newsreader Arend Langenberg and technician Ruud Doets empty their studio fridge of beers.

The Norderney had only been back at sea for a few weeks after her beaching and spirits were very high. Visits between the Caroline and Veronica crews became frequent and were a welcome respite from the boredom that so many of the Mi Amigo crew had to face that Summer.

Summer Programming

Within a few days more DJs were available, including Johnny Jason, who had lots of experience in Australian Top 40 radio and was a welcome addition to the team. Steve England too returned to the ship after a long break and within weeks the station had additional pre-recorded shows from Michael Lindsay and Roger 'Twiggy' Day, one of the DJs on the Mi Amigo on that fateful day in March 1968.

Michael Lindsay was an old friend of Chris & Kate who recorded his programmes in London, where he worked as a record label executive for Deep Purple's own label. Michael was invaluable as Caroline's London representative, collecting new music from record labels for the ship and collating the Caroline Countdown of Sound. Sadly, a lot of the music on the chart was not available on the ship; by the third week on the air, only nineteen of that week's Top 40 could be found on board, so the weekly Caroline Countdown chart programme had to be abandoned. The chart was full of Mud, Sweet and the Osmonds, though the DJs had free play of Motown, reggae, soul and album cuts..

Quite a contrast to the diet of Frank Zappa, Pink Floyd, ELP, ELO and other even more progressive artists heard overnight on the 259 service, which by day had lush easy listening from the like of Ray Conniff, Diana Ross and Frank Sinatra. The Dutch DJs were very laid back in their presentation style; the pipe-smoking Henk Meeuwis was usually enveloped in a cloud of pungent smelling tobacco fumes which seemed to help give his voice an edge. He and fellow journalist Leo de Later hosted some excellent shows as *Nieuwslezer op drift* (Newsreader adrift) while future superstars DJs Bert Bennett and Joop Verhoof were heard on most days, sometimes with shows recorded in The Hague. They were all produced by Andy Archer who was in charge of the Dutch service, which carried quite a good commercial load.

Jimmy Hoolihan
Carl Mitchell

Other staff are needed on a radio ship; with the two transmitters now running 24 hours a day it was decided to get Peter Chicago some help. The ship still needed a cook as these duties were being undertaken on a temporary basis by Ronan's strong arm man, Jimmy Hoolihan, who had a far more important job on the ship to attend to. Jimmy was there as a security guard to look after the ship as there had been several threats, not the least from the disgruntled owners of Candy magazine.

Bob Noakes was a radio amateur with some studio experience at the BBC and in Ireland who was now living in South London. His flatmate heard the announcements recruiting radio engineers and urged him to apply immediately, which he did. Two days later he got a telegram asking him to call Caroline House, reverse charges. He was destined to become one of the ship's real characters, with his rather formal style of radio presentation. A few months later, he was to join a plot to move the ship from the Dutch coast which was discovered. News of the intended coup was relayed to Ronan who promptly called the ring-leaders and pricked the bubble of dissent.

One of the unique aspects of Radio Caroline was the station's preponderance towards what is today called multitasking; the most ideal recruits could play records, cook a meal, handle a welding torch and be proficient at celestial navigation. Caroline was a "can do" organisation, in the vein of Ronan's own "why not" job description. Largely out of necessity, the station encouraged and cajoled many of its team to abandon formal job descriptions and try their hand at other skills. Many have consequently taken up ways of life they never envisaged before joining Caroline.

The Mi Amigo was a popular destination for several visiting boats. Being only four or five miles offshore, it was a pleasant trip out for people and a popular destination. Due to the usual insurance problems and danger is in getting across, not to mention from exposed live antennas on the ship, visitors were not normally allowed on board.

Another major danger was the flue from the generators which was always one of the hottest things on board and at hand height, next to the galley. At the other end of the deck the feed for the antenna was only fended off with the most rudimentary barrier and getting within inches of that could give a very nasty shock of several thousand volts.

Four Seasons of Caroline
Radio Caroline now broadcast no less than four distinctly different services on the two wavelengths. The 389 frequency carried the Top 40 or pop music service as *Caroline International*, although it also played a lot of rock, soul music and reggae too. Over on 259 listeners heard the programmes Radio Caroline, a Dutch language easy listening music service during the day.

After Dutch Caroline closed at 6pm, the 259 channel broadcast a few hours of classical music. This was presented by whichever DJ could read German as all the music came from a library of German albums that the ship had inherited. Paul Alexander spoke German and, as the classical library was all German albums, he did some of the announcing, which was simply reads from the album covers. No one on board listened to it but a few days later lots of mail began coming in for the shows.

Paul had covered up his lack of musical knowledge by suggesting that listeners wrote in with a short list of their favourite classical music pieces. Programme Director Andy Archer lectured the enthusiastic youngster that, “soliciting mail for classical music just is not the done thing” before dropping him from the rota for spinning that programme.

After 8pm the classical music was slowly upped in tempo, and semi-rock cum classical music (e.g. ELO, The Nice, Focus, etc) until, by 9pm when Norman Barrington normally took the chair, the station was playing alternative rock and progressive music. After midnight it went totally free-form with a never-changing mixture of totally ‘way out’ all-album Rock Music service through the night. The last hour between 5 and 6am was more laid-back material, to get listeners ready for the easy listening Dutch MOR / easy listening service.

There was no proper ‘branding’ as no one had any time to plan that, there were too many other things to worry about, but Andy Archer and Chris Cary’s intentions seemed to be to call the four channels:

- **Caroline International** (Top 40 pop) on 389
- **Radio Caroline** (Dutch easy listening)
- **Caroline Classics** – non-stop classical music,
- **Caroline Rock** - alternative & progressive music

The intention was to have the English service at high power and run 24 hours a day, but lack of staff and materials delayed implementation of the changes necessary for this. Initially, the 389 service just relayed the 259 ‘progressive’ programmes overnight.

These shows usually featured some pretty *avant-garde* material. This was matched by some quite surreal continuity between the music, thanks to the unusual presentation skills of Dick Palmer. He would first imbibe various herbal substances to broaden his mind which was often reflected in his distinctly odd style of delivery.

Dick's attempts to communicate with the audience were marred by a combination of his lack of dexterity and the occasionally reluctant ancient turntables. Caroline's output would be punctuated by strange sound effects, raucous laughter and fits of giggles from the other DJs, who would congregate in the tiny studio to try and disrupt Dick's show.

Two comical Dutch crewmembers, Peter and Jaap, would stand in as interpreters, supposedly translating the proceedings into Dutch, or so they claimed. In fact, their explanations were the most humorous sayings one could imagine. Much of the translation they offered Dutch listeners for Dick's mumblings seemed to be laced with sexual references – Dutch listeners must have imagined that Dick was a sex therapist or instructor! That's the kind of fun activity that usually passed for sport after midnight!

By day, Dick was one of the most interesting people in the entire Caroline organisation. He had managed a fort-based station in the 1960s, Radio Essex, where he had combined his duties of hosting the station's daily RnB programme with a role of substitute parent to a number of very young DJs, away from home for the first time. Now, on the Mi Amigo, Dick had more young trainees to care for, plus some older but often even more immature crew members. As a practical and sensible individual, Dick invariably tied his long curly black hair back with a wide yellow headband, a cross between a ribbon and a bandana. It looked very distinctive and gave him a unique character.

Dick's brief on keeping everyone on board safe wasn't limited to advice on the dangers of some of the equipment, but he felt obliged to dispense a constant stream of healthy eating advice. He was Radio Caroline's fountain of wisdom and he saw his duty to be to sow those seeds among his colleagues with lesser knowledge, who he felt were a right bunch of Philistines. Everyone's consumption of pre-packaged food was met by a tirade of disparaging sermons of how the stuff was "totally plastic" and dire warnings that "you will all die of heart attacks".

Dick was not only the ship's captain he was also highly entertaining host of the overnight programme called, quite appropriately, *The Night Trip*. Like many Caroliners, Dick was quite an armchair philosopher, enthusiastic vegetarian and a part time yogi. We now know that his predictions about food were mostly true and uncannily accurate.

Perhaps the best new face to arrive at the new Caroline House that June was the station's star advertising guru, Terry Bate. Strictly speaking he was still under contract to Radio Caroline since 1966 and despite his involvement in several bids for independent radio station licences in the UK, had come over to give Radio Caroline the boost she now needed.

Terry and his assistant Alex immediately felt at home with Chris Cary and together they set about dreaming up new advertising initiatives for various potential clients. A deal with a car rental company was immediately struck, although it didn't last long when the three cars that were provided to the station as part of the arrangements were each returned bent and broken. One of these problems was broken suspension joints after trying to carry a heavy transformer from the harbour for rewinding.

Veronica's radio ship, the Norderney, was only a kilometre away, which took ten minutes in the Veronica speedboat, but about an hour rowing in the Mi Amigo's lifeboat! Among the most hospitable were Arend Langenberg, a newsreader and José Groningen, an engineer, but all the Veronica team were very friendly and helpful. Among the Caroline staff who were headhunted by Radio Veronica were Dutch newsreader, Leo de Later, who later achieved TV fame on the RTL4 channel.

The ship was 'permanently' moored with a huge anchor just outside the Dutch territorial waters, about four or files miles from the Dutch seaside resort of Scheveningen. The town also had a couple of harbours and it was from the *Tweede Binnenhaven* (the second inner dock) that the radio ships were serviced, by a couple of companies.

Radio Veronica used their own dedicated tender boat, the *Ger Anna*, which sailed every morning at 9 am bringing supplies and new programme tapes out to the Norderney. RNI used the Trip Tender company who operated several different workboats, including the Eurotrip which had towed the Mi Amigo away the previous December.

Radio Caroline of course was different and used the biggest and best tender company on the Dutch coast. Their fleet, their crews and activities deserve a book of their own.

Rederij Vrolijk - Sportfishing and Tendering!
Radio Caroline contracted with a very experienced Dutch company called *Rederij Vrolijk*. Cornelis Vrolijk ran this small fleet of 'Sport Fishing' boats. The biggest of them was the *Zeester;* it could take two hundred people out at a time.

The sister ships the Morgenster, the Martina and the Dolfijn were quite comfortable, always had beers for sale and the skippers did good business by taking along radio enthusiasts on tender trips that Caroline had already paid for. They left from a small building on the Lelykade quayside that also doubled as a waiting room and café. It was a popular rendezvous, often with a curious mixture of sailors and radio enthusiasts, or anoraks as they were now becoming known.

A two and a half hour cruise took in not only the three radio ships, but also a trip around the REM Island, just off Noordwijk another 8 miles to the north. This structure was a small steel platform installed to transmit radio and TV programmes in the sixties and now only used as a weather station. Relatively inaccessible it was the haunt of several thousand gulls, a mini seabird colony.

In her last few months off the British coast, the Mi Amigo had only a sporadic service from the Wijsmullers using their Offshore One tender, sailing from IJmuiden. Off Scheveningen however, things were very different. It only took about forty minutes to get out to the ship and there were lots of small fishing boats in the area and pleasure craft, many of whom were welcomed at the Caroline ship.

More experienced crew could easily hitch a lift on a passing boat, but most days one of the Vrolijk ships would tie up alongside, sometimes as an official Radio Caroline tender. Kate Cary tried to get the regular tenders organised to a schedule but all often, extra trips were needed to deliver urgently needed equipment to the Mi Amigo.

The Vrolijk fleet, always ready for Sport Fishing and radio ship tendering!

On at least one occasion the Mi Amigo had no less than three tenders in one day! The first one was fuel and water, the second was a personnel change and groceries delivery and the third was for various items that had apparently been forgotten on the other two trips!

At least one duplicate tender trip happened after Chris decided that it was so urgent to get some programme boxes out to the ship with new commercials on them and he didn't want it to wait until the long Customs Declaration form could be completed for the food and other stores that the Dutch Customs officers insisted be completed for each trip. Some were very obliging and happy to turn a blind eye to Radio Caroline, though others were typical civil servants; officious, over-zealous and with no sense of humour.

The officials Dutch weren't looking for smuggled goods without duty being paid, as the British customs would confiscate (tobacco and booze don't bear such punitive taxes in Holland as are levied in the UK). TheDutch were looking for such illicit items as two-way radio telephones. Although the official 'ship to shore' stations would not handle traffic to radio ships except in emergencies, it was important to remain in communication with shore, so unlicensed radios were used..

Peter Chicago would repair and line up pairs of two-way radios on the Mi Amigo and then send one ashore for use by the office. One day he fell off the gangplank from the tender and into harbour, still clutching the radiophone. Chicago got a soaking but was fine after a change of clothes. The equipment couldn't be seen, but a sailor offered to get it out for 100 guilders at 6pm. Chris agreed and was amazed on his return to watch as the sailor walked down the harbour steps and picked it out of the mud. Much easier when the tide had gone out!

Generator failure

The replacement generator obtained for the Veronica transmissions was a used one from Carl Bart that began spluttering and spitting. The engine driving the generator was overheating and its intercooler was blocked. Ship's captain Dick Palmer and chief motor engineer Jaap de Haan cleverly found a way to spray cool water over it, enabling it to run a while longer, but it wasn't expected to last more than a few days.

At tender time one Thursday afternoon, at the end of June, a pow wow was being held in the large 389 studio. Paul Alexander announced "You're tuned to Caroline International, the station that's way ahead of its time, on 3 8 9. And if you don't believe me, listen to this . ." Just as the jingle started the transmitter cut out, due to the falling voltage.

Paul Alexander & Andy Archer in the Caroline International studio

"That f***ng generator, it's knackered my links again" he said in exasperation at the fourth failure that day. The fall in supply voltage from the generator had tripped the transmitter out, seconds before the lights dimmed in the studio and the sound failed. The studio didn't monitor 'off air' and Paul thought his appalling expletives had gone out on air. No one swore on the air in those days! Kate Cary and Andy Archer were in the studio and were at first shocked and then just laughed at his embarrassment. They assured him that he wouldn't be sacked for it.

It was to be the last time 389 was heard on the air for a couple of years. The 259 service had gone off the air at the same time but was in the middle of the 'Caroline Classic' service at the time, so the audience may have been quite small.

The downtime was not wasted and the crew were set to disconnecting the offending generator in the engine room to make way for a new one. It had been well-butchered by then so was decreed useless and hoisted by hand from the engine room. The work took quite few hours as it weighed over a ton. Eventually, it was held suspended over the side of the ship while Michael Wall-Garland read one of his poems over the now silent beast, as a prayer. With a splash the generator was consigned to the deep (engineer Teun Visser called the process a soak test!).

Algreco generator

When replacement generators arrived, they were rented from a big firm called Algreco who gave a guarantee – they supplied two for the price of one, but only one must be used. Some hope of that! As these were too large to be installed in the engine room, they were mounted on the stern deck, just behind the wheelhouse.

To protect the generators from the wave sand the weather, a framework was built around them and later most of it covered in. It never suppressed the sound though and a careful ear could usually hear it when the microphone was opened. It became a sound unique to Caroline, although millions of listeners may never have recognised it.

16. Return to Atlantis

Early in July Radio Caroline was offered a contract to broadcast a Flemish service, to be called Radio Atlantis. The station was not connected in any way with the Radio Atlanta organisation who had run Radio Caroline South nine years previously – this new station was owned by a Belgian businessman called Adriaan van Landschoot. He operated several companies, almost all of which were called Carnaby.

Adriaan's record and music publishing company were both called Carnaby. He also had a chain of boutiques called *Carnaby Jeans and Jackets* and other textile operations. He wanted to advertise on Radio Veronica but they quoted him such high fees for airtime that he decided it would be cheaper to open his own radio station.

Adriaan was also very keen to launch his own career as a singer and had his fingers in various other pies in the music business. He released several singles, not always using his own name.

One example was AD ROLLS, a name he used for the song *Taxi*. The cover of this Barclays Records single features his own Rolls Royce car, with his picture on the front and number plate with the digits '385' in it.

Adrian and a song about his Roller

Ronan was happy to rent out the air time on one of the two transmitters on the Mi Amigo and quickly agreed a deal for a hefty three month 'upfront' payment. The original deal was for Radio Atlantis to use the 389m wavelength which had just been proved to give good reception over the Benelux countries. The final work on the triangular mast went ahead and a pair of new generators were installed on the poop deck, right at the back of the ship. A new fuel day tank had to be added, but by the middle of the month the installation was just about complete.

New tubes were obtained for the 50kW transmitter but it could not operate on the 389m channel (773 kHz) in time for the big launch, planned for Sunday 15th July. As is the Radio Caroline tradition, non-stop Beatles music was broadcast throughout the test transmissions.

radio
385 atlantis

After a few hours, Radio Atlantis 385 took to the air at 12 noon but on 259m. This was probably the first time an offshore radio station had opened 'on time', even if it was the wrong frequency! The launch of the new Radio Atlantis went ahead on 259m, which infuriated Adriaan and his team. They were told that the 389 crystal had been misplaced on the ship after being used as a chess piece and seemed to believe that.

Many of the Atlantis programmes for the first week had been made with the wavelength quoted as 385m. Huge batches of car stickers and other publicity had also been started with 3 8 5 as the dial position, however the station was now up and running on '259' and there it stayed. Chris Cary calculated that this left the way open to restart an international Top 40 music service on 389, which got much better coverage per kilowatt of output power.

The station had also taken the P O Box 385 address in its home town of Oostburg in Holland, where they had studios in the Nieuwstraat. Oostburg is the first town of any size as you drive over the border from Belgium, which lots of fans did that summer to see the new superstars of the Medium Wave. One condition of the airtime contract with Radio Caroline was that Adriaan had to take on two of Caroline's DJs from the Dutch service, Joop Verhoof and Bert Bennett. They were joined by Belgians, Luc van Kapellen and Tony Houston.

The main Radio Atlantis DJ team

Also involved with the Radio Atlantis launch was Steve England, one of the best Top 40 DJs that Caroline had at the time and a master jingle craftsman. He made some superb stand-alone jingles but also produced many commercials and the station theme tune, which comprised various Radio Atlantis drop-ins over the Shadows' third instrumental hit, *Atlantis*.

Ronan then decreed that Caroline's Top 40 service be dropped, "Maybe we can put it back on the air next year, when we have made some money out of this Dutch relay service," he told disappointed DJs. He explained that he did not want the new customer Radio Atlantis to feel threatened by a rival Top 40 service in English, even if it was the real Radio Caroline.

Discussions at Caroline HQ in early July had centred on the return of the Top 40 service, which Chris and most of the other more commercially minded Caroline team felt would be a money spinner. Most of the team believed that this was a continuation of the Radio Caroline that had been snatched from them in 1968 by the Wijsmullers.

Chris Cary's view was that Caroline should not be simply a transmission service for other stations, but that the ship and all the hard work done should be broadcasting Radio Caroline. He had the backing of most of the English DJs who wanted to help return Radio Caroline to its pole position.

For Chris, the last straw was Ronan's agreement to allow the night time hours on 259 to be taken over by the people from *Radio Geronimo*, a progressive music station run by Hugh Nolan and Barry Everitt. They planned to launch another new station from the Mi Amigo.

This was an idea that had been precipitated by Tony Secunda, a well-known music producer and friend of Ronan's. He had managed several well-known groups from an office at Caroline House in the sixties, including The Move. Ronan encouraged them in a futile battle with Harold Wilson which involved printing thousands of postcards showing Wilson in a compromising position with his secretary, Marcia Falkender. The Move lost a libel case as a result and had to give all the royalties from the *Flowers in the Rain* record to Harold Wilson.

Over a lunch at *The Casserole* (the restaurant on the Kings Road where Ronan transacted most of Caroline's business), Tony Secunda had reminded everyone about Radio Geronimo. This was a short-lived radio station he had funded over the transmitters of Radio Monte Carlo. It played exclusively alternative and progressive music and used a studio in Harley Street with presenters Hugh Nolan and Barry Everitt.

Secunda persuaded Ronan that the name Caroline was out of date and should be dropped and a new progressive station substituted, called Radio Seagull. One of the key proponents of this radical change to Caroline's output was programme chief, Andy Archer.

your all night music station

RADIO SEAGULL

on 259 metres

Radio Seagull was named after Richard Bach's inspirational fable, 'Jonathan Livingston Seagull' and chosen because of its nautical theme. Chris Cary could not see any future for the ship just transmitting two other 'non-Caroline' stations. He felt strongly that Caroline should be popular and commercial, however he and Ronan could not agree. Radio Seagull was launched on the 24th July, without a fanfare – just some cool groovy music overnight.

"Ronan didn't really think the Radio Seagull project would succeed," explains Norman Barrington, who had now been with Caroline for six months. He favoured non-commercial music and album tracks and was easily able to fit into the Radio Seagull team. "Ronan agreed to the new programmes only if it used another name and so didn't tarnish the reputation of Radio Caroline."

Radio Atlantis' financial contribution was vital to keep the Mi Amigo at sea and operational. Ronan made it very clear to the staff that Radio Seagull should not even try to become a commercial success, which might have compromised the relationship between the Caroline organisation and Atlantis. Adriaan van Landschoot had signed a thirteen-week agreement with Radio Caroline for their programmes to be broadcast daily from 6am to 7pm for £25,000.

Chris Cary felt that he could not hang around unless Caroline had a commercial outlet so he and Kate returned to England in mid-August. Chris's secretary, Charlotte Ribbelink, assumed control of the office in the Hague.

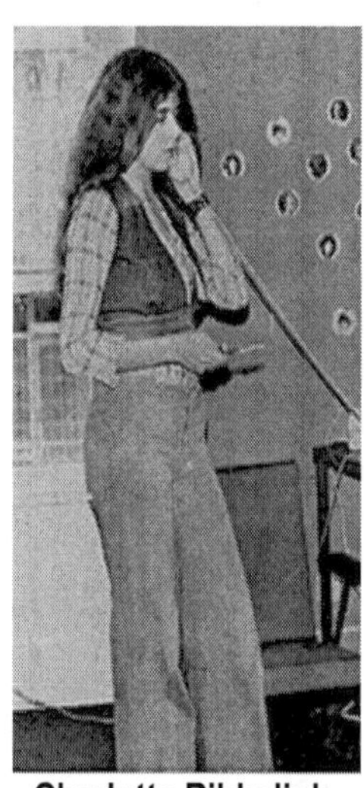

Charlotte Ribbelink
Peter Messingfeld

Charlotte, a pretty girl still in her teens, had only been with Caroline for six weeks but she was very sensible, capable and could turn her hand to most things. She became the Dutch representative of station owner Ronan O'Rahilly ,as she was multi-lingual and had good administrative skills that belied her young age. Elija van der Berg took over the vast Radio Caroline record library, managed some finances of the station, hired DJs for Seagull and liaised with the record companies.

Radio engineering on the ship was still in the hands of Peter Chicago along with his assistant Bob Noakes. The ship was still run by Dick Palmer but he left just after Chris and was replaced by Captain Meyer.

The ship's marine engineering and its vital pair of power generators were in the capable hands of Peter van Dyken, Jaap de Haan and Mike Phillpott. Reception with the completed mast and re-tubed transmitter was excellent across the whole of Belgium, the Netherlands and the whole eastern side of the UK. After dark the Radio Seagull programmes were widely heard across Europe and further afield.

Sadly, there were frequent breakdowns, to the annoyance of Adriaan van Landschoot, who had paid £25,000 to have the ship broadcast Radio Atlantis programmes. Radio Seagull received wide acclaim in some quarters for its *avant garde* sound and sheer difference to other stations, which relied more on playing non stop hits. The Times Newspaper gave it an accolade of "best station on the air', and there were more compliments and support from the music business.

John Witney was not so happy: he ran CNBC in the sixties was now MD of the new ILR station, *Capital Radio*. They were about to launch in London in a few week's time and he complained bitterly to the IBA that their allowing Radio Seagull and Caroline to continue broadcasting would affect his station's viability before they even got on the air. The IBA of course had no jurisdiction over stations on the high seas; they had in fact decided to put Capital Radio temporarily on the new Radio Veronica wavelength 538m. The frequency for 538m was 557 (later 558) kilohertz which was pretty clear in western Europe, until Capital's temporary usage spoilt it across a wide area.

Support for Caroline had never been higher and the 389 pop music version of Caroline was expected to be back on the air shortly. The Free Radio Campaign organised a huge rally in London for Sunday 19th August and distributed thousands of leaflets to advertise it.

Radio Seagull's name on the superstructure

Lion Keezer

A 'Caroline Stays Campaign' had similar ideals and was pressing the IBA for Radio Caroline to be given an ILR licence. At that time the IBA had not got any of its stations on the air, only some tests.

The Radio Atlantis programmes quickly won a large audience in Belgium, simply by being in the Flemish language and promoting local artistes. While Flemish is very similar to Dutch, there are many nuances and Radio Atlantis was much more welcome to the Belgians. Although the Belgian Government had a law prohibiting offshore radio, Radio Atlantis was able to circumvent this by recording its programmes just over the border in Holland where there was no such legislation. Many businesses bought air time on Atlantis using a couple of loopholes to avoid prosecution.

Calm seas means swim time for the crew
Ian Anderson

Station boss Adriaan van Landschoot had even more hits on his own labels, some of which became hits in Holland. He sent some of his artistes to compete in events like the *Eurovision TV* song festival with minor success. Several of the releases on Adriaan's labels feature his own vocal attributes, such as “Call Me a Taxi” which was played many times on Atlantis.

Many Radio Caroline DJs also broadcast on Radio Seagull, even the engineering team such as Peter Chicago, Dick Palmer and Bob Noakes. Even the admin manager, Charlotte Ribbelink, was heard on a few programmes, as was her assistant René van Spliff. It was all very ‘free form’ with no playlists at all, nor even a format really – this really was ‘free radio’. A total “free for all”!

Urgent maintenance often went undone as no one took overall charge. Many hadn't a clue about radio, some of them cared little. When an insulator began arcing, it was solved by a fool ‘technician’ chopping off the entire stay! The next event on board was inevitable.

Just after lunch on Monday October 1st, the newly completed triangular mast suddenly collapsed. The top three quarters of the 180 foot high structure hung doggedly over the port side of the ship, leaving just a 26 feet section standing. It put all transmissions off the air, for a while anyway. Dick Palmer was urgently summoned from his garage in Kent, even though he had officially left Caroline. Chicago returned from his holiday and they set about making a “quick fix”.

A temporary long wire aerial was erected running from the top of the first section across to the stern mast. It would not accept high power, but it did enable Caroline to complete the 13-week contract with Radio Atlantis.

Triangular mast is circumcised.
Lion Keezer

On board the ship at this time were Johnny Jason, Bob Noakes, Harry Bergman, Tony Allan and Ian Anderson, who had just left RNI and who later opened his own ILR station ion the Shetland Islands.

The Mi Amigo had now been back out at sea for just over a year but, by early October, had already broadcast under six names:

- **Radio Caroline** - part English, part Dutch Top 40 station
- **Radio 199** - a local service in Dutch and English
- **Radio Veronica** as a relay while their ship was beached.
- **Caroline International** - an international Top 40 station
- **Radio Caroline** - a Dutch language easy listening service
- **Radio Atlantis** -Pop and easy listening for Belgium
- **Radio Seagull** - international progressive / album station

Transmissions in October were identified using three further names:

- Joepie
- Station 385
- Radio Mi Amigo

These short tests were for a new client who wanted their own station.

Radio Atlantis often complained about even the shortest amount of downtime; these breaks usually went unnoticed on board the radio ship. Many of the crew were under the influence of various herbs and chemicals and few of them monitored the daytime transmissions. Few, if any, were commercially minded and were happy to enjoy the life on board, letting others worry about such mundane things as supplies.

Adriaan van Landschoot was unimpressed with Radio Seagull; he set up a recording studio for his DJs in Oostburg, near the Belgian border. He had been planning to set up his own ship and had already found a suitable vessel. He refused to renew his contract with Radio Caroline. He took his new ship to Germany for fitting out but it took them until Christmas to start transmissions and then only on very low power. It was a far worse signal than they ever had from the Mi Amigo.

A New Amigo

Bart van der Laar

Bart van der Laar worked for a Belgian music company called Start Records. He had bought some record plays for their artists on Radio Atlantis and Bart convinced his boss that Atlantis was very successful and that perhaps they should do the same and start their own radio station.;

Bart's boss was Sylvain Tack, a Belgian entrepreneur who not only owned the record company, Start Music, but other businesses too, mainly in textiles and confectionary.

Bart van der Laar was sent to investigate how Atlantis managed to transmit with such high power, when offshore radio stations were prohibited in Belgium. As part of his investigation, Bart bought time for some experimental programmes for a few hours in October. They were only short, one hour, programmes that Caroline had relayed in the early evening, after Radio Atlantis closed down for the day and before Radio Seagull opened.

On the first day, Bart identified the programmes as *Joepie*, the name of Tack's Belgian music newspaper. This was aimed at young people and run with the editor from the Pers Groep, Guido van Liefferinge. The paper had been set up by Guido and Sylvain Tack, as retribution against another music magazine that had insulted Tack many times.

The next day the station adopted a firmer identification and was referred to as *Station 385* (it seems that Bart still thought it would be the transmitter on second frequency, 773 kHz). Many of the records played in the 385 show were from *Start Records,* a music company owned by Sylvain. He was paying for these short test programmes because Radio Atlantis were charging too much money for plays of his records.

On the third night, a more formal name was chosen - Radio Mi Amigo. There was a favourable reaction to these trial broadcasts, and these convinced Tack to go ahead. He was very keen on having a full-time radio station of his own and a meeting between him and Radio Caroline was convened in the swanky restaurant at the top of the Japanese Okura Hotel in Amsterdam.

Charlotte Ribbelink had to act as an interpreter as Tack spoke almost zero English, about the same amount of Dutch that Ronan could manage! He was a successful waffle baker and music impresario and he offered 40 million Belgian francs to buy the ship outright.

Sylvain Tack

Charlotte knew that Ronan would never sell the ship as he was by now totally in love with the vessel, having first visited the Lady in Galveston ten years previously, in June 1963.

When Sylvain immediately agreed to the sale, Ronan panicked and claimed that an outright sale would take too long as it would involve lawyers in several countries such as Liechtenstein and Panama, who operated only very slowly. He suggested some other terms, including payment of two million Belgian Francs, paid within two days.

It took several hours to reach an agreement, but eventually a deal was done. Radio Mi Amigo would broadcast from the ship instead of Radio Atlantis. The only problem was, the ship no longer had an aerial mast. Ronan was able to talk Sylvain Tack out of a plan to fly over the Mi Amigo in his plane, to see the ship by telling him that radiation from the mast would attract the plane like a huge magnet and cause it to crash into the ship, if he flew close!

Adriaan van Landschoot was very angry that he had been usurped by Sylvain and vowed revenge by building a bigger and better ship for his station, Atlantis. The two station owners remained friends however and later Adriaan stood bail for Sylvain to get out of jail, and then bought into his newer ship, the Magda Maria, in 1978.

Sylvain Tack's initial payment to Caroline was used to invest in a new mast for the Mi Amigo. It was of sectional four-sided telescopic lattice construction. It was built by a company called *De Kerff en de Woel*, a wrought iron gates manufacturer.

The order was originally placed by Radio Atlantis who had also handed over a large deposit for the mast. When Mr Landschoot's agent tried to renegotiate a lower price, as they were now also having to buy a ship and transmitter too, the manufacturers refused. They then offered the mast for sale to Radio Caroline.

Charlotte Ribbelink and Koos van Duin quicky drove to the factory and handed over the balance due, in cash. Before van Landschoot's team realised what was happening, the mast was quickly moved.

Mast building

Ronan planned to complete the mast onshore and fly out to the Mi Amigo by helicopter, ready built. The urgency of the situation, the worsening weather and the possibility of any direct action by Van Landschoot convinced the team to take a more conventional route and ship the components out to the Mi Amigo using a regular tender. By the end of November five sections of the nine-section mast had been erected but strong winds and heavy seas prevented erection of the last few sections being erected. It was finally completed on Christmas Eve to its full 165 feet height and powered up. Caroline was on the air for Christmas Day, during which it also rebroadcast some programmes and the news from nearby ship, Radio North Sea.

By the end of the seventies the quayside price was hitting $900 a ton, plus delivery! Fuel oil prices can be very volatile, but the biggest headache for Caroline was often arranging delivery, which is why there were gaps in transmission when oil stocks on board ran low. Due to the volatile situation in the Middle East, OPEC reduced the world supply and the prices almost trebled within weeks. The quayside price had been less than $100 per ton earlier in the year but was now over $400 and there could be delays having it delivered out to the Mi Amigo.

Koos, Leunis and Ronan
Theo Dencker

Offshore radio ships can't simply pop into port and fill up (though Radio 270 did!) and regular bunker barges which deliver to most ships might be prohibited from serving radio ships from the nearest port.

Caroline had recently recruited two very experienced seamen: Leunis Troost and Koos van Duin, who had worked on RNI. They set up their own supply company and arranged for the Mi Amigo to receive a large delivery of fuel oil, at a time when this was in very short supply. Their "can do" attitude, their resourcefulness and flair for logistics was very useful in keeping Radio Caroline on the air through the mid seventies. The mast was soon up and ready for transmitting, just in time for Christmas.

There was no ‘hook-up’ as the previous year; RNI’s management had prohibited any such fraternisation on the air. The attitude of other stations to their competitors and even neighbours has almost always been one-way; Radio London did this, and Laser were later to do so, but most of the workers at the ‘coal face’ simply ignored the instructions from above, followed Ronan’s example and acted in a friendly and usually helpful manner.

The mast was the longest surviving of all radio ship masts and remained erect after the Mi Amigo sank in 1980. It was to be six years afterwards that the mast finally fell, and then only because the superstructure of the ship was corroding. A fine testament to the manufacturers.

Within a few days, test transmissions were under way in earnest for the start of Radio Mi Amigo, which opened at 12 noon on New Years Day, just six weeks after its scheduled start. Radio Atlantis reopened at the same time, with their ‘new’ ship, the MV Janine, from an anchorage just along the coast closer to Belgium, but its low power signal was no match for the huge signal from the Caroline ship on 259. One of Tack’s friends, Tom van der Linden sabotaged their equipment but Tack ordered him to leave Radio Atlantis alone.

The 50kW transmitter of Caroline was now pumping out a massive signal over the Benelux and the UK which attracted millions of listeners for the programmes of the new station which was named after the ship: Radio Mi Amigo. The station’s output was peppered with some news jingles, very professionally produced and which became a trademark of the station for the next four and a half years.

The Radio Mi Amigo jingles were produced by legendary Belgian musician Eddy Govert. An old friend of Sylvain, he was tutored and assisted by Radio Caroline DJ Steve England who had a Sonovox machine that added the distortion and modulation effects to audio.

Eddy Govert

The jingles were recorded in the Start Music studio in Buizingen which was owned by Sylvain. Most jingles were by singers on Sylvain’s label, including Norbert. A full library of jingles was made, many of which were destined never to heard on the air. The recording studio had been set up in the bakery near Ghent that Sylvain had bought for ten million Belgian Francs.

The biggest product from the bakery was by then *Suzi Waffles*, named after Sylvain's wife, Suzanne. She and Sylvain would often be found helping to wrap the waffles, which were the most expensive on the market. Suzanne explained that they made them to a set quality, never down to a low price. They are very sugary confections, covered with a layer of real chocolate and were incessantly plugged on the air. Suzi Waffles were the product that supported the Radio Caroline ship and kept it stocked for the next four years. Suzi commercials were well made, often preceded by a trio of coughs from character that sounded like an asthmatic Jimmy Savile!

Despite this, Sylvain himself never ate the waffles as he found them too sweet. They were laced with sugar and could be very sickly if you ate too many. Ronan O'Rahilly, was also no fan of Suzy Waffles. After first tasting them at the bakery, he confided to a few Caroline DJs "These must be the most sickliest things I ever tasted!"

Radio Seagull programmes continued for a few more weeks, using Radio Caroline DJs as the Radio Geronimo team had abandoned the project. Many well-known Radio Caroline names such as Bob Noakes, Tony Allen and Norman Barrington were joined by Americans Micky Mercer and Mike Haggler as well as Brian Anderson, who had worked for Caroline since the previous summer as a studio technician and for Radio Mi Amigo.

The more obscure album tracks were dropped from programmes before midnight and at the end of February 1974, the name Radio Seagull disappeared too, with the station identifying once again as Radio Caroline.

Eddy Govert also made many commercials for Radio Mi Amigo, including those now iconic Suzi Waffles commercials. Eddy's policy was always to add a short musical or sound effect that would make the commercials memorable. Many of the Radio Mi Amigo programmes for other advertisers were also made in a studio on the first floor of the Suzi Waffles bakery, but some production was still in the Hague. Andy Archer interviewed the Osmonds in Amsterdam and managed to get Donny Osmond to record a "Hi to Suzy Waffles" drop in, which delighted Sylvain Tack.

Eddy was also the man behind the global children's hit '*Kwek Kwek*',by Ronald Y Ronald. It's an energetic ditty that became an 'ear-worm', (so-called as you can't get it out of your ear) that sold millions.

Mi Amigo song with DJ sleeve

It was eddy who Eddy wrote the tune and lyric for the *Mi Amigo Song* that made the Belgian charts. The production was finished by Perre Kartner, better known as Vader Abraham.

The DJs were credited with the vocals, however they were so out of tune that co-producer Norbert sent them off to the bar with a bottle of Champagne while he and Eddy over-dubbed the chorus.

Radio Mi Amigo programmes were going from strength to strength and her main DJs becoming better known than the music stars they spun. Some were already known in Belgium, from previous careers as singers, or from stretches on other stations such as Radio Atlantis. Joop Verhoof started DJing on the Dutch service of Radio Caroline in Summer 73, as had Bert Bennet. DJ Norbert from Brugges was a famous singer with a high profile in Belgium.

Radio Mi Amigo featured its biggest plugs for a new record of the week every hour and called it the Lieveling (darling). Norbert chose as one of his personal Lievelings a track called 'The Hostage' by a new unknown singer, called Donna Summer. She turned up at the Radio Caroline office to thank him personally - this was before she achieved worldwide success with producer Giorgio Moroder.

A new music bed had been composed by three eminent Belgians to mark the daily transition from Mi Amigo programmes into those of Radio Caroline. The tune 'Bronx' was produced by Denis Desrouvres at Studio Damiens in Paris, it was a funky little instrumental (for 1972) arranged by Claude Vallois and conducted by Henri Decker. When it became Radio Mi Amigos filler, all three claimed composer rights.

Radio, the cockroach medium!

Some Radio Mi Amigo jingles and the theme for the popular daily *Baken 16* programme, were derived from la *Cucaracha*, a Spanish ditty about a cockroach. It's appropriate in that radio has been written off and 'counted out' by the press and popular opinion many times over the years. Radio has however, refused to die and has always continued to limp on, as strong as ever. It's survived TV, video and even the smartphone, still attracting the biggest share of the public's attention and consumption. The main reasons are its personality, (radio is perhaps the most personal medium), simplicity and the fact that it can be consumed and enjoyed while doing many other things – driving, work, etc.

At Easter 1974, Caroline was able to celebrate her 10th birthday, by replaying many highlights of the past ten years programmes plus a special interview with Caroline's first ever DJ, Simon Dee. He described Caroline's early days, the weeks waiting in Greenore to sail and those first broadcasts in an interview with Peter Chicago.

The music became more mainstream and the following month Caroline adopted a Top 40 Album format. Playing only tracks by established superstars, it attracted a bigger audience and one that was more appreciative and enthusiastic. By now, the junctions between the end of the Radio Mi Amigo programmes and the start of the Caroline shows in the evening were being filled by two of the technicians who were playing out the pre-recorded programmes; DJs Brian Anderson and Norman Barrington. They hosted programmes called 'Radio Mi Amigo International' for a couple of hours at teatime in English and, for a while, built up an audience larger than either Radio Mi Amigo or Radio Caroline achieved, attracting listeners from both the UK and the Benelux.

Norman Barrington & Brian Anderson
Rob Olthof

Caroline's daily station opener

Emmerson Lake & Palmer had become a firm favourite of many DJs. A new 'station opener' was adopted by Radio Caroline that Autumn: ELP's *Karn Evil 9* from their *Brain Salad Surgery* album:

> *Welcome back my friends, to the show that NEVER ends.*
> *We're so glad you could attend, come inside, come inside.*
> *Come inside, the show's about to start.*
> *Guaranteed to blow your head apart!*
> *By kind permission of Peerless Music Publishing - Keith Noel Emerson / Gregory Lake*

Charlotte Ribbelink was taken ill in 1974 and had to leave Caroline, which now came under control of two experienced Dutch mariners, Koos van Laar and Leunis Troost. They bought the MV Dolfijn which had been one of the regular Radio Caroline tenders and hired Captain Jacob Taal, who had brought the Mi Amigo safely out to sea again after she was hijacked by the previous captain, Will van der Kamp.

Eddy de Boeck took over as Head of Programmes when Andy Archer returned to the Mi Amigo to focus on the English shows. He was a key broker, liaising between the three Caroline leaders of 1973 – Ronan O'Rahilly, Adriaan van Landschoot and Sylvain Tack.

LOVING AWARENESS

Ram Dass,
Father of Loving Awarness

Radio Caroline increasingly referred to 'Loving Awareness' on the air, a concept that Ronan credited to Ram Dass, who was a spiritual teacher and follower of Timothy Leary. The idea behind Loving Awareness is that one has only positive thoughts, you show love towards all others and always have pure and honourable intentions. Ronan expanded the concept, rejecting Destructive Awareness (DA) which is the opposite to LA. Details about the start of LA can be found in the book 'Be Here Now'.

Ram Dass was previously called Dr Richard Alpert, and had been an eminent Harvard psychotherapist and psychedelic pioneer. His new name meant 'servant of God'. He offers many self-training courses and videos to his disciples and is very well regarded. By bringing his concepts to Caroline, Ronan was trying to foster a better world. It was an extension of the 'love' message that Caroline evangelised about in the summer of love, 1967, but the LA was going to be much bigger.

"Our brain has both loving energy and defensive energy," explains Ronan, an evangelist for the concept. "For many years now, we've tapped and used the defensive one and haven't yet fully explored the loving one. LA is about developing a loving habit. Love is, after all, our most natural emotion but it is the one we abuse most. If you give love to other people, they will love you in return."

To promote the somewhat abstract concept of Loving Awareness, Ronan found a group of suitable musicians who he planned to call the New Beatles. They were guitarist John Turnbull, bassist Norman Watt, keyboard player Mick Gallagher and drummer Charlie Charles. He sent them to cut an album in Palm Springs, a tourist resort in California.

After six weeks, the 'New Beatles' band emerged with a new mantle, the Loving Awareness Band and began a rigorous tour of Europe. They earned their stripes playing mainly small venues and emerged as a very capable rock ensemble. Two mop tops (George and John) gave their blessing and helped launch the band financially.

Ronan set up a new record label to promote the music, called *More Love Records*. The Loving Awareness album has since been rereleased as a CD on Ross Records in 1992 and once again, twelve years later, with some bonus tracks on SMC Records, a Dutch outlet for offshore radio memorabilia.

The album has been played often on Caroline ever since. It has a picture of the band and Ronan in a school classroom with Beatles and Kennedy memorabilia. They would later become Ian Dury's backing group, the Blockheads, but continued to perform some LA songs.

L.A. formed an integral part of the Caroline output for many years and is still referred to on the station today by some older presenters. It's now become much more than just promotion of the owner's philosophy and has taken on a life of its own. The idea of love and peace scared some of the team who wanted Caroline to be run on more commercial lines. A plot to take over the station by some former managers and crew was discovered and some of them hurriedly left the ship, including Bob Noakes who joined rivals Radio North Sea.

The station IDs were given a makeover by new American DJs Micky Mercer and Mike Haggler, with a variety of promotion pieces for Loving Awareness. One of the longest lasting has been:

> *"From a point at sea, to the circles in your mind,*
> *A new force is at work for planetary transformation*
> *A new radio for a new earth*
> *Europe's voice for Loving Awareness is Radio Caroline*

To celebrate midsummer, some Caroline DJs decided to promote a free music festival at Stonehenge. The event was talked up on Caroline each evening for a week before and many thousands turned up, according to the police. Mike Hagler was the main proponent: "It turned out just the way I wanted it, " said Mike. "On the Friday night we camped on the Army's property, but it was all totally peaceful."

"I was very pleased with the turnout to the Free Festival," said Ronan. "this was a mid-week event and many of the kids couldn't come as they had exams to sit." Former Radio Caroline DJ Steve England also promoted the festival on rival station Radio Atlantis where, in the spirit of World War III, he invited pensioners to take along their own deck chairs and bring some skinheads and Hells Angels to amuse them!

The Day the Music Died

In August 1974, the Dutch government announced that their new anti-radio ship law would come into effect in September. Three of the radio stations then broadcasting from ships off the Dutch coast made their arrangements to close on the last day of August, although the Act didn't take effect until 17th September. Radio Veronica, Radio Atlantis and RNI all closed down on 31st August, a date that became known to one generation in the Netherlands as "The Day the Music Died"

Radio Caroline of course was different. Very different!

Ronan planned to continue the saga of Radio Caroline. He had faced the introduction of punitive anti-radio ship laws before and found that no action was taken across on the British coast. He was confident that the same would happen again and that supplies for Caroline could be found. The Mi Amigo would continue broadcasting, much as she did before the Dutch legislation came into force.

The owner of Radio Mi Amigo, Sylvain Tack, decided that he too would remain with Caroline and continue his station. He now believed in the principle of free radio and Radio Mi Amigo had been making a lot of money over its short life. Sylvain's record companies and the weekly music paper *Joepie* had thrived thanks to the daily non-stop promotion on 259. His bakery product, *Suzi Waffles* especially, were now very famous across several countries.

Sylvain chose to keep a low profile, in contrast to his friend Adriaan van Landschoot who craved fame and released a flurry of records to mark Radio Atlantis' last week on the air. Sylvain he decided to not take any chances moved his entire operation out to Spain. The first office was to have been in Bilboa, a useful tendering port.

Caroline's Coming Home!

Just days before the end of August, Captain Koos van Laar arrived alongside the Mi Amigo with his sport fishing boat, the Dolfijn. As had happened in 1967, many Caroline DJs decided to leave; only Tony Allen and a few others would stay to battle on.

The Dolfijn tender

The Dolfijn had been one of the tenders used by Radio Caroline and part of a fleet operated from the Tweede Binnehaven in Scheveningen by Rederij Vrolijk. The fleet included the Morgenster, the Zeester, the Fortuna and the Martina. The Dolfijn was now owned by Koos and Leunis and usually skippered by Captain Jacob Taal.

The Dolfijn helped the Mi Amigo raise the anchor and then moved to a new position across the North Sea. Radio Caroline didn't broadcast any programmes that night when Radio Mi Amigo closed due to 'manpower problems'. The big difficulty was a sudden lack of DJs who were willing to move with the ship, into the unknown. Most of the well-known DJs declined the opportunity to stay on and continue broadcasting from an undisclosed location. Ronan had wanted the Mi Amigo to return to the British coast for the past two years, it had always been his intention to moor the ship close to London again.

The anchorage chosen was about 15 miles from the English coast. Comfortably beyond the limits of territorial Waters she would also be out of sight of land, which Ronan hoped might deter action from the UK. The Knock Deep was a clever choice as the ship was protected by large sand banks either side which almost always resulted in calmer seas. Being well into international waters, the ship was closer to the continent, which was potentially helpful for supply runs.

The thinking behind the decision to move the ship back to the UK from the Dutch coast was driven by several thoughts. Firstly, the Dutch Minister had declared that he would not tolerate any stations remaining on the air once the new law took effect, on 1st September. Secondly, it was clear that the second transmitter, to be used for an English service (as the Belgian Radio Mi Amigo insisted on being at high power) would not be strong in London from the eastern side of the sea, but it would be fine off the UK. The big 50 kW transmitter could easily cover its target of the Benelux even from the British side of the North Sea.

Other points considered were that the tender operators did not want the point of supply to be near their own coastline, as they might be closely monitored. 'Out of sight' would be more likely to be out of mind!

The UK had a new Labour government in March in a 'hung' parliament and it was thought likely they might leave Caroline alone this time. Sadly, Harold Wilson won a small majority at a further election in October which bolstered the Labour Party's attempts to kill Caroline off, though they held back from jamming or other direct action.

The Dutch legislation did not take effect until mid-September, as it had to be a fixed time after its publication in the official journal. However, to mark the point at which people thought the new Dutch legislation took effect, at midnight Caroline played the Beatles *All you need is Love* just as Johnnie Walker had done in 1967 when the British MoA took effect. Tony Allen told listeners that Radio Caroline loved them and would continue. The eternal message was:

Whatever the problem, **Caroline Continues**!
As the other three radio stations (Veronica, Atlantis and RNI) one by one closed down, Radio Caroline was left totally alone, with no friendly nearby country to allow the operation of supply tenders. She was now anchored in a lonely stretch of water closer to England but not so easy to reach. Maritime matters of the Mi Amigo were now handled by Koos

and Leunis who had between them skippered other radio ships and supplied most of the others. They were resourceful and very adept – ideal operators of an international radio ship moored out at sea.

The closest country that openly permitted offshore radio ships to be serviced was now Spain, so Sylvain Tack had closed the Radio Mi Amigo studios in Oostburg (south west Holland) and moved his base to Bilboa, later to the tiny resort of Playa d'Aro, in Gerona Province. Some shows were still made at a farm in Opbrakel in East Flanders.

Shortly after Sylvain's move to Spain, he came under a vicious series of attacks in AVRO's *Televisier* Magazine from journalist Wil Simon, which presented him as a big outlaw – a pirate! Like the British, the Belgians pride themselves on their maritime history and have some secret admiration for pirates and buccaneers, so this adverse publicity helped Radio Mi Amigo win more listeners and sell more advertising.

Many of the DJs did not want to move to Spain initially and continued to record their programmes at small studios in Belgium. They were then taken down to Spain on a regular coach and from then integrated with the programmes produced at the Mi Amigo studio in Playa d'Aro. This was constructed by Mi Amigo technician Maurice Bokkerbroek in the basement of Sylvain's villa in Mas Nou and the following year moved into a shop unit in the town where listeners were welcomed.

Radio Veronica's ship, the Norderney, remained at anchor off the Dutch coast for a year. Rumours abounded that she would be used by Radio Mi Amigo, or that Radio Veronica would return, based in Spain on the Caroline model, unless they were allowed time on the Dutch public broadcast networks.

Radio Mi Amigo DJ Norbert in the studio

Royal Mi Amigo!

Media reports helped boost the Radio Mi Amigo audience to be almost six million in the Benelux, by 1975. This was probably because anything 'a little bit naughty' can be assured of attracting a large audience of people, thanks to a human trait of curiosity. It was the cool thing to do, to have Radio Mi Amigo on in the car, in your shop, etc.

Radio Mi Amigo could even be heard at the reception desk of the European Parliament building in Brussels and on the internal feeds of VRT, Belgium's state radio and TV service. Prince Phillipe (who is now the King of Belgium) told fellow students at Oxford that, like all his schoolfriends, he listened to Radio Mi Amigo and some friends had offered him a trip out to see the radio ship on a supply tender!

As expected, a number of the established DJs left but there was no shortage of others willing to take their place and the station continued broadcasting. As far as the listeners could tell, nothing had changed, although the signal across the UK was now much better, and the station had a new mailing address at RADO, the headquarters of Radio Mi Amigo, in Gerona province in Spain.

Most of the adverts continued just as previously. While buying advertising time was illegal, it was quite legal for the station to simply read out information, from adverts in print media, including Sylvain Tack's own weekly pop music paper, *Joepie*.

Radio Mi Amigo had become popular during the first nine months of 1974 by the excellent production quality of its jingles, both those for the station and those for advertising spots.

In 1975 many tourists visited the small Catalonian town of Playa de Aro, to meet the DJ team, which now included Joop Verhoof, Peter van Dam, Stan Haag and his wife Michelle. Sylvain owned a large villa in the Mas Nou, a nearby enclave of millionaires, just inland from the harbour. Stan Haag too had a super villa close by and was visited by hundreds of his listeners, many who had grown up listening to his daily request show on Veronica. Some Mi Amigo shows were recorded in a retail unit in the town and, on weeknights, at the Pacha discotheque, just two km away.

Pacha night club near Playa de Aro

Douwe Dijkstra

By now Patrick Hendricks (Dubateau) had taken over a lot of the administration of the Mi Amigo operation. Patrick was the brother of Sylvain's partner Suzanne so, as a family member, he was trusted and conducted a lot of the financial and contractual arrangements for Radio Mi Amigo, usually transacted in cash and banked in Switzerland.

The "Goud Haantje" (golden chicken) company was one of Mi Amigo's most important clients and their advert was played up to three times some hours. The boss of Goud Haantje was Herman Kramer, who visited the Mi Amigo a few times, always filling up the ship's freezers with his chickens. The radio commercial was pressed on a 7inch single and sold in record stores, with an instrumental version on the B side. Copies still turn up for sale almost fifty years later!

Although sung in Dutch, the jingle was one of the catchiest ever heard on the radio. Translated, it promised that "in ten minutes time you could have something tasty in your room, vacuum-packed and roasted in butter." A direct translation of the ditty declared that "Herman's half-cock is simply not to be simply not to be despised!"

DJ Bart van der Laar was beginning to be falling out of favour within the organisation, thanks mainly to his non-stop partying. Bart would try every kind of drug, washed down with too much alcohol and became very unreliable. His taste for lurid sexual activities and orgies were well-known and brought the attention of the BOB (a division of the Belgian police, charged with hunting offshore radio people). Bart's song writing and record production activities helped to fund his excess. Eventually, in the 1980s, he was murdered, shot in the head in his Hilversum home. His killer was later acquitted after a lengthy investigation and court case.

Another route to get around the Belgian Marine Offences Act was to record programmes for one of several small legal radio stations in Spain that broadcast a few hours a day in Dutch (or Flemish) for tourists from the Benelux. It was claimed to be purely a coincidence that these taped shows somehow made their way out to the Mi Amigo and were played over the air. The contracts never mentioned it.

Johnny Jason and John Mair rejoined the ship just after the new Dutch law came in; Andy Archer also returned as Radio Caroline slowly built up a totally trustworthy team. DJs had to be people who could be relied on to not talk about the support network keeping Radio Caroline on the air. Although 'out of sight' off the English coast, the authorities were no longer turning a 'blind eye'. The heat was building as the UK authorities woke up to the realisation that Caroline was back, on their doorstep and once again pounding out Love, peace and Good Music.

The reason for the renewed interest in Radio Caroline was that the UK had started licencing local commercial radio stations and, having paid such high prices in competitive tendering process to broadcast, the contractors didn't welcome competition. They applied pressure on the British Government to silence Radio Caroline, that was 'stealing their audience' from the Mi Amigo, now sat just outside British waters.

Pressure from the BBC and the IBA was building in Whitehall, from where the civil servants carried out the will of Westminster. Broadcasting was controlled by the Radio Regulatory Department, a part of the DTI, with enforcement being carried on by the Home Office. A special department to thwart Caroline was known internally as Operation Zebra. Caroline's period of high visibility in Holland over the last two years meant that huge dossiers had been built up by the intelligence service. They knew who owned the station, who controlled things and his life in London, though were quite powerless to act.

Many of the Radio Caroline staff were amused by the way their leader often talked in riddles and used alternative names for items. Ronan encouraged everyone to use pseudonyms and not even refer to the Mi Amigo, except by her honoured name "The Lady".

The level of secrecy, of furtiveness and covert actions that Ronan preferred was not paranoia – the secret service really was actively watching his every move. Some of them took their job to stop Caroline just a bit too seriously and were over-zealous in their activities. As long as The Lady remained in international waters and was supplied legally then there was nothing the UK could do to stop her.

Supplies could be run from the large Spanish ports along her northern coast, such as Santander or Bilbao, but it's a three or four day voyage over the Bay of Biscay. Delta Diving took an ocean-going tug down to Bilbao and returned laden with enough supplies for three months. To be worthwhile the amount of fuel, food and other supplies would need to be for longer periods.

Unless an alternative could be found. There was great temptation to run supplies and people in and out of the UK, less than fifteen miles away. Arrangements were made to ferry the Mi Amigo's crew of DJs people directly into the UK and there was no shortage of willing boat owners who would make the trip from the UK or Benelux countries.

SEA CONDITIONS

In those days there was no way to know what the weather would be like at the anchorage, being so far from land and so out of sight of it. Tender operators did not want to make the twelve to fifteen-hour trip from the Benelux countries, only to arrive in the Knock Deep and find heavy seas running that prevented berthing 'alongside and transferring goods and people.

The crew on board the radio ship rarely knew when to expect a tender. The biggest vagary was the weather at the anchorage in the Knock Deep. To assure tender operators that they wouldn't be wasting their time, the hourly weather 'forecast' broadcast for listeners began including details of the sea conditions at the ship's anchorage. The 'sea state' reports continue hourly on all live broadcasts from Caroline's ship today, though it's now simply done as a tradition.

The Blue Meanies, as Caroline staff called the Home Office spies after the characters in the Beatles' *Yellow Submarine* cartoon film, had their first success only a month after the Mi Amigo arrived back off the UK when they intercepted a small boat at Burnham on Crouch. Radio Caroline DJs Andy Archer, Johnny Jason, John Mair and Clive Correll were all questioned under caution. They were warned that they may be prosecuted for offences under the Marine Offences Act.

The Home Office often made surveillance runs out to the Mi Amigo using various chartered vessels, often a police launch or a commercial tug. Up to ten officials usually manned such a run; they would circle the Mi Amigo for up to an hour before they got bored and steamed back to port. They took lots of reels of film, some did emerge and were slipped to Caroline by kind and sympathetic Home Office operatives.

Home Office picture of the Mi Amigo

Those on board realised they were being photographed and often appeared on deck in disguise or simply wearing paper bags over their heads which infuriated the officials, who will have endured about five hours at sea simply to see a ship harmlessly broadcasting music.

The Belgian authorities raided the Mi Amigo studio in Opbrakel, south of Ghent and arrested Patrick Hendricks, Tack's right-hand man, just a few minutes after he had arrived.

Sylvian fled to Spain that same day as he and Suzanne had planned to move there that weekend anyway. Patrick was held in custody and fined two million Belgian francs.

Another tender run was stopped and searched, with the occupants again being reported for breaking the MoA. Radio Caroline had a new radio link man in Essex, used to communicate with the Mi Amigo and he too was prosecuted soon afterwards for infringing the radio regulations. An engineer working for Capital Radio in London was fired from his job after providing technical help to Caroline, as was a BBC employee simply for exchanging information. The Home Office were plucking off the 'low hanging fruit'.

The supply situation improved as 1975 wore on with more small boat owners prepared to run supplies out from the UK. This was often done in the guise of taking out parties of anoraks to see the ship, which was not illegal. Albert and Georgena Hood organised regular trips taking out ten or so enthusiasts at a time.

Sometimes their sightseeing trips would go from Southend, sometimes from Brightlingsea – much depended on the availability of suitable boats. It usually took about four hours to get out to the ship's anchorage in the Knock Deep, a lonely channel between two sandbanks at the eastern extreme of the Thames estuary.

The English service of Caroline was doing well at this time, both for reliability and coverage and in March, popular Radio Concord DJ Don Stevens joined the station. In his trademark cowboy stetson, he cut a distinctive figure. Ronan and Tony Allan had persuaded Don to go out to the ship where his varied music taste and DJing skills proved to be popular with the listeners.

Ronan with Irish DJ Don Stevens and 60's legend Johnnie Walker

New all day English Service

With the stability and affluence brought about by the revenues from Radio Mi Amigo, and from record plugs and a few commercials heard on Radio Caroline now, more equipment was purchased to enable two stations to again be transmitted simultaneously. The 773kHz channel (usually referred to as *Caroline 389*) sprang into life again at the end of August. The ship stopped broadcasting for a couple of days to enable aerial riggers to make adjustments in the mast to permit, once again, use of two frequencies simultaneously.

The tests continued for several weeks, normally with continuous music being heard on 389, but by mid-September regular programmes were introduced. The power could not be raised sufficiently high on 389, as some equipment on the ship needed replacing. The second service stopped in mid-October to await new components but the main service on 259m continued, with a superb signal which brought in reception reports from all over Europe and occasionally even further.

The next month, Patrick Hendricks was arrested again in Brussels. He was collecting a package sent up from Playa de Aro containing tapes to be taken out to the ship. He was released the next day but his home was raided and searched on several occasions. He had to tell his seven-years old son that the prison was just a hotel. "I don't see myself as a criminal," says Patrick. "I am a fighter for free radio. Surely one should not go to prison for that?" Patrick also ran a football club called *FC Mi Amigo* in Halle, near Brussels.

Patrick is certain that he became the fall guy for his brother in law, Sylvain, who the courts felt was dodging his responsibilities for operating the Mi Amigo. The problem was that Sylvain had very publicly told everyone that he was the owner of the Mi Amigo and of the Radio Caroline ship itself. In fact, what Ronan had sold him back in November 1973, was simply the right to operate as Radio Mi Amigo, while the radio ship remained owned by his network of companies registered in Liechtenstein and Panama.

First MOA Prosecutions

The following month, the first ever prosecutions under the Marine Offences Act took place in Southend Magistrates Court. The charges related to the investigations of the Home Office's observation exercise Operation Zebra the previous year. In the cases, DJs Andy Archer and John Mair were fined £100 for broadcasting from Caroline. Former Capital Radio engineer Mike Baker was also found guilty of supplying records and boatman Walter Ord was fined £25 for taking DJs to the ship.

Caroline was by now running an experimental 'German Service' several hours a week. These were produced for long time Caroline organiser Dennis King, who arranged with Jack O'Brien for the shows to be recorded at the AFN studios in Berlin.

Adrift in the Edinburgh Channel

On the second Saturday in November 1975, the Mi Amigo lost her anchor and began drifting. She grounded on a sandbank for a few hours but as the tide rose she came off and began drifting even further.

Many thousands of listeners responded to Caroline's plea for help and called the coastguards. They were fully aware of the situation and had been tracking the ship's progress for some hours as she drifted across the Thames estuary.

The Mi Amigo's engine was running continuously but making little headway against the ebbing tide and a Force 8 gale which was pushing the Mi Amigo further south. Fearing they were about to drift into British Waters just after 10pm, Peter Chicago announced that Radio Caroline would be closing down for a while, as the situation on board was quite desperate but that everyone on board was safe. He thanked the coastguard for all their assistance and cooperation and beseeched listeners not to call the coastguards.

DJ Simon Barrett remarked to listeners that he was a bit nearer home that night as he sat in the studio wearing his lifejacket. Chicago assured listeners and the office in London that everyone on board was safe. There was no danger, but they were uncomfortably close to a navigational buoy and unsure whether they were inside UK waters. The crew were unable to drop the standby anchor until the early hours of the Sunday morning. A second emergency anchor was dropped in the late afternoon, by when she was in the South Edinburgh channel, about eight miles north of Herne Bay.

A 'Port of London Authority' vessel, the Mermaid, came by during the evening and pronounced the Mi Amigo to be a potential danger to shipping. The Mermaid was accompanied by a tug, the Sauria, which offered help, but Captain de Zwart feared that they might tow the ship into port and so rebuffed their help. The Mi Amigo remained silent as the captain believed that they could be just inside British waters.

Home Office intervention

On November the 13th, Caroline's tender arrived and towed the radio ship to a new location, about half a mile north of the South Edinburgh No. 3 buoy. Live programming commenced during the morning but a few hours later, two British boats came out and carried out a survey of the area around the radio ship. One of the boats spoke to the Post Office ship to shore radio station at North Foreland identifying themselves as Home Office officials and instructed that no further traffic should be handled from the radio ship, the Mi Amigo.

The following day, a fast launch brought out a party of 25 people, including police and Home Office officials. After forcibly boarding the Mi Amigo, officials stormed into the radio studio and wrestled the microphone from the DJ, who protested live on the air, as they cut the lead to prevent any further messages being broadcast.

The Home Office officials arrested two disc jockeys (Michael Lloyd and Simon Barrett) engineer Peter Chicago and captain Werner de Zwart. They were taken to Southend Pier and kept at the Police Station overnight. On appearing before the magistrates court the next day each was bailed in the sum of £1,000 and ordered to surrender their passports. When they appeared in court the following month, the Home Office sought permission to seize the ship, should she drift into British waters again, which was granted by the magistrates.

Simon Barrett & Johnny Jason outside Southend court.

The Lady remained at anchor but the skeleton crew of three who remained on board decided to stay off the air until help arrived. Only two days later the ship was adrift once again, and Margate lifeboat was launched to bring off two crew. It was to be six days before a tender reached the stricken radio ship and towed her back to the Knock Deep at a slightly new position, about two miles further north, where two new anchors were installed.

Simon Barratt published a book about his time on the Mi Amigo during the period adrift and subsequent Home Office activity around the ship. *SOS – Ten Days in the Life of a Lady* is long since 'out of print' but, if you can find a copy, it has a detailed look at life on board Caroline in the mid-seventies.

Radio Mi Amigo recommenced operations the same day and that evening Radio Caroline was back on the air, telling listeners about her travels around the Thames estuary and the drama of the last ten days.

A week later on the 1st December the top-most section of the mast fell off. This is a wheel of horizontal spokes that increases the electrical length of the antenna. Its loss caused a mistune and the station was off the air for a few hours while repairs were effected. The station survived the winter very well, with more listeners attracted to 259, following the extensive newspaper given to Radio Mi Amigo and Radio Caroline.

In February 1976 more DJs joined Radio Caroline, including 18 years-old Mark Lawrence recruited from land-based Radio Kaleidoscope. Mark was a genius at audio production and was soon one of the station's most popular voices. Mark was a roadie for Jools Holland's band Squeeze and is credited as producing some of their albums.

A Caroline Road Show was trialled at this time, appearing at a few specially chosen venues in Essex and Suffolk. These were initially on USAF bases, where one could be pretty confident that the Home Office investigators would not have any authority. They were operated by Robb Eden, Robbie Day and former Radio Luxembourg administrator Harvey The Rabbit. The music that went down well was the rock music heard on Caroline. As the events grew in popularity they were rolled out to other venues in many towns across East Anglia and Kent.

Radio Caroline was by now building a new reputation for offering a different kind of radio service to the many new independent local stations that were springing up in some towns. Terrestrial stations tended to rely on current chart singles to attract a reasonable size audience, almost competing with Radio 1 and Radio Luxembourg which followed the same sort of playlist in those days.

The content of most Radio Caroline programmes was album cuts, the DJs ignoring the most bland and over-commercial singles chart artistes such as Abba, who were 'played to death' on almost every other radio station. No one set down playlists for Radio Caroline DJs to follow, but none of them would play the most sugary and bland chart music. For most of them it was a matter of personal taste and their own credibility; all music was chosen wisely, which made for a more balanced station that listeners seemed to enjoy, and for longer periods.

On land however there were problems for Caroline supporters as far away as Liverpool. Ronnie Doyle, Jim Monks and John Jackson-Hunter were each charged with promoting the station or in fact a Roadshow. Mr Monks had simply been displaying a poster advertising the forthcoming event while the other two operated the disco that used the Caroline Roadshow name. All were found guilty but John took his case to appeal. His punishment was increased to a suspended prison sentence plus £500 costs. He served a 60 day prison sentence in jail for refusing to pay the costs of the appeal, and went on hunger strike.

This underlines the various hardships that many supporters of Radio Caroline on shore would endure just to show their support for the station. Caroline was of course, over the horizon, out of sight and in International Waters. The only link really was via the radio transmitters, over crackly old Medium Wave but still Caroline fans would go to the most amazing lengths.

Radio Mi Amigo programmes were by now at their most popular ever in the Benelux with no real competition. Jan van de Meer and Bart van Leeuwen headed a team of DJs that included Stan Haag, Peter van Dam, Marc Jacobs, Frank van der Mast, Michelle and Haike du Bois. Record companies were paying top prices for plug records on the station while the 'Mi Amigo Lieveling' brought in over 5,000 guilders alone for its once every hour promotion slot. The leading Dutch record companies were all supporting the station, it was giving essential exposure in the competitive Benelux market.

In Holland, Caroline support staff faced a few problems, after the Mi Amigo's drifting the previous November. Captain Jaap Taal who had previously skippered the Mi Amigo, was charged with helping the ship to get back into international waters and fined a thousand guilders. The owner of the tender used to tow the ship back, the Dolfijn, was Koos van Laar who was fined two thousand guilders.

Caroline was promoted in Belgium by the *Mi Amigo Drive In Show*, run by Patrick Valain from his office in Ghent. During Summer 76 it played at venues all over the Benelux, sometimes with guest live acts, but usually with a couple of DJs. The Mi Amigo Drive in Show commanded big fees from venues such as the *Casino* in Breskens, the *Boudewijnpark* in Brugge, *Der Heidens* in Oostvoorne and the popular *De Verenigingsgebouw* in Rockanje.

At some Mi Amigo roadshow gigs, DJs from the English service of Radio Caroline could be seen too; Nigel Harris and Tom Anderson were very popular while Norbert and Patrick Severs pulled the best crowds of the Belgian DJs as they would often sing live.

Norbert had several chart hits in Belgium and ran his own nightclub. Some nights the Mi Amigo Drive-In Show had three units out in separate venues and each of them were usually packed. In the first three months of 1976 they sold 20,000 T-shirts alone, plus a lot of other products, including records of the Mi Amigo jingles as well as artists of the Start Music company.

As well as the popular *Mi Amigo Drive In Show*, thousands of people joined the Mi Amigo Fan Club, which was operated from Vinkestraat in Wevelgem, near Kortrijk. Members could also obtain copies of the *Mi Amigo Fanblad*, a monthly mini magazine with details of DJs, artists and advertisers. It was also the source of the Mi Amigo Top 50, and the Mi Amigo *Lievelings* (darlings) which was the Belgian equivalent of a *Caroline Sureshot.*

One of the most popular radio shows ever began on Radio Mi Amigo in July 1976, Kassaspel (Cash Casino), which had been so popular on Radio Caroline in the sixties. "Win hundreds of guilders or thousands of Francs" ran the slogan, and many thousands of listeners joined in the cash game each Sunday morning (it later changed to Kassa Cash Casino). Listeners called Peter van Dam at the studio in Spain and had to guess a mystery sound – every error boosted the prize pot by a hundred guilders or a fifteen hundred Belgian francs.

The commercials heard from the Mi Amigo were just as popular as the records so were pressed up as 45rpm single records and sold in record stores. The five minutes of the week's top commercials played on one side while the B side played some Mi Amigo jingles.

Like the magazine, the record was called *PopTelescoop* and, was also widely available all over the Benelux. Excerpts from the record were played often by Radio Mi Amigo, which proved a good way to circumvent Belgium's law. When a client paid for their commercial there was never a contract saying it would be heard on the radio, just that the discs would be sold in record shops. It was a clever ploy to side-step the Belgian legislation that dated from 1962. Advertising space in the magazine commanded a premium price and was booked well in advance.

The Radio Mi Amigo organisation was not large enough to cope with all the interest and not from an office a thousand miles away. A lot of work in Belgium was done by the Mi Amigo Fan Club, run by Mireille Demeester and Fernand Moerman from an office in Wevelgem.

A weekly show called *Verenigen Vor Virije Radio*, (Friends of Free Radio) was produced each week by Baffle, a radio magazine headed by Jean Luc Bostyn, Frans Schuurbiers and others which is still active today and known as Radio Visie. When Mi Amigo's PD, Joop Verhoof left, the role was taken over by Peter van Dam, who replaced the actualities with music, on orders from Patrick Valain, who then replaced the club with his Maeva Road Show.

Being at sea was not all hardship and work. With only a small marine crew on board, the DJs had to help with the various nautical tasks: not simply painting and keeping the ship clean, but the daily grind of hand pumping fuel oil around the different tanks to ensure she stayed 'trim' and upright. Occasionally leaks had to be fixed, for the Mi Amigo was by now over fifty years old and the electrolytic action of the large RF current to the sea was corroding the hull in some parts, this was particularly a problem around the engine room, where a new section had been placed in the ship to extend her some years before.

Life could still be fun however and almost everyone who served on the Mi Amigo reports how satisfying it was to be bringing good music in a free atmosphere, free of control. The adventurous could take the ship's small dingy across to the two sand banks that lay either side of the Knock Deep. These dried out at very low water and it was possible to have a short game of cricket or soccer but there were many lost balls!

Peter Chicago was very brave and would sometimes go off on his own in the ship's dinghy, for fishing or simply to get off the ship. Once the outboard motor wouldn't start for his return and the crew called the coastguard saying they had seen a dinghy in trouble.

Chopper 166 winches Chicago back on board

Within minutes a Sea King helicopter from RAF Manston was overhead. They picked up Chicago and Frank van der Mast and winched them back onto the Mi Amigo.

When the matter of the ship being boarded came up in court, Peter realised that the Home Office had seized the logs from the ship which he had personally signed the previous year. He pleaded guilty to charges of maintaining the transmitters. DJ Don Stevens was fined £50 for making programmes although he had by then moved to Israel to work on the Voice of Peace.

DJ Johnny Jason was charged under the clause of the Marine Offences Act that deals with live broadcasts from the ship. When Johnny's barrister pointed out that it was impossible to prove he had broadcast live, the judge ordered the jury to find Johnny 'not guilty.' This was not to be the first time the prosecutors had tried to squeeze charges using an inappropriate clause of the Marine Offences Act.

At Southend coiurt Ronan O'Rahilly and several dozen Caroline supporters were in attendance. It was a very crammed courtroom that heard the Home Office demand that the ship be forfeited, despite her now being back on the High Seas. After some legal debate, the magistrates agreed that if the Mi Amigo was to be found broadcasting again in British waters without a licence, then the ship could be seized. A chilling thought!

Almost as soon as he got back out to the ship, Chicago began working on the new equipment that would enable a second service to be transmitted from the Mi Amigo. Instead of the 389m channel used for tests six months ago, the ten kilowatt unit was now retuned to 199m, Radio Caroline's first ever wavelength. These then moved down to Radio Veronica's original wavelength, 192m and intermittent non-stop music was broadcast for most of April 1976.

By the middle of May, everything was ready for a return of Caroline's new all day service of English language programmes on 192m, next to Capital Radio on 194m. DJ Tony Allan returned to the Mi Amigo to oversee the relaunch.

The Mi Amigo in her '319' days

Caroline's 192 service was sufficiently powerful be heard across southern England while *Radio Mi Amigo* continued at the full 50 kilowatts with its service for the Benelux countries. At night this transmitter also carried the Radio Caroline (English) service.

Caroline Homes

The first Caroline Home in Hackney

With some of the revenues from Radio Caroline, Ronan felt an urge to do something very philanthropic for his adopted home town of London. By the mid seventies, the cost of housing was soaring, meaning many young people were unable to get onto the property ladder. A small apartment then cost a considerable sum so Ronan gathered some of his contacts to help alleviate this problem.

One of those who was keen and enthusiastic to help was Sonny Karanjia, an architect heavily involved in the social housing world of the Housing Association movement. Ronan asked him to design a prefabricated home that could be built for £1,000, a sum that quickly turned out to be impossible. Sonny's immediate and expletive riddled response was not to waste his time, but as it was Ronan and, anything was possible in his world. He agreed to meet up, assuming he would soon get bored with this bizarre idea and move on to something else.

"Within an hour Ronan was at my office outlining his vision and half an hour later I was hooked and convinced that this was not as crazy as it sounded," remembers Sonny. "Ronan had somehow got involved with two 'larger than life' eccentric inventor/engineers called Mal Lewis and Victor Thomasson. Victor had the patented rights for a light-weight concrete with exceptional thermal and handling qualities called Slabcon. Mal, with questionable patent rights, had invented a moving floor which, through a counter balancing mechanism, converted into a wall. Ronan wanted me to take both these unique processes and mould them into a prefab home easily transportable and to high standards- and maintaining the £1000 build cost!"

Sonny being involved in social housing saw the huge advantages in taking this further forward as there was such high demand for low cost housing. That was the start of the Caroline Home Team!

Victor's invention was being tested on the Army shooting ranges at Hythe in Kent where it proved to be a huge success in its application as a fast track method of producing large scale light weight panels, only for them to need rapid replacement after destruction by Army shells. These panels were eminently suitable for production on a small-scale production line with simple techniques designed by Victor.

The Caroline Homes team by then included engineer Arthur Crowe whose role was to ensure that the proposed prefab unit would get approval, as new stringent rules applied after the aptly-named Ronan Point disaster in East London. Another recruit was Sonny's colleague Dinos Horratides who took on the task of getting the wall floor mechanism adapted to fit into the design development.

"Extensive research was done to establish the market competition in both the housing needs and pre-fabrication sectors. After a month, it was apparent that the ingredients making up the Caroline Home were well ahead of the market. The construction industry was very opposed to pre-fabrication due to bad press around concrete panel wall failures. The team felt that, with the right press exposure and branding, this downside could be overcome. There was no better market branding available than that achieved by Radio Caroline."

They formulated a solution and decided to press on regardless to the prototype stage. Builder Jeffery Davis was a perfect partner being a keen Radio Caroline addict. Enthusiasm was a key ingredient as everyone was still working on a 'pro-bono' basis; it was simply the excitement of the Radio Caroline branding, all roped together by Ronan's energy and optimism that ensured everyone responded to the project's needs with 'loving awareness'.

To help market the product, Ronan persuaded Hackney Borough Council through one of its senior officers Merlyn Williams to host the prototype. Through a friend's partner, Ronan secured permission to place the unit on some ground in the Conservatives heartland, on one of the 'old money' blue blood family estates.

"A coach was laid on to transport a contingent of Hackney councillors (mostly Labourites) to the solidly Conservative heartland of the Cotswolds - only Ronan could have achieved this," says Sonny Karanjia.

Schoolkids storyboarded the project (Caroline TV in the air, & LA abounds)

"Teetotal Ronan began to extoll the virtues of the Caroline Home to councillors, the majority of whom had imbibed vast quantities of liquid refreshments."

"I still recall the horror on the face of Ronan's friend as a mildly tipsy councillor stumbled head-first into a valuable, painting whilst holding on to a glass of vintage port!" said Sonny. "The viewing was however a brilliant success and the Caroline Home got its first seal of public sector approval."

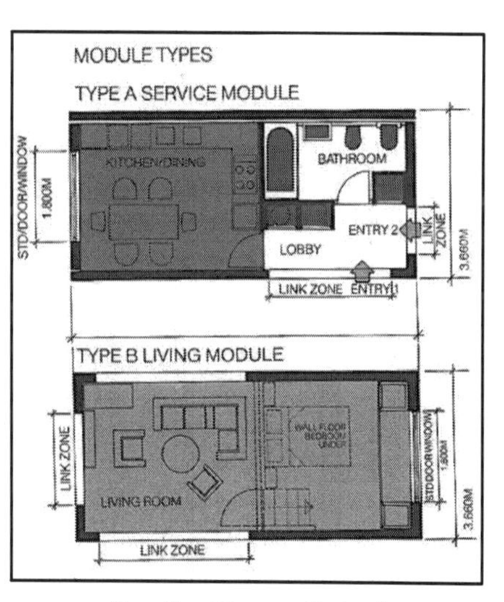

Caroline Homes floor plan

Hackney were so impressed that they decided to allocate a site of over an acre, close to their offices on Mare Street so that a real- life example of the unit could be erected. They also provided a young family from their waiting list so that they could be involved in the development process. The client could also choose décor and furniture early in the process, unheard of in local authority housing in the seventies. The young married couple were overwhelmed with the attention they were being given by the team and that they could select bathroom fittings and kitchen white goods.

The second prototype began at the Thomasson works at Hythe in Kent. The media were primed and seemingly the entire senior staff of the housing department at Hackney along with the full Council were invited to the opening. "On the way to Hythe for a pre-opening inspection of the unit, I asked Ronan which kitchen white goods he had managed to secure, and had they been delivered," said Sonny. "We were on a south London high street when Ronan realised that he had totally forgotten the white goods. Luckily (the luck of the Irish, no doubt!) we were right outside one of the showrooms of a national white goods supplier. In the heavy traffic, Ronan jumped out of the car and headed straight for the showroom. I park up and followed him in and find him in deep conversation with the store manager."

"We left a half hour later with Ronan not only getting all the white goods required, but not paying a penny for them! He had in minutes convinced the manager to put a shop sticker on all the goods as he would ensure they would get full TV coverage at the opening the next day." In Hythe, the supplier's van drove in with a set of white goods, fully supplier publicity sticker branded and ready for installation.

"O'Rahilly had done it again and said to me never question the 'power of loving awareness'," says Sonny. "He was beyond doubt the very best of the best persuaders in the hard-nosed world of construction."

The Council had decided not to publicise the launch but there was keen interest from passers-by. It was an unbelievable success with no adverse criticism from the press, only amazement at the innovative product that had appeared from nowhere.

The £1,000 cost per unit had however become a more feasible £25k per unit yet Hackney Council and some other boroughs still wanted to start placing orders. They didn't realise that behind all this was a small team with a tiny workshop in Kent that would be hard pushed to produce 20 units a year, let alone the thousands Ronan had promoted.

Much talk and strategy meetings followed immediately after the Hackney episode. Production numbers were being evaluated, costs analysed, factory site locations adjacent to a shipping outlet were being sought and within weeks if not months what had started as the first market fact finding exercise was being spoken about not only on national terms but on an International level.

"Regrettably, the ultimate investment required at the scale being envisaged was too high risk for the funding market," said Sonny Karanjia. "Ronan continued his efforts to secure the funds required but sadly, after six months, the Caroline Homes project was history. Had the investment been secured, the Caroline Home would have been developed much further and would have been the front runner by years in what, today, is a hugely successful prefabricated homes market."

Sonny Karanjia - Caroline Homes' architect.

Sonny has spent many years as a hard-working and much respected Housing Association Director in the social housing market. He retired after 29 outstanding years with the Paddington Churches Housing Association (rebranded as *Genesis HA*) by which time the association had in excess of 25,000 homes.

Many commercials were being broadcast on Radio Caroline. Jumbo Records of London were a production house offering souvenir recordings of the station's previous broadcasts. Campaigns for Levi's Jeans and Wrigleys Gum were also heard on Caroline, plus Coca Cola, Mazda cars, Martini aperitifs, Andy's record shop in Norwich and Budweiser beer.

Stuart Russell joined the station at this point, straight from school. Stuart has been one of the station's most loyal broadcasters and is still with the station today. He jointly holds one of the longest serving records with Roger Matthews having completed a stint of 14 weeks all buy one day on board the ship.

Later, Stuart wrote a lengthy article in the second edition of the Caroline Newsletter, in which he described life on the Mi Amigo, describing the dimensions of the ship in strides – fifty or sixty end to end and a width of fifteen strides.

Stuart Russell

"We all share the mess-room for food and recreation. There is always a lively, but happy atmosphere aboard," said Stewart. "Anybody who feels moody and unsociable can retire to their cabin and know that nobody will violate his privacy."

In the article, Stuart confirmed that normally there are no girls on board. "Our listeners regard this as one of our most pressing problems. Some picture us like caged lions, drooling hungrily, twitching our tails viciously and poised to launch ourselves overboard at the mere glimpse of a pretty girl approaching in a small boat," said Stuart.

"Others picture us as some kind of castrated saints, denying our beastly passions and embracing sexless, idealistic uplifting things. It's not like that at all!" When he left the ship in 1978 Stuart continued appearing on the Caroline Road Show gigs in the UK and, the following year, in Holland and Belgium, where he had built up quite a following.

On the 14th June, Tom Anderson was heard on Radio Caroline for the first time. He was to become one of the station's most popular voices in the 70s and 80s and was one of the four men rescued from the Mi Amigo when she sank in 1980. Tom was given the honour of being the first DJ on the air when Caroline resumed from the new ship in 1983.

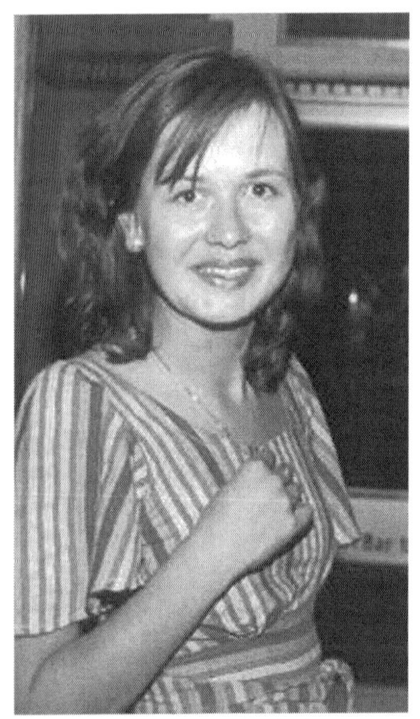
Samantha Dubois

The station had a trouble-free summer in 1976 with record temperatures being recorded on land as well as out on the ship. The DJ line up by now included James Ross, Kenny James, Stuart Russell, Steve Kent and Chicago's girlfriend, Samantha Dubois.

Samantha wasn't her real name; she had been born in New Zealand to Dutch parents and usually lived with her grandmother in the Hague. She was great fun on board and renowned for her frank observations on life and impeccable music taste on the air. She had worked on the ship since 1973 and was to return in the 1980s.

Samantha was popular among listeners and crew, a warm friendly girl with a bubbly personality. She never hid her feelings and was also well known in Holland, especially when she allowed her home address to be used by Radio Caroline for a time.

Earlier, several of Samantha's former colleagues who clearly bore a grudge, or wanted to protect their own positions, signed statements for the Dutch police confirming that she was working as a DJ on Radio Caroline. She was then fined a thousand guilders, with the alternative of being sent to jail. Samantha disappeared off out to the ship, but her Grandmother paid the fine on her behalf.

On 10th September a Force 9 gale blew up and sent a huge wave crashing over the side of the ship. It smashed the porthole in the studio used by Radio Mi Amigo. A deluge of water inundated the studio, damaging the mixer panel and soaking DJ Marc Jacobs. For a few days, their programmes had to come from the Radio Caroline studio.

During the Caroline programmes that evening the weather worsened and the Captain panicked and ordered the DJ broadcast for help. Chicago came on the air to announce that the appeal for help had been premature and things were fine. In fact, the ship was at that moment aground on a sandbank. A tender came alongside and Captain de Zwart left first, shouting to the Dutch to join him. Four Englishmen (Peter Chicago, Ed Foster, Tom Anderson and Mark Lawrence) stayed on board, baling out the ship by hand using buckets, as there was as much as six feet of water in some areas.

The tender remained nearby for a day and then sailed off to Ostend. An official boat came by to offer help, expecting to find the Mi Amigo abandoned. If so, they would have claimed salvage rights and taken the ship into port. The crew on the Mi Amigo offered the visitors a bottle of whiskey but their captain refused the gift.

After a few days two tenders arrived back at the Mi Amigo, with a new crew and captain. They also had a massive main anchor, a large reserve anchor and a release chute that was installed on the ship's starboard side. The main anchor held the ship securely for the next three and a half years. The Mi Amigo was sailed back to her regular anchorage, however the ship's engine finally seized up that day and never ran again. It was to be a week before the ship's two stations were able to broadcast again and a while longer before the daytime English service on 192m was back on the air.

Radio Caroline's latest DJ on the return of 192 programmes was Stevie Gordon who, like Tony Blackburn, came from the town of Bournemouth. He had worked in night clubs and bars in Scandinavia before joining Caroline. After a few breaks in Denmark, Steve was back on board the Lady and stayed until the ship sank in 1980, when his was the last voice to be heard from the ship.

Stevie Gordon

In November a National Opinion Poll published in a radio magazine suggested that Caroline now had an audience in the UK of almost 2.5 million. That made it easily the UKs second most popular commercial radio station. Radio Caroline also had around 500,000 listeners on the continent. As the polls don't count listeners under 18 years old, it is reasonable to assume that Caroline now had around five million listeners to the English programmes.

New DJs that month included Birmingham born Roger Matthews who came out to the ship as an engineer. He later helped run the Caroline Road shows in Belgium and had since appeared on stations in the UK, Ireland, Oman and Cyprus. Another popular DJ joining at that time was Mike Stevens who had only worked in hospital radio. He went out to the ship to supervise pre-recorded shows on Radio Mi Amigo but was soon presenting shows on Radio Caroline.

Carl Kingston

Carl Kingston had wanted to join Radio Caroline since his schooldays in East Yorkshire. His dream came true when Peter van Dam began using audio excerpts that Carl mailed to Spain where they were used as the International Pop News on Peter's shows on Radio Mi Amigo. Carl would later (in 1984) join Radio Caroline full time and broadcast live programmes from the MV Ross Revenge.

Late in 1976 some tests were undertaken from the Mi Amigo of another frequency, 962 kHz, which had been used a few years previously by Radio Atlantis when it left the Mi Amigo for its own ship. The test proved inconclusive but everyone was aware that there were problems on the 192m channel, especially after dark. The Caroline 10kW transmitter was insufficient to overcome foreign interference and, in some parts of the UK, especially in London, it was dwarfed by stronger stations.

There was a similar problem in reverse for radio listeners in Ipswich where a new local station, Radio Orwell, had been allocated 257m with a few hundred watts of power, but was swamped by the massive signal from Radio Mi Amigo on 259m.

It was decided to swap the transmitters around, moving the 50 KW unit used by Radio Mi Amigo from 259 to 192, a channel which would still be remembered with an element of nostalgia by listeners in Holland and Belgium. The Radio Caroline transmitter would move it's 10KW from 192m up to 259m, giving a marginal improvement in coverage for the English programme.

10kW and 50 kW transmitters on the MV Mi Amigo

The lower power signal on 259 meant that even the slight gain in coverage due to it being a lower frequency wasn't compensation for the strong signals that came in after dark on the frequency, which was shared with a station in Hungary, which had recently hiked its power. More head scratching was done about possibly moving the Caroline outlet elsewhere in the band, but first more research was needed.

The move also gave considerable respite for Radio Orwell's listeners in the Ipswich area. Ronan believed that this would be a good Public Relations exercise and might prove to the ILR bosses that Caroline was not simply a buccaneering nuisance, as had been suggested at a recent ILR conference. The frequency and transmitter swap took place just two weeks before Christmas, at the time of year when the nights were at their longest and the incoming interference was at its worst.

New Year's Day 1977 brought a special programme for Radio Caroline listeners, a Top 100 Albums of all time. This was drawn up from a poll of readers of Wavelength magazine and from votes from Radio Caroline listeners. Pink Floyd's *Dark Side of the Moon* topped the chart, while their "*Wishing you Were Here*" album was runner up and the Beatles' *Sgt Pepper's Lonely Hearts Club Band* third. The chart was published in Wavelength magazine and as a huge wall poster, available by mail order from the station.

Out in Playa de Aro, a big party was held for the third birthday of Radio Mi Amigo. It took place at Gringo's bar, a local hostelry run by Dutchmen where Mi Amigo and Caroline listeners were always made welcome. Many of the Mi Amigo team could be found there, new and old, including Stan Haag and his wife Nicky, who presented programmes on Mi Amigo as Michelle.

Peter van Dam

By the end of January, Peter van Dam was tired of living in exile in Spain so he and Lieve, his girlfriend, drove back to Belgium where they rented an apartment in Lochristi near Ghent. He had been planning to return to Belgium for some time and had already made some tentative but surreptitious visits for recording, etc.

Peter's programmes were still being broadcast from the Mi Amigo, but the problems he was experiencing, of living in an alien culture and having to record programmes two weeks in advance, were beginning to tell. Returning to the Netherlands, Peter settled in Kappellberg started his own drive in show and worked for the *Decibel Music Company* before returning to radio.

In the Spring of 1977, the Home Office sent a surveillance helicopter out to the Knock Deep and filmed a French trawler delivering food to the Mi Amigo. They sent the information and the film to their colleagues in France who were waiting when the trawler docked back in Boulogne. The crew were charged with supplying the radio ship and, to get bail, they gave the information about who had booked the trip.

When Radio Caroline secretary Oonagh was arrested in Boulogne, the police must have expected it was an armed terrorist they were looking for. They found instead a quiet gentle Irish lady, known to help people, when they arrived 'mob-handed'. "There were six policemen and a dog, just to arrest me! The whole thing was ridiculous," remembers Oonagh. "Especially as Bologne's Chief of Police at that time was a big fan of the station!"

French Court Case.

In Boulogne, the Captain and mate of the French trawler *St Andre de Flanders* which had been filmed by the Home Office spies in a helicopter while supplying the Mi Amigo, appeared in court a few months later. Captain André Fauchet pleaded guilty to supplying the radio ship with food and fuel, as did other members of his crew.

Also appearing with Captain Fauchet was Oonagh Karanjia, a close associate of Ronan's since Caroline began. The Procureur de la République alleged that Mrs Karanjia was Radio Caroline's chief administrator and Captain Fauchet gave evidence to say that she had chartered his boat to tender the Mi Amigo. The Prosecutor had asked for details of how Caroline was organised internationally, but Mrs Karanjia refused to give any information and was fined 4,000 francs.

The case was reported on national TV in France, in many newspapers and in the American music paper Billboard. The prosecution alleged that by taking supplies from France to the radio ship, the trawler was in breach of a 1965 treaty that outlawed international broadcasting. The French prosecution were being advised by the British Home Office, almost like puppets. They suggested that Radio Caroline had caused great hindrance to their British colleagues in breaking international agreements and evading the payment of taxes. It was an underhand attempt to discredit the defendants, none of them were being charged with any tax evasion offences.

Radio Caroline and the crew of the trawler were supported by the France Radio Club, organised by Francois Lhote and Chris Edwards of the *Offshore Echos* magazine. A few years later the France Radio Club participated in a French TV programme, *Talassa* and were the initial cause of its interest in the station.

Despite the persecution of a number of Radio Caroline associates in Holland and Belgium, mainly advertisers, revenue poured in, especially for Radio Mi Amigo. The Mi Amigo service was grossing around $90,000 per month and with, running costs of under $25,000, it was a very lucrative business.

Radio Caroline published a magazine for its many fans called the 'Caroline Newsletter' magazine which bought more revenue to the station, although the blue meanies at the Home Office did their best to stop this enterprise. They threatened to prosecute the printers and tried to have the mailing address at *British Monomarks* in London cancel the magazine's address.

In his article in the second edition of the Caroline Newsletter, Stuart Russell dismissed any listener's suspicions that the all-male community on board was a problem. He explained that "Samantha Dubois is one of our community, enjoying equal rights and privileges and neither expecting nor receiving favours. She is another of the *Mi Amigo* staff, her contribution being made at the microphone and all onboard bear for her the respect she bears for us."

In July it was decided to move the English service to 962 kHz; despite now being on 312m it was announced as Caroline 319 as it made good sense to stick with the tradition of having all wavelengths rhyme with Caroline. *Radio Mi Amigo* also moved, to 212 metres to improve reception in the eastern parts of Flanders and the Netherlands.

A survey in Wavelength Magazine showed Caroline's audience had dropped from 4 to 3%, perhaps as a result of the frequency changes and some listeners not being able to find the station. Radio Caroline was no longer heard after dark on the 50kW transmitter. Two thirds of the audience though were in the 15-24 year old demographics, meaning that the station was certainly attracting new listeners.

The Caroline and Mi Amigo Road Shows were doing well in the Benelux too and usually had one Dutch and one English DJ appearing. Joining the road show operation in 1977 was Nico Volker, who later hosted programmes on Radio Caroline as Piet de Prater. In 1984, Nico would help launch Radio Monique with Fred Bolland and later he worked for Holland FM on the radio ship *Communicator*.

The Home Office visited the Mi Amigo in August 1977 on board the tug *Vengeance.* Half a dozen officials took pictures of the ship from every conceivable angle. The DJs all congregated on deck in a show of force but no attempt was made by the Home Office officials to board. The photographic exercises seem to have been pretty futile and were to see if they could tie in particular faces on the ship to those appearing at roadshows etc, but this evidence would only have been circumstantial and hardly likely to help secure a conviction.

A much bigger visit to the ship took place a week later using the Scottish paddle steamer, *PS Waverley*. It had been chartered to make a trip around the Mi Amigo with over 800 fans on board. Many Caroline DJs, past present and future were also on board.

Even Radio Caroline's biggest fan, Buster Pearson made the trip with Chicago and Paul Rusling carrying him down the steps. Sadly, the Waverley's trim was affected by all the fans rushing to one side of the ship as they came alongside the Mi Amigo. The ship tilted alarmingly with one of her paddles thrashing away madly while out of the water, so the trip was quickly aborted. Her captain set course back to Clacton and Southend, arriving back well after midnight.

Buster and Chicago on the PS Waverley

A few days later, Ronan O'Rahilly and other off duty Radio Caroline staff attended *Flashback 67*, a celebration of offshore radio to mark the tenth anniversary of the Marine Offence Act becoming law. The event was organised by Music Radio Promotions, the publishers of *Wavelength* magazine and many of those attending were interviewed by Radio Caroline's Admiral Robbie Dale.

The recording was rushed out to the Mi Amigo where it was produced into a special programme that was heard on Radio Mi Amigo and Radio Caroline. This was billed as a special live link up to the Flashback venue, the Centre Airport Hotel at Heathrow. About an hour later ten Home office officials swooped on the hotel but found that most of the participants in the 'live broadcast had left. There was no equipment or link transmitter, the officials had been sent on a wild goose chase.

In September 1977 the team on board the Mi Amigo was already one man short as Tony Allan had left in the rubber boat. When DJ Steve Kent, fell ill. He had to be taken by lifeboat to the shore, which left only two DJs, to run the station around the clock.

Roger Mathews and Stuart Russell made a sterling effort to keep Radio Caroline running but needed the help of some of the Radio Mi Amigo team and eventually had to play some old taped shows and occasionally non-stop music to fill the gaps so they could eat and get some sleep.

At one stage Stuart Russell played out the *Tamla Motown Story,* a documentary programme telling the history of the legendary record label. It had some of the labels best recordings and was interspersed with interviews with the stars and Motown's background team. When he finally got ashore after a record-breaking thirteen-week stint on the ship he was told he was fired. For playing music and talk about one of the most important record companies in the world?

The authorities were looking hard at the Radio Caroline operation and regulators from the UK, Belgium, Holland and France met several times to discuss the station. They considered a join monitoring exercise to try and stop supplies reaching the ship, but this was beyond the resources that they had available to them. The civil servants conceded that, so long as the Mi Amigo remained in International Waters, then there was no conceivable action that could be taken.

The DGA (Belgian administrative police) and officers of the SGR (military intelligence) raided the Z592, a trawler called the *Hosanna*, in Zeebrugge and discovered on board her many programme tapes and new engineering components for Radio Caroline. The Hosanna had often run supplies to the Mi Amigo for Radio Caroline. It was now run by Germain Ackx. who had fitted additional large tanks for carrying extra fuel and water out to the Mi Amigo.

During a tender visit in the middle of August, 1978, Germain and his son engrossed the Mi Amigo's crew in some chat and drinks in the mess, while his crew stole the compass and the wheel from the bridge from the wheelhouse. This meant the ship couldn't move anywhere but would also be potentially dangerous in an emergency.

"Rarely have we touched on topics like this," said Marc Jacobs, one of Radio Mi Amigo's biggest DJ names of 1978. "Peter Chicago talked about it with me during a programme the next day." This was in the 'Baken 16' programme (Beacon 16 was a nearby navigation buoy).

"Peter said that the lack of the wheel could lead to big problems because the ship was no longer seaworthy from that moment on. So we announced in 'Beacon 16' that we had been robbed of some important items. We said that we would notify the authorities of the ship in question, and of the crew had robbed us, if they would not return our belongings immediately. That wheel was of vital importance to the ship. "

"Unfortunately, Germain did not care," said Marc. "In the program we mentioned that we were making an emergency provision, in order to avoid problems." When the Hosanna was sunk near Dover two years later, Ronan was certain this was the bad Karma coming down on them, as payback for robbing the old Lady!

The helm (a wheel that operates the rudder and steers the ship) and the compass, mounted in a binnacle on the bridge, which shows the direction the ship is pointing, never were returned and the old lady saw out her final 18 months without those two essential items. One of Marc's friends saw one for sale for sale in Niekerk (near Hilversum) so bought it for his friend, but it turned out to be a fake.

As with so many on radio ships, Marc Jacobs was not Rob's real name, but it was the name of his grandfather. He began his career on the breakfast programme 'Ook Gooie Morgen' and then became far better known for his afternoon show, 'Baken 16'. Marc was very concerned about the condition of the Mi Amigo and tried to persuade Sylvain Tack to pour some of his millions into replacing her. When Tack refused, Marc and Frank van der Mast quit the job. A few months later he was back on board "I just missed the old girl so much, it was my life." By quirk of fate, his was the last voice to be heard on Radio Mi Amigo from the ship only a few months later.

Marc Jacobs

He was back on the air for the Dutch Radio Caroline the following year but left for a career on land based radio and then television. He is still active in the media, with his *Dam Op* programmes and others.

The Hosanna's sister ship, the *Vita Nova* (Z588), was stopped the previous month sailing into Lowestoft, when Caroline's Chief Engineer, Peter Chicago, was found on board.

On the morning of Friday 11th November 1977 both Radio Caroline and Radio Mi Amigo's programmes were interrupted many times by the generator having problems and by lunchtime the two stations had to close down. Severe storms battered the Mi Amigo over the next few days with gales of up to Storm Force 10 being recorded.

The Mi Amigo was silent for a few days and although the coastguards at Walton said that there had been no calls from the Mi Amigo, it wasn't long before journalists were filing copy suggesting that a disaster had occurred. There was rabid press speculation predicting that this time it could be the end of Radio Caroline.

There were the usual stories about Caroline running out of money; even a wild tale that the ship's magnificent mast had fallen into the sea! All that had happened was that fuel had got very low (which is why the generator had been running poorly; when the levels in the tanks is low the fuel filter gets blocked and the engine shuts down.

The crew knew that a tender would not be able to get alongside due to the bad weather, so transmissions were stopped to conserve what little fuel they had, to keep the ships lighting running and have enough fuel to cook hot meals. In fact, food supplies were so low that the crew on board had only potatoes, rice and spaghetti left, so they lived on dry soup for a week. The weather improved and supplies were taken out to the ship, enabling Radio Caroline and Radio Mi Amigo to resume broadcasting again ten days later.

The following month it was necessary to reduce the hours of Radio Caroline to being night-time station only. Radio Mi Amigo would move to the 962 kHz channel ("319") as this was much clearer, so Radio Caroline would once again become a 'night-time only' service. Radio Caroline's round the clock service was suspended but listeners could now hear "Europe's first and only album station" from 6.00pm until 5am every night.

The Caroline Roadshow was, for a while, billed as the Caroline Rock Show. It was run by Robb Eden and Robbie Day, with a lot of help from Barry James. They played gigs in Kent, London and East Anglia, sometime with a live band but always with the best in rock music.

A range of Caroline T-shirts, caps, posters and other memorabilia was available at the gigs, which became very popular with Caroline fans and sold well

The authorities regularly attended the Caroline Rock Shows; they were easily spotted, often they were the only ones wearing a jacket and tie and they would lurk in the shadows making copious notes every time the radio station was mentioned. The road show was very profitable and, some a while, provided the only revenue generated by the English programmes.

In 1977, following a two year investigation costing over a hundred thousand pounds, the Serious Crimes Squad at Scotland Yard charged directors of *Wavelength* Magazine, Nik Oakley and Mike Baron, with publicising Radio Caroline. The offences concerned their selling T-shirts with the Radio Caroline ship and wavelength being shown on them. After they were found guilty at Marlborough Street Magistrates Court, fines of £50 were levied on each of half a dozen charges, plus costs of £21,000.

The costs were to be the final nail in Wavelength magazine; the Home Office vindictively suggested that the magazine was being used to fund Radio Caroline. Bailiffs seized the company's stock and froze the bank accounts. In fact, the magazines had their roots in a concept that supported the principle of free expression and freedom of the press and was never a part of Radio Caroline.

In the New Year, Radio Caroline began transmitting an album chart show. Although the programme was weekly, the chart actually changed every other week. The programme was called the *Caroline Countdown of Albums* and it was broadcast on Monday evenings so the station could reflect new chart placings from the official UK chart published the previous weekend.

On Easter Sunday, 1978, Radio Caroline celebrated its 14th birthday by broadcasting another *All Time Listeners Favourite 50 Albums* chart. This chart was compiled from the regular Listeners' Top 30 features. Two hundred of the listeners' personal charts were collated to produce a Top 50 chart of everyone's favourite tracks. Led Zeppelin's *Stairway to Heaven* headed the chart.

In early Summer, Sylvain Tack took steps to distance himself from the Radio Mi Amigo operation and the quality of supplies dropped alarmingly after he appointed new agents to represent Mi Amigo in Belgium. He told the Spanish Ministry of Culture that he was no longer legally connected to the ship. He was not however willing to totally break the links completely as hoped to sell the name *Mi Amigo*, which he said was worth about five million francs.

Two of Caroline's best-loved DJs had joined the station for the summer: Tom Hardy arrived on board in June and Richard Thompson (now much better known as Bob Lawrence and still with the station) came on board in August. He was given the nickname 'Buzby' by Dutch DJ Marc Jacobs, on his first day on the ship. It's one that's stuck.

Around this time a motor engineer with a workshop in North London began helping Caroline with various tasks. Peter Moore had become good friends of some of the DJs who frequented his local pub, the Black Rose in Highgate. One of Caroline's engineers, James Kaye, lived next door to his workshop.

Peter was a very hard working, but also hard drinking carburettor expert whose business acumen and mechanical skills were very useful to the Caroline organisation. He had been a supporter of the radio station for a dozen years or more and was generous to the station's staff who frequently found themselves at his home in a London suburb. His local pub, the Black Rose, was often the venue for Caroline staff meetings.

Peter originally came in to help out with a few jobs and began doing more and more. A keen boat owner, Peter increasingly threw himself into helping keep the Mi Amigo at sea and the Caroline lines of contact open. Some years later he found himself in at the deep end, often left alone to manage the ship and eventually running the entire Caroline organisation. While delivering a barge full of fuel to the ship he had to navigate it back to Richborough in Kent when the captain banged his head and was concussed, leaving Peter in command.

Hans Knot tuned in at Zeezenders
Jelle Knot

A big reunion of former Caroline staff was organised in Holland in July at the *Zeezenders* 20, which marked the start of European offshore radio in 1958. The event was organised by *Music Radio Promotions*, the company behind the Flashback '67, held in London the previous year.

MRP had lots of help from leading Dutch enthusiasts Hans Knot, his brother Jelle, Ton van Draanen, Marc Jacobs and Frans Schuurbiers. The conference was held at the Leeuwenhorst Congress Centre, at Noordwijkerhout.

A new magazine was launched at the Zeezenders conference called the *Freewave Media Magazine.* It was edited by Ton van Draanen and Hans Knot, who had been a keen Caroline supporter since the sixties. In the first edition of Freewave, Caroline DJ Stuart Russell wrote: "Life on board the Mi Amigo is generally good. There is plenty to eat and we have a good cook called Kees Borrell. Now summer is here, I'm looking forward to getting a nice suntan to show off when I get ashore."

Sadly, the Mi Amigo was off the air due to a technical fault and could not be heard, although the ZeeZenders 20 event was such a success (over 350 attended) that it was decided to stage this again. In following years it was given a special name - *RadioDag*, or RadioDay. Many Radio Caroline DJs, engineers and crewmen have appeared at the events and many radio awards have been presented there. Full details can be found on the *HansKnot.com* web site.

The following week, a high-level meeting was held in Paris between the authorities of the UK, the Benelux countries and France. Their goal was to combine forces to close Radio Caroline. During the meeting they discussed a report that the radio ship was now in very poor condition and possibly dangerous.

The Belgian police had received some financial reports that showed the Radio Mi Amigo side of the operation had grossed almost 80m Belgian francs. They also knew that several of the most popular DJs had left their Spanish retreat in Playa de Aro and were back living in Holland and Belgium. A careful watch was being kept on the supply boats that plied from Belgium, although two or three of the official observers were in fact keen Radio Caroline fans and happily turned a blind eye to movements.

The Dutch police reported that they had attended the *ZeeZenders 20* convention and collected a lot of intelligence. They had so much data that it would take some time before a fuller report could be made. An article jointly written by the DJs aboard the mv Mi Amigo in August was published in the sixth edition of the *Caroline Newsletter*. The article also mentioned the *Zeezenders 20*, which Caroline DJs had attended.

Londoner Stevie Lane was a night club and land pirate station DJ who made her first trip out to the Mi Amigo at this time. She also joined the Caroline Roadshow and brought a touch of glamour to the proceedings as well and helped organise trips out to the radio ship. A few years later Stevie became even more involved in the Caroline operation on land and eventually was heard DJing on the Caroline Overdrive service.

DJ & organiser Stevie Lane

There were several breakdowns of generators in September that year which often silenced Caroline and Radio Mi Amigo for several hours at a time. One day the programmes had to be all produced in the Caroline studio after a turntable burned out in Mi Amigo's studio. DJ Marc Jacobs handled this very well, with help from Ferry Eden.

The Caroline Music Bus was meeting a good response in towns it visited to help promote Radio Caroline, so talks were held to expand the tours onto mainland Europe. A deal was done to have this handled by Patrick Valain and Serge van Gisteren.

Sylvain Tack was becoming more demoralised that many of the Flemish DJs did not want to live in Spain. Just after Easter, the Belgian police suddenly raided offices and homes of advertisers. They took the address details of about 5000 members from the Mi Amigo Fan Club and the following day stopped a coach with 39 Belgians heading for Playa de Aro. The Belgian press was inundated with letters of support for Mi Amigo. They also reported on Tack's comments that cigarette adverts would soon be heard.

Stories about the high level of income from the Dutch programmes had reached all parts of Caroline's organisation and there was increasing pressure for extra payments to be made so that the radio ship could be replaced. The Mi Amigo was getting a bit tired and generators needed urgent replacement. News of the profits reached other ears too and other radio people wanted to get involved in transmissions.

Radio Hollandia
During September, Caroline boss Ronan O'Rahilly had several discussions with a Dutch company called *Radio Hollandia*. They made an offer to replace Radio Mi Amigo with their own taped programme. These were recorded legally in Holland, ostensibly for closed-circuit systems in stores and restaurants.

Joost De Draaijer

Radio Hollandia was run by former Radio Veronica star DJ Joost den Draaijer, who helped launch the Dutch Radio Noordzee. His colleagues Tony Berk and Veronica DJ Will Luikinga were also involved in the plan.

A large deposit of 25,000 guilders was paid over by Radio Hollandia to Ger-Jan Smit, the Dutch advertising associate of Radio Caroline but no programmes were ever transmitted. The Radio Hollandia plan to transmit from a transmitter on Sealand (Roughs Tower fort) was also abandoned. Word soon reached Sylvain Tack about the plan, which leaked in the Dutch press. Tack had already been plotting to launch his own ship but told Radio Caroline that he would fight tooth and nail to retain the position of his radio station and warned that the ship and its transmitters were contracted to his station.

Tack now had several businesses in Spain, a waffle bakery (in partnership with the Mayor of Playa de Aro) a boutique and two bars. Despite the huge income that he now had, the payments for using the radio ship became ever slower. The contract called for payments to Caroline of $28,000 per month for use of the transmitter plus the costs of tendering. Cashflow was slowing, so it was impossible to replace the generators, much less replace the ship. Sylvain Tack decided he would secretly equip his own radio ship, quite ignorant of how to do so.

High seas and some ferocious storms in October caused the only remaining generator to complain. The Dutch DJs on board the Mi Amigo by this time included Herman de Graaf, Marc Jacobs, Rob Hudson and Johan Visser while the only pre-recorded shows were by Haike Dubois and Ton Schipper.

An hour of dense black smoke one morning signalled that some piston liners had blown. Running the engines with low oil levels also damaged the 'big ends' at the bottom of the engine and once again the Mi Amigo was off the air. There was nothing Chicago could do to even keep the generator limping along, so Radio Mi Amigo hastily closed down just before 12 noon, after a few brief words from Marc Jacobs.

The awful weather that Autumn often prevented tenders sailing and conditions on board the radio ship deteriorated even further. Tack claimed that he was being hounded by the Spanish authorities, and assumed an alternative identity with a false passport, claiming that the Spaniards had invoked a Marine Offences Act. This was not true and at least three more radio ships were converted and equipped there, without any legal action.

The Spanish government later confirmed there was never pressure on Radio Mi Amigo to leave and that they had a lot of support from the Catalans who welcomed the extra business that Radio Caroline and Radio Mi Amigo attracted. The welcome afforded by the Spanish was investigated by three other former members of the Caroline team who decided to put together another ship and test the Spanish waters for themselves.

Mutiny and Piracy.

Eventually a tender did arrive to the Mi Amigo and the Dutch DJs were covertly given news of Sylvain's secret plans for their own ship. They kept this news to themselves and, after some secret meetings in the cabins, they decided to leave on the tender. This left the ship with just four English DJs on board who were immediately suspicious that no fuel had been delivered.

After pulling away from the Mi Amigo the tender suddenly headed back at full speed and almost rammed the Mi Amigo. Presumably, it was hoped that this might bring down the mast or somehow incapacitate the ship so no one could broadcast from the ship any longer. The tender then went to the bows of the Mi Amigo and tried to cut through the radio ship's anchor chain. They were unable to complete the sabotage as a British police boat appeared with its blue light flashing to investigate what was happening and cashed the tender for a short distance.

More details of the day's other events can be found in DJ Stuart Russell's excellent book describing his career with Radio Caroline. In his book, *Ships in Troubled Waters*, Nigel Harris (DJ Stuart Russell) explains more of the dark days in the Mi Amigo's history.

Caroline's ships have been attacked on several occasions but never by members of her own crew. Taking such potentially dangerous and destructive action is indeed piracy on the high seas. It's terrorism. To endanger the lives of others who were unarmed and unable to defend their ship is unforgivable, worse than the worst acts of war!

New radio ship, the Deep Diver

While all the drama of takeovers, and expiring generators was taking place on the North Sea, another radio ship called the 'Deep Diver' was equipped in Belfast. The ship would host Radio Sunshine and was the brainchild of Chris Cary and Dick Palmer. Chris managed Radio Caroline in 1972 and 1973 while Dick was captain of the Mi Amigo. They were offshore radio experts and were convinced that offshore radio would be successful off the coast of Spain.

There were two obstacles to mooring a radio ship off Spain: first, the water is very deep, several hundreds of feet so difficult to anchor in. Secondly, there are already many commercial radio networks and independent stations. The idea of running an offshore station off the Spanish coast was clearly a non-starter as it would have been very expensive and unlikely to make much money at all.

The Deep Diver had been built in 1945 as a supply vessel for the Admiralty. Less than 100 feet long she had a more powerful engine than the Mi Amigo. The plan was to anchor on the Costa Brava and was part financed by Philip Solomon.

Engineer Bob Noakes came close to being given a concrete overcoat after he threatened to report the project to the authorities, the money ran out and the ship seized by her owners. She was sold complete with lattice radio masts and, after a name change to the *Salamander*, she was beached at Espinho (Portugal) where she remained for eight years, embedded in the sand as her cargo was plundered by locals.

Radio Sunshine's MV Deep Diver, berthed in the Scilly Isles with the mast is telescoped down for the voyage to Spain

Dick Heuff

Caroline crew fight on

With the Mi Amigo now silent and in urgent need of supplies and crewing, not to mention a new generator, Radio Caroline went back to Radio Hollandia to try and reopen the negotiations. They would not however put up a large advance payment to get the Mi Amigo operational once again but were prepared to rent the facility if the station could be made to broadcast again. The Mi Amigo needed a generator so had to remain silent for a few more months.

Yet again, the long silence and rumours spread by Radio Mi Amigo had journalists busy again and newspapers wrote their usual "Radio Caroline is finished" stories. Even the quality press sensed blood and assumed the Mi Amigo was lost and Radio Caroline was finished. The *Daily Telegraph* carried a leader article, congratulating Caroline for a long, glorious and successful career.

Out on the Mi Amigo, the main two MAN generators needed urgent attention or replacing. Diesel fitter Albert Hood offered to strip both units down and rebuild one good one from the best parts. A scheme to take one of them ashore for rebuilding was firmly rejected by Chicago, who remembered the occasion when a previous machine went to Holland for reconditioning and never returned.

The ship also had a serviceable Henschel generator which could run a low power transmitter; it had a new coupling shaft that needed fitting properly so Albert set about lining that up correctly. The problem was, simply getting it balanced correctly, once done it was problem-free.

The 'powers that be' were reluctant to take any firm action so the ship remained silent with just a small Faryman unit running, for lighting. It only used a third the amount of the Henschel but was not powerful enough to operate a transmitter. Within a week it broke down, its alternator had simply disintegrated.

The 962 kHz frequency became semi-obsolete in November when all the radio frequencies in Europe were shifted by at least one kilohertz, in an attempt to rid the band of the awful 'off-channel' heterodyne whistles heard after dark. Many stations swapped frequencies and made bigger adjustments; some better slots were observed by Caroline engineers but, being off the air, there was no opportunity to take immediate advantage of them.

Talks were then held with Radio Delmare to broadcast their programmes instead. Gerard van Dam wanted his station on the air around the clock, a full 24 hour service, but Ronan refused.

A deal was done by Fred Bolland for Caroline to borrow a large generator from Delmare but it took many meetings to arrange. Eventually a bright yellow skid-mounted Cummins generator was loaded into the MV Epivan in Scheveningen and just before Christmas was delivered to the Mi Amigo. It could simply be loaded onto the ship, connected up to fuel lines and the power distribution board bus-bars and the station was then ready to broadcast.

As Christmas 1978 came and went, 962kHz was still quiet, despite Gerard having put some Radio Delmare DJs on the Mi Amigo and expecting to launch by then. Life aboard the radio ship was becoming increasingly unpleasant. Fuel supplies were so low that the power was only switched on for three hours a day - just long enough to cook a meal. Without power, the food in the deep-freezer began to rot.

In January, Peter Chicago went ashore to try and organise some supplies, leaving Roger Mathews, Tony Allan, Tom Hardy and two crew on board. The weather deteriorated still further in the New Year and the heavy seas caused some of the rivets holding one of the steel plates of the ship's hull to pop.

With the Mi Amigo now taking in water, a small generator had to be run non-stop to provide electric power for the pumps to keep pumping the ingress of water at bay. Eventually by mid-January even that last emergency generator expired with a splutter and the ship was again quiet. No active pumps running meant that the water level in the bilges began to rise. The waves were getting higher and when winds reached Force 7, the DJs began to fear for their lives.

On Thursday 18th January, the Mi Amigo was listing badly and the amount of water on board was causing her stern to settle quite deeply. Waves were occasionally rushing along the gunwales and up onto the stern deck. The DJs took to the bridge and sent a 'Mayday' call on 2182, the international distress frequency.

A helicopter from RAF Manston investigated the situation and confirmed that the ship was in a very dangerous position. They could not help due to the Force 7 winds now blowing and the bows having risen up into the air meant the mast and rigging were now obscuring most of the ship, which meant it would be almost impossible to send down winchman to help. Three other ships in the outer reaches of the Thames estuary came to the help of the Mi Amigo: the *Cambrai*, the *MayCrest*, a 500 ton coaster based on the Medway and the *Sand Serin* – a dredger from Ipswich that was often seen in the area.

In mid-afternoon the Harwich lifeboat was launched in failing light to the Mi Amigo. It took three hours battling against heavy seas, around the Long Sand Head to reach the Mi Amigo, well after darkness fell. She took off the Mi Amigo's five DJs and the ship's canary, Wilson, and set course back for Essex. The crew (and Wilson the pet canary) were taken off and the ship was left to the elements.

This was the first time that the Mi Amigo had been completely abandoned and many thought she might not survive on her own in the heavy seas. Even if she did, there was always the possibility that a passing ship might throw a line on her and make a salvage claim, or that the Dutch crew might come seeking to take control.

Chicago to the Rescue

The Mi Amigo's Chief Engineer, Peter Chicago, had gone ashore a week previously to try and sort out supplies. He anxiously watched the weather conditions all night and the next morning he and Richard Thompson persuaded a coaster from Sheerness to take them out to the ship and see if there was anything that could be done to save her. When they arrived in the Knock Deep the wind was abating, but it was still too rough to board. Peter took to a small dingy and paddled himself across to the Mi Amigo.

He managed to scramble on board and the dingy was then pulled back and forth multiple times, carrying the emergency supplies. The ship had by now settled out to an even keel and the bows were no longer pointing upwards. Peter had got petrol across and one pump running. She now clearly lit, was obviously manned and not abandoned.

The Caroline organisation managed to book a trawler from Ramsgate for the following day and a dozen crew plus supplies were taken out to the Mi Amigo. It took a long time for the poorly equipped trawler to even find the radio ship as she had no radar and only a very insensitive Loran receiver.

Eventually they found her, and six other crew joined Peter to help with the mopping up including DJs Tony Allan, Roger Mathews and Tom Anderson. Once again, the Mi Amigo had survived. Those on the salvage trawler were stopped on returning to Ramsgate, but they argued that the Mi Amigo had been a ship in distress, so was exempt from the Marine Offences Act, by virtue of section 7 of the Act.

The next big job was to get the ship cleaned up after being semi-submerged, find a good generator and a reliable source of diesel fuel. A deal was finally done with the Radio Delmare people and a large yellow skid-mounted Cummins generator delivered to the Knock Deep.

This was installed on the back deck of the ship and a suitable canopy built over it. On board the Mi Amigo a small dedicated team of mainly DJs worked day and night to slowly dry out the areas of the ship that had become submerged. The cabins and record library downstairs had suffered most, but nothing was a write off.

An abandoned barge was found that could carry ten tons of diesel per trip out to the Mi Amigo. It needed a lot of work to free her from the mud grave she was sat in on Margate beach.

Behind the scenes work had been going on to set up a new Dutch language Radio Caroline station. To this end, Ben Bode had been recruited along with former Radio Delmare partner Fred Bolland. Ben was a very capable Dutchman from the Hague who coordinated finance and supplies, while Fred had many contacts in the music business via his record shop. It was Fred who set up the original meetings with Ronan. He had been a long time follower of Caroiline, since he first visited the two ships in Amsterdam with Andy Archer and Hans Verbaan in 1971.

Three well known Benelux DJs joined the new Dutch Radio Caroline: Herman de Graaf, Johan Visser and Rob Hudson. The team was assembled by two Hague residents, Ben Bode and Fred Bolland and some DJs from Radio Unique, an Amsterdam pirate.

The media, as ever, were happy to print Radio Caroline's obituary but, to many loyal fans, abandoning the Mi Amigo in January 1979 really did seem like the end. We should all know by now that Caroline never ends, there is always a way back onto the airwaves.

While Caroline was having some difficulties at sea, a magazine aimed at the listeners, *Caroline Newsletter*, was having several problems with officialdom on land.

The police warned the printer that if they agreed to print the seventh issue of the magazine they would be liable for prosecution under the Marine Offences Act. The circulation manager June Sutton was threatened too. Fortunately, no charges followed and later, in a special edition of the newsletter dated Winter 1979/80, June was able to reveal to the readers what had been going on behind the scenes.

19. I saw three ships

A few weeks before Easter, in a bid to extend Caroline's coverage, Chicago decided to try a much lower frequency. 557 kHz had been a very successful channel for Radio Veronica five years earlier. Capital Radio had covered most of the south east when the IBA had sat them on it with only five hundred watts power. The transmissions were also to prove that the ship was once again operable and used the higher-powered Cummins generator. Non-stop music continued all morning and was heard over a wide area.

The semi-derelict barge at Margate had now been dug out of the mudbank where it had ran aground and was loaded up with ten tons of diesel for the main generator. This would keep the station on the air for a month or more. It had a serviceable engine and would sit well down in the water so be not so noticeable as other craft. It finally made it out to the Mi Amigo late on Easter Saturday. By working all night, Chicago had transmissions going out on the new 963 frequency by first light the following day.

Easter 1979 was Radio Caroline's 15th birthday. The station had by now been off the air for almost six months. Despite this, thousands of fans regularly tried to tune in to 963 kHz ("319 metres" as it was known, although the frequency had moved one 1kHz upwards). Many of Caroline's faithful listeners tuned in almost habitually. Just in case she had popped back - and they were not disappointed. There was a signal. Caroline was back in business!

By mid-morning non-stop music began and programmes resumed at 11am. Tony Allan re-opened the proceedings: after The Fortunes' theme tune had died away, he taught the doubters a lesson when he played Chris Rea's *Fool, If You Think It's Over*.

Tony Allan relaunching Radio Caroline

Tony told listeners that he was shaking, as it had been such a long time and that all on board were glad to be back on the air. "Although the radio station launched at the end of March, we think of Easter as being our real birthday. Like all queens we at Caroline are entitled to two birthdays; make of that what you will!"

Tony announced the names of all the Dutch DJs who would be providing Radio Caroline's new Dutch service and introduced Herman de Graaf, who later did the first show. The English team on board at the time of launch were Tony, the two Toms (Anderson and Hardy) and John Moss from Ipswich, a young sailor and engineer who was determined to make it as a DJ.

John was given some airshifts and adopted the name Steven Bishop. He was often known as 'Emily' in Caroline circles due this adopted surname being the same as Emily Bishop on Coronation Street, although he looked nothing like her! In later turns on board Caroline, Steve adopted the name Johnny Lewis.

Radio Caroline now seemed unstoppable with a Dutch service by day and English at night. The following week Caroline broadcast the first *Caroline Countdown of Album Sounds*, which was hosted by Tom Hardy and topped by Supertramp's Breakout in America. Runner up position went to Squeeze for their Cool for Cats album while George Harrison saw his self-titled album at No.3

Despite using the Radio Caroline name, the Dutch output was a separate concern. The English programmes continued in the same way as in previous years.

A frequency change of 962 to 963kHz was necessary by the Geneva Frequency Plan which had come into effect in November while Caroline had been off the air. Most Caroline listeners wouldn't have noticed any difference and the station still identified as Caroline 319.

During early May the station closed early most evenings, eventually settling on a 10pm closedown. The following month the schedule was augmented by a number of sponsored shows, mainly evangelical, taking up as much as two hours of airtime a day.

How Your Mind Can Keep You Well in a Moment of Truth was a discussion programme hosted by Roy Masters for an hour in prime time every evening. Jewish-born Roy gives advice to his listeners on a wide range of topics and, invariably, his controversial style could be compulsive listening. Roy was born in London and began work as a diamond cutter in Brighton. He served in the British Army before emigrating to Texas where he set up a school of hypnosis.

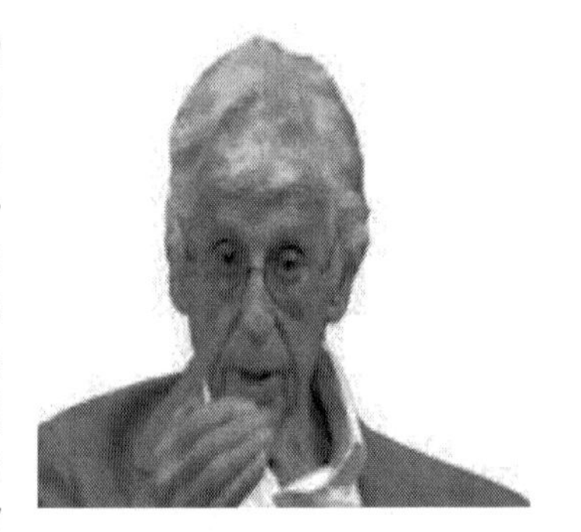

Daily dialogue from Roy Masters

Roy began a talk radio and counselling show in the sixties and continued to broadcast on many stations until recently. Roy's payments to Radio Caroline kept the Mi Amigo afloat for several years.

Although perhaps an intrusion into Caroline's usual station sound, the speech programmes brought in over £100 an hour. This was much-needed revenue for the Caroline coffers, depleted as they were after an expensive winter off the air. Programmes were recorded by around twenty radio evangelists, mostly in the USA but also some in the UK and the Netherlands. The most popular Dutch religious programmes were presented by Dominee Toornvliet and Johan Maasbach.

Dom. Gerrit Toornvliet

Just along the coast from Scheveningen is a little Dutch resort called Zandvoort and just outside it there is a small 'Sundays only' low power station called Radio Bloemendaal. From here, Dominee Gerritt Toornvliet ran a breakaway church and his radio foundation. As well as his own transmissions on 270m, he also bought time on Radio Luxembourg and Caroline to carry out the Lord's work.

Johan Maasbach had been one of the first evangelists on Caroline in the seventies and recorded his daily half hour shows in The Hague. They were a mixture of Dutch and cod-English and often featured Johan soliciting funds, letters and offering to pray for those who wrote in. He enjoyed responses from a million listeners and his *Blessing Church* and *JWM Wereldzending* work is now undertaken by his son David.

Although the station was now called Radio Caroline,day and night, the Dutch shows sounded very similar to those of the late Radio Mi Amigo, and few missed the incessant commercials for Suzi Waffles! Not much money came in initially so Ben Bode took control over this, along with Danny Vuylsteke and his DAVU music company. Danny had held a similar role with Radio Mi Amigo and knew all the advertisers, especially in the Flanders part of Belgium.

Soon there was enough fuel on board the Mi Amigo to use the big 50kW transmitter once again. Advertising was soon flowing in from the Dutch programmes "thick and fast", mainly thanks to Danny Vuylsteke. He had previously organised sales of Radio Atlantis, which 'broke away' from the Caroline family in 1973. Danny specialised in bringing in retail advertising, particularly from the furniture emporiums that experienced a resurgence in the Benelux at this time.

Danny Vuylsteke
Ben Bode

Originally from Kortemark in West Flanders, Danny was a big man, well known over the border in the Netherlands. He had a printing business in Brussels and was adept at setting up new deals and businesses across Flanders.

Other income continued to be raised in the UK by The Caroline Roadshow, a mobile rock disco which played successfully all over Essex, Kent and East Anglia. The events were organised and run by DJs Robb Eden, Barry James and Robbie Day, all aided and abetted by a former executive from Radio Luxembourg. He was known as 'Harvey The Rabbit' as he spent all his time chasing the girls!

The road show team were supposed to be in charge of supply runs from the UK to the ship but seemed to be very disorganised with no means of communication and apparently not a watch between them! The anorak boats that visited the Mi Amigo, such as the *Lucky Lady* and the *El Chiparon* from Brightlingsea organised by Albert Hood provided a first class service. Albert even found time off from work to help on board with generator repairs while his wife Georgena was an excellent coordinator.

Barry James had always been a keen supporter of the station and helped out with some of the covert tender runs from the UK and helping with sales of merchandise which raised even more income to help keep the ship afloat. He later presented programmes on the station and has been associated with Caroline for over thirty years.

The Caroline headquarters in The Hague became so well known that they had to be moved to a top secret address in Belgium. The key organisers of Caroline and the ones responsible for the station being able to return to the air were Fred Bolland and Ben Bode.

They had been involved with Radio Delmare, which was hopelessly under-funded. Fred and Ben however recognised that to be successful needed a powerful signal, such as Caroline's. The Dutch office in the Hague too over the tendering of the ship, done using several fishing boats from Dutch ports. Operating Caroline cost up to £5,000 a month, but it was soon producing three times that amount. Most was from spot advertising and a little sponsorship.

An important supporter was Greenpeace, the global environmental campaigner, which has its HQ in Amsterdam. Their legendary boat the MV Rainbow Warrior made several very welcome calls to the Mi Amigo and brought much needed supplies, in return for Radio Caroline's on-air support. The audience response to the publicity for Greenpeace on Caroline brought significant support for their campaigns.

The Rainbow Warrior arrived alongside to deliver some fuel in late July, expecting a long hose to pump it through, but it wasn't long enough and the two ships had to lay alongside. "As we pumped oil the two ships rose up and down, not in any synchronity," remembers Peter Wilkinson.

"It caused a few hairy moments with grating metal and squealing fenders," says Peter, who produced the show along with host Tony Allen. "We shared a few beers and had an enjoyable meeting. A few days later they broadcast a one hour programme to promote our campaigning activities. Long Live pirate radio."

The Rainbow Warrior's name comes from an old Indian legend "when the earth is sick and the animals disappear the Warriors of the Rainbow will come to protect the wildlife and heal the earth." After taking part in demonstrations against whaling off Iceland she went to protest about French nuclear testing in the South Pacific.

Agents of the French secret service, the *Direction Générale Sécurité Extérieure (DGSE)* boarded it in New Zealand and bombed it, killing a much-loved photographer. Several leading figures denounced this action as terrorism, including the Prime Minister of New Zealand. When two French agents were arrested and convicted, the French threatened to have the European Union ban all imports from New Zealand which would have crippled their economy.

After widespread public outcry, France paid Greenpeace $8.6 million, which was used to build Rainbow Warrior III, which had electric motors and a wind-sail for propulsion. Neil Young, Jackson Browne and Graham Nash performed in a benefit concert in New Zealand to top up the funds. Twenty years after the outrage, French President Mitterrand conceded that he personally had authorised the bombing.

A 'new' rival radio ship

During the summer of 1979 Caroline was not alone in the North Sea, as both Radio Mi Amigo and Radio Delmare briefly returned from new ships. A massive resurgence in offshore radio – three ships on the air!

Sylvain Tack had tried to buy the Peace ship, which broadcast as *Voice of Peace* in the east Mediterranean, but the asking price was too high. Tack's partner Patrick Valain and an associate, Germain Boy, bought an old coaster called the Centricity in Cyprus. The conversion to a radio ship in Athens took ten months! This lengthy delay enabled Radio Caroline to restart its transmissions, beating them on the air by several months, which helped to secure several of their advertisers.

Their 'new' ship was renamed the MV Magdalena, after Patrick Valain's wife. It was part funded by Adriaan van Landschoot, fitted with a Gates BC10H (10 kilowatt) transmitter and anchored off Zeebrugge.

In June, the 'new' Radio Mi Amigo started test transmissions on 1100 kHz (272 metres) from the Magdalena, off Zeebrugge. Two DJs who had broadcast from the Caroline ship the previous year, Ton Schipper and Ferry Eden, joined the new ship. Reception was marred in many areas as BBC Radio One used an adjacent frequency.

Many had great expectations of the new Radio Mi Amigo because the organisation had been very high profile in its period from the Caroline ship and many of her old team were still involved.

Radio Mi Amigo's replacement - the MV Magdalena

Wim de Groot

The Mi Amigo fan club and the Drive-In Show had grand plans, including a huge Fan Club Ball to celebrate Mi Amigo's fifth birthday in the Boudewijnpark in Brugges. Their artwork was based on the Caroline ship, not their own vessel! Perhaps they knew that they still needed the magic of Caroline's ship? They certainly suffered by not having her powerful 50 kW transmitter. Radio Mi Amigo II had poor reception, despite mooring close to Zeebrugge.

Within weeks their ship, the MV Magdalena was in trouble. She was adrift at least six times, and on her final 'tour' of the North Sea, she grounded on a sandbank. With no captain on board or engineer capable of starting the ship's engines she began to take in water. Eventually, an official Dutch boat took her in tow and towed her into harbour, where the ship was arrested.

The new Radio Mi Amigo 'organisation' seemed almost non-existent and she certainly had few friends. This was such a pity, as quite a lot of money had been poured into the 'relaunch' of Radio Mi Amigo by many, including Radio Atlantis founder, Adriaan van Landschoot. The Magdalena was quickly sold for scrap, a sad end for the 20 million Belgian Francs invested into a project. Had the operators invested only at tenth that amount in the Caroline ship the previous year they would still have a powerful station covering Belgium.

The original Radio Mi Amigo was never heard again from the North Sea, although there have been several small scale and short term re-enactments of the station. In 2014 and 2019 the remnants of the Mi Amigo team reformed for festivals celebrating the life of the station.

In 2015 German 'Captain' Kord Lemkau, a colleague of Dennis King at Radio Caroline much earlier, set up an international station from Spain, using the name ***Radio Mi Amigo International***. Using a dedicated 10 kW licensed short wave transmitter in Germany, the new station is named after the ship, not the radio station, and has become very popular with fans of AM and the traditional styke of broadcasting.

After Captain Kord died in January 2018, Lion Keezer who had helped set the station up, took over the daily operations. They now have several former Caroline and Mi Amigo staff, including Paul Graham, Johnny Lewis, Steve Foster, Emperor Rosko, Lion Keezer, Hans 'ten Hooge' Hogendoorn en Johan Vermeer. In 2019, RMAI opened a studio on the pier at Blankenberge.

Third time lucky for Radio Delmare?
Radio Delmare was the latest offshore project of Gerard van Dam, who had been the person who had saved the Mi Amigo from the scrap yard in 1972 and helped relaunch Radio Caroline. After a time running *Weekend Music Radio* he helped launch Radio Delmare the previous year from a small ship called mv Aegir.

Two replacement boats later and Radio Delmare now had the use of the MV Martina, a Dutch trawler of the type seen in Scheveningen and Katwijk. She had previously tendered Radio Caroline during her days as part of the Vrolijk Sportvissen fleet and was bought by Radio Delmare for a generous price. Delmare finally launched in early June with a mixture of live and pre-recorded shows.

Among the station's new backers was Fred Bolland from the Hague who owned a record shop where he met Hans Verbaan who took him on a trip to visit the two Caroline ships in Amsterdam. It was Fred who had loaned the Cummins generator to Ronan the previous Christmas and arranged it to be delivered to the Mi Amigo on the MV Epivan.

Anchored just north of Belgium, off the Dutch coast of Goeree, Radio Delmare had a bright, young, enthusiastic sound. Sadly, she had only a weak signal, perhaps a kilowatt or so. The third vessel of the Delmare project was now at sea and transmitting but the programmes could only be enjoyed by listeners in Zuid Holland, disappearing into the noise towards Rotterdam.

A ten kilowatt transmitter was offered by Caroline DJ Roger Matthews and some English 'pirate' operators including Chris Cortez and Leon Mitchell. The plan was to broadcast English programmes at night.

Radio Delmare ship, Aegir 2, off the Dutch coast
Jelle Boonstra

In late July, Gerard was hospitalised after being beaten up by the captain of the boat, Leo, over some infidelity involving their partners. The station deteriorated rapidly with two DJs forcing an engineer to help them take over the station. This piracy was quickly foxed by Gerard immobilising their car and stealing the tender's trailer. He had to go into hiding in Belgium after it was revealed that Delmare's Italian front company did not exist and suggestions were made about 'mob' connections to his Dutch company, *Prodihaag*.

At one stage in late September, there was only one person left aboard, Johan Rood. An enthusiastic engineer, he was running the station single-handed, maintaining the ship and all the equipment, presenting some programmes and running the tapes. Supplying the ship had become problematic with authorities raiding small tenders in harbours along the Dutch coast. The Delmare team usually put off from remote beaches near Goeree-Overflakkee, then the closest point to the ship.

Eventually it all became too much work and, after one hundred days broadcasting, the station closed down on 28th September after a bid to sell the station to Radio Mi Amigo fell through. In October five people were arrested in Stellendam while trying to take supplies out to the ship. They had managed to set sail but were unable to find the Radio Delmare ship in the thick fog and were apprehended on their return.

A further tender run by *Radio Benelux*, a Hilversum pirate station, was stopped by the police as it supplied the radio ship in October. They caved in under intense questioning and gave the police details of all the Delmare team. When the police visited Delmare's new owner, Ad, they threatened to make a tax investigation of his snackbar in Breda.

Another tender enabled Johan to escape ashore and his place was taken by the ship's owner, Hans Keers. After running out of food, he set sail for shore. To disguise the ship's identity, he painted over her name. On the way back his engine died and, on 31st October, the MV Aegir 2 was towed into Stellendam. She was later impounded in Rotterdam, with the two earlier Radio Delmare boats.

Never ones to give up easily, the DOO (as Delmare was now called) decided to try again and equipped yet another former Scheveningen fishing boat, bought from Vrolijk Sportvissen. This was the *Morgenster*, which also did some supply runs for Radio Caroline. Some new funding was obtained from a well-known Rotterdam musician's manager. Sadly, the Dutch authorities raided that ship just before sailing time and scuppered Radio Delmare's return to the air, so the DOO team began to court Radio Caroline.

All alone again

By the autumn, Radio Caroline was on her own again at sea. She had always had the strongest signal and a more reliable schedule than her rivals of 1979, Radio Mi Amigo and Radio Delmare.

In September, Radio Caroline had its first "death at sea": the ship's pet canary, Wilson, passed away. He was buried at sea with due solemnity and was replaced by another bird, who was given the name Wilson II.

During October, Caroline was experiencing some problems with money and supply boats from Holland; the activity by the authorities in arresting a tender and crews of the radio ships had scared some of the Caroline suppliers in Scheveningen. Arrangements were made to switch the tendering route to a port in Belgium but "loose tongues" resulted in a large amount of supplies being intercepted and seized by the authorities.

Lack of regular supply runs and disagreements about wages from Holland caused the Dutch DJs to strike for a few days. All had been paid at varying rates, with Marc Jacobs paid most at 1500 NLG a month. When the Dutch left the ship, two English DJs, Stuart Russell and Tony Allen, took over the daytime shows for ten days until the supply line problems were resolved and the striking DJs were all fired. This interruption to the normal service was prolonged by the Belgian authorities intercepting a loaded trawler in Zeebrugge harbour carrying food, fuel and new programme tapes.

Also in October, a new service from Radio Caroline was begun, in French. The ship had always enjoyed good reception across the whole of the Benelux and well down into France. Supplies had often come from Boulogne and the new programmes were an attempt to try and get some advertising support from France. Sadly, this never generated enough response to be economically viable and Caroline broadcast her final French service shows early in 1980.

Many of Radio Caroline's programmes were recorded at New Caroline House, a pet name for Ben Bode's jingle company, *Probe Score* in the Nieuwestraat in The Hague. This was just a couple of hundred yards from the Prime Minister's office and the Council of State in the Kneuterdijk, which is where the authorities planned their action against Caroline.

New Caroline House in Den Haag

In November, Radio Caroline began running a daily pre-recorded two hour show called *Space Play*, made in Los Angeles by Mike Hagler, who was by now using the name Michael Light. Mike had been involved in programming of Caroline in 1974 and recorded station IDs and other voice overs. Many of these extolled the virtues of Loving Awareness and are still broadcast occasionally today.

The Caroline schedule now continued until 2am each day with full 24-hour broadcasting just before Christmas. The all-night programming continued after the festive season was over, although in January the service was slightly reduced by half an hour, to allow engineering checks to be done each day at 5.30am GMT. The ship was using only one generator and it needed checking over and oiling daily.

Listeners would not have realised how bleak life was becoming on board the Mi Amigo, as programmes were usually presented with the utmost professionalism. Radio Caroline was now using the same name, day and night, with English and Dutch shows.

A young Ben Bode in his Den Haag studio

It was a very hard winter for the boys on the Mi Amigo, which was now in urgent need of repairs. A new Belgian manager was in charge of the tendering and he placed on board a crewman who did many idiotic things that annoyed his crewmates. One was to strip the wood panelling in the messroom back, to simply replace a fuse! For many of the crew it was just too much. It caused one of Caroline's best loved DJs, Buzby to leave, which he did in January 1980.

After a few months ashore, Buzby was refreshed and ready to go back out to the radio ship at the end of March. He made plans for the impending Easter birthday celebration of the Radio Caroline. Peter de Vries hosted the breakfast show on Radio Caroline until early March 1980 when he took a short break to record more novelty records.

There was some confusion at this time as the 'secret codes' used to get messages off the ship to the offices in London and The Hague got mixed up and for some time the Dutch had the wrong information, although no one realised this for some time. They were not even aware that the 'code record' warning of problems on board the ship was The Fortunes hit *You've Got your Troubles*.

The Old Lady's swan song

By March 1980 the situation on the Mi Amigo was settling down nicely with almost all the daytime output being taped in the Netherlands, played out on board the Mi Amigo using just one Dutchman. Overnight English programmes comprised a couple of hours of religion, plus the English programmes, using three or four DJs, presented live on board.

On Wednesday 19th March a crew change took place. Ben Bode had begun a system of splitting tender crew changes so the incoming team arrived on one run and those departing left on a later "pick up". For some reason, the incoming team did not all arrive and the crew remaining was only Tom Anderson, Stevie Gordon, Nick Richards and Dutchman Hans Verlaan, who had only arrived on board that day, replacing Hugo de Groot who left on the same tender. Hans would attend to playing the Dutch programming, Stevie did the English shows while Tim and Nick looked after the ship.

At lunchtime, the anchor chain snapped and a combination of the tide and north easterly gale took the ship towards the Long Sand. It took about three hours for the crew to release the emergency anchor, which they finally managed to do just as it was getting dark. The Mi Amigo had by then grounded on the sand, just four hundred yards from the territorial waters limit. Sheerness lifeboat, the Helen Turnbull, had been called by the Coastguard who were aware of the ship's perilous situation, however the million or so listeners heard only non-stop music, punctuated by hourly coded reports.

Messages to shore had for some years from Radio Caroline been sent as a group of numbers, covering such notices as the supply situation, location of the ship and the urgency of any help that was required. This step was taken not to exclude listeners from the drama that often unfolded around the radio ship, but to prevent responses overloading the emergency services.

Radio Caroline always had very responsive listeners, some of whom hung on the station's ever word. They would faithfully respond to every cause for concern and immediately call the appropriate emergency service. This was invariably the coastguard, an under-resourced public body who would be inundated with phone calls. After every emergency message, Radio Caroline would always have to ask listeners not to call the coastguards, who were usually aware of the predicament that the ship might be in. The ship was equipped with both MF and VHF radio and could usually speak direct to the Coastguard and other ships in her immediate vicinity.

Thames coastguards kindly called Radio Caroline's local boatman Albert Hood and kept him appraised of the situation. By the time the lifeboat arrived in the Barrow Deep, the Mi Amigo she was settled firmly onto the edge of the sandbank and in no immediate danger, just as she had experienced many times before. The crew decided to await a tender to take them back to the normal anchorage and fit a new anchor.

By mid-evening the tide began to rise, as did the easterly wind until it was a Force 9. This is what meteorologists call "a strong gale", with speeds of around 50mph. It continued to blow from the north east, the quadrant from which the winds have the longest 'fetch' and which have most power in the Thames estuary. This piled the incoming tide into very heavy seas resulting in waves that lifted the Mi Amigo up and then let her crash down again onto the sandbank.

The ship seems to have been sat over what was left of the anchor chain and, as she was bounced around onto it, water began pouring into the ship. The chain was literally punching holes in her already thin bottom. All the bilge pumps were set to work but the level of water in the bottom of the ship kept on rising.

The station was still on the air; Caroline's music had continued throughout the evening from tapes, but eventually the crew had to admit defeat and agree to be taken off by the lifeboat. Just before they left the Mi Amigo, Stevie Gordon opened the mic for some final announcements:

> *"Well, we're sorry to tell you that, due to the severe weather conditions and also to the fact that we are shipping quite a lot of water, we're closing down and the crew are at this stage leaving the ship.*
>
> *Obviously we hope to be back with you as soon as possible, but we'd just like to assure you all on land that there's nothing to worry about, just for the moment we'd like to say goodbye. Tom? "*
>
> *"Yeah, it's not a very good occasion really," responded Tom Anderson. "I'll have to hurry this because the lifeboat is standing by. We're not leaving and disappearing, we're going onto the lifeboat, hoping that the pumps can take it. If they can, we'll be back, if they can't . . well. I don't like to say it."*
> *"I think we'll be back one way or another'" suggested Stevie.*
> *"Yeah I think so," said Tom.*
> *"From all of us, for the moment, goodbye and God bless."*

Down in the Mi Amigo's hold, Nick Richards' final task was to switch off the transmitter for the final time and once again, the Mi Amigo was silent, but still wrestling with the waves as her crew desperately assembled in the gunwales and prepared to abandon ship.

Sheerness lifeboat made no less than thirteen attempts to get alongside the radio ship and take off the four man crew and Wilson II, the canary. Once safely on board, they were bunded below to the safety of the cabin for a change into warm clothes and hot drinks.

"The lifeboat guys were brilliant," said Tom Anderson. One minute the lifeboat was twenty feet above us and then it would be maybe ten feet below us. For them to get alongside at all was great seamanship." The cox of the Helen Turnbull, Charlie Bowry, was later awarded a Silver Medal for the rescue.

Twenty minutes later the lifeboat crew reported that all the lights on the Mi Amigo had gone out. Tom, Stevie, Nick and Hans realised that this meant the main generator had failed, possibly submerged and so her many pumps would now stop running.

Back at the lifeboat's home port of Sheerness, the crew members were questioned by police and officials from the Home Office but no action was taken. At first light, rescue chopper 166 from RAF Manston reported that the ship appeared to have sunk *in situ* over the sandbank and a plane flown out by ITN confirmed this. Journalists from the world's press were now gathering to report the news that the Mi Amigo seemed to have finally succumbed to the waves.

"All you could see of the Radio Caroline ship this morning was the top of her wheelhouse and her huge 200 foot tal mast pointing above the waves," said avid Caroline listener Carol Barnes in the lunchtime ITV news bulletin. It showed film of the Mi Amigo, still defiantly refusing to sink below the waves.

Carol was a long time Radio Caroline fan who had often helped the station. The following day she interviewed Tony Blackburn who said: "Well, it's such a shame as it's the end of an era. To me it gave me everything I have and I owe my success to my time on Radio Caroline. It gave everyone such a lot of pleasure and there can't be anything wrong with that in this day and age. It did revolutionise broadcasting in this country. If it hadn't actually started, we would still have Mrs Dale turning over the pages of her diary."

Two days later, some of Caroline's key staff went out to the Long Sand to see if there was any way of salvaging the ship, but it was a hopeless task due to her position on the sandbank, and the fierce tides which swept the channel next to her. Uncannily, in the immediate area of the ship the waves were becalmed.

Mi Amigo's mast and marker buoy

The aft part of the ship was beneath the waves, which swirled around the top of the wheelhouse. The Mi Amigo's bowsprit was reaching out into the air, as though inviting someone to take her in tow and return her to the Knock Deep! The mast was defiantly pointing towards the heavens, a symbol of her life. It was to stand proudly erect for another six years.

The story of the sinking was given hours of radio time and press coverage. Debates over her future ran for months afterwards. Thanet District Council in Kent discussed paying for the ship to be salvaged and brought to either Ramsgate or Margate as a tourist attraction however doubts over the ship's true ownership and worries about her condition after being partially submerged for a couple of months soon made this initiative impractical.

The ship had been gifted to Peter Chicago by Ronan some years previously however there were no ship's papers or ownership documentation. Some papers had been issued at the auction in 1972 to Gerard van Dam, but his subsequent sale to Ronan was mainly a verbal agreement with only a scrap of paper. Without proof of ownership there is little that can be done with a ship; her legal status is vague but this situation also side-steps the responsibilities of liability.

Divers visited the ship but were unable to retrieve much due to the murky conditions and the silt. They tried to bring off some output valves from the transmitter as these are the most valuable components and unlikely to be affected by sea water. They reported that the ship was already filling with silt and that the wooden doors to the cabins had swollen making it impossible to open them.

20. Caroline's Revenge

The Radio Caroline management team had in fact been looking for a replacement ship for the Mi Amigo for about a year before she had foundered. The core of the Caroline team set about trying to raise new funding and to identify a suitable ship. One suitable contender that was considered was the *Lord Nelson*, a large factory trawler that was laid up in Hull. While looking around her, a guide suggested to Chicago that they look at another de-commissioned trawler, the *Ross Revenge*, that was maybe even more suitable and was the biggest side-winder (a method of fishing) even built.

The Ross Revenge had been built in Bremerhaven, Germany in 1959 and fished out of Iceland for a few years before being bought by the Ross Group. She broke several fish-catching records and was probably the pride of the Ross fleet. They became a huge multinational food company before being bought out by United Biscuits.

After the Cod Wars the UK pulled its ships back from many traditional shipping grounds and many sidewinders were replaced with stern-fishing factory vessels. The Ross Revenge was retired and taken to a ship-breakers yard at Cairnryan, a small harbour near Stranraer in Scotland. At the last minute she was rescued from the cutting torches and locals told that she would be converted for survey and rescue work. Her new owners were a mysterious company represented by veteran ship broker, Captain Silas Victor Oates, who rejected all approaches to speak to the Caroline staff. Now long retired from the salvage business, he's still reluctant to discuss the Ross Revenge.

Contact was made with Captain Oates' bankers by Ernst Kuntz, the Liechtenstein-based agent for Radio Caroline. The bank had been funding the conversion and now that the work seemed to have come to a halt, they were keen to get the ship off their books. Herr Kuntz made a cheeky bid of just £28,500, only a little more than had been paid for the original Caroline ship, the ferry Fredericia, almost twenty years before. The bank were delighted to get any money back and quickly agreed to the sale.

An entrepreneur with a keen interest in Radio Caroline joined the organisation in 1980; Vincent Monsey was to play a key role in expanding Caroline into North America where deeper pocketed investors and very lucrative advertising revenue could be found. Vincent' and his partner Anthony Kramer became integral parts of the newly reconstituted Caroline organisation and provided substantial funding at the most crucial time to "start the ball rolling".

Vincent had long been interested in radio and was preparing to launch a project called *Radio Amanda*. He was fitting a ship out in the West Country and when DJ Nicky Horne prematurely ran a news magazine feature about it on Thames TV. This was seen by Ronan O'Rahilly who was keen to help. Ronan contacted Vincent and offered him a role in the new Radio Caroline.

Vincent Monsey

Vincent's first foray into offshore radio was as *London International Agency,* making and selling T-shirts and other merchandise for Radio Northsea in 1970, while still working as a civil servant. He was a wealthy young man with bags of energy and was made a partner in the new Caroline project. He became President of one of the Radio Caroline companies in 1980 and stayed until 1987, being responsible for contracting with programming and sales people, mainly in the USA.

Ronan formed a new company called *Caroline Communications,* with Vincent Monsey, who invested a substantial sum into the venture. This umbrella company was advised by John Leonard, a lawyer in New York and Ernst Kunz, the Liechtenstein agent for the overall owning company. Vincent also brought in one of his business partners, Anthony Kramer but he remained in the background.

Six months after the loss of the Mi Amigo's, the trade paper *Campaign* announced that a major New York agency had been appointed to represent Caroline there. Reporters were told that the station had secured enough equipment and a suitable vessel to relaunch in 1981.

All the items of equipment (generators, studios, transmitter, etc) and the new ship were purchased by a new Liechstenstein company, *Simor Establishment* and then ownership was transferred to a new Panamanian company. The incorporation documents called it *Grothan Steemship Lines Inc.* a common tactic, that worked when attempts were made to clone the name in Holland; they misspelt the main two words!

Ronan had decided that the new Radio Caroline would have a huge tower capable of putting out a high-power signal on a low frequency, so that wide coverage could be achieved. The lowest frequency that

Caroline had ever used was 557 kHz, the previous home of Radio Veronica andm temporarily, Capital Radio in London. It was now quiet but was being eagerly scrutinised by the BBC, who had a long-term plan to use it for one of their local stations.

At Easter 1981 a deal was struck with a Spanish tug, the Aznar Jose Luis, to tow the Ross Revenge south. Access was arranged to a dock in a quiet area of Solares, near Santander on the north coast of Spain for fitting the mast, generators and transmitters.

A lot of the discussions were of a sensitive nature which ruled out using the very public Carlton Tower Hotel, so Caroline Communications moved into a small office in Beauchamp Place, just off the Brompton Road and right opposite the IBA's headquarters!

Occupying an adjacent office was Paul Hodge, who had worked in insurance in the City and was now running a music management business. He was a member of one of the worshipful guilds, a Lloyds underwriter and very well connected in the City.

Paul Hodge was soon persuaded to become a member of the new *Caroline Communications* cabal. The funds he invested were used to pay for the two huge MAN generators that were installed on the ship. They were six-cylinder water cooled monsters, together capable of half a million watts from their Stanford alternators. One of them is still in use today.

One of the MAN generators in the ship

Caroline Communications signed a deal with a money broker called James Ryan. His role was to persuade wealthy investors to buy shares in the radio station. He deftly used Radio Caroline's reputation to assemble a consortium of investors, who would pay for the new ship to be refitted, offices to be established and the station to become operational.

"Caroline will return at Easter with a dramatic new sound," promised station spokesman Vincent Monsey from the New York office in March1981. "Many of the DJs from Radio Caroline's illustrious past would be returning," he said, listing Johnny Jason, Tom Anderson, Johnnie Lewis and Mike Stevens among those who could be expected to be heard in the first week's transmissions.

'Pan European' advertisers?
The trade press, including *ADWeek* and *Campaign*' quoted Warner Rush, the head of *Major Market Radio* saying: "We are targeting international advertisers, particularly companies who are heavy users of radio in the USA, but haven't yet advertised in the UK. Our lawyers have looked carefully at the Caroline set up and are satisfied that the *modus operandi* is completely legal."

A rate card for air time on Caroline was produced by Major Market Radio, a time booker owned by movie star Gene Autry. A small office was provided by MMR for Caroline, pending them getting their own premises.

MMR proclaimed that the station was appealing to "the Imagination Nation" and that some of Radio Caroline's best friends are advertisers. They said that "the Caroline keynote was a relaxed and easy-going style that offers the best in contemporary music with regular news and public service bulletins." The blurb promised a series of special programmes featuring areas of today's popular music that wasn't currently available on British radio, such as futurist and synthesiser rock.

"Musically, Radio Caroline has always set the pace; where she goes today Britain and Europe will follow tomorrow. If Caroline's success can be attributed to any one factor, it is this – she is the spirit of freedom and loving awareness in an age of conflict and petty restriction. She is the flagship of anyone who wishes to be truly free."

Three transmitters were shipped from a station in Arkansas in the USA by used equipment suppliers *Besco International* in late Summer but some of the paperwork mysteriously disappeared and more delays ensued, causing them to languish in Rotterdam for a few months. The main rig was a BTA50H, an old RCA Ampliphase 50kW transmitter. It must surely be the most photographed broadcast transmitter in the history of radio and remains the 'must see' item on the ship for all visitors, even though it's now over fifty years old.

The studios on the ship were hand-built by Peter Chicago and Tom Anderson. They carried all the timber from a local woodyard near the harbour to the ship. It was they who did the design and layout of the ship to convert her into a floating radio station.

Radio Delmare's fourth attempt

Across in Holland, radio listeners had lost Radio Mi Amigo, Radio Delmare and the Dutch service of Radio Caroline. There was now no commercial radio of any kind in the Netherlands, only the state NOS services (which carried commercials) and a few low power pirates who popped on and off the air for a few hours, mainly at weekends.

Despite having lost three ships already in a series of raids and arrests, the Delmare team were still keen to relaunch the station. Yet another of Radio Caroline's former tenders became available in early 1981, the MV Morgenster - which is Dutch for Morning Star.

Morgenster at the quay in Maasluis
Leendert Vingerling

Rederij Vrolijk only wanted 37,500 Guilders for the boat, so a deal was done for the manager of Rotterdam singer Ray Statson to part fund it. He didn't want the station's key man to be involved, and Gerard had lost his interest anyway, so he took on a new career in a discount clothes shop and left the radio world behind him, refusing to even discuss it.

After many months of hard work preparing her, the *Morgenster* was raided by the Dutch radio police in May as she waited for a bridge to be raised to leave Maasluis port. Only a studio was found on board so no charges could be brought but the case took almost two years to progress though the legal system, causing lots of problems and anguish for the team of owners, now led by Leendert Vingerling.

On the Morgenster's navigation charts were two little marks, which the RCD claimed were "evidence" of its intentions. One crew member broke down under questioning and confessed, so the boat was confiscated and brought to the customs harbour in Rotterdam.

After a trial lasting for two years the boat was given back to its owners. It was then sold to someone from Harlem, so that the financier finally got a part of his 120.000 guilders investment returned, but the days of Radio Delmare were now over. Some of the Delmare team were to become involved in the new Radio Caroline, taking shape in Spain.

Caroline in Paradise
The Radio Paradise project was assembled by Ben Bode, who had operated the Dutch part of Radio Caroline so successfully in 1979 and 1980. His associates were Danny Vuylsteke and A J Beirens, a well-known free radio supporter. They had advertising links with Patrick Valain who had engineered the breakaway of Radio Mi Amigo and was known on the air as Lieven Colijn. Together they now operated the *Mi Amigo Drive-in Disco*, a very successful mobile discotheque operation.

Ben Bode leased a base for the station in The Hague above a bank, which partly funded the new radio ship, along with record company plugging deals. These were primarily from Basart and from Red Bullet Productions, a label owned by former Veronica and RNI DJ Joost de Draaijer. Over £1m had been invested in the project, some of it was collected in the last few days before the Mi Amigo sank!

Ben and his team bought a ship in Krautsand, Germany called the *Lieve* but Danny Vuylsteke tried to recruit a ship's captain and told him that the ship was to be a replacement for Radio Caroline, even showing him pictures of the Mi Amigo! Unfortunately, the man he tried to recruit was a captain of a police launch; the authorities suddenly took a keen interest in the ship, so it had to hurriedly leave port. En-route to Ireland the MV Lieve was damaged during a storm and towed into Southampton, but eventually it reached Dublin where work to convert her into a radio ship continued.

Hans van Velsen and former Radio Veronica chief engineer, José Groningen installed the transmitters: two 10 kW AM and a 30KW FM transmitter from Broadcast Electronics. These were installed in Dublin, with a mast over 200 feet tall, erected by Sammy Prendergast's team.

The ship was supposed to be home to four radio stations

- ***Radio Europa*** an easy listening service on FM,
- ***Radio Paradijs,*** a rock music station for the Netherlands
- ***Radio Monique*** Dutch language music for the Netherlands. (backed by several Dutch record companies).

The ship's captain (Ben Bode, wearing another hat!) told customs officials that the transmitters were special fish surveying computers to be used in the Persian Gulf. An Irish newspaper, the *Sunday World*, got wind of the ruse and was ready to run a 'Irish Customs Are Fooled' story that weekend, so on the 15th July the ship set sail in a bit of a hurry. Sadly the antenna mast had not been finished and The Prendergast team had only few hours to add precious little rigging.

With only a skeleton crew on board, the ship, now renamed the MV *Magda Maria*, slipped out of Dublin and headed south down the Irish Sea. Only a few hours into the voyage, about 125 feet of the mast fell into the Irish Sea.

Radio Paradijs off Noordwijk, Holland (with the top third of her mast missing)

Hans Joachim Backhus

The ship was due off Holland early on Saturday; Her team of DJs waited at sea all day on board the tender, the Bizon, but there was no sign of her. They had to return to shore, despite paying 10,000 guilders for the trip, because the Bizon, a party boat, was booked for a dinner cruise that evening for a local government department.

During the event, the call came from the ship to shore station that the Paradijs ship was offshore awaiting her supplies so Fred ordered the Bizon to immediately sail to the rendezvous, complete with dancers and revellers, resplendant in evening dress and eating their meal. Probably the first time a radio ship had a live orchestra performing during a tender run! "We told the party it was an emergency and a ship needed urgent supplies or she might sink," remembers Ben.

Suitably replenished, Radio Paradijs tests commenced on 270m MW, although the station identified itself as Nova, 88FM! The ship's engineers used old tapes of Nova FM for a few days and then on the 26th, Radio Paradijs DJs began announcing the programmes.

Selected representatives from the Dutch media went out on the next tender and former Radio Caroline DJ Rob Hudson made a superb feature for NOS TV, seen on the national news at 7pm that evening. It showed that the Radio Paradijs ship was well equipped, fully stocked with records and had all comforts that star Dutch DJs expect.They had a full set of customised station ID jingles, which were a re-sing of PAMS series 49, *The Modulaters*.

A national Dutch newspaper carried some photographs taken from a plane they flew out to the Radio Paradijs ship. In the front page pictures, some cable drums of guy wires left on deck. They looked a bit like satellite dishes and were erroneously reported as such.

The following day, the Dutch Parliament debated the new arrival and a Minister ordered that action be taken against the Magda Maria. On the first of August, as dawn broke, a Dutch Roofdier class frigate, *HNLMS Jaguar*, F822, pulled alongside, boarded her and found several failings in her status. The ship's name had been changed from *Lieve* to *Magda Maria* without corresponding paperwork being on board and there was no qualified captain in command.

Although it was a technical 'fault', this was just enough for the Dutch navy to seize the ship, pending resolution of the irregularities. They towed the ship into Amsterdam and began removal of the radio equipment. The navy were ordered back to sea again to collect the anchor system for the ship, which was very expensive and newly laid.

News of this raid and seizure of a radio ship on the high seas had immediate repercussions for Radio Caroline. It certainly spooked some of the Caroline investors and precipitated a lot of discussions and meetings between Ryan and Caroline's management, culminating in an attempted overthrow of the organisation in Spain.

Radio Paradijs station director Ben Bode fought the Dutch authorities in the high courts of the Netherlands. It took over a year to reach a decision but eventually the court agreed with the ship owners that an illegal act had been committed by seizing the vessel while on the high seas. Lawyers acting for *Naviera Panlieve SA*, the Panamanian company which owned the equipment, began legal proceedings against the Dutch government.

At further hearings in the Dutch high court, the authorities accepted that they had been wrong to arrest the ship and remove her from the High Seas. They had to agree that the ship could leave port but the owners decided to "go for goal" and pursue the government for costs and compensation for their losses while the station was not broadcasting. The case dragged on for about fourteen years, racking up enormous legal costs – Radio Paradijs' costs alone were 50,000 guilders a year.

By the time the case was settled in 1984, the moment had passed and Radio Caroline was back on the air from a new ship in the Thames estuary. Several key Radio Paradijs people were about to launch a new service from the Ross Revenge, which was well away from Dutch waters. That station was to be called Radio Monique.

Ben Bode however was content that he and the investors had been paid all their costs and compensation for the amounts of profit they could have made while the Paradijs was under arrest.

Caroline makes progress.

While the Paradijs lawyers tussled with the Dutch authorities, Radio Caroline's team in New York were forging ahead, though the project was cloaked with a considerable degree of mystery and intrigue. In Summer 1981, Vincent did a deal with veteran American radio executive Al Ham to broadcast his *Music of Your Life* programme to Europe using a 50 KW transmitter on the new Caroline ship. His was a popular music format on American stations and would perfectly complement the rockier '*Caroline – your Imagination Station*' output that was to be transmitted simultaneously on another frequency.

Al Ham bought a 50 kilowatt transmitter from the Texas transmitter broker, Besco International, to carry his service. This was flown to Holland in August 1981 but seized when it arrived in Rotterdam. Eventually it was released and transported down to Spain amidst great secrecy as, only a month earlier, the Radio Paradijs ship had been arrested in the North Sea off Noordwijk and towed into Amsterdam.

Vincent also brought in James Ryan, a well-known arranger of financial deals, who introduced Radio Caroline to half a dozen wealthy investors. One of these turned out to be a mob member who was managing his investment into the project from his jail cell in the USA! That association led to Caroline severing all ties with Ryan. Like all fraudsters, Ryan had seen the Radio Caroline project as simply an opportunity to get his hands on other people's money, by managing the transaction and skimming a huge slice off the top.

Another signing by Vincent was Roy Lindau. An advertising rate card was devised by Ryan and Lindau based on what a 50 kW clear channel station might achieve in the USA. They sliced up the air-time and sold the slots to investors, promising them returns based on the amount of air-time that could later be sold to advertisers during their slots. They were effectively signing over blocks of Caroline's airtime to the investors on the hope that Lindau's company would later be able to sell the advertising spots within those blocks.

James Ryan's method however was little more than a 'Ponzi' scheme, as they double-sold some slots and practiced various other dubious rackets. Ryan already had previous convictions for fraud and had even been forbidden by the courts from holding a bank account. His financial japes had to be conducted using his wife's maiden name. Ryan was also demanding that any second station operated from the new Caroline ship be called Radio Ursula, named after his wife.

A Wolf on Board!

Vincent Monsey was now building a team that could maximise the potential inherent in the reputation of Radio Caroline. He arranged the signing of some of the biggest names in the world of radio to broadcast on Caroline. The first of these was Wolfman Jack, an American DJ who truly was "a living legend" after appearing as himself in George Lucas' blockbuster movie *American Graffiti*. Wolf had broadcast across the Americas for almost twenty years adopting the persona of a real pirate, border blasting on huge stations over the border in Mexico.

Wolfman Jack signs for Caroline with executive Vincent Monsey

The other big star signing for Caroline was Johnnie Walker, who announced in January 1982 that the station would relaunch later that year. Johnnie had been left high and dry in Amsterdam when Caroline was abruptly towed off the air in 1968. After a year hanging around in London awaiting the return of the station, he succumbed to the offer of a gig on BBC Radio 1.

After becoming a big star with a daytime show, Johnnie rebelled against the bland cheesy pop music style of the station and refused to play teenybopper music. A reflection of his refusal to play plug records on Caroline a few years earler. Johnnie had gone to the USA and enjoyed several years at KSAN, a freeform station in California.

Johnnie also introduced a young lady DJ called Vincenta Licata to the proposed Radio Caroline line up. He told a journalist in London that the ship was being renamed the *MV Imagine*, to honour John Lennon, who had been gunned down in New York just a year before. "We very much want to keep going the philosophy that Lennon was putting forward in his life," explained Johnnie. "We've got some amazing stuff that John gave us – in the sixties he wanted peace and everyone moaned about it."

"I've been attracted back by Radio Caroline's policy of free-form radio, playing a round the clock mixture of all genres, singles and albums. We won't be hampered by petty rules and long lines of bosses that have wrecked British radio. Out at sea you are free, with no pressure to hit target audiences for the advertisers," explained Johnnie. "We will be the radio equivalent of 'Ready Steady Go', the old TV programme that launched so many careers and was essential viewing for kids in the sixties."

Johnnie by the Ross Revenge

Now with offices on Madison Avenue and central London, Caroline was beginning to buzz. Some of the new Caroline team lived in Kent which is where Johnnie Walker and other DJs scheduled to join the Ross Revenge were billeted. Johnnie moved into a small flat in Ramsgate before heading west to join Radio West in Bristol. A quarter of a century later, Caroline is still waiting for him to rejoin the station, although he is now back with the BBC. He now hosts a rock show on Radio 2 and has made guest appearances on Caroline.

Roy Lindau was the VP of MMR, a company owned by legendary actor Gene Autry, that represented radio stations in 32 markets with offices across the USA. He claimed to have worldwide representation rights in Radio Caroline, a claim that was vigorously opposed by Ronan and others who were also appointed to sell time on the station.

Major Market Radio claimed that "Caroline advertisers could efficiently cover the entire UK and Western Europe with one radio buy on one station." The vaunted Easter relaunch came and went without a squeak being heard on any of the regular Caroline channels, apart from a few land pirates seeking to get an audience.

Throughout 1981 and 1982 Ross Revenge made steady progress toward becoming a radio ship. Some substantial amounts of funding had been raised but it came from people who caused delays and problems. The consortium led by James Ryan were becoming very disgruntled, not only with Radio Caroline, but among themselves. Ryan tried several times to hijack the entire operation. He didn't mind how he got control and tried both court action and even brute force.

Ryan had his eye on catalogue revenue streams and he wanted to have four offshore stations in a network, all on board ships which would sell space in the catalogues. One of his projects was for a TV channel on board a former bulk carrier that was laid up in Connecticut.

The plan was to anchor it off Eastbourne and using a 1200 high tower, to beam in a UHF signal to London, pre-empting MTV's launch in the UK. The plan was to call the vessel *The Iron Lady*, after Margaret Thatcher. Part of the team for this was Carl Gjerpen, a Norwegian ship owner who lived in considerable luxury in Norwalk, Ct. He had commissioned conversion plans for the vessel and had booked time at a shipyard in Norway to commission the work.

Another Ryan scheme involved Allan Weiner who established a multi-band offshore station off Long Island in the mid 80s, broadcasting to New York. The FCC swung into action and closed the station down within a week, whereupon Weiner appeared on the Ross Revenge for a couple of months. He was part of the plan to launch World Music radio on short wave from the Ross Revenge.

Ryan had tried using a method similar to that used in London in the 1960s by the Kray twins called 'the long firm'. Legitimate start-up business are funded and build up good lines of credit and a reputation before the firm's inventory is sold off in a 'fire sale' and the company goes under, with all the product having been obtained on credit. A patsy (front man) then takes the blame for the problem. James Ryan tried recruiting several British radio entrepreneurs with the same method, including Ronan O'Rahilly and Radio Caroline.

Ryan had been appointed Finance Director of Liechtenstein company, *Simor Establishments*, that had originally bought the new radio ship and owned the radio station. The lawyers battled for months to remove Ryan from any involvement with Radio Caroline or any of the Liechtenstein companies, including Simor, early in 1982, after several dubious practices were discovered.

Ryan had falsely told several people that they owned part of the Ross Revenge, when he knew that this was incorrect. He then prepared a Power for Attorney giving a British agent, Paul Hodge, the authority to go to Honduras and reregister the ship there. Ownership of the Ross Revenge had been vested in a Panamanian company, *Grothan Steemship Lines*, but another company had been incorporated in the Netherlands with an almost identical company name, *Grotham Steamship bv*. It was clearly dreamt up to be used in a "passing off scam" on investors using Radio Caroline's good name.

Trade newspapers reported that around half a million pounds of investors backing had mysteriously gone missing and that the resulting court case was now the main cause of the delay in getting the new radio ship out to sea. The real story however was somewhat different: some of the American investors, particularly Elaine and Thomas Morrison, were dismayed to discover that they were buying only a few hours of airtime to sell and not control of the full radio station, as had been falsely represented to them by Ryan.

Some huge disagreements over the station's output had arisen, with one group of professionals being determined that the station should broadcast a contemporary hits format to get the largest audience possible, while Ronan and some of his team were keen to have an "all albums" format, an alternative to BBC Radio 1 and the Top 40 market which the ILR station were happy to chase.

Ryan was by now out of the picture, with an FBI posse hot on his trail for a variety of offences. So too was Roy Lindau and Major Market Radio. The FBI were busy mounting a 'sting' operation to prove that the fund-raising for Radio Caroline had been fraudulent and Ryan was their main target. The wheels of justice turn slowly and it was to be another seven years before Ryan was finally convicted and jailed.

After a failed appeal, he was sent to jail for five years. The charges covered many fraudulent dealings Ryan had perpetrated using the money of some of the eight or so investors who claimed to have funded the return of Radio Caroline. One of those who gave evidence against him was a notorious mobster, who had already been given a fifteen-year sentence for racketeering!

There were also rumours of a takeover of the ship by a rival faction, which resulted in some violence on one occasion. The entire affair was argued and debated in the Spanish high court, which resulted in further lengthy delays.

PINK SHIP

It had been decided by Ronan some time previously that once the ship was ready for sea she would be painted pink, which is the colour of healing. He had become increasingly aware of various healing ideas and remedies and was a keen proponent of alternative medicine.

He also decided that the ship be renamed *Imagine*, in honour of John Lennon. Not everyone was enthusiastic about the proposed colour scheme, including some of the 'straight' crew members who felt it might send out the 'wrong signals' about the crew's sexual orientation.

The Norwegian captain who was engaged by Radio Caroline to skipper the ship on her return to the North Sea was not happy about Ronan's plan to have the ship painted pink and renamed the MV Imagine. "He just packed his bags and walked off the ship, without saying goodbye or anything," reported Carol Maszka, the girlfriend of Peter Chicago. He left a simple note that said: "I refuse to be the captain of a pink ship." Carol was the last to see him, struggling with his bags along the gangplank.

Meanwhile the ship had been dry-docked, transmitters had been obtained, shipped and installed. These were now in place in the Ross Revenge and the 285 feet high mast was in place and fully rigged. The ownership of the vessel was still a subject of a court hearing that would take an extra $150,000 in legal fees alone to resolve.

General Arrangement

The conversion work to the ship was quite extensive. The studios were built onto the level just below the bridge, with the former ships hospital on the starboard side being extended to form Caroline's Studio 1. Through a double window could be seen Studio 2 which became used for news and then for Radio Monique. It had previously been the First Mate's cabin. Twenty years later it was to be reconfigured once again and re-equipped; it is now used for the Radio Caroline North programmes on Manx Radio.

For'ard of the two original studios, overlooking the main deck, the captain's accommodation was converted to the record library. Down on the main deck, and towards the rear of the ship, a further studio was built in the former vegetable store, on the starboard side. This third studio was used for the Caroline Overdrive service. A tiny room opposite was used to play out the taped religious programmes. Known as the God Studio, someone had given it the number 666 on its door.

Initially, the plan was to produce the Caroline programmes from two studios mounted on the stern deck of the Ross Revenge. The cabin was craned on board and welded to the ship, as the marine architect had directed. Solid steel bracketing held the cabin in position.

Studio cabin installed on stern deck

Vincent Monsey

The Portacabin's windows offered an excellent view from the studios in almost all directions and equipment for the two was installed. They contained Russco turntables, Collins Cart machines and Revox open reel tape recorders. These were controlled by a large Gates mixing console.

The idea of studios in Portacabins was abandoned however just before the ship sailed to the North Sea. Access would have not been easy, especially when the weather was a bit wild, and some feared that the structure may have been blown off the ship completely! The insurers had decreed that anything on deck that wasn't original equipment would need rigorous sea trials before it could be approved.

The ships main fish hold had several feet of concrete poured in to act as ballast, as a counterweight for the 285 feet tall mast. The bottom section of the mast would also be mounted within that huge concrete 'brick', which weighed around 500 tons. The area above that was divided to form a separate section toward the bows, with enough room for three huge generators and the usual kit needed to service them, and a transmitter hold midships, directly underneath the tower.

Broadcast equipment would not work from the power generated by the ship's usual power plant, which gave DC. The new generator room had powerful alternators and was adjacent to the transmitters while being sufficiently well away from the crew's accommodation. The ship had numerous fuel tanks, all inter-connected and enabling the ship to run for several months without re-supply.

The transmitter hold was the heart of the ship. Steel mounting frames were installed here to hold the transmitters firmly in place and all the high voltage components (such as aerial matching coils and capacitors) located behind them. These were surrounded by steel cages to stop anyone stumbling onto them.
The transmitters on the original Caroline ship and the Mi Amigo were of the Doherty design, made by Continental Electronics of Dallas. They had been chosen by the original users of the Mi Amigo, *Radio Nord.* Those that would be obtained for use on the Ross Revenge were different.

In 1981 Besco International had offered Peter Chicago several suitable RCA transmitters. Their design can give a better, cleaner and brighter sound, if it is set up properly, although many lesser-experienced radio engineers have shied away from them. While some early examples had a reputation for overheating and catching fire, the one selected by Chicago was very reliable.

In RCA's Ampliphase transmitters, the signal is split into two, each out of phase with the other by 135°. These two branches are then independently phase modulated, amplified and then they are recombined in a summing circuit in the final stage. There were three of these on The Ross Revenge; one of 50 kW power level, a 10kW and a smaller 5kw, which was later upgraded to the 10kW level. Each was totally independent of the others, enabling the ship to transmit on three different frequencies simultaneously.

Tower sections craned on board.
Vincent Monsey

A Spanish company was found to design, build the huge now tower that Ronan had designed by a university. The new mast was to be of triangular construction, and 91metres (285 feet) in height. The design was done by the engineering department of the University of Barcelona. Once fabricated, it was professionally installed on the ship while in dock in Spain. Most of the sections were bolted together on the dockyard and then the entire structure hoisted into position by a large dockside travelling crane and held while the steel guys (stays) were fitted.

The mast was of triangular lattice structure from tubular steel and around 10 feet across each face at the bottom. It tapers gradually towards the top where it is less than 2 feet across. The tower itself is at ground potential at the base and supports an array of cables which form the 'antenna proper'.

The mast was assembled on the quayside in two halves, with the necessary guy wires. The 90m tall structure was then hoisted onto the deck of the Ross Revenge using a specially hired crane, with assistance from heavier lift quayside cranes with shorter reach.

A view up inside the mast
Vincent Monsey

New Finance

Eventually, in early 1983, the Spanish courts decided in Radio Caroline's favour but the legal battles had proven very expensive. The stay in the dock at Solares was also expensive and some of the accounts were racking up interest. The Caroline organisation was once again almost penniless. Ronan had to hit the streets once again in the quest for funds. It was something he was adept at and soon there were new offers.

Richard Branson was very well known in the 1980s for his success in various businesses. He had dabbled in activities as diverse as airlines, perfume, wedding dresses, vodka and even his own brand of cola. He had deep pockets and Ronan was certain that he would would have no difficulty in helping get Caroline operational. Branson had watched the Caroline journey carefully for many years and had even got involved in some record deals with them in the seventies. He was now keen to have his own radio station. He would invest, but only on his terms, which called for a large measure of control of the station's output. The terms and loss of control were too much for Ronan to stomach and he walked away from the offer.

In early 1983, another wealthy Irishman who wanted his own radio station approached Paul Rusling to help. With a new pub in Whitstable to run and with a new born first child, Paul didn't really want to get involved in an offshore radio project, so he spoke to Ronan O'Rahilly and suggested a merger. After some lengthy meetings, Ronan doubted that the prospective Irish investors would be suitable for Radio Caroline and said that he wasn't keen on having European investors in the station.

Nelson Skalbania

Alex Waterhouse

Fortunately, help for Caroline was at hand in the form of a wealthy Canadian investor, Nelson Skalbania. He was an international entrepreneur from Vancouver in Canada, active in many fields, from ice-hockey to environmental projects in which he had an excellent reputation as an innovative professional engineer.

Nelson had a strong reputation and track record for launching high profile, valuable companies and was often described as a whiz-kid and a mercurial entrepreneur.

While Nelson is a wheeler-dealer with nerves of steel, he is also a most generous man. There are countless examples of his philanthropy, particularly in the fields of art, culture and sport. Among his recent activities has been that of a resort developer, a plankton harvesting business, renewable energy and cold fusion.

Former Radio Caroline North DJ Mick Luvzit, a Canadian who got married on the ship in 1966, knew Nelson well and lived in Vancouver too. He was asked to advise Nelson about Radio Caroline before he invested the money. "I gave Ronan a glowing reference as he was always supportive of all the DJs on the ship, he made sure we were paid on time and was a man with extraordinary vision," said Mick.

The funds that Nelson provided as a result was sufficient to allow completion of the technical work on the ship and pay off the legal costs in Spain. Grothan Steemship Lines gave Nelson a mortgage over the ship to cover his loan of $500,000, although Nelson never called in the debt. A gesture that was typical of Nelson's generosity.

A large sum was also owed to MRK, a marine financier, who Ronan was always terrified might call issue a write if the ship came inshore. During May 1983 the court decision was handed down that the Ross Revenge was the property of Caroline once again and she was free to leave Spain. A huge effort was made to get the ship ready.

The portable building on the back deck complete with studios was hastily removed after it was realised that it would not pass any maritime regulations and it might even be dangerous. They were moved into the Captains cabin inside the wheelhouse. The ship was taken into dry dock and given a coat of bright red paint; she already had the pink undercoat. The stern deck was painted green and the large "LA–319 CAROLINE" legend applied on it, visible to aircraft flying overhead.

As the project neared fruition, Ronan recruited Annie Challis to manage the station. She was a lady who had impeccable contacts in the music business; she remains a close friend of Elton John, Rod Stewart and his wife Penny Lancaster. "For many years Annie has been someone I can rely on, I really treasure our relationship," said Rod Stewart to leading entertainment business publication, *Variety*.

Expert programmer Annie Challis

Annie believed in Caroline's mission and agreed to act as Station Manager, organising the "on air" team and be Head of Programming. This was to be an important role, liaising with the music business who would be providing exclusive programming, but it all had to be done professionally. As well as the programming items, some leading British celebrities and musicians donated funds to cover Caroline's expenses,

Caroline Gold?

There was an agreement that the station would transmit with the full 50kW of power on 558 kHz and be a mainly 'Gold' service, playing the cream of artists and their known hits, in order to attract a large audience. This was key to getting the financial support and other help that would be needed to keep Radio Caroline on the air.

A gold service in 1983 would have been innovative for the time as none existed. Radio Caroline DJ Crispian St John introduced a Gold format on a land pirate in south west London that year which proved to be very popular. It attracted a lot of interest, from listeners, from other radio people and especially from the music industry. When the authorities closed the land pirate down, Crispian rejoined Radio Caroline and assumed a new name, Jay Jackson.

"I was certain that a well-presented Gold programme would work from Radio Caroline," said Crispian, on many occasions. He had launched the UK's first such station as an unlicensed station in London. "People don't always want educating and most don't take music seriously at all, they simply want to be entertained. I always thought that music should be relaxing but maybe with some excitement too."

"When we grafted away in 1972 to get the Mi Amigo back to sea, we had endless meetings and agreed on this – Caroline should be for everyone, and not narrowcast," explained Crispian. "Focussing on only one genre of music or demographic group of people is not the way to make a commercial radio station work."

Capital Radio and several other ILR stations launched their own 'Gold' services very shortly afterwards. They too proved to be very successful, with the AM only Gold services of some smaller stations as popular as their FM outlets.

The Gold stations tended to attract a more mature demographic but also a lot more loyalty. A missed opportunity for Caroline; how might the station have handled becoming outrageously successful at that time; certainly the radio industry and the British Government would have been outraged to be shown up and probably taken action sooner,

This happened later when Laser, a new station, arrived and, by quickly winning huge audiences, made them look a bit amateurish, or worse.

Annie's instructions were ignored and all her hard prep' work for Caroline were wasted when the station launched while Ronan, instead of being angry was merely 'bemused' and failed to act, telling one journalist that "It seems that this time the lunatics really have taken over the asylum. Maybe we should see how it turns out, its only music. Caroline is more than that, its freedom- that's our message."

Annie eventually moved to the USA and has lived in Los Angeles for the last 30 years, working as a broker and realtor. Who knows what levels of success could have awaited the station had her instructions on programming been followed?

"The biggest problems arose because Ronan would never give the full go-ahead to programme the station in a way that would make us to be number one in the market," said Howard Rose. He was an experienced DJ who, as Jay Jackson, became Head of News on the ship.

Howard Rose, aka Jay Jackson (formerly Crispian St John)

Peter Harmsen

"It was almost as though he was afraid of allowing the station to become too successful. Annie Challis was in tears and eventually walked out, as any professional programmer would do if faced with such insurrection and disobedience by the DJs and a station boss unable or unwilling to put it right."

Howard was a larger than life character who arrived into the world of Radio Caroline in 1972 as DJ Crispian St John. After a period running other radio projects, including the UK's first all-gold station, he rejoined Caroline as DJ Jay Jackson, to start a news service, sponsored by Newsweek magazine.

On leaving Caroline, Howard worked for some ILR stations, and even set up a local radio station, as one would expect. You just can't keep the radio affinities out of these guys' hands, it is in their DNA! Howard launched the UK's most successful weekly trade paper aimed solely at the radio business, which gave substantial coverage to Radio Caroline and its case.

21. Revenge at sea.

During the last week of July the ship was almost ready and needed only two certificates to leave. Captain Martin Eve of Ipswich was hired to supervise sailing arrangements which included different lifeboats, at the insurance company's insistence. Leaked reports in the Irish press almost banjaxed the departure when the British authorities responded to press enquiries that they could jam the station if she reappeared off the British coast. It was decided to get out of Spain as quickly as possible and by the afternoon of 4th August, the Ross Revenge was ready to leave.

On the day the ship left port, Peter Chicago's girlfriend, Carol Maszka had dressed the ship overall with bunting and flags. Sadly, there wasn't any time to finish the studios before the 800 miles voyage. Towed by a Spanish tug she was followed by a small flotilla of other boats. This was headed by Ronan O'Rahilly on a small ferry boat that he had chartered. She left to cheers from holidaymakers on the piers and beaches of Santander as she was towed into the Bay of Biscay.

The tow from Spain to the UK by a Spanish tug had been decided to avoid insurance complications and as a security measure; there was less chance of interference in the busy shipping lanes of the English Channel by any official boats while under tow. Nevertheless, there was intense interest shown in the rather odd-looking ship with the big mast. She was tailed by a French destroyer for half a day and buzzed by a fighter plane, which peeled off when it saw it was the legendary Radio Caroline.

Ross Revenge's original mast

It took only four days to reach the Thames estuary, anchoring off the Kentish Knock overnight and then the following day travelling the last few miles into the Knock Deep on the 9th August. The first test transmissions of 1kHz test tone on 963 kHz, 319 metres, were made that same day. The plan was to launch on 14th August, a poignant remembrance of the same date in 1967 when the Marine Offences Act had outlawed offshore radio for Britons. Sadly the deck insulator blew and it took a few days to get a replacement out there.

The world's press once again descended on Radio Caroline as preparations were hurriedly made for the start of broadcasts. Stories about the return of the station were carried in hundreds if not thousands of publications all over the world. The ship had left Spain without a single studio being ready and DJs were pressed into service as technicians to connect up equipment. ITN's team on board showed viewers the huge RCA transmitters. Test transmissions of non-stop music were soon under way and it was announced that regular programming would commence at 12 noon on Saturday 20th August.

Superb Audio Quality

The station's output was processed with a unit made by Orban Electronics. The model's trade name, *Optimod*, was a clever combination of optimum and modulation. It was mentioned so many times on Radio Caroline that the word became a generic one used for all kinds of processor, although there were by then half a dozen similar types available.

The device boosts the amount of audio possible in the transmission by compressing selected parts of the audio, and passing through the most intelligible bits of the audio spectrum. This made the station sound much louder, which made listening at the farthest edges of the reception area possible. It also made the station stand out loud as listeners tuned along the band.

Caroline had several technical advantages in addition to the audio processor: the antenna was an excellent match to the transmitter, which could therefore send its power all into the antenna and out into the ether. The antenna was not the mast itself, but three wires running alongside the mast and connected into it at a particular height above the deck.

By feeding into the mast at that point (it's known as a delta match) the maximum radiation was sent out from the combination of antenna and mast. It also meant that the mast or tower itself need not stand on insulators and was instead brought down through the deck and mounted directly onto the keel of the ship. This was useful in many ways, such as grounding the mast giving less likelihood of it being struck by lightning.

As the antenna was over the sea and the antenna system properly grounded to the hull of the ship, a near perfect connection to 'earth' was obtained – the paintwork on the hull is not a barrier to RF signals as it works like a capacitor. Reception reports in those early days came in from literally all across Europe due to the selected frequency being almost clear across the continent.

The frequency chosen was 963 kHz, which, in the Caroline tradition, became called 3-1-9 metres. The choice of frequency was mildly annoying for a dozen or so flea power stations on university campuses who had been allocated the 963 channel by the British authorities. It was widely conceded that the allocation had been done purely to block Radio Caroline from ever returning to the channel, which otherwise was clear throughout western Europe. For the university stations to change frequency was a few minutes work and little more than a minor nuisance. After all, few of the campus stations had many listeners and the installations served purely as a training ground for media students.

Caroline had started on 963 kHz as it had not been possible to tune the large 50kW transmitter to the preferred 558 kHz frequency as many more components were needed, including some large inductors. The transmitter was of a special configuration, *Ampliphase,* a proprietary design of 'outphasing' that RCA had developed many years before.

In RCA's Ampliphase system, the RF signal of the transmitter is split into two separate channels, which are then fed out of phase in the final combining network. When correctly set up the path is purely linear resulting in a faithful or pure modulation of the carrier.

Another aspect of the Caroline set up that made the signal much better was the lack of audio filters which European stations normally apply to reduce the bandwidth. These suppress the higher audio frequencies; on Caroline the transmitter was American and had different filters on the audio, letting the treble frequencies out better, which makes for a less muffled sound on radio.

On the first day of broadcasts the Ross Revenge was joined by a flotilla of pleasure vessels They were not disappointed by their trip out to the Knock Deep and could now be among the first hand to see the impressive ship in all her majesty. Painted bright red with white superstructure and topped by her 90 metre fully-rigged mast, she looked simply magnificent.

Some of the launch team climbing the mast
David Kindred

Sadly, many of the DJs who had been preparing for the special relaunch of the station had been forced to get employment elsewhere, Johnnie Walker among them. Tom Anderson, who had been one of the last voices heard from the Mi Amigo in 1980 returned. He was joined by Robin Ross, Tony Gareth and a singing DJ called Dixie Peach, who stayed for only for one tour of duty before joining BBC Radio 1. Andy Archer too joined for a while and became one of the first DJs to be stopped while popping ashore. He decided to join the BBC.

A Musical Journey

The next phase of Radio Caroline began at 12 noon on Saturday 20th August 1983 with Tom Anderson welcoming listeners:

> *Good afternoon ladies and gentlemen and welcome to Radio Caroline on 319 metres, 963 kilohertz. I'm Tom and for the next hour I'd like to take you on a couple of musical journeys through the past two decades.*
>
> *We're going to start with the Zombies and "She's Not There" and follow that with the Yardbirds with "Heart Full Of Soul."*
>
> *Caroline, on three one nine*

There followed simply 'three in a row' segues of album tracks. Tom conceded that it was a bit of an inauspicious start and not something he is proud of. It was to be several weeks before jingles were heard on the station, even the Caroline Bell was not sounded until mid-September when Caroline also started a news service at peak times.

"I couldn't wait to get out there, it had been my goal for many years to work on Radio Caroline. and got my chance though my friend at Radio Aire, Peter Tait," said Carl Kingston, a DJ from Hull who had been a Radio Caroline fan since his schooldays. Carl had previously voiced the English Pop news reports for Peter Van Dam's shows on Radio Mi Amigo by post.

"Our station identification was 'Radio Caroline, Europe's first and only album station' and we simply did our best to play great music," remembers Carl. "There was a wonderful atmosphere on the ship, we never got hassled and the station did pay my wages regularly as I had a wife and two young boys back home in Hull."

Looking in the various media archives around the world it seems that there cannot have been many publications anywhere that didn't record the rebirth of Radio Caroline that August. Ronan gave dozens of interviews to radio, TV and the press.

"The beauty of Caroline is it's totally a relationship between the station and the audience; the audience is the absolute decision maker," he said. "When the audience don't want to listen to us, if they don't want to tune in, then there's no ball game. But we never had that problem. I think we're going to have an enormous audience."

It seems that Ronan still believed the prophesies of Roy Lindau, the advertising 'expert' from Major Market Radio, as he continued with the promise: "There's an enormous amount of international advertisers who are very enthusiastic about using us," said Ronan. "We will supply the ship direct from Spain and make sure that Caroline is run in strict compliance with all of the legal local legalisation in all the various European countries."

Responsible for communications between Ronan and the ship was another Londoner, PR agent Mike Plumley. He ran a company called Blurb Promotions and later began production of a film about Caroline with Hans Fjellestad, with contributions from Roger Daltrey, Mick Fleetwood and Richard Branson. A keen reggae fan, Mike also made a brief appearance on Caroline, standing in for Tom Anderson for a couple of nights on the Overdrive service.

With help from Robb Eden, Mike was responsible for hiring DJs and liaising between the London office and the ship. Others helping in this role at the critical time of the Ross Revenge relaunch of Caroline was Stevie Lane who occasionally hosted some programmes.

The Authorities in the UK immediately took a keen interest in the ship and intercepted some supply boats ferrying DJs and other crew in and out of the UK. Andy Archer was among the first apprehended and charged as an illegal immigrant!

A Caroline veteran, Andy's return to the ship in 1983 was heralded as a triumph for the station and provided an element of continuity as he had been lured from the safety of a gig at ILR station Centre Sound in Leicester. Andy was leader of the hippie contingent in 1973 who had started the 'all album' format.

Radio Caroline did attract a large audience in those first few months as not everyone was satisfied with pap purveyed by ILR and Radio 1, which excluded many types of music. That there was a massive demand for an alternative is apparent from the large number of listeners who also listened to the land-pirates that were now mushrooming on tower blocks all the UK. Many of them played a limited range of music, usually funk and soul, but it was a large mass of listeners who were being ignored by the BBC and ILR.

By 1983 the 'all album' format had become known in the American radio business as AOR – adult oriented rock, where it was quite successful, though nowhere near as much as Top 40, oldies, country or talk.

The reasoning behind the adoption of an Album Rock format on Caroline was not only that it was something that wasn't available elsewhere, except for perhaps two hours a week on some other stations. Ronan believed that by Caroline not being overtly commercial and highly successful, the authorities might leave the station alone.

Not everyone in the Caroline family was quite so convinced that the authorities might give the station an easier ride. That had not been the case just before the Mi Amigo was lost; evidence had come to light since that the Home Office were building up a dossier on the station's associates and may have been ready to pounce and knock the station out forever, until Mother Nature stepped in and rid them of the ship.

There were endless debates in the messroom on the wisdom of making Caroline a commercial success and everyone had their own idea of which way the format should lean.

The first mailing address for Radio Caroline was a P O Box number in Los Angeles, which was the office of Dan Kelly, who managed Wolfman Jack. The station also used an address on Madison Avenue in New York from where Vincent Monsey sold the airtime. No commercials were broadcast for the first few months but there were several record plugging deals done in the UK and in Holland.

A Gallup Poll was commissioned about 8 weeks after launch. It showed that *Caroline 319* had an audience of around 4 million, which was 7% of the adult population, and probably a further half a million in the Netherlands. These were very encouraging results and the station extended its broadcasting hours to offer ‘round the clock’ operation by mid-November.

Neighbours join Caroline

In the last few days of 1984, the Ross Revenge got a neighbour in the Knock Deep – the MV Communicator. The ship was the proposed home of Laser, the project that Ronan had rejected the previous year when Paul Rusling had offered another Irish investor. When Ronan rejected the new funds, the project was taken over by his enemy from the Ryan days: an advertising booking agent called Roy Lindau.

The Communicator was now almost ready to broadcast but needed to raise its antenna by a large helium balloon, an inflatable dirigible. Designed to hold aloft a heavy antenna cable about 350 feet above the ship, the balloons needed careful handling, especially on a ship and at sea. Keen to start broadcasting, the Laser management ordered the ship to raise the antenna and not wait for the balloon experts from their American supply company.

The first balloon lasted only a short time before flying off, dropping the aerial cable back onto the deck. The following week, the reserve balloon was hoisted and stayed on the air for less than a day, before being wrenched from its tether lines by near gale force 9 winds in a blizzard. Replacements would take weeks to obtain, and the owner was losing his patience with the Laser project, which had now cost him almost a million pounds.

The engineering team left on board were instructed to get the Communicator operational in some way without an aerial. A very short antenna could be rigged between the existing ships masts but vital test equipment was needed to make this happen. Paul Rusling was heading the team on board the Communicator and he called Ronan O’Rahilly on the Communicator’s satellite phone to solicit his help.

Ronan agreed to allow Paul to borrow some vital test equipment from Radio Caroline and help launch the new station. Without Ronan’s help, her owner would have pulled out and the Communicator would not have launched. It wasn’t the first time Ronan was generous with his competitors; it reinforced his long-held policy to ‘always be helpful’.

Caroline Commercials

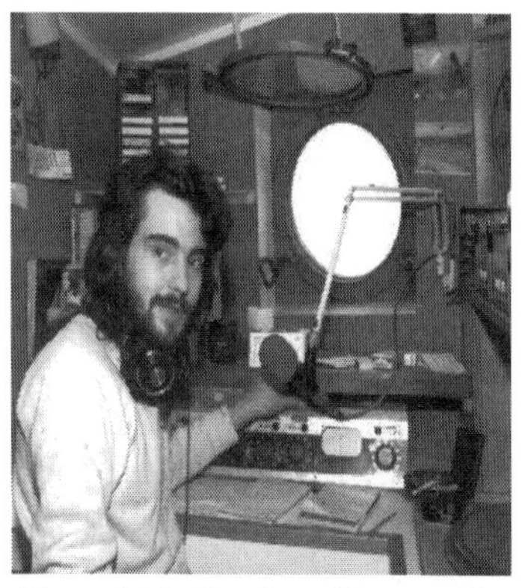

'Cosmic' in the Overdrive studio

Just after the New Year, Caroline aired its first commercials which were for Bet Canada, a lottery ticket agency. The deal for the sale of lottery tickets was arranged by the Canadian who had been bearing the costs of the operation for nine months and who had made the 'escape from Spain' possible. Nelson owned several professional ice-hockey clubs and a variety of other businesses including an hotel and an art gallery.

The biggest support then came from the Caroline Movement, a London based group that did a lot to help the station and its staff. Among the CM's activities were running sightseeing trips out to the ship and publishing a magazine, the CM Bulletin. The editor was CM member Andy Johnson who had also been heard on hospital radio and on a couple of London land pirate stations, SES and Radio Amanda.

Andy was delighted when, just before Easter 1984, he was invited to join Caroline to give a break to Caroline's hard-pressed News Editor, Jay Jackson who had been on board for three months. As a keen rock music fan Andy was soon pressed into hosting programmes too where he was often known by his nickname 'Cosmic', as he was a self-confessed hippie. After a few years on the Ross Revenge, Andy took up a shore role helping Tom Anderson to run the Caroline office. In London. This was now located in Rose Street, Covent Garden. Some time later, when Tom left Caroline after giving her twelve years of his life to the project, Andy took over as Station Manager.

He was famous for his driving prowess and was a mine of information about all kinds of vehicles, especially those from eastern Europe. Cosmic loved driving and would happily tear about all over the country in a succession of vehicles that eventually all were totally wrecked for the Caroline cause.

Andy / Cosmic was one of the kindest people one could ever hope to meet and always willing to help out, which is how he usually arrived in various jobs. Working 24 hours a day for Radio Caroline would however ultimately cost Andy his home and his girlfriend so he had been sleeping at the Caroline HQ. Eventually he could take no more and Peter Moore took over the role, but that's for a later chapter.

Around Easter the Caroline programmes began to take on a more commercial sound and began winning back some of the audience the station had lost to Laser, which was experiencing lengthy periods of 'down time' due to its flimsy aerial masts collapsing. The changes were directed by experienced American programming consultant, Lee Abrahms, who also founded the *XM Sirius* satellite radio network, where he was Chief Programming Officer.

Caroline celebrated her 20th birthday on the North Sea with a Top 500 listeners all-time favourite tracks being played out. The special milestone was acknowledged by Anglia TV, on the BBC World Service and on BBC2 by the 'Old Grey Whistle Test,' with a special contribution from Johnnie Walker. The top tracks selected by listeners were *Imagine* by John Lennon, *Stairway to Heaven* by Led Zeppelin and *All You Need is Love* by the Beatles.

By May Laser was operational and its 'hit radio' format, professionally presented, drew in millions of listeners. It became even more popular than Radio Caroline, and despite the Laser manager's instruction to the Communicator crew to have nothing whatsoever to do with Radio Caroline, there was considerable contact between the ship's crews, with Caroline staff using the Communicator's superior 'home comfort' facilities and much sharing of various resources.

Caroline had planned a second service for some time and was keen to be on as low a frequency as possible. It proved impossible to convert the big transmitter to transmit on a low frequency, not without a lot more parts and considerable downtime. It was decided therefore to use a smaller 10kW and by mid-July it was ready to be used on 594kHz.

The IBA (Independent Broadcasting Authority, the UK body responsible for commercial radio and television) were testing on an adjacent frequency, 603kHz, in Canterbury and they increased power to counter any possible interference from Caroline. Other nearby frequencies such as 585 and 576 were also tested by Caroline at this time and it was the latter that was finally brought into service in August.

The 576 frequency was said to be to give better reception in the middle of London where the some of the concrete-clad, steel-framed buildings shielded the 319 signal. Despite a lower power level, Caroline's new 576 signal was a huge improvement and covered almost as large an area as did the big 319 kHz service, except in Germany where two co-channel transmitters proved a little bothersome at times.

When the IBA issued licences (more like franchises, for the use of the Authority's own transmission network) these were strictly on a non-competing basis for a particular coverage area. i.e. they had virtually promised the operators that they would not face any competition. Worse, the authorities had imposed draconian rules on the stations with strict limits about what programming they could broadcast.

The UK's commercial stations were mandated, for example, to have a minimum of fifty per cent or their output as "meaningful speech". The quota did not include inane DJ patter or record requests. Meaningful speech had to be substantial dialogue, which was expensive to provide. But worse than the cost, it drove away audiences. Without audiences the ILR stations could not charge advertisers for their commercial time.

Radio Caroline and Laser were able to programme as much music as they wanted. Laser purposely kept its links short and snappy with dead air strictly discouraged and promised that listeners were "never more than a minute away from music". Laser only played hit singles and didn't allow its DJs to indulge themselves by playing their own favourites. It enforced this rule by having all music played in from cartridges, making it difficult for staff on board to add music not approved by their managers in New York.

Radio Caroline had considerably sharpened up its presentation style and pace of delivery after Laser launched and cut back on lengthy pauses between the music, although it still gave lots of airtime over to playing album tracks. Oddly, Radio Caroline was attracting quite a lot of commercial traffic and some of the spots were around a minute or so long.

Laser meanwhile had hardly any advertising spots on the air, despite its New York manager insisting that he would be bringing in lots of big name advertisers – "very soon". It later transpired that selling air time was not his speciality, he was more an administrator of air time blocks. It seems that Radio Caroline had a lucky escape from Lindau when they dropped him!

Lotto 6 - 49

Among the advertising heard on Caroline were *Jordache Jeans, Arabian Sands Holidays and Bet Canada*, a promotion of the Bet Canada promotion, Lotto 6-49. This was a perfectly legitimate gamble, not in any way a scam. The adverts aired twice an hour and offered listeners in the UK the opportunity to buy tickets in the Canadian Lottery. Entrance was by selecting six from 49 numbers, with entries sent to the Lotto 649 office in Vancouver, Canada. Caroline was paid a small commission on every ticket sold.

Thousands of Brits bought tickets for the weekly Bet Canada lottery and tuned to Caroline for the winning numbers. There were many winners too, and lots of people won a few hundred or thousand dollars in the draws.

Running a lottery in the UK was prohibited at this time, it was not to be until late 1994 that the UK allowed lottery tickets to be openly sold and then only for one government-controlled monopoly. Many people took part in lotteries while travelling or on holiday and this seemed a harmless form of gambling, very similar to the 'football pools' which offered similar size prizes.

Another unusual advert was aired during November, for the *TROS Kompas* magazine. The TROS organisation grew out of the of Radio Noordzee operation of the 1960s and had over 100,000 shareholders in the Netherlands. The operators of their weekly TV listings magazine calculated that it was cheaper to advertise on Caroline and pay any fine because the extra sales would be worth the risk and fine.

Both the 963 and 576 frequencies were used for Radio Caroline throughout the Autumn until 16th December when the 963 became the home of a new station for Holland, **Radio Monique**. This was a direct successor to Caroline's Dutch service of the late 1980s. Radio Monique was named after the wife of the station's new director, Fred Bolland. One of his partners in Radio Monique was Nico Volker, who had run the Mi Amigo road show in the 1970s. Radio Monique was heavily backed by Dutch record companies and had previously hoped to be on the air from the Radio Paradise ship, (see Chapter 19) the Magda Maria, in 1981.

Supply Tenders

Caroline had operated in the 1970s by having the Dutch service providing heavy supplies of fuel, food and water in return for their transmission time. This became the basis of the operation in the 1980s, with Radio Monique running the heavy supplies to the Ross Revenge from 'the near continent'.

The first regular boat to supply the Ross Revenge was the *Zeemeeuw*, a Dutch converted fishing boat owned by Danny Vissers. Danny's father was an English soldier in WWII whose family name was misselpot by a civil servant in Belgium. The Zeemeeuw carried fuel and water as well as visiting anorak parties and was replaced by the *Windy*. She was named after Fred Bolland's dog and owned by *Waipuna*, a Liechtenstein anstalt. She was built in 1921 and skippered by Captain Willy Wormenleyton, a popular sailor who was also a good engineer. He played a key role in erecting the new masts on the Ross Revenge.

By 1986 Willy and Fred Bolland were usung the MV Poolster, owned by Danny Visser before Fred and Ronan together chartered the Bellatrix, a fine former pilot cutter. She was almost as big as the Ross Revenge and very comfortable for the nine hour trip out to the ship.

The Bellatrix lying astern of the Ross Revenge

The Bellatrix not only brought supplies but also carried sightseers too who would pay handsomely for a trip to the Thames estuary where they could now visit not only Radio Caroline's ship the Ross Revenge, but also the enigmatic Laser 558 on board the MV Communicator, moored just two miles away. The Bellatrix charter was later taken over by Danny who stopped tendering just before the 1989 raid and took the Bellatrix down to Tenerife. The Poolster and the Zeemeuw followed there too, sailed by Leendert Vingerling and Captain Willy. All those ships are now scrapped.

The Caroline tenders were all classified as 'pleasure' boats and thus exempt from a lot of mercantile rules and regulations and they flew the Honduran flag. They sailed from Belgian ports such as Zeebrugge or Nieuwpoort and from Dunkerque and Boulogne in France quite openly. Some tender runs were made from Bilbao in Spain, using an ocean-going tug operated by Delta Diving, although these were rare events. None of the crew were happy with the quality or type of food brought over from Spain and another factor was that fuel is cheaper in Belgium!

The customs and harbour officials knew that the tenders were serving the radio ship but were happy that the business was coming through their ports. Fuel was normally put on board in Oostende in Belgium as it was much cheaper than in France. The French harbour officials never worried about its destination.

When the Greenpeace ship *Sirius* visited the Ross Revenge it was to carry out (and back!) a TV camera crew from Veronica TV, for their programme '*Der Grote Verwarring*' (the great confusion)

As well as the larger boats that serviced the Ross Revenge from the Benelux ports, many boat owners were still prepared to put out from Kent and Essex to keep Caroline supplied. They operated despite official warnings by the DTI that supplies from the UK were illegal.

It was always important to have an excuse to be out in the estuary; fishing was the usual one. Secondly, if carrying items that linked to the radio ships, these were always in bags or cartons weighted down with concrete so they could be jettisoned and not become evidence if the tender was boarded.

Graham Croft

Bob Le Roi

The best cover story was that the boats were simply taking sightseers out to see the ship, which was not illegal. Among the most reliable Caroline supporters were Alex from the Medway and his *Galexy* boat, Dave Turner from Ramsgate on his trawler the *FV Fairwinds*, and Graham Croft, who was also the Whitstable harbourmaster who commanded the launch *Henrietta*. Howard Beer sailed from too many ports to mention!

The longest serving boat trip organiser was Albert Hood. A diesel engineer and fitter, Albert and his wife began organising trips to the Mi Amigo in the 1970s, usually from Brightlingsea on the board the Lucky Lady. Albert's spanner skills were soon pressed into use on board and he was encouraged to spend long periods repairing the ship's failing generators. Whenever the Caroline organisation could arrange the funds he would do the shopping for the ship too and arrange its delivery, so his was always a welcome face alongside the Mi Amigo.

In April 1985, Forbes Magazine, the periodical for high net worth individuals, gave a long report about the fortunes of Radio Caroline. It reported that Caroline had now repaid its $1.3m start-up costs and was turning over around $25,000 per month.

Attempts were being made to launch new services: a Punjabi programme called *Kalsi Voice* was aired for a while and one night after midnight a new service called *Anorak Radio 558* was heard, presented quite unofficially by 'Bert Twigworthy', which turned out to be Simon Barrett!

Caroline programmes continued on 963 after Radio Monique had closed for the day and in time these were a separate stream of programmes. The line up on Caroline at that time included James Day, Fiona Jeffries, Jay Jackson, and Nick Richards. The 963 shows featured heavier music than was heard on 576, the 24 hour all English service.

By Summer, 963 had a couple of hours of talk programming each evening which brought in valuable revenue. The segment between 6pm and 9pm was now known as *Viewpoint 963*, and carried various religious and other programming. Among these was the *Roy Masters Foundation of Human Understanding*, a thought-provoking discussion programme recorded daily in Los Angeles. After 9pm, a new service called *Jamming 963* had music focussed on reggae and dub. It occasionally included some jazz and 'world' music from Africa, the content depended on who was on board the ship at the time and what they wanted to programme.

Expo 86 was another event promoted heavily by Radio Caroline. It was an official Canadian Government event. They were aware of Radio Caroline's status and had taken legal advice in the UK and in Canada, which assured them that it was quite lawful for them to advertise. The deal had been arranged by Nelson Skalbania's business partner, John Chambers, who sold the airtime through the Vancouver office of Baker Lovick, a large and well-established advertising agency.

Mail to the ship continued to flow freely via addresses in New York and California, but personal mail between the DJs and their families was handled by Hans Knot. He had a secret PO Box 685 address in Groningen and had mail couriered to the ship via Belgium.

Mess Room on the Ross Revenge

Rob Olthof

22. Eurosiege

In early August 1985, the UK's Department of Trade and Industry mounted an intense surveillance exercise to discover how the two radio ships were being supplied. They were spurred into action by the UK's commercial radio stations, many of whom were losing money. The ILR stations blamed their problems on the radio ships, Caroline and Laser, claiming that the radio ships were stealing 'their' listeners!

The UK ILR lobby had learned that Caroline was obtaining some supplies of music from the UK by a number of small boats putting out from non-customs posts in Kent, Essex and Suffolk, although its major supplies of food, oil and water came from the near continent courtesy of the operators of the Radio Monique, with whom it shared its ship.

Laser however had all its supplies ferried out by a tug company on the Isle of Sheppey. Investigations had not so far revealed any firm evidence of this, due to various canny methods. In order to prove what was happening, the authorities needed evidence that the ships were being supplied from England. This would be necessary If any enforcement action were to be taken.

The surveillance was dubbed 'Eurosiege' by staff on the radio ships. I took the form of a launch being chartered by the DTI from Trinity House. Called the Dioptric Surveyor, it was manned by a bunch of civil servants, many of whom turned out to be Radio Caroline supporters and friends.

In true government style, they began their working day in port and didn't arrive alongside the radio ships until mid-morning, returning home in good time for tea! Eventually their bosses twigged that supplies were generally being run to the radio ships at night and weekends so the surveillance period was extended.

The Dioptric Surveyor was quite a responsive craft and could easily nip from one vessel to another (originally the Laser ship was over 2 miles south of Caroline) but normally desk-bound civil servants were not suited to working offshore and were unprepared for the sea.

The ships supplying Radio Caroline from the continent were professional seamen whose ships were flagged in exotic places such as Honduras, so they didn't mind the Dioptric Surveyor taking all the photos they wished; the British ministry men had no jurisdiction across in the Benelux where the supply boats were running from and voyages were carefully planned to always have a good reason to be there.

The blockade of the radio ships was costing around £50,000 per week and relied on a small army of civil servants on board the sea going launch, the Dioptric Surveyor. A well-found craft she was not however suitable for remaining at sea for long periods; the land-lubbers on board soon found her to be very uncomfortable, not at all like their plush offices with padded chairs!

Some of the Laser DJs were vociferous in denouncing the surveillance exercise. Unable to take any direct action against any non-British ships in international waters, the DTI simply mounted close observation on both Caroline and Laser. Radio Caroline was a less vocal in its response and a spokesman commented "The blockades are a massive a waste of public money when all we are doing is legally providing a music service, which is enjoyed by millions of listeners." Caroline's supplies were all ferried to the ship by the Bellatrix which was registered in Honduras, a central American country. The Hondurans were not interested in helping the British authorities, only in the well-being of ships flying their own flag.

The Dutch Department of Justice seemed powerless to act against Radio Monique, saying: "It's impossible for us to take direct action against radio ships. We are trying to stop them by some indirect action through advertisers, but it's impossible to trace them usually." Unlike the British officials, the Dutch authorities were not being egged on by any commercial radio stations as the government there had not licenced any, only the state NOS ran radio services and they were funded by the taxpayers.

Popular tabloid newspaper the Daily Star tested the blockade by delivering champagne, the papers own T-Shirts, a journalist and cameraman to the Radio Caroline and Laser ships in mid August. They were not stopped but when the article subsequently appeared in the paper, the DTI said they would be reported for prosecution. Supplies for Radio Caroline continued arriving at the Ross Revenge as usual, the DTI's team found it impossible to keep track of the many small boats that visited the ships from England, although a few 'Anorak Boats" carrying tourists were chased by the DTI and threatened with legal action. So long as they had not delivered any supplies to the ships, they had not broken any laws.

News bulletins were now being carried on Caroline half hourly at peak times and weather forecasts were given around the clock. Caroline also started a 'Quit Coughing' campaign during Eurosiege that encouraged listeners to send in their favourite remedies to stop smoking.

Captain Tony Haggis

Captain Tony Haggis joined the Ross Revenge during Eurosiege. "We went out on the Windy, a small ship that sailed from Belgium usually. The DTI were there with a boat called the Dioptric Surveyor but it was hopelessly unsuitable. We always managed to stay one step ahead of them, so they were not very successful, not considering they were costing the taxpayers £50,000 a month. The two stations on the Ross Revenge, Radio Caroline and Radio Monique at that time only cost £3,000 a month to run!

"It was an unusual life on board the ship as I was skipper of a ship that, all being well, didn't go anywhere," said Tony. He was known as Captain Campbell on board the ship as that was the name that Ronan chose for him. "My main job was to just be there in case she came off the anchor and began drifting. I spent my time cooking for the crew!"

"There wasn't always a lot of 'Captain's work' to be done on board a stationary ship like the Ross Revenge," explains Captain Campbell. "Ensure the anchor chain is secure is a must, but the rest of the time I was in command on the Ross Revenge, I acted as cook and occasionally as a nursemaid to the more inexperienced members of the team." It's a fact that some DJs were so young and inexperienced of life in general that they were unable to look after themselves, even down to making a cup of tea!

The family of radio enthusiast Ian West visited the Ross Revenge in September. The DTI and Caroline office were aware of the trip, which was not to run supplies to the ship, but to scatter Ian's ashes from the deck of the ship. Ian had been a long-term member of the Caroline Movement and this was his dying wish when he passed away some months before from cancer, aged just 24 years old. His family donated a ship's bell in Ian's memory which has hung in the mess ever since.

Unlike Caroline, Laser ran all their supplies via the Isle of Sheppey and experienced financial problems when the price was increased to reflect the danger. Initially the tender trips cost only £600 per run, but once the Eurosiege blockade was in place the price rose to £2,000. This was "the straw that broke the camel's back" and was to lead to Laser's closure in November 1985.

The DTI mounted a road show around the south east to explain why they were spending so much money to close down the two radio ships. "These stations put out so much power that they are jamming out both the frequencies they are using," said Dilys Gane.

Ms Gane clearly hadn't a clue what she was talking about as any station 'jams out' the frequency it is using, otherwise no one can hear it at all. The highest powered offshore station was Radio Monique, which only ran with 17 kilowatts, while Laser was transmitting with only 12 kilowatts and Radio Caroline somewhat less than that level. These power levels could be compared with the nearby BBC station on Orfordness which pumped out half a million watts on the 648 channel but still caused no problems. Or so the authorities would have everyone believe. A few months later a case of severe interference was solved by the ships sequentially switching off for a few minutes. It was proven conclusively that it was the BBC station causing the problems.

"We've had numerous complaints from helicopter pilots trying to land on oil rigs in the North Sea because their directional beacons are being jammed by radio ships; instead of getting the signals to help them land, in those very dangerous conditions they're hearing pop music," claimed the DTI's Ms Gane.

The DTI's spokeswoman was either very misinformed or simply lying. The main aeronautical contractor had stated that they never had any problems on the rigs. Helicopters don't need the NDB beacons to help them land (they are used for reminding them of the direction of a rig). Its only once they find the rig that they would try and land, using visual sightings, not NDBs. Also, the helicopters don't fly when the weather conditions are dangerous. Someone in the DTI had wantonly built a package lies which were now being spouted by them who clearly had no practical experience of the topic they were talking about.

The DTI team never produced any evidence of a single instance where interference was caused by either Radio Caroline or the other ship. In a separate attack on radio ships, the Foreign Office said they had asked their Panamanian counterpart to withdraw the registration of the ships, so that action might be taken. The Panamian government simply instructed its Bureau of Shipping in London to not discuss any matter relating to the two ships with anyone but the owners; as long as they continued paying dues and licence fees there would be no action by Panama.

Some trouble causers had often suggested that Panama had withdrawn the flag of the Ross Revenge making the ship stateless, however this was not true. It is not mandatory for a ship to fly its colours on the high seas, unless it was entering into battle. Caroline was never interested in any battles, it was a ship of love, peace and good music!

A country does not ordinarily withdraw the registration of a ship while it is at sea, but only while in a port. So long as a radio ship remains at sea, no country is likely to withdraw its flag. Nevertheless, the name was painted onto the ship's stern and the Panama flag proudly flown.

Laser lookalike, the Gardline Tracker

The DTI replaced their surveillance vessel the Dioptric Surveyor early in November with a much larger vessel, the Gardline Tracker. She was under charter from the firm of Gardline Surveys, the company who had supplied Laser with the Communicator. In fact, she looked almost identical to the Communicator and she was well equipped to remain on station longer than the smaller launch that had now scuttled back inshore.

While delivering supplies to the Ross Revenge in November the Windy got some rope around its propeller, immobilising her. She remained tied to the stern of the radio ship for many hours but eventually had to be towed into Harwich for repairs by the RNLI.

Communicator surrenders

After just a few days the crew on the neighbouring ship of Laser 558, the MV Communicator, decided to throw in the towel. Having had no supplies for several weeks and unable to get an answer from their office, the captain and the chief DJ upped anchor and headed for shore. The Radio Caroline crew invited them to leave their valuable transmitters on the Ross Revenge, an offer that was declined. The Communicator was arrested by the Admiralty Marshall acting on writs from disgruntled creditors. The shipping inspectors prepared a lengthy list of repairs, while the DTI and HM Customs had a full 'rummage' oof the ship that took several days to complete.

Peter Chicago was sure that Laser wouldn't be back for a while and changed the frequency of Caroline's 10kW transmitter to 558 kHz. This was a clearer frequency and brought Caroline to a couple of new areas, as well as to the many millions of pairs of ears who tuned in that morning expecting to hear Laser 558.

A new face who appeared during the night of the frequency change was Dick Palmer, who had been captain of the Mi Amigo in 1973; he quickly busied himself sorting out problems with the anchors and generators on the Ross Revenge. Dick had spent many year helping to train officers in the Omani Navy and quickly brought some semblance of order to various mechanical contraptions on the ship.

After escorting the Communicator into Harwich, the Gardline Tracker returned to observe the Ross Revenge. When a tender came out from England, the DTI tried to prevent her tying up alongside the radio ship by deploying two fast rubber dinghies. A show of force by the Caroline crew, led by Mike Barrington soon dissuaded them and they sped off back to their 'mother ship'.

The following week, Caroline changed format, ditching a lot of the reggae, heavy rock and album music and replacing it with more Top 40 and Gold music, which helped attract a lot of the listeners turning in to 558 and expecting to hear Laser. Only tracks from 'featured albums' were heard but not long afterwards the rules were considerably relaxed and Caroline output began reflecting the personal tastes of each DJ.

One interesting new voice who appeared on Radio Monique was Otto de Winter, who many visitors will have recognised as the main tender coordinator. Leendert Vingerling and his wife Marjo organised many sea trips from Belgium for over a thousand visitors in the eighties, as well as running Radio Delmare for a while.

Leendert Vingerling and his wife Marjo

At the end of November, the first short wave transmissions were heard from the Ross Revenge, when Caroline used one of the old ship's communications transmitters to test in the 49m band. The power was only around 500 watts and reception wasn't great. Vincent Monsey at Caroline's New York office confirmed that Caroline planned to use a higher power transmitter on short wave from the following year. It was planned to use two transmitters in order to guarantee continuous transmission as this was to be a revenue earning service.

All alone again

The DTI 'observation boat', Gardline Tracker suddenly left the Knock Deep after a couple more weeks. Its real job, to drive Laser off the air, had been accomplished. Caroline was left alone to continue pumping out love and peace, as well as the music! The surveillance exercises seemed to be over, although the coastguard and police boats came by every couple of weeks, apparently for camera practice.

Jamming 963 disappeared from the dial at this time and a short-lived country music format of music was heard on 963 each day after Radio Monique closed. On New Year's Day *Overdrive 963* was launched. This new service was dreamt up by Tom Anderson; he had become unhappy with the direction of the daytime programming of Radio Caroline and strongly felt that Caroline should have a rockier sound.

Ronan gave Tom Anderson his head to establish a Caroline rock service on 963 after the radio Monique and 'The God Squad' (which became known as *Viewpoint 963*) had finished for the night. Tom's new *Overdrive 963* service was initially programmed just by Tom and Fergie MacNeal. They were later joined by Mark Matthews and Nigel Roberts. Overdrive was a more traditional programme of rock albums, while the pop service continued unabated on *Caroline 558*.

The regular day time Radio Caroline 'pop' service on 558 was supervised by Peter Philips, a professional broadcaster who had joined Caroline after a career that included stints on the Voice of Peace and Radio Jackie, where a much more 'poppy' sound had won them a large audience and a lot of respect. After telling Ronan that he thought that Radio Caroline had lost its way musically he was invited to take over programming the daytime service, a task he shared with Kevin Turner.

January was rarely kind to Radio Caroline and for the third consecutive year, gales tore the ship from her anchor. After broadcasting the code numbers to tell those ashore of the problem, the transmitters abruptly left the air as the ship was rolling heavily and there were concerns that the Force 8 north easterly was sending her into British waters. Lifeboats from Margate and Sheerness were launched to help the twelve man crew.

Eventually the crew managed to start the engine when just past the Tongue lightship and in danger of hitting the nearby Tongue Sands fort, a substantial concrete and steel structure. Escorted by the Sheerness lifeboat, the Ross Revenge head back into deeper water. The lifeboat stood by for several hours until an emergency anchor could be lowered in the early hours of the following day.

The DTI warned tug owners (after monitoring conversations from the Ross Revenge on CB) that they could be prosecuted for assisting Caroline. This action was entirely misleading as the MOA explicitly excludes ships in distress; provision of service or assistance to a ship is permitted if in distress. The DTI showed that they were clearly not working within the law and would resort to tricks to achieve their aims.

The new *Caroline World Service* that was promised from February, was delayed due to the bad weather and staff shortages. The promised five kilowatt transmitter had not arrived at the ship and Chicago set to rebuilding an old RCA Ampliphase unit that was on board.

Caroline FM ?

Less than six months after the format changes to *Caroline 558*, the station was said to be attracting over five million listeners in the UK alone. A technical appraisal by the Harris transmitter company predicted that a 25 kW FM transmitter high on the Ross Revenge's 90m mast would reach much of London, although some Caroline staff were sceptical. A proposed regional FM service for the south east was abandoned as over £140,000 was required for materials alone.

This had attracted the attention of new backers, both for Caroline and for some new projects. *Stereo Hits 531* had a large modern ship in Southampton with transmitters on the way from Philadelphia. It set sail to Bilboa in northern Spain to have its 240 feet mast erected and transmitters installed. Internal wranglings over finance led to the departure of the project's leader and chief engineer who moved on to join another offshore station being assembled in the Bahamas.

The Bacardi project was a European marketing plan that was aborted after an internal family battle. The partially completed ship was later sold to Sir James Goldsmith after his plans for six hours a day of overtly political shows was rebuffed by Caroline. Sir James wanted to promote his new Referendum Party at a General Election but he was later dissuaded by lawyers and simply paid off the entire crew, rather handsomely. The Referendum Party's intention was to campaign for the UK's withdrawal from the EU, an early 'Brexit' campaign.

There was considerable discussion in government and establishment circles about offshore radio during 1986. The Prime Minister's deputy, William Whitelaw, had more than some sympathy for Caroline and the idea of opening up the airwaves. His boss Margaret Thatcher brought considerable pressure to bear on the IBA for national commercial radio licences to be offered and it was suggested that Radio Caroline might bid for one of these. Ronan was not enamoured by this suggestion as it would mean relinquishing control.

During the last week of July 1986 the mast on the sunken wreck of the MV Mi Amigo finally collapsed into the sea. The break in the mast was at the top of the first section and divers later found that the mast was still lying along the deck of the ship. Shortly afterwards, the navigation authority, Trinity House, issued a Notice to Mariners advising that the mast was no longer visible. The following month they laid a canister buoy just a cable from the wreck showing its location, to avoid anyone steaming into it. The obstruction has been marked on all the hydrographic charts issued since.

American engineer Alan Weiner spent some time on the Caroline ship, supposedly getting equipment ready for the new Short Wave service but no further tests were made in 1986. Caroline tried a 24 hour service for a few weeks, but maintenance and other factors led to this being curtailed to a 2am closedown the following month.

BBC Radio Essex laid a further claim to the 558 frequency for their launch in late 1986, but Caroline rejected requests for them to relinquish the channel, which had now given Caroline not only her best listening figures for two decades, but the most stable period of her life. BBC Essex were allocated 729 kHz, a frequency which a couple of years ago was said to be impossible when Laser tried to use it. It gave BBC Essex extensive coverage over a much wider area than just the county they were supposed to be serving.

Ria Valk – Monique hostess

Radio Monique was going from strength to strength at this time. They had a studio facility on the Vartweg in Hilversum and the operation of the business was being organised from The Hague by Rob Holland. One of the DJs was legendary Dutch singer Ria Valk. This Eindhoven-born 'national treasure' is well known from her many rock and roll hits, comedy songs and TV appearances. She hosted a daily show on Radio Monique, which was recorded in Hilversum

Radio Monique continued to be responsible for providing the bulk supplies of food, oil and water, that enabled both their station and Radio Caroline to operate. These major supply tenders usually operated from Calais in France, Nieuwpoort in Belgium or Vlissingen in Holland, although other ports were used from time to time to avoid any official intervention. The service from the Windy and the Bellatrix was now reliable and things were going well for Caroline.

UK Territorial Waters Extended
In May 1987 the British Parliament introduced new legislation to extend territorial waters. Instead of extending just three miles from the low water mark, British waters would now be up to 12 miles from the coast. This dastardly deed was regarded by many as the maritime equivalent of the government deliberately moving the goalposts!

This made the closest reasonable anchorage much further out to sea. Ronan and the tender skippers travelled out to the Ross Revenge and conferred with Peter Chicago in the newsroom. After poring over the Admiralty chart 1610 (Thames Estuary south) the closest spot was found near the South Falls Head which was outside the new limit. There was even a convenient sandbank that gave a little lee from the heaviest seas.

The stations from the Ross Revenge were really flying; Caroline had an audience of around four or five million and over 2.5 million people tuned to Radio Monique every week. This meant the station could get good prices for both record plugs and regular spot commercials as it was still the only private commercial radio station heard on the air.

The Ross Revenge sailed to her new mooring a few weeks later, accompanied by a Belgian salvage vessel, the *Onrust* which often helped the Ross Revenge. Leaving the Knock Deep at breakfast they heading south towards the Tongue fort and then headed east to a new position, by the South Falls Head. Safely outside the new twelve-mile limit, the new anchorage was more exposed but closer to shipping.

The following day was a General Election in the UK. Irish Head of News Steve Conway and Australian DJ Jackie Lee spent many hours collating and reading the results. Olau's daily ferry service from the UK to Holland passed very close by. Her captains usually announced this on the ferry's public address system to passengers.

Many of them lined the rails on the German TT Line owned Olau Britannia and Olau Hollandia and waved to the DJs; Caroline won lots of new listeners as a result.

Olau ferries pass within a few hundred yards of the Ross Revenge twice daily
Fotoflyte

Most Olau crews were supportive of Radio Caroline, especially the Radio Officer (Fergie) on the Olau Hollandia. The ferry would slow down to allow the Ross Revenge's inflatable to pop across and transfer various supplies gifted by the crew on the ferry.

The Communicator returned to moor near Caroline in the Knock Deep and broadcast as *Laser Hot Hits* for a short time but failed miserably due to a series of management errors. Former Caroline fund-raiser James Ryan took control of her, while still dodging incarceration after his conviction for stealing Caroline funds. The Communicator moved closer to France for the convenience of supplying.

Caroline 558 began using a new package of ID jingles at this time, based on the LA message, and ran promotions for the World Wildlife Fund. The former Laser ship, the MV Communicator joined the Ross Revenge at the South Falls Head for a week and then returned to the Knock Deep in late August, in a move to demonstrate her abilities to prospective new investors. A test broadcast was made at the end of October, using the name Radio Sunk, hosted by one of Radio Caroline's longest serving DJs, Johnny Lewis.

Cable rival

The only competition to Radio Monique was Joost de Draaijer's new initiative of cable radio, a medium that was available in over 90% of Dutch homes. The government thought that this was yet another ruse being used by Radio Monique to record programmes in Holland. *Cable One* used a U turn construction to 'broadcast' ostensibly from London as their government decreed that private radio studios were prohibited in the Netherlands.

Cable One's studios appeared to be in London, from where shows were uplinked to Holland via a communications satellite and then relayed on the cable networks. In fact, the originating studios remained in Hilversum and the DJs produced all Cable One's programmes there, with a convoluted transmission route. To avoid being Dutch, Joost set up an English company and some coverage in Glasgow and Berlin. Leading Dutch DJs Linda de Mol and Yvonne Keeley used a new language devised by Joost called Eurowaals (a mix of Dutch and English) and the old Luxy slogan "Your Station of the Stars".

The system worked well and *Cable One* soon built a big audience, but legal action by the Dutch state broadcaster, the NOS, led to their closure. The natural successor was a copy; a fully legal and British Sky Radio, which was managed by the last Dutch DJ to leave the Mi Amigo when she sank in 1980, Ton Lathouwers, known as Hans Verlaan.

That Autumn, Panama's shipping inspectorate announced that all vessels flying their flag over twenty years old must have a further inspection. Believing that flags would not be withdrawn while at sea, no action was taken to meet this new rule, a mistake that was to have severe repercussions a few years later. Panama did allow inspection to take place while at anchor out at sea; the Communicator was surveyed by their approved inspector while in the Knock Deep in early 1987, in order to update some of her papers. The Inspector confirmed that he often carried out the work at sea.

The Ross Revenge's new location did mean that supplies were much easier, weather permitting. The new anchorage was a little closer to the continent, where the French and Belgian harbour authorities were pleased with the extra trade that servicing radio ships brought. The ship saw fewer visitors from the UK but those who did make the longer journey out to sea were heartily welcomed and often invited on board.

In September and October the short wave transmitter was finally brought back into use, and several frequencies around 6.2MHz, just above the 49m band, were heard over a wide area.

After an eventful summer at sea, both Radio Caroline and Radio Monique looked forward to an easy winter, but it was not to be. In the early hours of the 16th October a hurricane hit the UK. This was a very rare event, technically needing a cyclone over warm seas to generate, but the deepening low moving so fast towards the UK created winds that were certainly of hurricane force (74mph plus). The BBC TV weatherman, Michael Fish, said he had been asked by a viewer if there would be a hurricane; he dismissed the idea as silly!

The winds overnight were much stronger than those in a hurricane, about one and half times stronger! The hurricane force winds brought down thousands of trees in southern England and a large cross-channel ferry was swept onto the beach in Kent. As well as the uprooted trees, roofs were torn off, electricity cables snapped and BBC and ITV masts felled. On the Ross Revenge all seemed well, although those on board (including Steve Conway, Tim Allen, Ad Roberts, Dave Cox and Chris Kennedy) had quite a night, pitching, yawling and rocking as the foaming North Sea tossed and turned the radio ship at her new location. Regular anchor checks were made throughout the night but the chain held firm.

Peter Philips began his first programme at 5am the next morning as usual, but not realising that Caroline was one of the few radio stations available on the dial for British listeners. Peter woke newsman Steve Conway with the customary mug of tea, saying "Oh, by the way, it's a trifle rough out there this morning!"

Peter Philips in the newsroom

"The ship was pretty stable even in the face of the hurricane," remembers Steve. "The only change was the white wall of foam that seemed to be enveloping the ship. It was an incredible sight, as high as the top of the bridge, the view from every window was a white out, like a blizzard. Although it was only a few feet from the bridge windows, you couldn't see the mast, just a few flashes of blue every now and then as the water shorted out thousands of volts."

"There was nothing on the TV, which I thought must be our TV aerial on the bridge roof, never expecting that all the TV transmitters across southern England could be down. There was nothing on the FM band either, so I tuned to the Radio 4 Long Wave service, I was astounded to hear of the devastation from weather ashore. The BBC was only on the air thanks to emergency generators and the police were warning people not to travel anywhere!"

The Ross Revenge wasn't rolling much, but the mast itself was moaning like no one had heard before, as the wind rushed though its lattice structure. Eventually one of the stays on the mast broke loose, a common occurrence in high winds. They often needed replacing, but that was not a job for windy conditions! When the loose stay started hitting the aerial and causing showers of sparks, Peter decided to stop transmitting for a few minutes and try to fix it.

Tethered to ship's rail he bravely climbed onto the roof of the bridge and eventually was able to catch hold of the stay which he secured safely to another part of the railings. Peter was used to climbing the mast and would often go aloft to carry out minor repairs. Not many DJs can add that to their curriculum vitae!

Another mast stay came loose in the afternoon and was whipping around the other stays and the mast, so Radio Caroline and Monique both had to close down early. This was a safety precaution, to allow some of the more experienced crew to fix it.

Engineer Mike Watts and head DJ Peter Philips were soon climbing the mast to address the worst of the damage to the stays and aerial feeder. Peter made it to the very top of the mast, which was still describing large arcs across the sky as the ship was tossed and turned on the waves. Eventually he was back down on the deck again and the transmissions resumed next morning.

Radio engineer Mike Watts
Chris Edwards

It was clear to those on board that the mast and its stays needed some attention as they had clearly been loosened in the hurricane. A full report and urgent plea for the riggers to come out was sent to the office. This was quickly dealt with and two experts who knew the mast very well were despatched the following Tuesday on the MV Eilleen. She was not a regular tender and, when she arrived alongside, it was evident that the skipper, Sammy, had not been properly briefed of his role.

The instructions were for the tender to remain alongside, or at least in the vicinity, to give the two mast riggers a chance to go aloft and carry out any maintenance that was necessary to the rigging. Tender skipper Sammy didn't want to remain at sea long. As soon as the supplies had been passed to the crew on the Ross Revenge he pulled off. He didn't give the riggers chance to even get on board the Ross Revenge, much less carry out their work.

Those on board the Ross Revenge didn't even realise that any mast riggers had been on that tender and were still expecting some help to arrive "any day now" while those on land in the office believed that the urgent work had been done. This was to be a classic example of a gross breakdown in communications causing the biggest problems.

The move to 819

In recent months, reception to the Dutch service, Radio Monique was increasingly difficult, especially after dark. This was due to a co-channel station in Finland having increased its power sixfold, to 300 kilowatts which badly affected coverage in the Benelux.

The 50 kW transmitter was retuned to 819 kHz (369m) which was not so prone to interference. This was used for Radio *Monique* during the day, for *Viewpoint* programmes in the early evening and then for *Caroline Overdrive*. Reception improved, which helped bringing in a new customer who was interested in buying Radio Monique.

23. Mast Overboard!

On the 24th November, a ferocious wind tore at the ship in her new exposed position. The weather was increasingly rough and most of those on board had stayed up late. Peter Chicago was on the bridge sending a message over his private telex ink to shore, reporting that some stays were a problem and that the weather was very rough.

Caroline was still on the air and DJ Pat Brooks was in the middle of playing a track by the hooters called *Satellite* when, just before 3am, the antenna feeder cable was torn out and tangled around some mast stays, putting Caroline off the air. Two decks below, in the mess room some DJs were sat around discussing the weather, Stuart Russell was making a video in the record library. Suddenly, there was an almighty crash and clattering that resounded throughout the ship

Out on deck, pieces of porcelain from shattered insulators were raining down and dozens of steel guys were scything through the air. Chris Kennedy was in the wheelhouse and saw the mast go: "It was as though it was walking sideways, across the deck and towards the sea," he described it. When they went on deck, the crew saw that everyone's worst fears had come true; the mast had snapped off near the base and fallen over the starboard side of the ship. Nothing could be done until dawn broke, which showed the ship to be in danger.

Fortunately, the ship now had on board a very experienced mariner: Chief Engineer Ernie Stephenson from Hull. A down-to-earth former trawlerman, Ernie had seen all kinds of weather off Iceland and had been a group engineer for the Ross Group, looking after several ships. He marshalled those on board to their muster stations and allayed any fears they had. Morale was at a low ebb and most were scared.

Ernie realised that the motion was causing the top of the mast to bang on the seabed, only fifty feet below. It was still tethered to the ship by guy wires, causing a bad list. It was impossible to retrieve the 90 metres of tower which weighed over 12 tons. Reluctantly the crew set about cutting through the many stays still holding it to the ship. Once the structure was relinquished, the ship rode the seas much better.

Back in London, Peter Moore organised a crisis meeting to get a tender organised as a lengthy shopping list came from the ship of the items needed to get back on the air, in addition to a new mast! As usual, most people now wrote Radio Caroline off as no one ever expected her to be able to climb back on the air from such a blow.

As Jesus Christ said: "Oh Ye of little faith!"

Ronan refused to believe that the ship's tower had all gone and was distraught. This turned to anger as suppliers of replacement masts demanded upfront payment and several of his ideas were dismissed by the Caroline team. His proposal for a tower crane from a building site, complete with a lift, was denounced impractical.

It took just nine days to string up a temporary antenna between the small foremast and the funnel and the station resumed transmissions on only one frequency, 558 KHz. The power was low as any more caused the antenna, far too short for the frequency, to arc and spark in the damp conditions.

Only two broadcasters were still on board the ship when Caroline returned in early December, Chief DJ Steve Conway and his brother, Chris Kennedy. It really was an all-Irish Radio Caroline, for a while with the brothers doing some long stints to keep Caroline on the air for twelve hours a day.

Brothers in Arms
Chris Kennedy and Steve Conway
John Burch

As Peter Philips was in the USA for a holiday, Steve took over the duties as Programme Controller, which meant compiling all three playlists. Steve even managed to reintroduce the *Caroline Newsbeat* service by the winter solstice as by now Mike Watts had rebuilt the newsroom, refixing everything to the walls and floor. The ship was rolling around quite a lot now as she had been ballasted to cater for the huge mast. Now that was gone, she was well out of trim.

The crew of four struggled on until they were joined by reinforcements on Christmas eve, comprising a cook, an engineer and an extra DJ, Mike 'Coconut' Dixon. After another week's work the antenna was lengthened and soon the power was increased, but still only on the one frequency. The Dutch transmissions were, for now, off the air.

The captain of the supply boat *Windy* had been jailed in November for running supplies to the Caroline ship after being caught two years previously when the propeller of the Windy became fouled with a rope. Another crewman, Howard, had pleaded guilty and Southend Crown Court jailed him for nine months, the first UK incarceration for such an offence. Howard was later freed by the Court of Appeal freed, who agreed that the jail sentence imposed was absurdly long.

New masts and aerials

By now, the Dutch service was in complete disarray. The Monique operators had been planning to move to another ship anchored closer to Belgium and so had sold their rights to the time from the Ross Revenge to a new owner, Alfons Ravelli. He was in the tobacco business in Amsterdam; the *Texas* cigarettes brand advertised on Radio Monique was just one part of his operation.

Alfons intended to call his station *Radio Noordzee*, but only later, once it was able to broadcast with the 50 kilowatt transmitter again. In the meantime, a temporary Dutch service would be renamed **Radio 819.** Listeners would not have noticed much difference, but for the lower signal strength, perhaps.

The previous three Januaries had been very unkind, but out at the Falls Head as 1988 broke, conditions suddenly abated, which enabled the crew to get on with building a temporary system of two masts, with an aerial wire strung between them. The Bellatrix arrived with more mast sections, lots of other engineering supplies and more crew members, including Peter Chicago and marine engineer, Ernie Stephenson. The tender was contracted to lie alongside until the mast building was completed, so that its crane could be used to hoist up mast sections.

Eventually, a new steel lattice mast was erected on the stern deck with four sections of mast each 15 feet high. At the same time, the fore mast was increased in height to around 90 feet, by adding parts of the old loading arm and lengths of steel pipe onto the former ship's mast. It looked ugly, like most things on the Ross Revenge, but it worked. A much stronger signal could now be radiated on 558, a couple of kilowatts was emanating, although an elaborate loading network was needed to make the new T aerial work.

Ronan had a master plan that had three stages. First, the crew would build two one hundred feet tall masts and hang a T-aerial between them. Then the old mast would be rebuilt midships and finally a hundred foot tall carbon fibre section would be added to the top, giving the Ross Revenge a four hundred feet high aerial, plus a small standby system of the twin 100 feet tall masts. He had already ordered two carbon fibre masts from the factory in Canada.

Ronan had thoughts of constructing a copy of the original tall mast in France and have it flown out to the ship by helicopter, complete. All it would then need was bolting to the deck of the Ross Revenge and connecting up. The idea was simply too expensive, probably impractical and so it was quickly abandoned.

On land the Dutch authorities were carrying out surveillance against the Radio Monique team, including the main director, Fred Bolland. They also tailed Captain Willy Wormenleyton, who had previously been responsible for the supplies to the ship. They sold their interest in Radio Monique and refused to do any more tendering of the ship except for cash, paid upfront, which wasn't always easy.

The Dutch authorities also had in their sights Gert-Jan Smit who had arranged many of the adverts heard on Radio Monique. Most of the evidence they collected however was not admissible in court as it had been collected illegally, by the investigators claiming that the entire Radio Monique operation was involved in drugs. No drugs were ever found in any searches and no one was connected in any way with drugs, so the entire case collapsed as their 'evidence' was not allowed to be put before the court.

Work continued into February on erecting the back mast while the now returned Peter Philips was busy aloft up for'ard, rigging the cod liver oil piping, scaffold poles and an odd length of mast into a hundred feet tall structure to match the rapidly growing mast astern. These new masts were both reinforced, having two doubled up sections for the two lower segments to add strength.

A fuller description of the mast building can be found in Steve Conway's excellent story of that time, called *Shiprocked*. (see the bibliography on Page 506 for details)

Doubled up lower mast sections

Caroline listeners had a Valentine's Day present in 1988 – the return of Caroline 558 at full power once again. A proper relaunch of Radio 819 as well as Caroline 558 proved impossible without a higher mast, however the *Caroline World Service* on Short Wave service was a possibility as it also needed a much shorter antenna. By getting this outlet operational there would be revenue from the religious output that had previously bought time on the *Caroline Overdrive* programmes.

90 feet high Carbon Fibre Aerial made by Valcom for 819
Paul Graham

Transmissions took a couple of months to refine but, by May 1988, a new American-owned short wave station was operating from the ship. *World Mission Radio* had a mixture of Dutch and English programmes, with the regular Caroline shows used as a sustaining service. The income from this would help funds and increasing the height of the masts meant the restart of a Dutch service on 819.

At Easter, the a long-promised and somewhat revolutionary new carbon-fibre antenna finally arrived from the Valcom factory in Canada. It was a helically wound antenna around a fibre glass pole. These antennae are in use at hundreds of locations around the world, but usually with only low power beacon signals transmitted from them. The manufacturer was sure they could build a stronger one that would handle the 819 signals with a few tens of kilowatts.

The fibre pole antennas were usually free standing when erected on land but on board a ship at sea it would need some stays. It was mounted towards the stern of the ship. Without any stays it was never still and looked as though it was waving to passing ships. Erection was eventually completed by the crew on the ship and test transmissions from Radio 819 could begin. At first only very low power was used and then the power was turned up, ready for a grand start with high power.

The helical antennas are fine with a single tone, that is – a narrow bandwidth signal but with the *AmpliPhase* transmitter at its widest settings, the narrow bandwidth (and correspondingly high 'Q') Valcom aerial simply could not cope with even a fifteen kilowatt signal. It was in fact designed for only five kilowatts, but that information had been mysteriously erased from its nameplate!

When an aerial has high 'Q', the voltages become quite fierce and so the device began to melt. It did work for a few weeks at low power but as soon as this was increased to even a moderate level, the trouble began.

A couple of hours after opening as Radio 819 the antenna simply burst into flames, causing the transmitter to trip out. The Valcom aerial just kept on burning however then suddenly it split in half around the top and spat pieces of carbon fibre around the deck! It was an amazing spectacle as discs of carbon were flung around, still hot to the touch. Mike Watts tried to make the stump of the Valcom aerial work by attaching a cage of wires from its tip across to the foremast, but this was unsuccessful.

It was vital to get the revenue earning Dutch service back on the air as soon as possible and Caroline relinquished the 558 transmitter to the Dutch service who began multilingual programmes, this time as **Radio 558**. It could be heard well over the Netherlands and Belgium and accrued a sizeable audience. Dutch listeners were used to hearing music at that end of the MW, on Radio Veronica's old frequency.

"Good Morning Europe, it's exactly 9-00. Live from the North Sea" were the first words spoken by Erwin van der Bliek on the 9th July, instead of the normal Caroline 558 programmes. Station manager Nico Volker was annoyed to hear the early start though, as he had planned a full launch with jingles, a full book of adverts and some star DJs. One of the Dutch DJs was totally inept and had to be taken off the air, but eventually more proficient DJs such as Walter Simons and Elly van Amstel arrived at the Ross Revenge and brought a professional sound to Radio 558.

The planned one month of Dutch language programmes on 558 turned into several as the antenna was not yet finished and Caroline's English programmes stayed relegated to night time hours. The crew worked hard to complete the masts so that both 819 and 558 could transmit.

Twin masts taking shape on the Ross Revenge in 1988

Most of the programmes were presented by Dutch DJs live from the Ross Revenge and Radio 558 was heard all day, while Caroline 558 continued at night. The station offered not just Dutch programmes, but also Radio Caroline international news bulletins twice a day in English. Dutch evangelist Johan Maasbach too was heard on the air in the Radio 558 schedule, which played music targeted at the Netherlands more than Belgium.

Radio Caroline had a heavy commercial load that included Texas cigarettes, a couple of travel agencies, Atari computers and of course the Canadian Lotto 6/49. The Dutch service also carried commercials for the cigarettes which were in abundance on the ship. Literally thousands of them were brought out to the Ross Revenge, which helped all those with a nicotine habit to stay a bit calmer!

The Dutch news reports were obtained by SW telex but this had to be stopped after a while when the transmissions from the ship's own *World Mission Radio* caused interference. The following month this was restarted once a new telex machine had arrived on the ship. The SW transmission also broke through onto some items of studio equipment, making odd sounds, and several changes in frequency had to be made before this was rectified.

Some of the regular Caroline DJs took jobs on shore-based stations as there was little or no money coming into Caroline by this time. 'Dangerous Dave' was one of Manchester's most famous DJs. He arrived on Caroline in July 1988 and presented many programmes as Dave Miller. While on board the Ross Revenge he became enchanted with the Laser project and later bought the *MV Communicator* and set up a new station called the Superstation in the Orkneys. Full details of the vessel can be found in the book *Radio Adventures of the MV Communicator*; see the bibliography on page 506.

Sexy-voiced Judy Murphy

Judy Murphy was a Canadian DJ who met Radio Monique's Herbert Visser while travelling in Europe and joined the ship with Dave Miller on the day that Radio 558 began. She stayed for less than six months before joining Radio Luxembourg where she used a new name, Jodie Scott. While on Caroline Judy put her voice to great use, not just in programming but in production and recording of commercials.

Among those commercials for which Judy did a superb job on were those for *Bet Canada*, the Canadian Lottery. The original spots had been running for three years; Judy did a sexy twin voice production with Steve Conway using Alison Moyet's "That old Devil Called Love" as a bed. Now living in the UK she works as an actress, as a voice over artiste and a vocalist.

Steve Conway took a break from the ship and on his return he presented a late night programme on the now nocturnal Caroline 558. He also wrote and presented the afternoon news programme in English. "I found being on the air late at night was far more satisfying than hosting programmes during the daytime," said Steve. "You are somehow in much closer contact with the listeners, maybe because the audience is smaller."

In August, Chief Engineer Ernie Stephenson had to leave the ship for his son's wedding in Hull. It was to be some time before he returned as he contracted tuberculosis and spent several months laid up.

A period of serious mast-building on the ship took place using twenty foot long sections of lattice mast brought out by a variety of clandestine methods, including some delivered on board an open-top bus, emblazoned with the LBC logo. A truck carrying mast sections would be noticed heading to a port, but on the open topped bus they would be invisible to other road users and passers by, especially at the coast in summer. A Dutch DJ called Arie Swets was a keen mast climber. Arie was almost as nimble shinning up the mast as Peter Philips.

Arie Swets

The lower sections of the fore mast were doubled up using extra sections brought out from Belgium and later the aft mast was doubled up similarly. At one stage Mike Dundee brought out accessories on a tiny inflatable dinghy. He went to carry out repairs and attach the end fittings to the Kevlar stays. During a disaster with the fuel pump, stood up to his waist inside the diesel tank and filled buckets to be taken to the generator in a chain gang, until the pump was fixed. Several others made enormous sacrifices and put their lives in danger, just to keep Caroline on the air and the music flowing out.

It took until another three months to erect an aerial suitable to diplex both the 558 and the 819 signals into it but eventually, in late October,1988, the Dutch shows were switched onto 819 while Caroline 558 got its old slot back again.

Long serving offshore DJ Ad Roberts made the return of 819 his last day. Nico Volker became the chief liaison man between the Dutch DJs and the Radio 819 station owner, Alfons Reveile. Normal programming began once again on Guy Fawkes Night 1988, almost a year since the mast had been lost. The ship could now transmit five stations once again: Caroline 558 in English, Radio 558 in Dutch, Viewpoint 819 and Caroline Overdrive and World Mission Radio on short wave, although three of them time-shared the same transmitter.

During December the crew on the Ross Revenge were let down by the Dutch tender operators and the management of Radio 819. They arrived with no water and almost no food, just fuel.

The English DJs and engineering team were despondent at being treated in this way when they had worked so hard to get the Dutch Radio 819 on the air. Supplies were at a critical stage, and by Christmas Eve it looked like dinner the next day was to be rice and a few sausages.

The DJs on Caroline 558 went onto a Winter Fast to raise funds for the Clapham Rail Disaster, where a commuter train had run into the back of a stationary one in south west London. 35 were killed and almost 500 injured, just two weeks before Christmas. The programming on Caroline was very sensitively handled and helped raise thousands to support the families who had lost a bread winner – the message of Radio Caroline was always to help people. Few realised that the boys on the Ross Revenge also were in dire need of help themselves and, as darkness fell on the 24th, they all felt they had been forgotten.

Around 7am on Christmas Day the bell was rung that signalled "tender approaching". Everyone sprang out of bed to see Dave Turner's 'Fairwinds' approaching from Ramsgate with station manager Peter Moore on deck, wielding a Christmas Tree and Christmas cheer for everyone! The turkey was immediately put into the oven and that evening saw the crew enjoying fine wines, sparkling conversation and some very welcome treats sent out by the Caroline Movement. Ronan and Mike Plumley had persuaded Peter Moore to "cover the tender run" (meaning pay for it) including the supplies.

The following day, the 26th, the Poolster was alongside, with the much-needed fresh water and even more mast sections. It had been decided to extend and strengthen the masts to enable more power to be used on both the 558 and 819 channels.

The New Year was celebrated with a top 100 tracks of the year, chosen by all the crew; top position for the best track of 1988 went to the Pet Shop Boys' track *Domino Dancing*

A legal case was started by Caroline against Valcom, the antenna manufacturer who had supplied the carbon fibre helical antenna. The action was lost due to the supplier's technical advice being vastly exceeded, which voided not only any warranty but any legal obligation to be "fit for purpose".

The first days of 1989 began with a flurry of mast building, beefing up the existing masts. It was however to prove one of the most decisive and certainly one of the most devastating of the Ross Revenge's stay at sea. Mast erection was usually done without any interruptions to transmissions; both Caroline 558 and Radio 819 continued as normal. The weather and sea conditions out at the South Falls Head could be kind, some years! Extra height and stability were added to both masts to enable the aerial array to accept higher power on both frequencies.

During January the old Caroline Overdrive service was put back on the air once again on 819kHz after the Dutch programmes closed for the day. After the departures of Tom Anderson and Cosmic Andy, the late night rock service would be run by Rob Harrison, Paul Shelton and Bruce Williamson (aka Colin Mueslibar) and have a new name - *Caroline 819, the Overnight Alternative*. It had a slightly rockier feel and was more avant garde than the 'poppier' Caroline 558.

Evidence that the station's owners meant business came in early February with the attendance of a huge tug that topped up every tank on the ship. Over a quarter of a million litres of fuel meant several months operation was possible with no problems, while the ships water tanks and plumbing was flushed out before refilling with sweet water.

New recruits Nick Jackson and Caroline Martin arrived on board at this time; having a woman on board was always good for morale and improved attitudes and manners no end. In preparation for the big birthday bash to celebratre Caroline's jubilee, lots of journalists were invited out to the ship to prepare their stories and see life first hand.

BBC Visitors

The BBC eagerly took up the invitation to visit the Ross Revenge and sent out a team of twelve to film a short piece for their 'Daytime Live' programme. There were camera hands, soundmen, lighting experts, two note-takers, even two make up girls, plus a union officer to ensure that no one did anything that was outside their normal job description.

The BBC staffing levels were quite the opposite to Radio Caroline, where everyone did at least two or three jobs and was expected to help out with all manner of tasks. Caroline was running three separate channels (identified as five stations) as well as running a ship and its own engineering with a team smaller than the BBC had sent out for a short piece just a few minutes long!

Silver Jubilee

At Easter 1989, the station celebrated its Silver Jubilee with some special events. A 25th birthday is very special and Caroline broadcast two separate Countdowns in celebration. On the *Overdrive 819* service, Rob Harrison and Paul Shelton hosted a Top 200 listeners all time chart, while across on the pop channel, *Caroline 558* offered listeners a Top 1001.

It was discovered that a local station in Essex was trying to steal Caroline's thunder by running a Top 1000 chart over the same Easter weekend, so Caroline went one better and had a Top 1001, and without a thousand commercials either! The information was collated by Steve Conway using a computer to average out the Top Tens that had been sent in by Caroline's audience. The tracks were interspersed with the vast range of jingles from each era of Caroline, plus all the instrumental themes that were so popular in the days when Radio Mi Amigo broadcast, just as Radio 819 was doing in 1989.

The first 250 positions in the chart (1001-751) were played on Good Friday, then 750-501 on Easter Saturday, 500-251 on Easter Sunday, and the final 250 counting up to the Number 1 on Easter Monday. Steve hosted the main programmes jointly with Caroline Martin and duos were established for the other peak time segments too, giving the Caroline sounds a new dimension that it didn't usually have.

Speech was limited however to the music and memories that each track invoked, as the music was after all the key dynamic, as that had been the heart of the station over the past quarter of a century. The format also lent itself to incorporating Ronan's idea of 'pleasure points' where two sounds went well together and would magically segue into one another.

The entire weekend's programming was run like a military operation, with special 'record pullers' detailed to have the necessary albums ready for play and alternatives worked out. While it was widely expected that the Fortunes' Caroline would top the chart, it was felt that this had been a bit overplayed. Another possibility was John Lennon's 'Imagine', once intended to be the name of the ship, but this had headed the Top 500 chart on Caroline's 20th birthday.

The other really huge favourite and unanimous choice of the number one was Bob Dylan's '*Hurricane*'. Rarely heard on any other station, it was a song not about the wind that had wrecked Caroline's magnificent tower almost eighteen months previously and almost finished the station off, but about justice, freedom and liberty, all key parts of Radio Caroline's goals and philosophy.

Planning what probably was Caroline's best ever weekend, was undertaken by a 24 year old Irishman, Steve Conway. It mirrored the work assembling Caroline in the sixties by another 24 years old Irishman, Ronan O'Rahilly. Caroline had always given the opportunity to young broadcasters to change things, encouraging their new ideas and rewarding initiatives as the older hands moved on to shore stations. This usually happened when regular wages became more important to them or getting home every night!

The 25th birthday was also marked with a very special event; the *Olau Britannia* ferry had hundreds of Radio Caroline's supporters on board, some of them seeing the ship for the first time. They were also surprised to meet Ronan O'Rahilly on board the ferry, out at sea celebrating with them.

Ronan and the CM's JB cut the 25th birthday cake

Julian Wellings

Ronan and some Caroline DJs who were also on board spoke to many of the anoraks and cut a huge 25th birthday cake as they sailed past the Ross Revenge. He was assisted by the Caroline Movement's John Burch, the organiser of the event. On Caroline 558AM, after playing a five minute montage of jingles from the station's quarter of a century on the air, Chief DJ Steve Conway rang the Caroline bell and said:

This is Caroline 558, your all day music station, now 25 years old. Thank you to all our listeners, thank you to all the people who've been involved, especially Peter Chicago and the Silver Fox.

The start and the finish of the special birthday broadcast was relayed on Radio 819 and included three special songs that described what Radio Caroline is all about – The Beatles' anthemic *All You need is Love*, *The Voice of Love* by the Loving Awareness Band and *Fool if you think it's Over* by Chris Rea. BBC local radio station *GLR* had a

party on a Thames river barge, hosted by former Radio Caroline DJs Tommy Vance, Johnnie Walker, Mike Ahern and Gerry Burke.
Caroline's new Dutch station Radio 819 was not faring as well as its predecessor *Radio Monique* had. One reason was the still inferior signal; it wasn't possible to transmit with high power on the 819 frequency which was not strong in many parts of the Netherlands.

The Dutch station had also lost several of its star DJs and now had competition from other stations on cable and some local public outlets. For some weeks she became the more topical *Holiday Radio 819*. The partners in the Dutch operation pressured Caroline to move the ship closer to the Netherlands or Belgium; when they were told that this was not feasible, they threatened to join one of the two other ships nearing completion and planning to broadcast to Holland and Belgium.

Morale among the Dutch DJs on board was low due to poor management. Tenders were less frequent and supplies ran very low, especially the tobacco and beer. Telephone calls were now possible onto the ship on the mobile phone, but "incoming only" after some enormous bills were racked up. Calls at this time cost 35p a minute 'local' and over £1 for non-UK calls. To have some start a call, the ship would play Abba's 'Ring Ring' over the air and hope for a response.

Laser's old ship, the *Communicator* had been bought from her Essex interests and Ryan by Fred Bolland, the owner of Radio Monique. He planned to refurbish her to broadcast several different stations from the ship. After spending some time anchored near the Sandettie Bank and then close-by the South Falls Head, the Communicator was taken to Portugal dry-docked and her masts installed.

During this move, the Dutch authorities had become aware that two Germans were to be the operators of one of the new stations and fronted by the "Underground Church." They had previously been jailed for raising mercenary armies in Germany (illegal in that country since World War II) and had other equally shady links to organised crime in the Netherlands and Romania.

The Dutch BVD (a national intelligence and security agency) were very concerned and persuaded their Portugese equivalent, the SIS, to take immediate action against the MV Communicator. During her dry-docking a lot of work had been carried out on her. One mast had been erected on her stern and all the transmitters were safely stored in two shipping containers on the dock.

MV Mia Migo, formerly the Nannell

Radio 819's core team of Walter Simmons, Erik Beekman and Mirjam Verhoef held things together well even though their boss Nico Volker told them that the station would soon move to the MV Nannell. She was now anchored off Blankenberg without a mast and also had a new name that might sound familiar – the *MV Mia Migo*!

It was originally to broadcast as *Stereo Hits AM* from the ship which was even larger ship than the Ross Revenge. She had finally left the Spanish port of Santander in June and assumed the name Mia Migo. While crossing the Bay of Biscay she rolled a few times and lost her superb 240 feet tall telescopic antenna mast. The crew had ignored the requirement for guying or stays and believed that a few spots of welding would hold it upright!

On arriving off the coast of Blankenberg (a Belgian seaside resort) the Mia Migo made a few short test transmissions on FM and was then silent for three months as everyone was very worried about official action. Eventually, the ship sailed to Southampton where many of the crew had connections and she was later scrapped there, never having started regular broadcasting.

Caroline's Dutch customer, Radio 819, would have to remain on the Ross Revenge and they immediately redoubled their efforts to get the twin masts built on the ship, which would enable both 819 and 558 to broadcast at higher power.

The France Radio Club at this time persuaded French TV programme, *Talassa*, to cover life on the Radio Caroline ship. A crew and the programme host, Isabelle Moeglin spent several days on board the Ross Revenge, filming everyday life of the Caroline family. The film crew then travelled to London to interview Ronan about his reasons for Radio Caroline carrying on, despite the problems of legality.

The TV programme gave wide publicity to the Radio Caroline cause and during the several days that they spent on the Ross Revenge, they shot many hours of film. The period they were on board included the erection of the carbon fibre helical antenna, which was seen in their report. The coverage was fronted by Isabelle Moeglin who also spent extra time on the Ross Revenge, conducting background research into Radio Caroline's story.

24. Government piracy

During July, the crew on the Ross Revenge noticed an official-looking patrol boat anchored close by for several days. It seemed to be simply monitoring the area and didn't make any contact with them. As a tender approached, the boat sailed up close and two photographers appeared on deck to video and photograph the transfer, but again no action was taken. A French navy patrol visited twice but made no contact with the ship, it later turned out that they had followed a tender, which had abandoned its course when it realised that it was being followed.

The following week, as the fuel tender came alongside the Ross Revenge, two British police launches appeared out of the mist and warned the ship's master that he was breaking international law. They did not take any direct action but did photograph everyone who ventured on deck during the fuel transfer, which took about an hour.

Over the ensuing week helicopters and small planes would often appear and it was clear they were making a very thorough photographic record of the ship. They even attempted to photograph the DJs in the studio through the windows but were thwarted by the use of curtains in the studio.

Observations during that investigation gave even more concern to the BVD who were keen to supress the transmissions from the Ross Revenge. They publicly denied to the Dutch press that direct action was being contemplated when door-stepped by journalists on the Tuesday 16th August however, on the following day, the authorities raided twenty addresses in Holland and seven in Belgium. They detained some key Caroline associates for questioning.

A DTI clerical officer in the UK (a former policeman called James Murphy) telephoned Peter Moore and tried to grill him further "about the radio ship you operate" which showed his ignorance of the situation. Murphy claimed: "I have invoked an exclusion zone around your ship" and invited Peter to 'give himself up". Knowing that Murphy had no such authority, Peter declined the 'opportunity' to surrender.

A chartered cutter the Landward, with a posse of Dutch and UK officials on board, set off from Ramsgate the following day. The launch's captain and DTI officials htalked with the Ross Revenge's crew and DJs by shouting between the two ships; Caroline DJ Bruce Purdy went onto the official boat to be briefed on the situation. The DTI officers told him that Caroline's onshore organisation had been 'immobilised' but that anyone who left the ship now could still escape prosecution.

It' seems that they were referring to the two stations planned to launch from the *MV Mia Migo* or the four stations planned for the MV Communicator as both ships had criminal links. None of the new stations were connected with Radio Caroline at all but the mention of criminality it was typical of the devious ploys practiced by the DTI.

The crew of the Ross Revenge said they wanted time to consider the situation. They needed to urgently contact the Caroline organisation in London which proved impossible, though that was not unusual. They believed that the authorities might be playing tricks to get them to leave the ship. The officials on the Landward pulled away and said they would be back the following day for an answer to their offer.

Contact was made with associates in the UK, who tried to pass on messages and get some instructions, or news of the situation. Seven telephone numbers in use only recently were, inexplicably, not answering or just unobtainable. During the evening, the Radio 819 DJs decided that recent events suggested that some action had been taken, especially as it proved impossible to contact anyone. They were reluctant to continue broadcasting until they knew more.

Peter Chicago who had been on land guessed that some direct action might be about to take place. He sailed out alone from Broadstairs in his small dingy to the radio ship and spent several hours hiding various piece of vital equipment in places around the radio ship.

Saturday 19th August dawned with smooth seas and a shroud of thick mist enveloping the ship. Programmes began as normal on both *Caroline 558* and *Radio 819*.

The DTI team (Murphy, Allison, Hawkins and Innes) returned on the Landward and suggested to the Caroline team that others in the shore operation were involved in matters more serious than just a radio station and claimed that they were hardened criminals. The DTI men insisted that both Dutch and British crew must all leave the vessel as one group, but this was rejected by all on board.

It's likely that they were referring to the two stations planned to launch from the *MV Mia Migo* or the four stations planned for the MV Communicator. None of the new stations were connected with radio Caroline at all but the mention of criminality it was rather typical of the increasingly devious ploys practiced by the DTI at that time.

The atmosphere on board was very tense and a coded message to the office signified to colleagues ashore that something was very wrong on board the radio ship or in the vicinity.

Neil Gates took over programming and both *Caroline 558* and *Radio 819* were combined to one output, with the name changed to simply *Radio Caroline*. The 49 meter short wave service of *World Mission Radio* ceased just after midday; Howard Rose of the Radio Magazine had passed on a warning about this to Peter Moore who advised the ship the previous evening. Ronan insisted on "business as usual" and Chicago steadfastly maintained that it was a good clear channel.

Dutch government raiding ship, the Volans

A short time later, a large Dutch ship, *the Volans,* appeared out of the mist. She was a large well-equipped vessel that had helped fight the major fire on the Mebo II some years before. She often used by the Dutch government and on board her on this occasion were her crew and several dozen men including uniformed police. An urgent call to the UK's 'ship to shore' station at North Foreland from the Ross Revenge was ignored, a most unusual response. It was clear that they had been instructed to not take any calls from the radio ship.

A man on the Volans who identified himself as being an officer of the Dutch Water Police asked for permission to come on board and inspect the ship's papers, which was refused as the police had no jurisdiction in international waters. The police officer repeatedly maintained that he had sufficient authorisation and demanded to see registration papers. Peter Chicago, as the acting captain of the Ross Revenge, refused to comply with the request, as was his prerogative.

After a while the men on the tug grew impatient and the largest jumped onto the Ross Revenge. When Peter barred his way, the police officer confronting him went for his gun. "You're surely not going to shoot me are you?" Peter asked the officer, who then punched him on the chin, knocking him over.

"They had no warrant, papers or badge, no papers from any court," explained Peter later. "I asked them repeatedly to show me what authorisation they had, but they just refused and wouldn't even show a badge of office." The police officers told the crew that they had orders to board the ship and dismantle the transmitters and studios. They asked for the crew to comply with them and not stand in their way which might result in harm or damage to the equipment.

Caroline Martin in the 558 studio

Faced with over thirty armed invaders the 15 men and women on board the Caroline ship had no option but to surrender. The atmosphere was very heated but the peace-loving Radio Caroline team were helpless in such circumstances and totally out of their depth. Their home, the Ross Revenge, was being literally invaded by armed thugs who were now becoming menacing and aggressive. This was probably Radio Caroline's worst ever moment.

English DJ Caroline Martin was indecently assaulted when she tried to bar the doorway to the ship's transmitter room. While she was not physically hurt she was affronted and left shaken by the outrageous behaviour by the man, who simply sneered at her.

Several DJs tried to keep listeners informed, playing significant radio and peace songs, their impassioned pleas getting more and more urgent. Radio 819 switched to relay the Caroline output in time for listeners in Holland to hear Chicago make the following urgent plea:

> *This is a special announcement from the Radio Caroline ship, Ross Revenge. At the moment we have a large Dutch tug, the Volans, . . they seem to have the intention of taking this ship from the High Seas. We've had previous warnings, that some kind of action was contemplated.*
>
> *On the starboard side of the Ross Revenge we have the Dutch tug, the Volans, which seems to have the intention of taking the Ross Revenge from her moorings in international waters of the South Falls Head. We'll try and let you know what goes on as the programme continues but I have an idea that events will move very quickly.*
>
> *Anybody hearing this broadcast could perhaps help us by telephoning the coastguard to register a complaint, possibly by contacting anybody in authority that you think could help us.*
> *This is the radio ship Ross Revenge."*

Caroline continued playing music in between the increasingly desperate pleas for assistance being made on the air. The tracks played were the most emotive Caroline all-time favourites and peace anthems – Imagine, Lady in Red, and the station theme by The Fortunes. This was done to attract attention from listeners who were asked repeatedly to call anyone in authority they knew and the press.

Just after 1pm both 558 and 819 transmitters carried the last announcements from DJs Chris Kennedy, Dave Richards and Nigel Harris who had now taken to the studio and given up the deck which was swarming with the Dutch invaders from the Volans. The thugs had no idea how to switch the transmitters off and summoned across the British DTI technicians to explain the controls to them.

The final announcement made over the air immediately before the raiders shut off the equipment was:

> *We will be leaving the air at any moment now, the boarding party are trying to get into the transmitter room. They are going to dismantle all our transmitting gear, take the studio to pieces, dismantle our generators and then in incapacitate the ship totally, they also intend taking all the staff off with them.*
>
> *We just can't fight them, there are too many of them. We will be back. 19th August 1989, the day on which the UK, Great Britain, became a totalitarian state.*

Bruce Purdey spoke to the coastguards on the VHF and told them "Everything is A-OK here sir" when it clearly was not. His purpose on the Ross Revenge has always been in doubt and it was no surprise when he hitched a lift back ashore with the DTI officers. His last words on the air were to invite one of the intruders to speak. Before anything further was said, both transmitters fell silent.

Caroline was, once again, off the air.

The crew on the Ross Revenge could now see who they were up against. The raiding team comprised a posse of Dutch Water Police, some members of the Dutch secret service, some Dutch PTT engineers and a dozen additional 'security men' who were simply heavies or thugs hired for the occasion by the tug operators. About a third of the men were armed and others were simply menacing.

They were also accompanied by three officials from the British DTI who had arrived on board the Landward, normally based at Gillingham pier. Although they did not take part in the handling of any equipment they demanded to see everyone's passport and wanted British crew members and DJs to give them full statements describing why they were on the Ross Revenge. They had no right to do so, nor even come on board the ship. Their HQ denied that any of their people were on the ship, but around twenty witnesses confirm that they certainly were.

The invaders had not expected the Ross Revenge to contain so much equipment and they were somewhat overawed at the size of the transmitters. They brought sledgehammers and angle grinders on board and set about smashing up the ship's generators and tried to cut down the two masts by hacking at the stays. Chicago pointed out that they and others might get hurt if they did that, so they resorted to tearing down the 'T' antenna radiator slung between them and threw that onto the deck of the Volans.

"It was just sheer mindless vandalism, heart breaking and quite numbing to watch but there was nothing we could do against such overwhelming force," said Peter. He advised that without any generators the ship could not be kept lit, so one of them was saved.

Over the next four or five hours the invaders systematically chopped away at the contents of the generator hold, the transmitter room and the studios, taking every item possible and throwing it into large cargo nets on the deck of the Volans, which lay tied up along the starboard side of the Ross Revenge.

Dutch thugs and their booty!

No care at all was taken with any of the equipment, they simply hacked out most of the wiring looms from the transmitters. Many fragile ceramic and glass vacuum capacitors and expensive valves were maliciously destroyed. The thugs were also drinking beer from bottles, despite many of them being in uniform.

During a meal break Peter organised the Caroline crew on the Ross Revenge to gather up key components and hide them all over the ship. Large valves were immersed in the oily black water in the bilges under the engine room plates, and a mixing panel from the studios was secreted in the funnel. The many components that the crew squirreled away would enable Radio Caroline to get back on the air as soon as possible.

After a meal break the carnage continued until the Volans was called by an approaching boat; it was the *FV Fairwinds*, Dave Turner's fishing boat, which had tendered the Ross Revenge on many occasions from the UK. Dave claimed that his boat was full of journalists; Mike Dundee claimed to be from Reuters, at which news, the Volans gave a toot on its horn and took off into the mist.

The Dutch policeman in charge of the raid (Martin Rouman) said as he left that he was sure that Radio Caroline would be heard again, but so long as it had no Dutch broadcasts then they would not have any further interest. The Volans took off all the Dutch DJs who had been offered immunity from prosecution.

That evening, Dutch media historian Hans Knot was interviewed on Holland's Radio 1 where he stated that both the Dutch and the British authorities had acted illegally. He anticipated that Radio Caroline would fight back to redress their rights and get their property back.

In a statement to the press the following day, the officials tried to excuse their action by claiming that there had been complaints about the transmissions from the ship, though no details were given. The Dutch Minister of Justice, Mr Mijnsen, said they were concerned about rumours of two more radio ships, the *Mia Migo* and the *Communicator*. The direct action had been planned some time ago and had taken over a year to prepare. The purpose of the raid was to deter any new operators, as well as to close Radio 819 and World Mission Radio.

Radio Caroline instructed expert London maritime lawyers, Richards Butler, to pursue a legal case against the Dutch authorities as well as the British DTI, claiming that their action was illegal. There was considerable 'case law', in so much as acts in international waters were covered at all, to back up the claims that the raid had been unlawful. A recent precedent was the action against Radio Paradijs ship off the Dutch coast in 1981; the authorities had been found to be in breach of their powers and the owners of radio of the station had received substantial compensation.

British civil servants at first lied about their part in the raid, even issuing a statement claiming that no British officers were present during or after the raid! In fact, the logs of the Landward proved that they were and that they had remained tied up alongside for the duration of the raid. The DTI said their officials were on another vessel, just keeping surveillance.

The DTI investigators had invaded the Ross Revenge too, uninvited, and taken statements of some crew and DJs. Strangely enough, the names didn't correspond with names heard on the air, so no prosecutions were possible. Later, the DTI admitted to their officers' presence and agreed that they had given assistance to the Dutch officials, claiming that was only to render the equipment safe!

Journalists who arrived on the Ross Revenge in the late afternoon spoke to a DTI official on the radio ship who identified himself as Jim Murphy, an officer in the Solicitor General's office of the DTI. He did so while he was in the middle of interrogating her crew, thus proving beyond any doubt that he and the DTI were being untruthful.

Photographic and video evidence exists of the damage done during the raid. Some of the raiders were also drinking heavily and left behind a large number of empty bottles which have now been removed from the ship. Radio Caroline had these bottles tested for fingerprints, for use in legal action against the authorities and individuals concerned.

Many of the crew and most listeners were utterly despondent following the raid and were mentally shocked that any government could take such action against a peace-loving ship whose only purpose was to offer Love, Peace and good Music.

Fleet Street journalists worked that Saturday evening to prepare the Sunday newspapers, in which Caroline would have been assured maximum exposure. That was not to be, as the story was usurped by a disaster in London late on the Saturday resulted in 51 young people drowning when a pleasure boat was hit and sunk by a dredger.

A Press Statement was issued on behalf of Radio Caroline by Peter Moore. It read:

> *The Canadian directors of Radio Caroline said they were shocked and horrified at this act of piracy. They said they had taken urgent legal advice and that they would be bringing charges of piracy, assault and criminal damage against the authorities and against individuals concerned. It seems that both the British and Dutch Governments are now involved in a deniability exercise'.*

The Ross Revenge was silent, her three studios had been stripped of all the audio equipment and record library was now bare. The transmitter cabinets remain but denuded of parts. Chicago was sure that at least one transmitter could be rebuilt from the remaining parts and various components that he had hidden away. He marshalled the remaining crew into working parties, tidying the ship to get her ready to go back on the air quickly.

In London, Peter Moore organised a protest rally to which Caroline's supporters were invited to bring along a token gift. This was interpreted by listeners as being food and records, plus items of electronics. One French radio station made a donation of £2,000 which became the core of a fighting fund.

Many former Caroliners now staffed both ILR stations and the BBC. One of the first tenders to the Ross Revenge following the raid was funded by staff at a station in Kent who sent out a complete studio! Tenders were not apprehended as, technically, the Ross Revenge was not a radio ship; her 'distressed' status allowed supplies to be delivered unimpeded. Peter Moore agreed with Ronan O'Rahilly that Caroline would stay off the air to allow supplies to be stockpiled on the ship, in case of a future siege.

Warwick Armstrong was a gregarious Australian who had previously been heard reading the news as Mike Dundee; he had really come out to fix an poorly generator. He started making hazardous supply runs of fuel out to the ship, alone in a rubber Zodiac boat. This was the only fuel route now as the Dutch tenders melted away, fearing prosecution.

Peter Moore felt that Caroline should get as much fuel out to the ship before there was any blockading of supplies. Moore believed that they might not bother taking any action against a now silent radio ship.

While Peter Moore urged the team on shore to quietly arrange fuel deliveries, on board the ship Peter Chicago was following a different set of instructions. Ronan had told him to get Caroline back on the air as quickly as possible, fearing his beloved 558 frequency might be hijacked by the IBA, the BBC or other organisations preparing ships.

Legal Procedings

Ronan was busy pursuing legal proceedings against the authorities and a fighting fund was started by supporters to finance this. The case was taken to several law firms, only to find that each one mysteriously pulled out of the action after a while. He was furious when Moore persuaded Christopher Chalker from a small firm of lawyers to act "The Government will laugh at us he said and insisted they use Richards Butler, who charge 'City' rates. The supporters' funds were soon gobbled up, some in trying to obtain a back-dated set of registration papers when the law firm said any claim was worthless without a valid certificate.

Acting for *Grothan Steemship*, the Panamanian owners of the ship, Richards Butler wrote to the British government and the Dutch Embassy in London seeking compensation for various offences committed by the raiders the previous year, including assault, battery and false imprisonment as well as an indecent assault.

Philip Bush was the lawyer responsible for the case and he moved to another firm(Jackson Parton) where Caroline was instructed to provide trading history to support the claim for losses.

Ronan refused to do so, claiming that Radio Caroline was a major international station. When the lawyers ranted at Ronan demanding to know "How much have you lost?" Ronan stalked out, claimed the lawyers were traitors and paid off by the British Government. The case was dragged around more law firms, including *Clydes, Swepstone Walsh* and *Stevens Innocent*, but they too wanted quantum evidence.

Knowing that the ship's owner (Grothan Steemship) had no assets in the UK, the Government demanded a bond to cover the costs, in the case Grothan lost. An unsuccessful attempt was made to have the case covered by Legal Aid as the funds dwindled. Several benefactors contributed, including Peter Moore and Howard Rose but by now only a small back street law firm would manage the case. A couple of young barristers pleaded the case at the Royal Courts of Justice but the judge struck the case out on grounds of time and that the owners had produced no information of the trading history.

The Ross Revenge suddenly sprang back to life on 30th September with low powered transmissions, though initially with only two DJs on board: Caroline Martin and David Asher. The DTI were incensed that a station they had seen smashed to bits only six weeks before was now back on the air, defiantly pounding out its 'Love, Peace and Good Music' to the UK. The power level was very low as the makeshift aerial was fed through an upturned water barrel on the deck of the ship, instead of a ceramic insulator. Being plastic, it was a good insulator, until it got coated in sea spray when it would catch fire and acrid wafts of black smoke and the most pungent fumes.

A large amount of diesel oil was ready to be sent out on board the MV Galexy, a former Tyne ferry funded by the Caroline Movement, who used it as their HQ. When the Galexy's captain, Alex Pluck, heard the station back on the air he wouldn't sail, as his immunity was gone. Two parts of the Caroline team were working to different agendas, a situation that was to develop into a deep rift and simmer for a long time.

As the licensing agency responsible for allocation of radio frequencies, the DTI announced that 558 kHz had now been allocated to a new station serving London. New entrant *Spectrum Radio* was selected to try and jam out Radio Caroline by allocating them the same frequency. Many of Spectrum Radio's staff were admirers of Radio Caroline and they were not at all amused that the DTI was using them to try and silence Radio Caroline. Spectrum's owners took legal action and the authorities were forced to give them an extra temporary transmitter on another frequency. Despite that, the blocking of Caroline on 558 went ahead, proving the spite and vindictiveness of the civil servants.

Radio Caroline was soon broadcasting various religious programmes under the Viewpoint banner. While appearing to be almost 'back to normal' with 24 hour broadcasting, the depleted team of backroom staff were finding life difficult with telephones being tapped and rumours of more direct action being planned. On the Ross Revenge extra security measures were taken; access to the transmitter room was sealed off from the deck and many ordinary doors had tougher locks installed to keep out any further boarders, whether another official raid or the several rival groups.

Listener support groups kept the team on board the Ross Revenge supplied with domestic necessities. They also helped restock the drastically depleted record library and the slow trickle of new material meant that Caroline 558 became more AOR than before the raid. A news release to the press on the 1st November announced that Caroline was now back on the air with religious programming. *Caroline Viewpoint* was on the air at 6:30 each evening and their office could be contacted at either the BCM Box 66 address in London, or at Torre Avenue in Cupertino, California.

Early in the New Year, the output power of Caroline was increased five fold, meaning that the range went up to several hundred miles. This was vital in order to retain some of the religious programmes, whose UK agents monitored coverage and the response rate. The same month a breakaway group of former broadcasters lobbied for the station to come ashore and seek a licence to broadcast within the UK. This divergence of views about future activities caused further rifts in an already diminished Caroline organisation. Some wanted to bring the Ross Revenge into port and focus solely on getting a licence.

Pretenders to the throne?

Yet another group had registered a UK company as *Radio Caroline Ltd* in 1987. Led by Richard Hilton, a prolific writer of letters to the press, they applied for a national licence for a rock station but made it clear that they were not connected with the offshore Radio Caroline. Another group announced that they would apply to relaunch Radio Caroline on a satellite channel, taking Caroline into a modern era. They were nothing to do with the original Radio Caroline organisation and were simply bandwagoners.

Ronan responded that "They are pirating our name just to win a licence we don't want. Never, not ever! Any on land licence would have to be over my grave. The idea of The Lady broadcasting with a licence issued by a government just sickens me to the pit of my stomach," he proclaimed. "The ship will remain at sea, where we have now been for over 25 years," he promised.

At the same time, the lack of revenue from the Benelux countries was beginning to show and Caroline was forced to rely more on funds provided from Britain. This too was very depleted as the DTI had taken to calling advertisers and record companies threatening dire consequences if they were found to be supporting Caroline.

The ship was being battered by harsh conditions for the rest of the winter. Since the mast had been lost she was not so stable. The irregularity of supply runs to the ship took their toll on the broadcast staff who began to complain bitterly on the air about a perceived lack of concern being shown by the station's management for their well-being and welfare.

On one occasion the first tender they saw in a month had brought only some new studio equipment, which had been donated by members of the France Radio Club. The FRC also raised 34,000 French francs to help pay for more supplies.

The FRC and Offshore Echos team later organised the publication on a book by Caroline's station manager, Peter Moore that produced additional revenue for Caroline at time when precious little other funds were forthcoming.

Peter Moore's fund raising book

The title "*Breaking a Butterfly on a Wheel*" that Peter chose for his book is one that was used in a Times editorial in 1967, criticising the sentencing of Mick Jagger for possession of a small amount of amphetamins.

The expression originated in a work by Alexander Pope in 1735, Epistle to Dr Arthubuthnott and referred to a medieval form of torture, in which victims had their long bones broken with an iron bar while spun on a Catherine wheel. In many ways, Caroline was a beautiful butterfly. The book tells the inside story of the organisation and focussed on those who were working their socks off to keep the ship broadcasting. The story includes the period of rebuilding the masts on the Ross Revenge after the big tower crashed down in November 87, including the debacle over the wholly unsuitable carbon fibre aerial supplied by Valcom. Included in Peter's story is how sections were transported to the coast at one stage by an open top tourist bus by John Buch of the Caroline Movement.

IBA jams out Caroline

In May 1990, on orders of the DTI's Radiocommunications Agency and the IBA, Spectrum Radio's programmes were transmitted on 558 kHz from a site in Fulham. This made reception of the ship's broadcasts impossible in central London. Caroline issued a press statement that was regularly read on the air, explaining the situation. The decision to transmit another station on a frequency already in use by another is something that is simply 'not done'; the authorities were certainly "bang out of order" and this was clearly a desperate move to jam Caroline.

Spectrum Radio abandoned their planned launch on 1st June and announced that they would be taking legal action against the IBA. Both Spectrum and Caroline had warned the DTI and the IBA that there would be huge problems if they persisted in use of the same frequency.

Broadcasting Act 1990

In Parliament, the Government's latest Broadcasting Bill 1990 was passing through various legislative stages prior to becoming law in 1991. At the bill's first reading in the House of Commons, the new laws didn't seem to offer a problem and the threatened 'beefing up' of the clauses that applied to radio ships didn't appear.

When the Bill was read in the House of Lords however, at the last minute, a whole raft of new regulations were added. They were the most threatening and beyond Radio Caroline's worst fears. One new clause, number 159 of the new Broadcasting Act would permit armed service personnel to board any offshore radio station in international waters and use force to close it down. As well as giving them the power to arrest crew of offshore radio stations and seize any equipment the clause also gave the automatic immunity from prosecution or claims for damages done while carrying out such acts.

The proposed powers were widely considered to be a completely "over the top" and a completely unnecessary, not to mention draconian measure. Such measures were not even available to stop a ship running drugs or smuggling people.

Lord Monson made a lengthy speech about his reservations to the 'anti Caroline Clause in the Bill. "This clause has alarming implication for international maritime law and for civil liberties. The powers which Her Majesty's Government are seeking against Radio Caroline are very much greater than the powers which they have, in the past, sought and obtained against hijackers, smugglers and drug traffickers."

Addressing the upper House during the second reading the Bill, Lord Annan, who knew a lot of radio broadcasting having chaired a Committee into the Future of Broadcasting in the 1970s. He and his wife had even been out and had lunch on a radio ship in the sixties. He spoke very eloquently on Radio Caroline's behalf:

"I particularly dislike the extraordinary amendments aimed at Radio Caroline. They will enable the police, the Army, Customs officers and anyone who is authorised by the Secretary of States to board and seize these foreign ships and seize their documents. I realise that the Home Office regards Radio Caroline as a maddening wasp and is infuriated that its attempts over the years to swat it have failed.

However, surely this station is not a wasp but a common or garden cabbage white? Why break a butterfly upon the wheel? Why run the risk of an embarrassing diplomatic confrontation? This could perfectly well happen if the vessel turned out to be under the American flag."

Lord Annan

Lord Annan described the boarding powers being sought in Section 7A of the bill as being quite extraordinary and reprehensible. Ferrers retorted that offshore stations often offend against and infringe the laws of the country. Lord Monson tabled amendments to dilute the powers of the Home Office but his motion was defeated.

Protests by 29 peers who had sympathy for Radio Caroline's plight were voiced during the reading. Some members of the House of Lords called the clause "a sledgehammer to crack a walnut" and, at one stage, it seemed the clause might be withdrawn. It was however passed in November 1990 and took effect early in the New Year.

Responding for the Government, Earl Ferrers promised that "the powers will be exercised with moderation and restraint in the case of foreign-flagged vessels to avoid a diplomatic confrontation." He went on to claim that the new laws were provided for in the new UN laws of the seas convention and ignored the fact that this was not yet in force nor was the UK yet a signatory to it.

All the protestations in Caroline's favour, and in the name of freedom and liberty, were all in vain as the bill entered the statute books and became law in early 1991. Probably one of the most undemocratic piece of legislation and one that tarnishes the name of Great Britain.

The arguments continued for several hours' among the comments made were the following, that were made in Caroline's favour:

---

is it not beneath the dignity of Her Majesty's Government to make such a proposal? That is high-handed and bullying. It reminds one of other instances in which the Government use power when those it is used against have no power to resist it.

I have a feeling that the Government will regret passing a measure of this kind. They are trying to bring down a mosquito with artillery fire. I know also that they are trying to bring it down by illegal means.

After the Act became law, the Ross Revenge Support Group reached an agreement with the authorities over the supply of the ship on the strict understanding that no help would be given for broadcast operations. At that time the RRSG was a part of the Caroline Movement.

At the time it appeared that there may have been discrepancies in the registration of the Ross Revenge with Panama. This had been made in 1981, There was a scandal involving the officers at a Panamanian consular office in Texas which issued the certificates, which went some way to explain the lack of certain paperwork for the ship.

The Support Group raised a further £9,000 for various needs on the ship before it split from the Caroline Movement and became the *Radio Caroline Support Group.* A substantial amount was also raised by individuals and by the France Radio Club, the publishers of Offshore Echo's magazine.

Caroline's management had always kept a very low profile and they steadfastly refused to discuss matters concerning the ship's legal status, for a couple of very good reasons. Some busybodies, claiming to be supporters however took matters into their own hands. Without any authority from the Caroline organisation, they began besieging the Panamanian Government for details of the ship's registration.

Whatever motives the busybodies had for stirring up long-buried paperwork in Panama City, the authorities there received so many enquiries about the registration that they began a far-reaching internal inquiry. This showed that there had been some level of corruption in Panama's ship registration activities, although that was not the fault of Radio Caroline.

The Panamanian authority revealed that the original ships registration had not been completed satisfactory. In fact it appeared to have been issued by a breakaway representatives in Houston, Texas, although the ship's owner maintained that it had been taken out in good faith. Panama said that, if broadcasting resumed from the ship it may ask the British government to take action to ensure the ship was silenced.

At the end of June, the threatened Spectrum Radio programme transmissions began; they were simulcast on both 990 and 558 kHz, which resulted in a loud buzz being heard behind the Caroline programmes over a wide area. Within half an hour Caroline 558 closed down "for essential maintenance." She was off the air until the end of July, when transmissions resumed but with only non-stop music.

Some of the crew on the Ross Revenge in 1990
Ricky & Tracy Jones, Christian Colby, Steve Conway and Neil Gates

Bob LeRoi

Ronan firmly believed that the station should not give up the 558 frequency without a fight as there was a principle at stake. Some members of the team wanted the frequency shifted slightly, perhaps to the old 576 channel, which Peter felt they should at least try, if only to show good faith. Ronan thought this would also be jammed.

On the first anniversary of the raid, Caroline 558 broadcast a special programme, "Remember the Raid" following which the station closed down again. No transmissions were made for another three weeks when Caroline 558 returned. Transmissions of non-stop music and the Overdrive programmes were made for several days but reception was not good in many areas and the response was poor. Many of the evangelists had threatened to withdraw their support for the station, meaning one of the few sources of income would be lost.

The ship was now being supplied on a clandestine basis by several small boats based in the south east, including a very hairy delivery of a generator engine to the ship by the Ross Revenge Support Group. An inflatable boat used by Warwick Armstrong was sabotaged, while the *Dreamboat Annie* and the *Fairwinds*, Dave Turner's trawler based in Ramsgate, were both raided. Finally, two larger boats in Kent owned by Peter Moore were boarded too. The authorities seemed to be having a last attempt to silence Caroline.

Despite the difficulties, transmissions of Radio Caroline continued. Suddenly at 2pm on the 14th September, DJ Ricky Jones announced that the patrol boat Landward was circling the ship. Those on board the coastguard cutter limited their activities to taking photographs of the ship from every conceivable angle. Ricky Jones played a series of significant music and dedicated the tracks to the DTI solicitor's clerk James Murphy who was on board the launch, the Landward. It had been chartered for the day at a cost of over £6,000.

The patrol boat remained nearby for four hours and then disappeared towards Ramsgate. Caroline 558 kept the transmitter operating all night in case the authorities returned and it was needed to make an emergency call for help. The following evening Caroline announced every half an hour that the station would be closing down at midnight for some time in order to enable positive steps to be taken for the station to continue.

Two weeks later Radio Caroline returned on 819 kHz but there were frequent interruptions to programmes which were being broadcast to maintain an audience for the Overdrive programmes, now Caroline's main income source. The news service was suspended towards the end of the month and increasingly lengthy periods of non-stop music were heard, usually due to a lack of staff on board the ship.

At the end of October 1990 Ronan O'Rahilly attended a Press Conference in Calais organised by the *France Radio Club*, while on his way to Paris to meet with another country's embassy who were interested in helping. He was interviewed by French TV about Caroline's plans. A large amount of supplies was collected by FRC for the ship and Warwick Armstrong made a trip to Calais to collect them.

Final Transmissions at sea
In early November 1990, the DJs were still in good spirits with Rico and Caroline Martin both making light of what was increasingly a desperate situation out at the South Falls Head. After the Viewpoint programmes on 4th November, Neil Gates presented a programme until 1am when *Caroline 819* closed down for the night.

The last record that Neil played was, rather fittingly, *Pilot of the Airwaves* by Charlie Dore. No one realised at the time it was to be Caroline's last transmission form the Ross Revenge in International Waters. A severe lack of fuel in the ship's tanks meant that they were unable to generate enough electrical power to broadcast much longer.

Neil Gates left the ship in the control of Rico Marks a few weeks later to join the search for new funding for Caroline. Life on the ship was now dire and the crew were desperate as, without fuel, the ship could not be lit or heated. The starter batteries for the main generators had failed to take a charge so they could not be run.

During one Force 10 storm, heavy seas had swept the ship's reserve supplies of petrol off the deck where they were stored, while Rico was knocked unconscious while trying to save the little Honda petrol generator from being washed overboard. After two more hellish days and nights in the middle of a blizzard the trio called the coastguards and asked for a lifeboat to bring them ashore.

The ship's batteries had insufficient life left to even power the ship's marine radio kit but a link was made to a contact on land by CB. 'Dave the Fish', in Ramsgate was able to confirm to the coastguard that the ship's crew urgently needed assistance.

The high seas out at the anchorage meant that transferring crew down to a small lifeboat would be impossible. A SeaKing helicopter from RAF Manston airlifted the three crew members off the ship in a dramatic midnight rescue. On reaching shore, DJs Caroline Martin, Rico and Cliff Adams were questioned by police for hours and then released.

A DTI chartered vessel came alongside and shone lights on the abandoned radio ship to illuminate it and avoid a maritime catastrophe. The following day, Trinity House managed to put a man on board the Ross Revenge to check on her condition. Attempts by Caroline crew to board the ship over three days were made difficult by mountainous seas in mid-December but eventually Peter Chicago and Rico managed to get on board. It was just in time, as a few hours later two tugs arrived wanting to take the abandoned ship for salvage.

An important truce
Peter Moore obtained agreement from the UK authorities that the ship could be supplied once again overtly from Ramsgate in return for a guarantee that no further transmissions would take place. It was an important truce as Caroline's management had been advised that a full-scale boarding of the ship was planned to take place early in the New Year.

An attempt to block the new Broadcasting Bill becoming law was made in the European Parliament in November by French MEP, Mme Elmalan of the French *Coalition de Guaches* party, who questioned the UK's authority to stop and search foreign ships in International waters. A few weeks later the French Green party laid down a similar questions asking that the law be blocked from taking effect. Member Frederic Sevriere spent a few weeks on board the Ross Revenge getting background information before briefing his colleagues and making Caroline's case to the EU parliament.

The Broadcasting Act came into effect as New Year 1991 dawned, but the Ross Revenge remained on station as moves were being undertaken ashore to find alternative ways for Caroline to broadcast.

On the ship, a new crew headed by Caroline News editor and DJ Steve Conway set about cleaning up the ship, which had got into a sorry state over the past few months. All the navigational lights were repaired and over a period of weeks more fuel and other supplies were delivered.

Reviewing the ship's log for the last few months she was at sea, it's harrowing to learn of the awful situation the crew were in. Depleted supplies of fuel, food and even water meant they were poorly fed yet still spent many hours squeezing the last gallons of fuel for the generators. This meant getting inside the filthy tanks themselves and hand scooping rust and debris out. Unable to wash properly, it was very unpleasant. Worse was that the broadcasters could not even practice their art, which was totally demoralising. The six strong crew deserve a Caroline medal for their service in that last year at sea.

The ship welcomed an unusual visitor on 9th October in the form of Sea King 166 from RAF Manston which sought permission to land as part of a training exercise. Captain Steve Conway spoke at length to the helicopter's pilot on the VHF radio, and eventually gave permission for this, on the strict understand it was for training purposes only. The chopper asked if it was safe with the transmitter on. He was surprised to be told that Caroline was off the air, as he could receive music clearly on 558. (It was the 'local station' Spectrum he could hear, audible loud and clear so far from the middle of London!

Radio Caroline Support Group

Most of the supplies were sent to the ship by the Ross Revenge Support Group, an organisation whose aims were to preserve the Ross Revenge at sea, to provide essential equipment and supplies, to keep the Caroline name in the public eye and to research any ways by which the station might be able to legally resume broadcasts. This eventually became the Radio Caroline Support Group.

The new group continued to be financially supported by the Caroline Movement and the France Radio Club. The CM's Thanet branch was managed by John and Jenny Knight who had been running a local branch of the Caroline Movement from their home in East Kent for many years and provided much comfort and support to visiting Radio Caroline DJs. They also ran a regular magazine called Horizon, which was edited by the Knights and Bill Barnes. Kevin Carylon usually paid for the printing of the magazine, which helped bring in more funds for the station and kept supporters informed.

Dave Richards, Stuart Russel, Jenny and John Knight and Neil Gates.

The Ross Revenge Support Group raised valuable funds by a variety of methods, including a toll telephone line service that relayed latest news to interested radio enthusiasts. Sadly, this was diluted by a North London land pirate who had been rejected for a DJ job on the ship.

In February 1991, the legendary Irish lager brand Harp made an award to the Walton lifeboat in recognition of the valuable service it had provided to Radio Caroline and other radio ships over the years. The presentation was made by former Caroline FDJ Johnnie Walker. He was joined by Ronan and several other Caroline alumni for the event in Walton on the Naze.

Third World Licence

Sadly, 1991 also brought the confirmation that the ship had been deleted from the Panamanian Ships register four years previously to comply with a new Panama law to prohibit broadcasting from the country's ships. The large cash amount that had been paid to guarantee this would not happen was a fraud practiced by unscrupulous registration agents on the Caroline team.

This brought new urgency to the quest to find a licence from a 'Third World', to include the necessary ship's registration. Caroline's lawyers had confirmed that there were still loopholes in the new Broadcasting Act. One of these lacunas meant that if a sovereign nation licenced and flagged the ship then it could still broadcast legally from the North Sea, or any other international waters. The problem was to find another country that would award such a ships registration certificate and a broadcast licence. Perhaps an impoverished 'third world' country would oblige, one that wasn't worried about its relations with the UK.

There were almost 200 sovereign nations, many of whom registered all kinds of 'slightly dodgy' vessels; the flag of convenience was a common route for all kinds of questionable maritime operations. Hopes were high that a suitable licence could be obtained from one of these. Since the introduction of coordination of MMSI, MID and other international ships registration details, a vessel can no longer choose not to reveal its identity. SOLAS regulations have now been adopted by most nations and there were only a dozen possibilities. Any flagging must now be done correctly and in compliance with a country's laws, which raised the costs.

A former *Caroline International* DJ was now working in Eastern Europe as a broadcast consultant. Paul Rusling had negotiated with the new government of Lithuania to provide a licence for Baltic Radio International. This was a powerful AM station (500 kilowatts) broadcasting across the Baltic into Sweden, which at the time had only state-controlled radio.

Lithuania was in the process of escaping the yoke of the Soviet Union and keen to do joint ventures with any western company that could bring enough US dollars into their country! Rusling set up meetings with the Lithuanian representatives and Caroline which went well until they suddenly retracted their offer. They had been advised that support for Radio Caroline would jeopardise their own relations with the UK. At that time their office off Kensington High Street was their only overseas base and they were at a delicate stage with the UK's foreign office.

Ronan held further talks at the time with Cuba and its representatives in London; this was followed up with officials at their Embassy in Paris. Originally it seemed they might be willing to issue a licence for humanitarian broadcasts but it seemed they also wanted all the programmes to include some very left wing messages.

Eighteen months later, while working on another project, Rusling brought the Liberian High Commissioner to Caroline for talks. Their country was in the middle of a civil war and relations with London were so poor that the embassy's telephone and telex had been cut off by the newly privatised British Telecom!

The Liberian High Commissioner was reduced to having to operate his office from home but he could still issue ships certificates. His demand of an immediate down payment of £100,000 plus an ongoing monthly licence fee of £10,000 was beyond Caroline's capabilities. There was simply nothing left in the kitty and all other known sources wanted too much control over the output to be acceptable. It would be too much pride to swallow to have Caroline diluted and operate commercially or give any control over the output.

One of the evangelists whose programmes were carried as part of the Overdrive service put the station in touch with a government minister in Equatorial Guinea. Historically, it was a poor small African country of barely a million people, a quarter of its population had fled to neighbouring countries when gangsters took over its government. President Obiang was wanted by French courts to face charges of plundering the country's finances. They too wanted a large sum of money before they would issue any permits at all but the amounts were way beyond the capabilities of Caroline's now severely depleted resources.

Some Radio Monique team appeared in the Belgian courts over the channelling of adverts through the right-wing magazine *Topics*. They were found guilty and fined for diverting the magazine's advertising money to keep Radio Monique on the air. The magazine was owned by Eddie Heerema, whose family had been involved with the sixties Radio Noordzee and had built the REM Island, but he was acquitted of the charges he faced. Some of his team did not fare so lightly however.

Caroline Confusion

There was good news in March when former DJ and station manager Chris Cary donated more satellite air time to Radio Caroline. He had tried to set up a sustaining service for ILR stations using well known DJKs, and had some time left over at the end of contracts.

"Ronan warned me not to take the offer, saying it would all go wrong," remembers Peter Moore. "He was right as Chris Cary ignored our programmes and put in his own DJs and offered his own 'Caroline' merchandise. His satellite Radio Caroline also carried some of the religious programmes under the banner *Insight 738*." These produced valuable revenue although Caroline saw none of this. The channel carried its first ever phone in programme, called *Caroline Forum.* Some views were controversial; most of all the claim that Caroline didn't need a ship any longer and, as Ronan often said, "could bc anywhere."

The satellite relay from Camberley lasted only two weeks. On the final night, John Burch and Steve Taplin, both key players in the Caroline Movement, hosted the last shows live and threw the lines open. Calling in to the programme from a yacht in the Mediterranean, Chris Cary claimed that the satellite service was being closed down prematurely because the authorities had directed him to do so. "It's far better to close down now, with a proper goodbye programme, rather than have the plug suddenly pulled abruptly."

Chris relentlessly pressed on with his opinion that there was no point in Radio Caroline retaining the Ross Revenge at sea and they should get rid of her, perhaps by bringing her in and selling her for scrap. It was a view that a view that did not go down very well!

"The Radio Caroline management wants to keep Caroline on the air," countered Peter Chicago in response to Chris's "get rid" suggestion "We are exploring various different possibilities that would enable us to do just that. We're not looking to break the law and go back on the air, if we can find a legal way of broadcasting from the high seas at the position where the Ross Revenge is anchored at the moment." Peter argued that at one stage every DJ on *Invicta Radio*, a Kent ILR station, was from Radio Caroline, as was the case with Contact FM in France, but that didn't make their stations Radio Caroline. "If you want a station in Camberley, then call it anything else, but it's not Caroline and it hasn't sounded like Radio Caroline," said Chicago. "I believe it's carrying the name of Caroline under false pretences."

After the anxious discussion programme, satellite 'Caroline' closed at midnight. The DTI refuted that they had suggested that it be closed. Ronan and several within Caroline felt that Chris Cary was trying to hijack the Caroline name and staff it with his own Radio Nova staff. Caroline was soon heard again from the Clarke belt via a station called RNI. This project was the brainchild of Dutchman Henk de Jong and officially came from Norway. RNI was on a sub-transponder of TV4, a Norwegian channel on one of the Intelsat birds at 1° west.

Further outlets were found for Caroline programmes during 1991. The France Radio Club organised for carriage of Caroline programmes over *Radio New York International* which had access to a legal Short Wave transmitter in the USA. With 100 kilowatts of power, *World Wide Christian Radio)*could be heard widely and they carried a series of programmes outlining Radio Caroline's extensive history.

Eight hours a day of Caroline programmes were carried by Norwegian satellite channel, RNI, which was owned by Henk, an offshore radio enthusiast. Two hour programmes were pre-recorded at Highgate by Johnny Reece and Nick Salomon, but listeners needed a huge dish to receive the weak signal on Intelsat.

Peter Moore was uncomfortable about the ship remaining at sea but Ronan wanted the ship to stay in international waters rather than seek sanctuary in a port, where creditors might seize her. He wanted her ready to resume broadcasts and produce revenue quickly when a licence was obtained. Knowing that the crew were inexperienced or self-taught everyone knew it would be difficult to provision the ship in winter. Major engineering problems included the rudder, which had worn loose; it swung so violently that it wrecked the steering gear. The anchor chain had worn thin at the bow roller so a new chain was bought, but it made it only as far as Whitstable.

The DTI were aware of the situation and had considered whether Peter Moore could be charged with negligent manslaughter of anyone died on the ship.

In June, representatives of Radio Caroline and the lawyers Richards Butler met with the Radio Regulatory Department. David Vick also attended as Director of Development for the *Radio Authority*. The *DTI* was represented by Barry Maxwell, the Director of the UK's Radio Communications. The meeting was an initiative of John Burch, a founder of the Caroline Movement. The regulators both confirmed that Radio Caroline could apply for a licence to operate a radio station from the Ross Revenge.

25. Aground on the Sands

A skeleton crew remained at sea on The Ross Revenge, still on her anchor half a mile from the South Falls buoy, about 14 miles north east of Margate. As darkness fell on Tuesday 19th November, a fierce storm blew up. Unnoticed by the six-man crew, the anchor chain parted with the constant heaving and stretching caused by the seas.

Acting Captain Neil Gates and a trainee DJ were up on the bridge and heard Dover coast guard calling a mystery ship heading south but didn't realise it was them, as the ship was behaving relatively normally as she dragged a long length of chain behind her. They didn't see any unusual buoys or other landmarks as visibility was so poor.

Dover coastguard had noticed the ship's progress however on radar and, not receiving any answer to their calls, had sent a helicopter to investigate. It reported that the ship was indeed the Ross Revenge but was unable to make radio contact with the ship. Just before 4am the crew felt a huge bang as she ran aground, stern first, onto the rapacious Goodwin Sands, known as a graveyard for ships. Over 2000 wrecks litter the ten mile long sandbank just a couple of miles off the East Kent coast. They were 16 miles from the South Falls anchorage, south of Ramsgate!

On contacting Dover coast guard, the captain was told the ship's position, which was on the notorious Goodwin Sands. Very few casualties are ever saved from the dangerous banks of sand, shingle and clay that stretch for about ten miles. They have long been such a hazard that they were marked by three fully manned lightships, one of which also foundered there. The Goodwins have claimed hundreds of ships and thousands of lives in modern times alone.

"It was the roughest night that I have ever known on all my years on Caroline," said Steve Conway, who had been in bed when first alerted something was wrong. "There was an enormous crash and we were flung out of bed onto the wall. Within minutes everyone was on the bridge in lifejackets. When we called the Coastguard they told us that we were fifteen miles from our mooring, and on the Goodwin Sands. I thought this would be the last dawn we would see."

"The memories are still vividly seared onto my brain, even all these years later," recalls Steve with a shudder. "It was the most terrifying moment of my life. I absolutely believed that we were about to die. That morning, and in particular that moment, has changed my life since."
"The sudden apparent end of Caroline in 1991 instilled in me a knowledge of the impermanence of states of being and ensured that

ever since I treasured each moment and drove myself to both give and take the maximum from every day that I worked there. In life too, I reach out with lust for living to take the most from each day, and push myself to do and experience more and newer things. Life after an experience like that is a bonus, and I am determined to spend that bonus to the full."

It was well before dawn when the *Dextrous*, a harbour tug from Dover ,was despatched to the casualty, as was Ramsgate lifeboat. A Sea King rescue helicopter from RAF Manston flew out to the ship but the crew said they would remain on board, to protect the ship from being seized as salvage.

As well as stand in skipper Neil Gates, the crew comprised Stuart Dobson, trainee disc-jockey Chris Wilson, cook Wendy Shepherd and broadcasters Ricky Jones and Steve Conway who had been Caroline's Head of News the past few years..

After three hours they realised the peril of their situation as the ship began to list dangerously and some parts began flooding. They found that the water ingress was from a broken porthole and that the ship hadn't been holed. "The ship kept pitching further and further onto her beam and we were pretty certain that she was going over completely a few times," said Neil Gates. "That would have been the end as she would have flooded quickly." As the tide dropped, the ship suddenly lurched to starboard at an alarming angle.The crew decided that the best option would be to abandon ship.

The seas around the sands were so rough that the Ramsgate lifeboat and its seven man crew were almost lost in the rescue. She beached on the sands when still about half a mile away and lost one lifeboatman overboard. Fortunately they were able to retrieve him, thanks to their 'always on a lifeline' policy in such situations but they were unable to get any closer in to the stricken radio ship to effect a rescue.

Dover lifeboat was then launched to assist both the Ramsgate lifeboat and the Ross Revenge. A tanker, the *Shell Marketer,* also stood by a mile away to render assistance but there seemed little that could be done as the Goodwin sands dried out on the receding tide.

By 7am and first light the helicopter was back overhead. "It was a very difficult rescue as the ship's aerial masts were slicing through the air, "said the chopper's pilot, Squadron Leader Paddy Hayes. "For us upstairs it made life a bit tricky." Eventually the winchman managed to to take off the five men and one woman from the stern deck of the ship.

They had to be winched up one by one in appalling conditions with the deck of the Ross Revenge bucking around like an angry bronco. "It was very sad abandoning her to the elements, although we really did fear for our lives," said Steve. "She was being swept over by the waves onto her beam and a few times we thought she had gone."

Wendy Shepherd, Steve Conway, Chris Cobley, Neil Gates, Stuart Dobson and Ricky Jones with FRC organisers John and Jenny Knight.

John and Jenny Knight from the FRC Thanet branch collected the shipwrecked crew from RAF Manston, who were clad in flying suits by the helicopter crew as their own clothes had been soaked.

A Dover Harbour Board tug, the *Dextrous* remained close by and she was then joined by a sister boat, the *Deft*. It appeared that the Ross Revenge would be lost when she seemed to list even further to starboard. All attempts that day to land a salvage crew on her failed but the following day some hardy sailors from the Dextrous scrambled on board. They later managed to get lines onto her.

The salvage crew from the tug decided to cut the ship free from the anchor chain that it had trailed onto the sandbank. Peter Chicago then arrived in the *Fairwind*, the Ramsgate trawler skippered by Dave 'the Fish' Turner. They were unable to get close in so Peter took to a dinghy and paddled towards the ship. As he was trying to get on board, the salvors threw links of chain at him and he had to withdraw.

It took two days to get the Ross Revenge afloat and she came clear on their last attempt and was towed the few miles south into the east dock at Dover. She became one of only a few ships to ever run aground on the Goodwin Sands and get off again. The wrecks of hundreds of ships are found there.

If the tugs had been unable to move her on that tide, the intention was to take the final option of puncturing her hull to force her to flood. This would stop her floating off on her own and becoming a danger to other shipping. Radio Caroline's guardian angel was again looking after the ships! Ronan was keen to remind everyone that she came in on a very significant date: the anniversary of the assassination of President Kennedy, the 22nd November.

The authorities immediately impounded the ship at Dover and carried out a full inspection which resulted in a long list of urgent repairs that would have to be completed before the ship could go back to sea again. The Ross Revenge Support Group and representatives from Radio Caroline's management began negotiations with the Dover Harbour Board, owners of the tugs that had rescued her. The salvors had full salvage rights and were looking for a six-figure sum for their work.

Three of the Ross Revenge crew had been at Dover to meet her in; Neil Gates, Steve Conway and Wendy Shepherd. They were allowed to move back on board and act as caretakers for the ship. Check Steve's *Shiprocked* book for more details of the dark days in Dover.

The ship was subjected to close examination by various bodies; first of these were HM Customs who originally took away many 'suspicious' items, but later returned everything. The only narcotics they found was some very old Texas rolling tobacco, left by one of the Dutch crew in the ship's Radio Monique days.

"Customs were probably disappointed not to find any drugs, but it's always been an absolute rule that no-one is ever allowed to take any drugs on board," remarked Peter Moore, Caroline's Station manager.

"I've always been adamant about this in the five years that I've been managing the station, and as far as I know this has always been station policy." Peter is vehemently against drug abuse himself, "The DTI are always waiting for us to put a foot wrong so they can pounce, " he says. "We just couldn't allow it; the enormous risk it would pose could jeopardise the entire operation."

The marine inspectors from the Board of Trade were not so easily satisfied as HM Customs. They gave Steve Conway a long list of repairs which were impossible to attend to in the time frame allowed (48 hours) so the ship had a Detention Order placed on her.

"The boat and all of us require a long holiday before she goes anywhere," said Peter Moore. Although the intention was never to bring the ship into port, the Caroline team were making the best of the situation. Everyone in the Caroline organisation as happy to have the MSA (Marine Safety Agency) provide a free ship's survey as it meant that the Ross Revenge would have a complete overhaul before facing the North Sea again.

Dover Harbour considered that their salvage efforts were worth £120,000, but on seeing the condition of *Ross Revenge* and the circumstances which surrounded the ship they soon realised that they were unlikely to squeeze such as sum from the owners, its operators or the insurers. The ship did not have a formally appointed agent who, in normal circumstances, liaises between the harbour authorities and the owners. The crew rescued from the ship on the Goodwin Sands were clearly destitute and penniless.

"Several people tried to negotiate with Dover Harbour Board, but they knew who it was unwise to talk to" said Peter Moore. Surprisingly, the DTI helped out and advised them that I was the correct person."

After discussion with Peter Moore, who put himself forward as the manager of Radio Caroline, Dover Harbour Board decided to settle for salvage costs of £20,000. This amount covered the harbour tugs costs in refloating the ship and towing her into Dover, plus a modest amount for wharfage costs. Dover is one of the most expensive ports in the UK to berth and not one that would normally have been chosen.

The only condition to the settlement was that the ship must be removed from Dover as soon as possible, as the hordes of curious visitors and others had become something of an embarrassment.

The *Ross Revenge Support Group* had by now built up some reserves under the careful guidance of Paul Hipkiss and Steve Taplin and a full fund-raising exercise among the station's supporters swung into action. The initial payment was made by John Knight, the Thanet CM organiser. Additional funding was donated by the *Foundation for Media Communication* in Holland and several individuals.

Peter Moore was very sad that Radio Caroline had to buy back its own ship for £20,000, which was the result of having the ship sat out at sea, wasting her time and all for nothing. The organisation had only very limited resources by this time but Peter felt that even these were being mismanaged. He blamed Ronan for not attending to the daily problems of keeping the ship afloat but only having time to chase legal action, which had been futile and cost serious amounts of money.

Ronan often had bouts of headaches and appeared to be slipping into manic depression. Peter now had to step in and lead the Caroline team in the absence of anyone else. Not for the first time was he being made a 'fall guy' after a bad decision turned out to make matters even worse.

Caroline's new leader, Peter Moore
Martin van der Ven

"I love Caroline very much and in her history are so many exploits of bravery, resilience and courage," he explained to *OEM.* "But let us be honest, there's been many instances of pig-headedness, ludicrous and sometimes devious decision making, plus glaring wastes of money and obsessions with unimportant issues, to the detriment of truly important ones."

The plight of the ship was suddenly front page news again and offers of help came from all directions. A Dutch satellite radio station offered a couple of hours a day as an outlet for Caroline, while across in France *Radio 6* in Calais broadcast a three-hour special recorded on board the ship in Dover.

The audiences for the satellite channel were small as the medium had only recently become available and few homes were equipped to hear satellite radio stations, much less had a clue how to tune to them. Compared to modern day platforms such as DAB and the internet, satellite was notoriously complex even to explain, it was costly and of course was fixed - totally unsuitable for listening in cars or on portables.

While the potential audiences were small it was a good morale booster, getting some of the Caroline team back 'on the air' again. A caretaker crew was permitted to live on board the ship in the Granville Dock in Dover.

After a spring cleaning exercise, they were able to offer conducted tours on the ship; the small amounts of funds raised from these help keep body and soul together for the small team. This was led by Steve Conway and Neil Gates who had each acted as captain of the ship during her last year at sea, off the air. Neil single-handedly cared for the ship for a couple of weeks in 1991.

Kevin Turner

One of the most professional Caroline's DJs in the 1980s was Kevin Turner. "What Radio Caroline did when it launched in 1964 was truly revolutionary," explains Kevin.

"It gave the British people the music they wanted, lots of music, all day long. That was something that no one had done before."

Kevin told an interviewer that his own memories of the station when he was on board the ship in the 1980s were generally very good ones. "Not all the times were good times; on my last stint, the three hundred foot aerial tower came crashing down, putting us off the air. That was a really hairy moment, it wasn't always as glamourous as the scenes shown in the movie The Boat That Rocked"

Kevin had a long career in ILR and out in the Middle East working on the Voice of Peace. He was even seen on BFBS TV for a while as continuity announcer and in the 21st century returned to Radio Caroline during its internet years. He has recently made guest appearances on the Radio Caroline North monthly weekend broadcasts.

Au revoir Luxy

At the end of the year, Radio Luxembourg's English service, the 'Station of the Stars', lost access to its 1.2 million Watt MW transmitter. The banking regime that had changed RTL into CLT ran on a financial basis and the German service were willing to pay more money for the airtime. The Great 208 was replaced by *Der OldieSender*.

The English language service continued on satellite for a year but without the AM outlet, it made almost no money at all, so that closed too. In its time it had used over a dozen Radio Caroline DJs in its line-up, such as Roger 'Twiggy' Day, Tony Prince, Judy Murphy, Mark Wesley, and Emperor Rosko.

26. Caroline in Captivity

The New Year saw the now retired, former Chief engineer Ernie Stephenson back on board. He had been persuaded to come down to the ship in Dover and see what help he could give on the many repairs that needed tackling. He was excellent at organising the fitter younger crewmen to do useful tasks and bit by bit, most of the repairs mandated by the inspectors were addressed.

The funding provided by the RRSG enabled the team to get the many essential materials to renovate the ship. Many thousands of hours of labour was given free of charge and at no cost to the ship by the Northern Support Group.

Chief engineer Peter Clayton

The lion's share of the tasks were carried out by members of the RRSG, and other supporters.

The group consisted of a dozen or so Caroline enthusiasts from West Yorkshire. Many of them are engineers, some with excellent skills needed to get the Ross Revenge repaired and back into compliance with the various rules and regulations.

At their own cost, they spent most weekends travelling down to the Ross Revenge and then working their socks off to get some of the heavy engineering completed. The Northern Support Group was headed by Peter Clayton, a renowned diesel engineer and motor mechanic from Leeds who eventually was to take over as Caroline's Chief Engineer from Ernie.

Peter was usually assisted by the team from Pudsey near Leeds comprising Tommy the Welder, Geoff, Carl, Graham and Alan. They did huge amounts of work, not just keeping the ship repaired and not just repairing. The restoration team also painted all the pipework in correct colours and installed new systems that the ship had never had in the past. Although the inspectors drew up a lengthy list of work they required doing before the ship could leave port again, most were straight forward tasks that could be remedied with "enough money and a great deal of hard work," as Peter Moore summarised.

Peter Moore was formally recognised by the Dover Harbour Board as a representative of the ship's owners, despite the fact that the ship's papers were almost all missing. "There is no problem at all with the state of the hull - it looks a little rusty and battered, but it's totally sound. The major problem is the ship's rudder and steering gear, which was already in poor condition due to the hydraulics failing at sea. Grounding stern-first onto the Goodwins did it no good at all; it is totally wrecked. This is an integral part of the ship and it's not something that you can just go into the chandlers and buy "off the shelf", like a replacement life-raft."

Radio Caroline was by now being heard via several outlets around the world: a Norwegian satellite channel, Radio Fax (a Short Wave station in Ireland), Radio 6 in France and Radio New York Worldwide all relayed the programmes.

Caroline RSL in Dover

One of Radio Caroline's DJs had investigated the possibility of operating a low power FM station from the ship for a 30 day period. Tony Kirk got the papers for an RSL (Restricted Service Licence) which was obtainable on demand from the Radio Authority, although the fees for royalties, engineering supervision and the administration of the licence by the Authority were quite punitive. Tony had calculated that if enough local interest could be drummed up then enough income might result to make a small profit for Caroline.

Caroline went ahead and obtained a Restricted Service Licence to broadcast on FM for a month from the ship for its birthday at Easter 1992, but as the ship was at sea level the FM channel offered would have had a very restricted coverage. The transmitter was placed at Dover Castle on the top of the iconic Dover cliffs and, as a result, was heard over a wide area, including by listeners in France. Programmes were micro-linked from the ship up to the FM transmitter, and attracted advertising from many advertisers in France, organised by the France Radio Club, and in Kent. The RSL was soon being repeated over a satellite channel to most of Western Europe. Several hundred visitors were given tours of the ship and many of them bought merchandise.

The RSL was to attract several prestigious advertisers: even National Heritage, a Government quango all bought time. National Heritage was chaired at the time by Jocelyn Stevens, who was one of the key people involved in the launch of Radio Caroline, in early 1964.

The 28th birthday of Caroline was also marked by Spectrum Radio who broadcast a special programme commemorating Radio Caroline. This was the station that the authorities had sought to pitch against the ship's transmissions in its battle to close Caroline. A very small mark of respect, but perhaps it can be seen as a small symbol of justice. Ronan visited the ship once while she was in Dover in an attempt to boost morale. The crew were unhappy as the living conditions were not very satisfactory, but they could not bring themselves to say so when Ronan asked.

A 'license' for Radio Caroline?

Throughout the years, while fighting for Radio Caroline's freedom, its founder Ronan O'Rahilly had always held the same view regarding the possibility of one day having a 'licensed' Radio Caroline. "No, No, No and definitely No!" said Ronan, whenever asked about the possibility. "The very idea of broadcasting with a license turned my stomach." Ronan's position was always the same during his lifetime battle for a free station at sea. Freedom is key.

"Caroline has come to symbolise a battle for individual freedom," said Ronan. We are probably the last institution on the planet that is absolutely free. The things that Caroline has done at sea can't be copied or reproduced on land. The spirit of freedom is in the blood of Radio Caroline and the station can't be under the control of governments."

"You can't create or institutionalise Radio Caroline," continued Ronan. "You can't lay down some Government's legislation to make a nice sanitised Caroline on land. You can't do it, and we never can."

Some of Radio Caroline's supporters and former members of staff were unhappy that broadcasts had been made using a legal licence from the ship. On several occasions, Ronan O'Rahilly's promise that the station would never operate with a licence was quoted. Ronan reinforced his opinion that he hated the idea of a licence, but conceded that Peter Moore had no other option.

Peter Moore had to constantly remind followers that Radio Caroline had no other resources with which to get back control of the ship. A way to broadcast and make some money was essential if the ship was to be reclaimed. Ronan did reluctantly agree that there simply was no other way except the legal routes to get Caroline operational again.

Many cared little for Ronan's philosophies but others remained steadfastly loyal. Neil Gates was the last ever voice to be heard on Radio Caroline from the North Sea in November 1990. His loyalty and devotion to the real and free Radio Caroline at sea, and to always defend her founder Ronan O'Rahilly has always been remarkable, if perhaps misguided and invariably misunderstood.

Neil Gates on the Ross Revenge
Offshore Echos Magazine

"I was so very sad to see Ronan apparently marginalized from his own radio station when it got 'taken over'. His requests to ensure Caroline's future were ignored. It went on without him, after all the decades of blood sweat and tears he put into Caroline. It's a very sad ending for such a great inspirational man," said Neil.

Neil remained at loggerheads with the shore based contingent of Radio Caroline for many years and bitterly complained that the organisation had lost its spirit and *raison d'etre* in following the regulations laid down by the various government bodies. He claims that Caroline was stolen from Ronan O'Rahilly and that some of the station management colluded with the DTI to keep the station off the air. Neil believes that the ship was kept short of fuel during its last year at sea to stop it from resuming broadcasts and that it was always operating profitably.

As with all arguments there are usually two sides. Peter Moore is an articulate and sensible, level-headed individual who has kept his own business alive for decades. He maintains that had Radio Caroline not taken out one of the RSLs issued by the Radio Authority for the broadcasts from Dover harbour, then she may have remained locked up in harbour for years, as had been the Mi Amigo and the MV Caroline from 1968 to 1972.

The usual remedy for a harbour authority to regain its costs from a ship apparently abandoned in its area of control is to send it for scrapping. That was in fact the fate facing the Ross Revenge when the low power short term licence was taken.

It's worth also remembering that, had Peter Moore not agreed that the Ross Revenge would not try to broadcast at sea in breach of the new Broadcasting Act, the DTI would never have allowed the ship to be openly supplied from the UK in 1991, when the organisation was at its lowest ebb and unable to fund the costs of covert supply runs from Belgium.

QEFM

From May, Caroline's programmes were carried on yet another satellite station. QEFM was one of the first station to broadcast direct to home using only satellite and had built up a following from its early days at the Cheltenham Music Festival. The brainchild and protégé of Roy Lichfield and Ray Pearson, it moved to the Radio Nova HQ in Camberley for a while and soon was attracting listeners across a couple of dozen countries. The station played light pop and easy listening and became home to many former Caroline DJs, including Tony Prince, Tony Blackburn and Dave Lee Travis.

Radio Caroline took over QEFM's overnight hours and had attracted a reaction from enthusiastic listeners. The station was persuaded by Eric Wiltsher to bid for its own satellite licence which was issued by the Radio Authority in July 1992. The programmes were carried on the Hot Bird satellite, as a sub-carrier on *Red Hot Dutch*, a soft porn channel.

FRC arranged for the Ross Revenge to attend a worldwide famous shipping even at Rouen, the Armada Festival. The organisers were willing to pay for the Ross Revenge's steering gear to be refurbished as part of the trip and cover all other costs of her attendance which would have been excellent publicity, however the Caroline management were not keen to let her outside the UK.

In August 1992, many stations commemorated the 25th anniversary of the Marine Offences Act which, in 1967, had made operating an offshore radio station illegal for British subjects. The UK's leading ILR station, Capital Radio, recreated 1967 using three former Radio Caroline DJs, Tony Prince, Mike Ahern and Tony Blackburn.

The BBC' local station BBC GLR hosted special programmes with two more Caroline stars, Johnnie Walker and Tommy Vance.

RESPONSIBILITY

During the first phase of Radio Caroline, both ships were chartered from another company, the world class Wijsmullers. Their ship management company had three hundred mariners under contract to them. Their cost of doing business that way of course was part of having such a large team available, many were idle most of the time.

The Caroline organisation didn't have to worry about hiring, training, managing or firing crewmen, captains and ship's engineers. Caroline also didn't have to worry about maritime regulations, compliance with safety measures, surveys or insurance. This was all taken care of by the Wijsmullers, for whom such matters were routine.

Offshore Radio 1584

The most adventurous of events to mark the 25th anniversary of the Marine Offences Act was undertaken by the Caroline Movement, a campaigning and support group. They obtained an RSL to transmit from a ship at sea and called it *Offshore Radio 1584*. The former passenger ferry Tyne Princess had been bought and used to run anoraks out to the Ross Revenge at the South Falls Head so she had some 'offshore history'.

Renamed the *Galexy*, she was equipped with a studio by a land pirate station in the south east and usually moored just a mile off Walton on the Naze, other times from the Walton backwaters. Even with just a watt of power, the station was audible over parts of Kent and Essex and helped publicise an Offshore Radio Convention in August.

The MV Galexy broadcasting 'Offshore 1584' off Frinton in 1992

The Offshore 1584 project was headed by the Caroline Movement's Publicity Manager, John Burch who had driven the talks between Radio Caroline and the IBA for licences to be issued to Caroline. Valuable publicity was obtained on Sky TV and in national press and the station rebroadcast the nostalgic words of Johnnie Walker and Robbie Dale from 14th August 1967, when Radio Caroline South became *Radio Caroline International*.

Offshore Radio 1584 broadcast many highlights of Caroline's radio career, including several recreations of the famous 'Frinton Flashing' that Johnnie Walker had staged on the ship most nights in 1967. Many hours of the output of the tribute station were rebroadcast over satellite stations bringing Offshore Radio 1584 to a very wide audience.

This was the first ever official offshore station, certainly the first to have a licence to broadcast from a ship at sea. John Burch and his team at the Caroline Movement worked extremely hard to make the month-long broadcast happen, an event that will be remembered for a long time. Some local boat owners cashed in and ferried hundreds of tourists out to see the Galexy, anchored out in the Wallet, where the Mi Amigo and other radio ships had been moored until 1968.

Mooring an offshore radio ship

There are many important essential considerations before embarking on the risky business of running an offshore radio ship. The following examples give some insight:

Since 1974 the Caroline ships had been anchored in the Knock Deep, a stretch of water between two sandbanks in the outer reaches of the Thames estuary. Although not always dried out, the shallow water above the sandbanks did afford quite a bit of protection from heavy seas. The seabed in the Knock Deep was quite good 'holding ground', meaning that anchors did not drag readily when correctly laid and the location was out of sight of the land. It was however quite easily reached, being around 14 miles out, from both Margate and Felixstowe. Choosing a good mooring location is a vital first step.

The ideal way of anchoring a radio ship is using the same method used for lightships and other craft designed to remain 'on station' for extended periods. Rather than two anchors, one for and one aft, as might be expected, and which is often seen in rivers and other inshore anchorages, radio ships are best anchored with one simple large anchor from the bows.

The anchor itself is not the main thing that hold the ship in place, rather it's the weight of the chain that holds the vessel in place. Generally, radio ships have around a ton or so or anchor chain put down, always laid out in a line, rather than just jettisoned in a heap. The Communicator (Laser's ship) when delivered to her mooring had regular 'Admiralty Pattern' anchor of half a ton, plus a five ton block of concrete as a sinker which was then hung onto the ship by around three hundred feet of chain, weighing another three tons.

The Ross Revenge had a large 'Admiralty Pattern' anchor with over four tones of chain. This broke after just five months at sea and was replaced by a heavier combination. The problem was always the chains snapping, often when they didn't have a swivel fitted and the chain twisted. This places enormous stress on the links, which a thousand tons of ship pulling at it can soon break though, unless the twist is 'unwound' by steaming the ship back around the chain again. In heavy seas when in a fast tide stream, it helps to run the ships engine at slow speed into the flow and reduce the strain.

The problem is not so much dragging the chain but the individual links in the chain snapping. Chain is invariably tested to many "tons of pull" and good quality chain always comes certificated. Sub-standard chain is literally "the weakest link" in any anchoring system and is the reason why it gets replaced quite often in professional organisations such as Trinity House.

Usually any craft at anchor hangs on just the one chain and as the direction of the tide changes, so the ship or whatever is on the chain, turns to face the opposite way with each turn of the tide. Usually one or two a swivel joints will be put into the chain to permit easier turning, to prevent the chain knotting on itself. This prevalence of chains becoming twisted is the main reason why two chains are seldom used – after just a few tide changes, the two chains easily tangle.

When the Caroline ships did end up adrift (even those sturdy anchor chains don't last forever and can snap when they have over 1,000 tons of ship hanging on the end of them) the first job the crew had to do was to get the main ship's engine running. It was important to get the ship under control, and not take the seas 'side on' as this could be dangerous. Riding the waves, either from the bows or stern, made for a much safer ride.

The next job was to plot the ship's position. This was vital as, if you don't know exactly where you are, there was little point in moving as you could easily be steaming into danger! This could be either into shallow water where there was a risk of grounding, or into territorial waters where there was always a risk of being apprehended and the ship taken into harbour.

Electric power on radio ships

Until the 1970s, most ships used DC (Direct Current) power for lighting, motors, etc. Modern studio equipment and broadcast transmitters are built for AC supplies (alternating current) which meant the installation of a different type of generator.

The amount of power is also vital – high power transmitters require substantially more energy than low power models. Radio Caroline only used ten or fifty kilowatt transmitters. The power load these presented to the generators varied with several factors – how much modulation was applied, how well was the antenna matched, etc. To convert the raw AC into radio waves, there are several processes.

Caroline's high powered transmitters were all valve based which are less efficient than modern 'solid state' models. They need various extra supplies for circuits as well as fans to keep components cool, which all take extra energy. Matching the antenna to the transmitter needs capacitors and inductors, all of which waste even more energy.

For a given power output, up to three times that amount will be consumed in producing it by the transmission plant. The ship also needs electrical power for lighting, heating and cooking, for studio kit and for communications. A ship's anchor winches, refrigerators and even the TV all add to the power needs. At a minimum 50 kVA (roughly the same as kW) and up to several hundred kVA is needed.

Food

Operating as almost like a hippy commune for many years, some expected that it would be better to let the crew and the broadcast teams prepare their own food, as and when they wanted it. This is a complete folly: letting everyone just dip into supplies as they wish is very wasteful. A good cook will manage food much more efficiently than a 'free for all' and ensure best use of the available galley resources.

From the earliest days, Radio Caroline had a good cook available. On the Radio Atlanta ship, the first cook was Irene, the captain's wife. The Caroline had a qualified ships cook and a steward to ensure the broadcasters ate well but that things were done economically. The cook in the sixties was always a Wijsmuller employee.

In the seventies, marine crews became far more expensive and manning levels were considerably reduced. This was largely for economic reasons, although concerns about their loyalty was also a factor. Cooks were not so easy to find and not the cheapest crew member. They also can be quite volatile and their emotions seem to be more sensitive than others, so they need to be treated with care!

Ships are always known as 'she' and, like ladies ashore, can easily be a bottomless pit. Maintaining them well and keeping them in good condition can be expensive, but is usually a good investment, in the long run.

Chatham RSL

At the same time as the *MV Galexy* was making radio history, Radio Caroline was making another RSL broadcast from Chatham, the historic dockyard in Kent. It had been hoped to bring the Ross Revenge into their drydock for a survey however, the authorities would not release the ship as some vital ship's paperwork was missing.

The Chatham RSL had already been paid for and some commercials had been booked so it was decided to go ahead using the Caroline studio in the town. A programme link was made across Kent to the Ross Revenge, still chained up in Dover docks. That link was a rather circuitous one, running from Dover to Brighton, then to London then back down again into Kent and out onto an FM transmitter in Chatham.

In a magazine interview the following month Peter Moore explained why Radio Caroline was still pressing on in its various broadcasting quests, given the difficulties that had often arisen. "You can't kill off a legend. Radio Caroline has become something that many people try to copy, but they never succeed. She is the world's best-known radio station, now offering high tech reception. Who else can claim that?"

Caroline lost a couple of the outlets late in 1992 when one Irish short wave relay closed and QEFM had to cut its hours of broadcasting, for financial reasons.

Return of plundered equipment

The Dutch Ministry of Justice announced that, despite its armed raid on the ship in 1989, it wouldn't press any charges against any crew. At a radio convention, former Radio Monique DJ Herbert Visser introduced Peter Moore to Martin Roumen, the Dutch officer who had led the raid on the ship. He claimed to be a big Radio Caroline fan and offered to return all the seized items, rather than try and sell them at a public auction, which was the usual official course of action.

Since the deposit was made on the salvage fee agreed with Dover Harbour Board, regular instalments had been paid; as soon as the final payment was made, a 'Deed of Release' of the *Ross Revenge* was handed to Peter Moore. This gave him control of the ship, although it did not transfer ownership. The ship was still subject to a Detention Order prohibiting her from sailing until essential safety regulations had been complied with.

In January 1993 the thousands of records and several tons of radio equipment stolen from the Ross Revenge in the piratical raid were collected from the Dutch radio police storage compound at Bleiswijk near Rotterdam. Peter Moore and Mike Dundee drove the kit back to the UK in a rented truck where they were loaded back onto the Ross Revenge, which was still detained in Dover. The van was rented by the Foundation for Media Communication from the revenue generated by sales of the CD *The Legend Lives On*, produced by Hans Knot,

Having the Ross Revenge accessible by tourists and visible to those travelling on the ferries using Dover had only marginal advantage, and there were ongoing costs. Suddenly an opportunity arose to move the ship to the Chatham Historic Dockyard and have her on public display there. This was an ideal opportunity to attract many more visitors and perhaps operate further RSL stations.

The problem arose that permission would be needed to move the ship. Every day that the ship stayed in Dover, the charges rose. A temporary RSL broadcast was tried in the Chatham area but ordinary RSLs from a building on shore were at that time common place and it was not a financial success. Whether a station was called Radio Caroline or not, unless it was from the Ross Revenge, to many of the station's followers, it was not really Radio Caroline. The ship seemed to add a magical air to the programmes, it made it easier to get publicity and involve sponsors plus it instilled a greater spirit in the team.

The ship's Chief Engineer Ernie Stephenson had been working the crew hard and this had paid off. They had now got the ship's main engine operational and at Easter it was tested. Peter Moore pressed the marine inspectors to survey the ship and release her from the Detention Order, but they refused as she was stateless and ownerless.

In early 1993, the Caroline Movement closed down as its main work was now being done by the Support Group. Some of its more active branches continued however, particularly those in Southampton and Leeds. They evolved into subsidiaries of the Radio Caroline Support group and continued to provide valuable sustenance and succour for the ship and the Radio Caroline team.

Several memorable events occurred in 1993, including the return of Johnnie Walker who was heard on Caroline the first time in 26 years. The Ross Revenge also left Dover and was towed to the Essex coast. This happened after Dover Harbour Board persuaded the MSA to survey and release her, just once. (The Marine Safety Agency was merged with the Coastguard Agency in 1998 to become the Maritime and Coastguard Agency)

Dented Bottom
A large dent in the ship's bottom was causing some concern among the crew who felt that it may have damaged several of the steel frames that hold the plates in place. It was to be the end of September before the final inspections could take place and a 'Load Line Exemption Certificate' could be finally issued. Such a document enables a ship to be towed after being 'sealed up' and no one on board, although later for later moves, it was deemed better if there were crew on board.

With the MSA's Exemption Certificate issued, the Ross Revenge could be moved from Dover docks. This was a temporary measure, enabling a cheaper mooring to be used as the dock charges in Dover were much too onerous at around £300 per week.

The Dover Harbour Board tendered a bill for £11,000 that by now had accrued in mooring and assorted other harbour costs. To show some goodwill, Peter Moore paid the Board £2,000 of his own money and promised payment of the balance in instalments, as he had done previously.

At last free to go, the ship left Dover under tow for River Bradwell in Essex. The Mayor of Calais had also offered a refuge for the Ross Revenge but it was felt that the Dover Harbour Board would not release her for an international journey, even though it was only 22 miles away. It was also decided that it would be difficult to manage the ship if she was in another country and fears about ownership and potential creditors determined it was better to be confined to the UK.

Almost two years after being rescued from the Goodwin Sands stranding, the ship finally left Dover. She was under tow by the tug Sea Challenge and had been fully sealed up at the instructions of the MSA, a normal practice. By the end of October 1993, the ship had been safely delivered to a mooring in the River Blackwater, near Maldon in Essex. She spent a year there while teams of volunteers spent long periods bringing her up to modern standards, decorating, refurbishing and generally making the ship more comfortable to live and work on.

The Dutch Government had been forced to issue some private radio licences, including five national networks; three AM and two on FM. Twenty seven applications were made, including one from *The Radio Caroline Partnership*. Sadly, that was unsuccessful, although former Caroline DJ Paul Rusling was successful with his bid for a national FM network on behalf of Classic FM. He was also involved with Radio 10 Gold which took over a 120 kW government transmitter on 675 kHz. The equipment was stuck on low power but after his reconfiguration it was persuaded to emit high power, the full 120kW.

A new voice first heard on Caroline at this time would be familiar to many as one of the key Caroline organisers. Steve Anthony has been a Caroline fan for many years and had joined the Caroline Movement becoming its Treasurer after his first trip out to sea in 1985. Steve was still working for a major bank so his links to Caroline had to remain low profile.

Steve Anthony

He made his first broadcast for the Lady during an RSL in 1994 from Bradwell. As Steve describes it: "I was broadcasting to the insomniacs and the sheep of Essex." After a break from Caroline for a few years, he was to rejoin after retirement from the bank and take up a very important role in the Caroline organisation.

The work to be done on the ship was not just cosmetic but covered the many items needed to get the detention order lifted. There were about a hundred 'faults' that the MSA had ordered to be completed. Before the end of the year, over 75% of the work had been done, however a couple of major items remained, including the steering gear.

Caroline's 30th birthday was celebrated by East Anglian Productions organising a large 'birthday bash' at a holiday camp near Clacton over the last weekend in March. The event was hosted by Andy Archer and included a gala dinner, plus a special performance by The Fortunes, who had recorded the song that became the Caroline theme tune.

On the same day, Southend ILR station *Breeze AM* devoted eight hours of their programmes to a special celebration of the station's life. DJs Peter Philips and Ray Clarke spun significant music from Caroline's past, many of the station's best known jingles as well as interviews with many leading Caroline participants, including Ronan.

The Ross Revenge hosted an RSL in May and June 1994 on behalf of the South East Boat Show from the location, between the marinas at Bradwell and at Tollesbury Marshes. The original intention was to move the ship into Burnham, the location of the show, but this proved impossible. Nevertheless, considerable publicity was generated for the Caroline case and even veteran DJ Johnnie Walker took part. This was the first time he had been heard on Caroline for over a quarter of a century.

At one stage the RSL broadcast was the target for a jammer; not the actual transmission but the link from the remote studio. Peter Moore complained to the DTI's Radio Investigation Service, about the interference who visited the site and found the jammer hidden in a hedge, close to the main transmitter. The DTI would not add a few extra days on the end of broadcasts to compensate for the loss of transmission time.

Caroline engineer Alan Beech

Chief engineer Ernie Stephenson had worked like a Trojan to get the many repairs completed but had to take more of a back seat after suffering a stroke in late 1994.

Alan Beech, a skilled radio engineer, did some sterling work on board the ship for the RSLs, not just on radio transmitters but on the various electric motors in the engine room and elsewhere throughout the Ross Revenge. He was also the leader of the ship's restoration crew for many years.

In December, Caroline organised an RSL of her own to broadcast over the Christmas and New Year period. This was the first time a full RSL had been broadcast continuously from the ship by Caroline since she had come into the UK. The small surplus from the operation allowed a further instalment to be paid to Dover harbour Board.

At the end of the RSL period, an announcement was made of Caroline's intentions whereby Caroline would continue to seek a licence from another country to broadcast to the whole of Europe. The UK's authority (the DTI) said they would only recognise such a licence if it was issued by a country that was a member of the ITU (International Telecommunications Union) and that no ITU member would get involved. Despite Peter Moore pointing out to them that a licensed radio ship would ensure responsible operation, the DTI position was that this would put them in a Catch 22 position, whereby if Caroline got away with it, others would follow suit, which they could not allow.

Caroline have so far not been able to persuade any ITU member country to issue the ship with a licence for a flag.

Veronica on the MV Communicator

The radio ship Communicator was now in the Netherlands to broadcast as Holland FM, but on the Medium Wave band. Her team included many from Radio Monique, but a few from Radio Caroline too. This was in fact part of a plan to return Radio Veronica to the air, but her status as a public broadcaster fettered her at that time. The following year, *Veronica Hot Hits* began transmissions from the Communicator, now safely moored on the IJsselmeer. With a new name and a hot-rocking format, *Veronica Hot Hits* was clearly heard all over the Benelux, thanks to a new 60 kW transmitter.

Caroline in Clacton

In 1995 the Caroline management noticed that the RSLs were by now producing less and less revenue, especially as the ship was off the beaten track and not easy to reach. The impact on listeners was beginning to fade. The MSA (Marine Safety Agency) eventually found that they could reclassify the ship as a coastal barge and issue an extension to ships certificate that allowed her to be moved to Clacton.

In August, after a tow from the tug *Horton*, the ship anchored off Clacton and transmitted on the old 199m wavelength. It was the first time the Ross Revenge had transmitted on 199, Radio Caroline's original dial slot in 1964. It was impossible to tie up at the pier as there was insufficient water for her draught. The broadcasts off Clacton were successful and adverts were run for MacDonalds and Barratt's homes.

Thousands of tourists visited a pop-up shop on the pier selling Caroline souvenirs and EAP's Ray Anderson noted a shop unit at the head of the pier, in which he later opened a Pirate Radio Museum. Sadly, it did not last very long. The footfall was very poor once Caroline had moved on and it closed down. The ship was then towed to Southend pier where there was a larger potential for audience and visitor footfall.

Caroline on the Continent

Regular Caroline broadcasts were still being heard via Radio 6 in Calais in cooperation with the France Radio Club, but these stopped in mid 1995 when a new owner took over the French station. Other relays continued via *Solar Sound*, broadcasting to Gibraltar.

. . and into London

In September 1995, the pressure group *Charter 88* offered to fund a trip to London for the ship to support their cause by way of an RSL. They are a quasi-political group made up from an assortment of well-meaning businessmen, whose goal is for the UK to adopt a written constitution. They had the financial wherewithal and political clout.

As predicted in 'Man's Fight for Freedom' by Johnnie Walker in 1967, (see page 193), Caroline's ship did finally sail up the river into London in 1996 with Johnnie on board and Ronan watching the ship arrive. The event received generous publicity on TV and in newspapers.

After berthing at South Quay in London's West India Dock, she broadcast for a month on behalf of Charter 88 which was proclaimed a success. Former Caroline DJs Tom Lodge and Mike Ahern joined the team for the RSL in Docklands, as did Tommy Rivers of *Laser 558* fame. Even Tony Allen returned to host programmes and Hans Knot presented an hour long special called 'The Legend Lives On'. Over 2,000 visitors trooped on board the ship to have a conducted tour, which provided much needed income to keep Caroline going.

The surplus generated in Docklands was enough to have the ship dry-docked, an essential step to having the detention order fully lifted. The Ross Revenge was trapped in London Docklands for a while, pending the settlement of yet another dispute being settled. One suggestion was to find a less encumbered ship and start Caroline again on that.

Eventually Peter Moore organised the release of the Ross Revenge from the West India Dock and she moved down the river to Chatham. Just after she sailed, a huge explosion caused by an IRA truck bomb tore through several adjacent buildings. Two men were killed and a hundred were injured in the blast which caused £150 million worth of damage. The Ross Revenge had again escaped disaster by the skin of her teeth.

Ross Revenge tied up in London Docklands.

Rob Olthof

The Future of Manx Radio

The Isle of Man Government considered the latest report into the future of Manx Radio, the first commercial radio station in the British Isles, licensed by the GPO. The 300 page report suggested leasing the station to Brian Kreisky, who ran a video production company called *Video Vision*. Part of Kreisky's plan was to hive off Manx Radio's 20 kiloWatt medium wave transmitter to Radio Caroline, who would run it as a billboard for the Island. This proposal was to wait over twenty years to come to fruition!

Members of Tynwald, the Isle of Man's parliament were not very keen and adverse publicity about Mr Kreisky persuaded them to ignore his offer and continue making an annual subvention of £700,000 towards the running of their radio station.

A former Radio Caroline DJ was awarded a new licence by the Isle of Man Government a few years later. Paul Rusling was CEO of a public company which successfully bid for a half million watts station on the island which would have covered the UK and Ireland on 279 kHz Long Wave, but disputes over share ownership delayed the station for many years and the station never launched. Among the plans were to build the transmitter on a man-made structure in Ramsey Bay, which was to be called Caroline Island.

Dry Docking

The Ross Revenge's move to Chatham for dry-docking finally took place in February 1996 and finally the long-awaited marine survey could be done. Once in the historic Chatham dry dock it was found that the thickness of steel in the ship's hull was still more than adequate to pass all the inspector's tests, although a large dent several plates wide was evident. It had been caused by her taking the ground on the Goodwin sands in November 1991. It was at first feared that this may have seriously damaged the frames that support the plates and if so, replacement could prove quite expensive.

Attention was paid to her sea chests and other areas that affect the watertight integrity of the ship. She was also given many replacement anodes and the hull was cleaned and painted.

After ten days 'high and dry; she was sailed out into the middle of the River Medway. Previous requests to moor in the Medway had been refused, but the Authority was now headed by Captain White who had been in charge in Dover. He knew already that the Radio Caroline were honourable people who paid their bills; Karma was finally working for the Caroline organisation!

In the middle of the river, the mooring fees were a lot easier to manage, but she was under detention, due to the lack of various appropriate paperwork. She was however allowed to undertake another RSL broadcast, this time on 107.4FM, during June 1996. The broadcasts brought a little more money into the coffers and helped keep the Caroline name in the public eye. Caroline had a friendly relationship with the MSA enabling them to go to most places within the Thames estuary, but the Harwich Harbour Authoritry put up so many barriers that it was realised they did not want the ship there and a proposed visit to Harwich for another RSL was not pursued..

Later in the year, a further RSL was organised in Bristol on 105FM by Radio Caroline stalwart, Steve Satan. Larger than life, Steve had been heard on Caroline during the eighties using various identities, including Andy Bradgate and Colin Mucslibar. He had represented Caroline at various music festivals such as Glastonbury and Womad and been responsible for organising several events.

Another RSL for Sheppey was beamed at the Isle of Sheppey on 1278 medium wave. Caroline had now been involved in more than half a dozen of these restricted broadcasts but they did keep the station's name alive and attracted many visitors. The mooring in the River Medway meant the public could come to see the ship while the live transmissions from the Ross Revenge helped for the team's morale.

Peter Moore shows DTI officials the 50kW transmitter.

Rob Olthof

Keeping the Dream alive

The RSLs on both medium wave and FM were limited to only a month and always had the power restricted so that only a very small area could be served. As they were infrequent, the star presenters whose careers Radio Caroline had launched were rarely interested in participating. This reluctance to be part of Caroline's humiliation is not surprising. Only the real stalwarts continued to support the station through these very lean years.

The Ross Revenge was incarcerated in a country which had been embarrassed by Caroline's broadcasts on so many occasions, and was now exacting the direst of retribution. Ronan O'Rahilly often suffered from bouts of depression leaving Peter Moore to manage the station alone. There were days when Peter felt like giving up, especially when he was attacked by Caroline supporters who simply did not understand how difficult it was to even keep the Caroline organisation operating at all.

Fortunately, there were some who believed in the Caroline ideals and kept the faith. "Keeping the Dream Alive", the title of a popular track by the band (Münchener) Freiheit in the eighties became a mantra for the hard-core anoraks who were determined to save Caroline for total submission. So long as man can dream – he can live!

Among those with whom Radio Caroline formed an alliance at this time was Peter Leutner who wanted to operate an ILR station in Kent. He took out a licence for a satellite station which was called European Classic Rock. It was based at the former TVS studios at Vinters Park in Maidstone. The station ran at a loss and sold some of its airtime to Caroline at a very reasonable price. Caroline eventually took over a lot more airtime on the channel when EKR crashed.

There was increasing interest in satellite stations but the only ones open to Caroline had been the low cost birds, more suitable for communications. The real goal was access via the Sky Astra satellites which were available in around 12 million UK homes. Listeners first had to accomplish a difficult battle with their equipment, tinkering with sub-carrier frequencies and the like, but most Caroline enthusiasts were technically inclined and managed to find the station on the sub-carrier quite well. Many of them became ambassadors for the station, helping neighbours and friends to tune their receivers to hear the new Radio Caroline.

Magical Merlin – Caroline's most powerful broadcast

The biggest ever Caroline broadcast was a special broadcast in 1998 hosted by Ronan and Johnnie Walker place to celebrate that the Marine Offences Act had failed to stop offshore radio. There was a tremendous response from listeners worldwide.

While the programme came from a makeshift studio in London's Gray's Inn Road, Caroline was heard all round the world using a network of transmitters with a total power of five million watts. These were controlled by Radio Merlin International, a management buyout of the transmitters of the BBC World Service. Half a dozen sites and literally dozens of 250 and 100 kilowatt transmitters all around the world relayed Caroline.

Eric Wiltsher controlled programming for Merlin and he filled the company's unused time with Radio Caroline programmes. The transmissions brought Radio Caroline to the ears of many former and lots of new listeners all around the world. Merlin tried hard to attract commercial air time but didn't manage to find enough clients to make it economically viable, so the transmissions had to cease.

To Sunny Southend

The Ross Revenge was still moored in the middle of the River Medway, where it was difficult to get access for the public and the Caroline crew. A trip across to Southend Pier was organised, with an extended berthing period. This allowed staff easier access and produced lots of revenue from extra visitors for the Caroline coffers. After the RSL, some bad weather threatened to dash the Ross Revenge into the pier, so the ship was quickly moved back to the Medway mooring.

The ship's next moved was to be back into London again, as a floating studio from which to relaunch Radio Luxembourg. Closed down by the giant RTL, the transmitters were still in situ, and used by day by Radio Luxembourg's German service. Eric Wiltsher dreamt up a scheme to relaunch Luxembourg's English service and needed a suitable focus in London for it. The Ross Revenge was deemed ideal and arrangements were made for an area of the West India Dock to be made available again.

Sadly, the new Radio Luxembourg plan didn't come to fruition and, on Christmas Eve, the Ross Revenge snapped the five mooring ropes holding her in position and she set off on a voyage of her own. She finally grounded on a sunken battleship near the *Thamesport* container terminal. The cost of having a tug pull her free and drag her back was eye-watering.

Online Radio

Virgin Radio and the BBC were among the earliest to develop radio over the internet, now called 'online', but Radio Caroline wasn't far behind them. The costs of getting established online were a lot more modest than on many other platforms, but it was roundly condemned by many in the media in the mid 1990s as at that time homes only had very slow dial-up internet access. The audio quality wasn't wonderful and those using the internet were paying to be online by the minute, so the audiences started out being very small.

Radio Caroline's satellite coverage was now very good, using a Sky sub-carrier, although listeners needed to know all about the complex instructions that were needed to tune it in on a satellite TV receiver.

The only way to get a bigger audience via this platform was to have a listing on the electronic programme guide which all the millions of Sky homes had available at their fingertips. Sky were no fools however and charged radio and TV stations a pretty penny for access to the EPG. Many Caroline team members and supporters were convinced that this was the only way to go, so a separate 'fighting fund' was organised to fund an EPG slot. Eventually Caroline had enough to get a place on the EPG, whereupon Sky tripled the cost!

Caroline coughed up the punitive initial fee and subsequently appeared on channel 0199 on the Sky EPG, hoping to gather in many more listeners and boost advertising revenues.

One of the Caroline fund-raisers, Mike Weston from Newark in Lincolnshire, discovered that some National Lottery funding might be forthcoming if an RSL was run to help raise money for other charities. The Lottery's Grant committee would also help fund a book about the Ross Revenge's long and colourful history, although they were unable to help pay for anything on the ship itself.

Mike subsequently published the book *Records at Sea* and this was promoted with the RSL, organised at the old ocean liner platform at Tilbury. The book is crammed with details of the Ross Revenge's career, from her launch as the *Freyr* in1960 through to her career in various locations of the South East as Radio Caroline. Mike's book also looks at the fishing industry, going back to the 16th century, and how it is organised in ports like Grimsby and Hull. (The book is still available in the Caroline webshop).

Radio Caroline had been approached by London ILR station Capital Radio to provide a standby transmission facility while their main AM transmitter at Barnet was closed for essential repairs and servicing. A location in London was really needed and many possibilities were surveyed. The only useful location was at Tilbury, where a large pontoon was used only for occasional cruise ships.

All the arrangements were made but Capital Radio suddenly pulled out of the deal, leaving Caroline committed to moving the ship to Tilbury. It was decided to go ahead with an RSL anyway at the cruise terminal, with a charity slant, which meant that was funding from the National Lottery was available to promote Mike Weston's book 'Records from the Sea' book and several other local deserving good causes too.

A mid river berth

Changes to the Medway Port Authority's berthing rules excluded older vessels after an old trawler almost sank at her moorings, and a restaurant boat sank without a trace. The owner of both those boats made themselves scare as the salvage costs were huge. The Port Authority invoked an age limit on craft anchoring in the Medway.

The closest option was to go into the main docks at Tilbury, who were not keen to have the ship as it tended to attract the public into what is a commercial operation. Tilbury made a couple of wharfage rent hikes to encourage the Ross Revenge to leave, but alternative mooring options were scarce.

Thanks to sterling work by Mike Weston the monthly harbour dues were paid and the ship remained at Tilbury. She was shunted off to a quiet part of the dock where barges were once moored that was no longer used commercially, just as a scrap yard. Radio Caroline were given permission to do some routine maintenance work and painting of the Ross Revenge. The ship was accessible by vehicle but protected from public access by security guards.

Caroline imposter down under

At the other side of the world, some New Zealanders formed a group to run a community radio station at Caroline Bay in 1995. When the licence came up for renewal, a London-based radio operator saw an opportunity to realise his lifelong ambition, to claim that he is Radio Caroline. He bid for the NZ licence. Companies House records are littered with companies that he has formed and dissolved using combinations of the name Caroline and several other offshore stations. In company with others he has tried again recently to acquire the rights to the name Radio Caroline and has even operated a station using other famous offshore identities.

Caroline to the Rescue

Caroline took its own satellite channel in 1999 to complement the round the clock broadcasts on the internet which were growing at a steady rate as more and more listeners migrated to online reception.

On the longest day of the year, the Ross Revenge was taken across to Southend by the tug Horton by her captain Andy Wood. After berthing at the pier head, the crew spent all week working to get the ship ready for visitors.

There were plenty of willing customers who would visit the ship wherever she went – it's surely become one of the most photographed ships by now? For just £3 admission, visitors can enjoy a conducted tour hosted by an experienced Radio Caroline DJ and see the famous Caroline studios, transmitters and other equipment. By the end of the month the ship was ready and Radio Caroline was back on the air for another RSL. Various memorabilia products including the usual T-shirts were available in the on-board shop.

Tours of the ship

Staying up to date with modern technology, Caroline also started selling 'mouse mats' at this time for just a fiver each; as you would expect, the proceeds from the sale of the mats went to keeping the Astra satellite service on the air. Listeners were writing to DJs at the time asking for a return to the Caroline schedule of the Personal Top 5 feature. It was decided this would take place on Sunday mornings.

While the Ross Revenge was tied up at the Pier, the cable supplying mains power to the shops and café at the end was severed. They faced closure until the break was repaired, but the Caroline ship being moored there saved the day. Engineers were able to hook up the restaurant and shops to the Ross Revenge's huge generators on board; Caroline saved the day (or three days).

The medium wave band allocated for this RSL was once again 1503 kHz, but again it was only one watt. Being at the end of Southend pier, the longest such structure in the world, out in the middle of the Thames estuary, the signal did travel a long way once again. Visitors could also see DJs broadcasting live, except on some really busy occasions when the studio in Maidstone was relayed, via an ISDN link to the ship.

Sarah Miles near the Ross Revenge

During the RSL at Southend, one of Caroline's latest DJs saw the ship for the first time. Sarah Miles had been recruited from a London local station, Liberty Radio and had also been heard on a station in Harlow, Essex.

"Radio Caroline has always acted as a proving ground for newcomers to the industry" station manager Peter Moore told The RADIO Magazine.

"We are delighted to be in the position to once more offer opportunities to new talent. Sarah's programme attracted a lot of response from our audience, and we look forward to hearing more of her in the future."

"Working for a great station like Radio Caroline is a dream come true for me," said Sarah. "I love the atmosphere at Caroline, the music has always been great and I have been totally overwhelmed by the number of people ringing in from all across Europe."

The ship arrived at Southend pier with Andrew Austin on board. He was an experienced travelling salesman of the old school, who responded to an advert that Caroline placed in the Guardian seeking volunteers. He felt his sales experience would help Caroline and offered his services, but was soon pitching in with many other tasks, including on air shifts./

A long-time fan of the station, Andrew's home in Rochester is convenient for the station's main studio and he is now a part of the furniture and a regular on Caroline Flashback and the North Service.

By December the DJ line up on Caroline included Johnny Lewis, Buzby, Graham Hall and Sietse Brouwer. *Medway FM*, an ILR station in Kent, carried some programmes live from the Ross Revenge, hosted by Bob 'Buzby' Lawrence and organised by Bob Le Roi. Caroline also got a special email address installed direct to the studio, as well as a telephone line, which for the first time the station had a regular means for listeners to contact the station live on the air.

The last month of the year ended well for former Radio Caroline legend Johnnie Walker. After a horrendous year in which his habit was exposed in the News of the world, and he was fined £2,000 for possession of cocaine, the BBC gave him a daily drive time programme five days a week.

Holland's rival Radio Caroline

Early in 2000 two entrepreneurs in the Netherlands started their own version of Radio Caroline. They obtained a licence from the Dutch authorities and began transmissions in late Spring on 1584 KHz. This is one of the two 'international common frequencies' at that HF end of the Medium Wave band which any country may use at low power levels.

The Dutch transmitter was located in Utrecht where they also had a small studio and could be heard in the nearby cities of Amsterdam and Rotterdam with mainly pre-recorded or automated programmes. There were complaints from the UK owners of the satellite station Radio Caroline alleging that the Dutch station's use of the name Radio Caroline was an infringement on its rights.

The name Radio Caroline had been formally registered in the UK and the certification presented to Peter Moore to hold on Ronan's behalf. Previously, the company names *Radio Caroline Ltd* and *Caroline UK Ltd* had been registered with the UK's Companies House in Cardiff. *Radio Caroline* had also been registered as a business name in the Isle of Man.

One of the operators of the Dutch service was Bob Noakes, who had served as an engineer on the Mi Amigo in 1973. He was also a presenter on Radio Seagull, but he had moved on to neighbouring station, Radio North Sea. Now in 2000 he joined with Ruud Poeze, who was previously a news reader at the Dutch government's overseas short wave station, Radio Nederland. The Dutch station calling itself Radio Caroline was not a commercial success and changed its name to Radio Paradijs after a short time.

Ross Revenge at anchor off Queenborough

Rob Olthof

In August 12, 2000, Radio Caroline returned to the airwaves, legally, to launch its entry into the high-tech age. Still afloat on the River Medway Estuary in Kent, Caroline was now embracing modern technology with broadcasts via satellite. She was also to be heard online and to mark the passing of the Marine Offences Act 33 years previously, she was heard around the world on several powerful ex-BBC short wave transmitters.

The 14-hour special broadcast also marked the 11th anniversary of the day that government officials had boarded the ship to try and close Caroline. It was paid for by the Dutch Caroline Support group and used a 600 kilowatt medium wave transmitter. Many emails, faxes and phone calls came in from all over Europe as a result of the transmission.

The following week a Caroline Supporters Day was held on board the Norderney, the old Radio Veronica vessel, in Leeuwarden, in northern Holland. It was attended by anoraks from Holland, Belgium and Germany, with station manager Peter Moore heading up a contingent from the UK that included Dave Foster and Barry James. Sir Hans Knot and Jelle Boonstra also attended, with ex-Monique DJ Herbert Visser known to most people as Herbie The Fish.

Another short term exercise took place in October 2000 from the lightship LV18 in Harwich. Once again the station was heard on 1503 kHz medium wave. Included in the line-up were Phil Mitchell, Paul Dennis, Colin Lamb, John Patrick, and Barry James. Although having a power output of only one watt, the RSL signal was received far and wide. Caroline received reception reports from listeners in Lincolnshire, Kent, Sussex, Norfolk, Northumberland, Cambridgeshire as well as many from the Benelux, Germany and Scandinavia!

Caroline recruited Rob Leighton in 2000, who was to become one of the longest serving hosts on the satellite programmes. Rob had dabbled in radio for many and joined the Voice of Peace in the eighties. After a period running his own Stafford Broadcasting Society, as an RSL and on short wave, he changed its name to Imagination Radio, renting time on 250 kilowatt former BBC transmitters in Cumbria. Rob was also a full radio amateur as well as a keen fan of most of the music that Caroline played and a generous benefactor too.

The British Radio Caroline also acquired a broadcasting partner on the French and Italian Mediterranean rivieras. Arranged by Mark Dezzani, who has broadcast in the Monte Carlo area for several years, the *Caroline South* group provided some weekend evening programmes for a while.

The shows were broadcast from Mark's home in Seborga, just over the border in Italy. Caroline South's programmes were heard on FM radio transmitters along the Riviera and hosted by Caroline DJs Grant Benson, Rob Harrison and Tom Anderson.

On the 21st of January 2002, a Dutch Caroline fan called Sietse Brouwer launched another Dutch Radio Caroline in Harlingen, on the Friesian cable networks, but this was largely independent of UK Caroline. Sietse and his chum Adrian Hondema intended to obtain an AM frequency from the Dutch authorities in 2003 when the country's medium wave frequencies were to be reallocated.

Sietse Brouwer launches the Dutch Radio Caroline

Pic by Rob Olthof

The event around the launch of Dutch Radio Caroline was a big media event and gave Radio Caroline tremendous publicity. It was attended by many of the UK Radio Caroline team, including Rob Ashard, Dave Foster, Steve Gordon and Graham Gill. The new Dutch Caroline failed to secure a high power AM frequency and the cable network service was discontinued because of lack of funds.

The Dutch Radio Caroline then changed its name to "Radio Seagull" and has broadcast ever since on 1602 kHz and on the internet, with a Stevie's was the last voice heard from the Mi Amigo in 1980.

The Dutch station's ID was:

Live on cable all over the Netherlands
And all around the world on the internet
This is Radio Caroline

The Dutch Radio Caroline was heard on the cable network from Essent, before being replaced by the broadcasts of *Radio 192* (a Radio Veronica tribute station run by studio technician Adje Bouman).

Stevie Gordon celebrates
Rob Olthof

Radio Caroline also got a regular outlet via a medium wave transmitter in Latvia, as well as weekend relays via satellite and online. Caroline then got transmission on a short wave transmitter and via satellite.

Listeners' Choice
A regular feature of Caroline's programming for many years was the Listeners Top 5s, extended to the Top 15 as fifteen album tracks usually fit nicely into a one-hour programme. Cliff Osborne and Pat Edison were responsible for assembling the shows for some years. It's an important part of keeping Caroline close to its listeners and of gauging exactly who the Caroline listeners are, and the kind of music they like. After all, Johnnie Walker promised in 1967 that "Radio Caroline is your radio station."

Pat constructed a web app to make the process easier. This enables listeners to type their choices into a form online, or simply select tracks from the *Caroline All Time Listeners Top 500.* The App automatically adds in the running timings from its own memory and whoever is building the programme can access this from wherever they are.

Roland Beaney
Chris Cooper

The Southampton Support Group hold an open meeting once a quarter which is often well attended by members and visitors. The members regularly raise money for Radio Caroline, with a variety of activities. The open club nights are run by Roland Beaney and have many former Caroline staff among their membership with others making guest appearances at the events, held at the Hamble Club.

Most of the money that the SSG raises goes towards the paint fund for the ship. The Ross Revenge always needs primer, white as well as the red. It's not just the paint but the paintbrushes, rollers, white spirit and lots of other bits and pieces; like most old ladies, she needs ever-increasing amounts of warpaint just to make her look good!

Restoration work continued on the Ross Revenge in Tilbury dock while transmissions settled down to a steady format. As with any family, nothing stayed still for very long and when Mark Stafford resigned, Steve Anthony took over his regular slot and Steve Silby's Friday afternoon programme.

Now that Caroline was now operating legally, with a licence, there was more administration work to be done, such as completion of the returns for the music royalties and Steve Anthony undertook those tasks too. With the increased regulatory requirements that follow all this 'legitimacy' there was all sorts of 'paperwork' things to attend to and Steve became a director of the company that holds Radio Caroline's Ofcom licence and other permits.

The Caroline connection with the Irish port of Greenore faded in 2002 when the O'Rahilly family sold their interest in the land and other property there for £14m; a good return on the purchase price of £12,500 in the sixties. Greenore continues to thrive under its new oweners, the Doyle Shipping Group, with considerable development since *An Bord Pleanala* (the Irish Planning Authority) decreed it to be one of the country's critical infrastructure assets.

Caroline Support in Germany

Another valuable group of friends to Radio Caroline are the German team led by Martin van der Ven, who run and attend the Erkrath Radio Day, held each year. It was originally run by Freddie Schorsch, who has now sadly passed away, but his legacy lives on. The events usually attract over fifty anoraks and a variety of special guests, invariably DJs from Radio Caroline, such as Roger 'Twiggy' Day.

DJ Roger Day at Erkrath

Chris Cooper

Album Zone

Caroline DJs Johnny Reece, Andy Brooks set up a separate station called the Album Zone with the help of Caroline's Calais connection, Radio 6. It expanded to include a dozen or so experienced presenters such as Keith Lewis, Lady Sam, James Barclay and Steve Leyland. They have provided programmes to many stations around the world, as well as their regular on Radio Caroline. It's still heard each weekend and remains popular with many Caroline listeners. The Album Zone has studios in the UK, Denmark and the USA

Worldspace

A company called *Worldspace* was set up to transmit programmes to Africa using a powerful satellite that could also be received in the UK, across Europe and most of Africa. It needed a specially adapted receiver to hear it, but these were heavily subsidised.

The basis of their 'business plan', for what it was, called for stations to pay (quite heavily) to be carried on the Worldspace satellite. As Caroline had no spare money for such a speculative investment, Atef Awad, the Chief Executive of the Worldspace allowed carriage on the basis that the presence of Caroline would be newsworthy and attract buyers for the receivers, which Caroline also agreed to promote. Listeners had to not only buy the radio, at quite a capital cost, but pay a monthly subscription too.

The Caroline Worldspace service duly started in late summer 2002. Caroline did sell quite a lot of the radios, which are still found in many homes even now, many years after the Worldspace service closed. For around six years Caroline was able to justly claim that it could be picked up across about a third of the world's surface!

In February 2003 Caroline was able to start a full-time digital service on the Astra satellite with round the clock broadcasting.

A team of divers reported back on the condition of the Mi Amigo after visiting her 'grave' in 2003. The wreck now seemed to be resting on her port side, half buried in the sand. The divers said that she appeared to be in the process of breaking into two halves, just for'ward of the bridge, in the area of the old generator hold. Two sections of the mast were still attached to the hull, but the remaining sections were not visible.

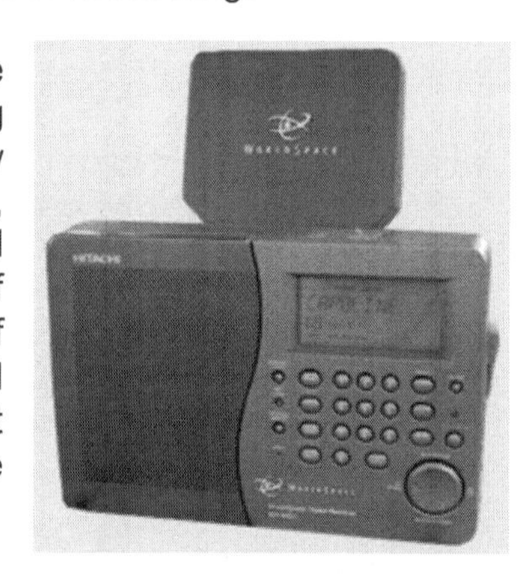

Worldspace portable receiver

The Mi Amigo is considered to be a difficult dive because the water moves very fast and in conflicting directions around the side of the Long Sand bank there. It can only be dived infrequently, a few times a year, and then only for a short time while there is slack water. Visibility is always only a matter of a couple of feet at best. The hull has remained pretty clear of any marine growth. This will be due to the scouring effect of the sand in the tidal stream which flows pretty fast thereabouts.

"Buzby" - Bob Lawrence

Bob Lawrence returned to the Caroline fold after a lengthy break working at ILR stations in the Midlands and London. Bob has worked in radio continuously since he left art school aged just 18 and was always popular with listeners, many of whom knew him better as 'Buzby'.

Having grown up listening to Caroline, Bob was keen to get involved in the new phase of broadcasting via satellite and the internet. A keen proponent of Loving Awareness, Bob was soon back into the swing and producing first class programmes, as well as performing some other very important tasks for Caroline.

Bob had seen more than his fair share of life and shenanigens while living on the Mi Amigo and began writing a book about some of the events. Reflecting on it, he felt that most readers would never believe even half that happened and he might get some people into trouble, so decided to change all the names (something that they often say it is done "to protect the innocent") and publish it as a fictional tale of love, hate, fear, joy, betrayal, guns, sex, drugs and rock n roll. The novel is called *The Last Great Adventure for Boys* and it's a great rip-roaring read. It's also good fun to spot who exactly is supposed to be who in the story!

The France Radio Club continued to wave the flag for Caroline in 2003 with their annual *Euroradio* event in Calais being a special presentation of called "Twenty years of the Ross Revenge". It was held in the town's George V Hotel, opposite the famous *555 Club* which had been the venue in previous years. The event was organised by François Lhote, Boudewijn Dom and Robert Magniez. It was attended by almost a hundred hard core Radio Caroline fans.

Star guests for their special event celebrating the Ross Revenge included Dennis Jason, Paul Graham and Peter Chicago. Dennis exhibited some of his fabulous collection of photographs, including those which he took from the top of the tower on the Ross Revenge before it was lost in 1987. The afternoon began with a slide show of the early days, fitting out the ship in Spain, with a commentary by Peter Chicago.

RIP Tony Allan

Stalwart Caroline DJ Tony Allan passed away in 2004, a huge loss for everyone in the Caroline family. He had tried to join the station in 1967 when he left Radio Scotland but Robbie Dale said he was too young. Eventually, he joined the station for the first time in early 1973 and, despite his poor health, was still pulling air shifts and training new staff until he passed.

Following sustained requests to have Caroline visible on the Sky EPG, Peter Moore wrote to all the station's supporters in December. Stressing that he personally had now worked for Caroline for about sixteen years without ever receiving a penny in wages, he asked anyone who wanted to contribute towards getting a place on Sky's EPG to send donations to a special fund set up for this purpose. It was administered by John Knight at Horizon Sales.

Several innovative fund-raising attempts were tried. One of these was a web site sold off by owner Dave Bullock. His *Radio-Caroline.org* domain was auctioned in 2004 to help raise money for the EPG fund. The successful bidder by Caroline DJ John Patrick and the proceeds donated to the EPG fund. The Caroline Society's Oliver Hicks now owns the domain.

Each time the Ross Revenge was opened to the public, there was considerable interest from ordinary members of the public. Everyone knew of the station, some hadn't listened for years and many didn't realise Caroline was still going. Many wanted to have a look around what is the most unique radio station in the world. Conducted tours by a Caroline DJ are a good revenue earner and remain so with trips out to the Ross Revenge, anchored on the River Blackwater now costing £25 per person. You get a nice cup of tea too in the ship's messroom!

In spring 2004, Radio Caroline contracted with RTL102.5 for some programmes to be carried on part of the national DAB system in Italy where it can be heard in Rome, Milan, Turin, Bologna, Florence and Naples. The programming was a mixture of Caroline's UK-produced material and the RTL locally produced material. Eventually Vatican radio made a better offer and took over the channel.

Another RSL broadcast ran from 7 August until 3 September 2004, with the ship moored at the cruise liner terminal jetty at Tilbury in Essex. This broadcast was part of the commemoration of the fortieth anniversary of Radio Caroline and promoted the station's legal internet and satellite programmes. The medium wave frequency used this time was 235 metres (1278 kHz) and the programmes were sent through ISDN landline to their Maidstone studio and streamed via the internet and broadcast on satellite. The supermarket chain *Asda* and *English Heritage* (headed by former Caroline MD Jocelyn Stevens) were amongst the backers for this event.

Some of the Radio Caroline North crew including Tony Prince and Mick Luvzit met in Vancouver for another Caroline reunion. An appropriate setting as Caroline's return had been made possible by a large investment from another BC resident, Nelson Skalbania.

Towards the end of 2004, China Radio International rented airtime on Spectrum, the station now occupying 558 KHz. This caused some disgust in the Caroline family; a country that jammed the UK's broadcasts into it's territory could be heard loud and clear in London on 558 KHz, which many listeners still regard as the home of Caroline.

One of Caroline's oldest presenters retired from radio at Easter 2005 to run a commune in the USA. Tom Lodge had joined Caroline in May 1964, before the merger with Radio Atlanta, and had been the main host of the Caroline ship's voyage to the Isle of Man that summer. He had become chief DJ and was responsible for reshaping Caroline South to be the grooviest station in London in the sixties.

Tom wrote an excellent book about his Caroline days called *The Ship That Rocked The World* which is obtainable from the Caroline webstore. His return to The Lady after she came ashore was a very welcome one and he was often accompanied by his son Tom on programmes, who continued hosting a Sunday night slot after his Dad retired. Tom spent his last six years, running a Zen retreat near Santa Cruz on the Californian coast.

The work on the Ross Revenge was now being overseen by some very hard working members of the restoration team: Peter Clayton, Alan Beech, Roland Beaney, Rockin' John Cronnolly and many more. Transmissions expanded again, making Caroline now available on Apple FM as well as a Sky channel 913 for two hours each weekday.

Caroline on 0199

In June 2006, Caroline purchased an EPG slot on Sky - channel 0199. No subscription or viewing card by the listener was required which many thought would make it a very attractive service. The service lasted five years but was a heavy drain on Caroline's depleted resources. It did however bring the station more easily to a larger audience and many new friends were made who hadn't realised that the station is still broadcasting. The cost of the transmissions (£2,200 a month) however did stop Caroline looking at the other advances then being made in broadcasting, which were many and several.

"In hard terms, our situation is simple enough," explained Peter Moore in Horizon magazine. "By being frugal, we can probably continue as we are. Our supporters are astonishingly loyal, but if they drift away, we may have to contract our activities, which would be very sad."

The Ross Revenge was still in Tilbury at berth no. 20 being lovingly restored by the usual crew, headed by Peter Clayton. Rockin' John Cronnolly was part of the regular team in those days too, as was electrician Dave Simcox from Scarborough. Dave later funded community station Radio Scarborough from his own pocket, a station that is still operating today.

A huge amount of painting was carried out on the hull at this time, the red and white areas, using scaffold towers. Others who gave freely of their time were Tommy Gerrard, marine specialist Steve Hedley from Newcastle and Gill Whiteley from Lowestoft.

Programmes continued to come from the main studio which was at the Maidstone studio centre (on the right) a large TV production facility owned by Flextech. Located at Vinters Park it had previously been used by TVS, an ITV regional contractor who lost their franchise. The studios are used by various independent programme contractors for ITV and other channels.

Radio Caroline's *Rockin Beerfest, Weekend* the 3rd, was held in Godmanchester near Huntingdon during August. Radio Caroline's programmes were relayed to the assembled drinkers and imbibers courtesy of the Worldspace link and the whole event organised by Dave Roberts and Chris, with volunteers Jim and Maria manning the Caroline merchandise stall.

Radio Caroline first began paying royalties for music played on the station in the sixties and one of the Performing Rights Society staff, Welshman Clive Thomas, took early retirement from there to join Caroline in 2006. Clive had previously been involved in hospital radio and RSLs in Essex but had harboured an ambition to join Caroline for 41 years. Radio Caroline in the sixties had first got him into music and radio when he was only 17 years old.

Alan Beech is one of Caroline's expert transmission engineers and has refurbished the ships original equipment and some smaller units that have been used for RSLs. He noticed that the latest unit that Caroline had acquired had been set up on 558 kHz; presumably it had been the one used to force Caroline off that frequency in 1990! Alan has also been working on equipment for Caroline's cousins at Dutch station Radio Seagull in Harlingen. This took over from the Dutch radio Caroline after it split from the UK headquarters.

Many other Caroliners have made the trek to Friesland to help on the Radio Seagull ship, the Jenni Baynton, which was bought by Sietse Brouwer and Radio Waddenzee after they won a Dutch terrestrial license. Radio Seagull broadcasts around the clock and which is taken out to sea for a few weeks most summers. Several transmitters have been installed by Radio Caroline engineer Alan Beech, Walter Galle and various assistants from the Support Group.

Radio Seagull's chief DJ is Stevie Gordon, whose was the last voice ever heard from the Mi Amigo, minutes before she sank beneath the waves. The Caroline DJs who have also been heard on the station is too long to list here but among the notables are Steve Conway, Norman Barrington, Mark Stafford and the delightful Mandy Marton.

The Ross Revenge remained land-locked and docked in Tilbury which enabled the restoration teams to continue various tasks. These are manyfold and encompass not just maritime matters, such as the continuous repainting that is always necessary on a ship, but replacement of most of the ship's electrical systems. Technology and the regulations governing it are forever changing meaning that many items constantly need upgrading.

Even simple lighting circuits on the Ross Revenge have now been upgraded, which takes time and investment. Fortunately, Radio Caroline can draw on a wide circle of 'friends' and helpers for most of the work, all that's needed is the materials and components. Many suppliers do respect Radio Caroline and all she has done for the radio and the music industries and many have been willing to supply goods and services at heavily discounted rates, or even free.

While the ship is made of steel, many areas are fitted out with wooden panelling. Timber will deteriorate over time and so many items have had to be replaced, particularly doors and their frames. If the walls and ceilings are not well clad they will make cabins and other areas very cold. The woodwork on the Ross Revenge continued to be given expert attention by the chippies, led by ace carpenter Steve Dack.

Ken Petrie and his company Sentek in Basildon supplied display and storage cabinets which were installed into Raffles' old dog-kennel. This is now a pleasant sales area where visitors can see the range of Radio Caroline merchandise and buys souvenirs of the station and the ship. The restoration team also stripped down and rebuilt the all-important anchor winch equipment, the huge mechanism used to lower and raise the ship's anchors.

News of developments on board the Ross was regularly brought to enthusiasts by a variety of supporters group, including the Caroline Movement and Horizon Magazine, the official journal of the Ross Revenge Supports Group. This was edited and organised by John Knight and Bill Barnes.

Caroline made several live broadcasts via an ADSL link to the Maidstone studio centre; probably the most notable was that from the Cambridge Rock Festival, which changed its name to the Rocking Beer Festival. DJ Barry James introduced the acts onto stage including Nine Below Zero, Eddie & the Hot Rods and Dr Feelgood.

Honoured at last

In Summer 2007 the BBC honoured radio's precious memories by running their own radio ship for a few days. BBC Pirate Radio has a studio on a former lightship in Harwich, transmitting over the MW outlets of local station BBC Essex. The event featured many former Radio Caroline DJs, including Keith Skues and Johnnie Walker. Producer Ray Clarke commissioned a jingle package based on old Caroline and Big L jingles and recordings of many Radio Caroline events and milestones were included in the broadcasts.

The Radio Academy, an association of people working in BBC and independent local radio, organised a half day celebration of offshore radio at the beginning of August. It took place at a restaurant in Soho and featured appearances by many Caroline luminaries, including Ronan and Chris Cary with many others who flew in from Canada and Australia to take part.

The event took place at the Sugar Leaf in the heart of Soho and focussed on the glory days of the 1960s. It completely ignored the seventies and eighties, even though Caroline's activities in both those decades were far more remarkable than anything that happened in the 1960s. No mention was made that Caroline continues to broadcast, except by Johnnie Walker. Ronan O'Rahilly was shocked to be inducted as a Fellow in the Academy as he doesn't enjoy such plaudits or public acknowledgements.

During the first session (Caroline, the Sound of the Nation) Roger Day made the point very strongly that UK radio had become so poor because the accountants had taken over and they didn't really have either radio or music in their hearts.

A more relaxed and longer event was Caroline's appearance at the annual *Cropredy Festival*, thanks to DJ Pandora and Radio 2's Bob Harris. The Caroline merchandise stand sold out of T-shirts on the first day, thanks to the hard work of Phil Meek and Alan Watts.

One of the station's most popular DJs, Alan welcomed the Levellers to the Maidstone studio in July where they did a couple of numbers live and answered questions about their lengthy careers and their studio in Brighton. The Levellers also donated packages of their CDs to half a dozen lucky Caroline listeners.

Financial matters continued to be a big headache for Caroline. In an edition of Horizon magazine in 2007, Peter Moore explained the financial position of the organisation: "Concerning the Caroline staff, since we all work for nothing, whether on air or behind the scenes, we are obviously not looking to line our own pockets. On the plus side however, we have no shareholders, no finance house and no merchant bank wanting to see a return on their money."

An extra Caroline stream

A lot of hard work had by now been put into the launch of a second service from Caroline. Dreamt up by Mike Brill, this was originally going to be called **Caroline Extra**. It would be an internet only service, with mostly pre-recorded shows or non-stop music. The music royalty collection bodies proved to be very difficult to deal with in this respect, but the team continued to progress the arrangements hoping that the service could be launched by the end of 2013.

Caroline in the movies

Legendary film director Richard Curtiss made a romantic comedy film called The Boat that rocked, based on life on an offshore radio ship. Some of the equipped they used was loaned by Radio Caroline and the film company were advised by several former Radio Caroline people, including Johnnie Walker. On its release, many criticised the film, for not being a documentary, completely missing the point that it was a fictional story, and not intended to be educational, or factual. It starred Bill Nighy and Philip Seymour Hoffman, and many Caroline personalities were reflected in the film's characters. The public release of the film *The Boat That Rocked* gave Radio Caroline considerable publicity, with film reviews on radio, TV and in the press remarking that Radio Caroline was the first and discussing the lack of music heard on the air in those days.

An independent film producer called Saskia Vischer visited the Ross Revenge and held advanced talks with Caroline's management about her plans to make a movie exploring the politics of Caroline's era.

"I had many discussions with Saskia who, being Swiss-Australian, has a most intriguing accent," remembers Peter Moore. "Her film was to have been a docu-drama, but far closer to the truth and much darker in content than *The Boat that Rocked*. Her interest pre-dated the Boat and she had a web site and a sheaf of scripts. However, as soon as Richard Curtiss came along with his track record in the industry, Saskia's project was at once quashed. She went off to some exotic place to live the good life."

Saskia's film wouldn't trivialise offshore radio, as *The Boat That Rocked* did, but would look at the impact of the station on music trends and tastes. It would be an inspiring story about rock and roll, social revolution and the fight for free speech, which are all aspects of the Radio Caroline lifestyle.

A third film that features Radio Caroline in some detail is *PIRATE RADIO – Taking Back the Airwaves*. It was produced by *Lionheart Filmworks* and is primarily a series of interviews with Caroline station manager Peter Moore, Johnnie Walker, Rosko, Keith Skues, Tony Prince, Hans Knot and a host of the DJs and others in the pirate radio movement.

The film has humour and tragedy, told by some of the people who were there, and their views about the film 'The Boat That Rocked'! The DVD has so far been unavailable in the UK but Caroline have imported a quantity and sell copies through the web shop.

After a gap of over a quarter of a century, the cry of 'News from the Caroline Road Show', once heard at the top of every hour in the Mi Amigo days, was scheduled to be heard in 2008 but nothing came of the plan.

Tilbury docks, being an operational private dock, did not cater for easy public access. Caroline was just as 'out of sight' as when she was out at sea, and to the majority of the public, that also meant 'out of mind'.

The difficulty with any good berth was that the cost would be huge, plus all manner of extra costs were likely to poke their heads above the parapet. Insurance, security . . the list is endless.

One of the biggest problems for the ship was the damage to the hull from her grounding on the Goodwin Sands in late 1991. The visible dent may be more serious and the repairs were quoted as being "potentially in the region of £80,000 if some frames inside the hull need replacing". Even a simple tow to a public shipyard with a dry dock, such as Ramsgate or Ipswich, would have cost in the region of £8,000, plus but they no longer have suitable facilities

The rent and other service charges for the Flextech studio at Vinters Park in Maistone continued to escalate in 2008 to a point where they were becoming unsustainable. As has often happened in Caroline's life, an innovative solution was found: a studio owner in Rochester had space available, fully equipped and with parking and the necessary connection to the WRN building in London. As it is fully serviced around the clock this would reduce the need to have engineering staff on standby for the times when things went wrong and there was even car parking immediately adjacent. Perfect!

To celebrate Radio Caroline's 44th birthday at Easter 2008, live broadcasts were made from the ship for several days. Featured were many DJs from the Mi Amigo broadcasts of the seventies, including Bob Lawrence, Kees Borrell, Cliff Osborne and Roger Matthews.

While the movie 'The Boat That Rocked' had reminded everyone of Radio Caroline's existence, it also prompted Tilbury's dock master that, somewhere in the vast acres of his yard, was the Ross Revenge, Caroline's latest ship. He began giving the ship more attention, some of which was not completely welcome. As is common with officials, he was keen that all the various regulations appertaining to ships be fully complied with. One of these was that the ship must have a proper gangway to access the vessel from the quayside. The crew had been simply clambering on board.

The harbourmaster wanted the access fenced off, with a secure gate and the insurance certificate be displayed at the ships' entrance. This caused a problem, as there wasn't one! He also began requesting that the Ross Revenge be moved out of his dock as soon as possible.

Worldspace's days seemed to be coming to an end as they were simply running out of money. They had spent millions on flashy offices and PR events, but attracted scant revenues. All revenue had was a small royalty on receivers sold by others, and a modest monthly income from subscribers such as Caroline listeners.

OFCOM steadfastly refused to award a medium wave licence to Caroline, maintaining that there were no AM frequencies available. This was utter nonsense, as there clearly were many empty spots on the dial. 'They seemed to be saying that we can't have it because we say so,' said Bob. "We believe Caroline is a special case, due to our longevity. We've given so much exposure to the music industry but we're not allowed to query their decision, or ask why not."

Forty years celebration

The fortieth birthday Caroline Reunion held in Mayfair at the Red Lion in 2004 had been so successful that it was decided to hold another one to mark the 45th in 2009. Caroline's birthday also coincides with Roger Day's too, so he had the job of arranging the event. The Red Lion was being refurbished into a grand town house, so Roger chose another legendary Mayfair hostelry, the Grapes in Shepherd Market. Over fifty former Caroline staff showed up from all phases of her history. The guests and attendees are too numerous to mention, but many lined up outside for a photograph by Sylvan Mason, who had spent a weekend marooned on the Mi Amigo in 1965.

Caroline's 45th birthday reunion at the Grapes in 2009

Sylvan Mason

Manx commemoration

On the west coast of the Isle of Man is the ancient city of Peel. As well as being the home port for the North's ship tender, *Essex Girl*, it is home to Harry Maddrell's family, an important part of Caroline North in the sixties and the location of the House of Manannan. This is a maritime museum dedicated to the old sea god Manannan.

In early 2009 a special exhibition was staged in the museum as a tribute to Radio Caroline North. Ronan attended the formal opening of the Manx exhibition in Peel along with many Caroline listeners and invited former staff of the station.

The event was organised by Andy Wint, a veteran radio DJ who has been at Manx Radio for many years. He also published a picture book telling the story of Radio Caroline North called *Manx Giant.*

Retuning the platforms

The audience for Radio Caroline was now growing and had soon shot up five-fold to reach 100,000 hours per month, all at very little cost. This was in stark contrast to the SKY EPG slot which took £2,200 from the meagre resources. It was decided to revert to the 'tune-in manually' service using the WRN satellite.

This created some problems in that the more modern satellite tuner boxes didn't allow for customers tuning to sub-carriers manually, meaning the loss to Caroline of a chunk of audience. As a platform for programme carriage it was proving very expensive and, while convenient to some to play Caroline around the home, it didn't seem to be expanding the size of the audience or have other benefits.

After lengthy deliberations it was decided to cut the satellite link completely and broadcast only on the internet. This cost very little and still meant that listeners could find the station, as by then an App had become available.

Mobile Phone App

The Radio Caroline Mobile Phone App allows listeners to find the Caroline internet transmissions with remarkable ease. Apps (its short for 'application', a mini piece of web software) were becoming the way forward as they remove the fiddly tuning in process of finding online stations. Apple led the way with this development and soon had thousands of apps available which became an industry in itself. Soon Android and other phone systems followed and led to a burgeoning 'smart phone' market taking over many aspects of people's lives, including the way they once consumed radio.

The Caroline app has allowed the station to grow and grow, with three channels and any number of bit rates, or bandwidth being available at the touch of a button. Later developments have included playlists and a link to email the studios directly. The Radio Caroline app now includes presenter profiles, programme alarms, schedules and a list of important events that happened on each day in music history.

While many apps are available to download without a fee, the really useful ones invariably have a cost. This can be from 99p up to $1,000, but for the Radio Caroline App, its only £1.99, to cover the costs of providing the service via the App Store, etc, and includes a small donation to keeping Caroline operational.

The App has been upgraded several times to incorporate an option to select varying bandwidths, thus saving on the cost of downloading the stream – very useful, especially when travelling abroad in countries where web access can be very expensive.

By limiting transmissions to the app and other online outlets, the pressure of crushing financial burdens was avoided. The audience was growing, week by week and response to merchandising covered most of the station's needs.

Occasional broadcasts were made by the 30 day RSL system, usually on bank holiday weekends with some extra publicity gained on the August Bank holiday 2010 being the fiftieth anniversary of the first voyage of the Ross Revenge. With such a colourful history strewn with landmarks, Radio Caroline and the Ross Revenge were never short of anniversaries to commemorate!

Caroline AM licence in Parliament

As a true Caroliner, Bob wouldn't be giving up so easily and he mounted an energetic campaign to have the matter raised with as many politicians and others as possible. He redoubled his efforts and wrote to every member who might be willing to support the idea of getting Radio Caroline an outlet onto traditional radio frequencies.

Tracey Crouch MP

Bob found a willing ally in Tracey Crouch MP whose dad had always been a Caroline enthusiast. She tabled an Early Day Motion in the House of Commons, which created a lot of interest. Over seventy other MPs were in favour and voted accordingly.

There is no doubt that this caused a rethink at OFCOM, who deliberated for a couple of years, and needed constant prodding to remind them of Caroline' s existence.

At one stage the head of OFCOM was literally door-stepped by one of Tracey's colleagues and asked bluntly why Caroline couldn't be given a frequency. The Head of OFCOM said that he often asked his team to see if a frequency could be found, a common way of kicking the ball into the long grass.

It was just before Christmas that Tracey Crouch, the MP for Chatham and Aylesbury presented her Early Day Motion to the House of Commons. The motion is worth stating in its entirety. It read:

That this House expresses its disappointment that, having pioneered commercial radio in the UK and for the past decade being a fully licensed broadcaster, Radio Caroline, a cornerstone of British radio history, has been denied by OFCOM the opportunity to secure a medium wave frequency from which to broadcast; regrets that as a result its devoted listeners are confined to listening to Radio Caroline via the internet and unable to enjoy its musical offerings in transit; and calls on OFCOM to exhaust all avenues in making the provisions available for Radio Caroline to celebrate its 50th birthday in 2014 by broadcasting on a medium wave frequency which, it appears, is unwanted by both BBC and commercial operators as a broadcast platform.

New Mast

No one could fail to have been impressed by the elegant 285 feet tall mast that adorned the Ross Revenge when she first arrived off the UK in the eighties. When this fell over the side a few weeks after the great hurricane of 1987, the ship's crew spent nine months erecting two replacement masts, each of just over a hundred feet in height. The insurance surveyor felt that as these were getting on for a quarter of a century old they were in dangerous condition and thus had to be removed. Further, one was over an emergency escape hatch that must be removed, which led to endless discussion and debate over what would be the best solution.

Many of Caroline's supporters were keen to see the original mast rebuilt, now she was in harbour and could easily call on the assistance of craneage but the cost was beyond Caroline's means.

The new mast from Radio Structures Ltd

Radio Structures Ltd, are a UK tower company who offered to donate a complete mast and put it up. The RSL engineers designed and fabricated a more modest mast, at their factory in the East Midlands, which they delivered to the ship and erected over a period.

To most people's eyes it looks just as pleasing and completes the look of the Ross Revenge. The stays are not insulated but as the mast wasn't intended to be used as a radiator, that didn't really matter.

When the original mast fell, just a few inches was left protruding above the deck. The original base insulator had been wrecked and had been replaced by a nice shiny new one, around which was fitted the base section of a new mast. Of more modest proportions, the total height above deck was to be 30.5m, or just under 100 feet high. Triangular in section it was constructed on deck from dozens of extruded pieces. The first four sections are 6m in height, topped by two 3 metre sections.

Caroline had been streamed on the internet since the 1990s and, in 2011, joined the *Radioplayer UK* project. This is an internet feed formed by the BBC, and the commercial stations that supplies a 'listen live' service of UK radio stations to listeners across the globe.

Caroline's audience developments
The SKY channel 0199 facility was removed on 1 July 2011 after failing to renegotiate costs with Sky and deciding not pursue a Freesat EPG slot. Surveys performed in 2008 and 2010 into the audience's listening habits showed that only a small percentage listened to Caroline via Sky and that satellite listening had dropped by 9% since the 2008 results, while on-line listening had increased by around 40%.

The audience for Radio Caroline has continued to grow, year by year. Some increases are modest but after each major milestone that attracts widespread press coverage, there is always a surge, as new listeners realise the station is still operational. Radio listening is very much a habit; once someone gets out of the habit of tuning in or has something more important to attend to, it's very hard getting them back into listening regularly again.

With internet listening increasing use of satellite for radio reception falling, listening. Caroline management had lengthy discussions with the satellite provider. They were not willing to help reduce the cost, so Caroline stopped the satellite service at the end of September 2013.

OFCOM invited expressions of interest in using MW frequencies during 2013, but then sat on their hands, repeatedly moving the time scale back. Bob Lawrence was growing tired of the procrastination by OFCOM over the pleas for a MW frequency and Cliff Osborne began to take up some of the relentless pushing and prodding to get a decision out of OFCOM.

After about three year's delay, OFCOM suggested that eventually a low MW frequency might be made available. They did warn Caroline that this would be a very difficult frequency to operate on, which made Caroline's engineers smile a little. They had successfully operated transmitters on low frequencies for some years.

The Port of Tilbury were by now becoming very insistent that, after an eleven year stay, the ship be moved from their dock, which meant extra insurance cover. To qualify, the Ross Revenge had to pass many new regulations that had since come into force. Altogether 29 pages of demands were made that all had to be exhaustively carried out. The ship's Stability Book had to be revised and updated, to reflect the various items of machinery, internal alterations but especially the new mast and the ballast.

Ronan is inducted with Candy Devine

Ian White Photography

In October 2012, Ronan was inducted into the Hall Of Fame at the *PPL Radio Awards*, which were held at the Lyrath Hotel, Kilkenny in Ireland.

Ronan, the late Gerry Ryan of the RTE and famous Downtown diva Miss Candy Devine all received their prestigious awards in a glittering ceremony, the highlight of the evening.

The backdrop of the stage was huge shot of Ronan in the new studio on the Mi Amigo in April 1966 when she returned to sea with the new 50kW transmitter.

Caroline DJ Mick Williams published his book *The Boat That Really Rocked* in 2014 which told the story from the DJs point of view. He is still heard regularly on Caroline under his real name of Ray Clarke.

Caroline Ownership and Trademarks

For many years, the Radio Caroline name was not registered, which left the door open for several 'chancers' to lodge claims to the name. Several variations of the name were registered to others who had no link at all to Caroline. This caused problems from time to time, so it became important to secure the rights to the name of Radio Caroline. The Radio Caroline trademark was obtained by Caroline's Tony Kirk in the early 90s when he saw it was not protected. This prevented the other chancers from using theirs.

The international nature of the Internet demands that multiple claims must be made in different territories, a tiresome administrative task. A battle was fought with one group of "wannabe Caroline" pirates who tried to demand that the real Radio Caroline's ISP remove it in their favour, as they had registered an EU name for the whole of Europe. Considerable resources was wasted in correcting this. Both *Radio Caroline North* and *Radio Caroline South* trademarks have now been registered with the Intellectual Property Office so they can no longer be hijacked by anyone masquerading as Radio Caroline.

27. A Golden Birthday

Caroline's 50th birthday celebrations in 2014 were held at a private event in Kent; some 'old salts' were invited, including Kevin Turner, Martin Fisher, Johnny Lewis and Ray Clarke, but many were excluded.

Station manager Peter Moore commented that the worst days of the station's history were the late 1980s and early 1990s. "The ship had become unseaworthy, we had insufficient budget to supply it with the various supplies that it needed and we had to use marine crew who were unqualified. Some had no marine experience – they shouldn't have been there. I shouldn't have sent them out there."

There was considerable pressure to move the ship from Tilbury and, for a while, there seemed to be a real possibility that she would be seized and sent for scrapping. There was potentially a berth on offer at the Essex Marina on the River Crouch but there were endless objections from the local harbourmaster and it was clear that the Ross Revenge wouldn't even be allowed in their river. Other locations were approached, again without success.

The Tollesbury Oyster Company who controlled the riverbed on the River Blackwater agreed to give sanctuary to the unwanted ship and, to show good faith, Caroline paid a year's rental fees in advance. Serious costs were expended in making the Ross Revenge seaworthy for the voyage with £4,000 spent on stability tests alone.

Finally, in late July, the insurers agreed to cover the tow for a premium of £500, the tug *Horton* which had towed *Ross Revenge* many times in the past arrived to be the shadowing vessel though really she was just there in case of any problems that occurred along the way. The *GPS Avenger* was lead tug and at noon on the last day of July, 2014 the convoy was ready to leave. "It was the most amazing experience, the weather was superb," says Steve Anthony, who was on board.

For a while the PLA who control all activities on the river seemed reluctant to give permission for the Caroline convoy of boats to venture out onto the River Thames. Eventually, the lock gates were opened, the ship nudged out into the Thames and then was tugged hard aport. At long last, the Ross Revenge could head towards the open sea!

Freedom for the Ross Revenge
Chris Dunford

After a couple of hours she had cleared the Sea Reach Number One buoy. With Southend now falling away to port and the Isle of Sheppey receding off her starboard quarter, the Ross Revenge headed off down the Barrow Deep. Three hours later and the tugs brought her about the head of the Gunfleet sand and into the Wallet.

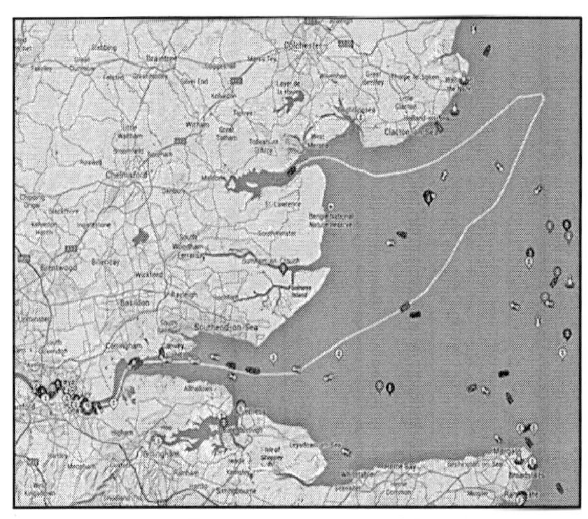

The Ross Revenge's voyage of Freedom from Tilbury to the Blackwater

AIS

Caroline supporters on land watching her progress on the *Ship AIS* traffic logging system held their breath for what seemed like an eternity as the Ross Revenge lingered off Frinton, the site of so many broadcasts that had emanated from there in the sixties.

Steve Anthony was one of the lucky passengers on this landmark move for the Ross Revenge and he suggested trying some 'Frinton Flashing'. A message was posted on the Caroline Facebook page. "We did try flashing with a powerful torch but sadly there was no response from the shoreline," said Steve. "We then realised that it was way past people's bedtime for the 60s generation who were probably tucked up with their Horlicks that late in the evening!"

This was the spot where the Mi Amigo had launched as Radio Atlanta and then as Radio Caroline South. It was the location that Caroline had become International, where Johnnie Walker and The Admiral Robbie Dale had broadcast into illegality on 14th August 1967. It was also the anchorage from where the ship had been towed away in March 1968.

After a few hours stooging around waiting for the tide it was time to make the final journey into the River Blackwater. The delay was essential to ensure that there was enough water to avoid grounding on the sandbanks that narrow the entrance into the river.

The Ross Revenge was carefully attached to a permanent mooring in mid-river, just upstream from Bradwell Marina. Initially, trips to the ship were made from Maldon, but recently the public visits on the *Razorbill 3* have been from the quay in West Mersea.

Extra Studio Consoles

Former Radio Caroline DJ Ian Anderson, later started his own station in the Shetlands Isles. SIBC is still the only full-time radio station operating in this, the most northerly of the British Isles. It was originally to operate on 558 kHz and cover a wide area around Shetland.

SIBC subsequently launched on FM and has operated for over twenty years. It's a respected part of the community and Shetland's infrastructure, with a good service of shipping information and weather forecasts. Due to Ian's constantly upgrading of equipment, SIBC was able to donate two 'top of the range' mixing consoles to Caroline.

Two commemorative events took place on the 28th March, in Walton on the Naze and in Harwich, which was opened by the town's Mayoress and their MP, Bernard Jenkin. The Walton events featured an open-air disco hosted by Paul Barber (who plays 'Denzil' in *Only Fools and Horses)*.

In spring 2015, Caroline decided to try an experimental second service on the internet, which became ***Caroline Flashback***. After several tests, Caroline's IT engineer Mike Brill had found that it would be possible to transmit a stereo audio signal from the ship using the now rapidly expanding network of 4G. Sending the signals as data by mobile phone did not add much to the cost of transmission once the capital expenditure had been made. This meant that signals could be sent to anywhere for onward transmission, via the internet or land-based AM or FM transmitters.

Caroline Flashback is online as well as via the Caroline App. It features a daily show from Roger Day and various specialist music feasts, such as Todd Slaughter's *Elvis Hour,* Bill Rollins, Graham L Hall and Barry James with his popular '*Forgotten Vinyl*' programme. Flashback was in answer to many requests from listeners, who felt that Radio Caroline should play the same music, pop hits, and sound similar to how it did in the sixties. Sadly it has been Caroline's best kept secret and rarely promoted.

Live Music on the Ross Revenge

On a cold November day, the Ross Revenge played host to American rock artists, the *Billy Watson Band*. The five-piece blues rock band were just finishing a tour of Germany and the UK and played a short set on the stern deck, which was filmed for use as a promotional video. Steve Anthony interviewed the band's leader, Billy, who told him about the time that he jammed with Bon Jovi.

The band were amazed at Caroline's record library and said they had never seen so much vinyl. After being filmed hamming it up as DJs in the main on-air studio, they adjourned to the mess for a more formal interview. This was an historic occasion, being 48 years since any musicians had last performed on a Radio Caroline ship.

With the Ross Revenge now safely on a suitable mooring it was hoped that public tours could commence again to earn more revenue, but it was found that the ship's insurance covered only workmen and crew, and, of course, third-party risks for damage to other ships if the ship was ever adrift. A new list of repairs and alterations had to be made before the public could be admitted. Among the requirements were the removal of trip hazards, fire-fighting kit including a Fire Plan, signage, life jackets, a defibrillator and a dedicated First Aid area.

Caroline held discussions with friends at Manx Radio in the Isle of Man. The station is owned by the island's government and has its own network of FM transmitters which covers their own audience quite well. Manx Radio also has a pair of 10kW AM transmitters which feed a directional transmitter at Foxdale. This is a two-mast site, just east of Peel, on the island's west coast. The signal caries well north and south of the Isle of man and is directional in order to 'protect' the coverage of several other users of the channel, such as BBC Radio Lincolnshire.

The Medium Wave service, on 1368 AM, is used for broadcasting some speech programmes, such as coverage of the Manx TT and the Grand Prix motorcycle races, as well as the monthly proceedings of Tynwald, the Manx Parliament, but usually they simply duplicate the Manx Radio FM programmes. It was agreed that Radio Caroline would provide a programme feed for these over one weekend each month.

The programmes would be produced live on board the ship and be called Radio Caroline North, a service that the Island had from 1964 to 1968, thus creating a nostalgic programme sound for Manx Radio at no cost to them and give Caroline a bigger audience in the Isle of Man. The transmitter on 1368 not only covers the Isle of Man, but a broad sweep of Ireland, Scotland and the North of England, thanks to its directional pattern. Initially, reception of 1368 over on the east and south coasts was spoilt by a local BBC station, but their ideas of modernisation saw these closed in 2018, which enhanced the coverage of Manx Radio's MW transmitter.

Radio Caroline North, from the Isle of Man

In September (2015) Caroline started the Radio Caroline North service via the MW transmitter of Manx Radio once a month. Programmes were produced and presented on board the Ross Revenge by Barry James, Steve Anthony and Kevin Turner. They began with simply a hard drive of music and jingles plus a very old computer installed in the port side studio, previously the home of Radio Monique.

This was the first time that live transmissions had been made from the ship for many years and, thanks to the link arrangements nurtured by Mike Brill, worked perfectly. Manx Radio's Programme Controller Mark Tylney and their long serving DJ Chris Williams were special guests on board the Ross Revenge for that eventful broadcast.

From the ship, the programme is sent using a 4G circuit to the Caroline control centre at the Rochester studio. From there tan online feed is picked up at Manx Radio's studio centre on Douglas Head, where any extra programmes can be inserted, before being transmitted on their 1368 AM transmitter at Foxdale, a few miles west, on the Peel road.

The programmes of Radio Caroline North are presented from the ship by a carefully selected group of Caroline's best DJs. The line-up usually comprises Dave Foster, Peter Philips, Johnnie Lewis, Ray Clark and Steve Anthony. These are all capable of slick programming and invariably they use an up-tempo pace of delivery. The programmes are usually heard over the final weekend of each month and from Friday evening for about 48 hours, finishing at the start of Manx Radio's sponsored religious programmes on Sunday evening.

Each of the Caroline North weekends are sponsored and listeners are actively urged to enter a draw, broadcast on the station every thirty minutes or so. Participants must answer a qualifier question, invariably this concerns a piece of Radio Caroline's history. The winner is drawn live on the air on Sunday evening. The prizes are modest: a hamper of Tiptree's jams, or a voucher to be spent in the Caroline web shop.

American Streams

Caroline began offering separate streams in both the US Eastern and the Pacific Standard time zones. This has enabled listeners in the USA to wake up to Caroline's breakfast show as well as relax to the late-night shows, just as they are intended to be heard. The time stepping is only available in the USA and is available right across the continent by using a new iOS app in the Apple App Store. There is also an Android app available in the Google Play Store.

Caroline gets DAB Outlets

OFCOM suddenly dangled a carrot in 2016 suggesting that they might just find time to invite applications for 'AM community of interest' stations, though no one held their breath. More encouraging was the announcement that they would be awarding licences for some small-scale trial networks using the DAB+ format of transmission, to see how small these could be made and still be successful.

BFBS (British Forces Broadcasting Service) were involved in the same trial and the contact was initiated by Caroline presenter Chris Pearson who worked for BFBS. Caroline offered a feed of her programmes to several of these SSDAB outlets and was accepted as potential programme supplier by several. Some of them subsequently launched and the initial 'trial period' was extended for an extra two years and then eventually for five years.

The successful applicant groups covering Aldershot and Woking, Norwich, Portsmouth and then Glasgow and Brighton were each licensed and gave Caroline a channel. Reception is now possible on DAB across most of London. This brought the Caroline organisation to a much wider group of listeners. In 2019, the UK Parliament was to approve new legislation enabling the expansion of small-scale DAB transmitters, meaning Caroline could shortly be available to more listeners. Caroline's online audience continues to grow, with its initial 20,000 hours a month by now mushrooming to exceed 22,000 a day.

Raffles dog kennel becomes a shop

With regular visitors to the ship there is a good footfall for selling Radio Caroline merchandise on board, where better to buy Caroline goods? The Caroline shop is now located towards the stern of the ship, port-side. It's in a room that has a bit of history of its own. It's known as the Dog Kennel, as it was the home of the ships dog, Raffles, who lived on board throughout the 1980s.

Raffles was an Alsation cross bred who was rescued form the harbour in Spain by Peter Chicago after he had been thrown into the harbour by some Spanish dockers. He grew up on the ship, was often mentioned in many programmes and attracted quite a lot of mail from listeners over the years! Raffles roamed freely over most of the ship, although there were one or two places he wouldn't venture into.

Raffles eventually went ashore at Margate for a veterinary check up and saw out the end of his days at Chicago's home in Margate, where he had the run of a lovely garden. After Raffles went ashore, the dog kennel became an aerial tuning room for the ill-fated Valcom antenna.

Trips to the Ross Revenge

The insurance company underwriting the cover for the Ross Revenge produced a list of essential work and upgrades to allow the public to visitors on board, the first of which was that the ship must have a Fire Plan. Most of the documentation for the ship had been lost or misplaced over the years so, to remain in compliance, it was important to have these all redrawn.

The Support Group has an ongoing programme of carefully measuring every corner of the ship and producing plans, which are available to interested parties to download.

Once the necessary work for insurance cover was completed, Radio Caroline was able to invite members of the public to visit the ship. She was still mid river and trips were arranged from Maldon and from West Mersea, usually aboard the *Razorbill 3*, a small pleasure craft. Visits include a conducted tour of the ship, by one of the radio station staff and cup of tea in the messroom, the scene of so many events in Caroline's history. A shop in Raffles' old room has many souvenirs..

The trips were organised by Albert and Georgena Hood until 2019 who by then had been coordinating visitor trips out to Radio Caroline for almost forty years. They have now retired from daily Caroline roles and trip bookings are managed by Paula Shaw, a long time Caroline enthusiast who lives locally.

Albert and Georgena have also developed Caroline's merchandising operation, which provides valuable income for the radio station. The goods offered cover a wide variety of products: books about the station, videos and DVDs, apparel of all types and, of course, tickets for the boat trips. They can all be bought online from the Radio Caroline web-shop, which is managed by Ollie Hicks and the important financial support being handled by Mike Weston.

Mike wrote and published the book *Records At Sea* which is the definite story about the Ross Revenge. It told the story of the ship from her days off Iceland, how she was bought by Caroline and the layout of the vessel.

28 An AM licence for Caroline

Finally, in 2016, the UK regulator OFCOM invited interested parties to register their intentions and plans for new community radio licences. Caroline carefully constructed the necessary documentation and this was submitted in October 2016.

The proposal was for an AM licence to cover the counties of Essex and Suffolk, which is the original heartland of Radio Caroline. No one else seemed to be interested in applying for a licence for the area, which was encouraging as it meant the applications would not be subject to a 'beauty parade' as happens in areas where there are many applicants chasing only one or two frequency allocations.

It was a long anxious wait that winter as OFCOM deal with community radio business "as and when" they have staff available to do so. They had received several dozen other applications for various areas around the UK, most of them for urban areas. On 17th May 2017 Ofcom informed Caroline that the application for an AM licence had finally been approved and that a licence would be awarded. All the work begun by Bob Lawrence and Tracey Crouch MP seven years previously was finally paying dividends!

The basis of the Caroline application was that the station's original coverage area and its traditional heartland was Essex and Suffolk, where the signal from Caroline were strongest heard when the station began in 1964. The intention was to allow listeners in that area to hear music radio on the band they knew (AM) and presented in a style they remember.

During the Summer Caroline was able to announce that one kilowatt of effective radiated power was to be allowed on 648AM. A solid-state transmitter (right) made by Nautel was obtained and tuned to the allocated frequency. This was a 3kW unit for two reasons. Firstly, it is better to operate a transmitter below its rated power output as components 'under-run' are not under such stress and usually last much longer.

Secondly, most antennas need matching components to make them perform better. These are coils or capacitors. Any component added to an aerial circuit will add losses, meaning that more power needs to be pumped into the circuit to achieve the assigned amount of radiated power.

The original site in Suffolk was offered to Caroline at a generous cost. But it had no existing facilities, meaning a complete build. An alternative was offered using the omni-directional standby antenna at the old BBC World Service site on Orfordness.

The old BBC site was surrounded by water and away from homes, etc. Better still, it had an existing mast that can carry up to 250 kilowatts, so the 1KW licensed to Caroline presents no problems. There was even a ready built transmitter building close to the mast, although it was huge compared to Caroline's needs. Suitable rental terms were agreed with the owner of the site and test transmissions began in November. They proved that everything was operating within the terms of the licence and to the satisfaction of Ofcom.

Finally, just a few days before Christmas Caroline's new 648 service was formally launched with a special programme lasting ten hours. Over Christmas, Caroline was operating on two medium wave frequencies and several online channels offering a variety of bandwidths. A superb achievement for a radio station that so many had written off so many times in her past.

OFCOM published a map that shows the predicted coverage of Caroline's 648 signal in north Essex and Suffolk. It illustrates the area in which it's likely that good, 'city-grade' reception can be had.

In fact the 'usable reception' area of the transmitter extends much further. The location on one of the east coast's extremities ensures an easy sea water path to a wide area. Good reception is possible for a considerable distance inland from Southampton around to the Yorkshire coast as well as across to Holland and Belgium, where it is the strongest station on the MW band most of the day.

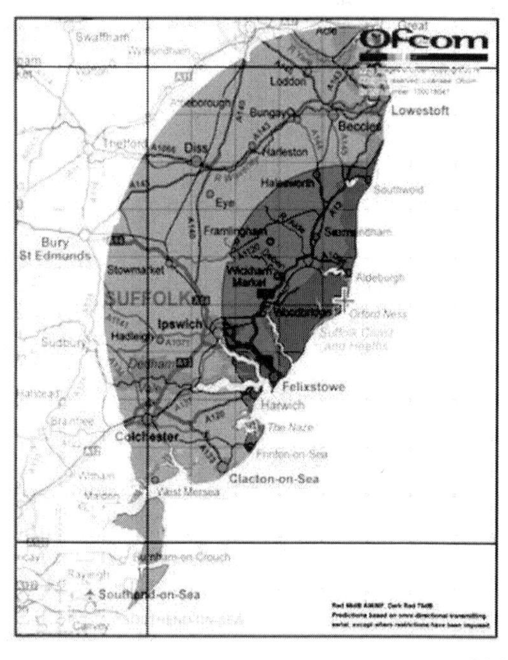

53 years
to get a licence!

Caroline's origins marked

In late summer 2017, a commemorative plaque was unveiled in Felixstowe commemorating Radio Caroline's launch off the resort in 1964. The unveiling was attended by many Caroline stars, from newcomer Andrew Austin to old hands Alan Turner, Albert Hood, Tony Prince, Roger Day. They were accompanied by many local celebrities and civic dignitaries, including the Mayor.

Several hundred supporters thronged the streets to see the amazing spectacle parade through the town. Star of the show was Emperor Rosko, now resident in Los Angeles, who had travelled to the town in a motorcade of Mini-Mokes.

Plaque commemorating Radio Caroline's launch

Brian Nicholls

The stone unveiling event was organised by Felixstowe resident Brian Nicholls and included the traveling exhibition of offshore artefacts by Chris Dannatt's *Pirate Radio Memories* and the *Felixstowe Offshore Radio Group*. The plaque is in Wolsey Gardens (a street close to the beach with an elevated view of the North Sea) and is a unique commemoration of Caroline's beginnings.

As the New Year of 2018 dawned, the BBC announced that many of its local radio stations would lose their medium wave relays. Among them were BBC Radio Lincolnshire and BBC Radio Surrey which had previously restricted the coverage of Manx Radio's 1368 AM outlet. With BBC Radios Lincolnshire and Surrey removed from the band, coverage of Radio Caroline North was greatly extended as Manx Radio's AM transmitter can now be heard over a much wider area.

The Radio Caroline North programmes usually begin their weekend with a few hours from Manx Radio's MD, Chris Williams, who has broadcast there, on the BFBS and on Radio Caroline for almost thirty years. His uptempo, jovial style of delivery sets the pace for some of the best of Radio Caroline's established DJs, including Johnnie Lewis, Ray Clarke, Peter Philips and Dave Foster. The music is well known hits of Caroline's glory years peppered with the usual banter and a competition that listeners can participate in simply by sending an email to the studio.

Caroline's Chinese Cousins

Talks had been held with Chinese media company *Muzen* who had visited the Ross Revenge for filming in 2017. Muzen Audio are a leading manufacturer of electronic equipment; their range includes some rather beautiful and clever radios, all based on vintage designs. Many of these combine an FM radio with a Bluetooth receiver, enabling users to feed their favourite online radio station to a speaker that can easily fill a room with quality audio.

They invited two Caroline executives to join them at an exposition in Paris where they discussed holding a 'crowd funding' campaign in the USA to raise funds for Radio Caroline. After the exchange of legal agreements, Muzen flew Caroline's Steve Anthony and Richard Lavelle to New York, where it was to be announced that Muzen and Radio Caroline were now partners.

Prior to launching Muzen, Jimmy Wang had founded Life Token Inc, which sells unique personalized jewellery. Jimmy has a passion for building brands and is driven by constant curiosity and expanding his knowledge about everything.

A big press launch was held in the Javetts Centre, a massive expo building on the banks of the Hudson River. "It did seem strange standing on the purpose-built stage, addressing an assembled crowd of press and industry people," said Steve Anthony. "Richard and I told the story of Radio Caroline which was a bit surreal, as not one of them appeared to have ever heard of us before!"

Caroline's Steve Anthony and Richard Lavelle hosting Caroline China

A few months later Caroline were invited to Beijing, China. 'The Second Radio Renaissance' was to be the repeat of an event Muzen held in Morocco the previous year. Lasting for three days it celebrated free radio, and featured 18 DJs including Caroline's Richard Lavelle and Steve Anthony.

Voyager space age studio in the Gobi desert

Around eighty invited guests were invited out to Dunhuang, on the edge of the Gobi Dessert. Muzen had built a studio modelled on a space ship and named 'The Space Voyager'.

And its mission?

To take music to the stars!

The highlight was *The Radio Caroline Show – The Best of British* which was presented live from The Voyager by Steve Anthony and Richard Lavelle.

"It was great fun broadcasting from that studio while looking out over a moonlit Gobi desert, said Steve. "Our hosts seemed to love what we did but more importantly, so did the listeners. It was an on-line station so the number of connections could be monitored which showed that we had just over three million listeners."

Comments on Chinese social media flooded in during the show which went out in the early hours of the morning, proving that many of them must have stayed up through the night to hear this radio phenomena.

"The response we got suggested that it all went rather well!" said Steve. "The entire trip was quite amazing and the memory of the broadcast will stay with me forever."

A special edition "Caroline Radio" has now been launched on Muzen's own on-line radio station in China which is named '***Radiooo Station***'. Each week they broadcast a two-hour Radio Caroline Show presented by Richard Lavelle. The show is heard by several million people across China and in the early hours of Saturday on Caroline's main channel.

Muzen made a reciprocal visit to London where they were shown the legendary Abbey Road studios and the Caroline ship, Ross Revenge.

Caroline studios upgraded

Early in 2019, Caroline's four-man studio team of Mike Brill (who is an IT guru), Rob Ashard (a master of mixers!), Steve Anthony and Dave Foster made big changes to one of the studios at the Caroline HQ in Rochester. The long-planned alterations saw the installation of two Alice 2000 mixing desks and various other studio kit donated by former Caroline DJ Ian Anderson's Shetland station *SIBC*.

The computers serving the music in the studios were checked and the studio area was laid out again. A lot of previously 'loose' equipment was properly installed into equipment racks along with a *Broadcast Warehouse* DSPX Mini HD processor. Everything now looks 'hunky dory', a lot more comfortable and easier to operate.

In March 2019, two Radio Caroline DJs, Peter Philips and Ray Clarke, visited the old home port of the Ross Revenge, Grimsby. At the town's Heritage Fishing Centre, they spoke at length to some former crewmen of the trawler from her days as one of the UK's best performing deep sea trawlers. The purpose of the trip was to get more information and be better informed of her fishing days so that Caroline can run better visitors' days on the ship.

"We have altered the ship as little as possible, but photographs of how she was would be good. Having self-funded the Revenge for 27 years, the time has come to make a plan," station manager Peter Moore told the press.

Caroline's MD, Peter Moore

"We have paid for a marine survey that has shown that the ship is still remarkably sound and have split our development proposal into three phases. First, we plan to dry dock her and repair the hull to give her another decade before more attention is needed. Secondly, we want to use the two levels of the forepeak, which is a substantial space, to create a museum or exhibition and education area of her two careers. fishing and radio."

"Thirdly, we want to make her 'operational' again, able to travel, albeit with caution, under her own power. This is a mighty undertaking but Caroline has a long history of achieving the impossible," said Peter.

Fast cars

Radio Caroline now supports motor racing again with sponsorship of races and of a car. The reason for radio stations promoting motor racing is usually a marketing one. Young adult males are a very lucrative demographic groups; think 'male grooming' products, beers and so on. Those products are high profit items with a huge mark-up; lots of competition mean the marketing spend is huge.

Caroline's sponsorship is mainly for races of historic touring cars, Classic Formula 3 and Classic Clubmans at Snetterton in Norfolk and at Brands Hatch in the summer. There is a regular programme of events arranged, including a nostalgia weekend at Croft, culminating in the finals at Silverstone in October. The motor racing events bring the Caroline name and display opportunities for Caroline to many new potential listeners. Radio Caroline was involved in such ventures in the sixties and at the Zandvoort circuit in the Netherlands in 1974.

Radio Caroline now has a branded car with the number 648 emblazoned on it. The BMW is in 'Ross Revenge red and yellow' and is piloted by David Cornwallis. It's been seen at many events in 2019 and finished well in a *Swinging Sixties* race at Silverstone

David Cornwallis, pilot of the Caroline 648 BMW.

Radio Caroline

Programmes continue on the main and Caroline Flashback channels with monthly broadcasts as Caroline North via Manx Radio's 1368AM frequency. Programmes are hosted by half a dozen Caroline old-timers from the Ross Revenge, Johnnie Lewis, Peter Phillips, Ray Clarke, Barry James, Nick Jackson, Grant Benson and Andrew Austin with guest appearances from others from Caroline's yester years.

RADIO MI AMIGO continues!

Radio Mi Amigo was rarely heard again from the North Sea after deserting Radio Caroline in 1978. An international version of the station transmits daily on short wave and online as Radio Mi Amigo International. It is popular with radio enthusiasts across Europe.

Over the Spring holiday weekend in 2019, Radio Mi Amigo was reborn at the Belgian resort of Blankenberg with live broadcasts from the MV Castor to commemorate 45 years since the birth of the station. The Castor is a sister ship of Caroline's former tender, the Bellatrix.

Named **Mi Amigo 45**, the event featured many of the Radio Mi Amigo personalities, some of whom had been heard on Radio Caroline, including Bob Noakes and Ferry Eden. Lion Keezer, who was involved with Caroline in the seventies, supported the event by a four day relay of the *Mi Amigo 45* output via his station's two short wave outlets, normally used for *Radio Mi Amigo International*. The celebrations were also heard on FM locally as well as on several of the small AM transmitters across the Netherlands and of course, online.

The programmes were all presented live from on board the MV Castor, moored in the Blankenberg yacht haven. Her studios were built by former Radio Caroline engineer Bob Noakes during the voyage from Rotterdam. Around 5,000 visitors came to see the ship, enjoy the barbecue and buy the Radio Mi Amigo DJs a beer.

Radio Mi Amigo International now has a new studio on Blankenberg Pier with panoramic views over the sea. Listeners are welcome to watch live shows hosted by the station's Belgian DJs and buy Mi Amigo merchandise. A series of live music performances is planned to take place during the summer months.

Radio Mi Amigo International's studio on the pier at Blankenberg

Radio Caroline also gets involved in several music festivals each year including the 'Todd in the Hole' at Stevenage in Hertfordshire.

The 55th Birthday of the station in 2019 (actually on 27th March, but it is usually celebrated over Easter weekend) was marked by various special programmes on the main channel, Caroline Flashback and on the Caroline North service.

A major "on air" fund raising campaign was organised to raise enough money to enable the team to take the Caroline project even further. Those who contributed £25 or more received a special 'limited edition' T-Shirt of the Caroline Bell logo, last used on the Caroline Roadshow almost thirty years before. Over £25,000 was received in donations from 77 new members, pledging at least £7.50 per month.

Caroline Road Show T-shirt, 2019

Caroline in the 21st Century

Over the last quarter of a century , Radio Caroline has gone from being shipwrecked and chained up by salvors and the shipping inspectorate, to running several radio channels and operating its remaining ship the Ross Revenge close to the shore, with a fully insured programme of events and activities, that members of the public can visit in a safe environment and fully insured.

Today, Radio Caroline continues as a listener-supported station and encourages supporters to make a regular monthly payment, or buy items of memorabilia and other merchandise, the profits from which helps expand the various services

Now available on the Medium Wave in Eastern England, in selected towns on DAB, around the Irish Sea on Manx Radio's transmitter one weekend each month and globally online, Radio Caroline has never been so accessible or so close to her listeners.

A remarkable achievement by any measure, that's Radio Caroline.

29. Caroline's future

Under Peter Moore's stewardship, Radio Caroline continues, with studios on board the ship and transmission facilities on land. As a legal British entity, Caroline continues to thrive and expand, a remarkable achievement when one considers its dire position at the end of 1991 when she was salvaged from a ships' graveyard, the Goodwin Sands.

What future is there for radio in the UK? Listening is at a peak (over 90% of people tune in) and the authorities are coercing a stampede towards digital transmission, meaning it can be controlled more easily. There seems to no longer be any room for small, privately-owned radio stations in the UK where radio is rigidly controlled by an oligopoly of a handful of major companies. The only alternatives are 'not for profit' community stations, which the rules prohibit from being successful.

Perhaps freedom lovers need Radio Caroline more than ever?

None of us live forever and Radio Caroline has been a lifelong struggle for Ronan. "Those close to Ronan say that the disasters such as the collapse of the magnificent 300ft mast on the *Ross Revenge*, the armed raid at sea and the shipwreck put an intolerable physical and mental strain on him from which he never truly recovered," says Peter Moore who took up the mantle of Caroline's manager, despite his own bout of ill health. "Ronan's problems were compounded by a long, futile court case against the British government for having raided his ship and the many attempts to obtain an overseas broadcast licence."

"By now being 'all out of rabbits' he still encouraged others to rebuild what could be rebuilt in both the Radio Caroline broadcasts and the ship. He shunned conventional medicine and relied greatly on the spiritual guidance offered by Dr Sharma and two other advisers"

Ronan has always preferred to be pressing on in new directions and has always been happiest when dreaming up new schemes and ideas and pursuing them.

His teenage ambition was to live life to the full in London. He has done that for three quarters of his life now, in Kensington, Eaton Square, Hay's Mews in Mayfair and in Paulten's Square, a leafy hideaway on the Kings Road in Chelsea.

Most of the business meetings concerned with Radio Caroline took place at a variety of restaurants nearby, such as the Asterix or the Dome coffee bar, though Ronan's favourite was always the Picasso Restaurant. It was much loved by so many of the Caroline family. It's since been sold and, like Ronan, is now predominantly vegetarian (it's called Rabbit).

Since the Ross Revenge ran aground, Ronan has increasingly left Peter Moore to his own devices to get the station back up and running once again.

Ines Rocha
Sean Kelly

Throughout the nineties, Ronan was often unwell and unable to contribute much to Caroline's management. His Brazilian girlfriend, Ines Rocha, took him to a succession of specialists and tried to arrange suitable treatment for him. There seemed to be little that could be done and she helped him escape London to live back in Ireland. The Radio Caroline management team helped with the move and to put Ronan's extensive collection of souvenirs and mementos into storage.

Initially they stayed in a seafront apartment at Bettystown, on Ireland's east coast, where he enjoyed long walks by the sea, playing an occasional round of golf and going horse racing. His doctor recommended long chats with friends, but this was difficult in such a remote place, although he continued to pursue one of his favourite hobbies - talking on the telephone.

Ronan was finally diagnosed to be suffering from vascular dementia, caused by restricted blood flow to the brain. This gradually causes problems with mental ability and eventually brain damage, explaining how he gradually became unable to communicate sufficiently well. He had to move into a nursing home near the banks of Carlingford Lough where he can receive the care that his condition demands. Ronan still listens to Caroline whenever possible and sometimes makes contact with requests for music, notably Ray Charles.

Perhaps Ronan's long held dream will now be fullfilled and he now be appointed the President, of Radio Caroline?

Peter has vowed to continue developing Radio Caroline and keep alive the dreams of those who launched the station in 1964. With the same spirit of 'Love, Peace and Good Music' the spirit of Caroline lives on.

The Caroline Family
Although a privately-owned radio station, the 'family' of Caroline has always included not just those who own or even those work in the radio station. Perpetuating a radio station like Caroline has depended on the active support and assistance of a wide and varied circle of people – those who have helped out for a very short time and a few who have been there since the beginning. The Caroline family includes an amazing selection of engineers, journalists, musicians and presenters, not to mention various administrators and organisers, all have played a vital role in keeping the Caroline spirit alive.

This book has tried to chronicle the major events and the important members of the family, but even five hundred pages has had to omit some. The interesting thing about the Caroline family is that there have not been too many 'black sheep'. This is why everyone is hired for a probationary period; if it looks like they could be problematic, they are simply not invited back. Ronan has always said that "Once we accept someone into the fold, they are never out of the family forever. You are always a part of the Caroline family; once you're in, you are in for life." As the Eagles sang in 'Hotel California', "You can check out any time you like, but you can never leave."

The story of Radio Caroline featured one person throughout most of its life, either figuratively "at the helm" or actually pulling the strings. It was of course bigger than any one person and needed many others, who are acknowledged earlier. Those who have steered the station and who are the most important:

60s *Allan Crawford | Jocelyn Stevens | Barry Ainley | Terry Bate | Philip Solomon*
70s *Gerard van Dam | Chris Cary | Sylvain Tack | Ben Bode | Fred Bolland*
80s *Vincent Monsey | Tom Anderson | Andy Johnson | Peter Moore*

and not forgetting some key assistants, who are quite irreplacable:
Oonagh, Frances, Joan, Pinky, Nan, Kate and the two Carolines.

Radio Caroline spawned hundreds of DJs but most important of all, and the biggest reason for Caroline's success and longevity are the millions of listeners. Without listeners, any radio station is pointless. For a small privately-owned radio station fighting against almost impossible odds, attracting over 20 million listeners is a remarkable feat.

Undoubtedly, Radio Caroline is a remarkable radio station!

Media Support
Radio Caroline has always provided plenty of copy for all media, with audio copy often being dramatic, visuals of the ships, studios and personalities often very eye-catching and even words quite unique. The story of Caroline has been reported in almost every country around the world, as was reflected in Johnnie Walker's 1967 strap line:

The World's Most Famous, the Nation's Number One

Some newspapers could be relied on more than others to carry news of Caroline's colourful life, while others only reported the problems and disasters, carrying only pessimism or the Government's line.

As well as the many authors who have published works about offshore radio, or Caroline in particular, mention should also be made of some of the many publications that have reported on the Caroline story.

Offshore Echos

Ronan, Chris Edwards and François Lhote discuss the FRC on board the Ross Revenge

By far, the longest running chronicler of Radio Caroline has been the *Offshore Echo's Magazine,* which was first published in 1974 by the France Radio Club.

Chris Edwards and François Lhote jointly edit English and French editions of this excellent glossy magazine which has been running for 45 years.

Available only on subscription, but sent to anywhere in the world, the Offshore Echos team carefully research their material. Most editions are about fifty pages in length and are printed on glossy quality A5 size paper stock. Each contains many photographs and copies of cuttings and items from archives not seen anywhere else. The FRC produces excellent quality DVDs showing almost every offshore station that has ever broadcast; details at their web site (see page 506)

One of OEM' hardest workers died in 2019 on the 51st anniversary of the Caroline ships being towed away, March 3rd. Boudewijn Dom had been suffering from vascular dementia disease, the same affliction from which that Ronan is now suffering. "He was a great friend, an excellent photographer and a true lover of offshore radio," said the OEM editor, Chris Edwards.

The key listener organisations have been the Free Radio Association, the Broadside Free Radio Movement, in the UK and the Free Radio Campaign in Holland. In recent decades, some consolidation has taken place with the Radio Caroline Support Group bringing together various organisations.

Dutch readers were catered for by a publication called *Pirate Radio News*, which often brought exclusive news of Radio Caroline developments, thanks to a young reporter called Hans Knot. He later edited the magazine as well as supplying news and articles on Caroline to such well known radio magazines as *Monitor* and *Anoraks Weekly* in the UK and *Baffle Radio Magazine* in Belgium, now called *RadioVisie*. Hans has written for *Offshore Echos* since the 1980s.

A glossy monthly magazine now called *Freewave Nostalgia* began life in 1978, thanks to Ton van Draanen and Hans Knot. Rob Olthof was a partner with Hans Knot in the SMC (Organisation of Media Communications) which organised many events and some maritime excursions out to visit the Radio Caroline ship in the 1980s, along with former Radio Delmare manager, Leendert Vingerling.

The **Foundation for Media Communications** has now published over fifty books about offshore radio, mostly edited and researched by Hans Knot. They also organised the successful *RadioDay* events in the Netherlands at which many Caroline personalities spoke.

The most prolific journalist and historian in the Netherlands is Sir Hans Knot of Groningen who produces regular reports on offshore radio as well as working for several publications. In 2009, he was awarded a Royal Knighthood in the *Order of Oranje Nassau* for his work in recording an important part of Dutch cultural history.

Martin van der Ven, Rob Olthof and Sir Hans Knot

For many years he and his colleagues, Martin van der Ven and the late Rob Olthof, organised *RadioDay* in the Netherlands. After a hugely successful event in 2014, they handed the reins onto others but so far only one event has followed, in Harlingen during 2017, run by Sietse Brouwer and Jan van Heeren.

Caroline's enemies

Even those officials who fought Caroline 'tooth and nail' in the sixties, the seventies and the eighties seem now to have given up fighting. Most adversaries profess they had a secret admiration for the Caroline family and the tenacity, its character and fortitude displayed.

They say "you can't please everyone" and its true about Caroline too. Some will wish to be a 'thorn in the side' of their opponent and relish having someone to lock horns with. They have some peculiar gladiatorial urge that probably goes back generations. Most peace-loving humans suppress it and enjoy life, but not the ones who hate.

Some civil servants working for the British Government have been zealous in their battle with Caroline, which can be part excused as wanting to do their job well. They are usually 'jobsworths', unable to create anything personally, so seek fulfilment by destroying others. Some of these civil servants are of course well-meaning and believe that they are working 'for the country'. They may well have been indoctrinated to believe that something free like Radio Caroline is a threat to national security. While a few original participants may have had subversive thoughts, for many years, Caroline has been staffed solely by a peace-loving breed of folk who wanted to do little more heinous than playing decent music on the airwaves. There can't be anything seditious in that, can there?

It now seems certain that one or two civil servants infiltrated the Caroline organisation and other embryonic offshore projects that had similar aims in the early 1960s. They may have acted as *agents provocateur,* but it can be excused for a state to operate intelligence gathering. We should be concerned if it didn't.

It's known that Harold Wilson had a vendetta against Ronan O'Rahilly personally and was increasingly rabid in his attempts to stop Caroline operating. Several of his cabinet shared his belief that the state (or was it simply 'the Party'?) should control all aspects of our lives – where we work, where we live, go to school etc, and what we hear on the radio.

Free and independent broadcasting is abhorred in the socialist dogma. They really believe that only the state should be allowed to speak to the people. They will lie, cheat and be irrationally dishonest in attacking any vestige of freedom. They're typified by John Stonehouse, a Labour minister who was determined to squash Radio Caroline but was later found to be dishonest and have been a Soviet spy for many years.

Caroline's enemies work for 'state control' and against the people.

Any new business that does well can expect to attract attention from a few who seem to be consumed with jealousy, an awful trait but displayed all too often. They may be impotent but will do their best to damage something fresh, fun and free like Caroline.

Few have tried so hard to denigrate the Radio Caroline name and the reputation of Ronan O'Rahilly, as a small group that claims that the original Radio Caroline finished in Autumn 1964 when the original backers lost interest, once Harold Wilson came to power. It's true that some 'original backers such as CO Stanley, of the Pye group and William Harvey of the BPC dropped out at that time but they were small investors and never key players. Others reputed to have triggered the launch of Caroline had only nebulous connections and there is no trace of them in shareholder lists and other records.

Those who have vowed to destroy the mythology surrounding Radio Caroline and to disprove the link between its various eras may have set themselves an impossible task as Radio Caroline has considerable longevity, having been around for well over half a century. Ronan O'Rahilly is the constant link between the station's four phases, the eternal figurehead of the Caroline family and someone who has led so many in the fight for free radio. It's unlikely he will be forgotten, no matter how much mud is thrown.

Some have claimed that Caroline contravened treaties that the UK was subscribed to, such as the 1949 Copenhagen Plan, which shared out the MW spectrum among states. As Radio Caroline was never a party to any such treaties, nor subject to UK law, then by definition it cannot have contravened treaties or laws. It didn't exist in the UK until recently, since when it has observed the various radio rules and regulations.

The name *Radio Caroline* was always simply a logo or call sign, used on the air to identify broadcasts. The Caroline spirit is now formally registered as a UK entity, and has taken steps to protect its trademark and the name, which is sound business practice.

A lacuna in the British legislation meant that the only ones breaking the law relating to offshore radio were the millions of British listeners, whose reception was outside the terms of their radio receiving licences. The Government had neglected to draft the legislation correctly, meaning that the GPO, originally set up to censor all communications, whether newspapers or broadcasting, actually had no real legal powers to regulate!

Always the same Radio Caroline?
Radio Caroline has always been privately owned, funded by several investors. One man has always admitted responsibility when others would only run and hide. As backers dropped out over the years he has become the *de facto* owner. As funding grew more difficult and the station became less profitable, obscure financial sources had to be accessed and unorthodox methods employed to raise funds.

At the start of the Caroline story, funding sources were deliberately veiled by shrouds of incorporation in several offshore jurisdictions. That was necessary to protect the identity of the owners for a variety of reasons. Those original funders were happy for someone to front Radio Caroline for them. Ronan did the job rather well, thanks to his training as an actor. His softly spoken Irish accent, his amiable cordiality and pleasant disposition usually delighted those he came into contact with, especially Caroline's many supporters and followers.

Some detractors claim that today's Radio Caroline is not the same as the team that launched in March 1964, ignoring that organisations evolve throughout their life. The BBC's team is not the same as that which launched the Corporation in 1927, yet they continue to adhere to Lord Reith's strictures and it remains the BBC.

When a football club is bought and sold, the name carries on. Many business names continue despite major changes in ownership and it happens increasingly in the radio business too. Changes in ownership of a vessel or the equipment doesn't signify a change in the radio station. Any claim that there is no link between the 1964 incarnation of Radio Caroline and today's is erroneous; the ownership was always vested in a Liechtenstein company; can anyone be certain that it isn't the beneficial owner of today's Radio Caroline? It's axiomatic that Radio Caroline continues to be Radio Caroline.

Radio Caroline has changed slightly over the years; the ships, the equipment and the programme format, but there are elements of continuity, particularly the spirit, the atmosphere and the campaign. It's that spirit which is the true Radio Caroline. Its intangible and can mean different things to various people, but it can be summarised as being a freedom loving, unfettered radio voice of entertainment, that cares for its listeners, is not aggressive or vicious and expresses itself with the best in music. While some of those points have been corrupted on occasion, usually due to *force majeure*, Caroline's slogan (or strapline as it's called in radio) has evolved to be

Love, Peace and Good *Music*

Radio Caroline's major events form four distinct phases:

	1963	Radio Caroline & Radio Atlanta
	1964	Radio Caroline North & South
A	1967	Caroline goes International
	1968	Radio Caroline International
	1970	Caroline broadcasts from the Mebo II
B	1972	Radio Caroline relaunch the Mi Amigo
	1980	Mi Amigo sank
C	1983	Radio Caroline revived from Ross Revenge
	1991	Radio Caroline grounded
D	1992	Caroline licensed in the UK
	2019	Caroline Continues! *On AM, DAB and online*

The above dateline shows how Radio Caroline's life covers four eras: A, B, C and D. Each of the first three eras encompass a particular decade: the sixties, the seventies and the eighties. Each era ended with a maritime disaster – a hijacking, a sinking and a grounding.

Caroline's current era 'D' began in 1992, the longest period of all. It began with a wrecked ship, crippling salvage bills and no way of getting back to sea. From that almost hopeless situation, Caroline was steadily developed, making irregular broadcasts at low power, to today's situation - on MW again, supplemented by DAB and audible over much of the UK as well as around the world online.

Ronan O'Rahilly is the common element throughout the life of Radio Caroline and its purely for health reasons that he has abrogated to Peter Moore all responsibility for the business of Radio Caroline and the ship. Peter Moore affirms that his values and intentions match those of O'Rahilly, so it seems entirely reasonable to say that, while the station's full cast of participants, its legal status and ownership has always been either nebulous or in a state of flux, the continuous involvement and participation of one or both of them reinforce the claim that the station remains as 'Radio Caroline'.

The Caroline team have managed to perpetuate a long running saga. Caroline has a story line almost as long as the world's longest running TV drama series, Coronation Street. There are similarities in that 'Corry' is the UK's most viewed TV drama, and Caroline also had the biggest audience at one time. With an almost unbelievable sequence of intrigue, takeovers, threats and battles, Radio Caroline has certainly seen more action. Caroline is very different – her story revolves around real people!

D

E

F

G

H

N

O

P

Q

R

S

T

U

V

W

Z

BIBLIOGRAPHY

These publications include substantial references to Radio Caroline. The list is not exhaustive, nor are any particular titles necessarily recommended.

Title	Author	Publisher
25 Years of Caroline Memories	Hans Knot	SMC/Monitor
Pop Went The Pirates	Keith Skues	Lambs Meadow
Shiprocked!	Steve Conway	Liberties
Poptastic!	Tony Blackburn	Cassell
Butterfly on the Wheel	Peter Moore	OEM
Wheel Turned Full Circle	John A Burch	Caroline Movement
A Nation's Station	Derek Winterbottom	Manx Experience
Far Out At Sea	Gordon Kelly	Radio Seagull
Van Atlantis tot Mi Amigo	Roger Henderick	Joepie
Radio Caroline – The Pirate Years	Ralph C Humphries	Oakwood
Life and Death of a Pirate	Susan E Moore	Fillongley
Radio Caroline The Boat That Rocked	Ray Clarke	History Press
When Pirates Waived the Rules	Howard Rose	NOW RADIO
Ships in Troubled Waters	Nigel Harris	My Way
Anoraks and Arseholes	Andy Archer	
Manx Giant	Andy Wint	MNH
SOS Ten days in the life of a Lady	Simon Barrett	MRP
Sylvain Tack	Sylvain Tack	Culemborg
The Ship that Rocked the World	Tom Lodge	Bartley
Whatever happened to Simon Dee?	Richard Wiseman	Aurum
Radio Caroline	John Venmore-Rowland	Landmark
Pirate Radio Illustrated History	Keith Skues & David Kindred	Amberley
Memories of a Dear Old Lady	Albert Hood	
Radio Caroline North	Bob Preedy	Preedy
From International Waters	Mike Leonard	Forest Press
Johnnie Walker, Autobiography	Johnnie Walker	Penguin
Last of the Pirates	Bob Noakes	White Noise / SMC
When Pirates Ruled the Waves	Paul Harris	Impulse

Sadly, many of these are long out of print, but some may be found via links on WorldofRadio.co.uk/RadioBooks.html

Internet Links

Radio and the internet continue to grow ever closer. You can find more information about current Radio Caroline activities and programme streams online at

www.radiocaroline.co.uk

OTHER USEFUL LINKS

https://WorldofRadio.co.uk

http://www.offshoreechos.com

http://RadioMiAmigo.International

http://www.radioseagull.com

http://www.HansKnot.com

http://www.offshoreradio.co.uk

https://Radio270.net

ABOUT THE AUTHOR

Paul Rusling studied radio engineering at college in Hull while working as disc jockey in night clubs. In 1973 he joined Radio Caroline as a disc jockey and hosted the station's breakfast programme. He and his wife Anne managed nightclubs and pubs and started their family at the Punch Tavern in Whitstable. In 1983 he converted the MV Communicator into a floating radio station, her role for the next 21 years.

Switching his attentions to other projects as a broadcast consultant, he has since been involved in 19 successful licence applications, mostly for large scale, national radio stations. His work has included programming, engineering and management functions at many stations across Europe and in the Middle East. Paul has also written for many publications and magazines and published several books on radio.

Email; paul@RadioCarolineBible.com

Worldwide Broadcast Consultants

WBC is a collective of experienced radio administrators, engineers, lawyers, DJs, programmers and other practitioners. The WBC team can help you establish your own radio station almost anywhere in the world. With skills and attributes including practical knowledge and first-hand involvement in the broadcast industry in over forty countries, they are aware of the many pitfalls best avoided. WBC can advise operators on any aspects of broadcasting and help to make your project a success.

Maritime Broadcasting

Some WBC staff have offshore expertise and relish unusual projects.
WBC use expert maritime lawyers to stay on the right of the law.
While nothing at sea is cheap, neither is it prohibitively expensive.
The utmost discretion and complete confidentiality is assured

If you think the prices charged by professionals are expensive, be warned - using an amateur can cost you even more!

For professional advice: https:worldofradio.co.uk/WBC

Serious enquiries only, to *wbc@worldofradio.co.uk*

You too could have your own radio station

More radio books by Paul Rusling

The thrilling story of how one radio ship was home to 11 radio stations during its 21 year career as a radio ship.

This is a fun-filled, action-packed tale of dramatic events and real-life adventure on the High Seas, told by those who were there. Amazing swashbuckling excitement and real life piracy ! Read how fortunes were made and lost too, how the audience built to around ten million at one stage. Sadly, it all ended in tears.

LASER pulled ten million listeners. Read how it happened. The format, program techniques, secrets, Laser's 'hot clocks' & etc.

The LRP book has biographical details of all Laser DJs and their photographs. It concludes a copy of the Laser 558 Operations Manual and gives details of other Laser activities since the 1980s.

Internet Radio 2016

Launch and Operate your own Online Station,

A comprehensive guide to how radio transmission has divided into two routes, Traditional 'ether' reception and online streams.

The book also describes all you need to set up your own station and where to source it. Available as a book or a Kindle, from Amazon.

These titles and more radio books are available from
https://WorldofRadio.co.uk/Books.html